Masters Of Anatomy is a subsidiary and registered trademark of 2387171 Ontario Inc.

ISBN:

Softcover - 978-0-9937929-0-8

Hardcover - 978-0-9937929-1-5

All rights reserved. No part of this book may be reproduced in any manner whatsoever without express written permission from Masters Of Anatomy.

Printed and bound in Canada

INTRODUCTION

The Project

Andrew Loomis created the Ideal Male and Female references over 70 years ago and since then generations of artists have used them to understand the complex proportions of human anatomy. But while the art world has evolved dramatically, these classic references have remained unchanged. We believe it's time for a refresh.

Masters of Anatomy: The Ideal Body is a collection of artistic anatomy bringing together the work of over 130 famous artists like Adam Hughes, Joe Madureira, Humberto Ramos, Francisco Herrera and many others that have worked for famous animation and comic book studios. Each artist recreates the Ideal Male and Female body illustrated in their own signature style and without the aid of external reference. The goal: to translate a decades-old sketch into something more relevant to a modern aesthetic. The result is a volume unlike anything that exists today.

Who is this book for?

This book is for any artist interested in anatomy as it relates to character design - animators, cartoonists, concept artists, game designers, comic-book artists and aspiring professionals. The 280+ pages of drawings will make it easier to narrow down the styles you like best. By studying the drawings in this book you will gain an insight into how anatomy can be deformed to produce more appealing designs. You can easily compare any of the drawings to find the designs that appeal most to you.

What will this book teach me?

The most important goal in becoming a successful artist is finding your own style. Simply put, style is a distinctive way of doing things. The aim of this book is to help you craft your own style by exposing you to the work of artists who have built very successful careers from their style of drawing. Every artist needs style, whether you're talking about a character designer, a dancer, a musician or a novelist. Your style is an extension of yourself and should be as unique to you as your own face. Think of how important a voice is to a musician, or rhythm is to a dancer, or prose to an author. How memorable would their work be if they lacked these necessary styles?

Most people learn by imitating their idols. Though it's a great place to start, you eventually need step out of that person's shadow and into your own spotlight. People love originality and there is something universally inferior about imitators. Spending too much time trying to be someone else can lead to an artistic dead end - especially if your work isn't as good as the original. Since this book provides you with a great number of original designs to explore you're less likely to devote your energy imitating one particular artist.

Having a mixture of both "contrasting" and "similar" design styles will help guide and refine the direction of your own art. Styles that appear alike still contain important nuances that tie them unmistakably to their creators. Being able to examine and compare these small but significant differences will allow you to more intelligently tinker with your own work.

In order for you to learn effective design principles you need to learn from the best. Audiences today expect a lot from artists. We are bombarded with examples of great design in every aspect of our life from car commercials to block-buster films to trendy home interiors - even the way our food is presented. That's why this book shines - all of the contributing artists are well known professionals at the top of their respective fields and many like Joe Madureira, Adam Hughes and J. Scott Campbell are world famous industry icons with millions of fans around the world. Their work puts food on the table, pays their mortgage and puts their children through college.

This book is an accumulation of all the years and decades of hard work and effort each artist has devoted to their personal style. Their drawing styles are a proven formula of success that will aid you in discovering your own voice.

The Artists

We solicited work from artists all over the world working in very different industries - comic books, video games, animation, illustration and even children's books. Each artist was carefully chosen for their style, appeal and underlying knowledge of anatomy. Together they have produced 260+ unique male and female anatomies with 780+ angles all beautifully drawn for you to examine and explore.

Thank-you!

We would like to sincerely thank everyone that supported this project from the earliest stages and especially all of our Kickstarter backers who made this book possible. We plan to continue delivering great character design books for you in the future.

THE ARTISTS

Adam Hughes
Alessandro Micelli
Alex Maleev
Andrew Robinson
Andy Park
Anna Cattish

Bahi JD
Ben Fiquet
Ben Li
Boris Matia

Celaoxxx (Marcelo Trom)
Charlie Bowater
Chase Conley
Chhuy-ing
Chris Sprouse
Chuck Pires
Cindy Yamauchi
Corey Smith
CreatureBox
Cushart Krenz

Dan Howard
Dan Panosian
Dan Seddon
Dani & Mafi

Daniel Araya
Dave Bardin
Dave Malan
David Rosel
Dean Yeagle
Derek Laufman
Devon Cady-Lee (Gorrem)
DJ (Dark Kenjie) Welch
Dusty Abell

Eddie Nunez (MiaCabrera)
Ein Lee
El Gunto (Guillaume Poux)
Emilie Decrock
Eric Guzman
Erin Humiston
Eugenia Nobati

Felix Sputnik
Flaviano Armentaro
Florian Satzinger
Francisco Herrera
Francisco Rico
Francis Vallejo

Genevieve Tsai
Guilherme D'Arezzo

Humberto Ramos

Ingrid Liman
Itaru Saito
Ivan Oviedo

Jae Hong Kim (tincan21)
Jaeyong Jo
James Harren
Jeff Wamester
Jerome K. Moore
Joe Madureira (Joe Mad)
Joel Jurion
Joe Olson
John Timms
Jon Diesta
Jon Sommariva
Joshua Covey
Joslin Jorjet
J. Scott Campbell
Juarez Ricci
Justin Rodrigues

Karioks
Kenneth Anderson
Kevin Keele
Kim Jung Gi

Lavah (Volta Ilustracion)
Lene Chavez (BezerroBizarro)
Linda Chen (Ying Chen)
Loish (Lois Van Baarle)
Loopydave
Ludo Lullabi
Luigi Lucarelli (Luigi L)
Luis Gadea

Mahmud Asrar
Marcio Takara
Mark Brooks (diablo2003)
Mark Crilley
Martin Abel
Mathieu Beaulieu
Mathieu Reynes
Mattias Adolfsson
Meghan Hetrick
Michael Bills
Michael Buffington Jr.
Mike Bowden
Mike Butkus
Mike Henry (Zatransis)
Milenko Tunjic
Minoh Kim
Mister Hope

Pascal Campion
Paul Renaud
Pedro Delgado
Pedro Perez
Phil Bourassa

Rachel Saunders
Rad Sechrist
Randy Bishop
Raul Moreno
Raul Trevino
REIQ
Rene Cordova
Riley Rossmo
Rob Laro
Robert Porter (Robaato)
RobbVision (Robb Mommaerts)
Roger Cruz
Ryan Hall (frogbillgo)
Ryan David Jones
Ryan Ottley
Ryan Woodward

Sam Nielson
Samantha Youssef
Sarah Mensinga
Sean (Cheeks) Galloway
Sergi Brosa
Shaun Healey (Endling)
Simone Kesterton
Stanley Lau (Artgerm)
Steven E. Gordon
Studio Qube

Terry Dodson
Tooninator (Matthew Boismier)
Tori Davis (ToriCat)
t-wei

Warren Louw

XAV

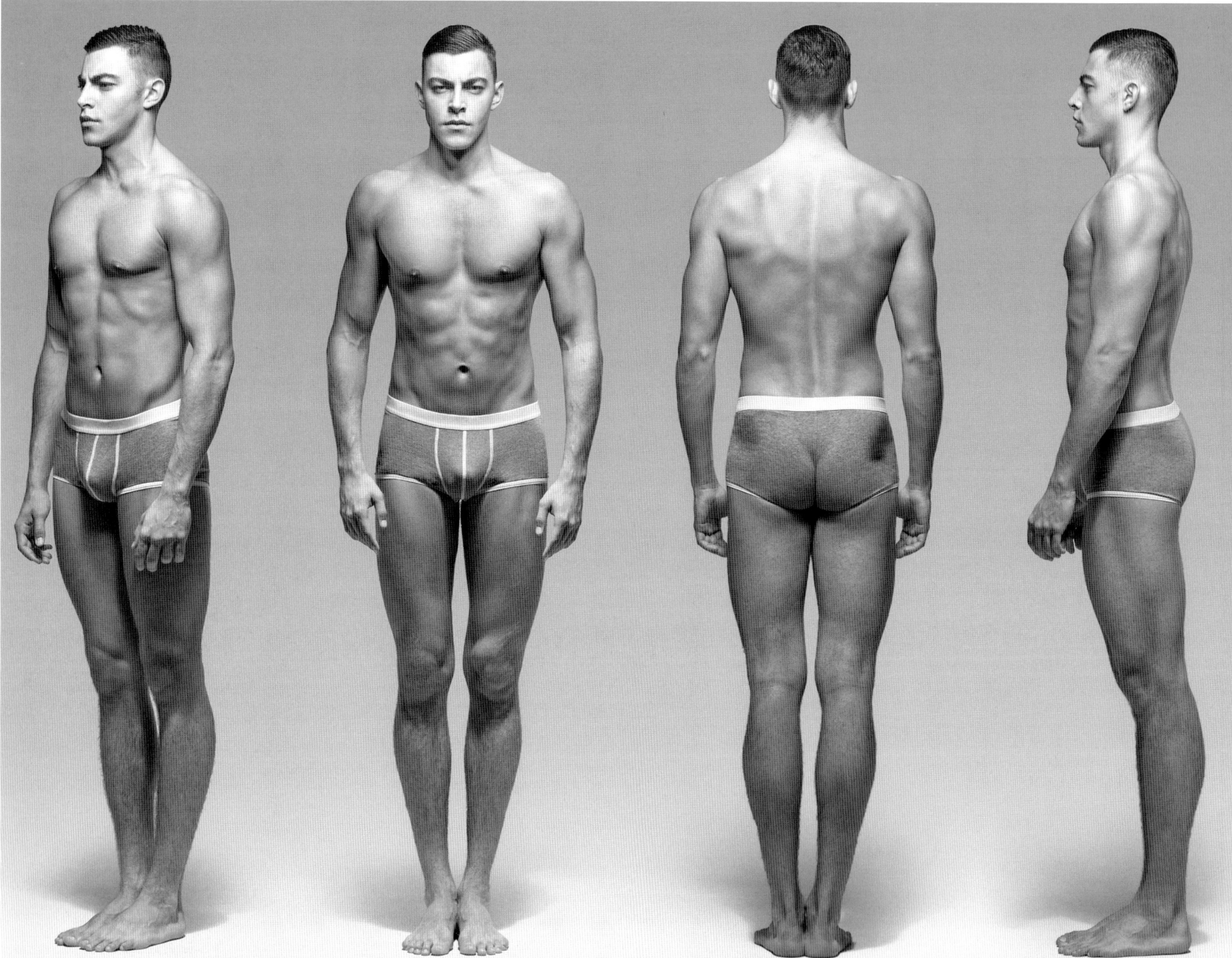

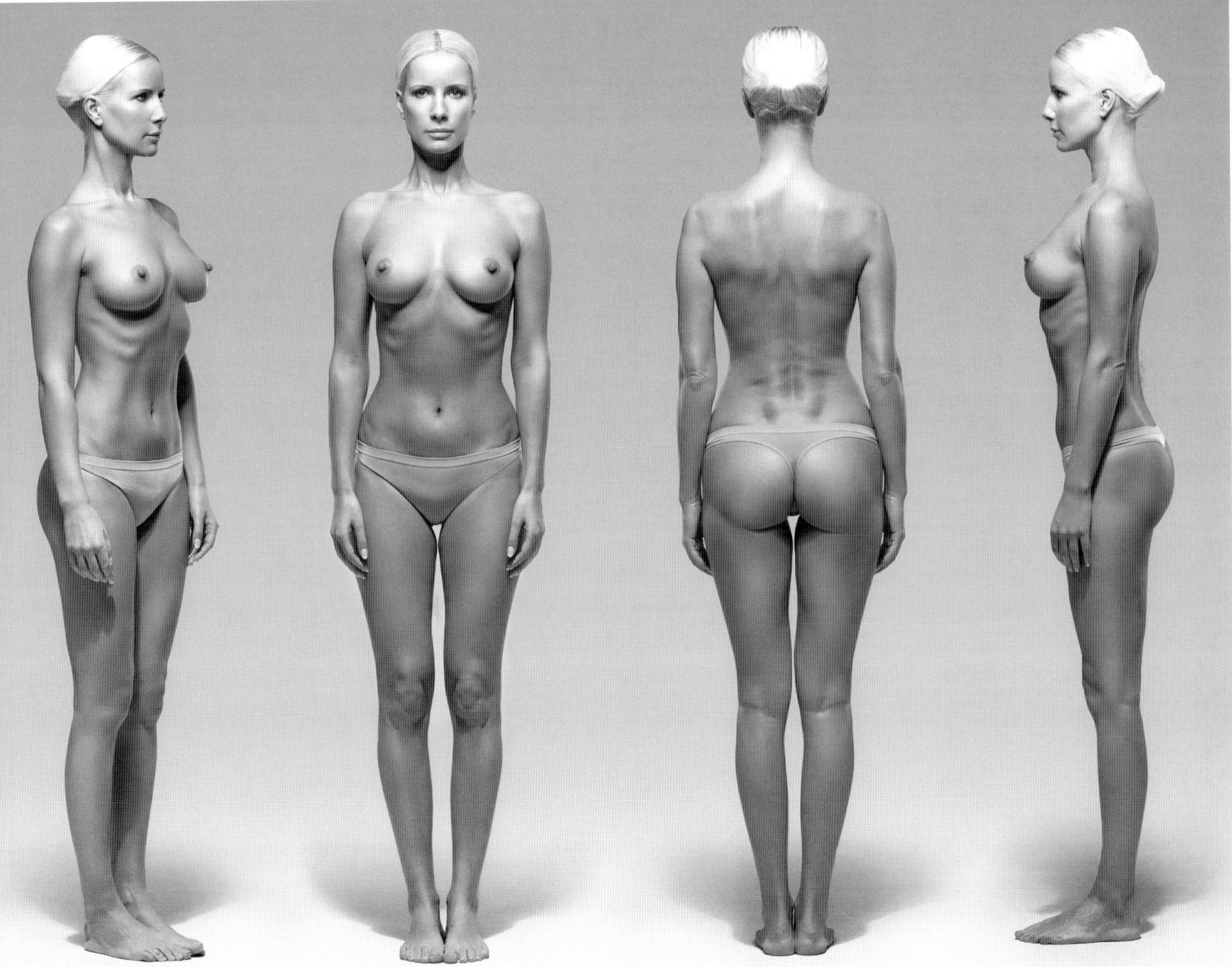

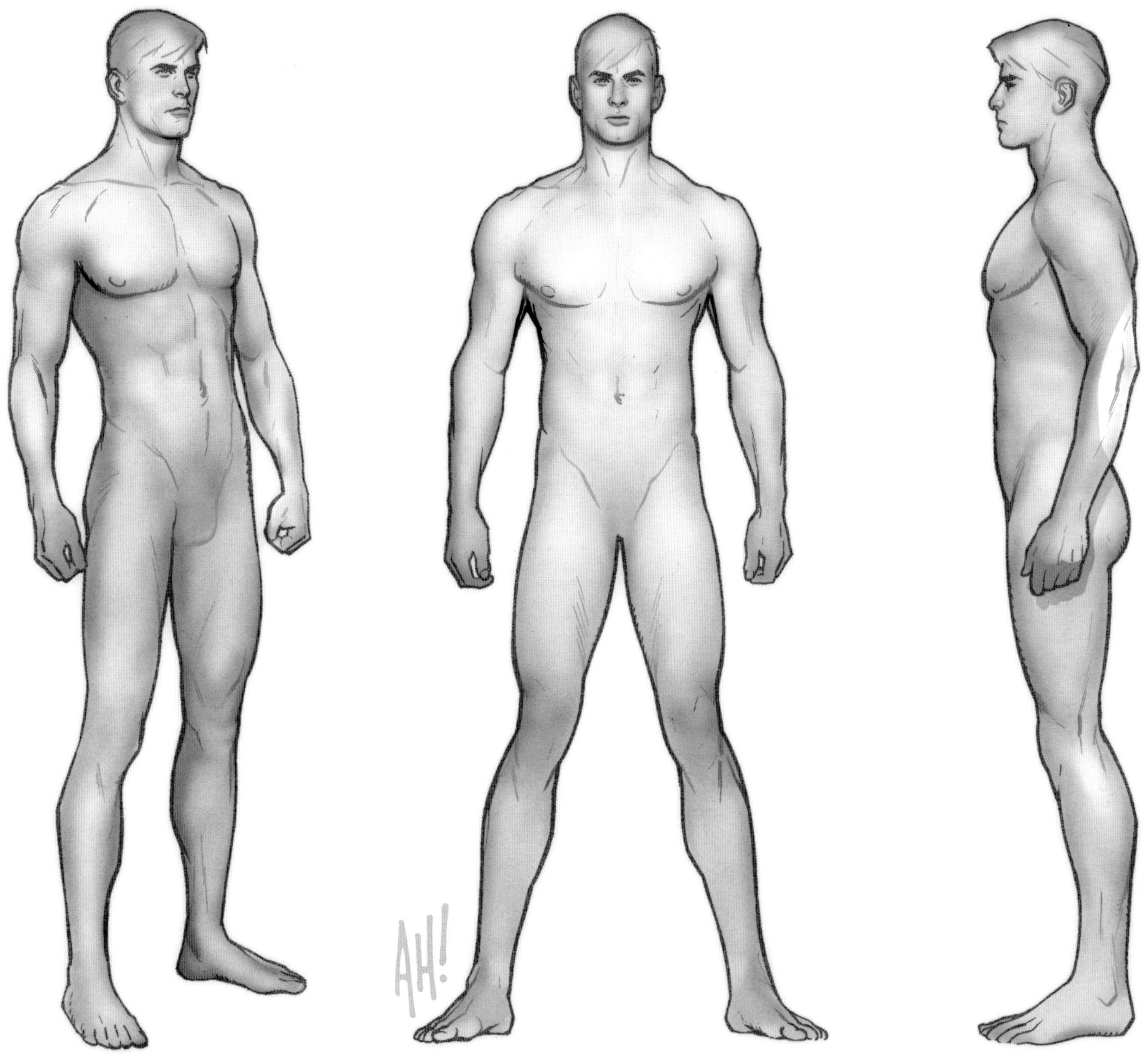

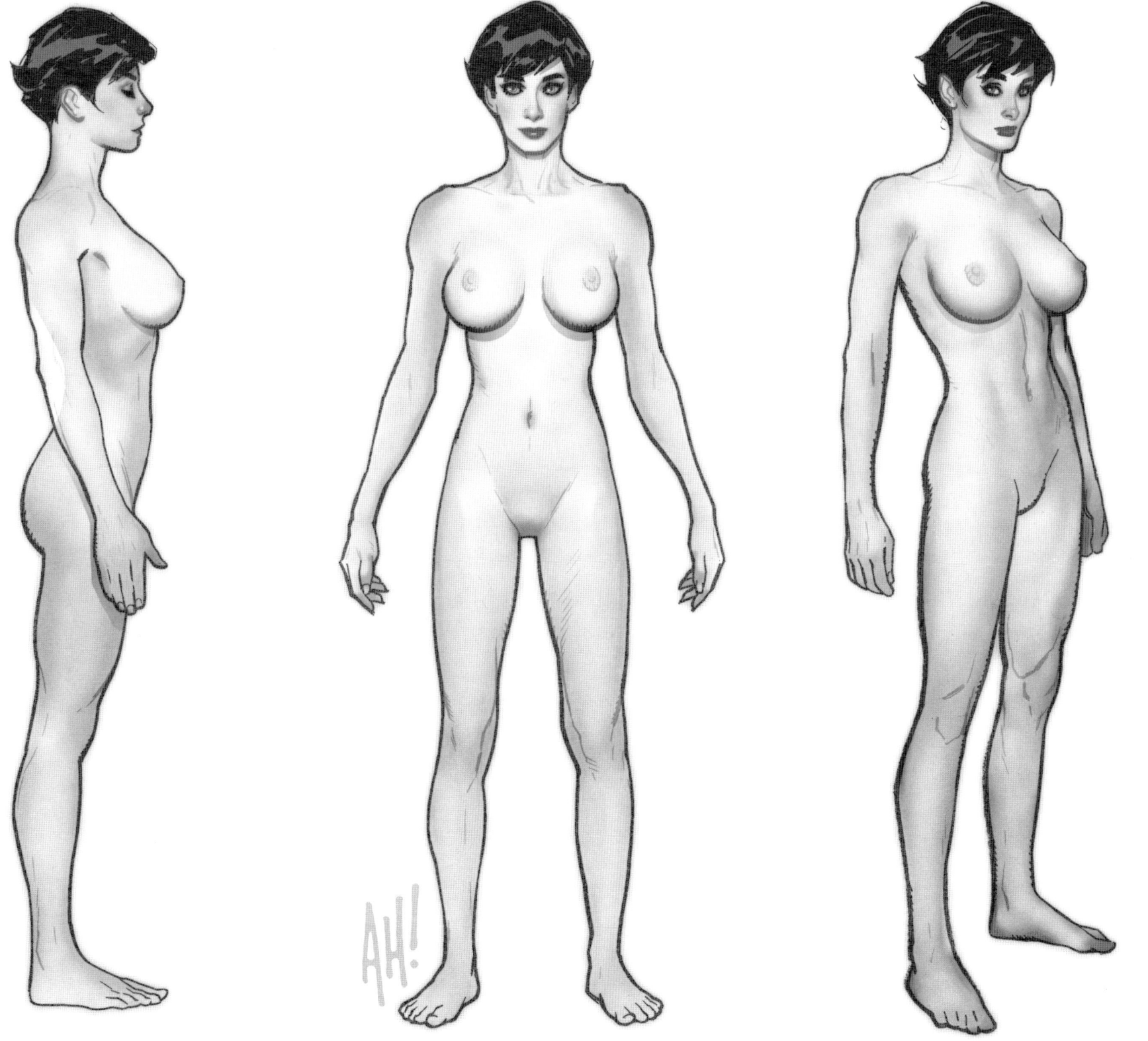

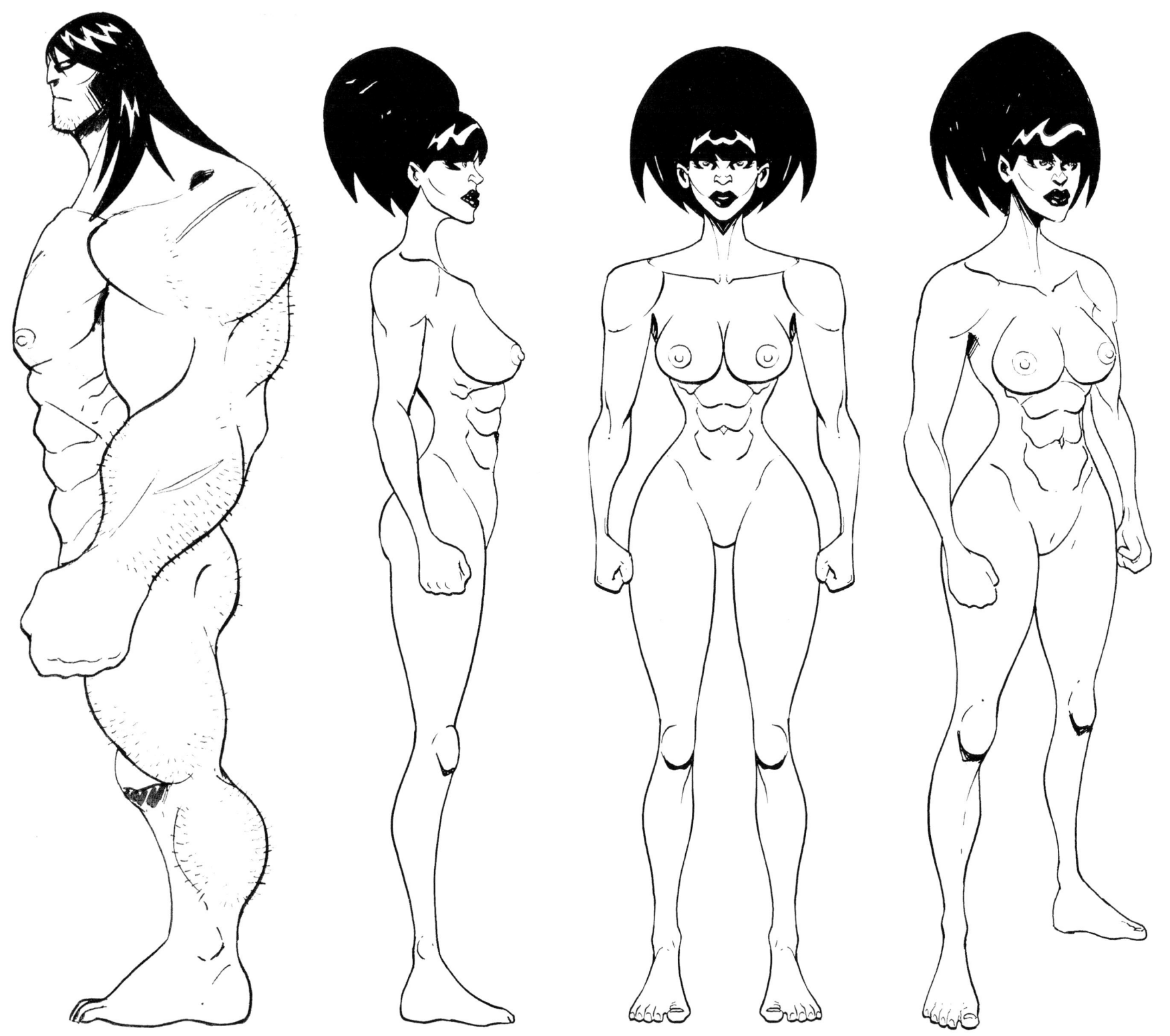

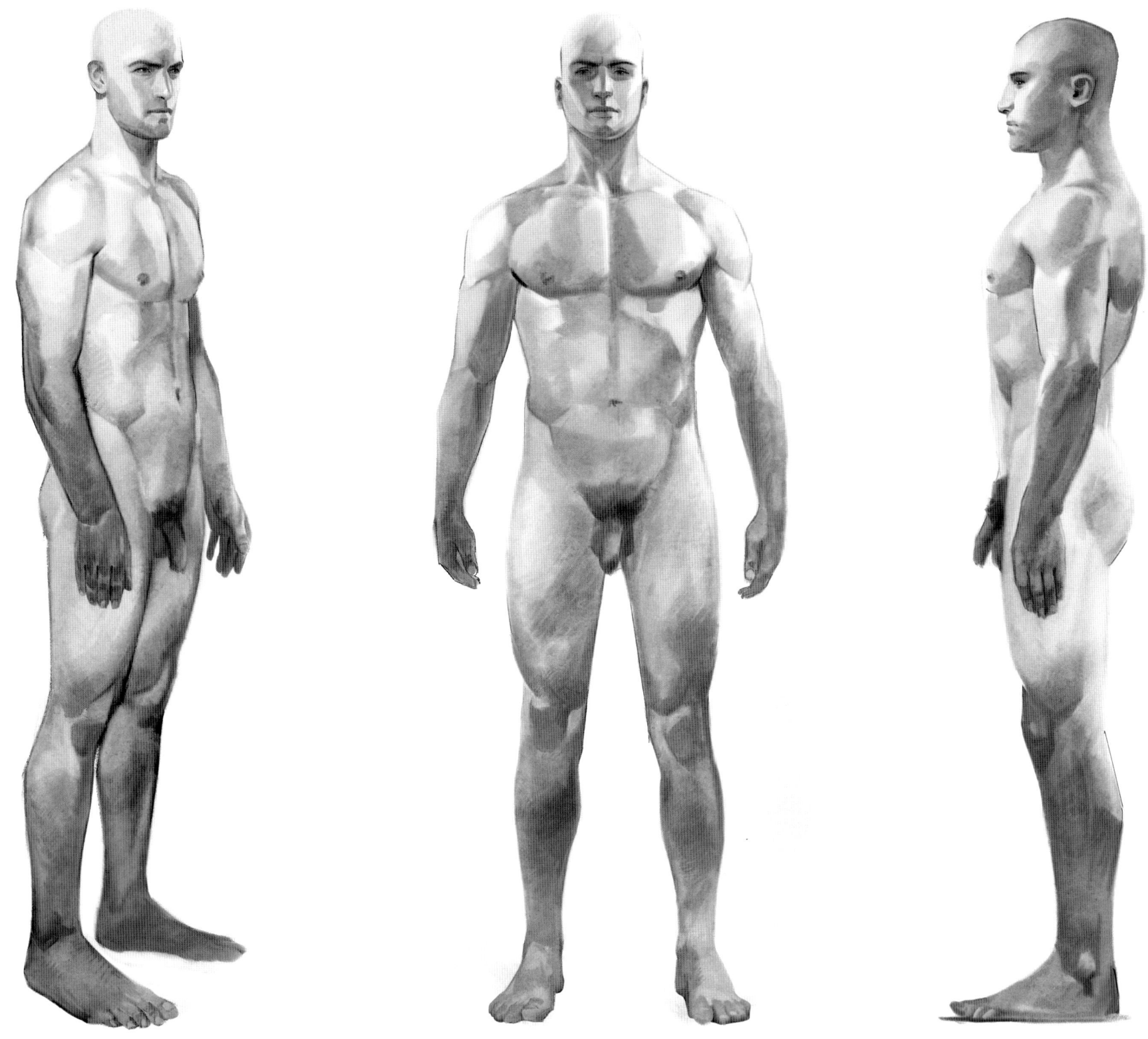

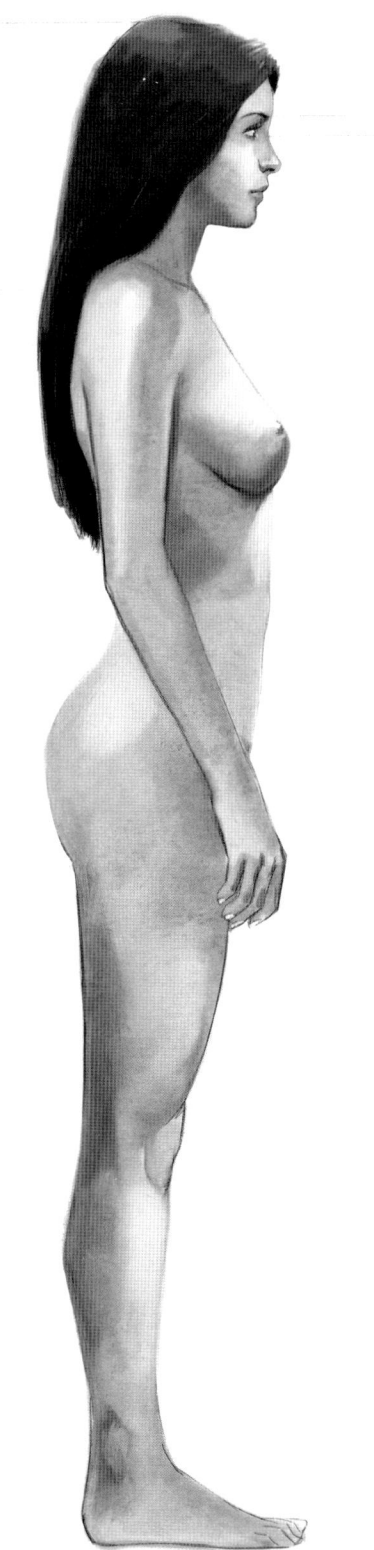
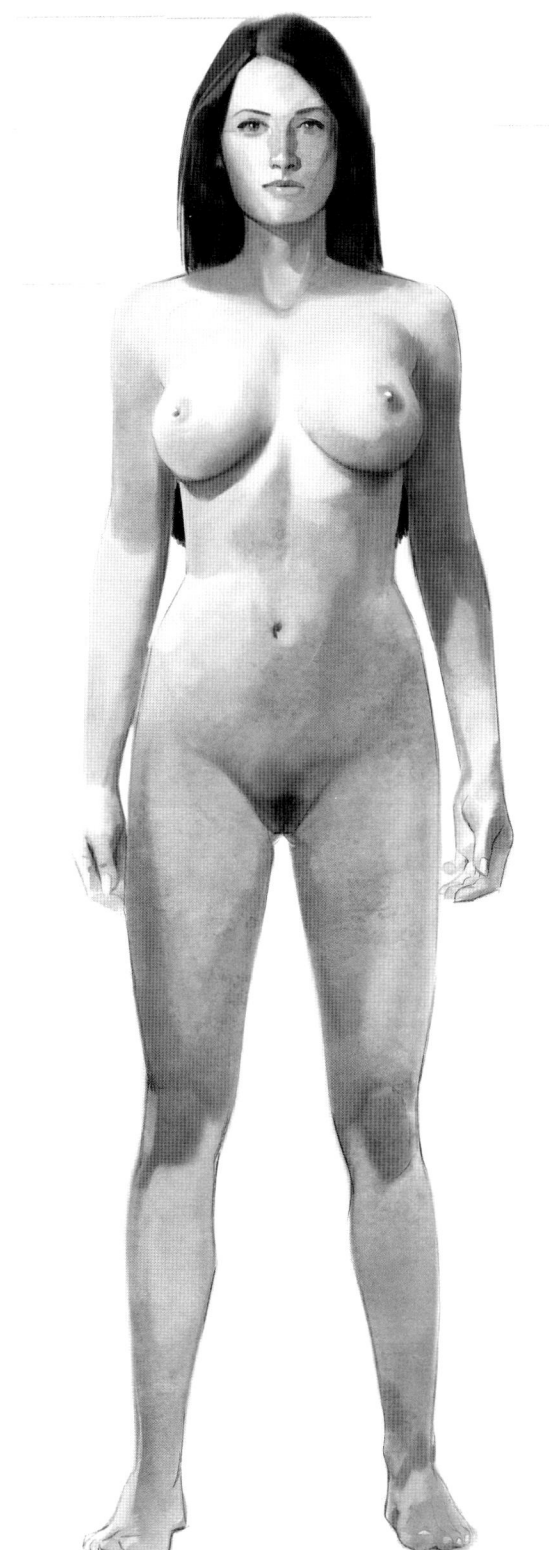
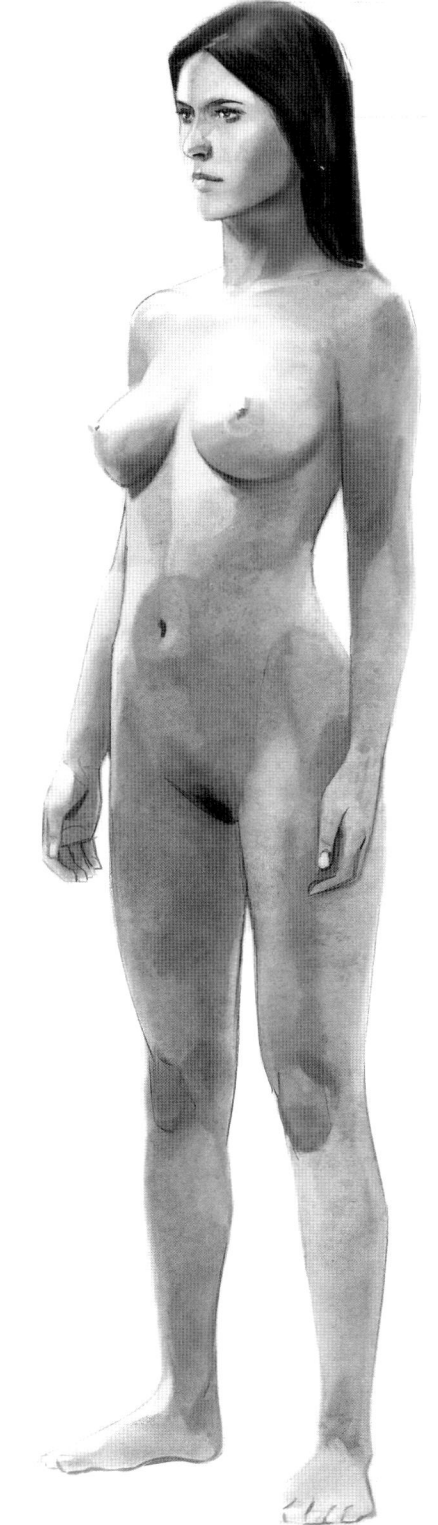

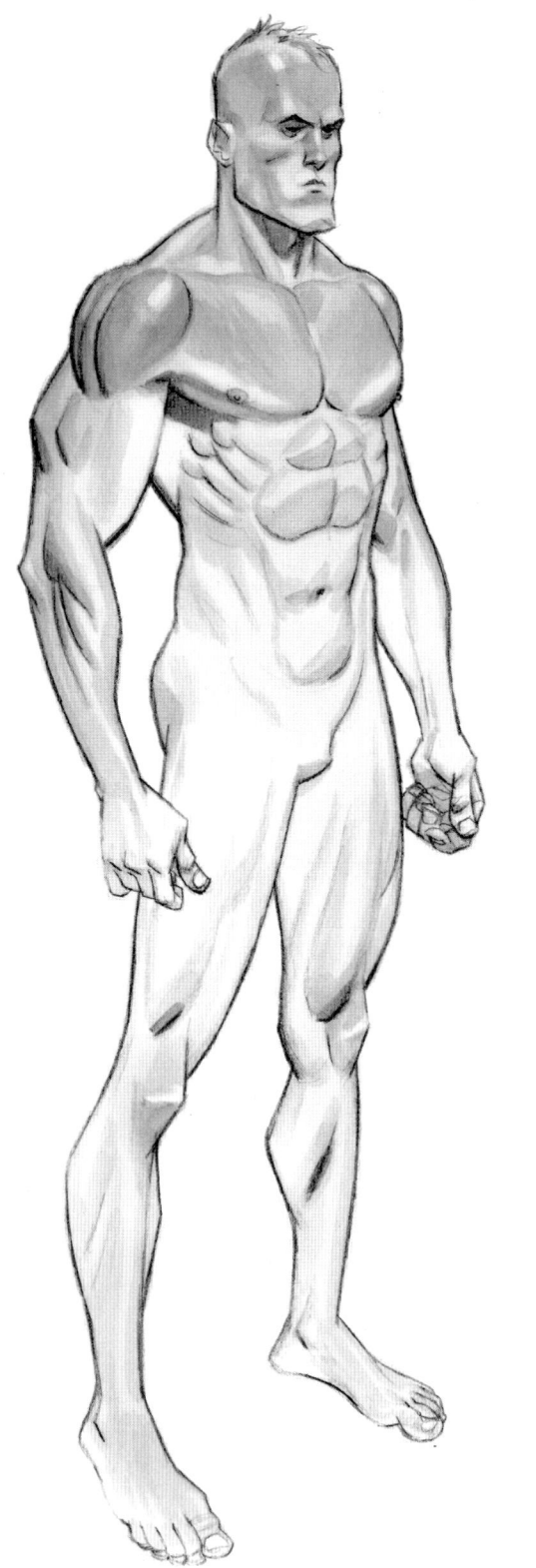
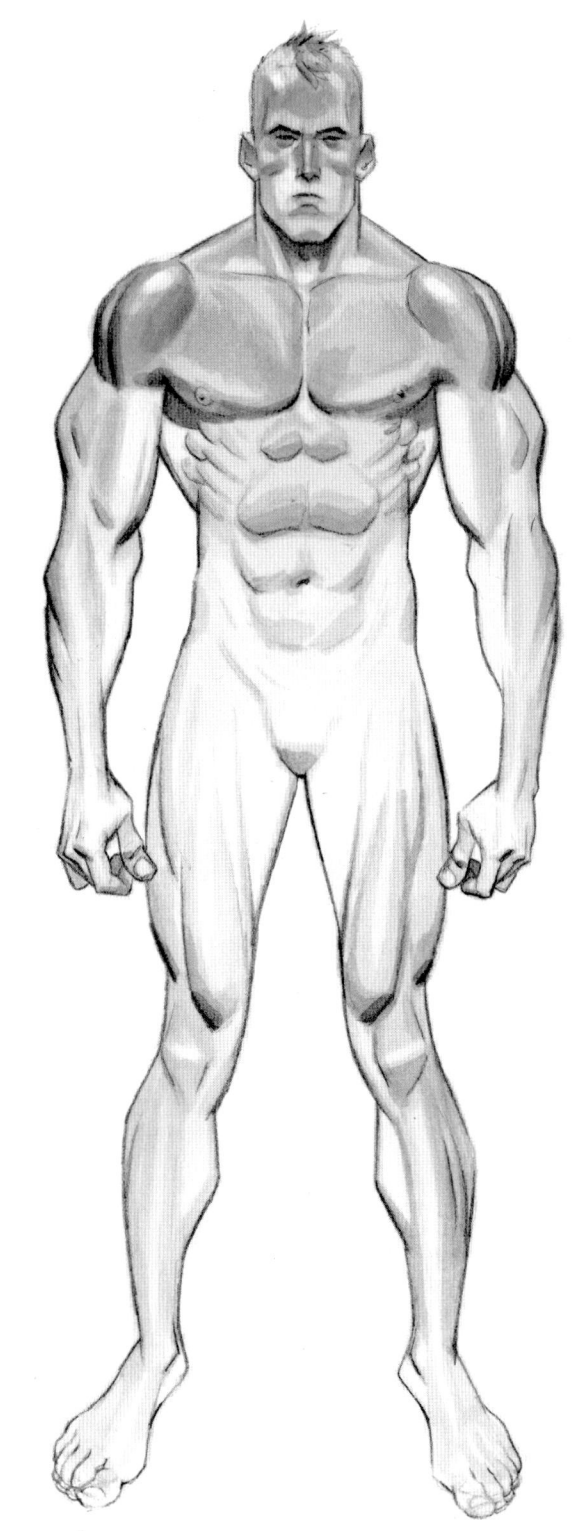
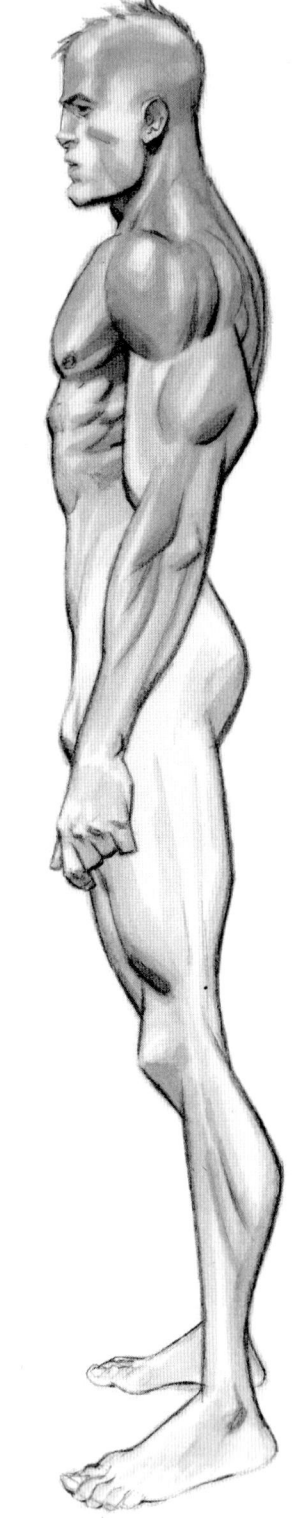

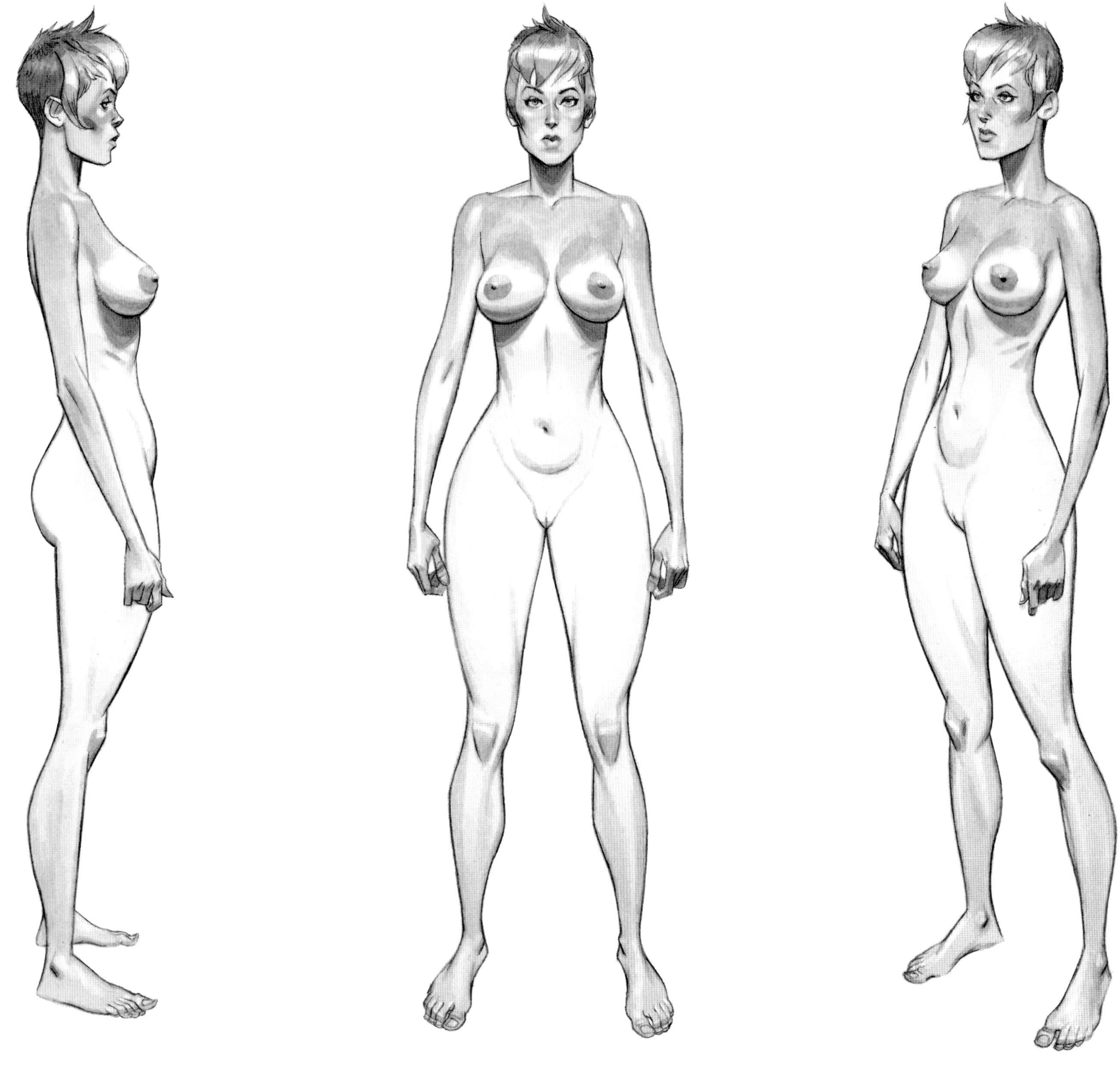

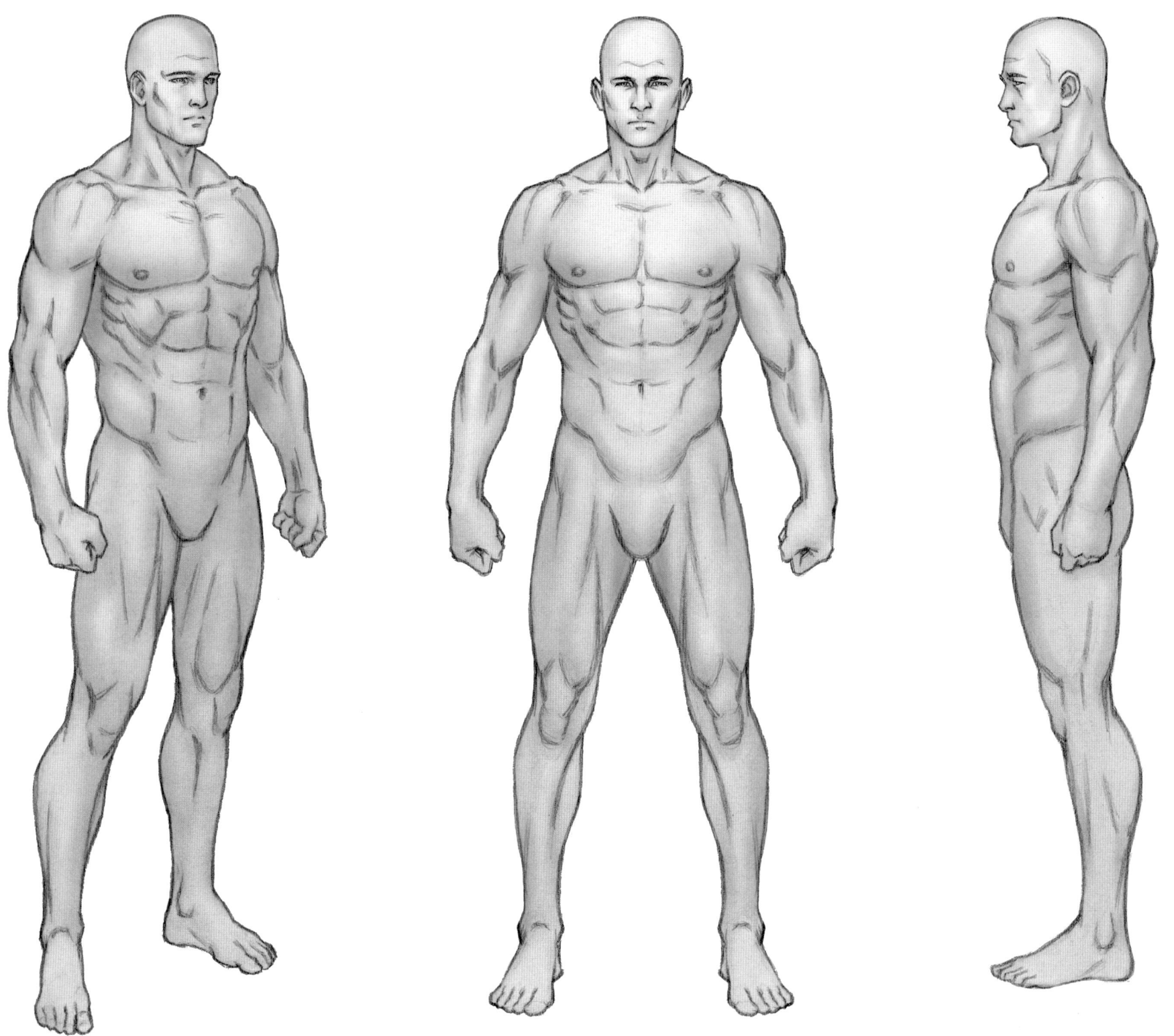

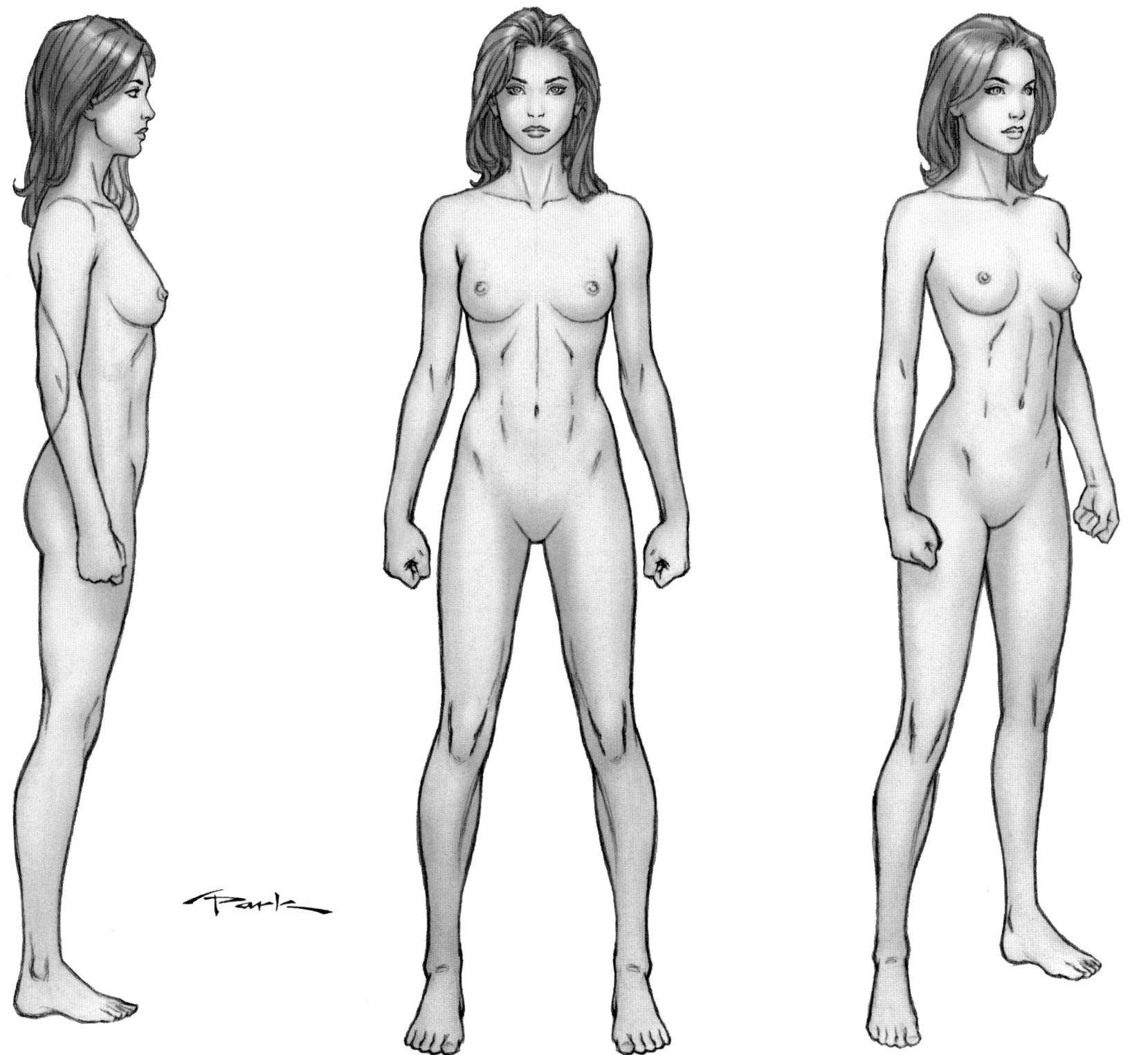

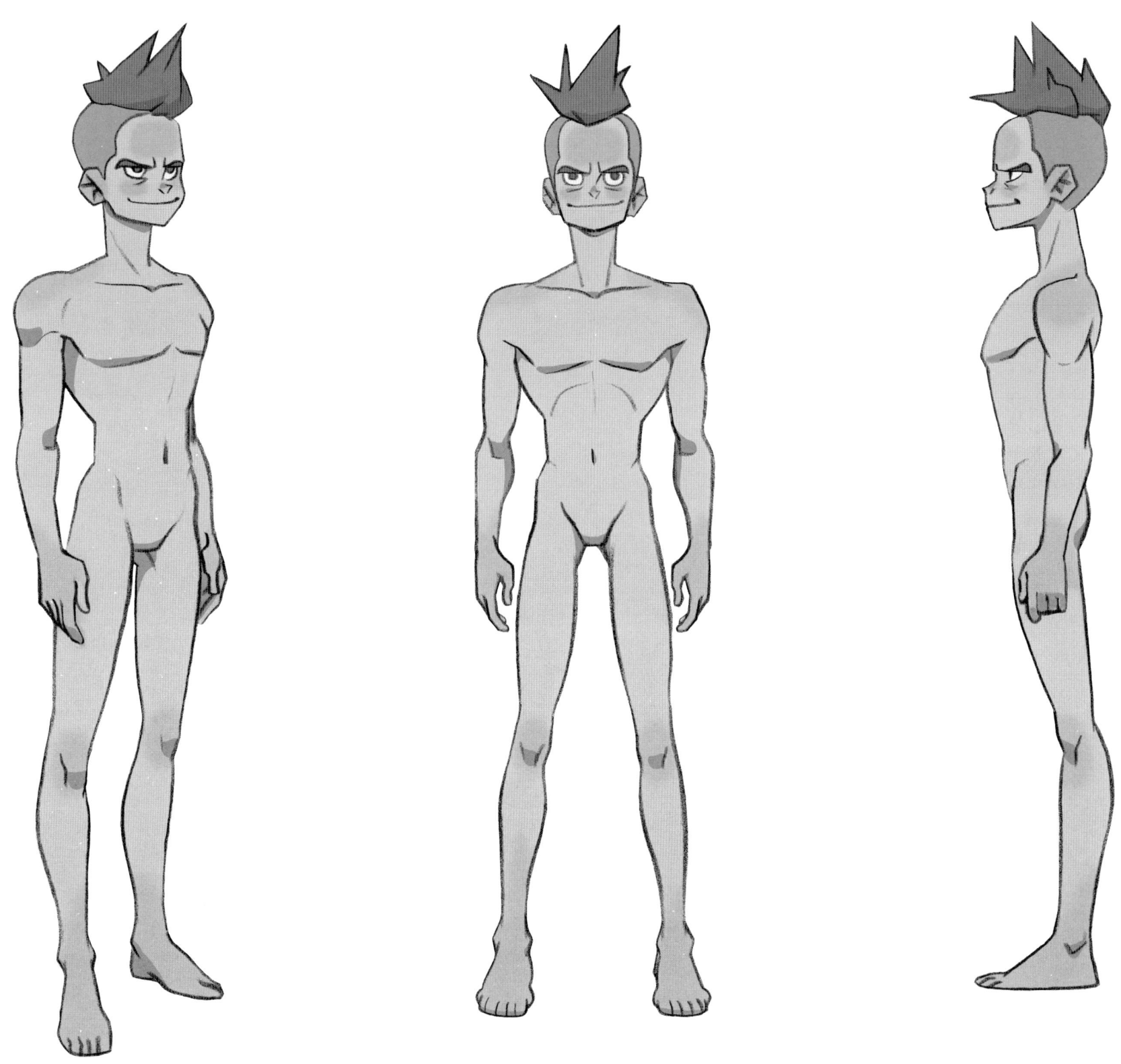

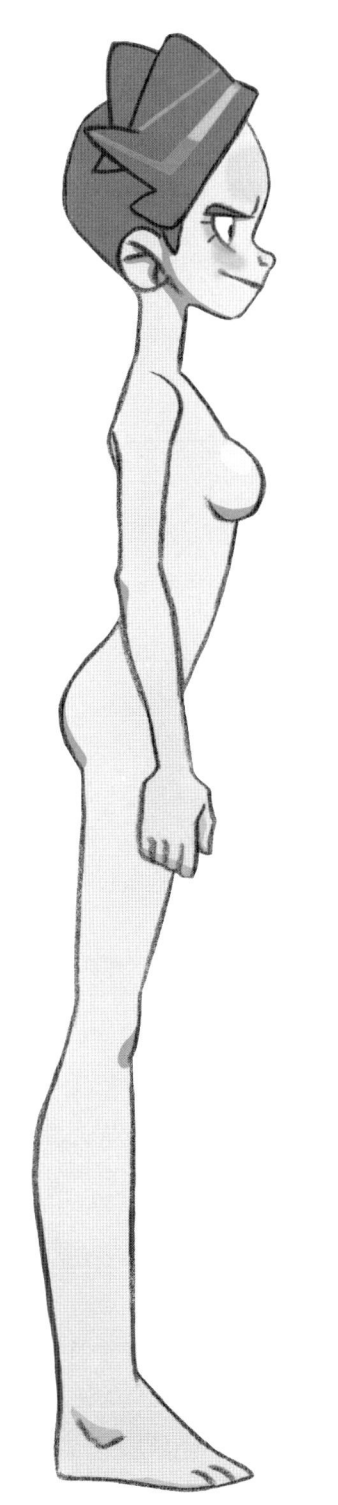
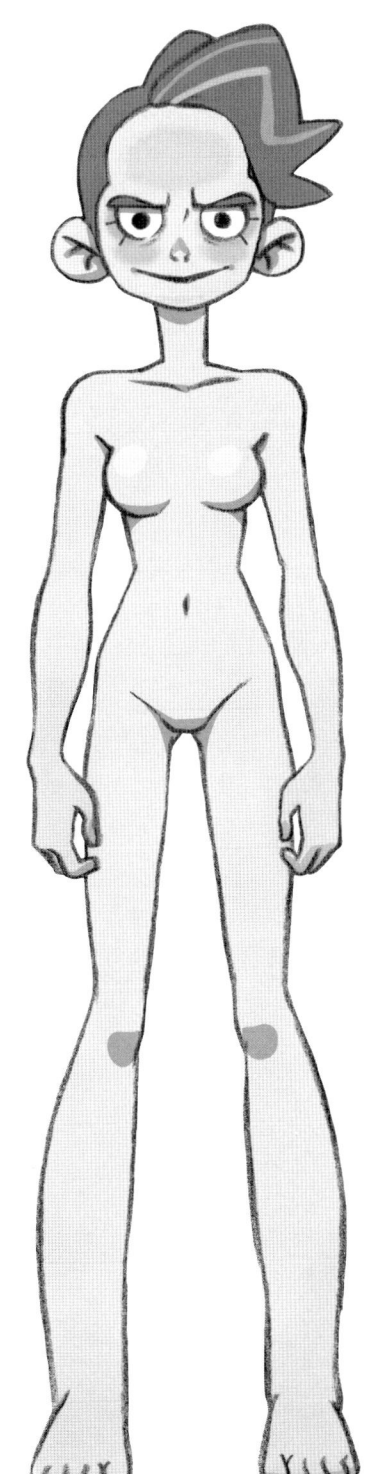
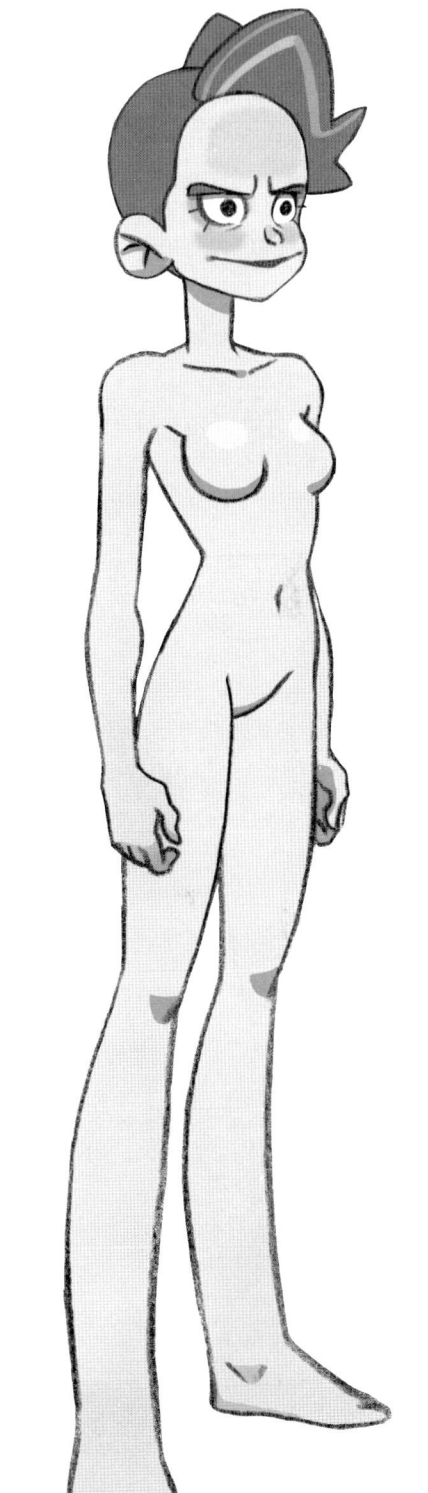

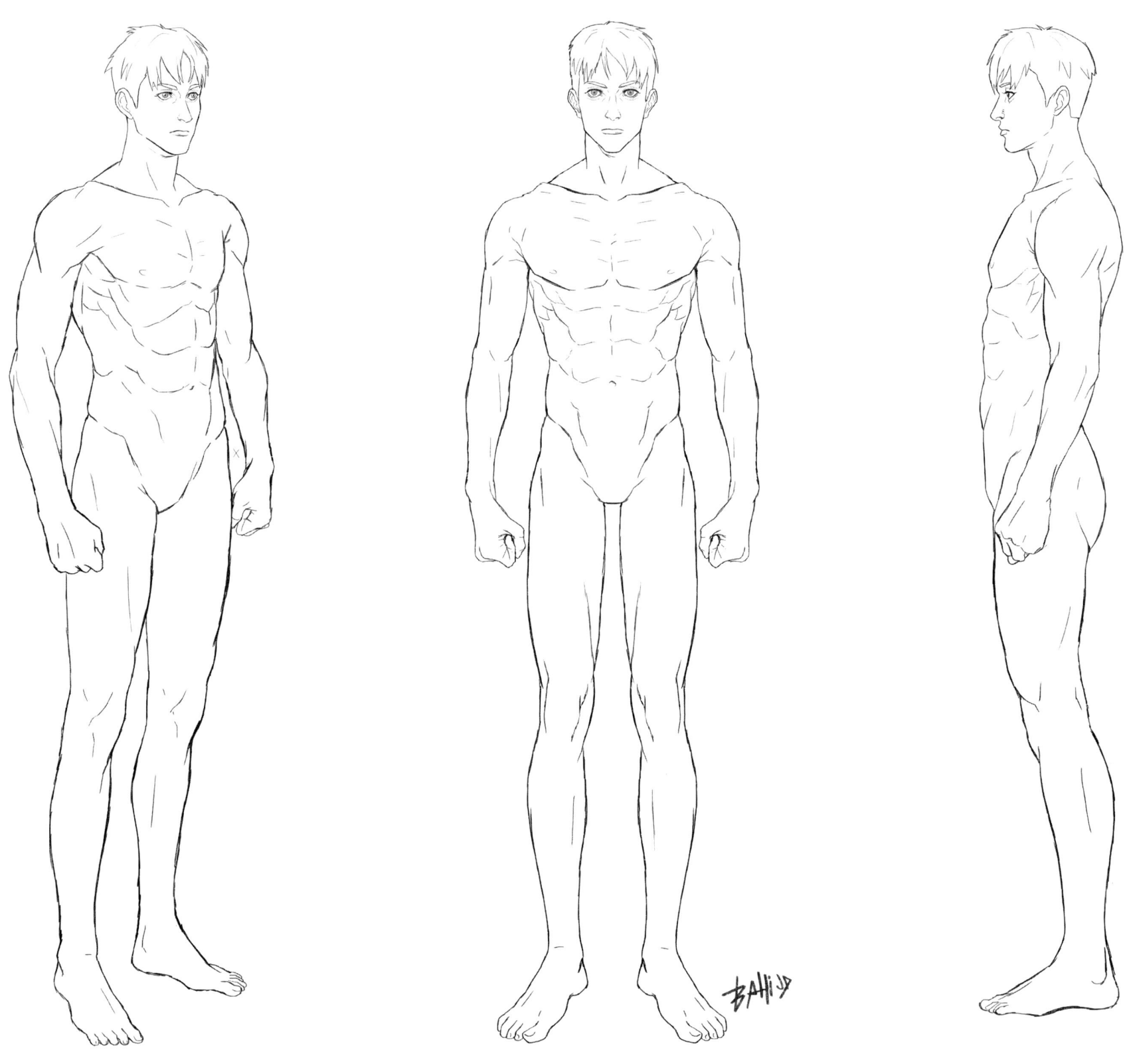

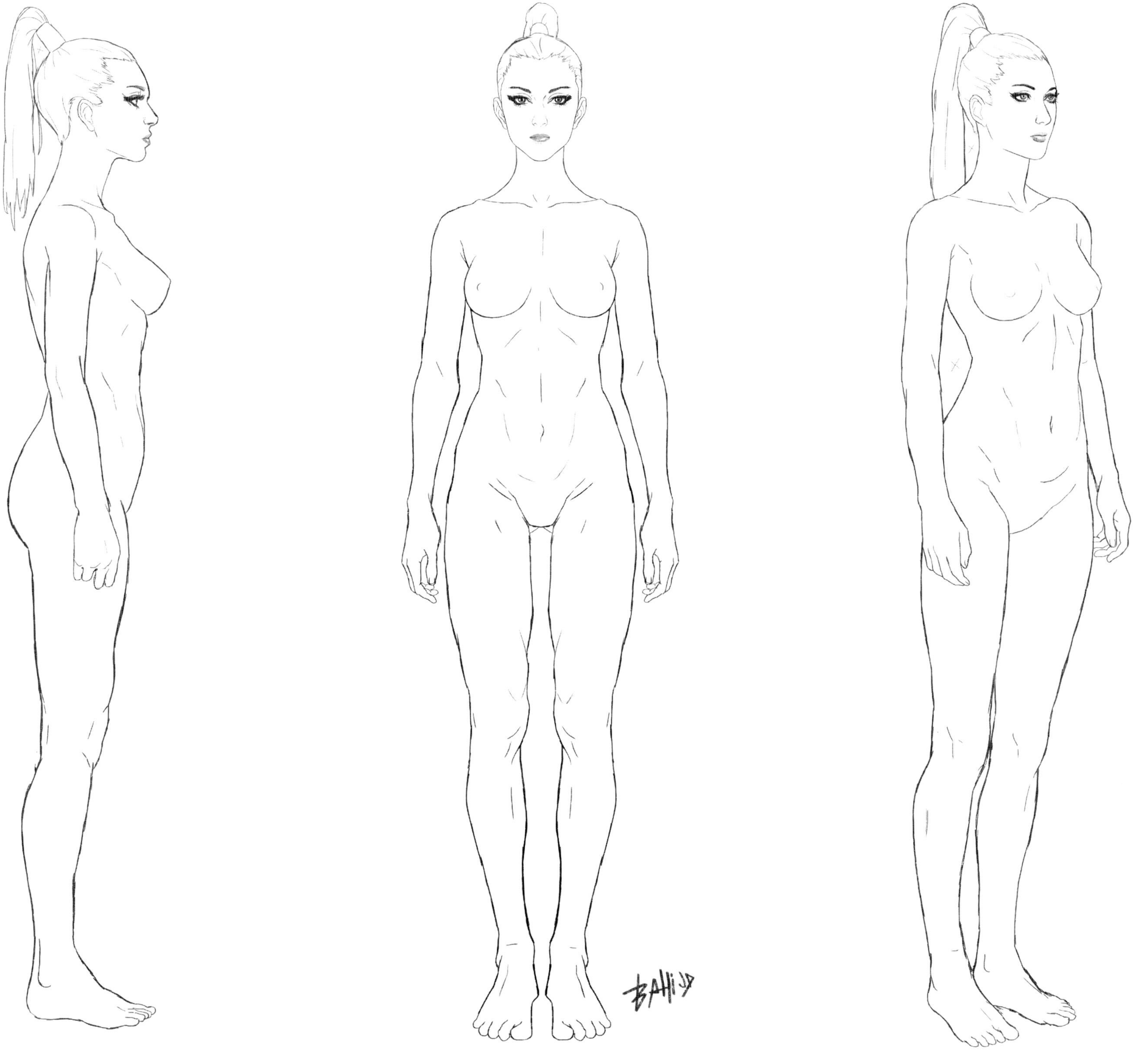

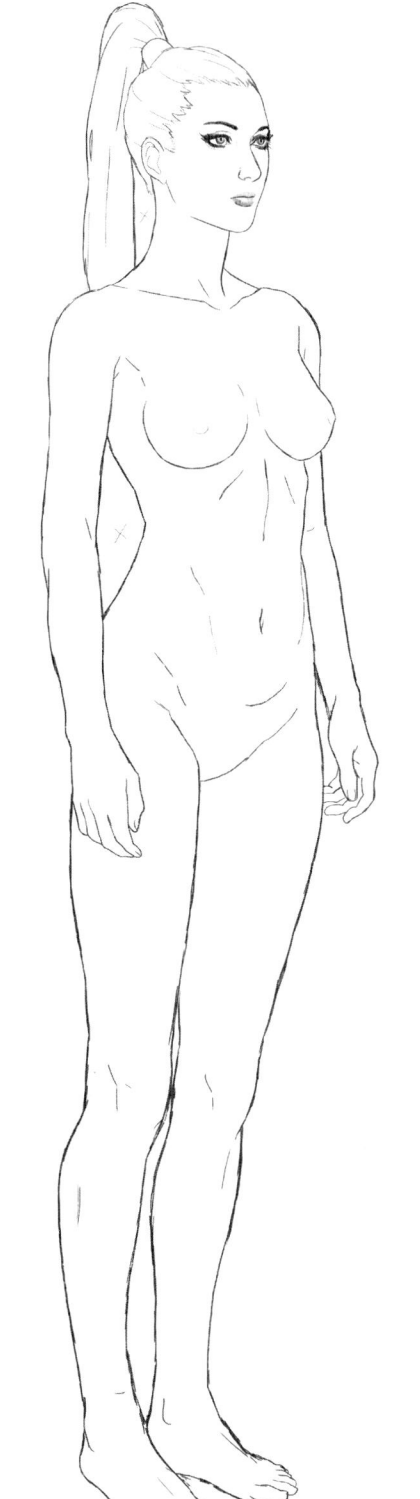

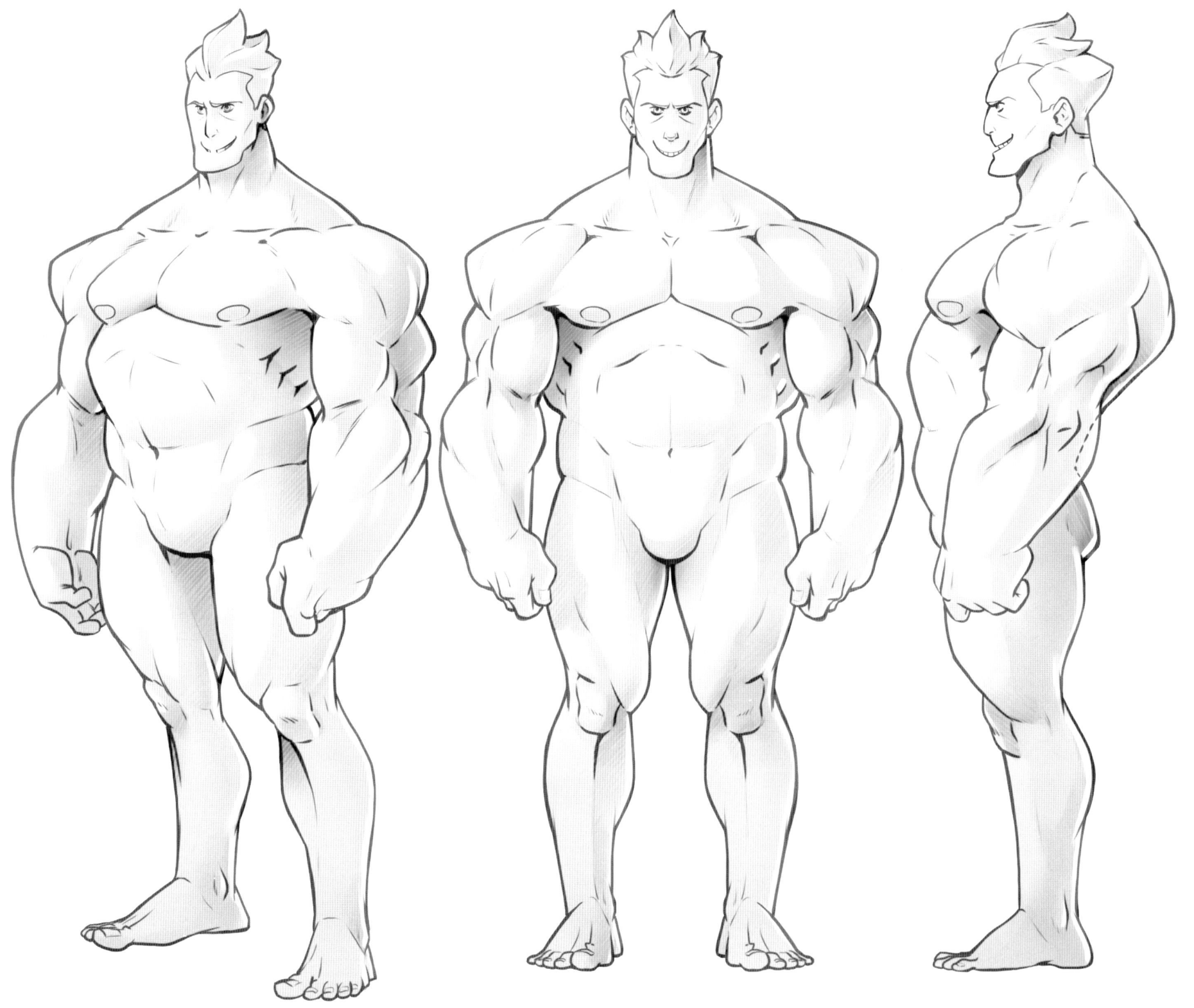

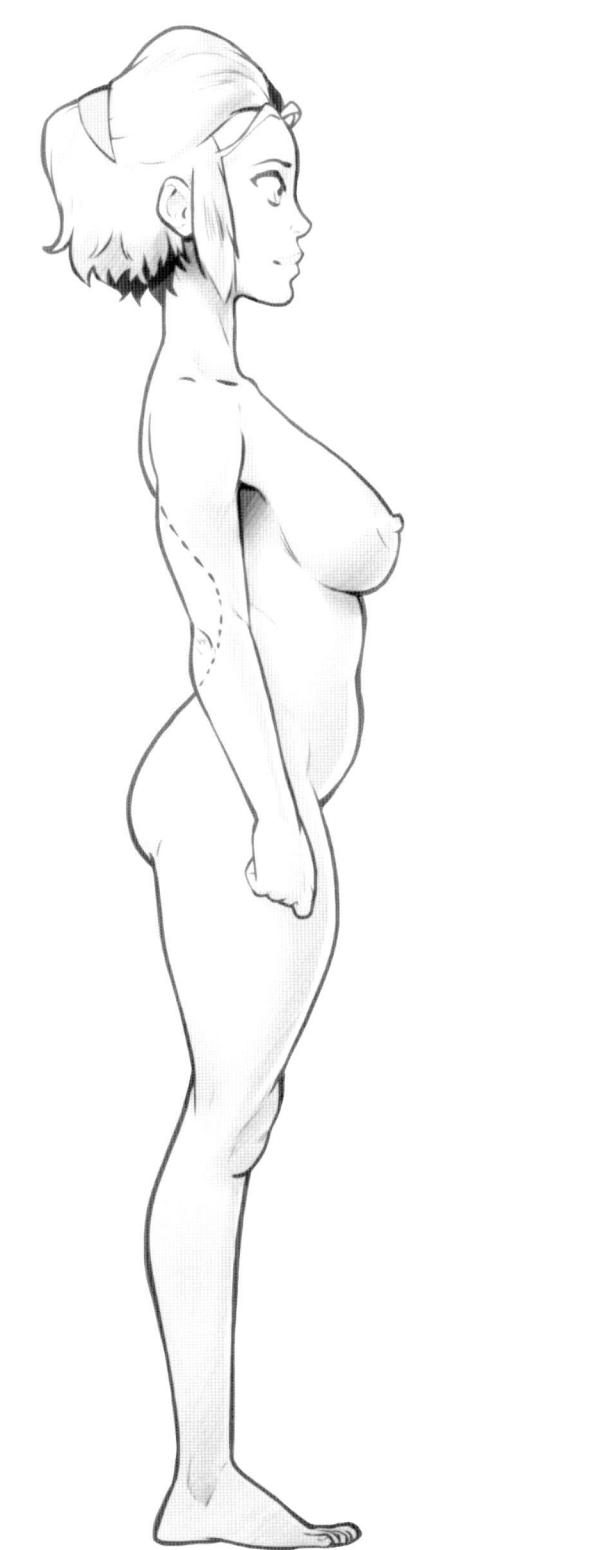
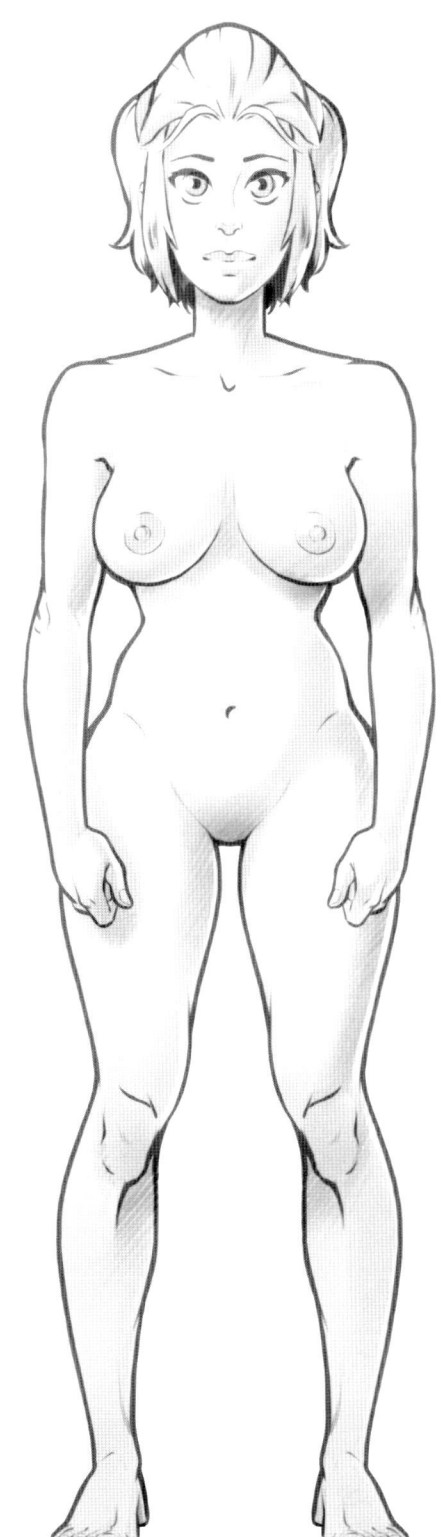

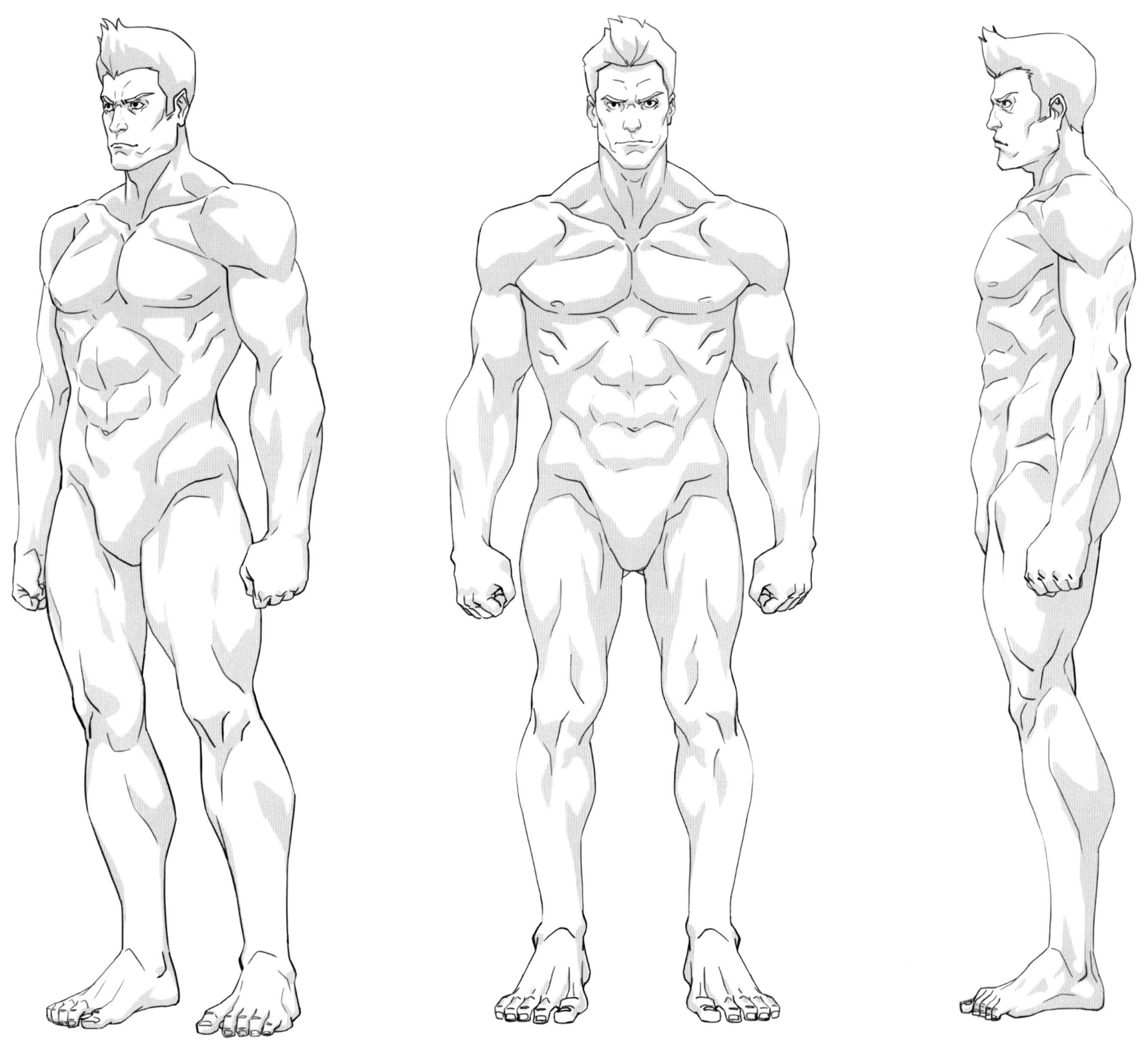

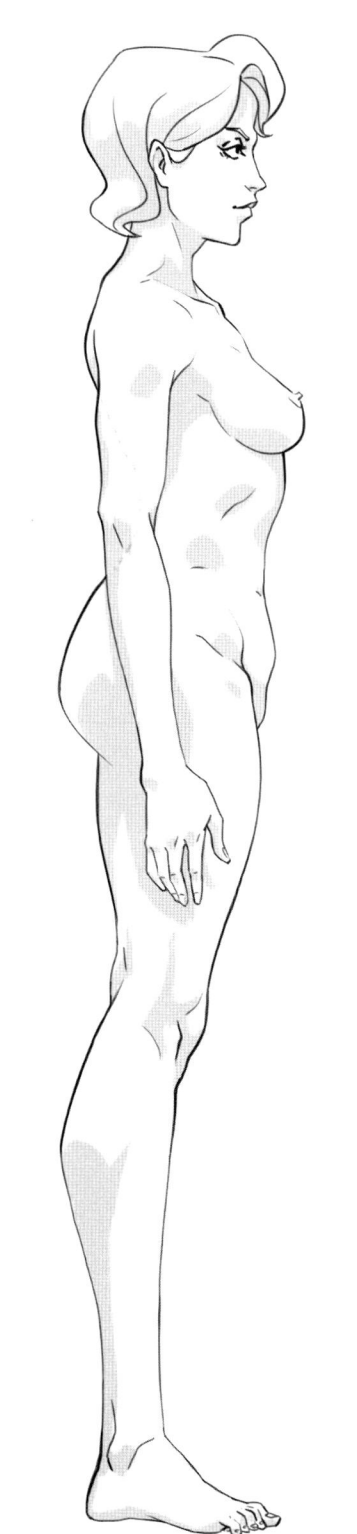
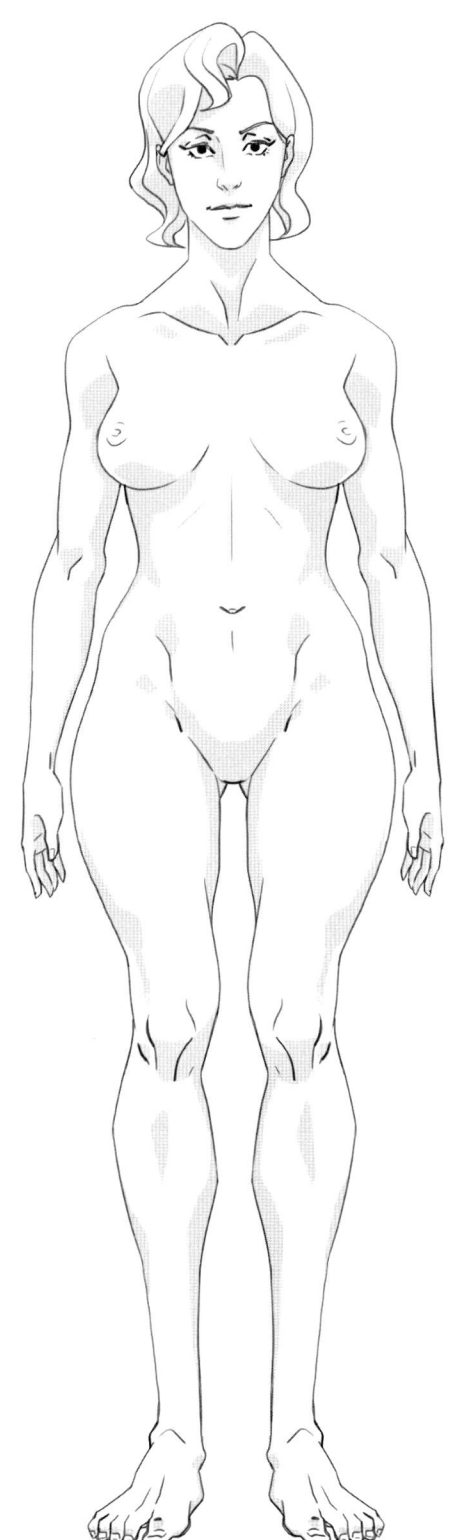
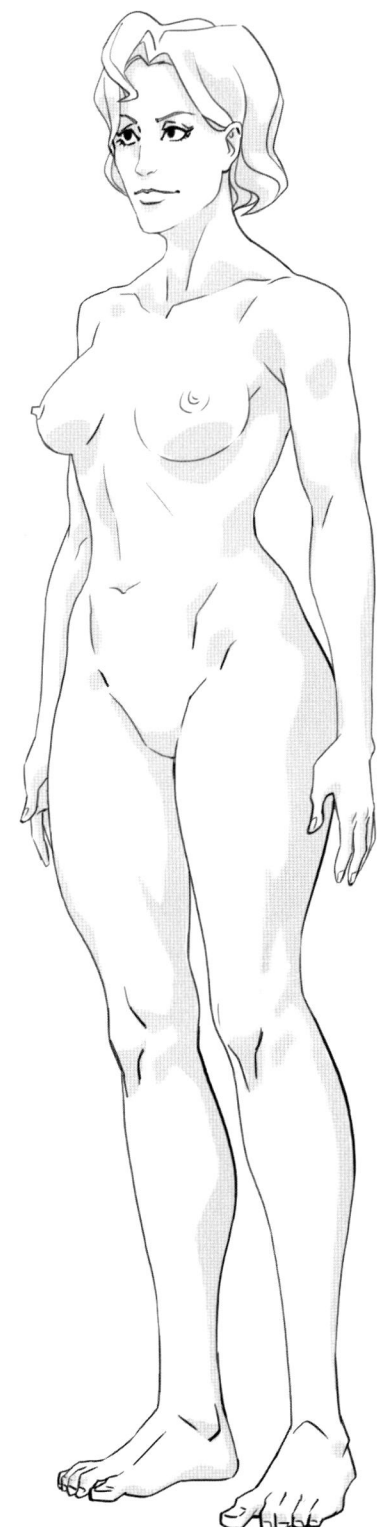

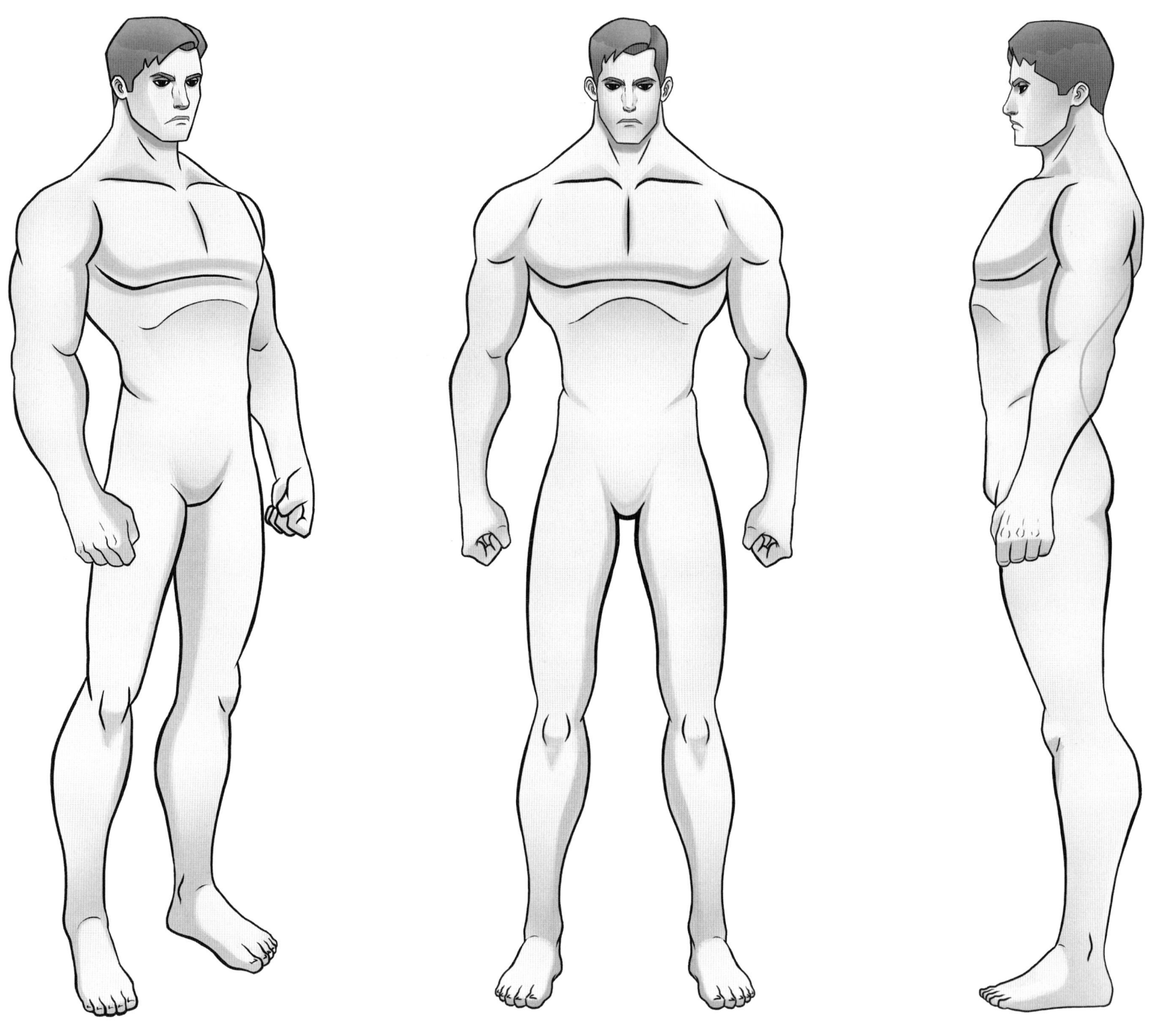

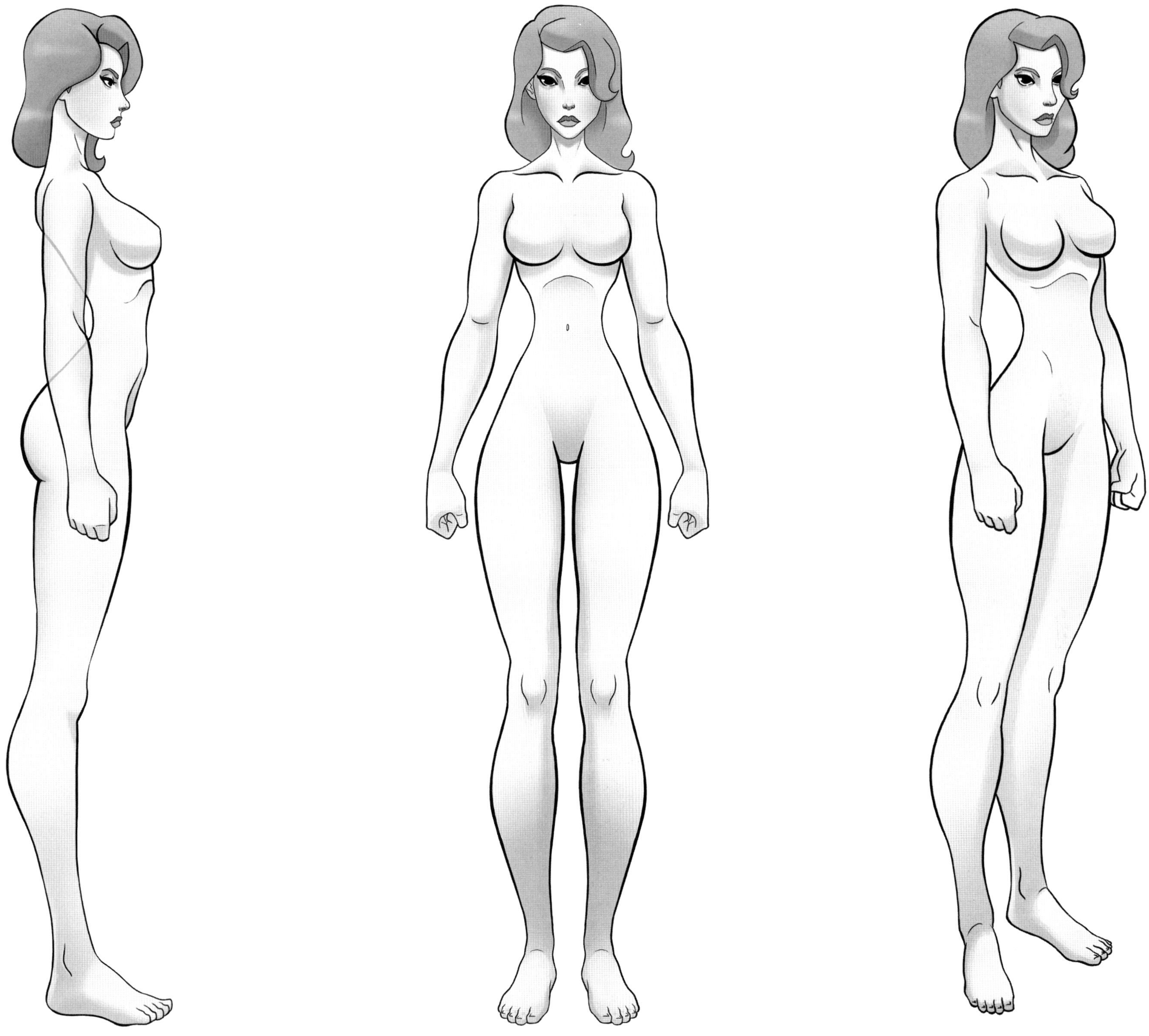

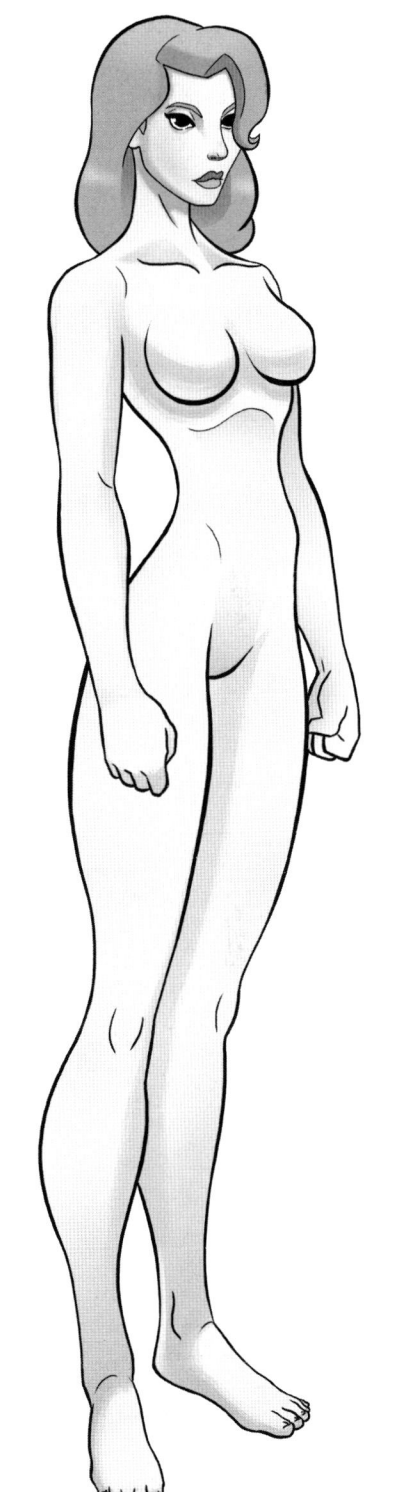

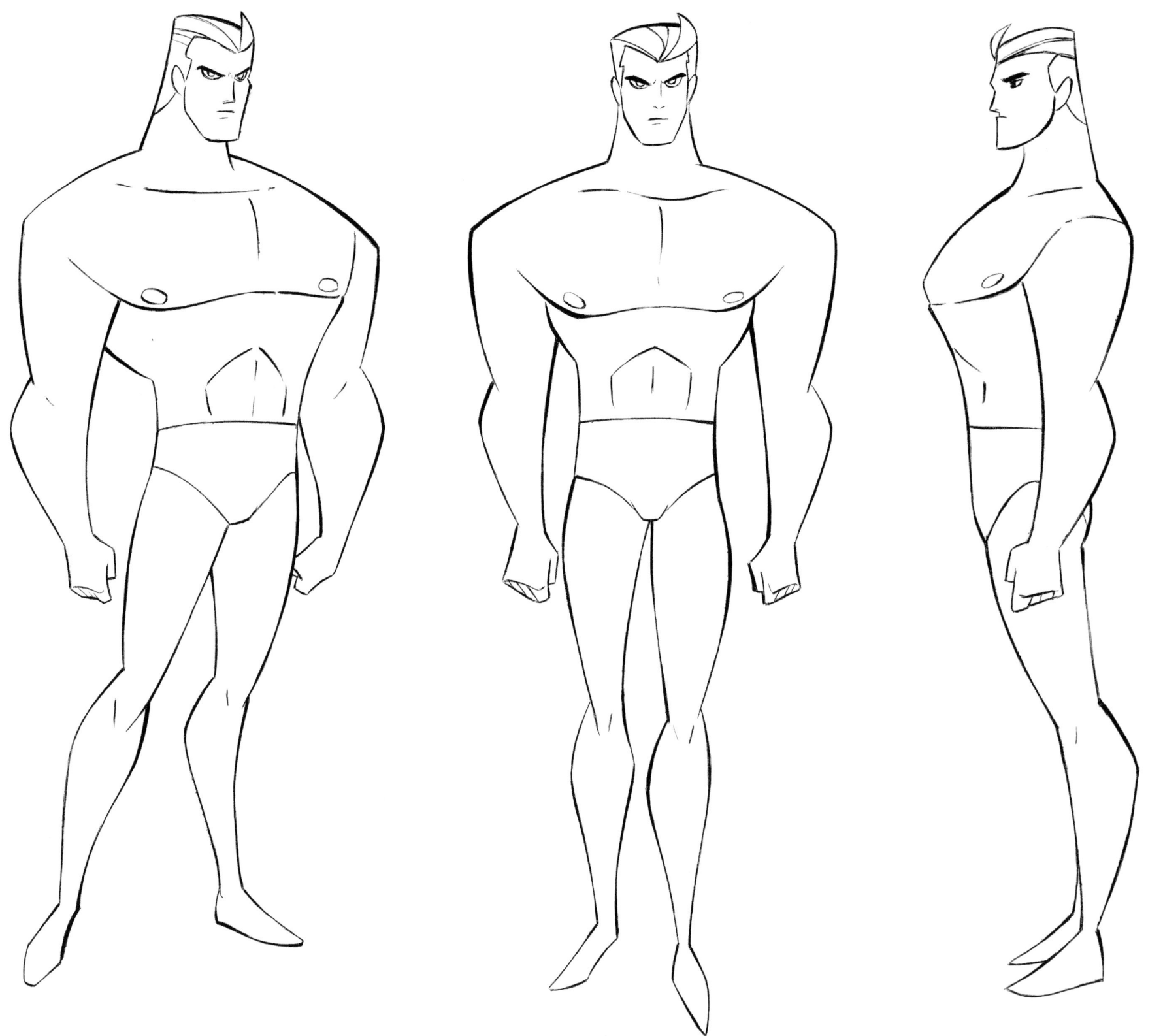

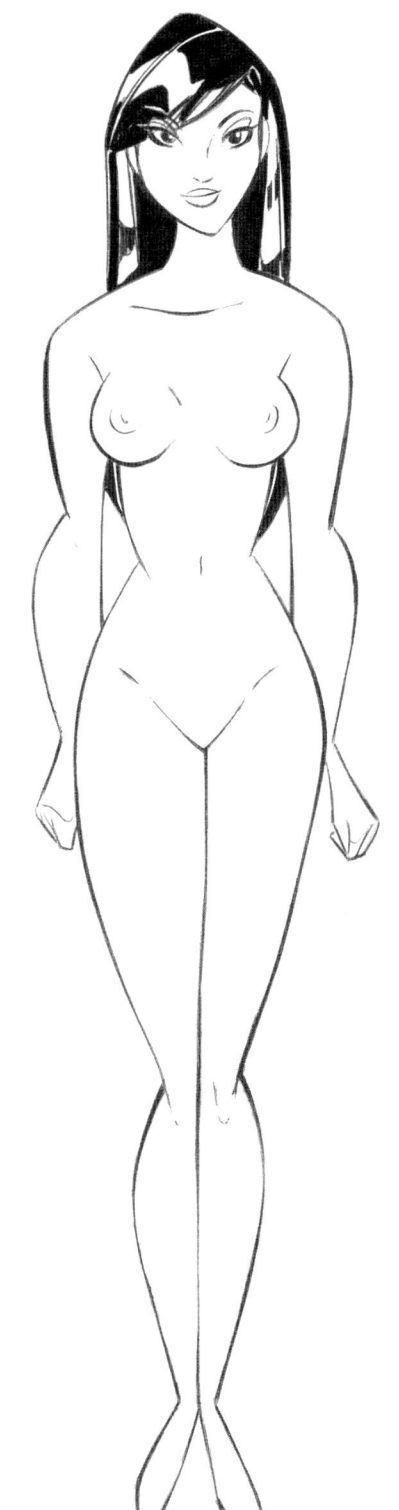
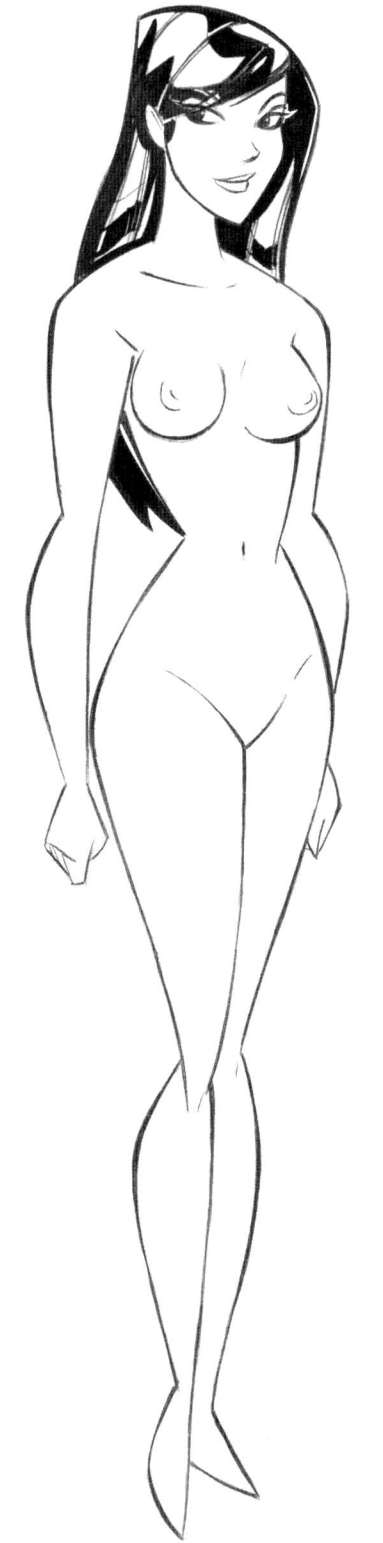

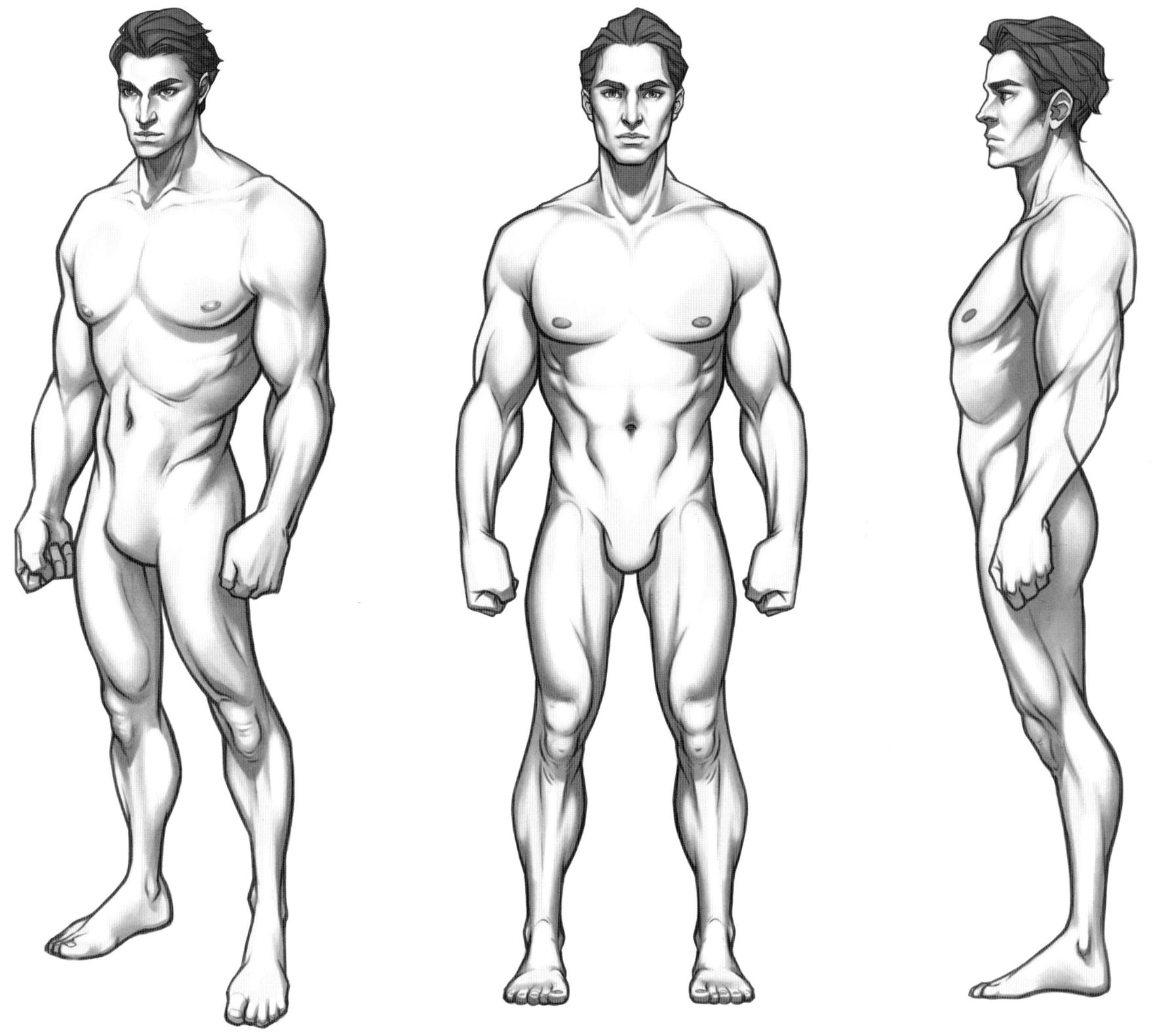

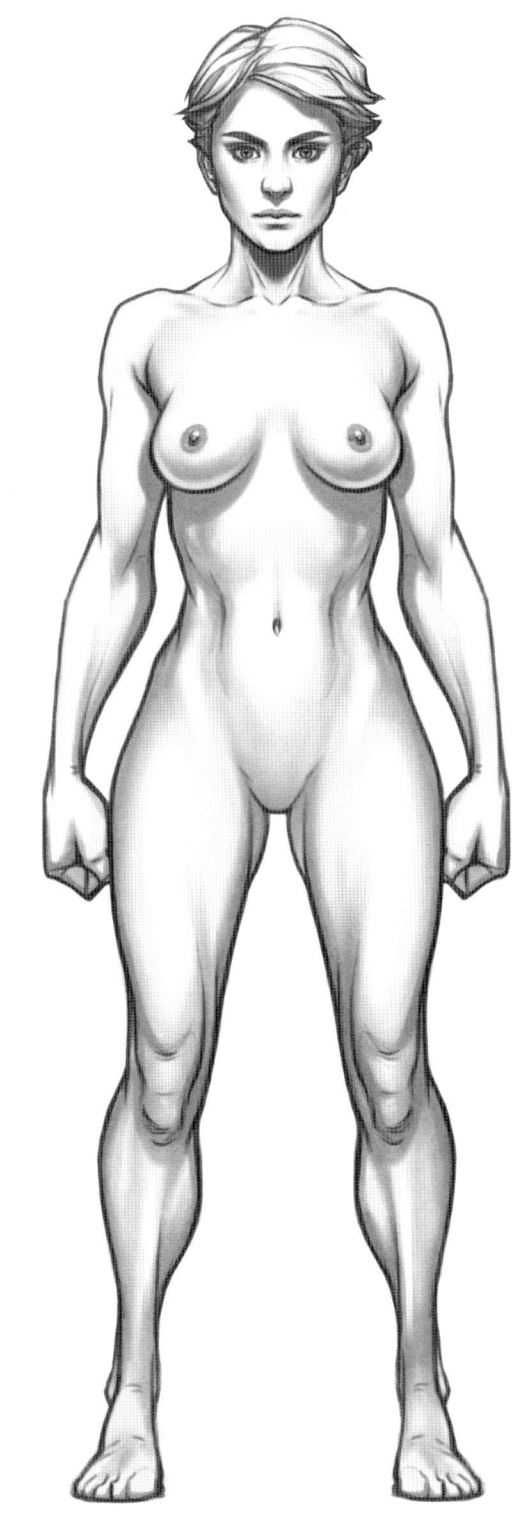
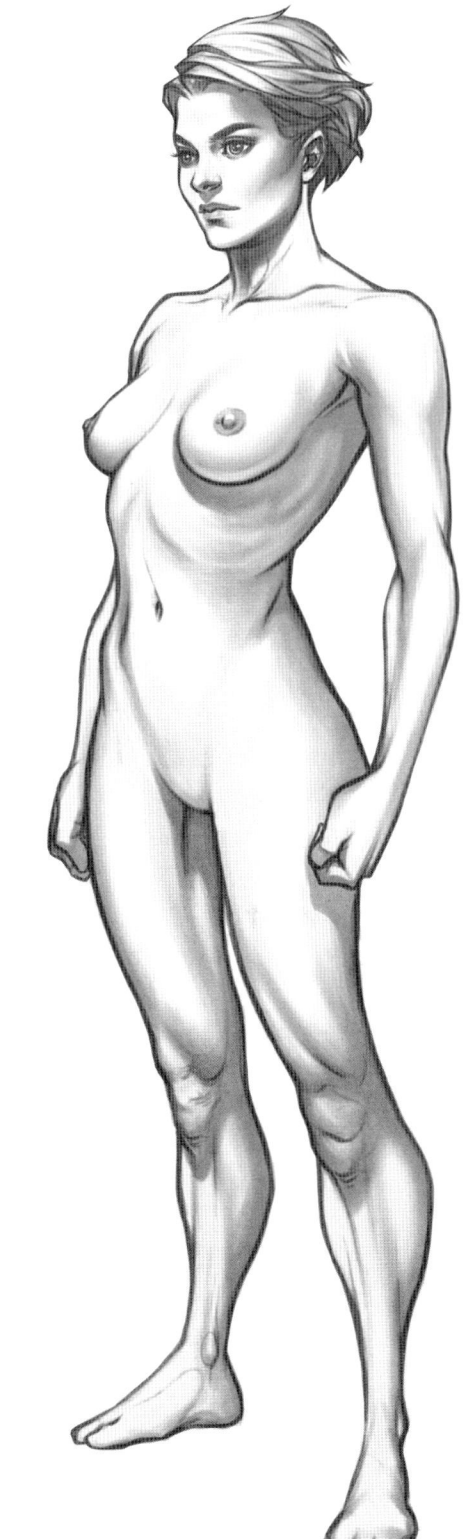

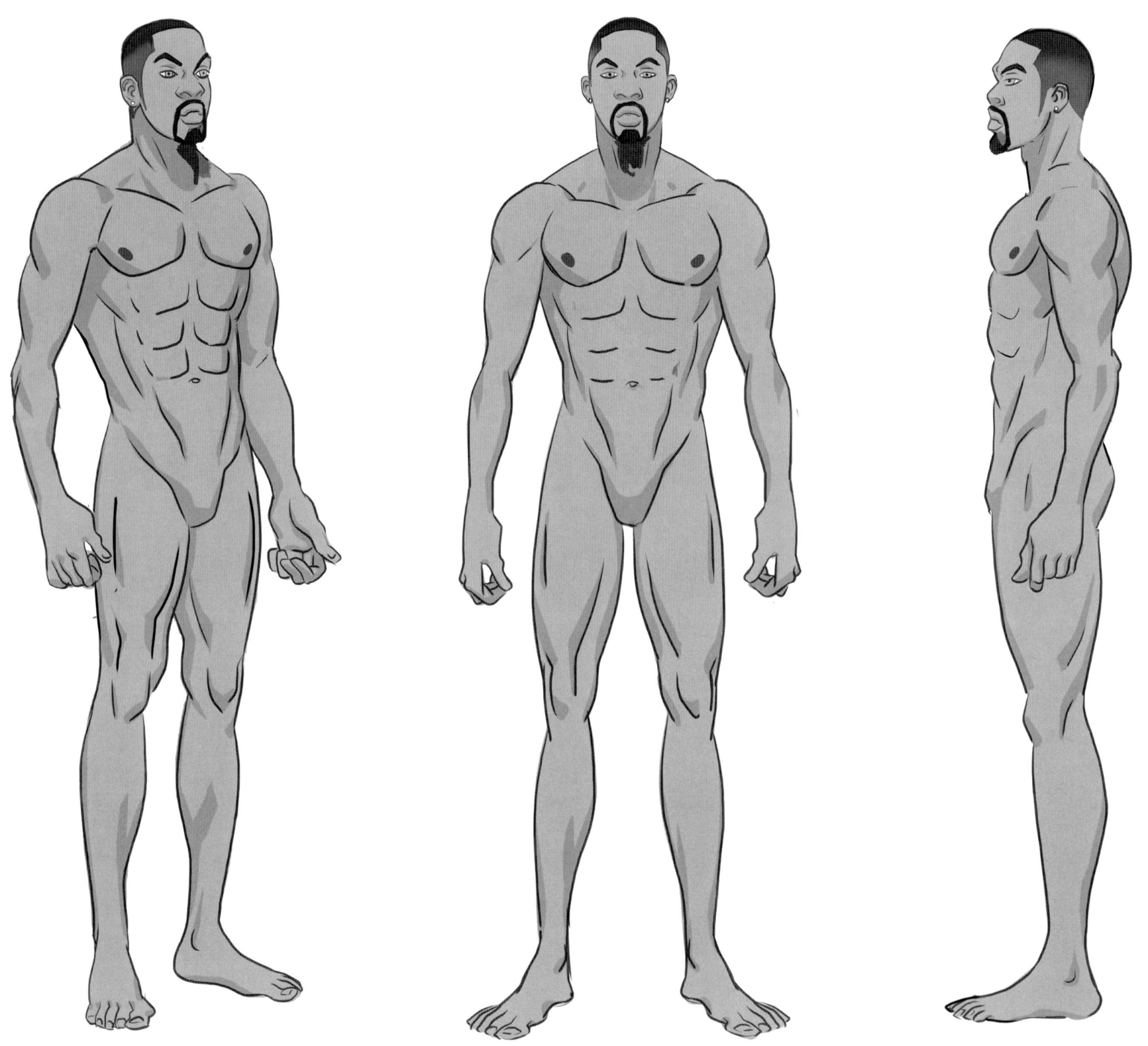

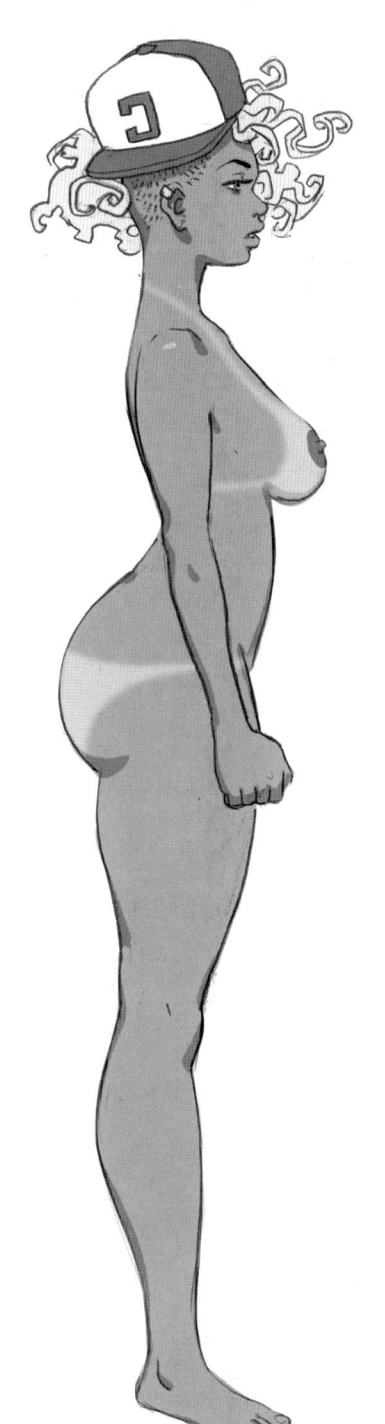
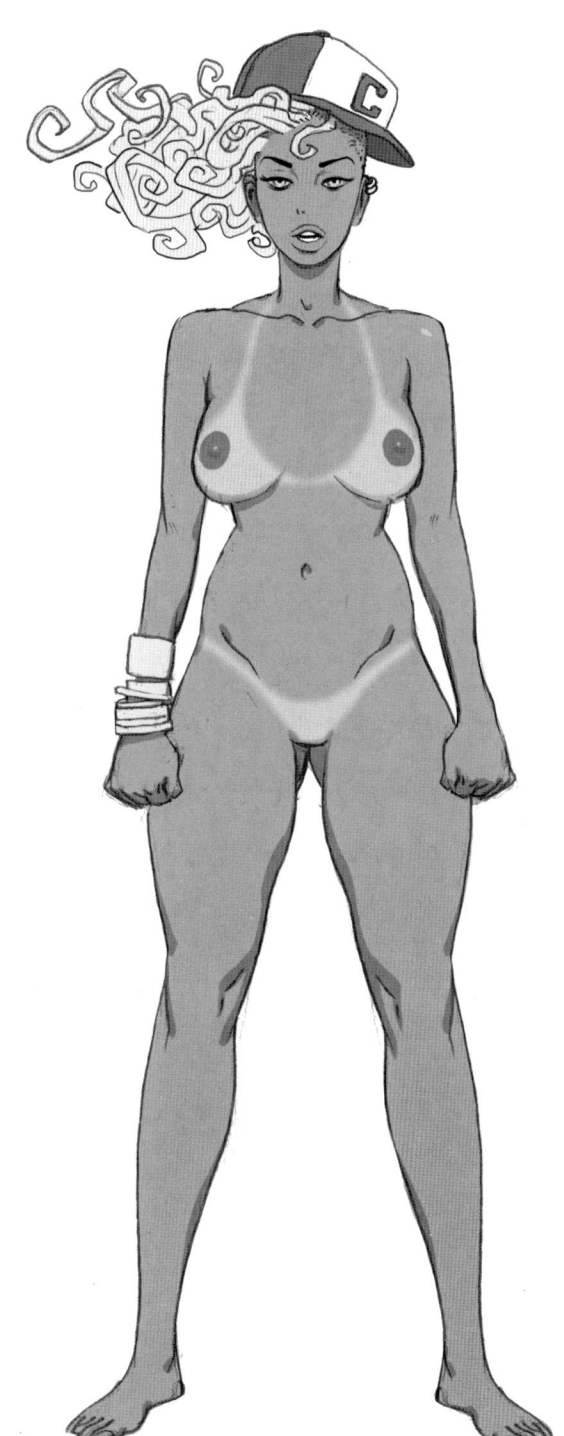
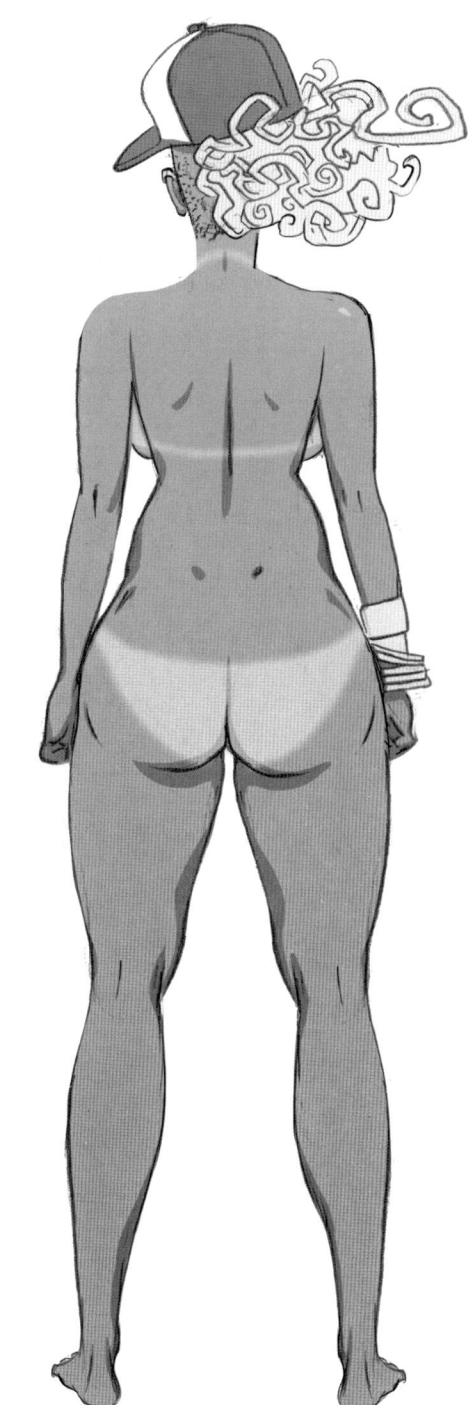

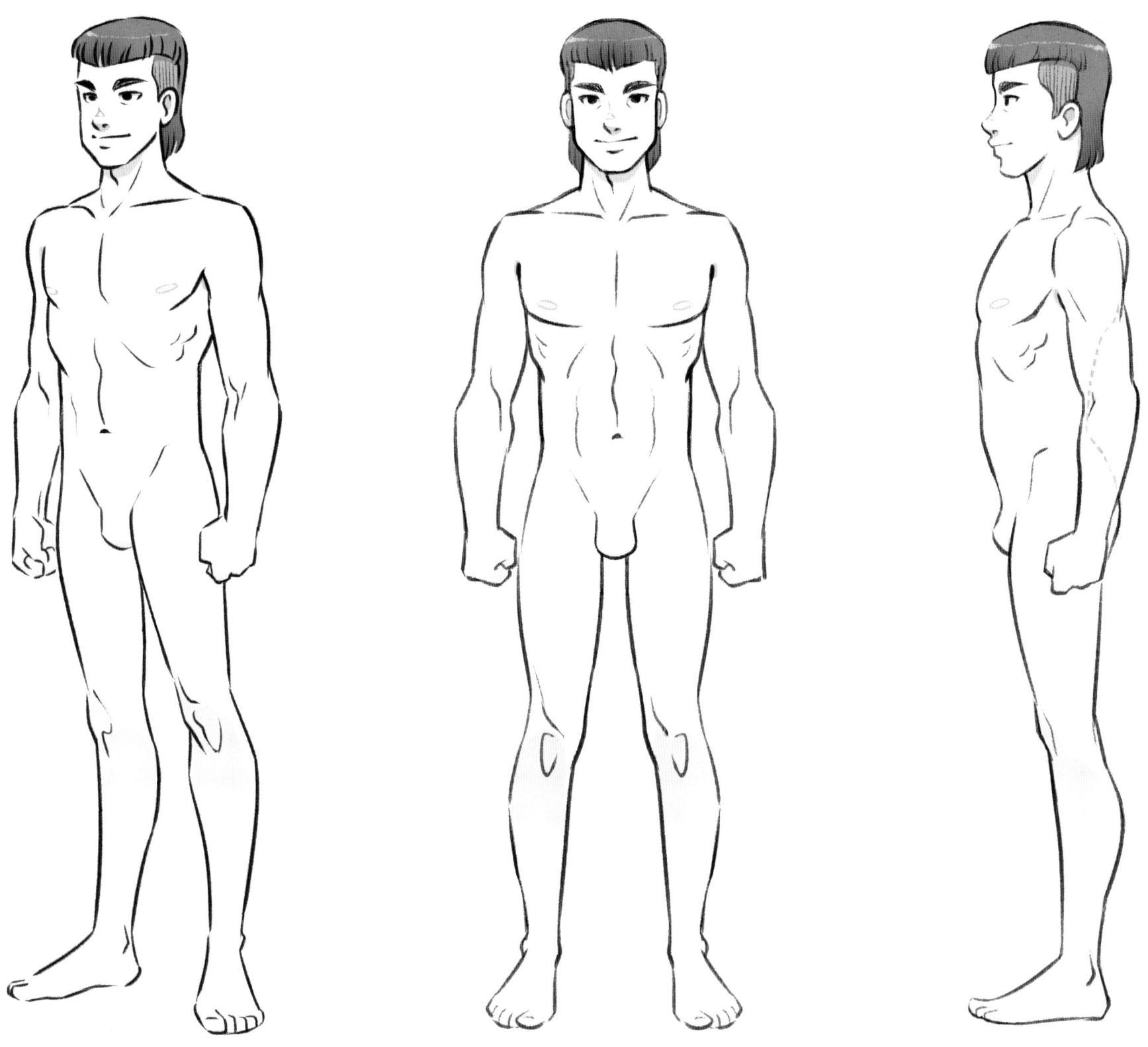

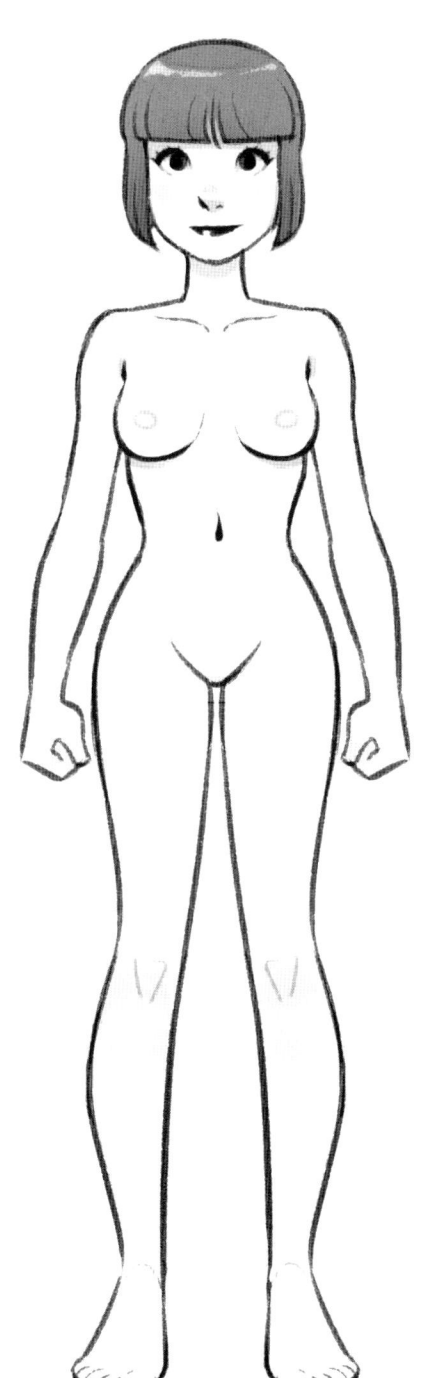

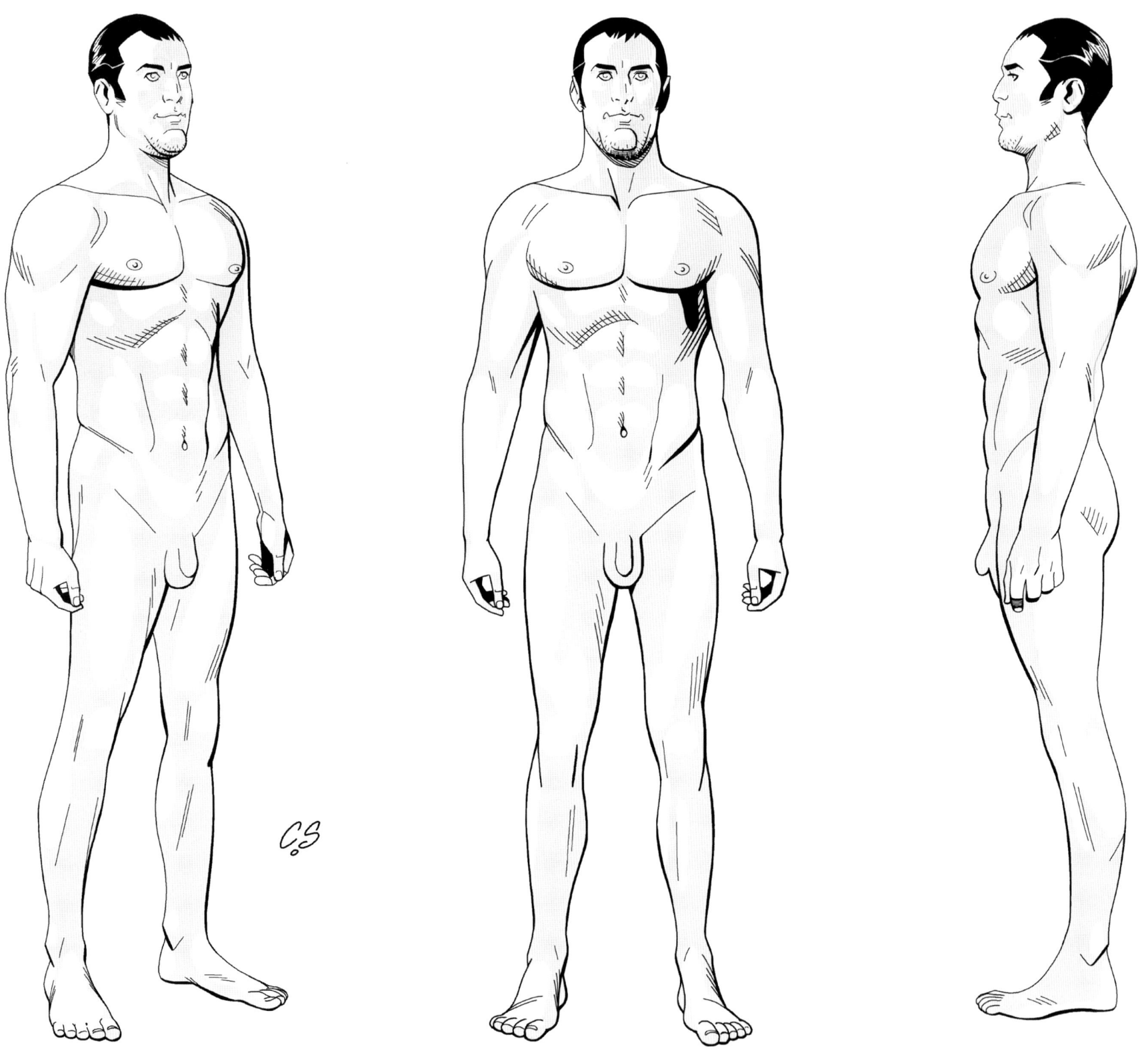

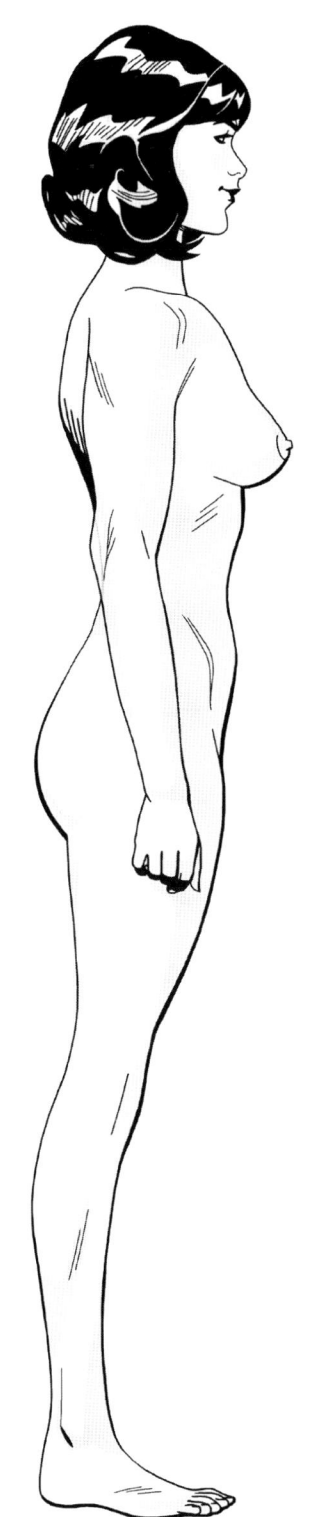
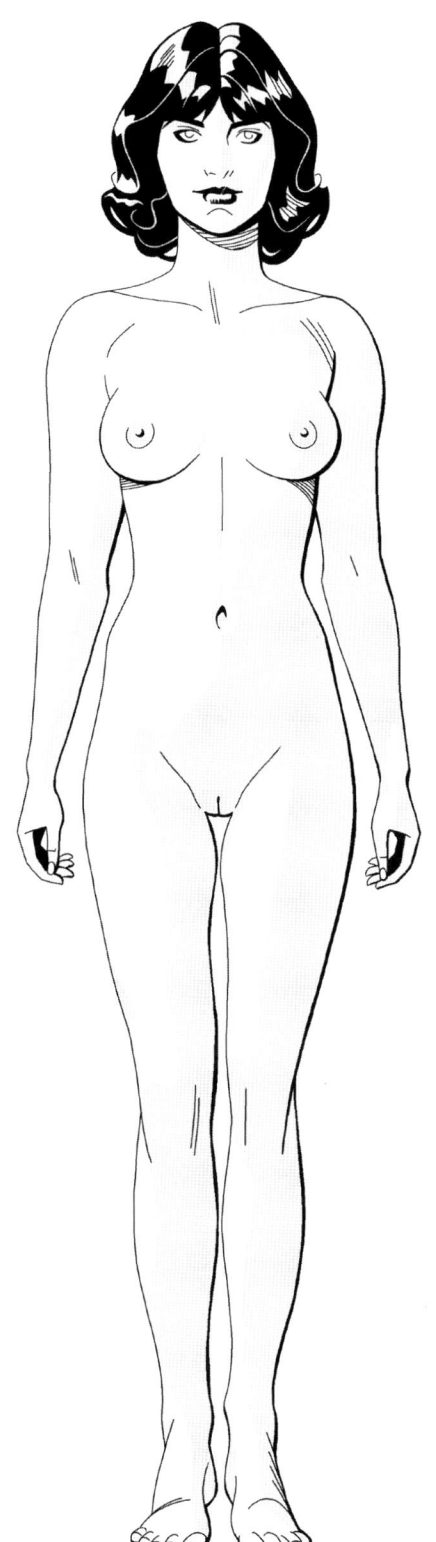
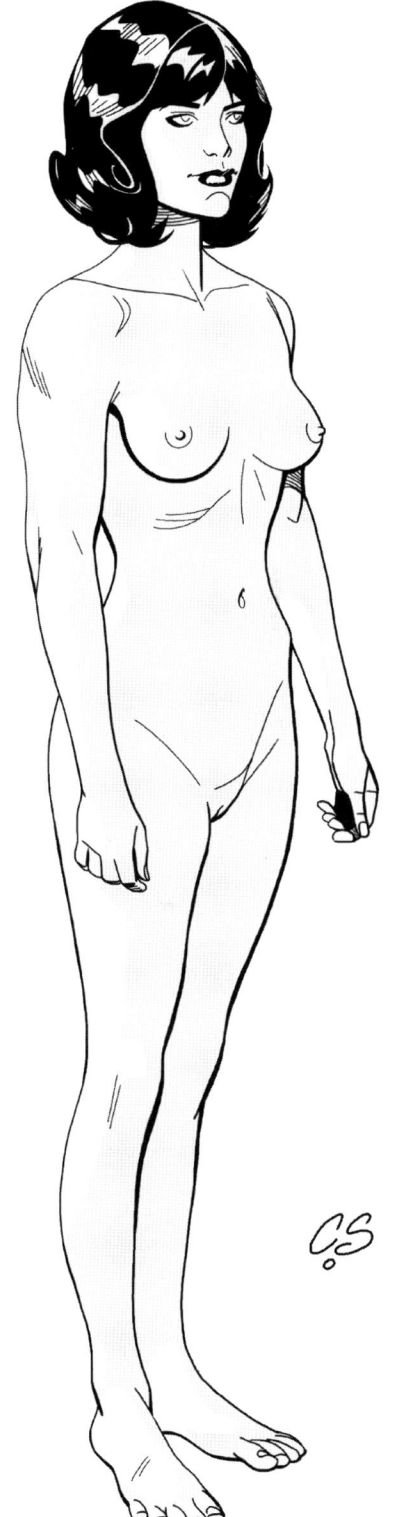

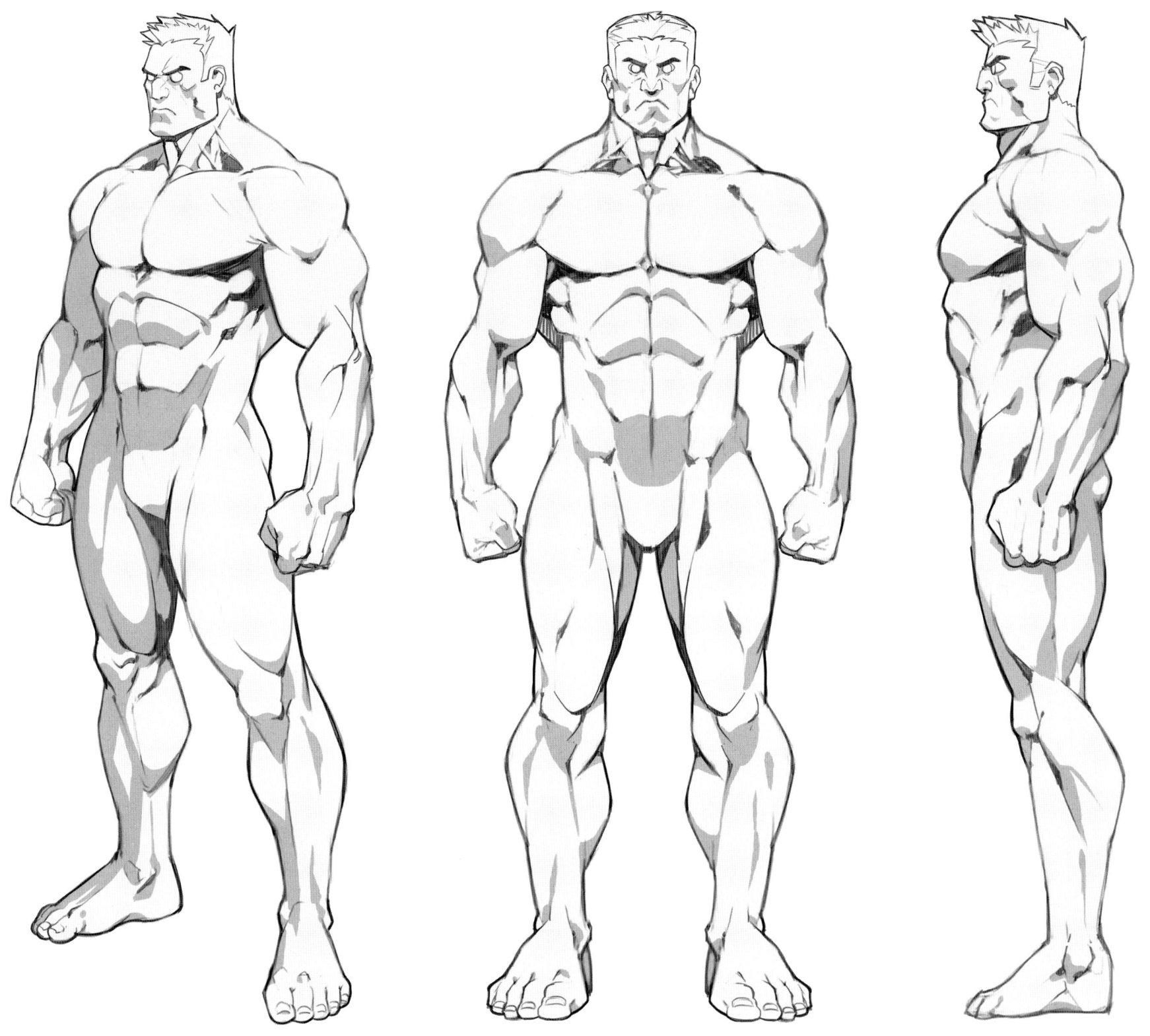

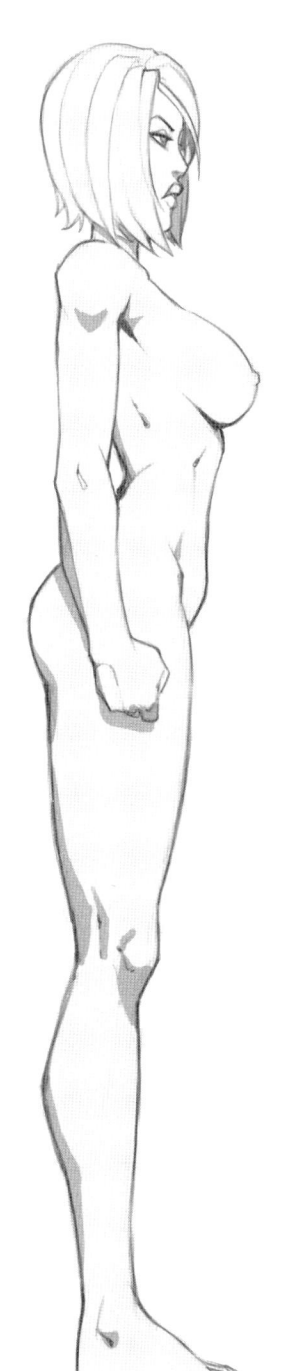
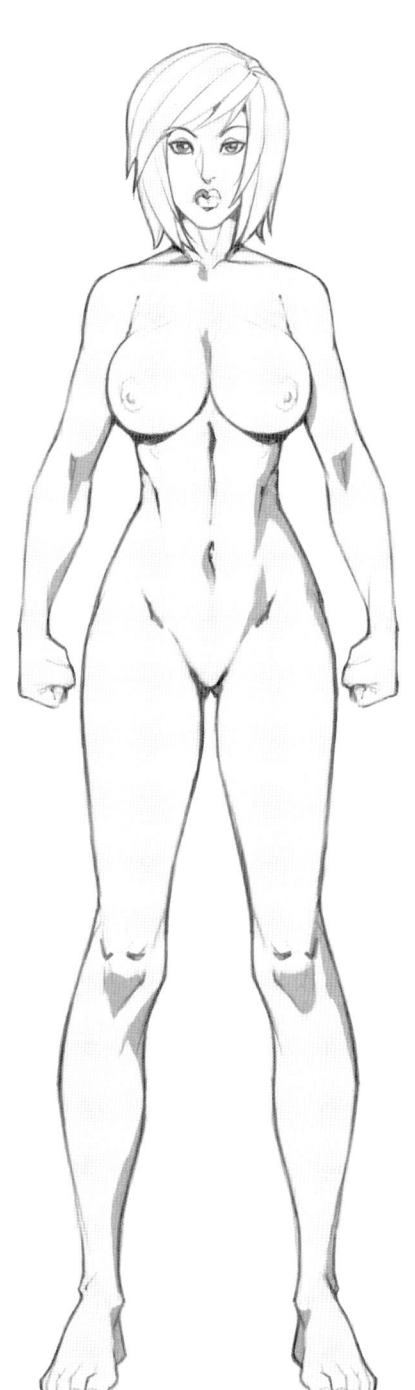
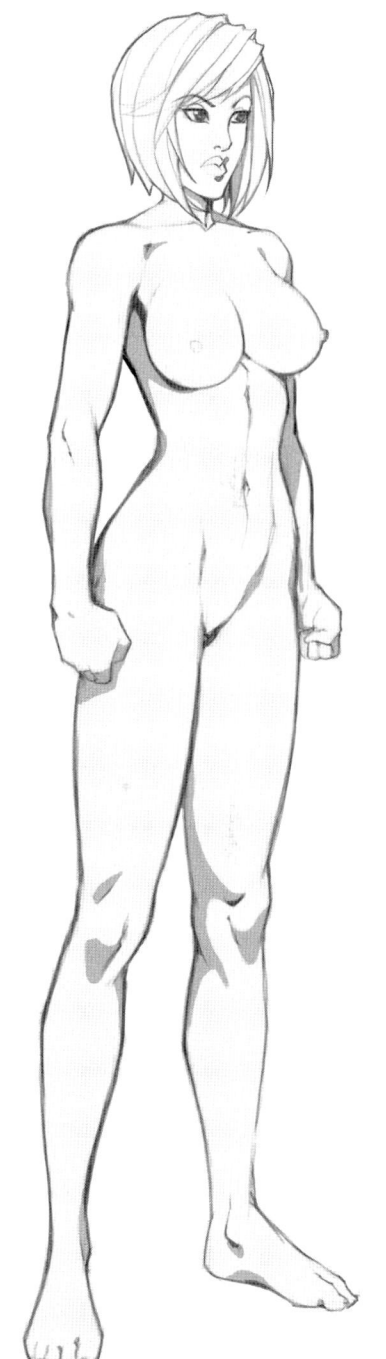

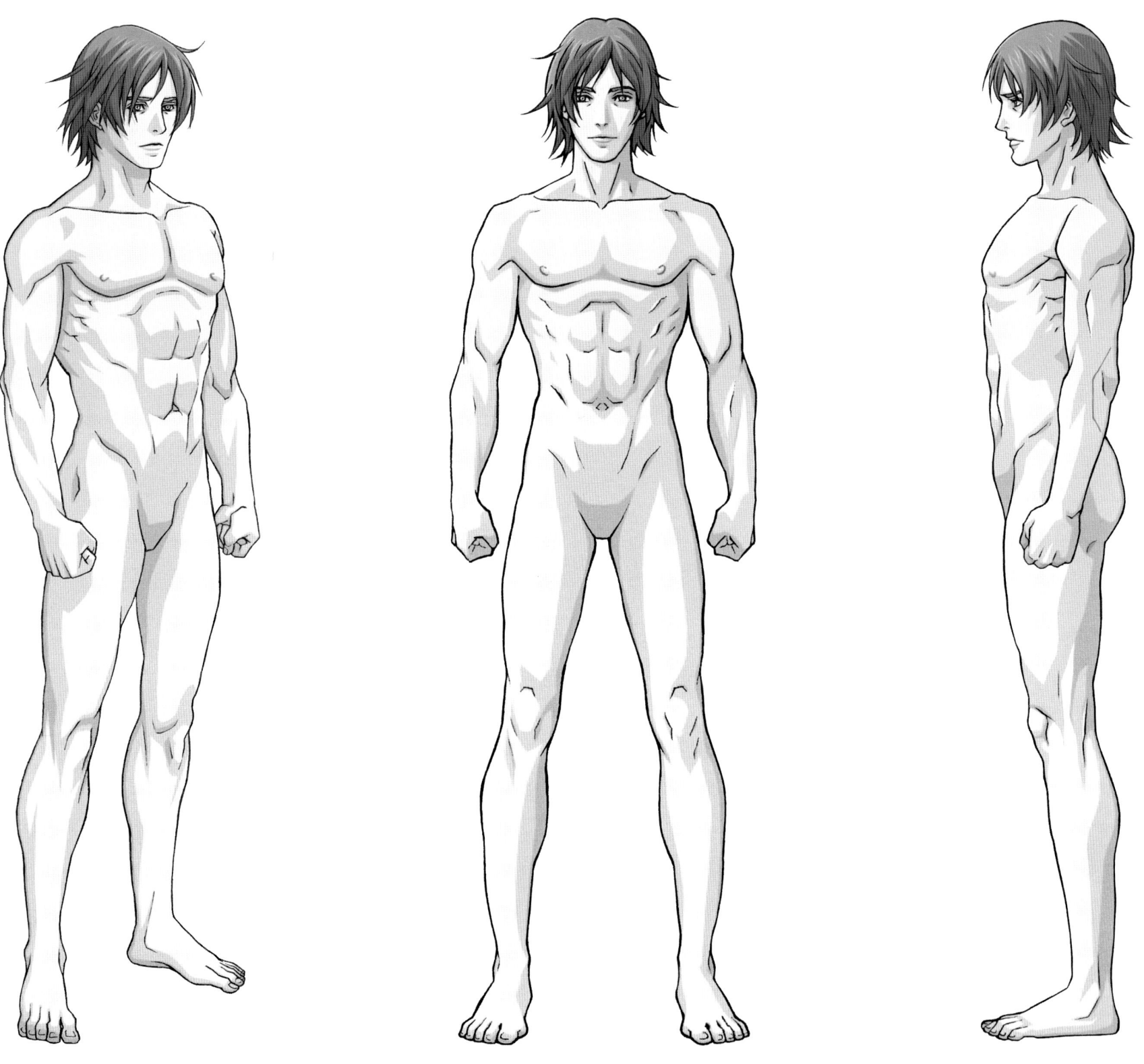

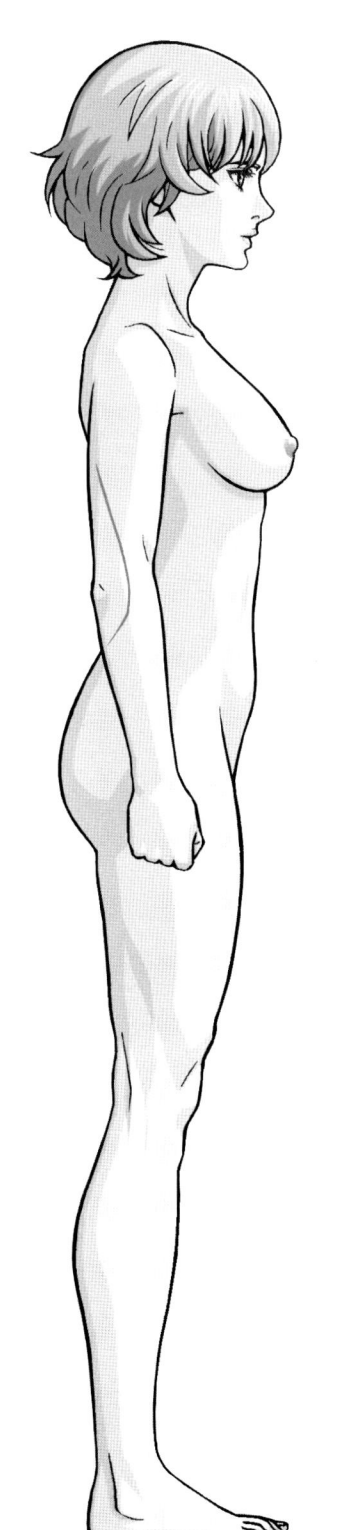
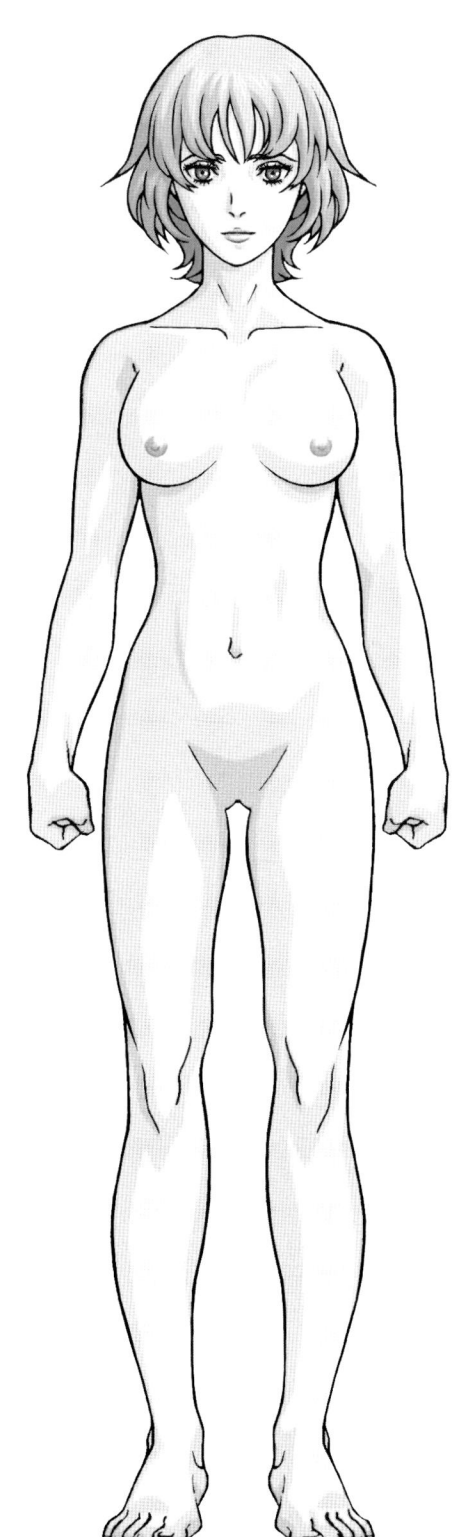
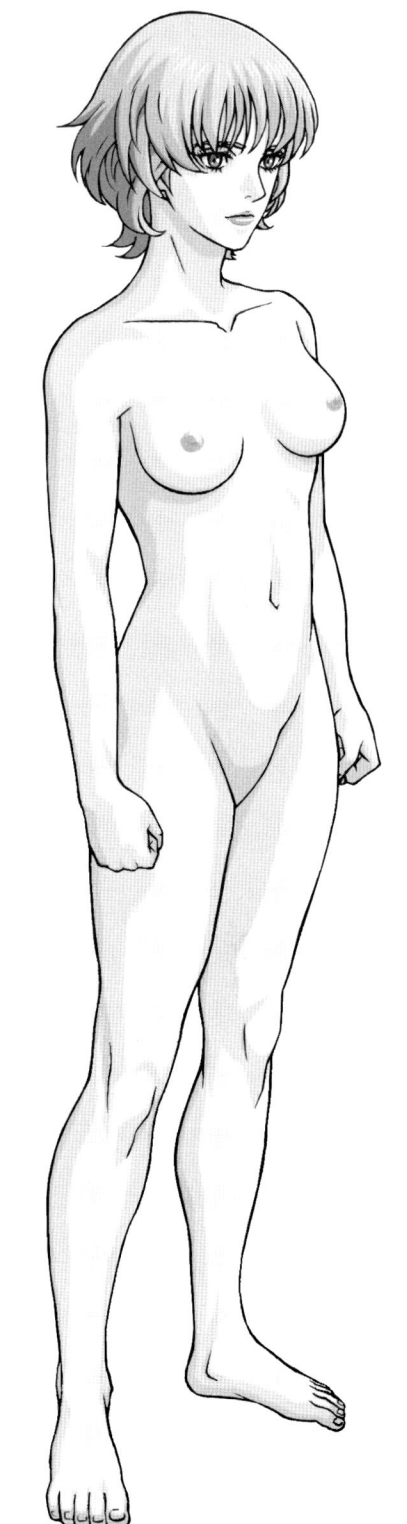

CINDY YAMAUCHI

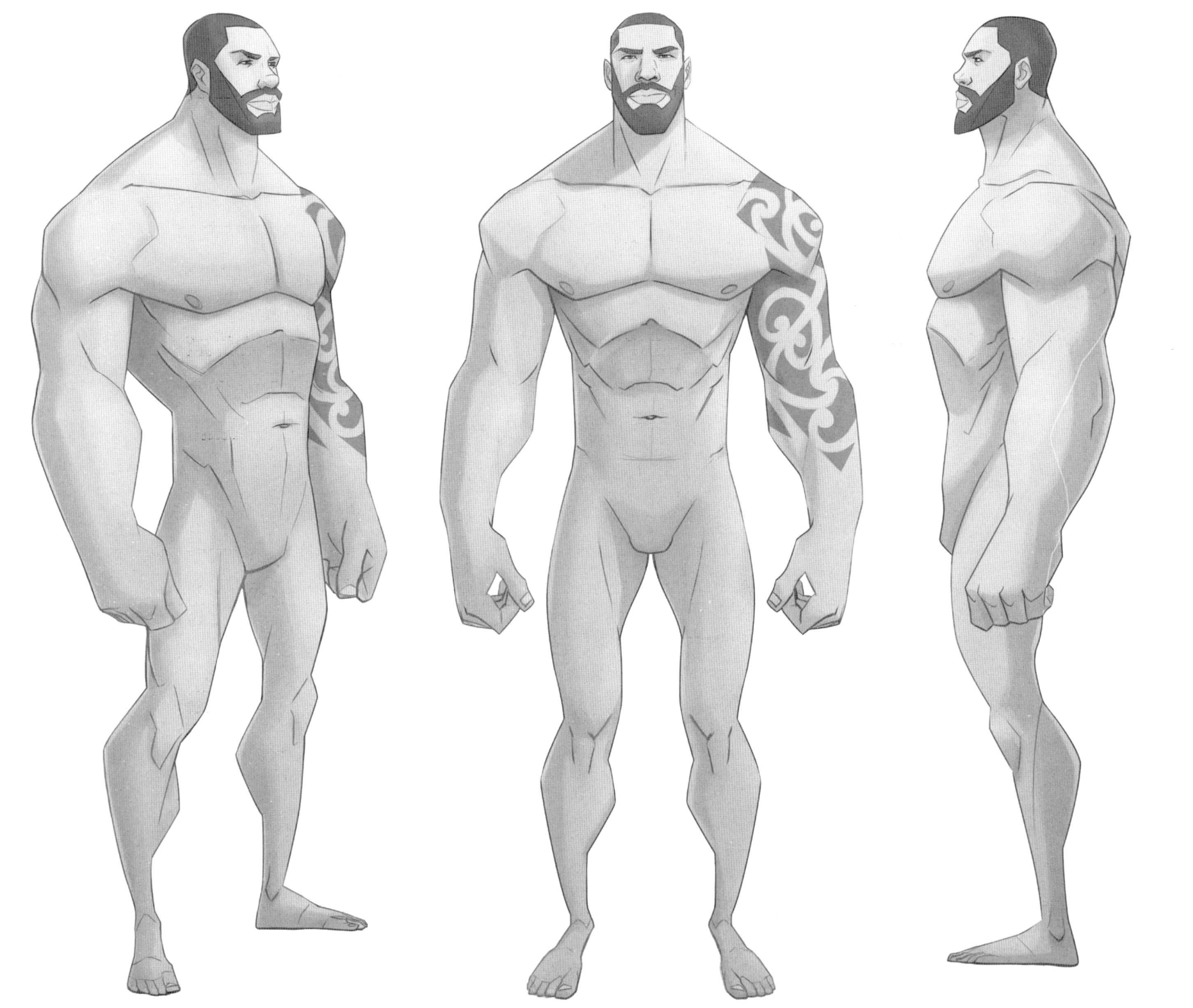

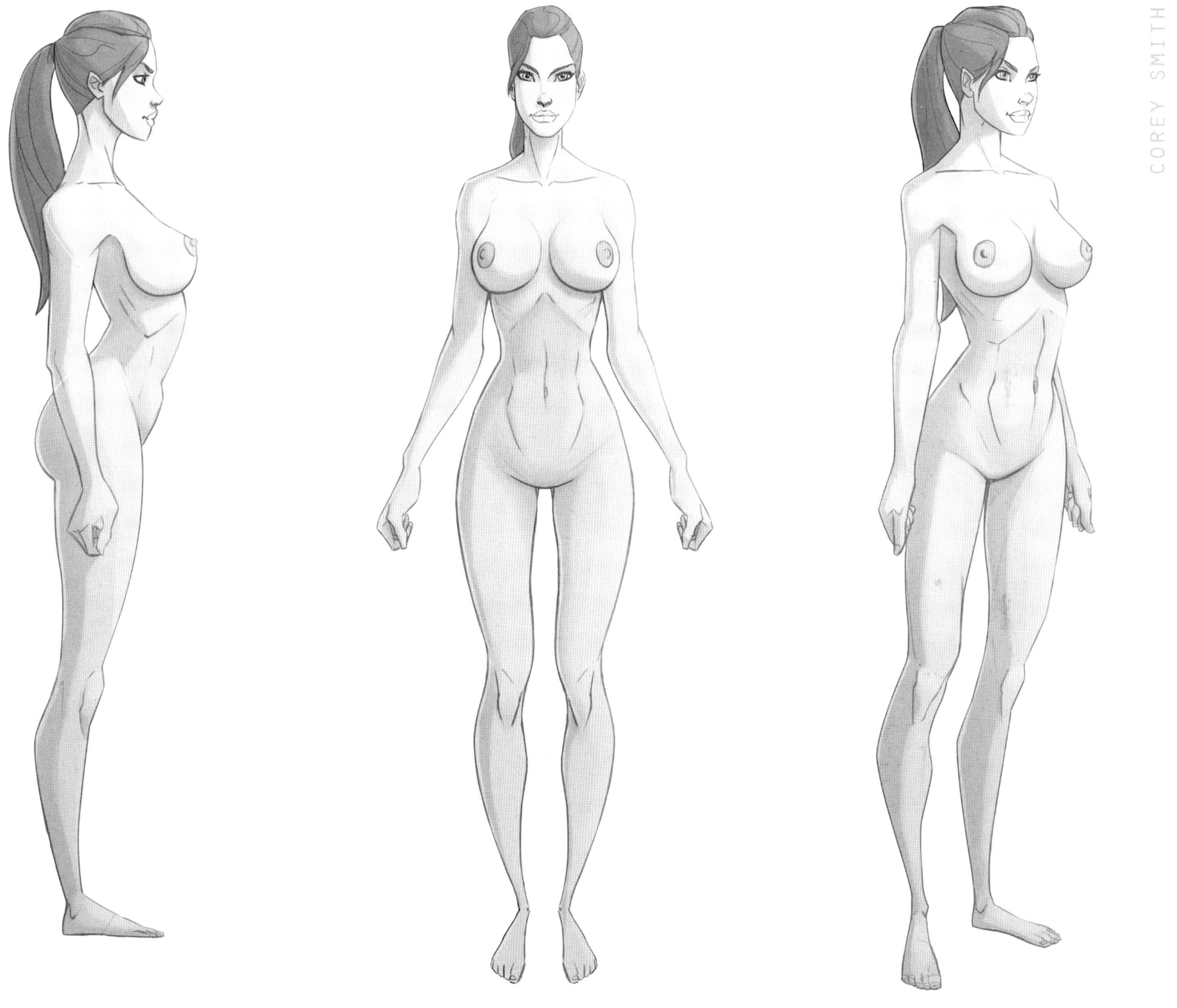

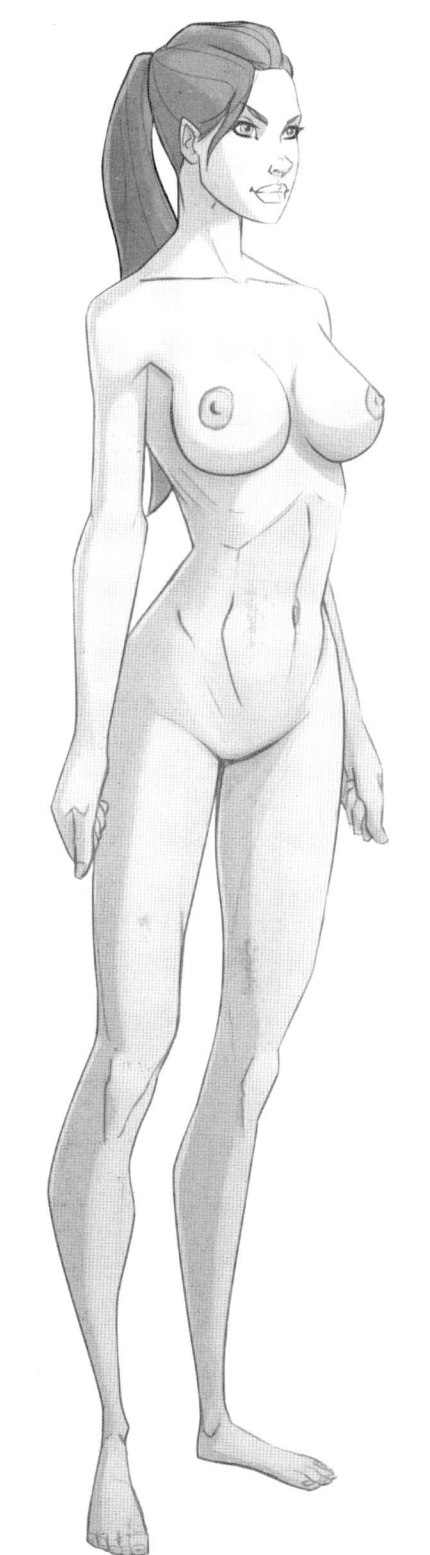

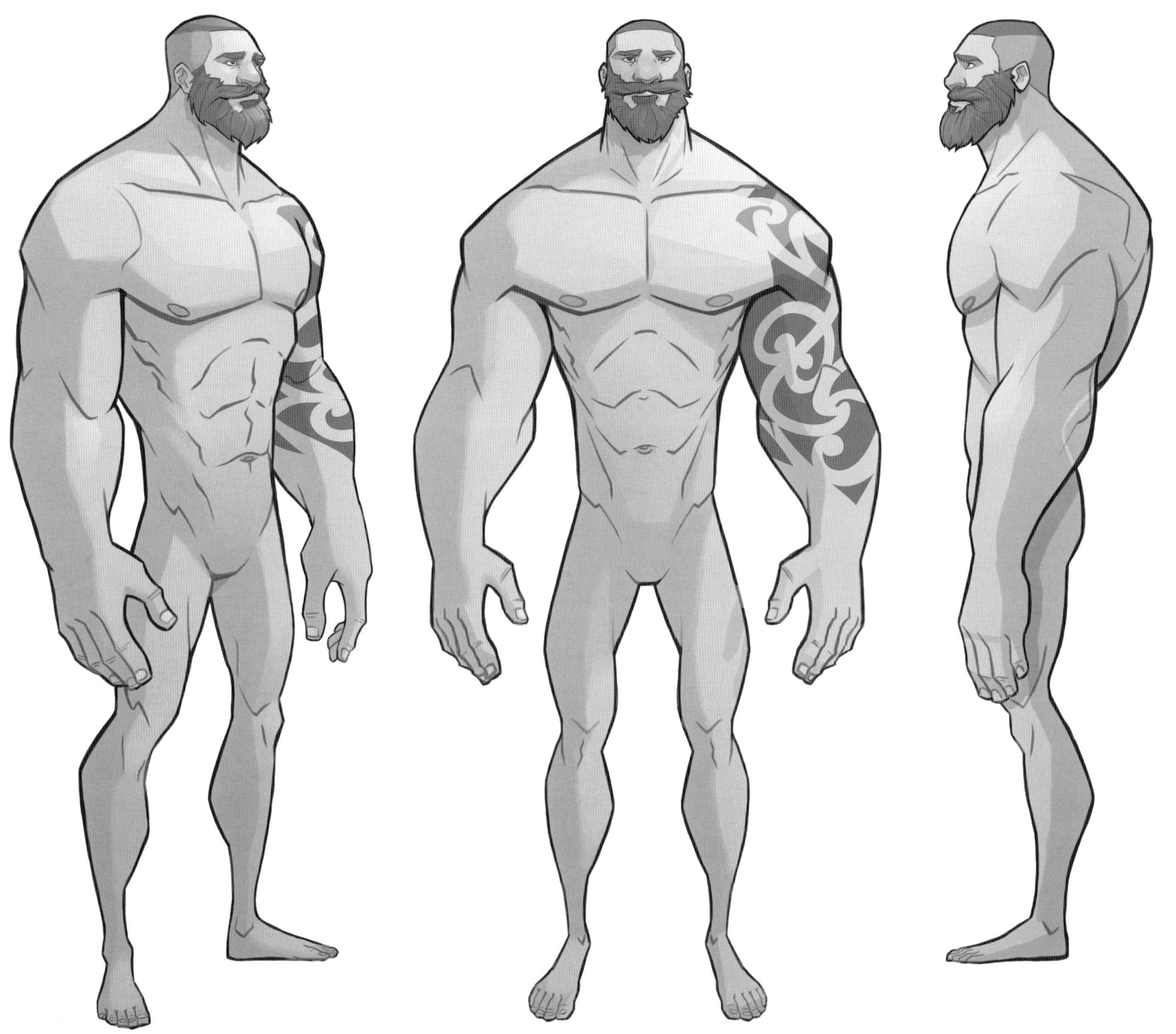

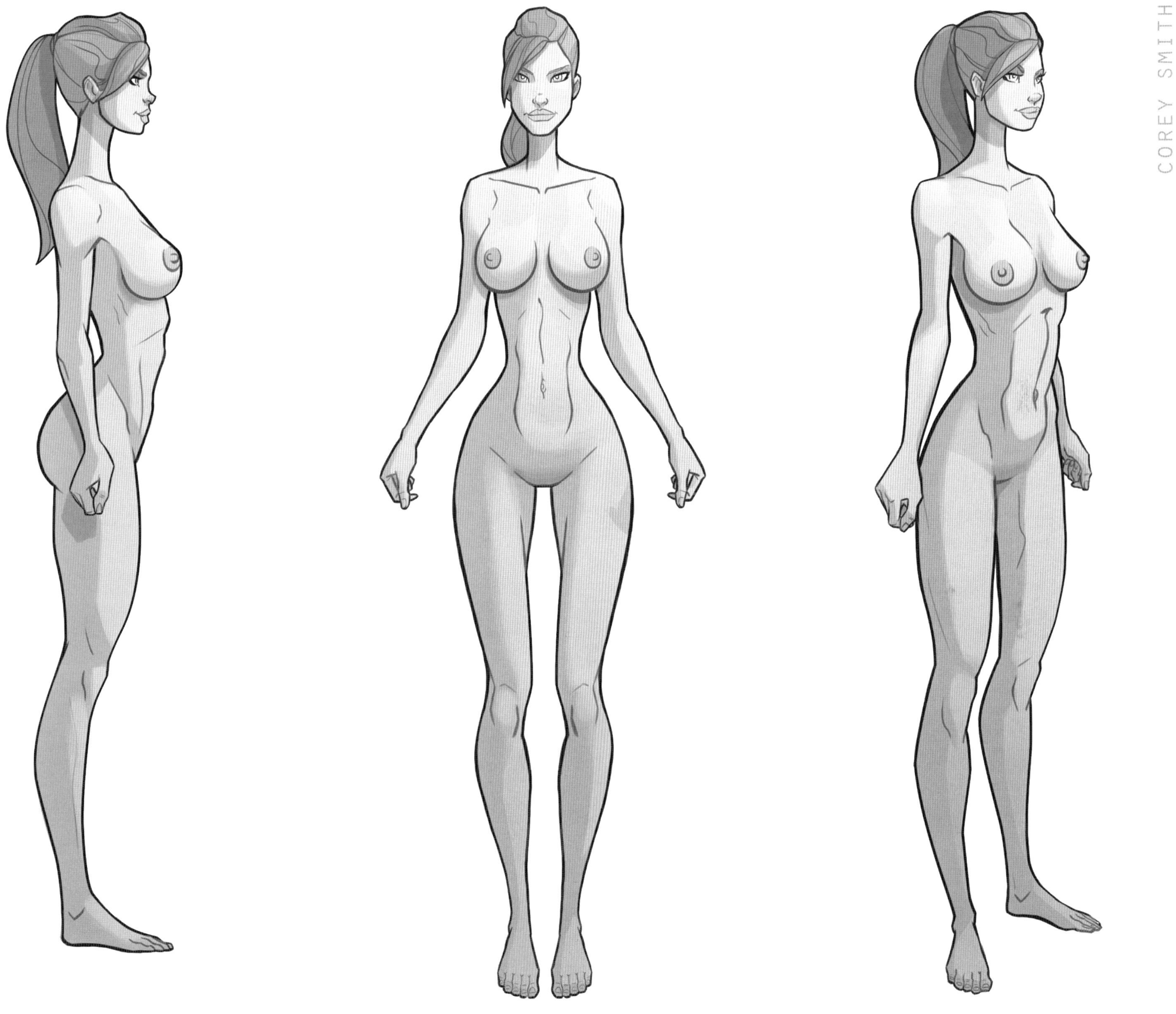

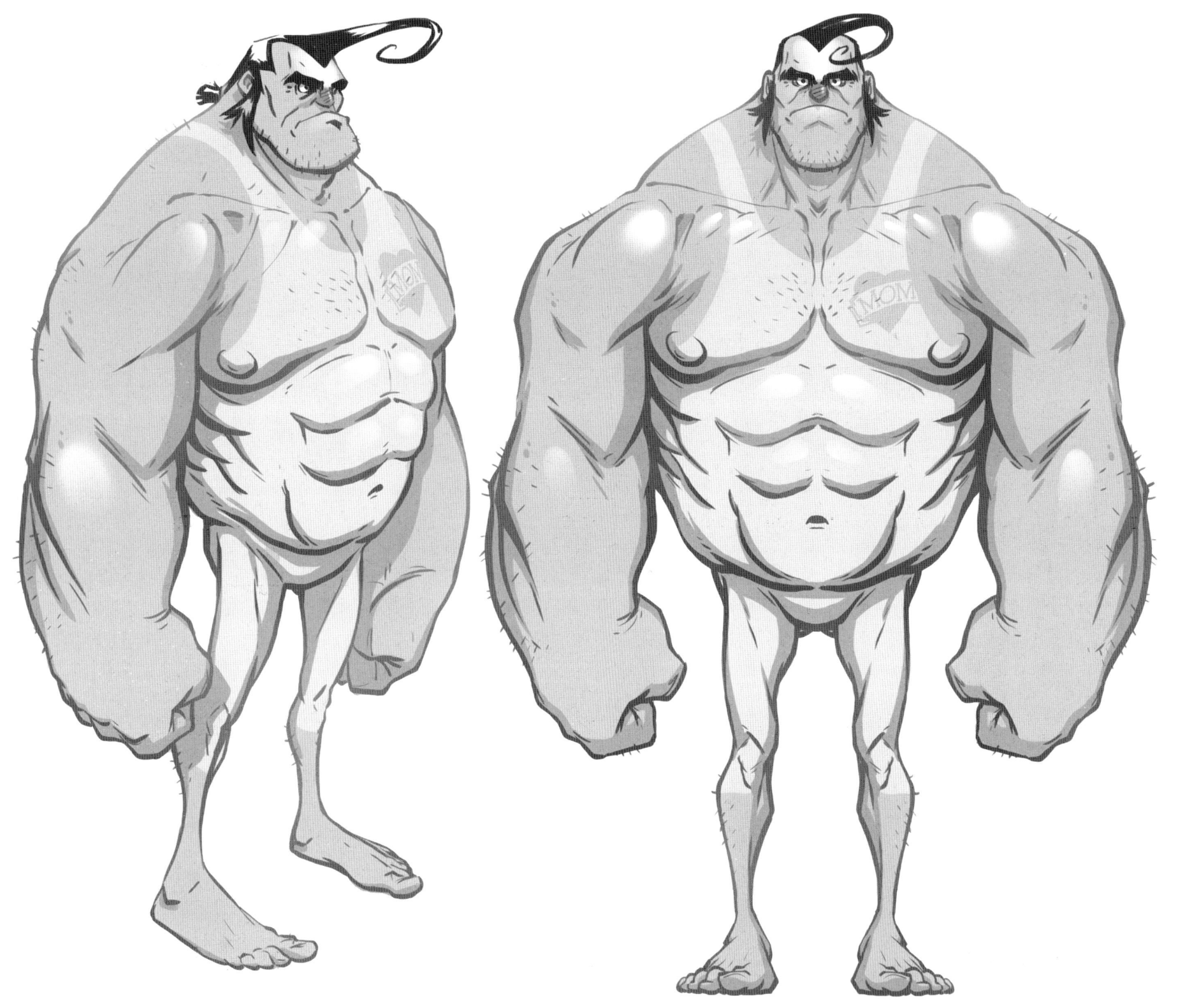

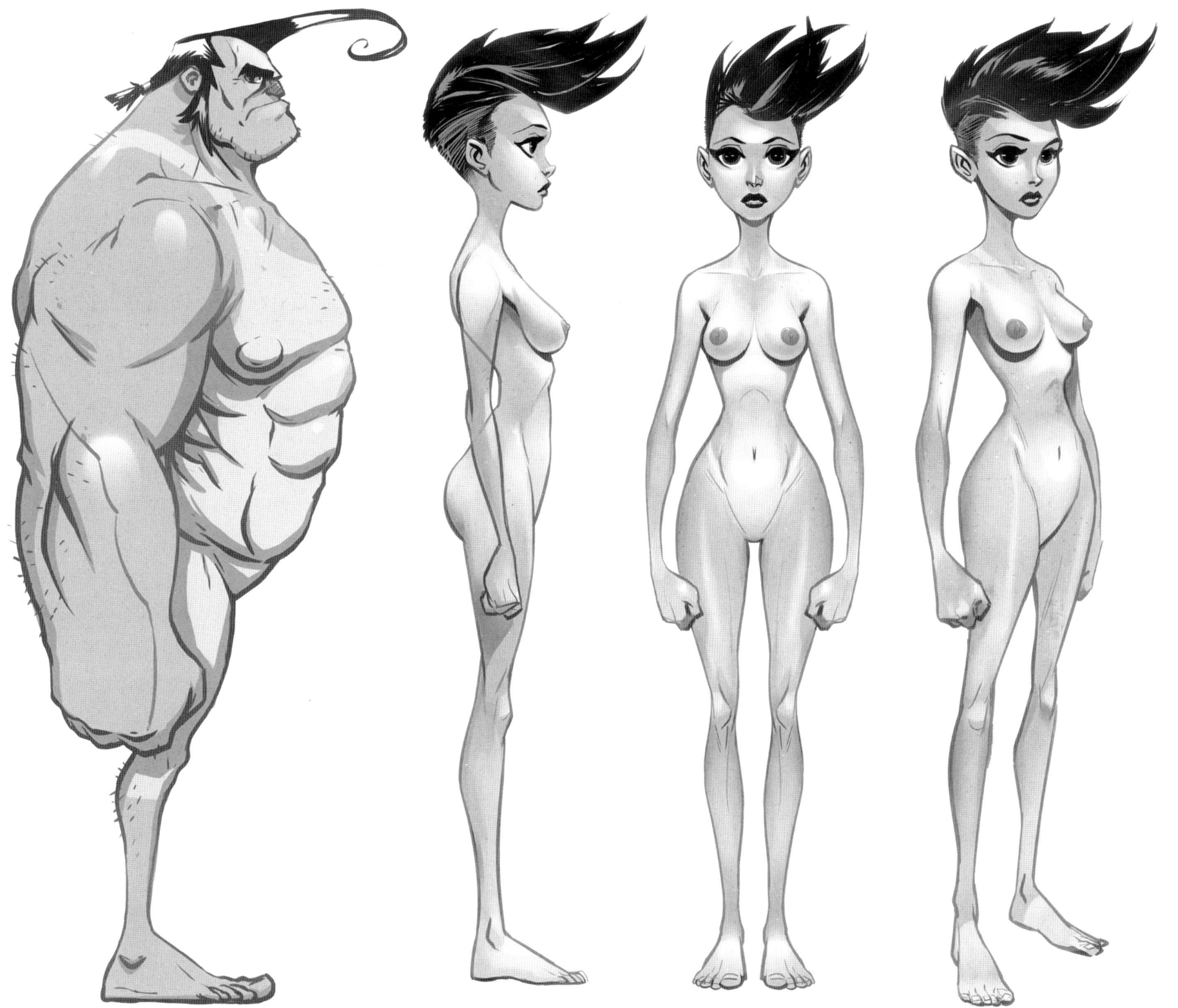

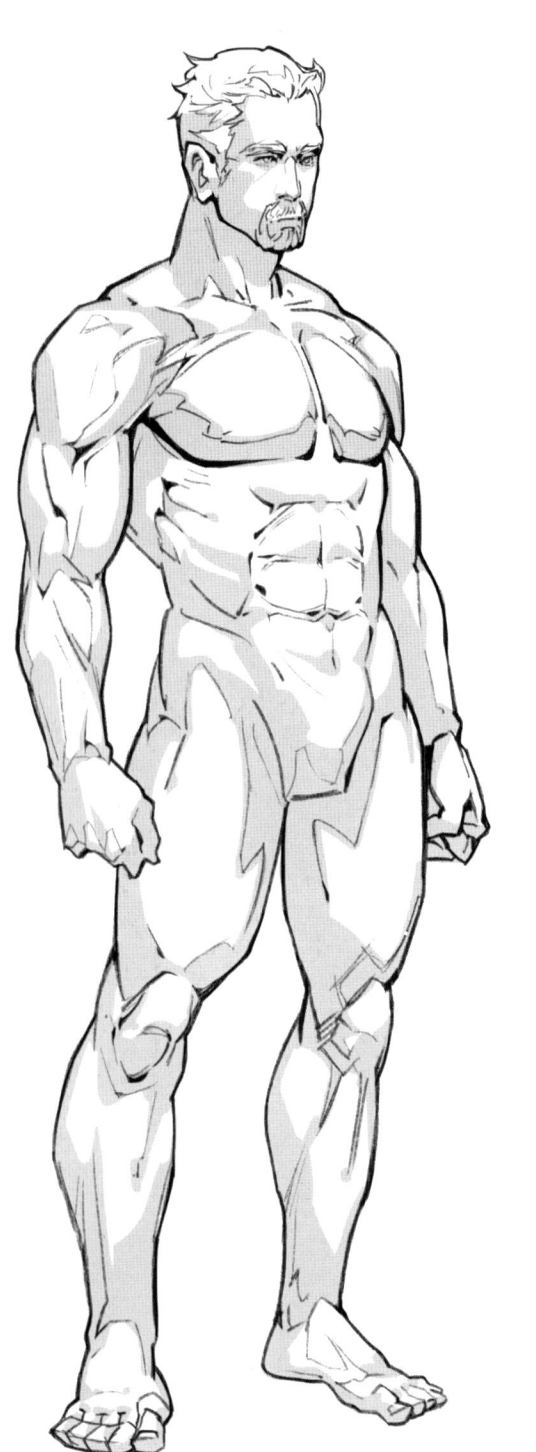
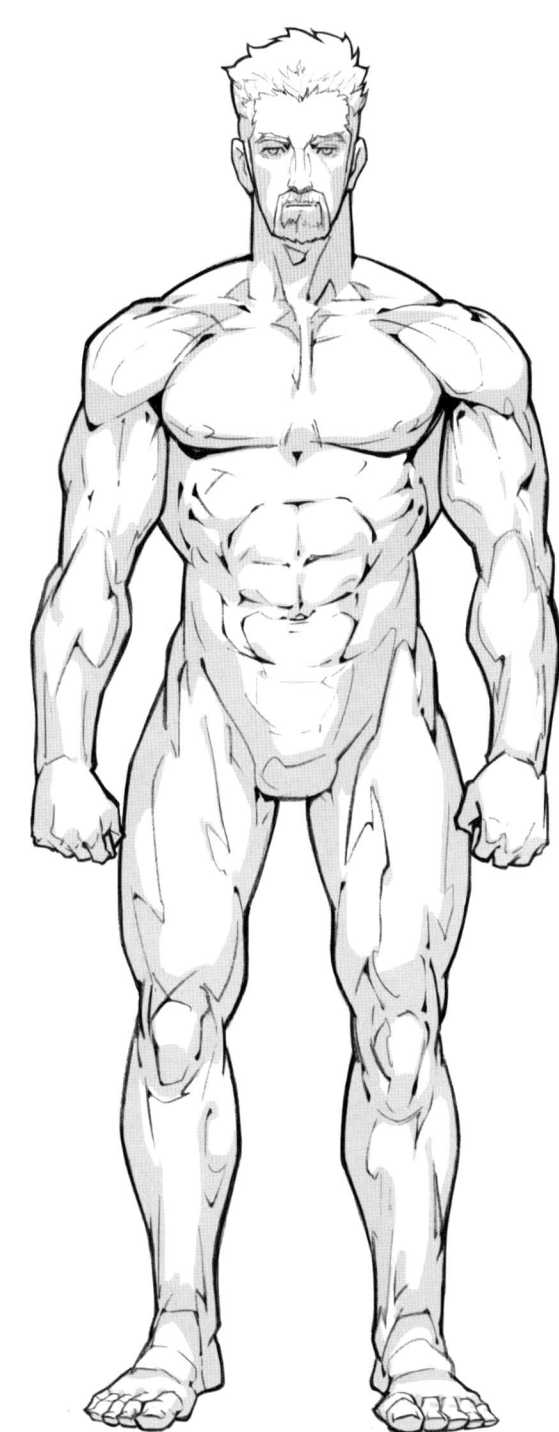
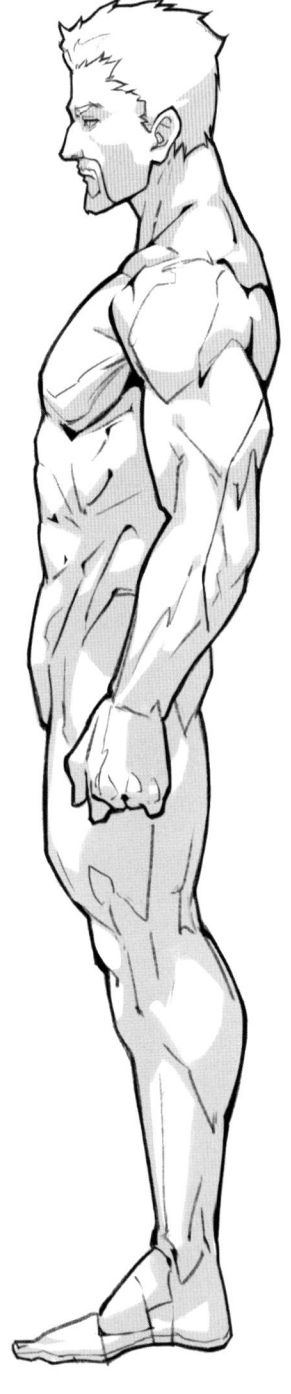

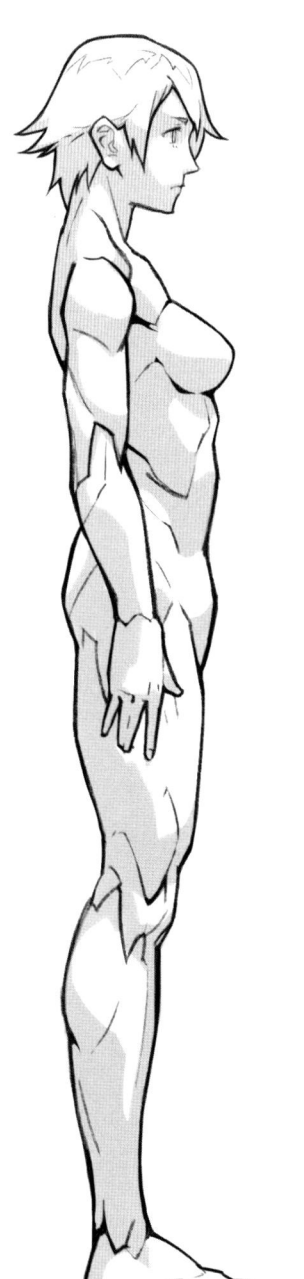
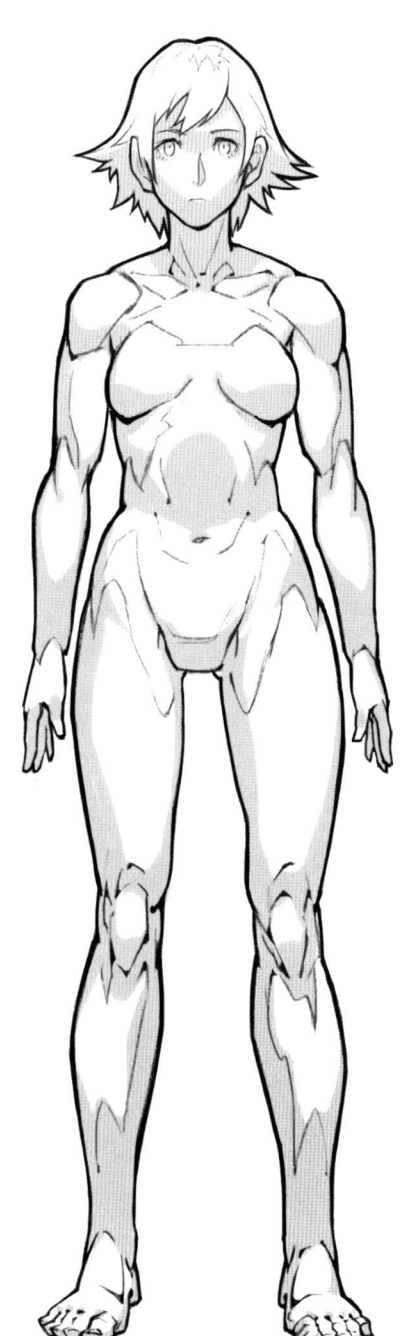
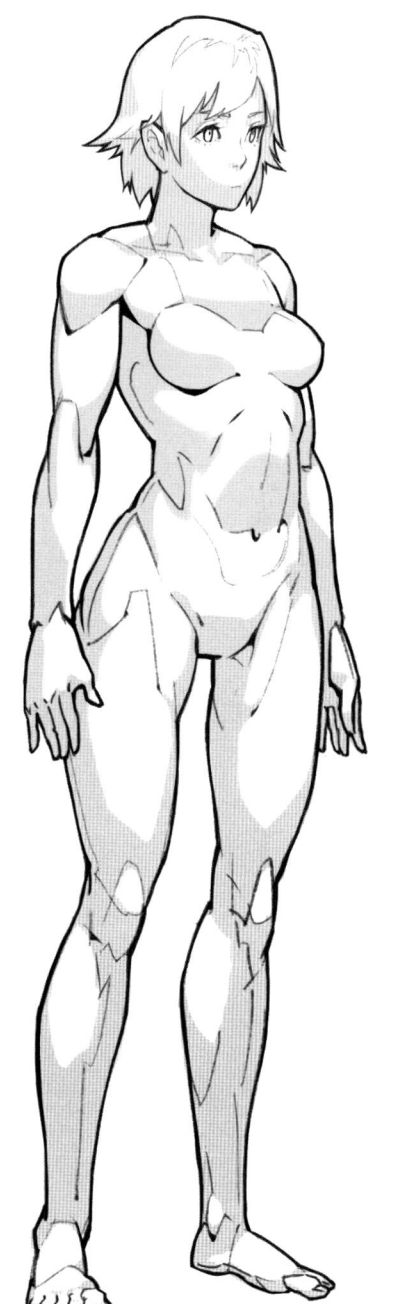

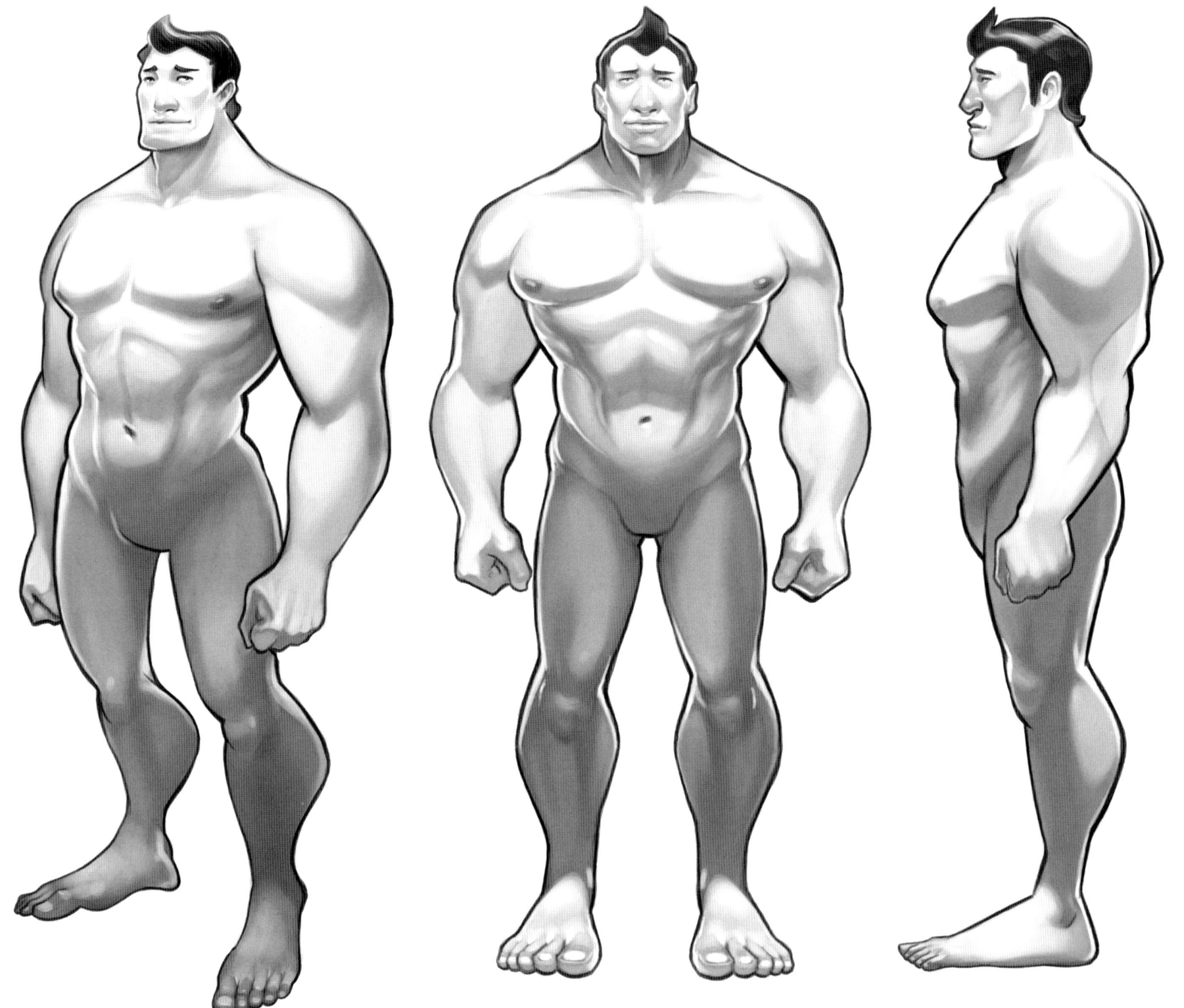

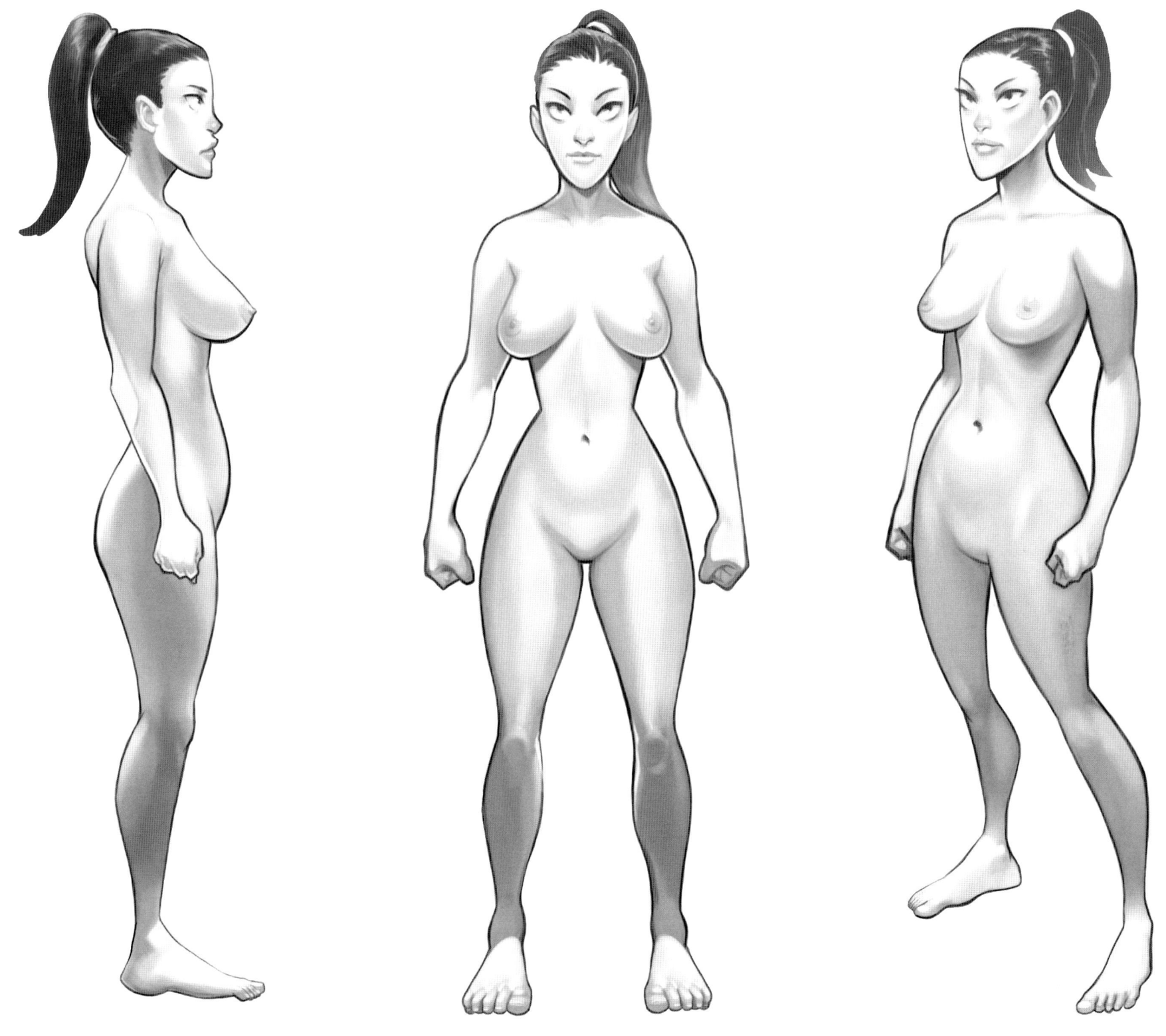

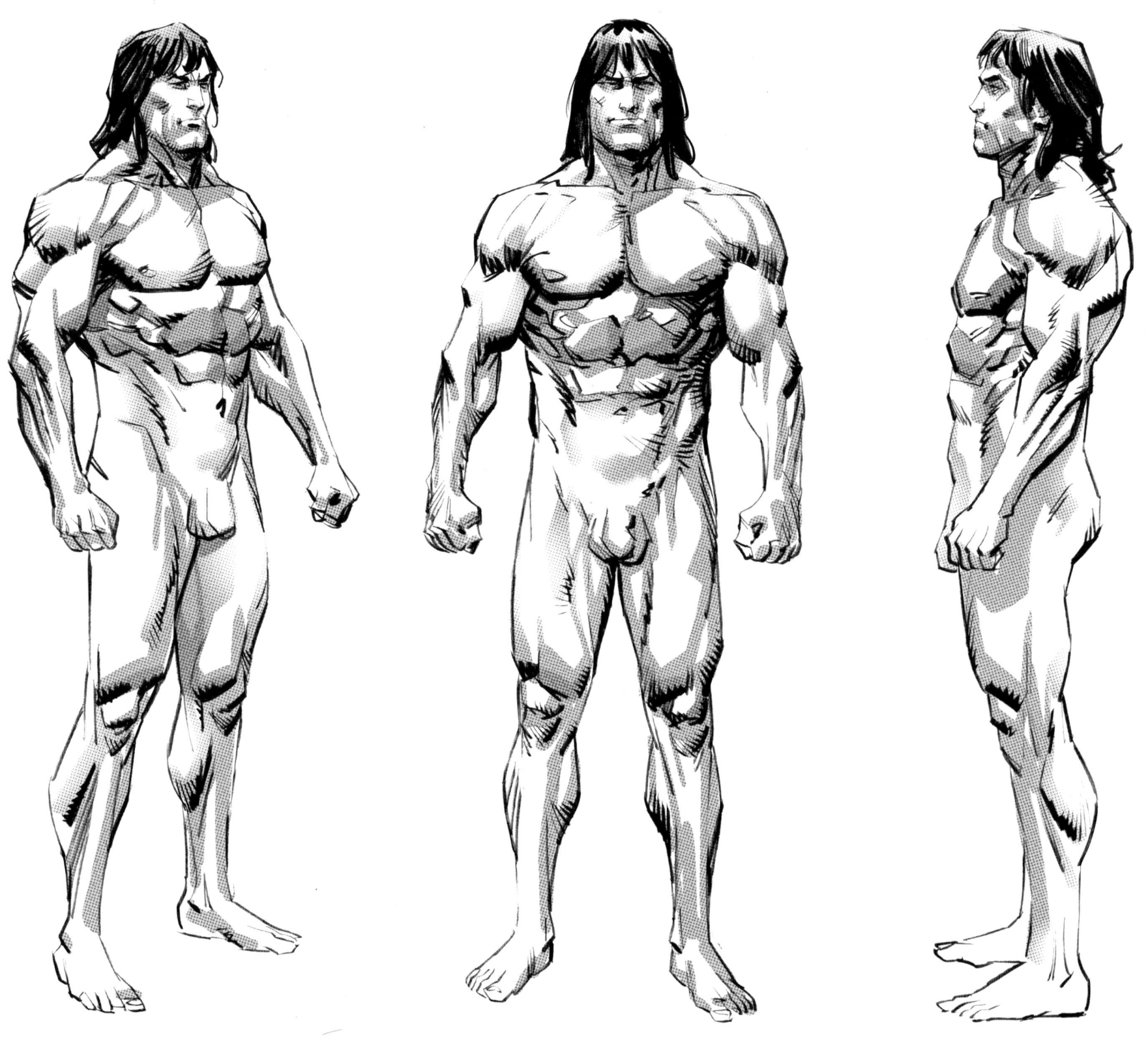

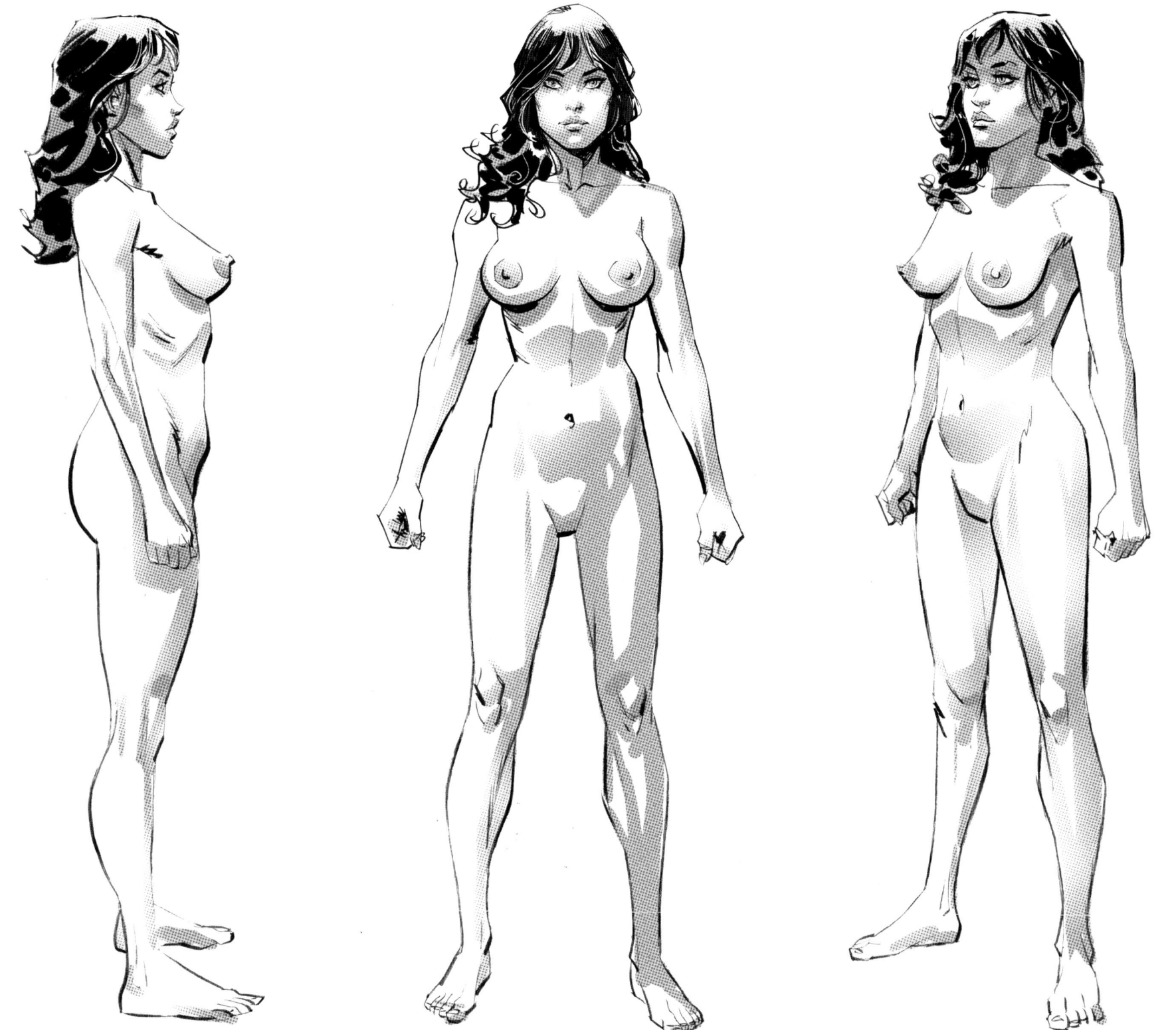

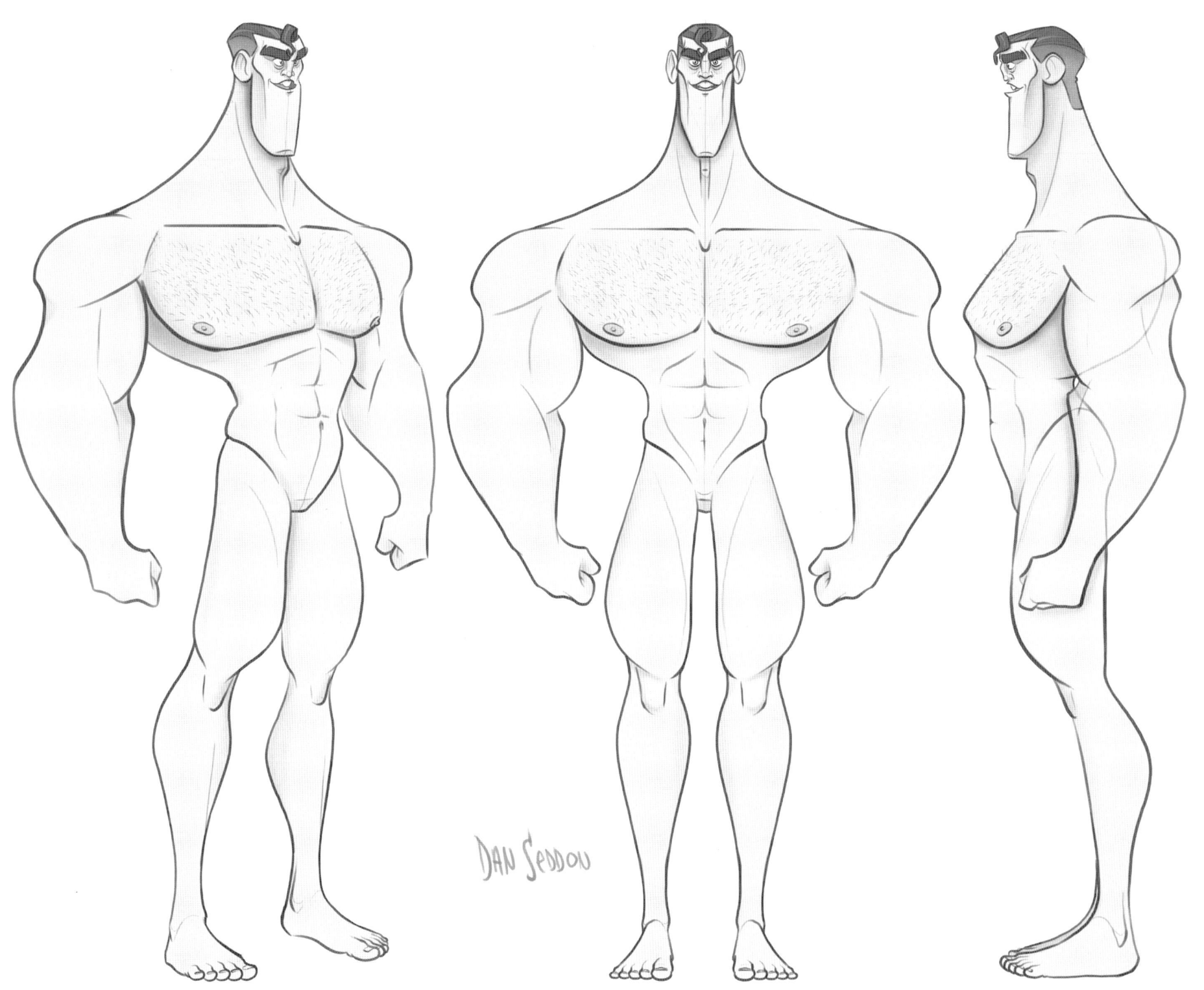

Dan Seddon

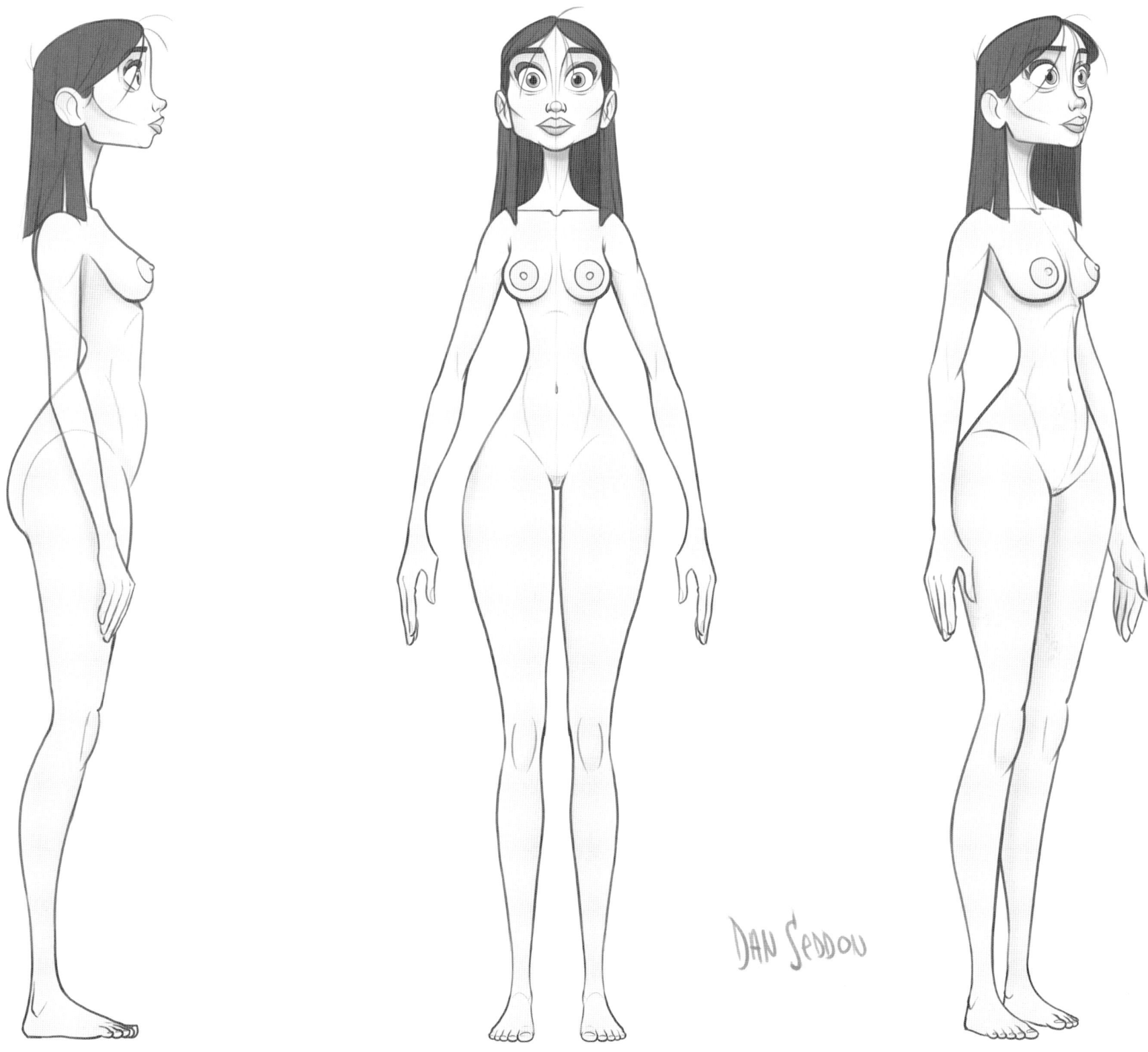

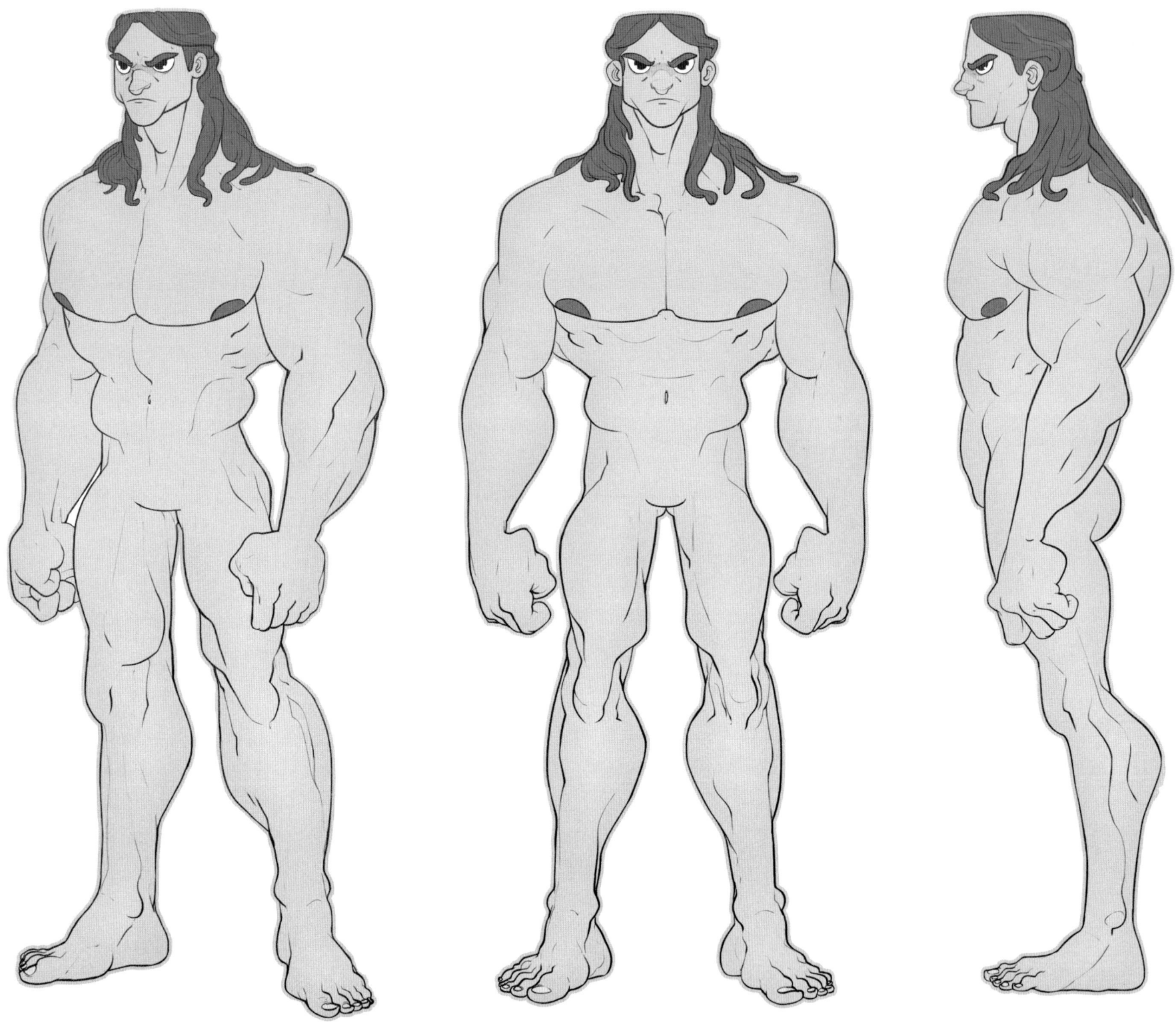

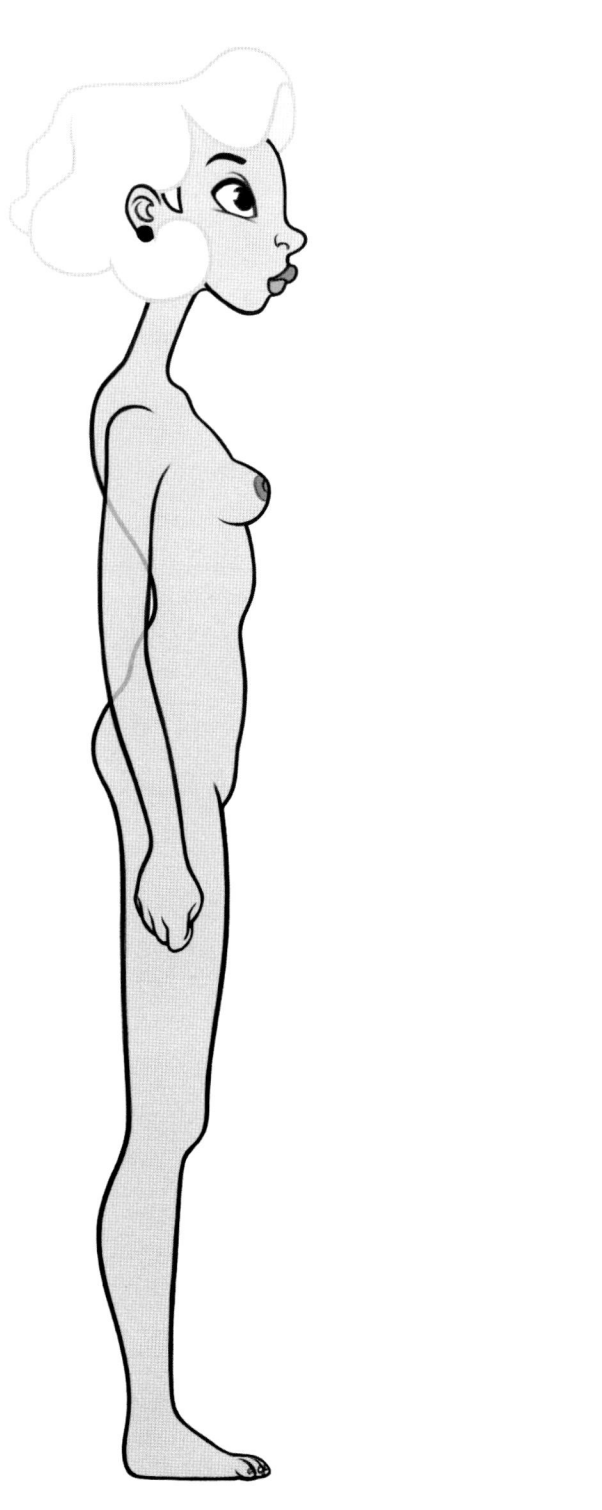
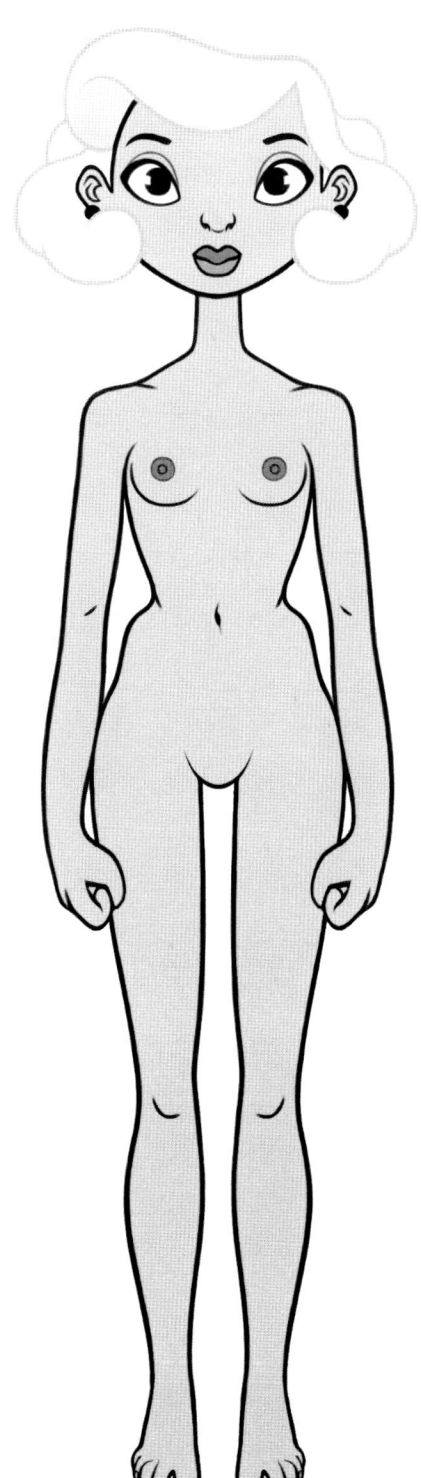
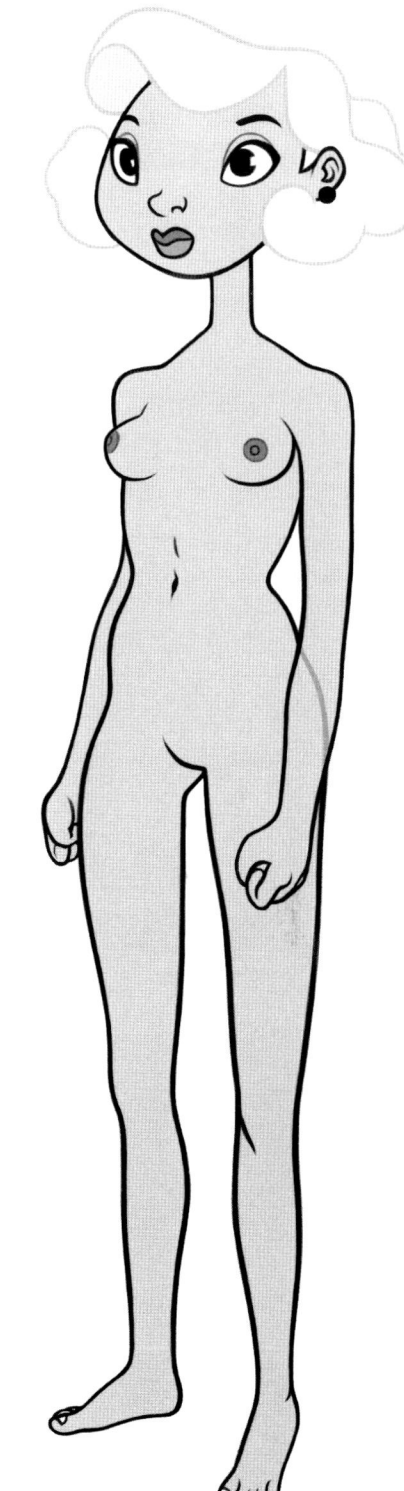

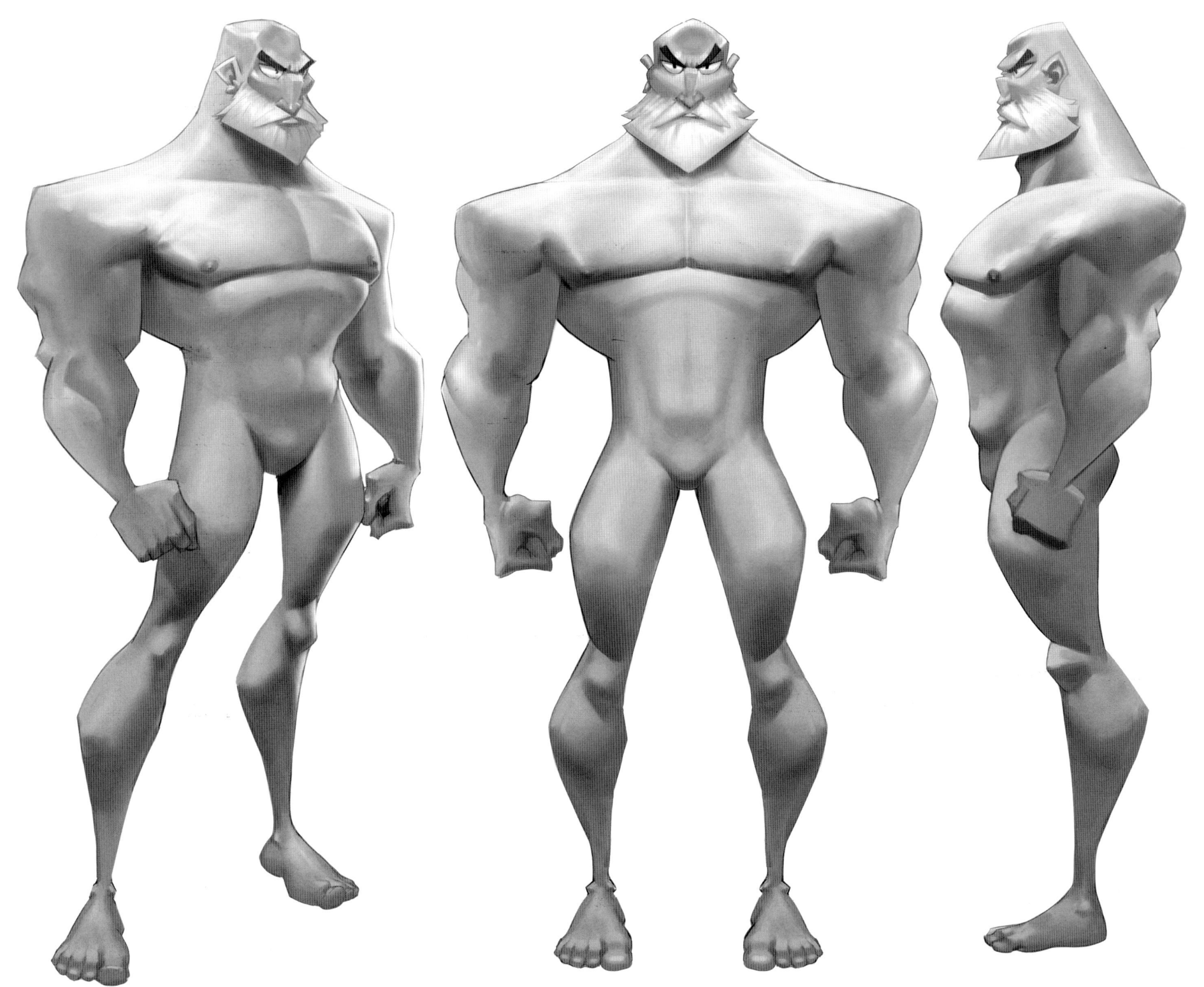

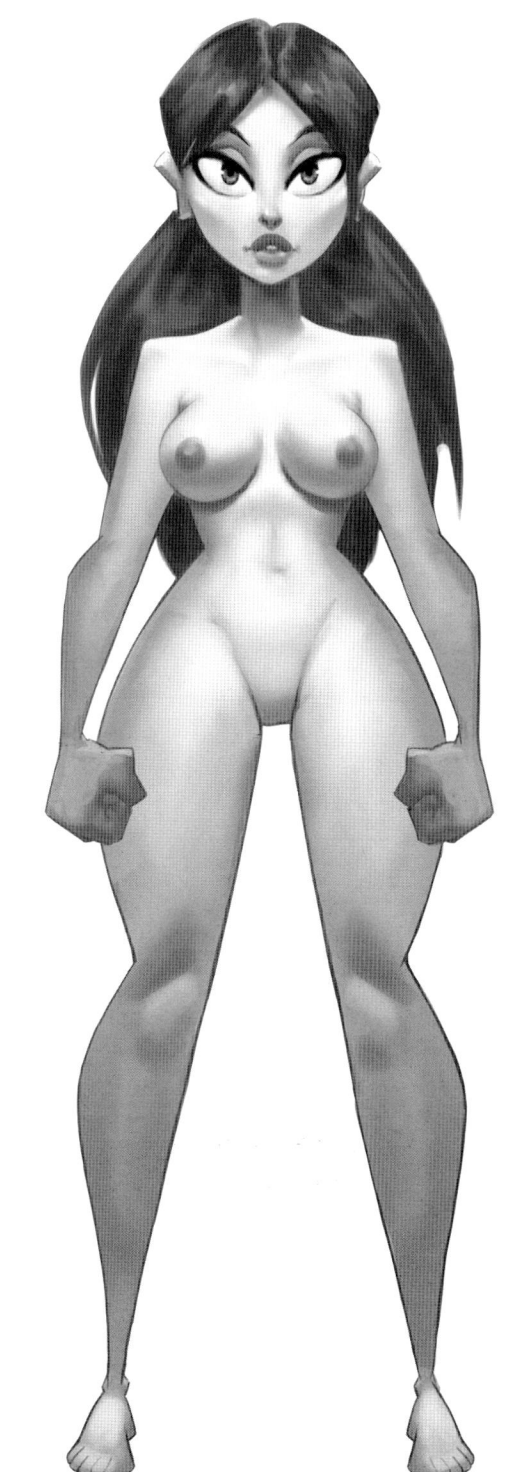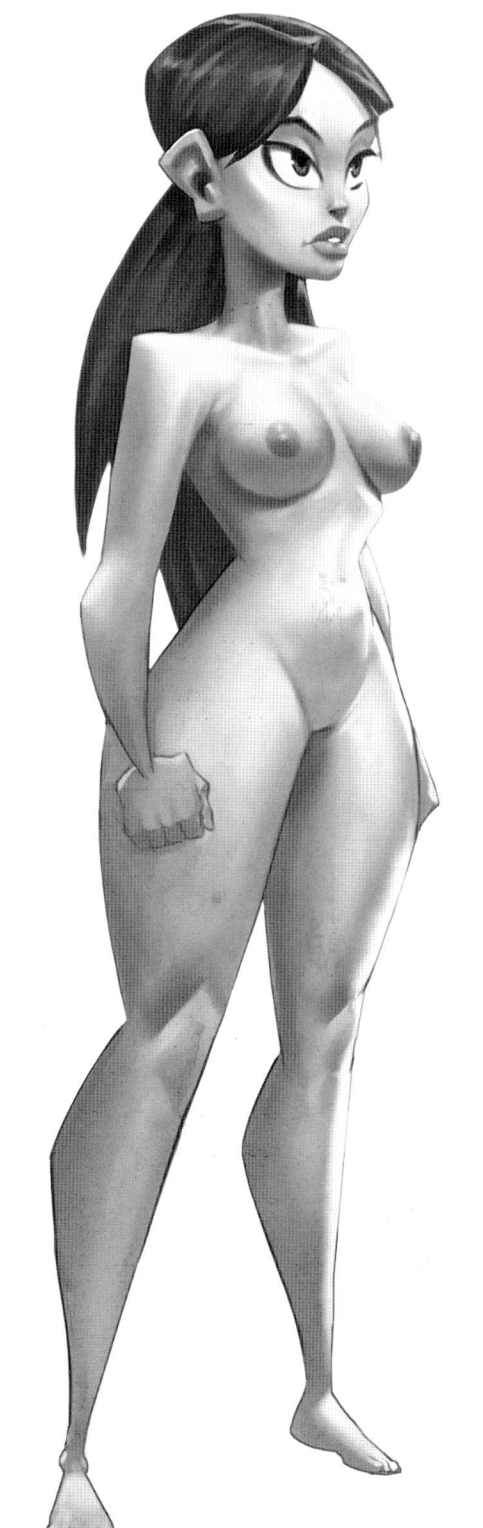

DANIEL ARAYA

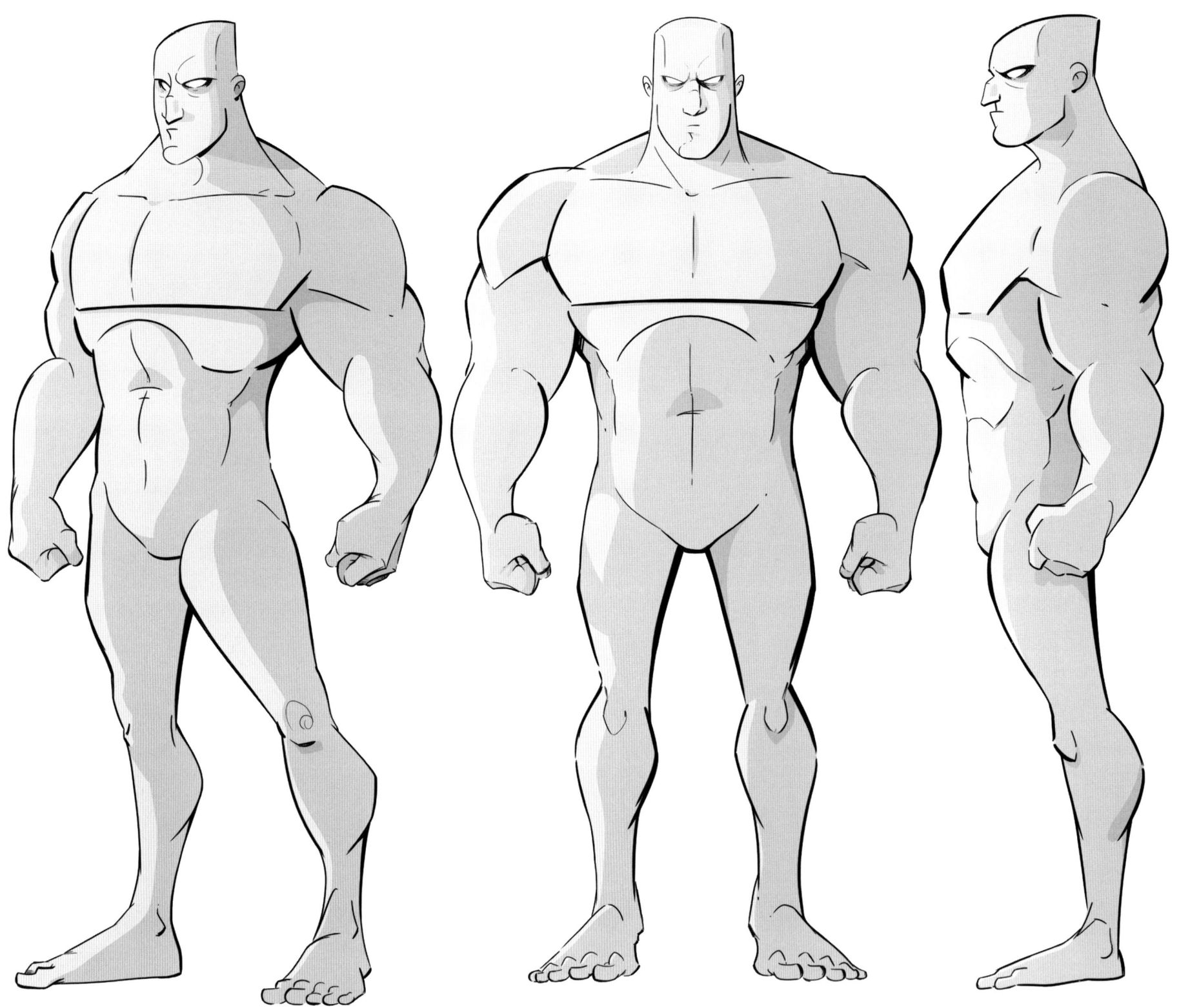

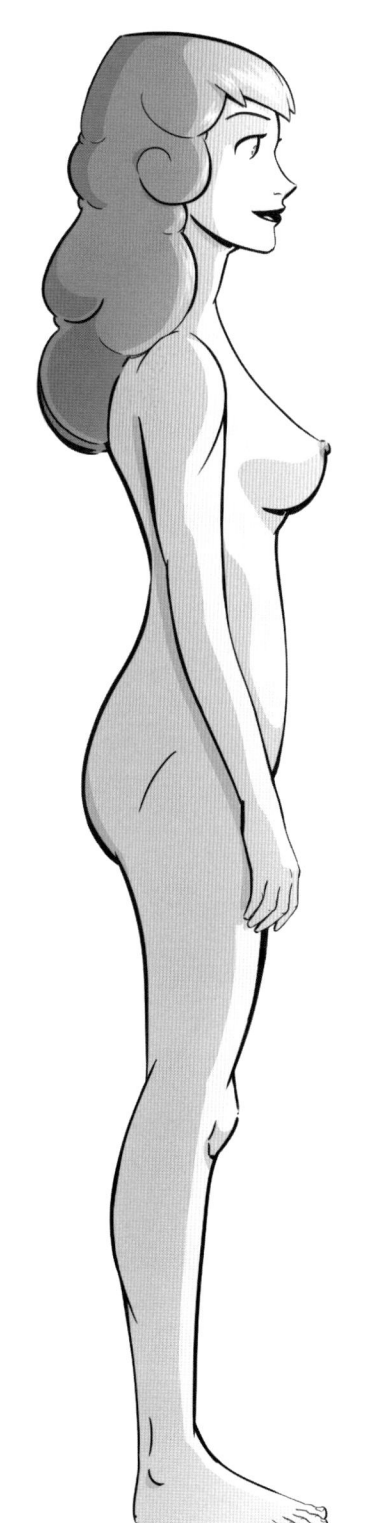
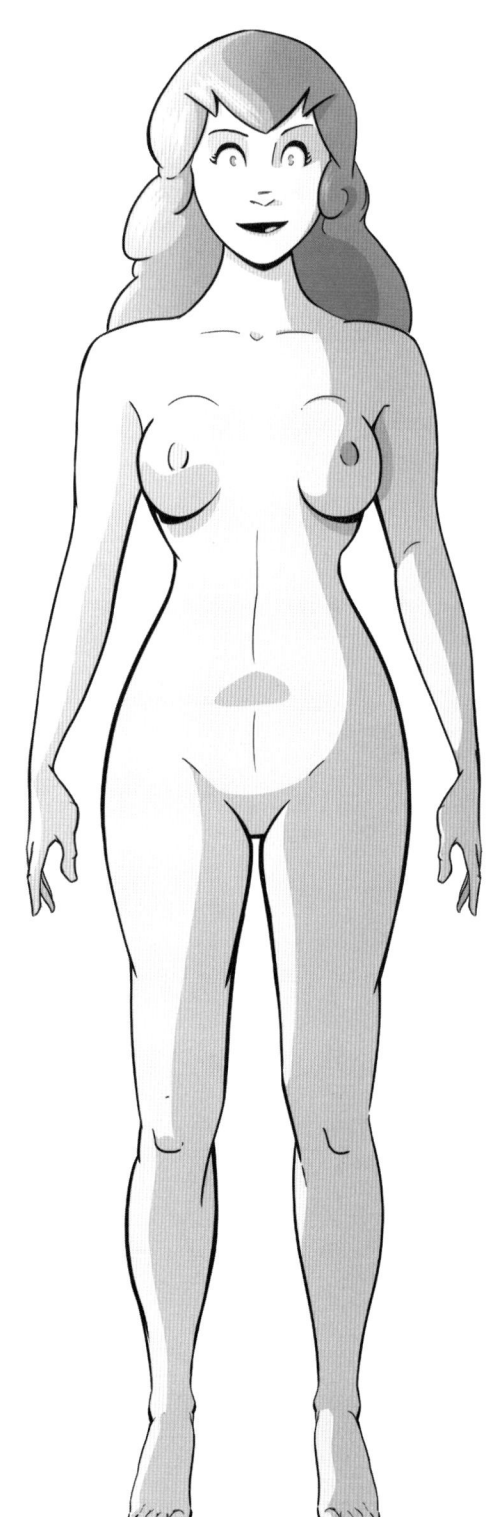
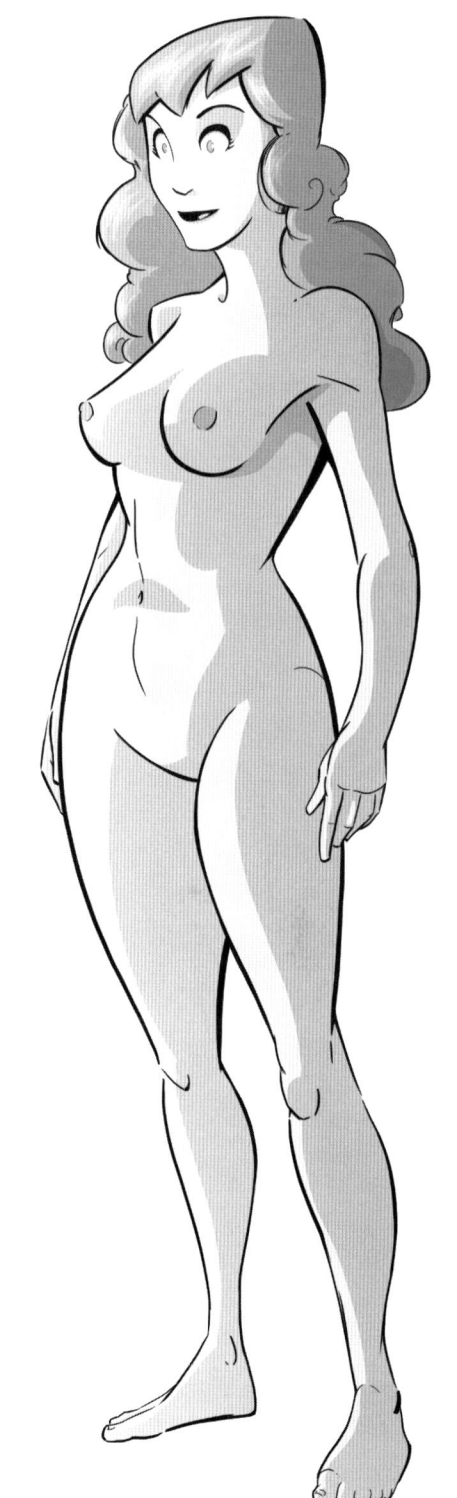

DAVE BARDIN

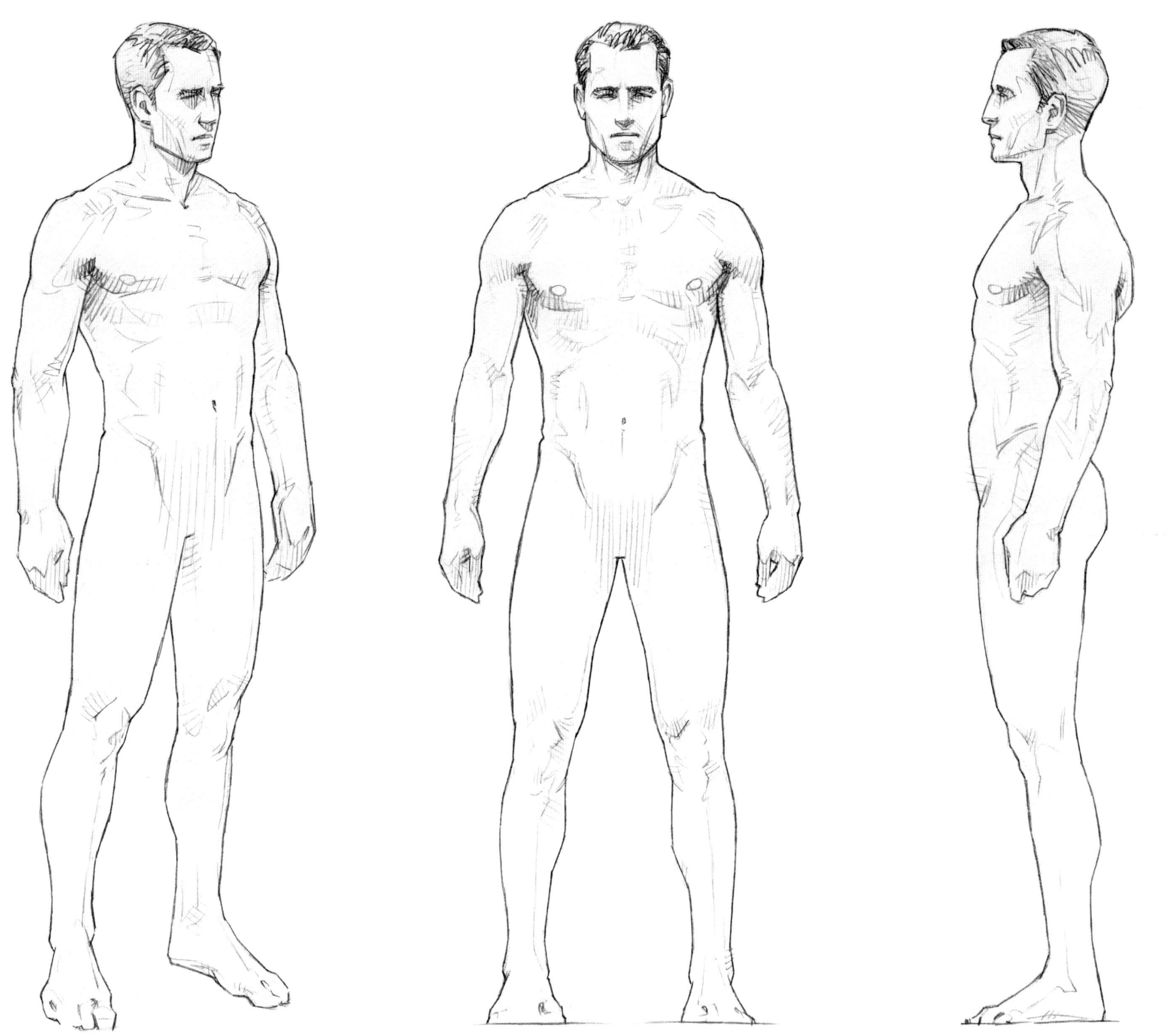

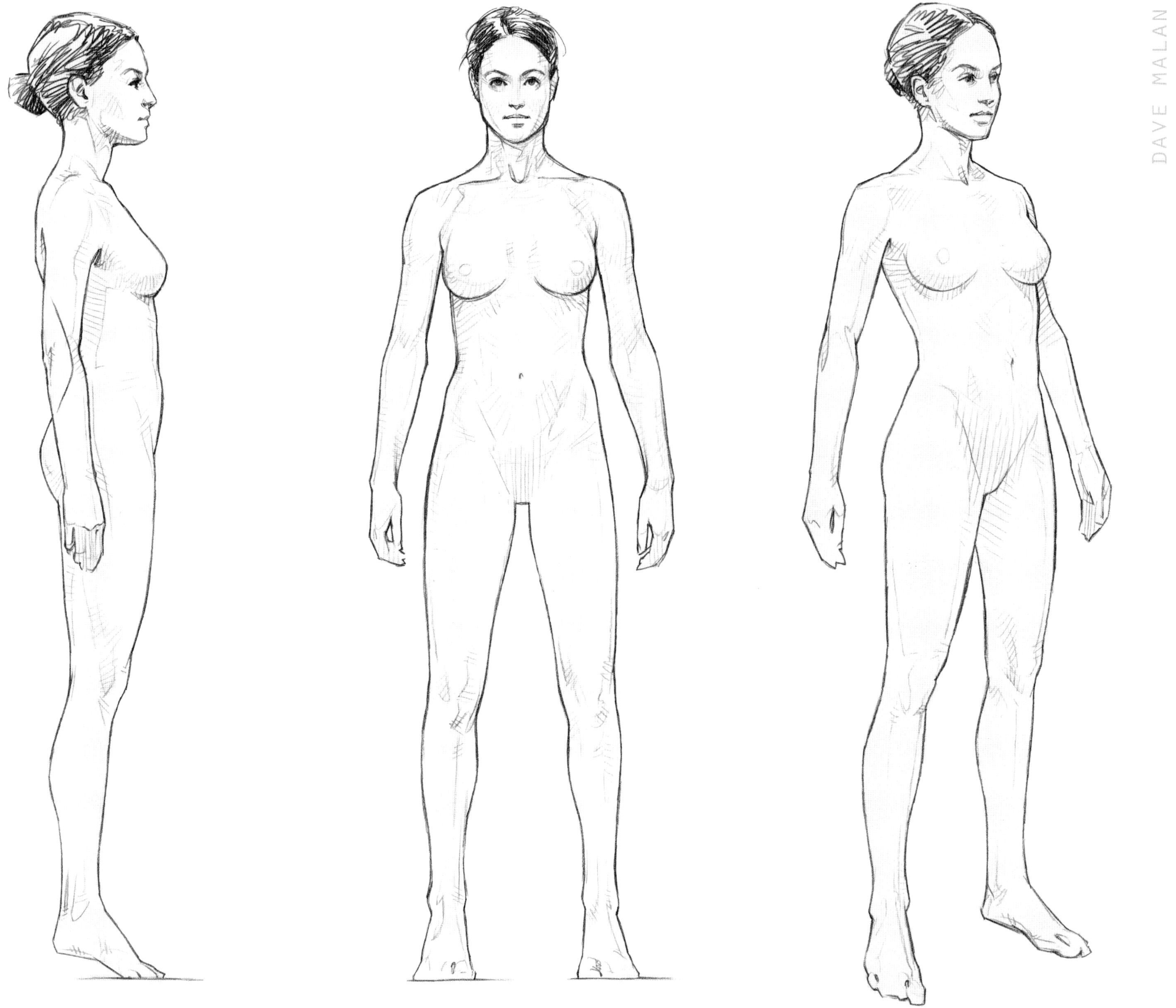

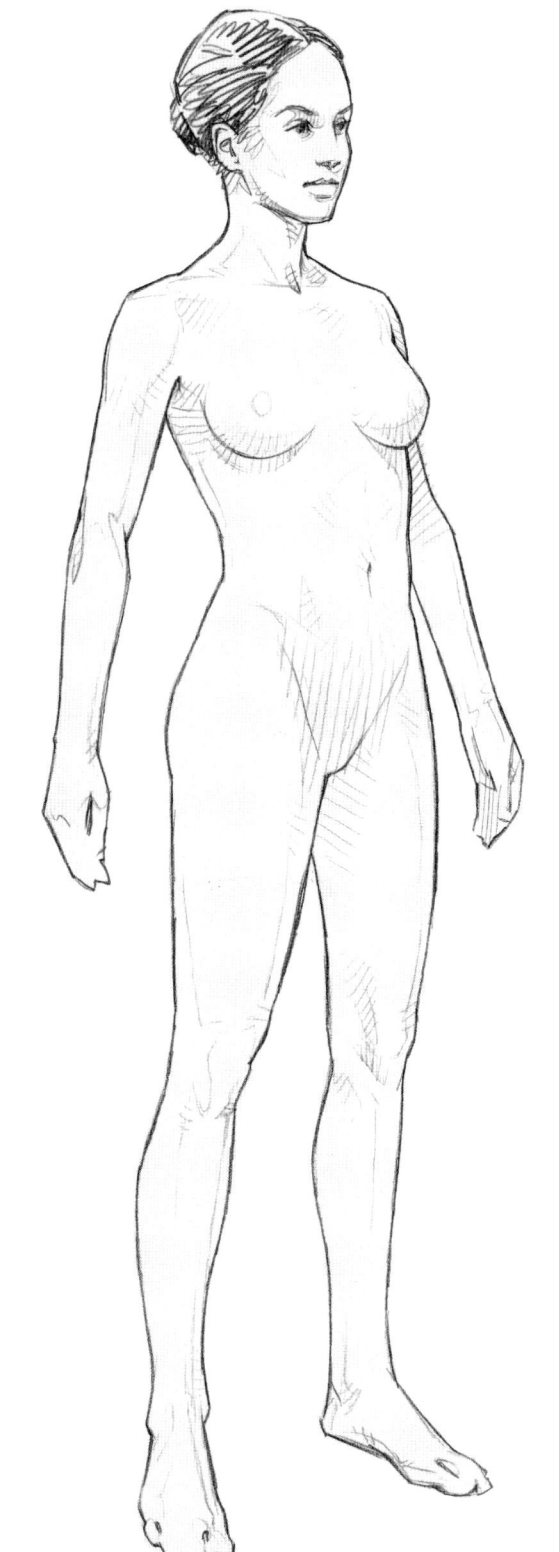

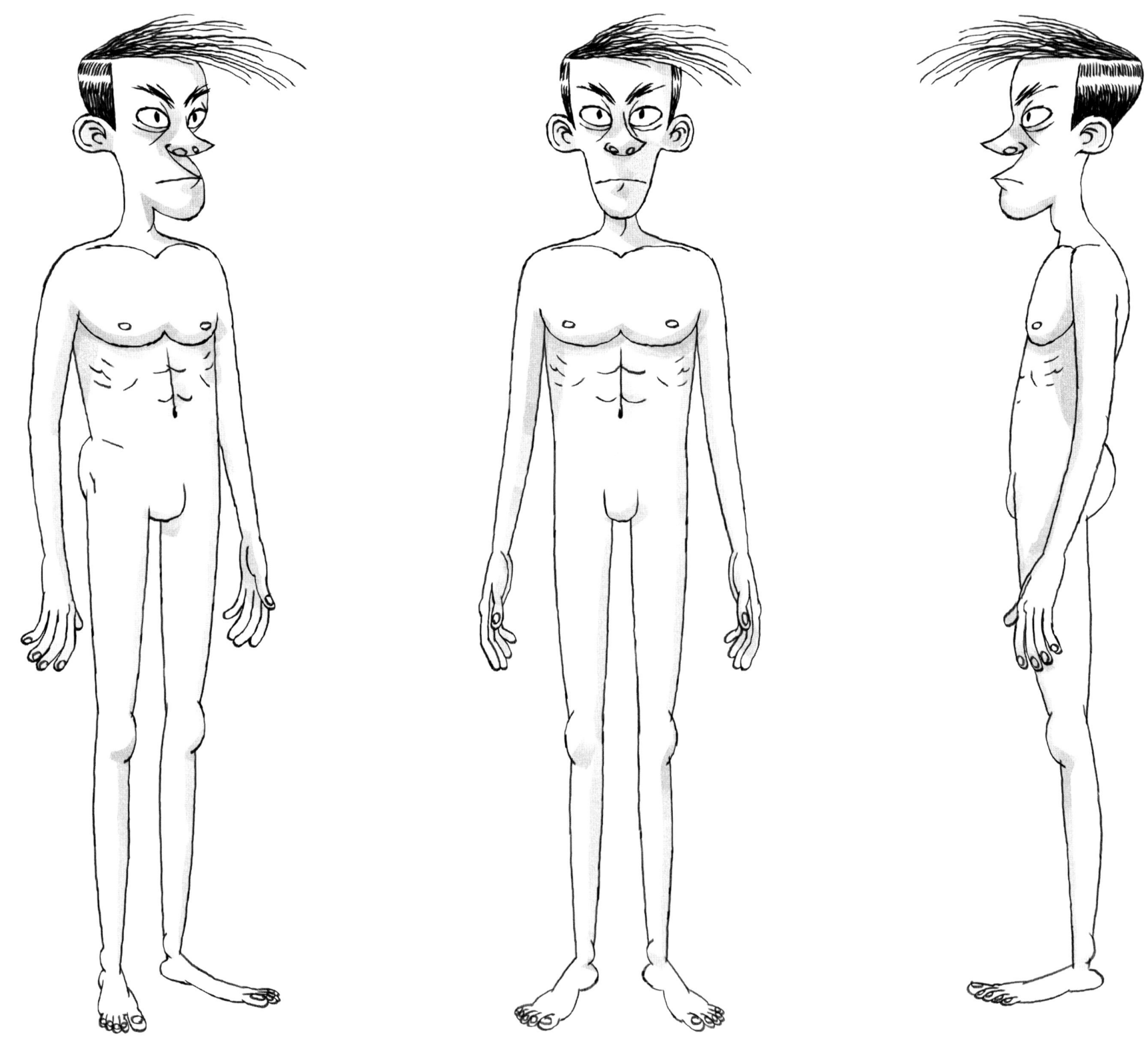

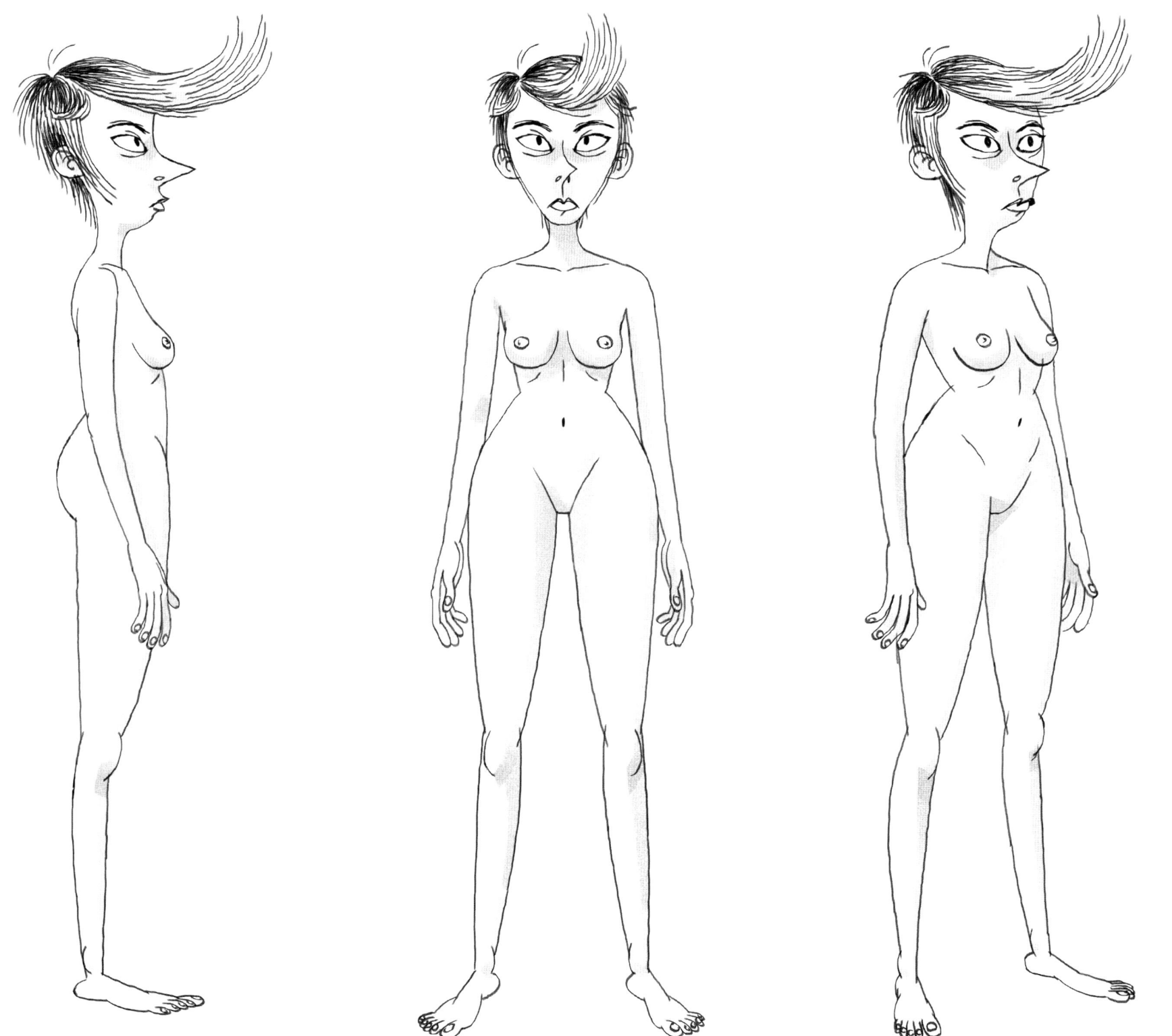

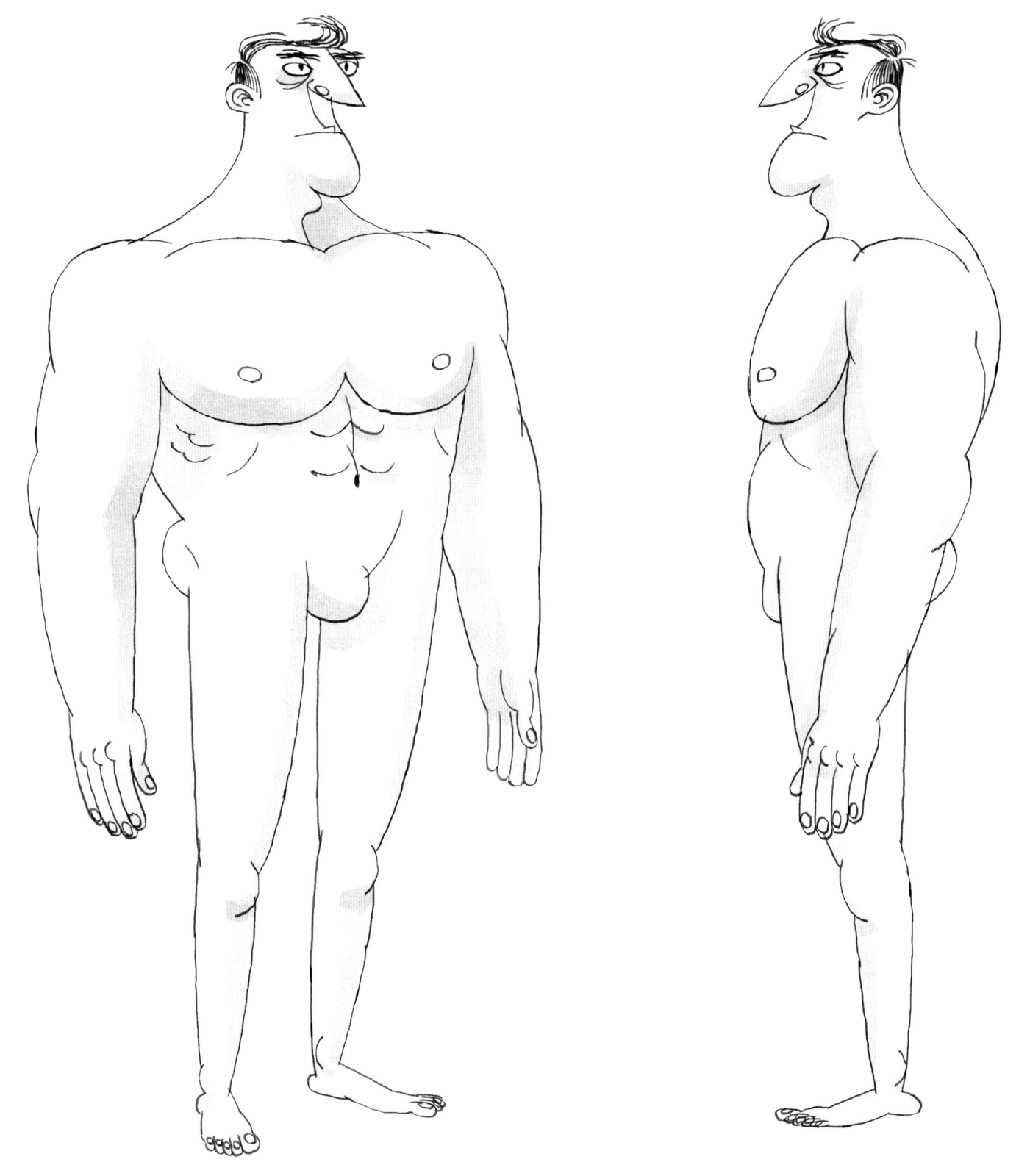

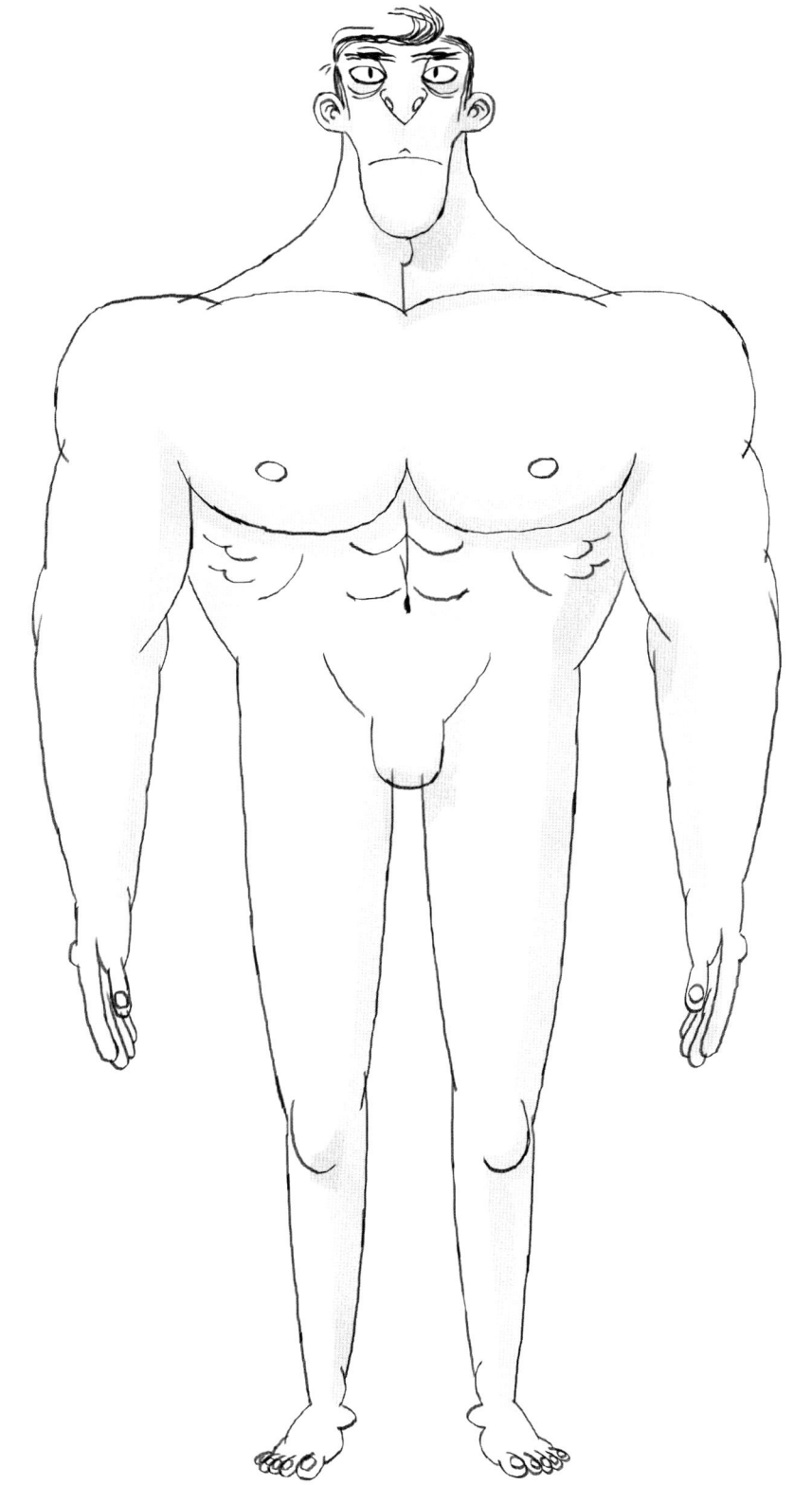

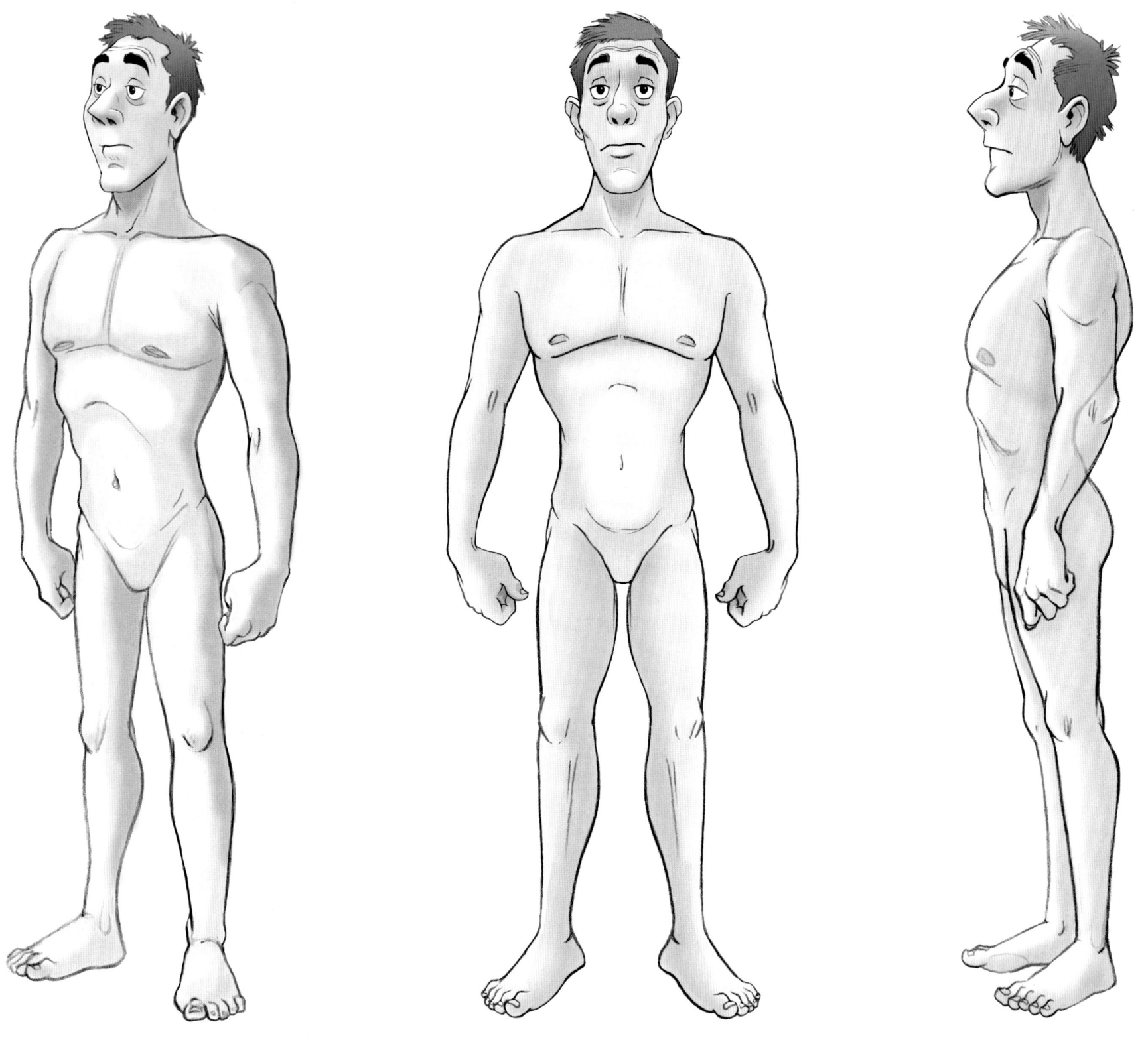

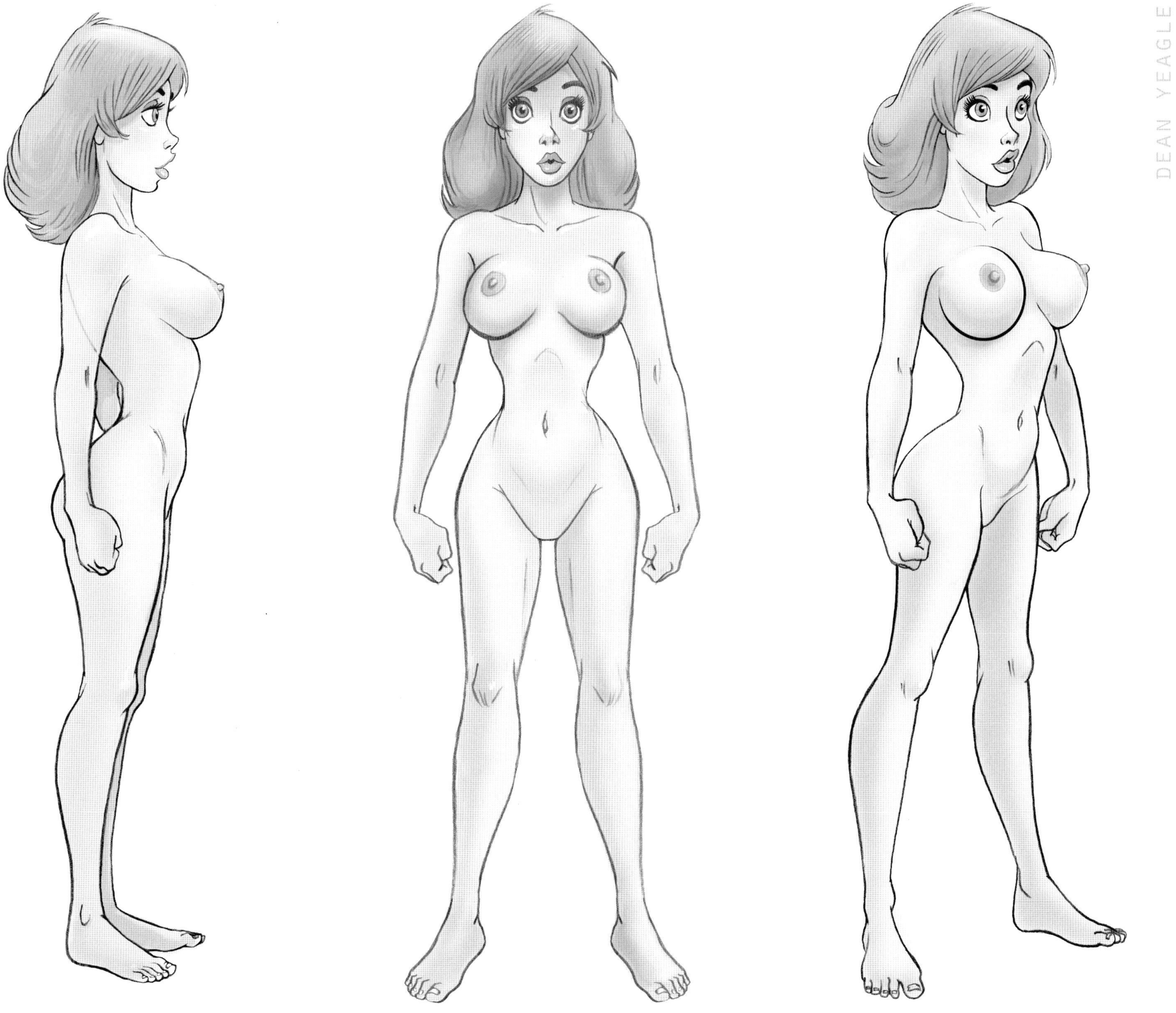

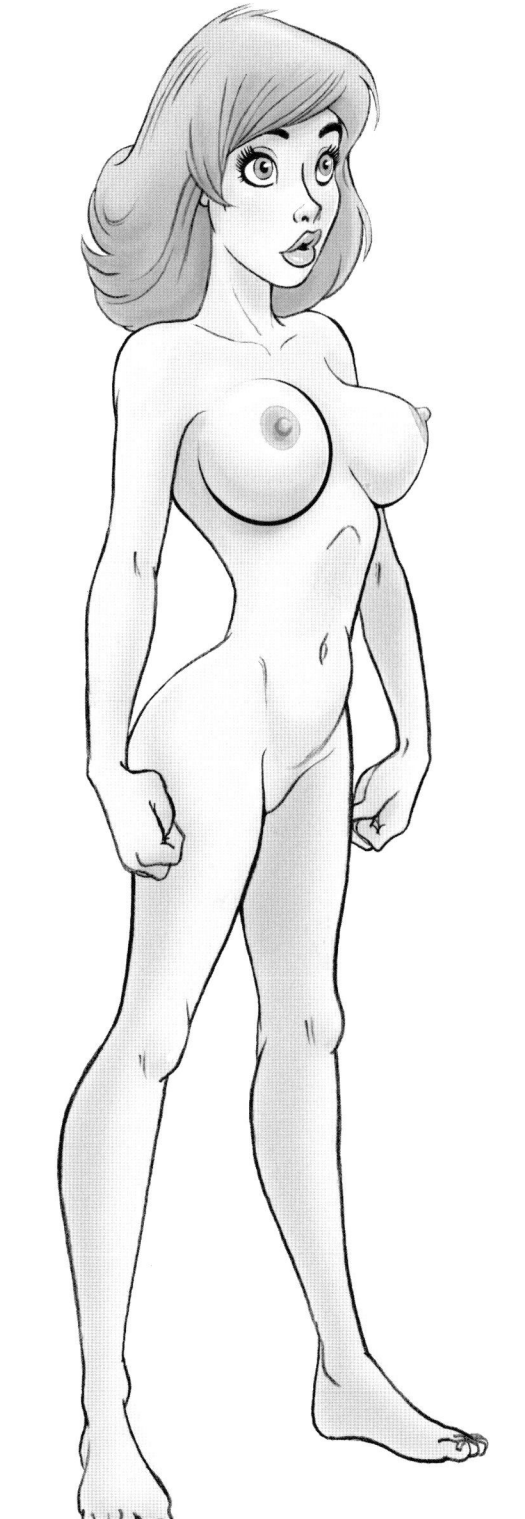

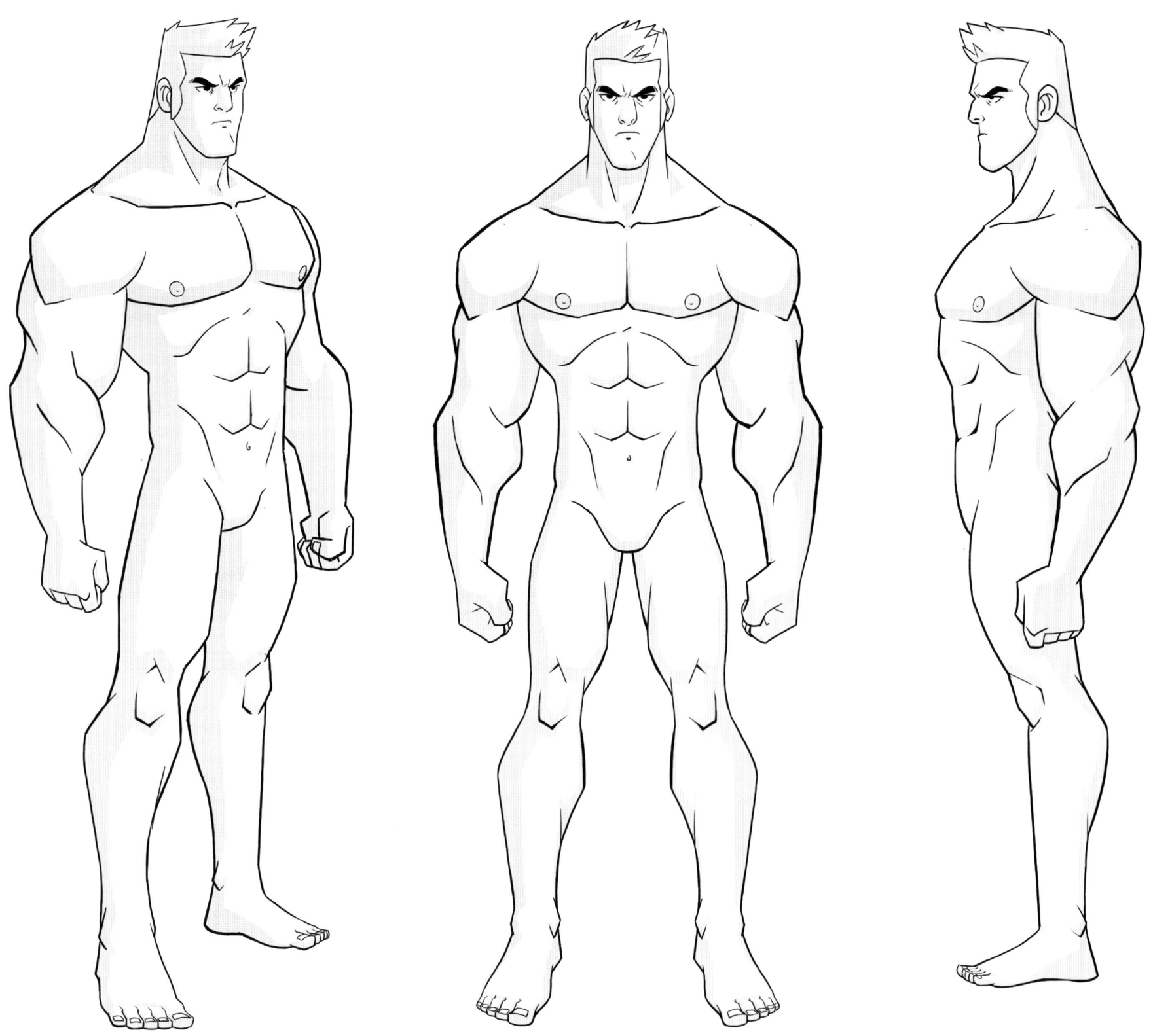

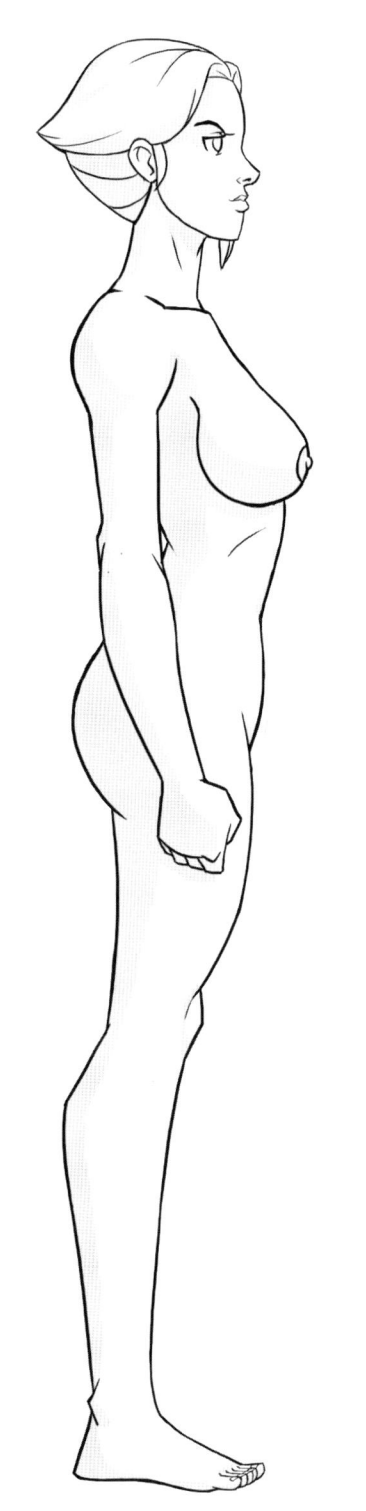
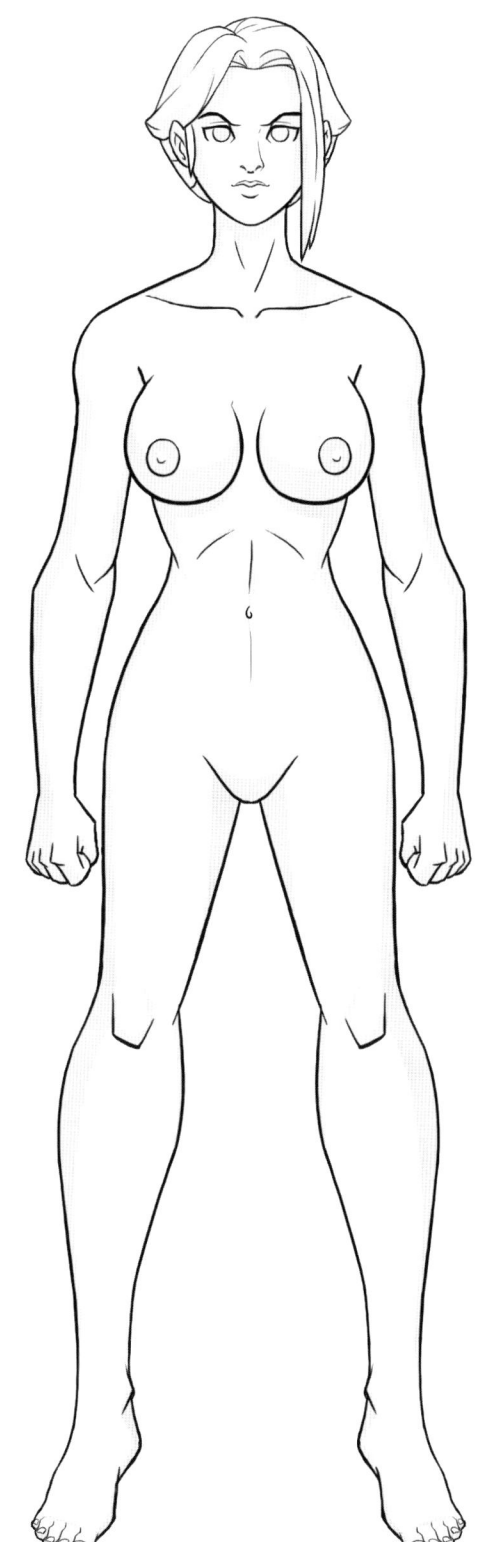
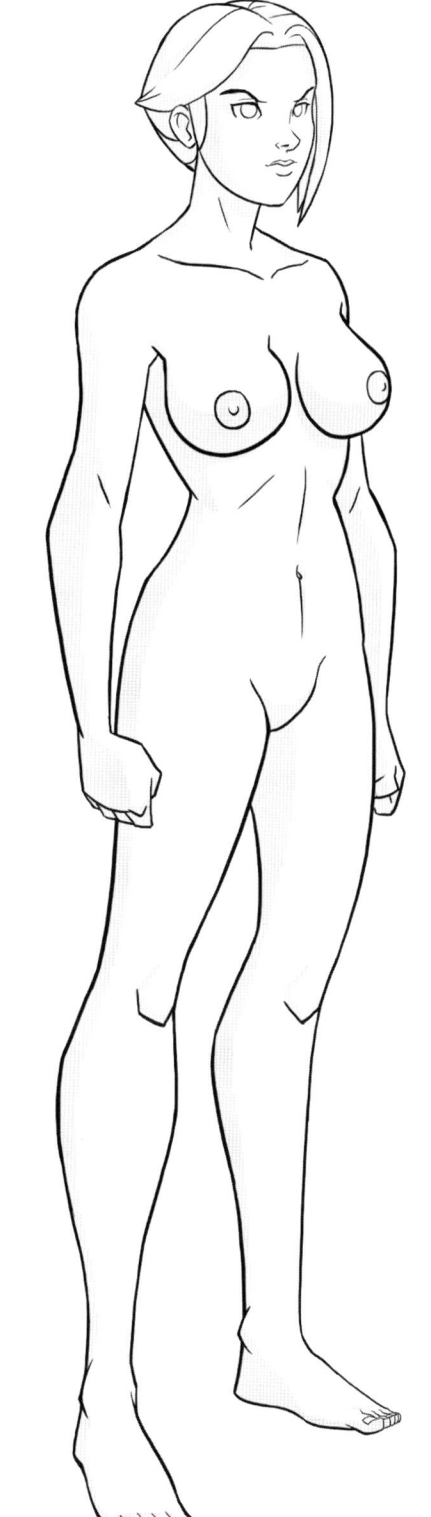

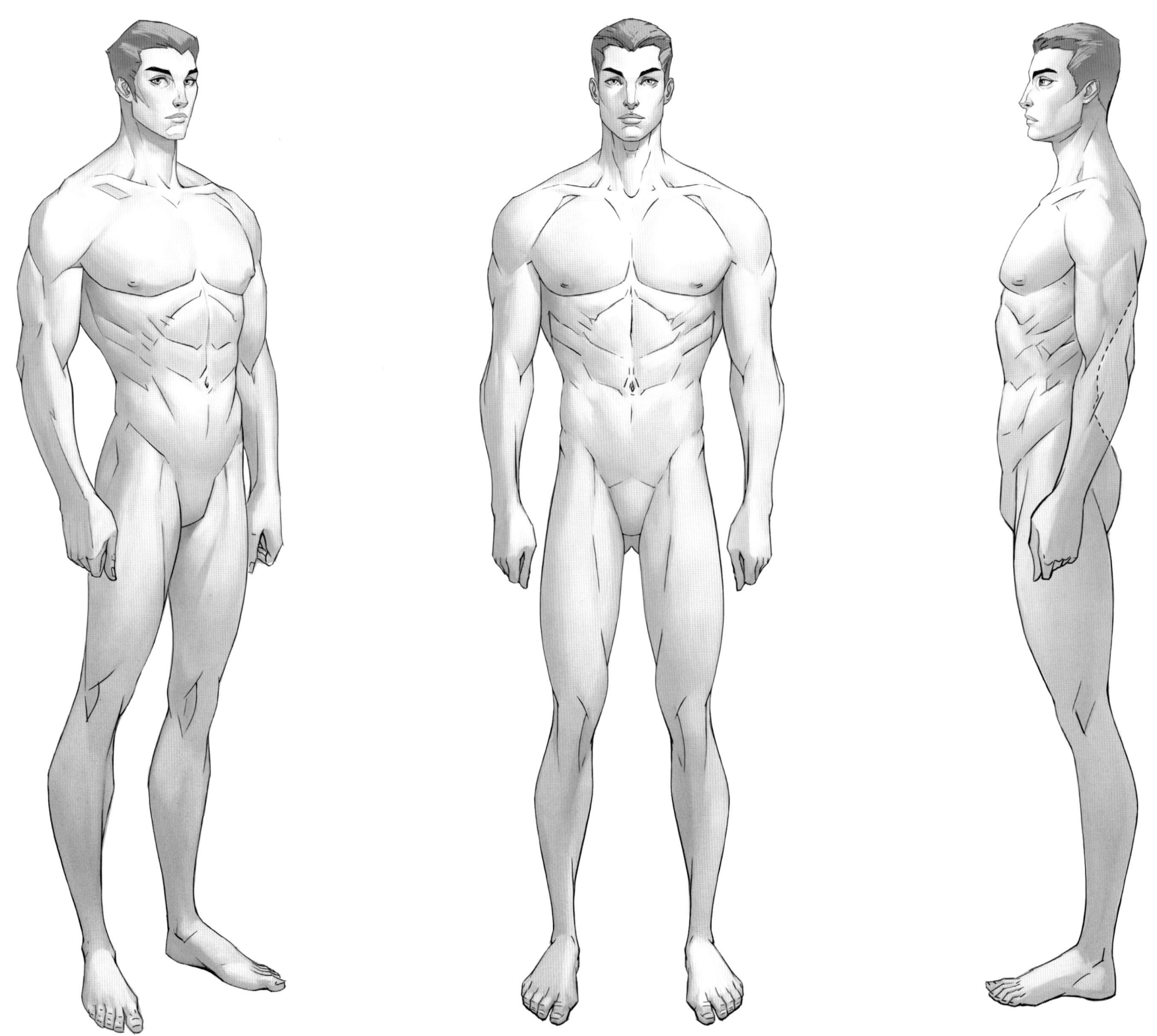

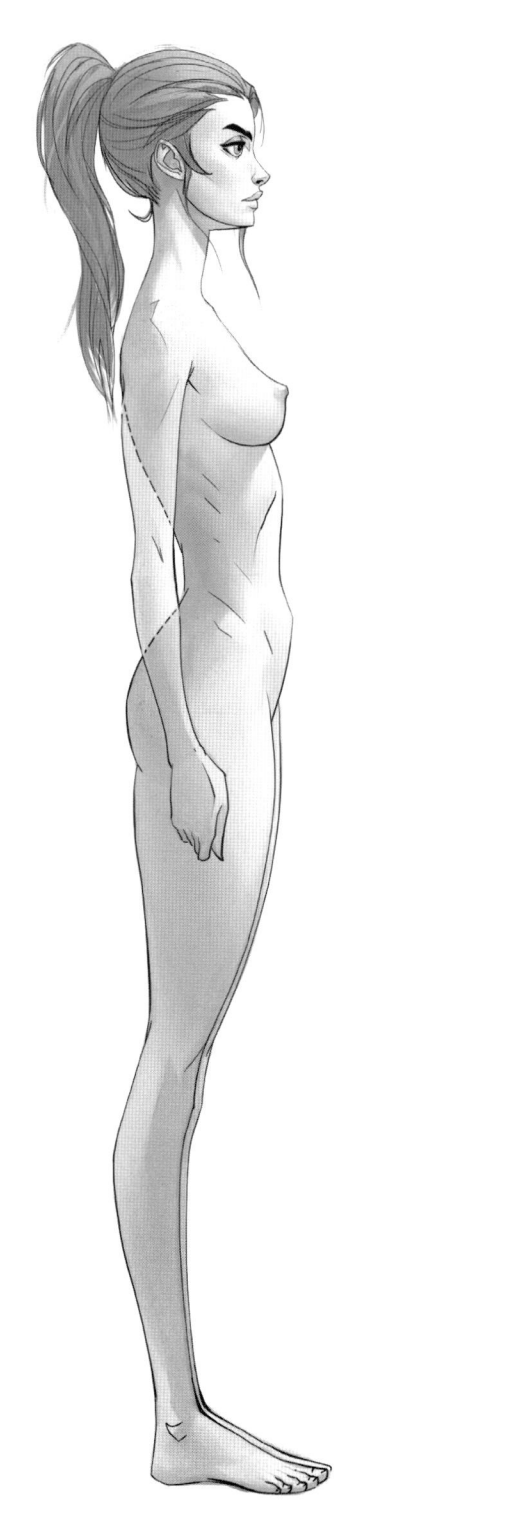
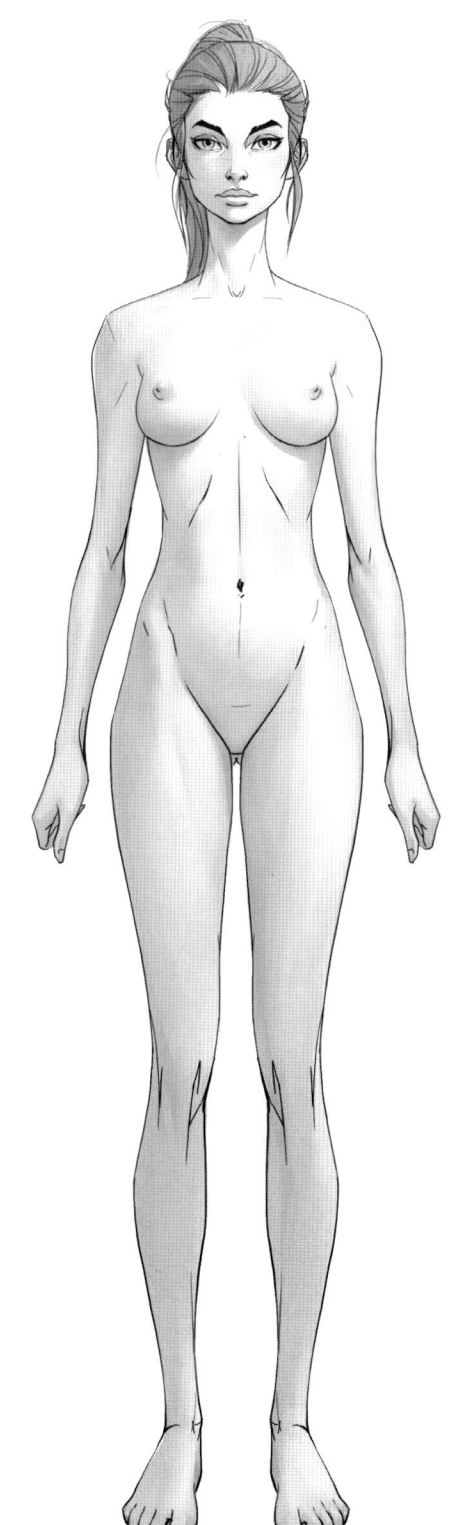
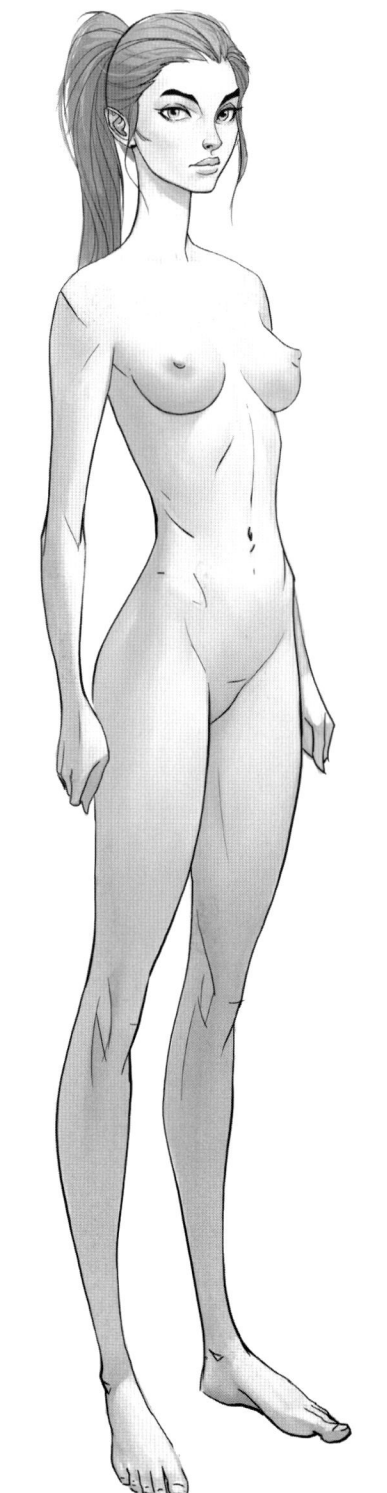

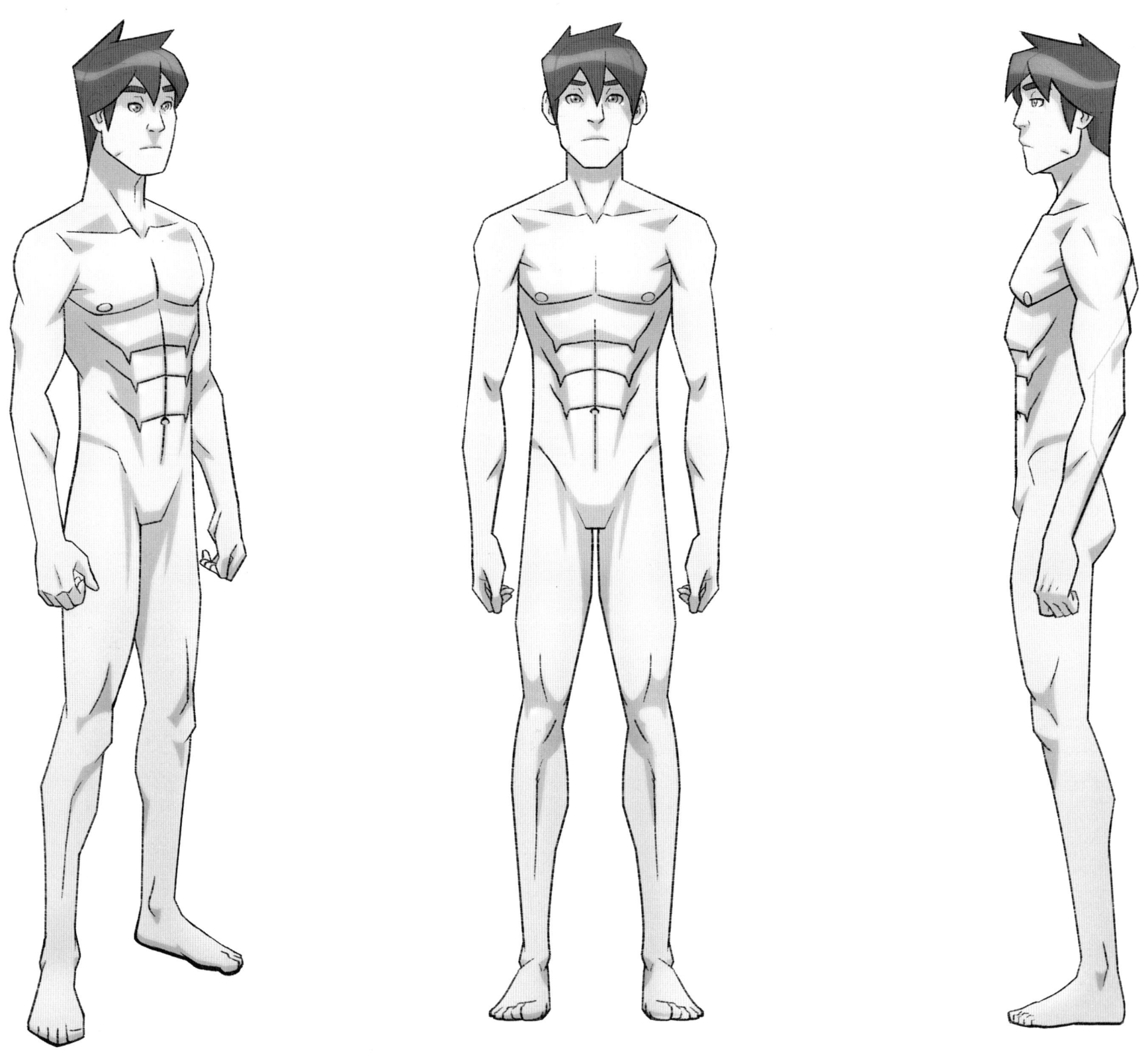

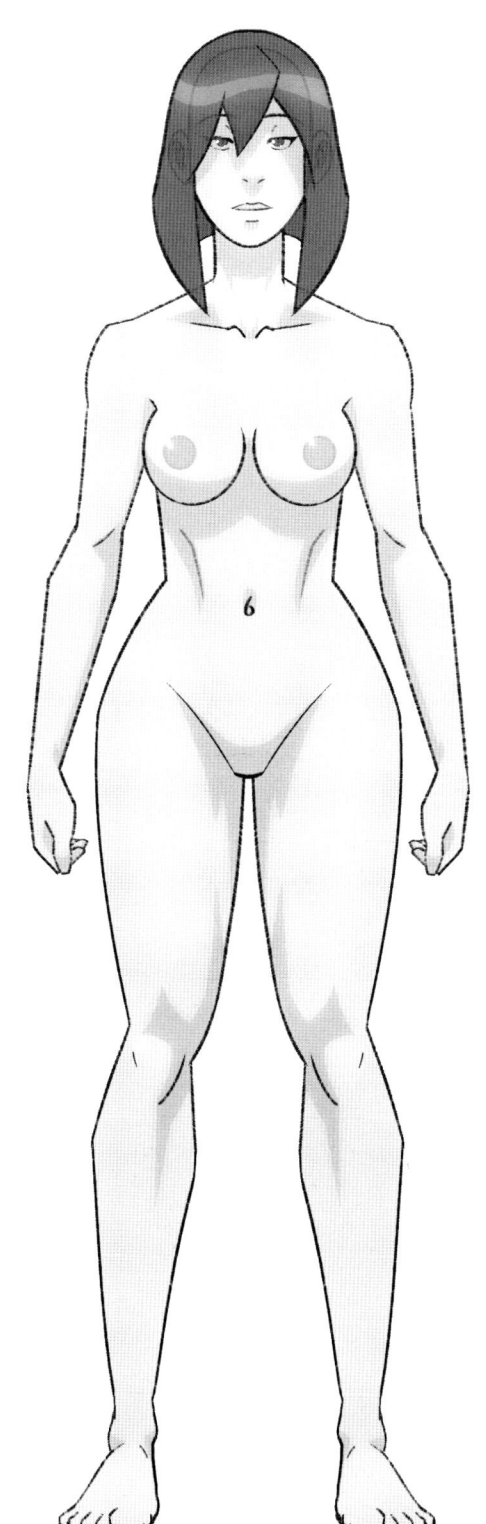
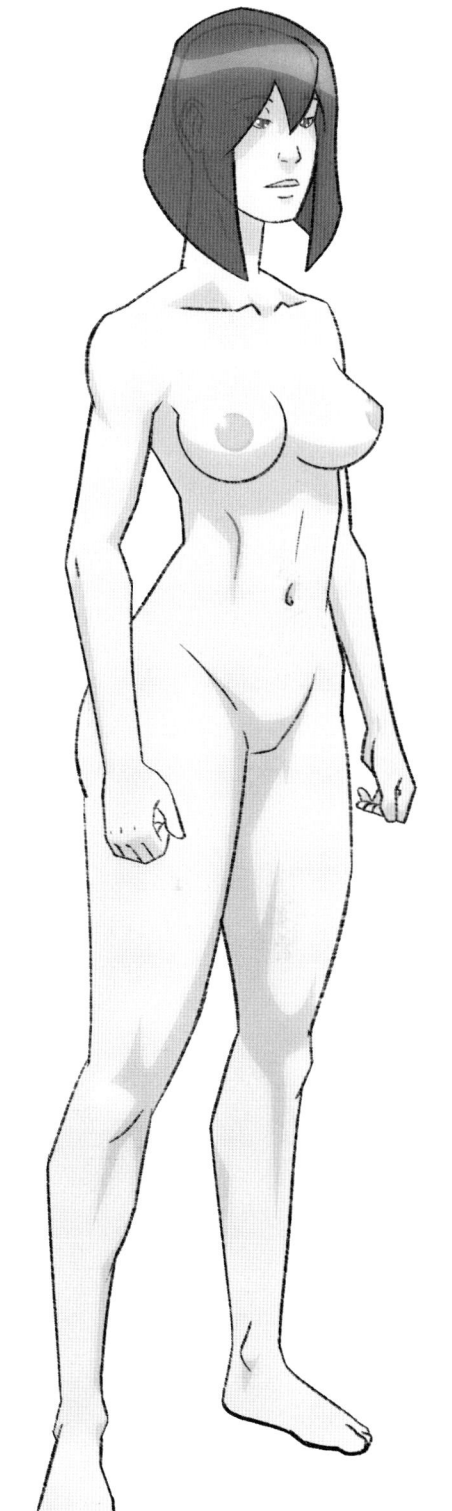

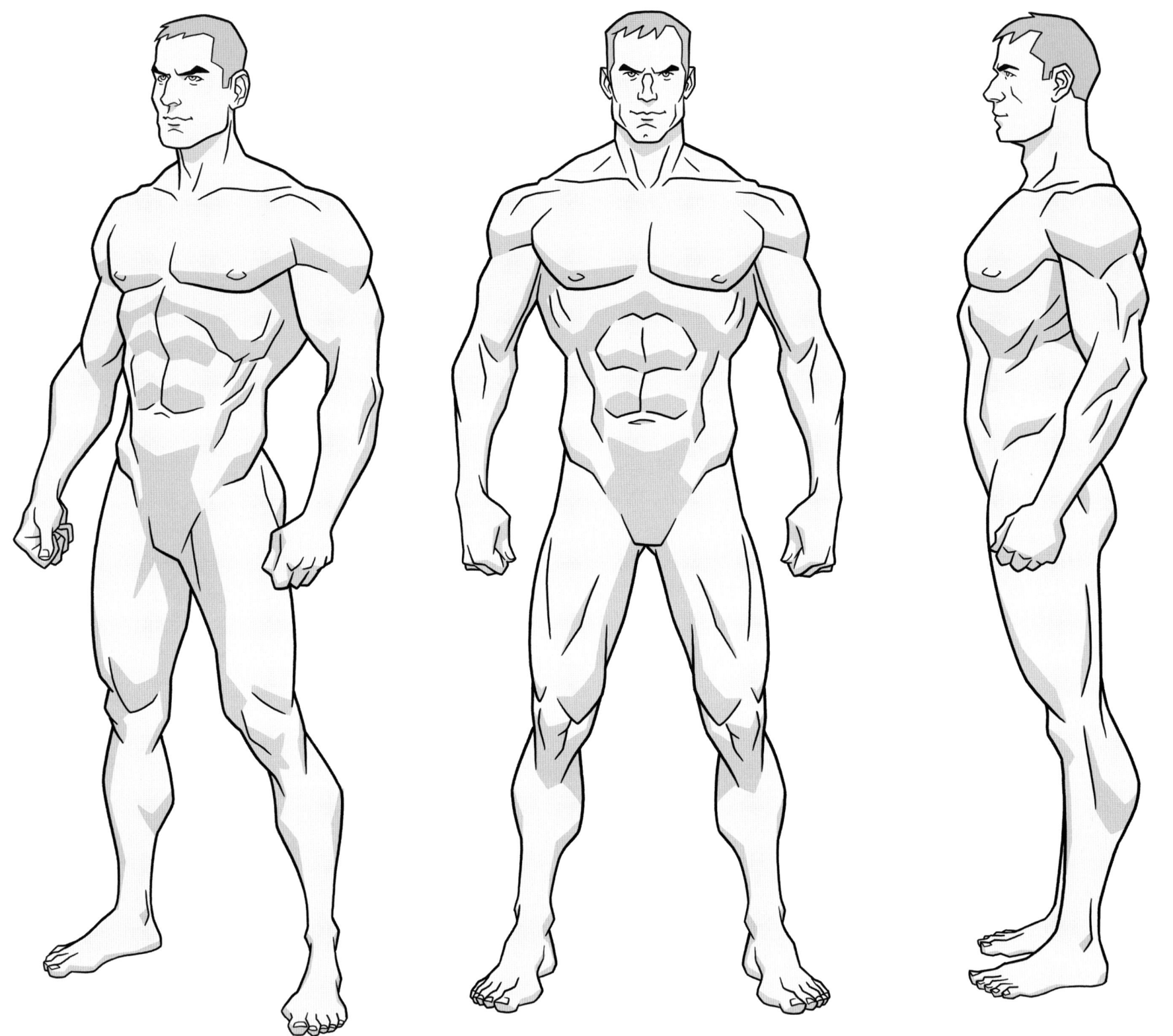

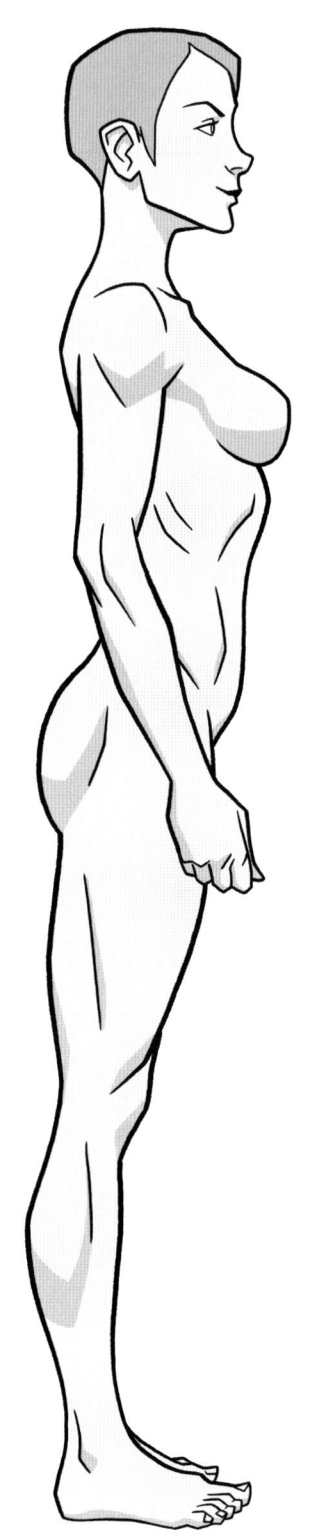
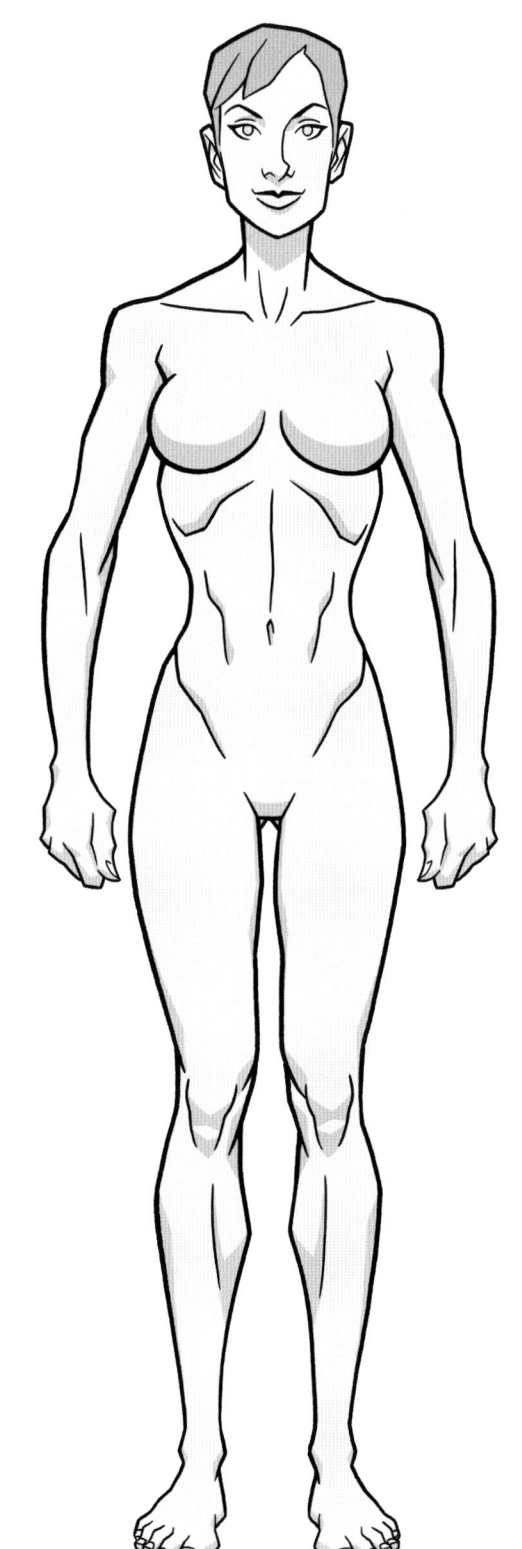
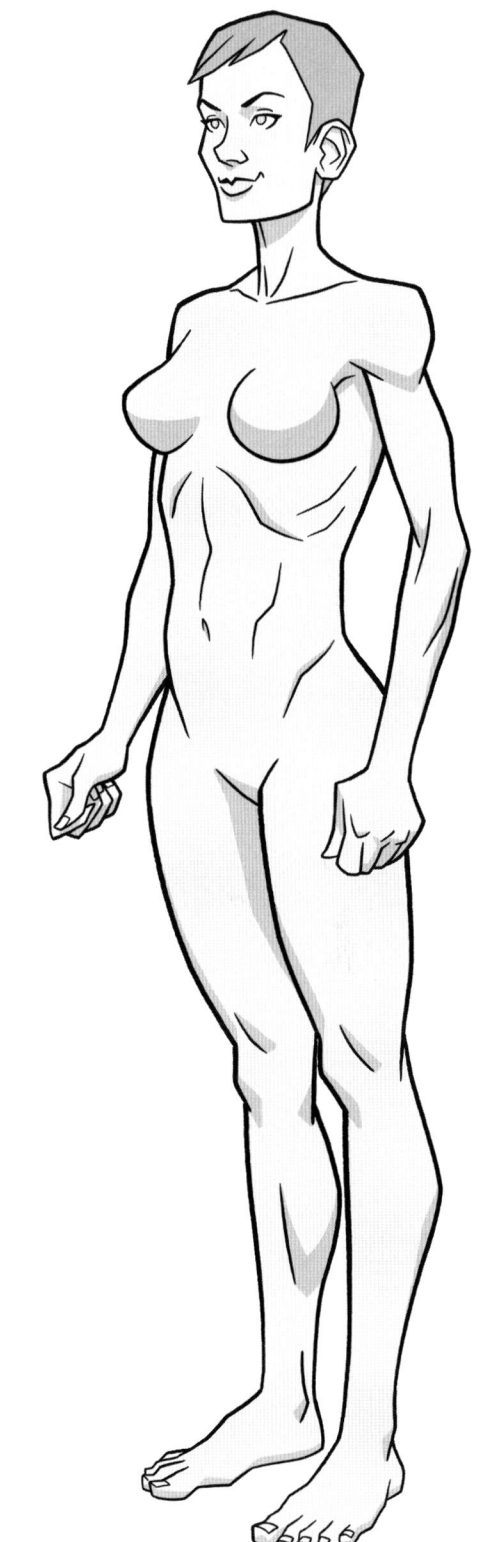

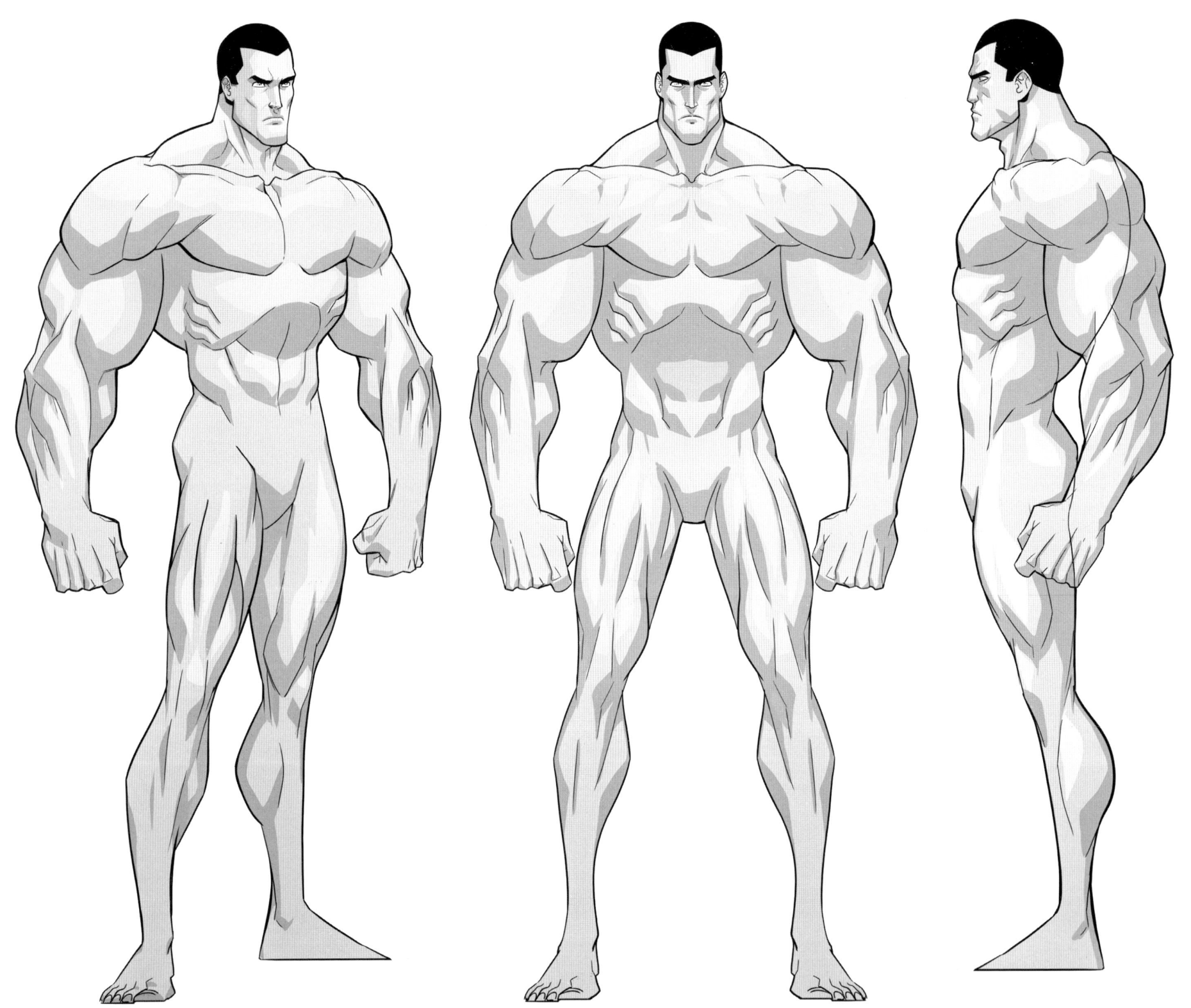

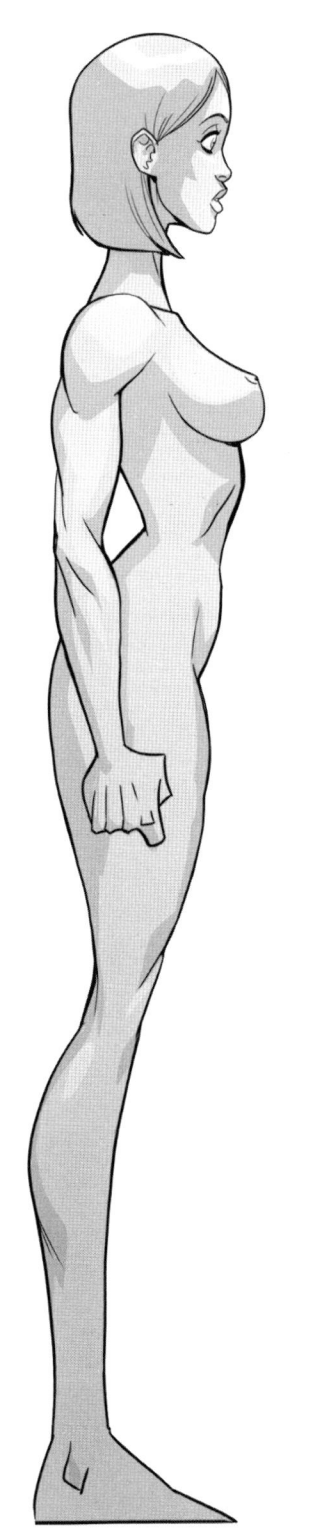
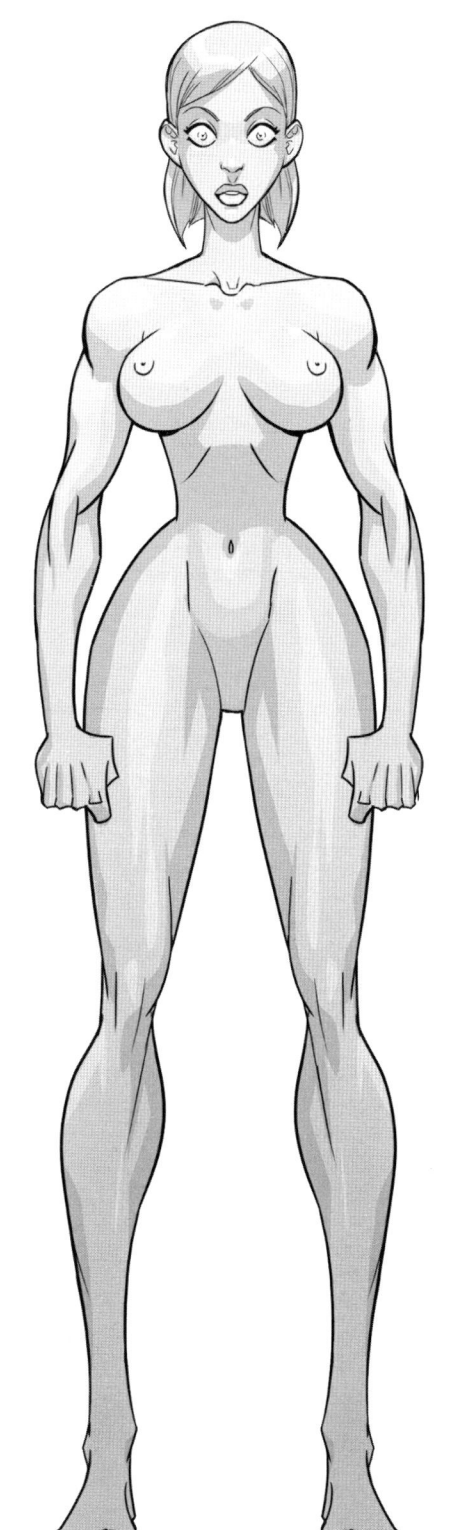
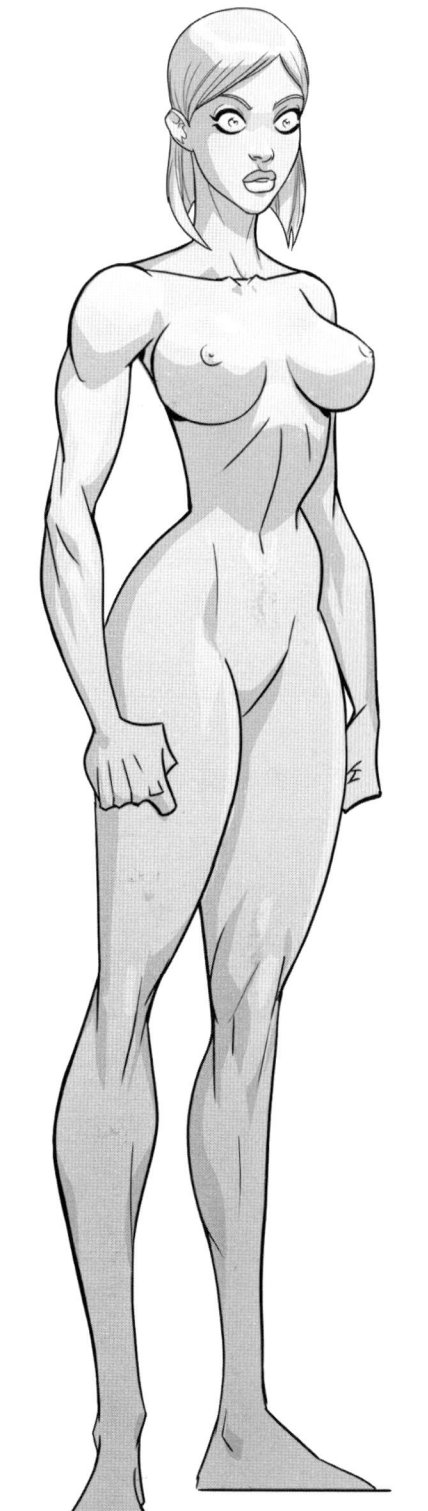

EDDIE NUNEZ

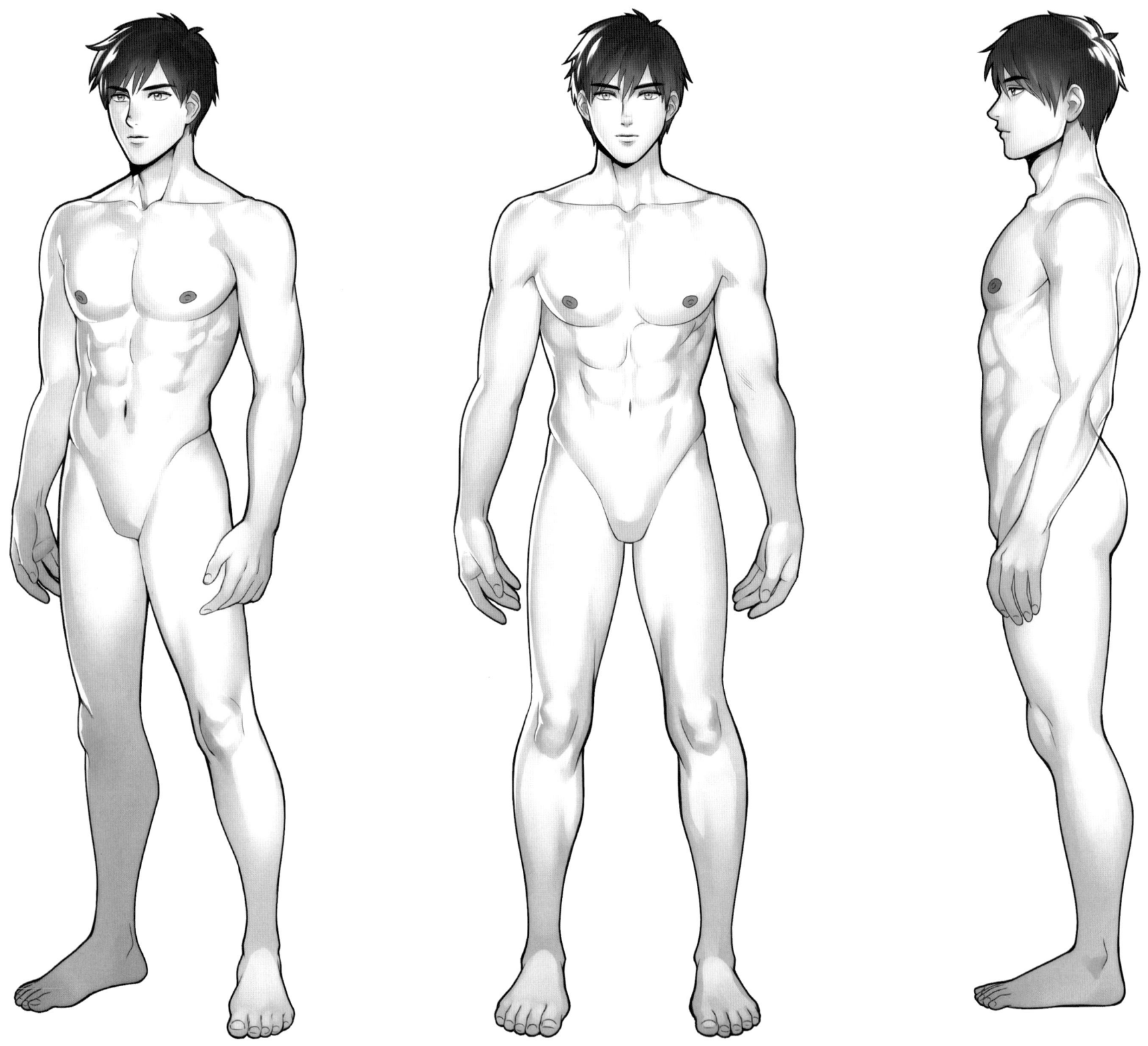

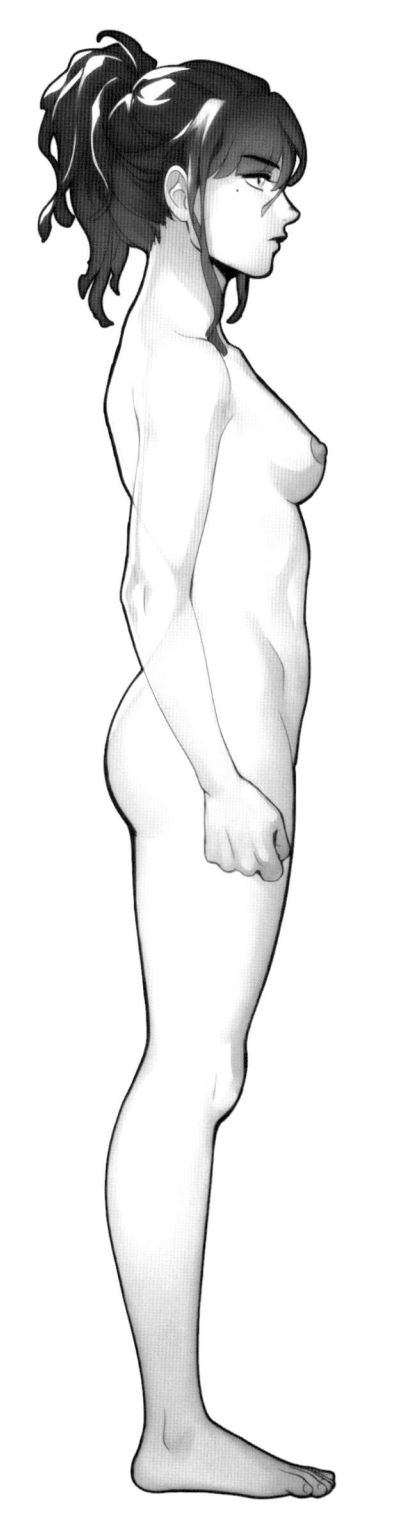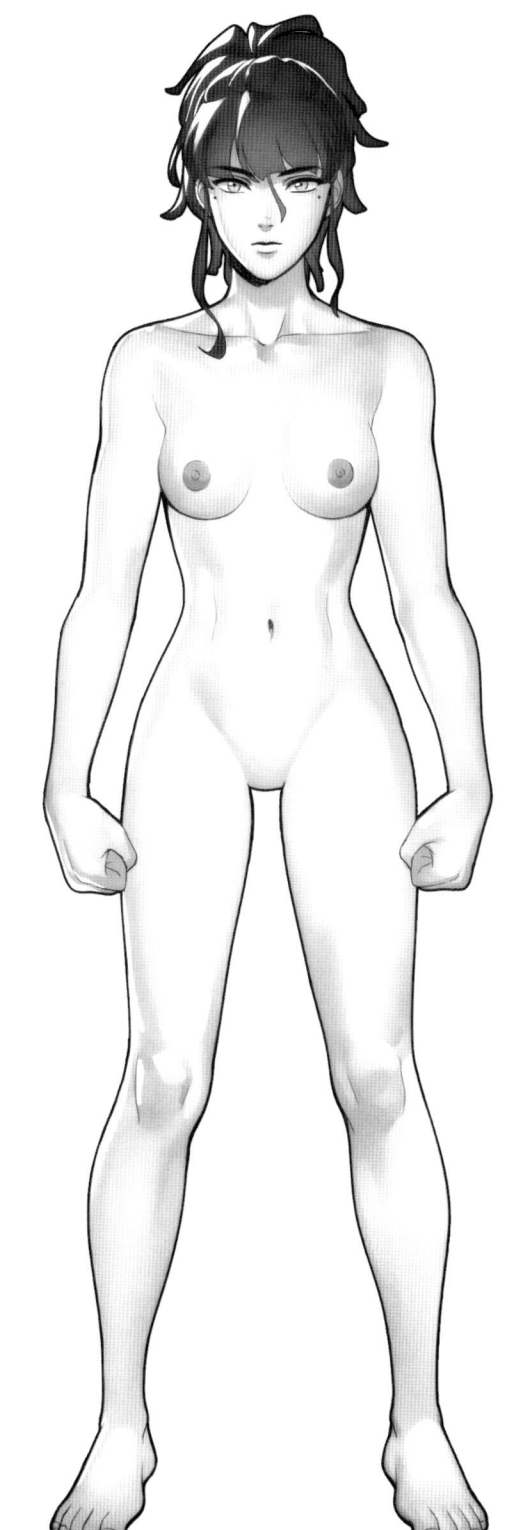

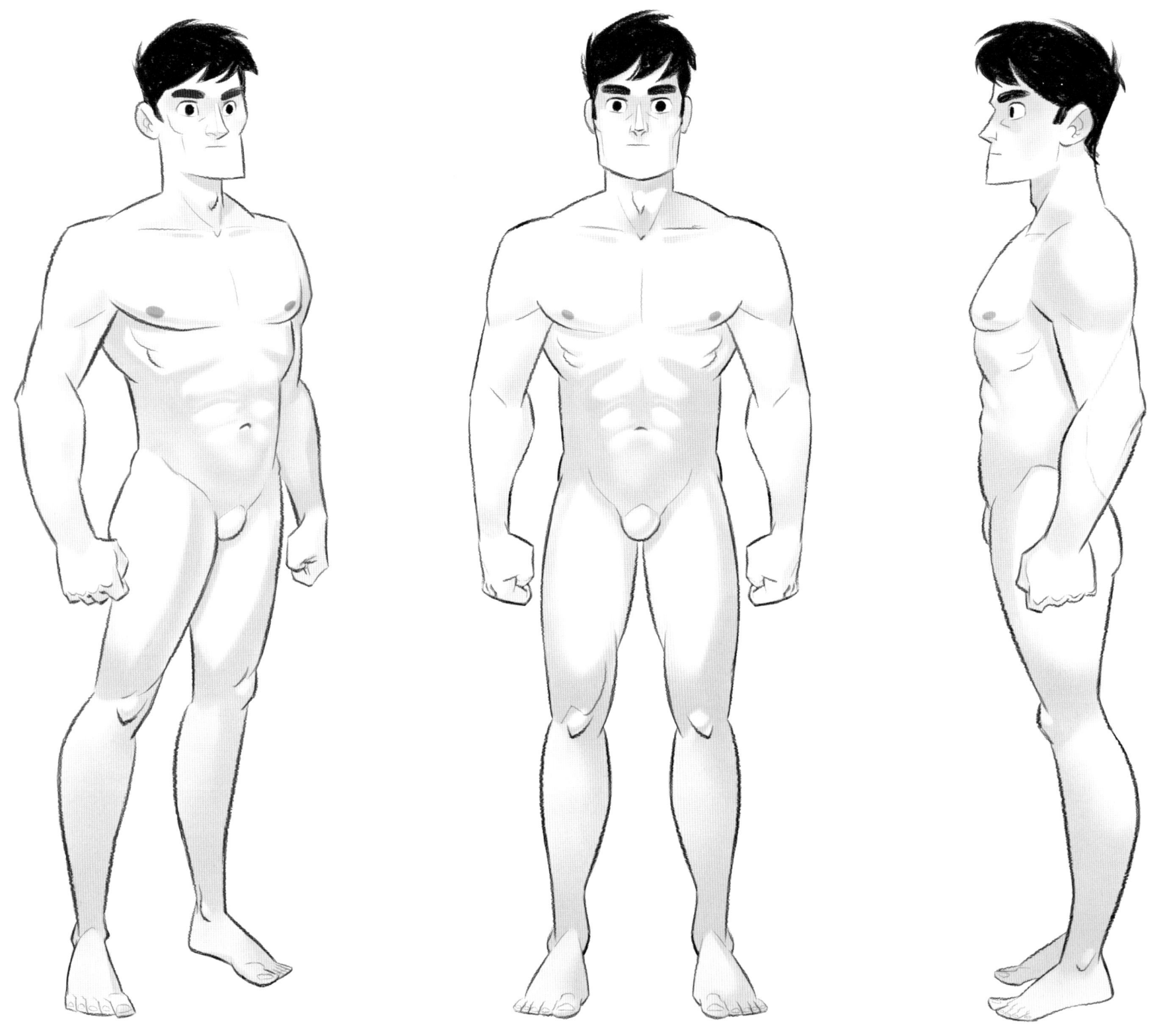

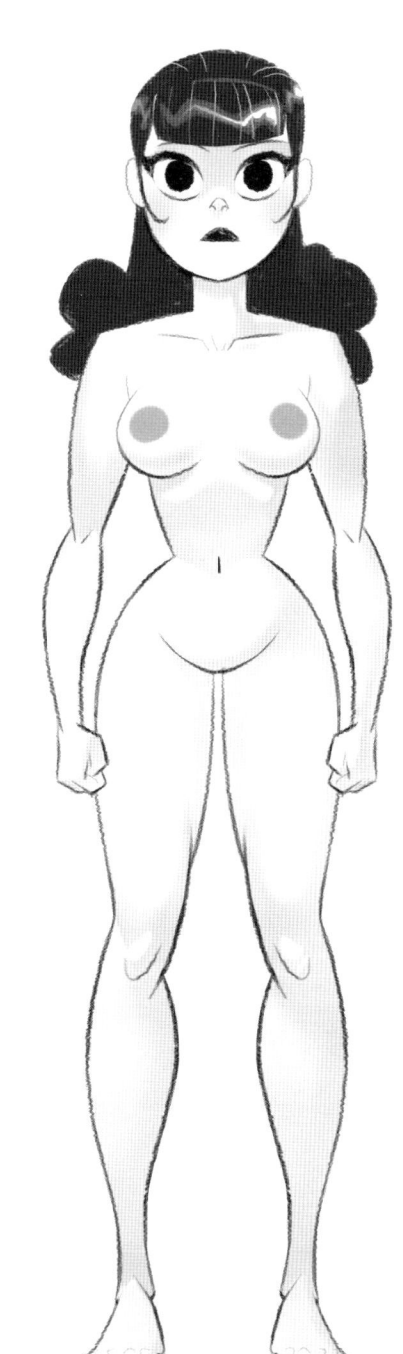
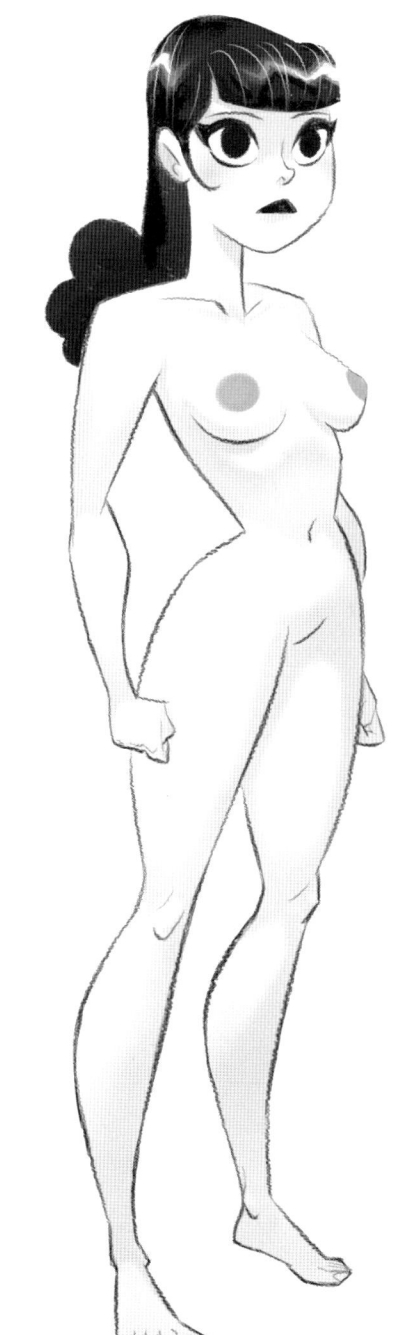

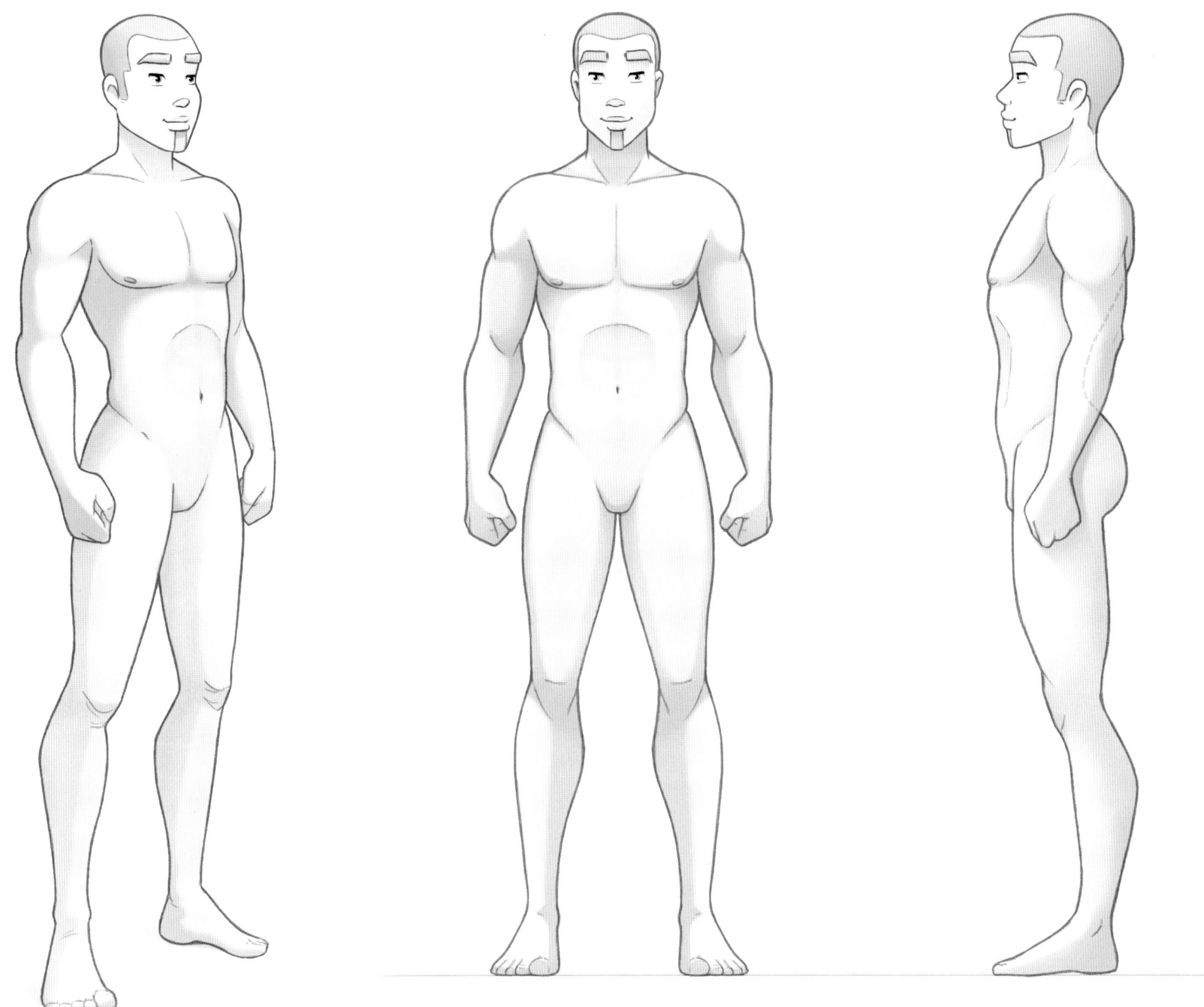

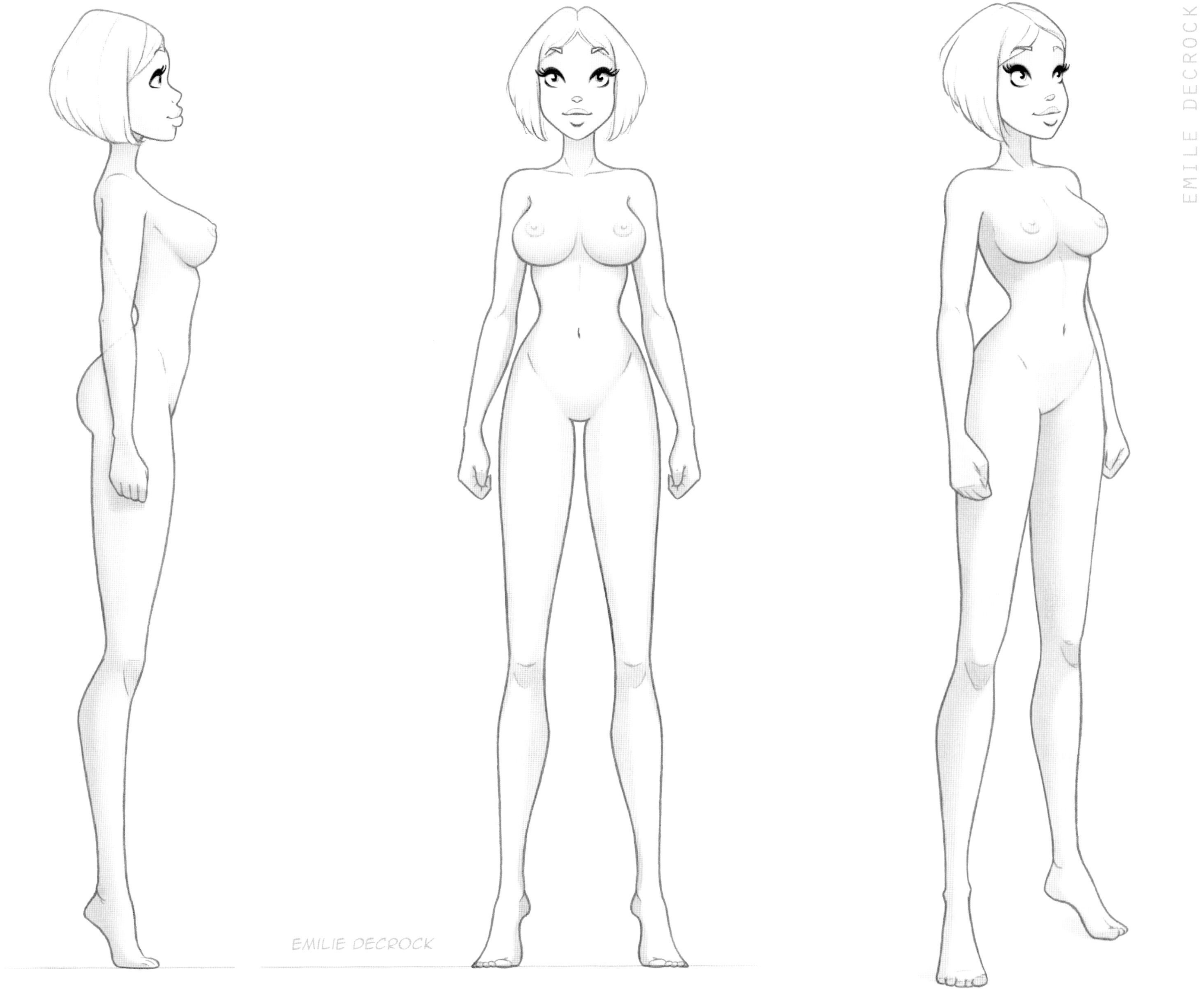

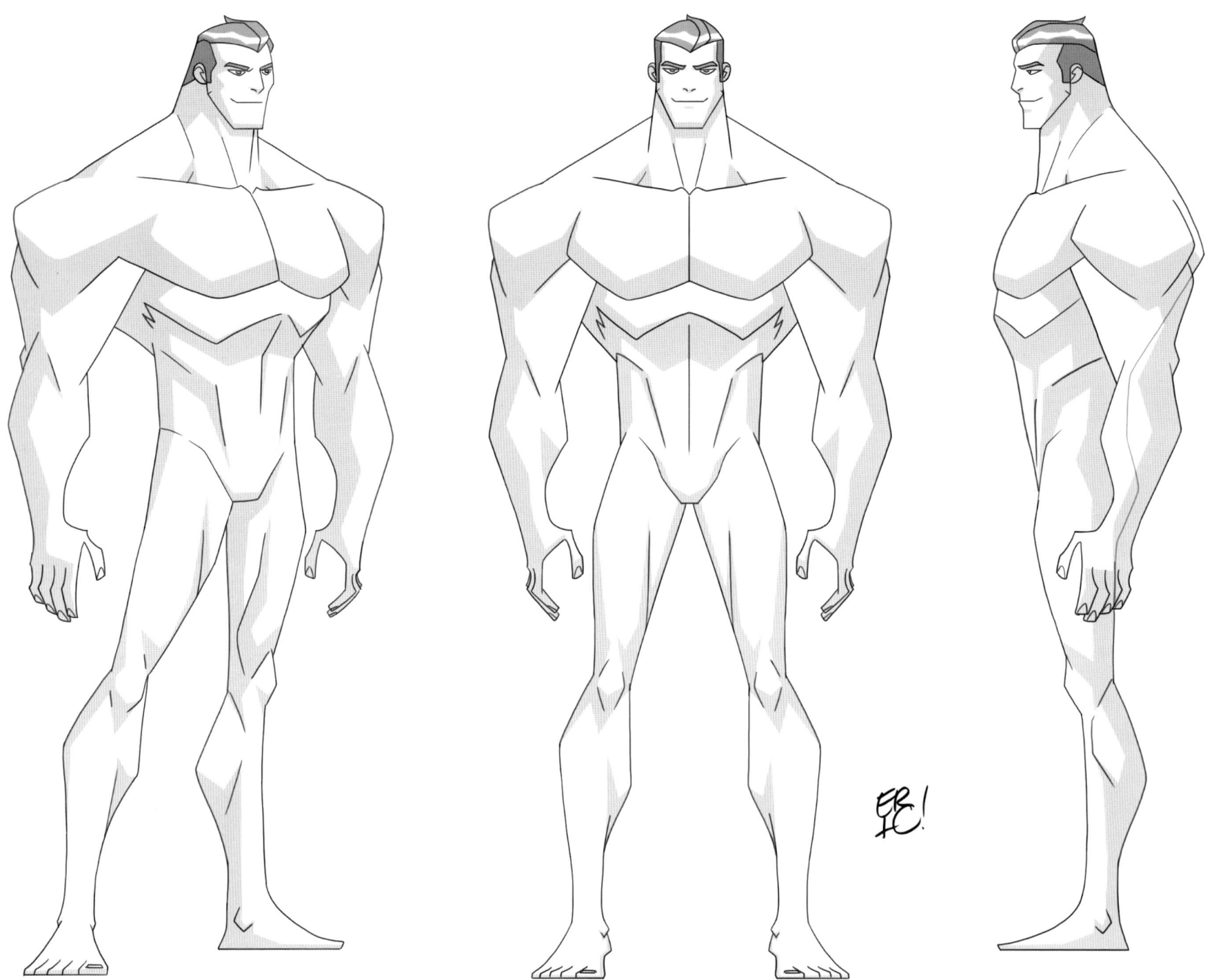

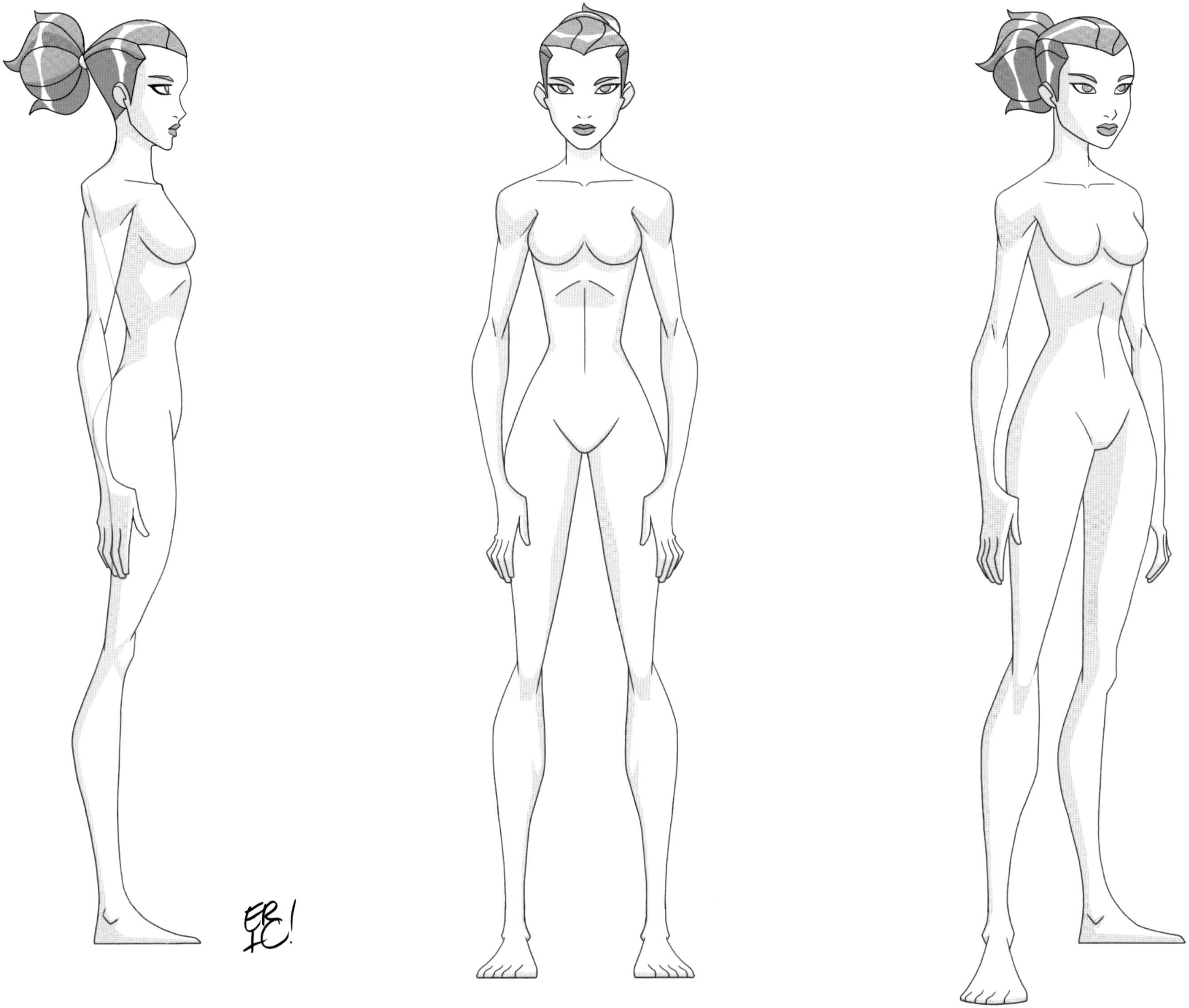

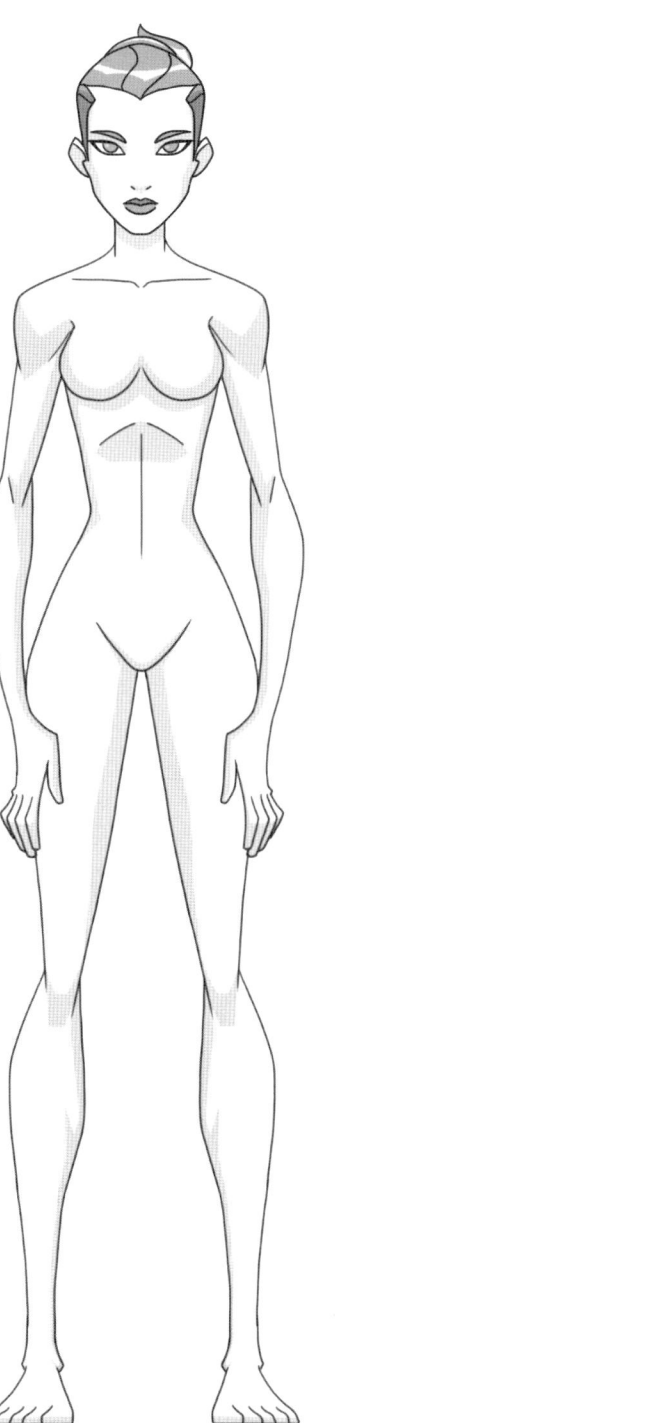
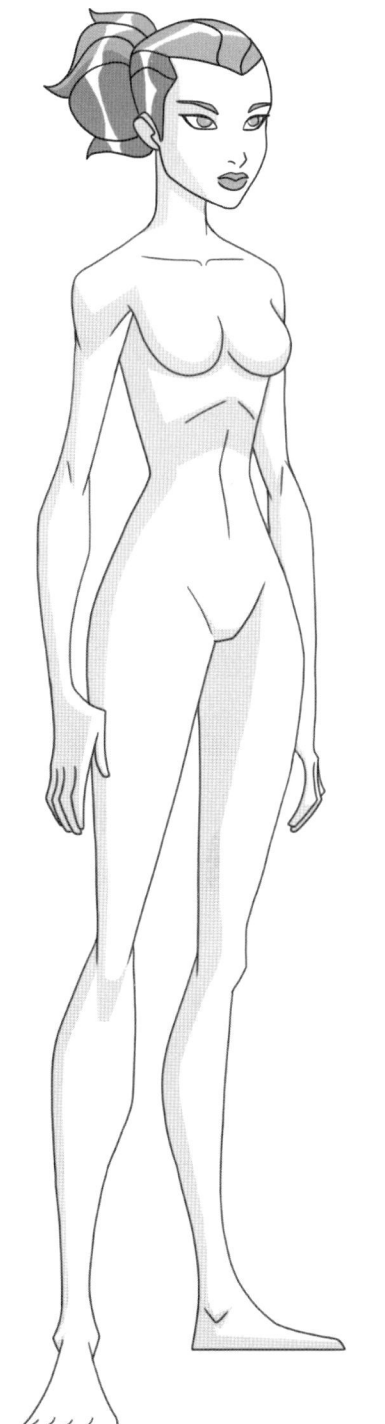

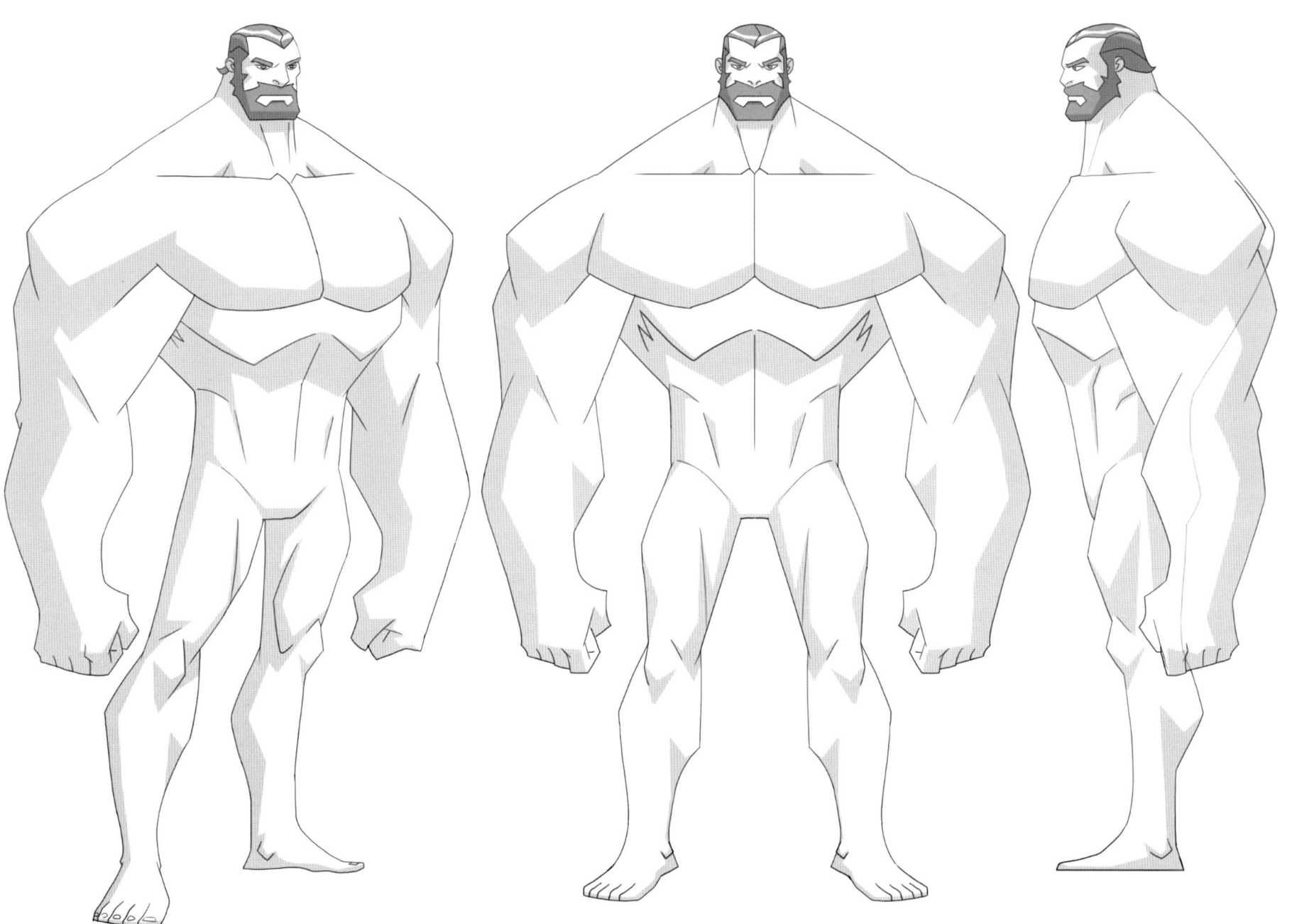

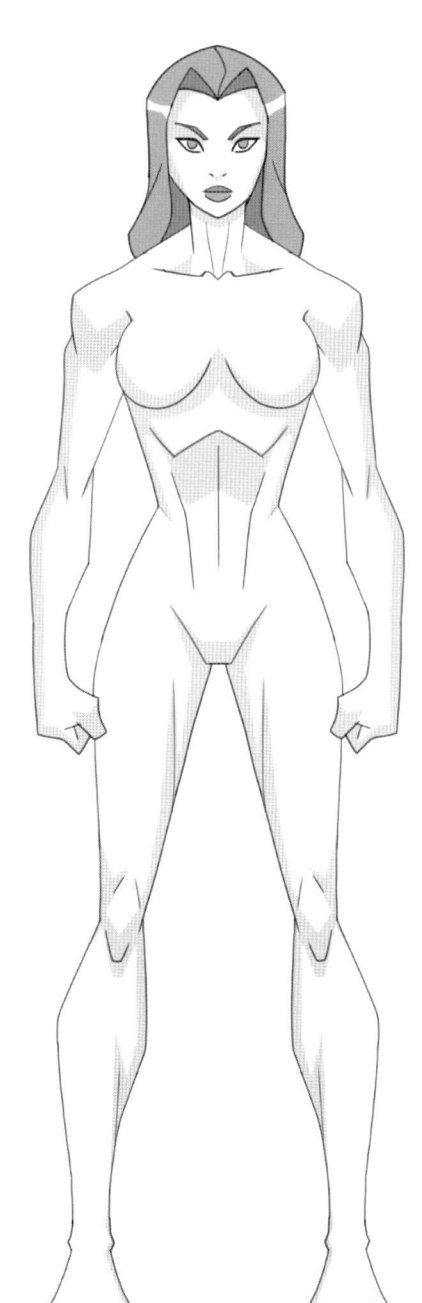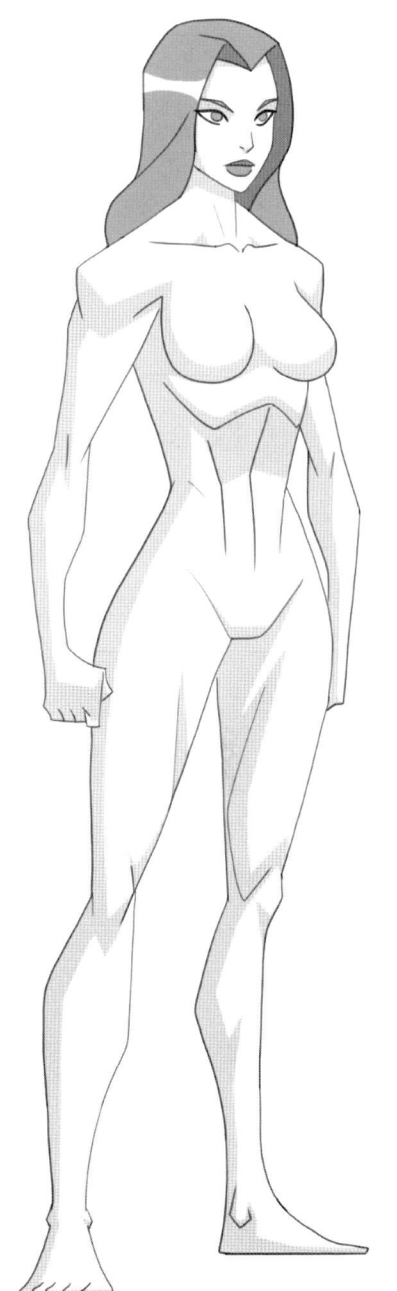

ERIC GUZMAN

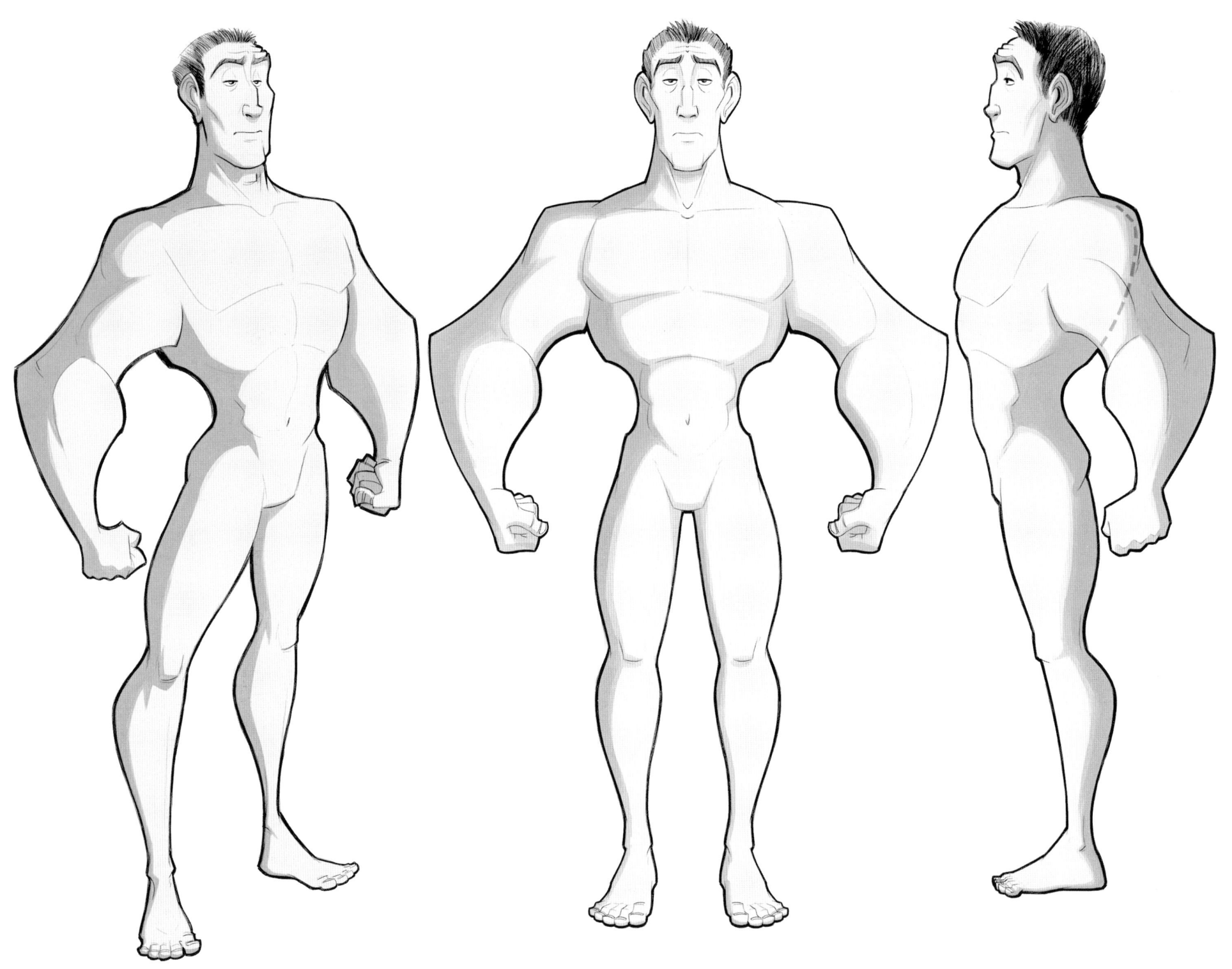

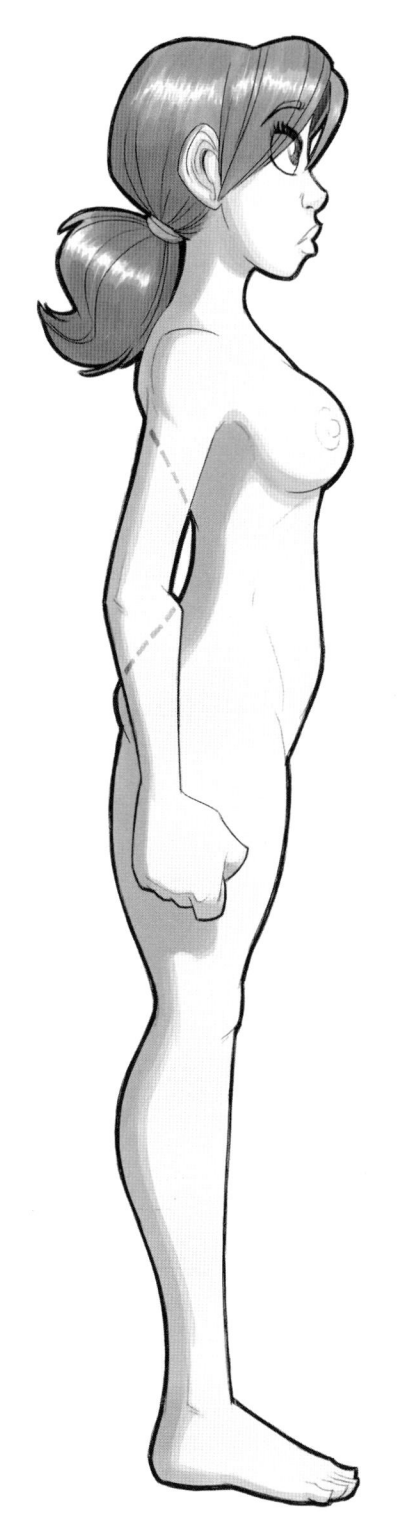
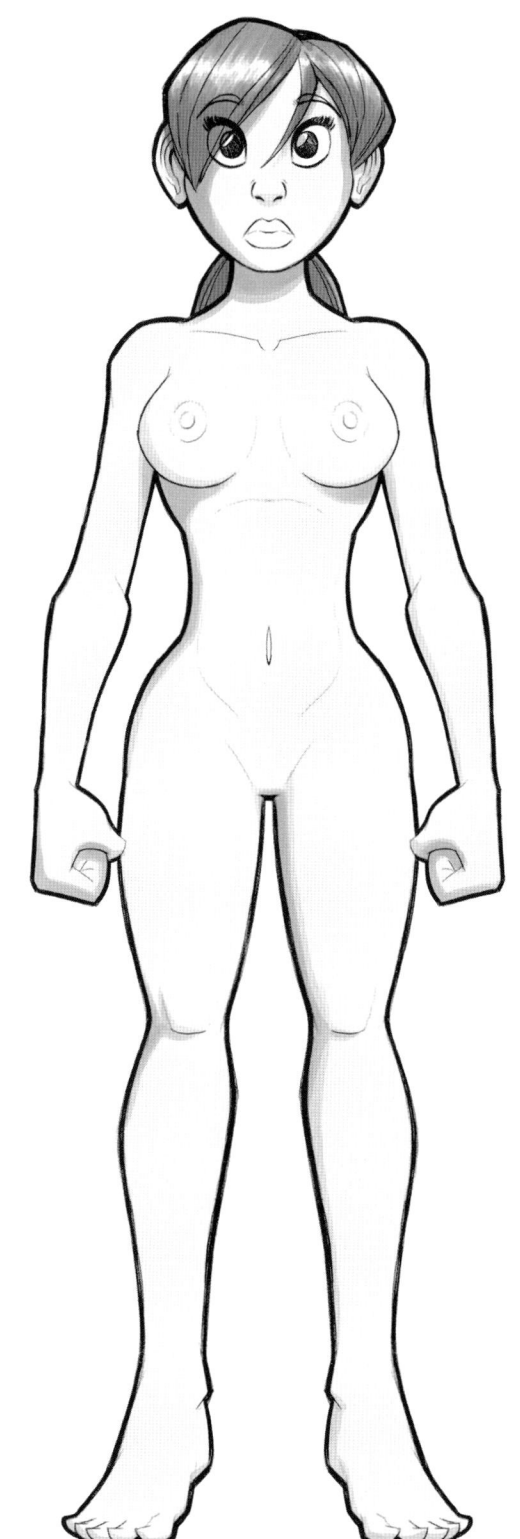
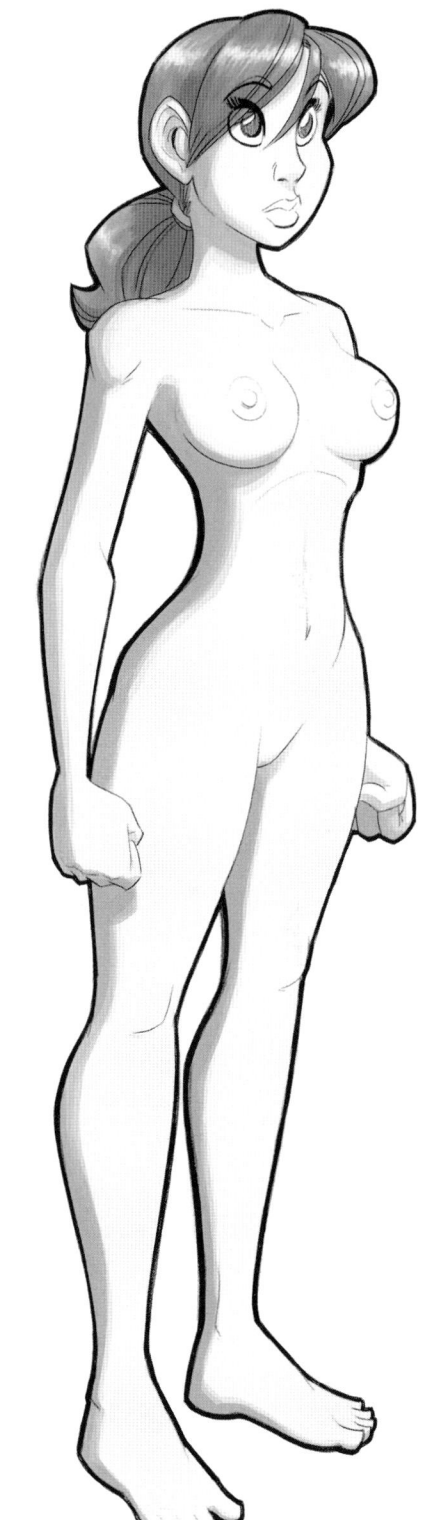

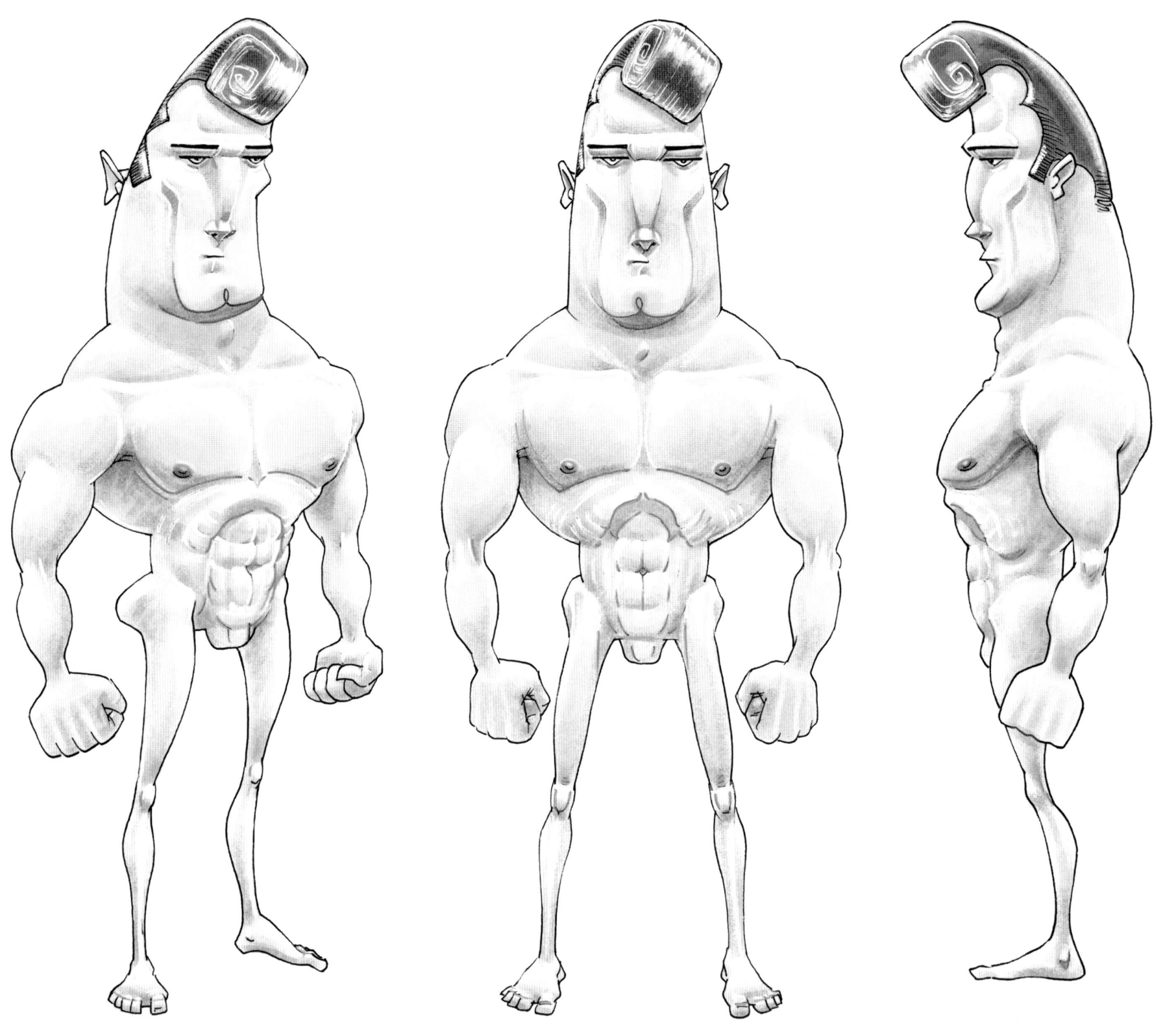

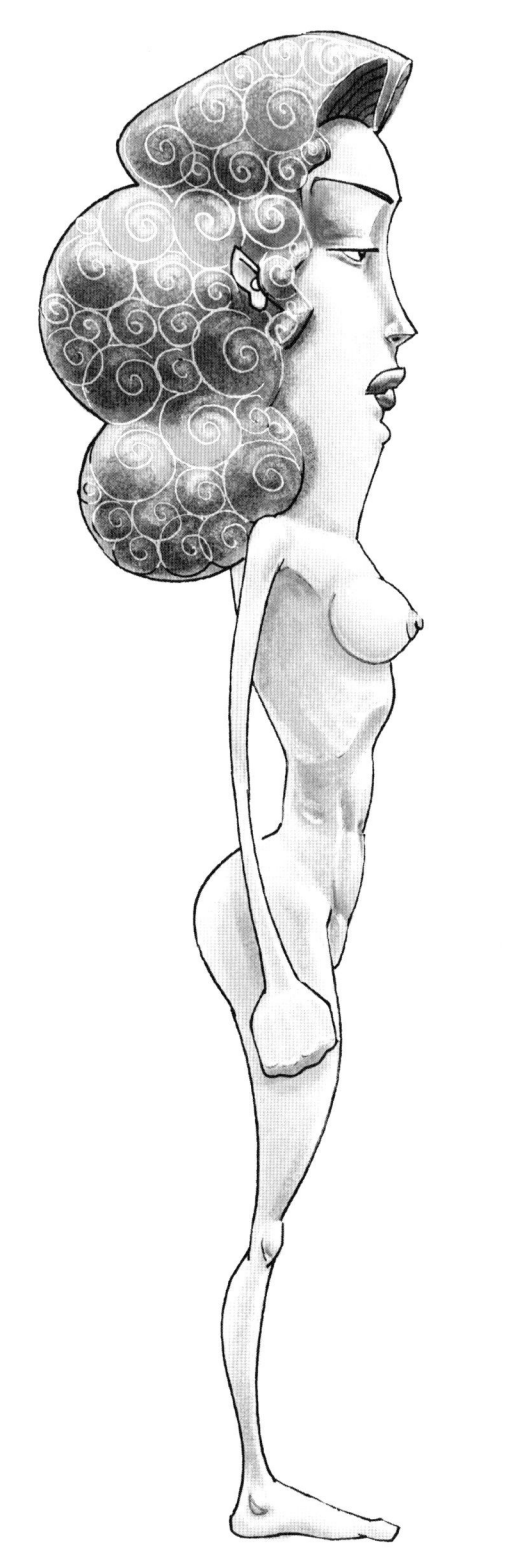
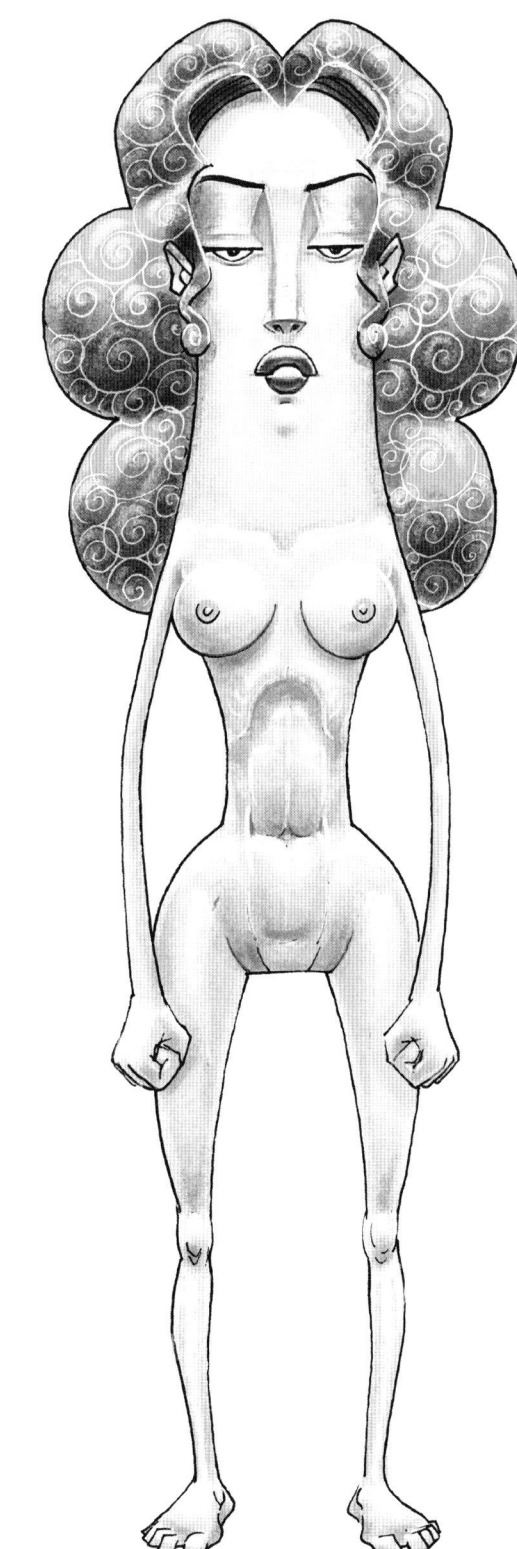
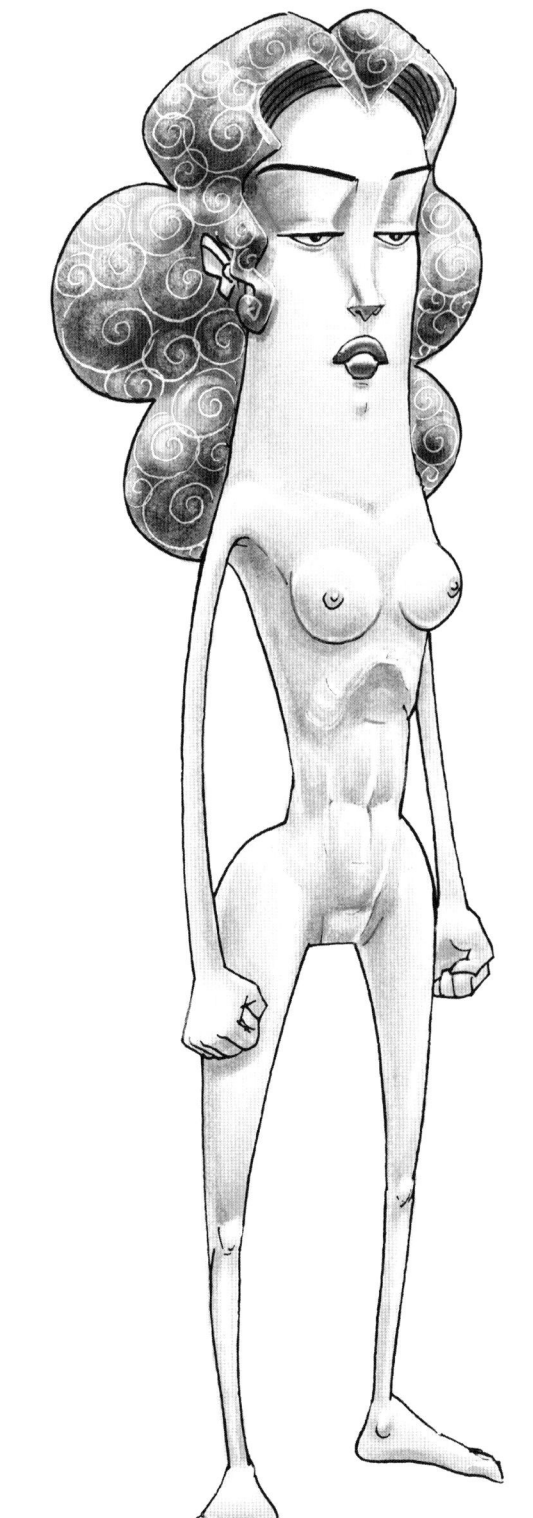

EUGENIA NOBATI

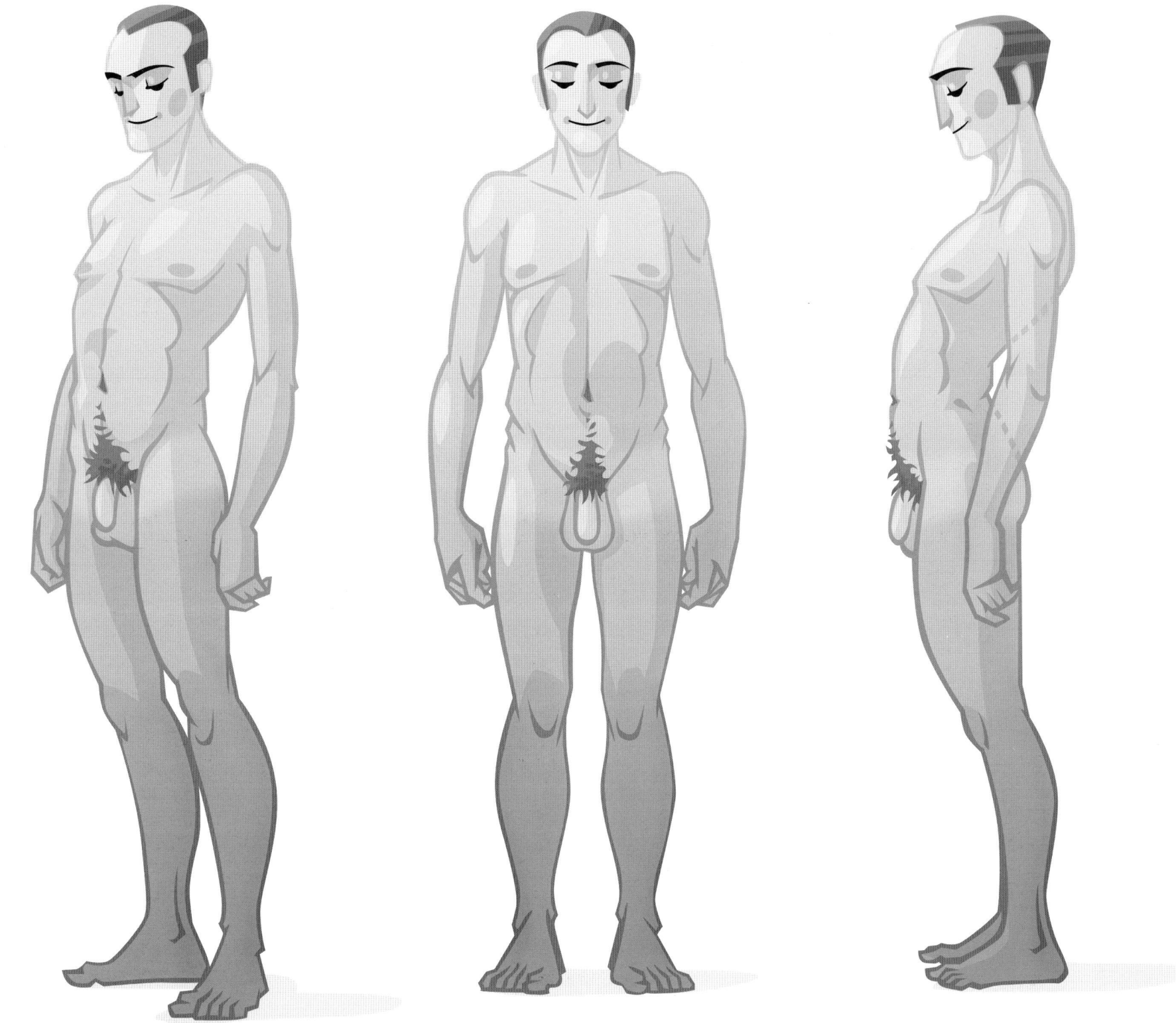

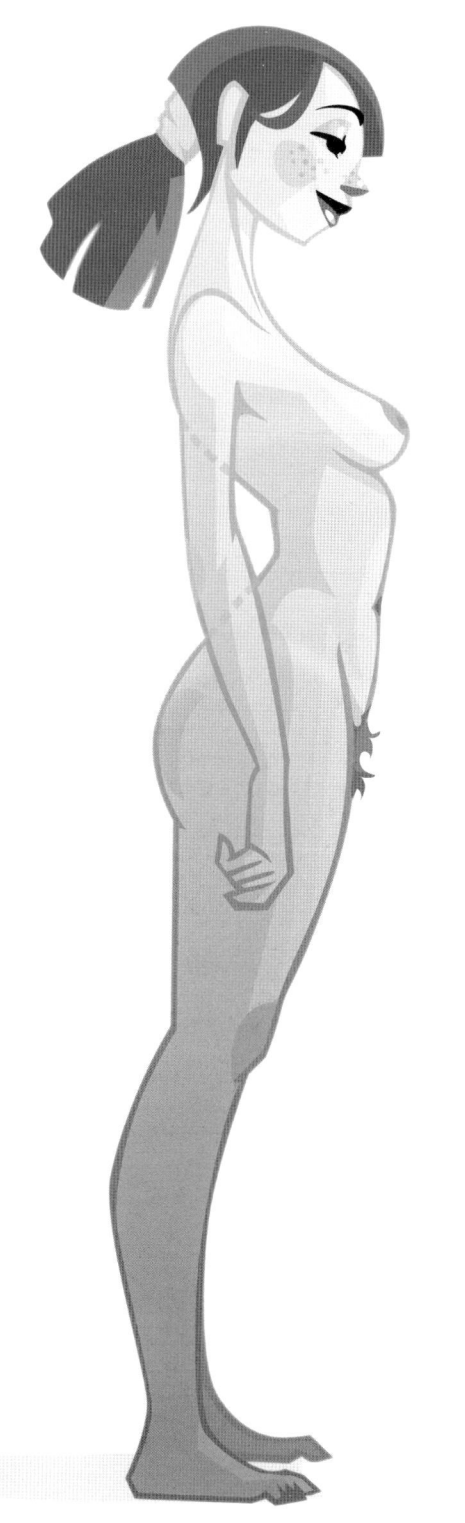

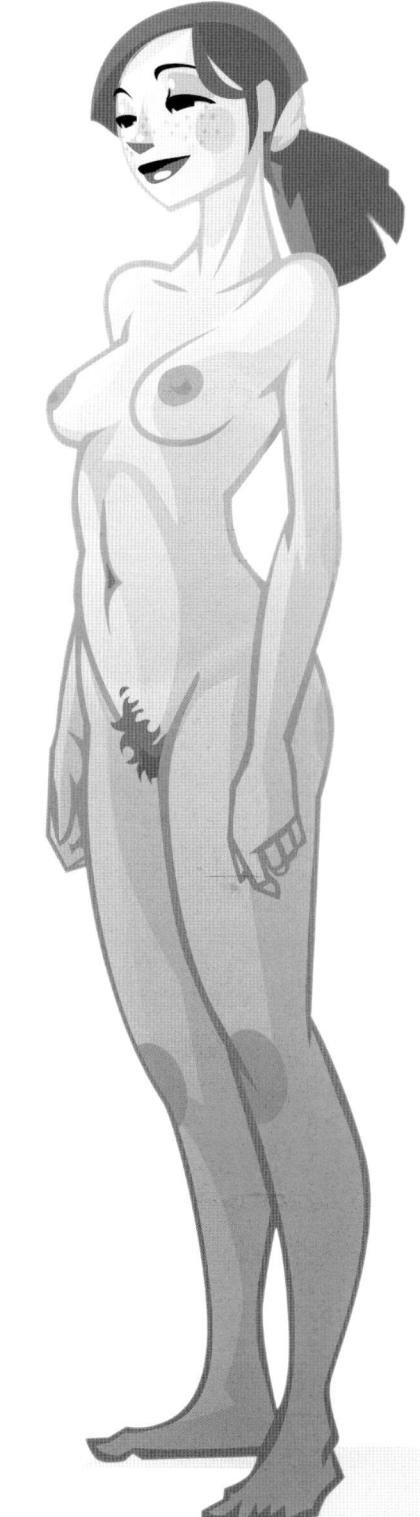

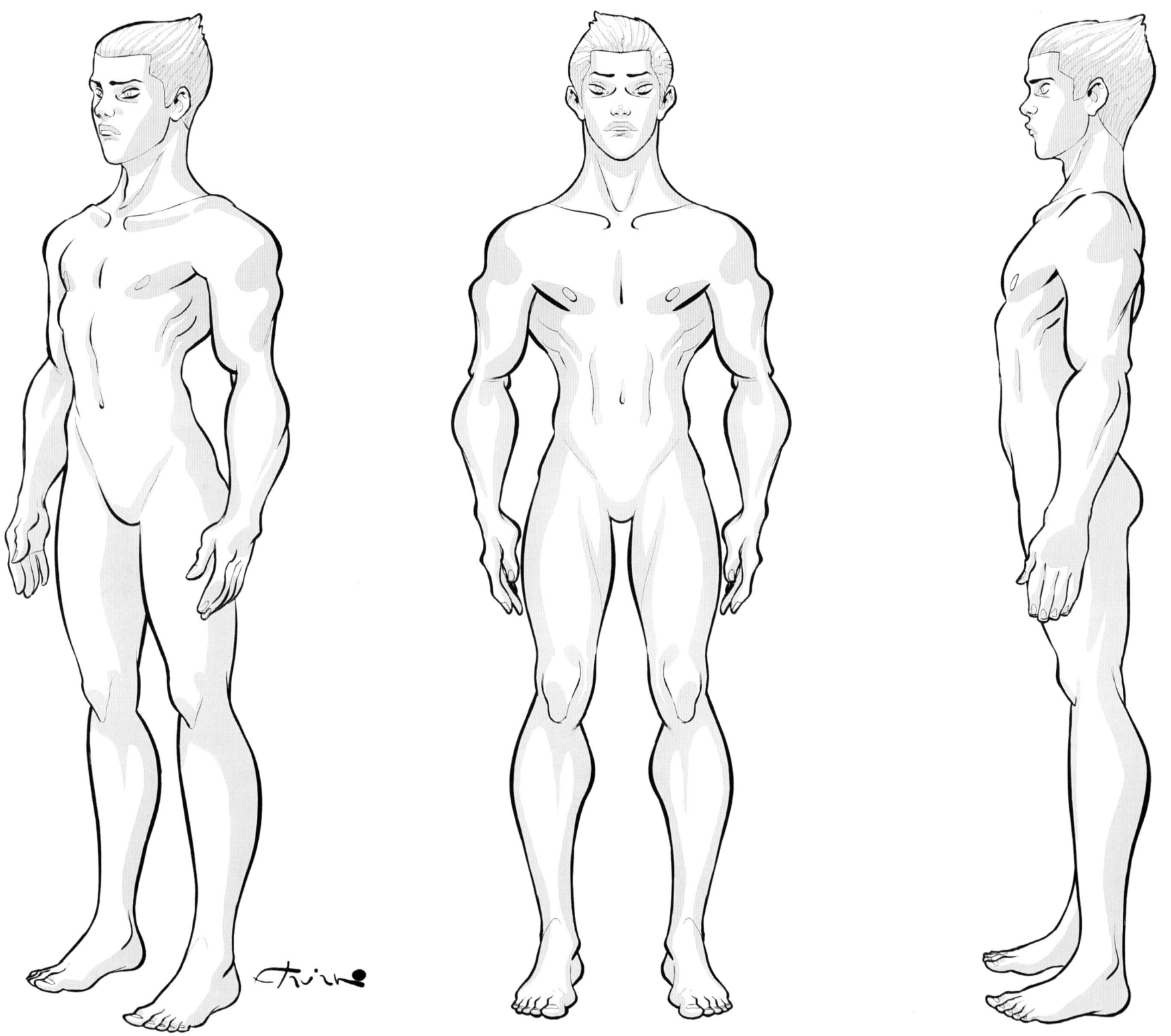

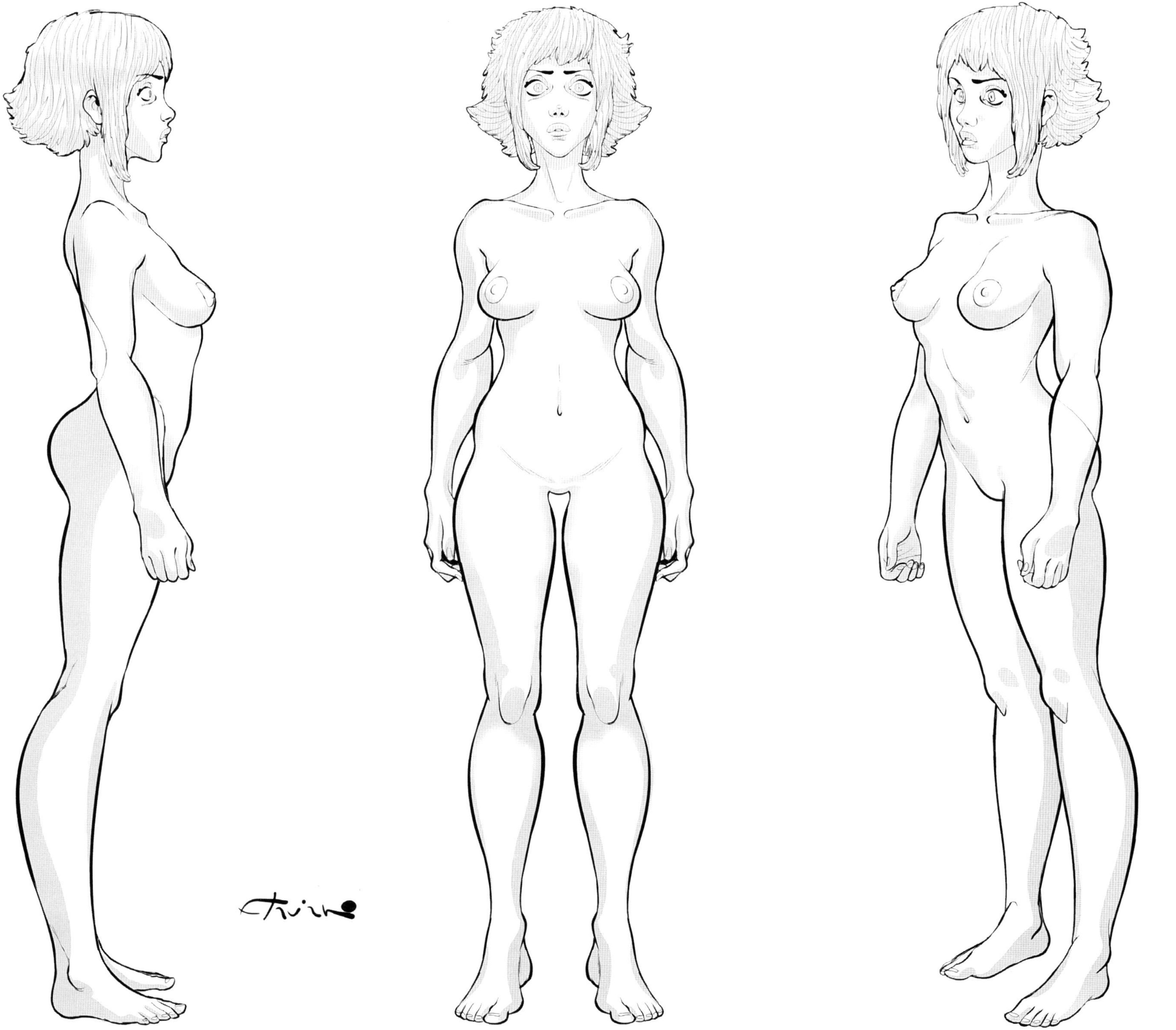

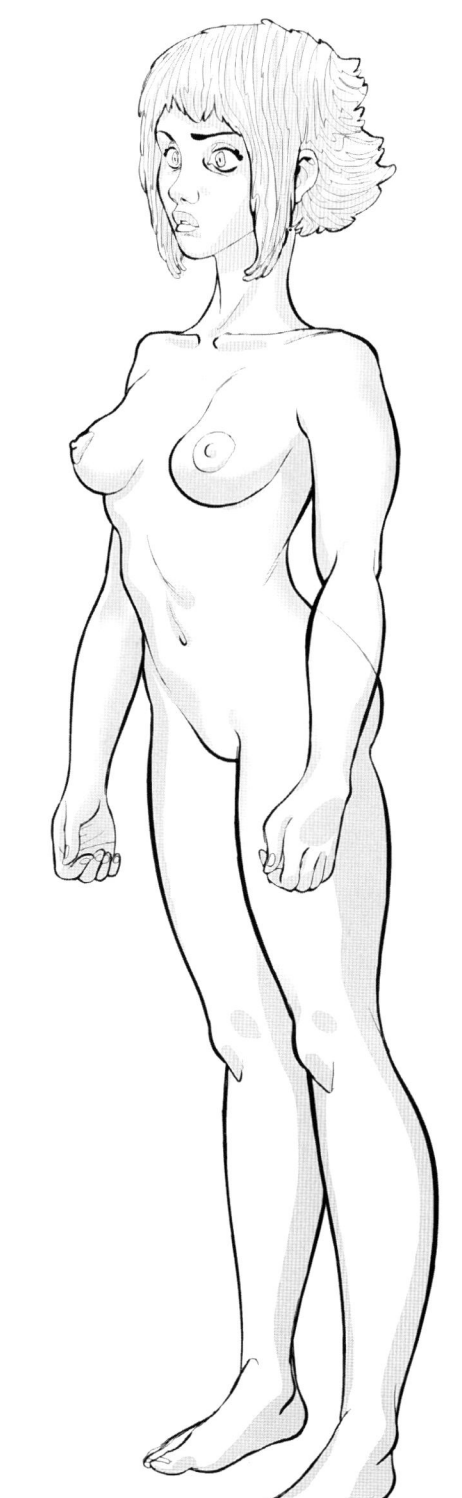

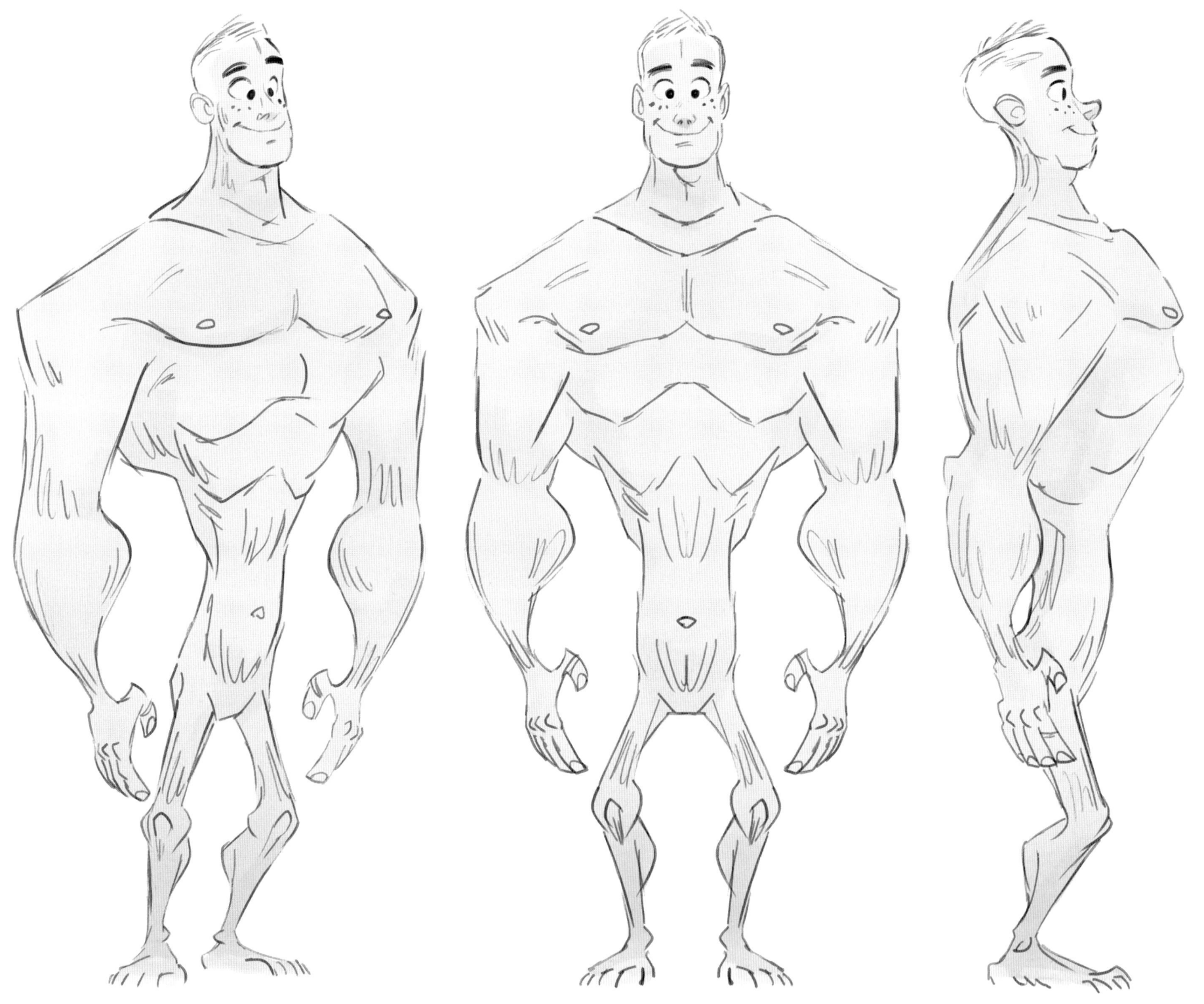

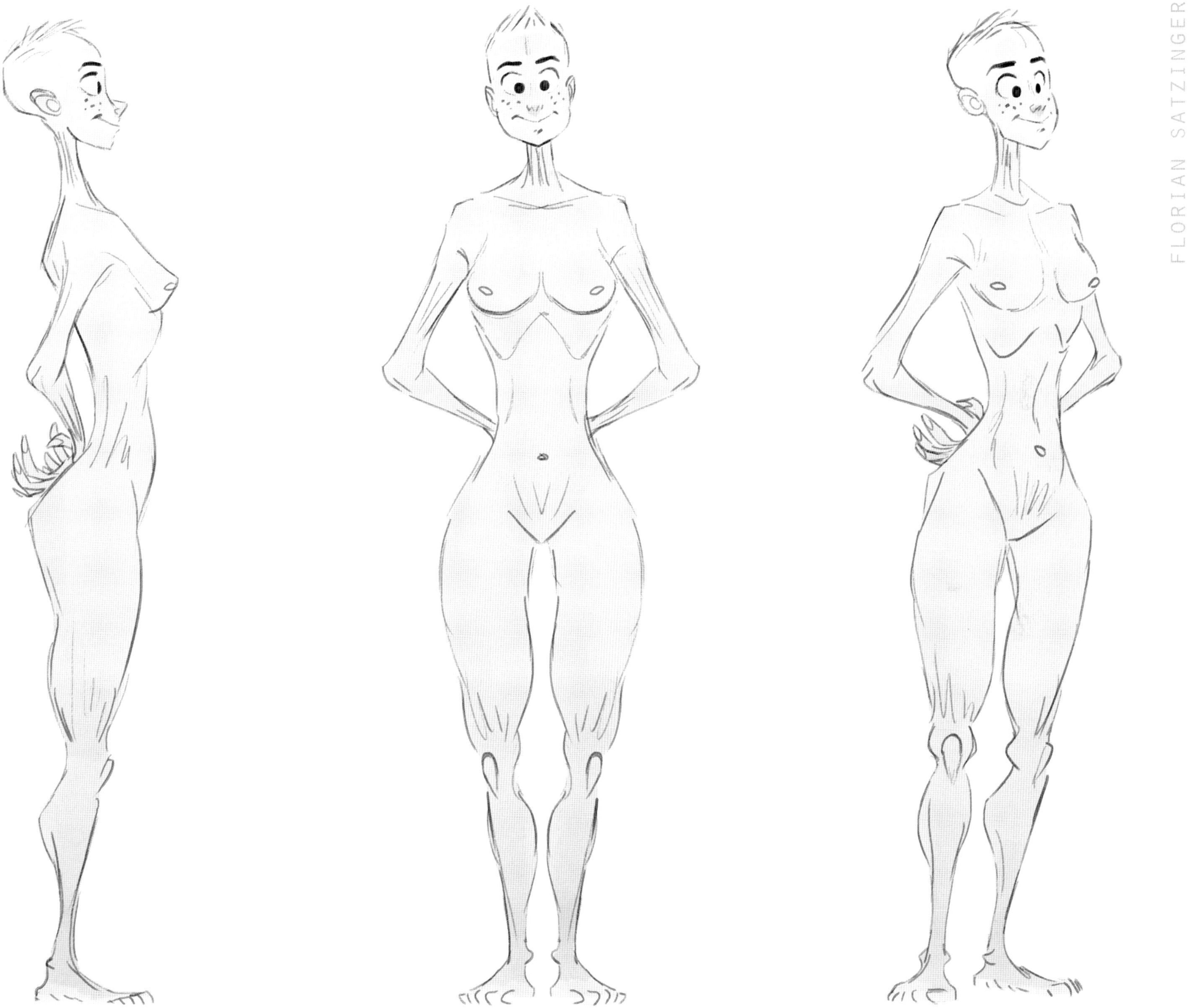

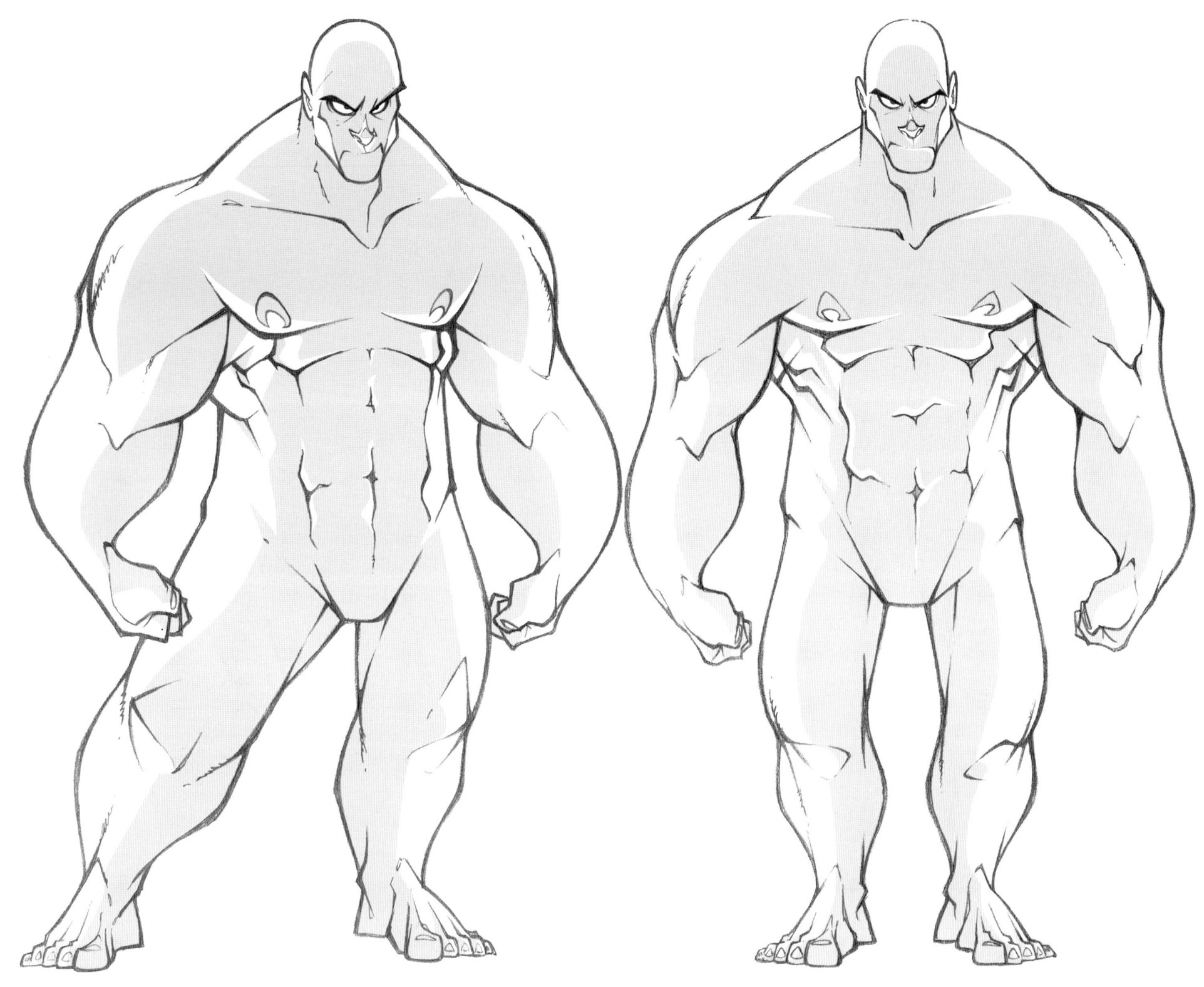

FRANCISCO HERRERA

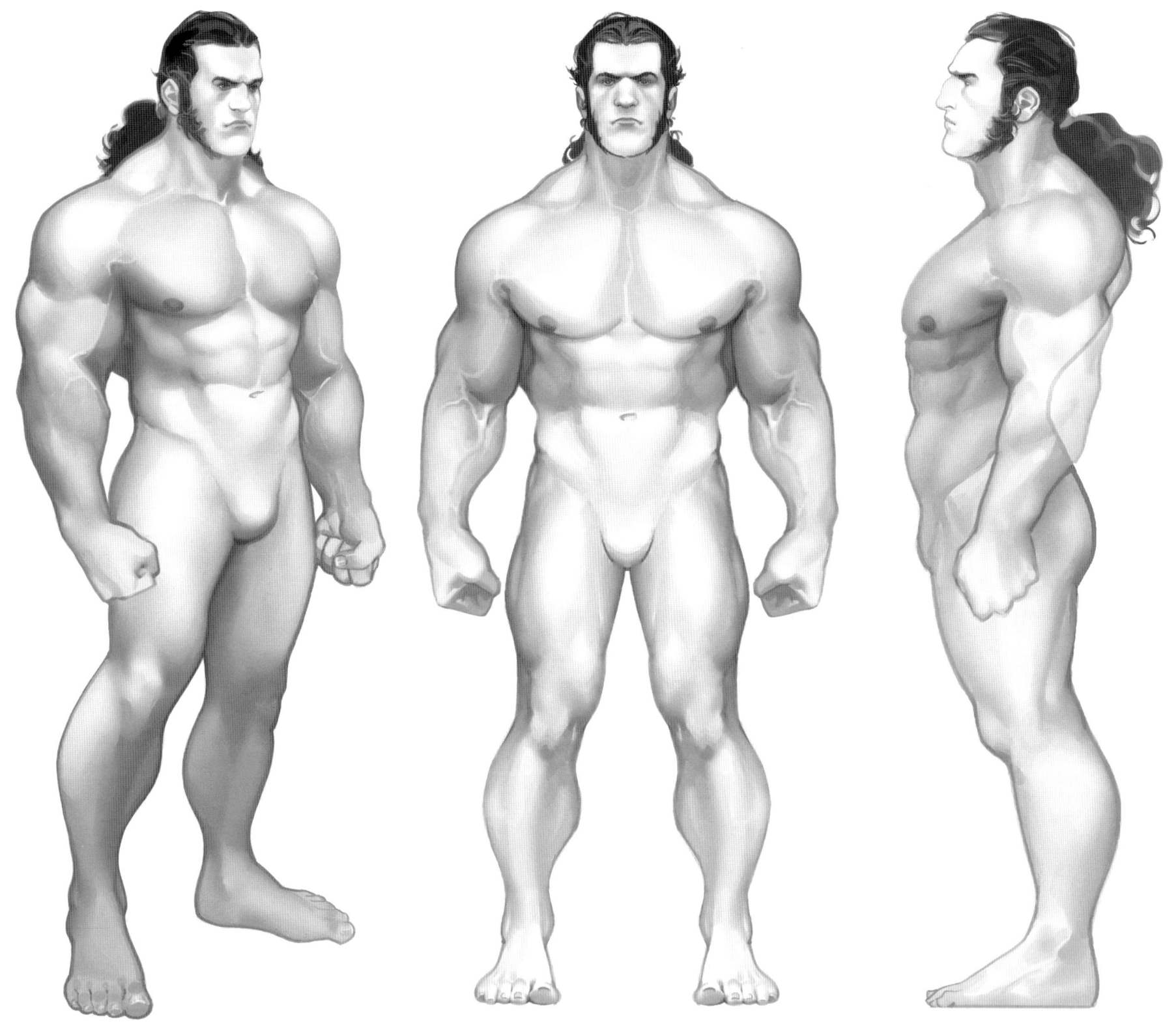

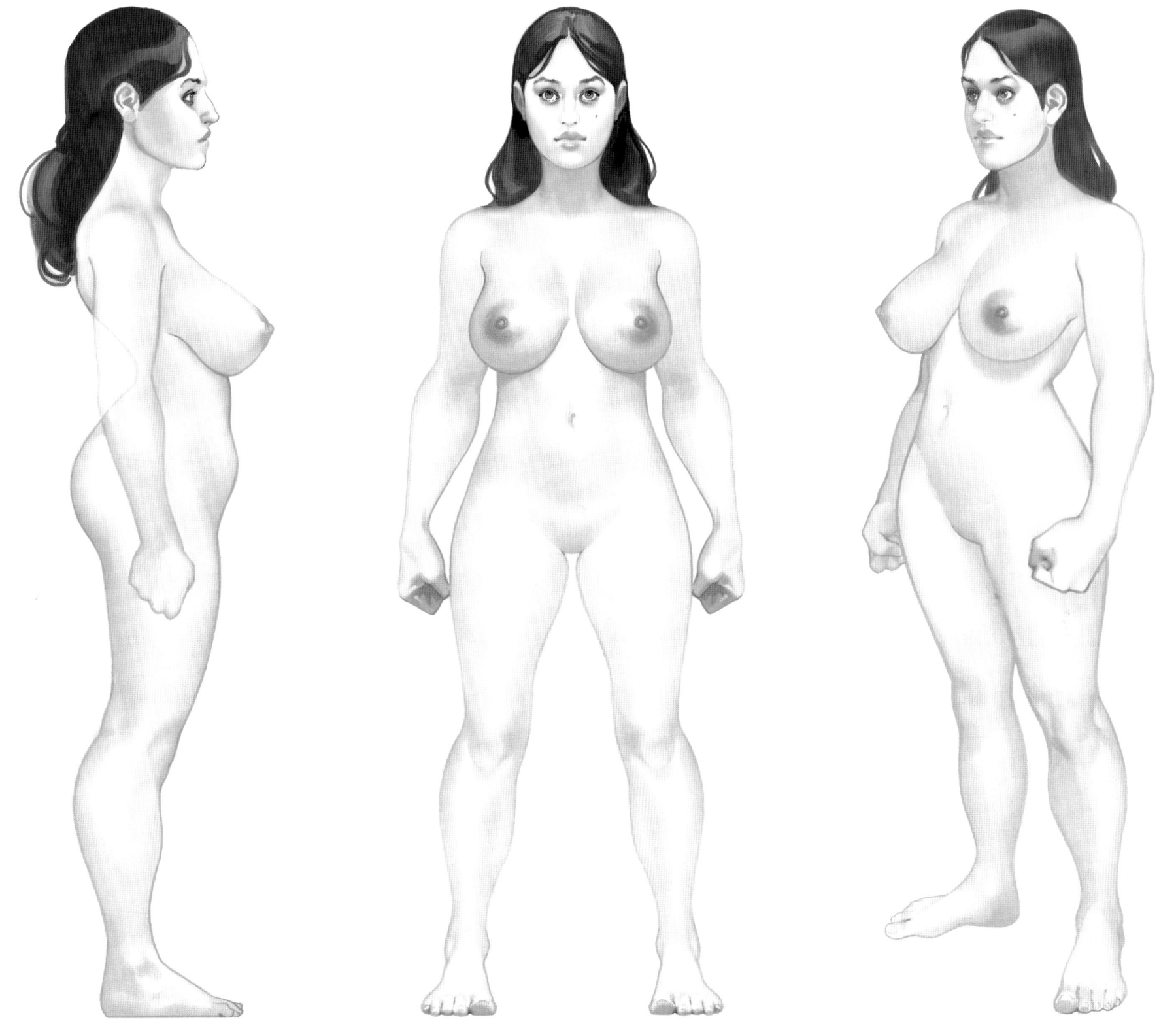

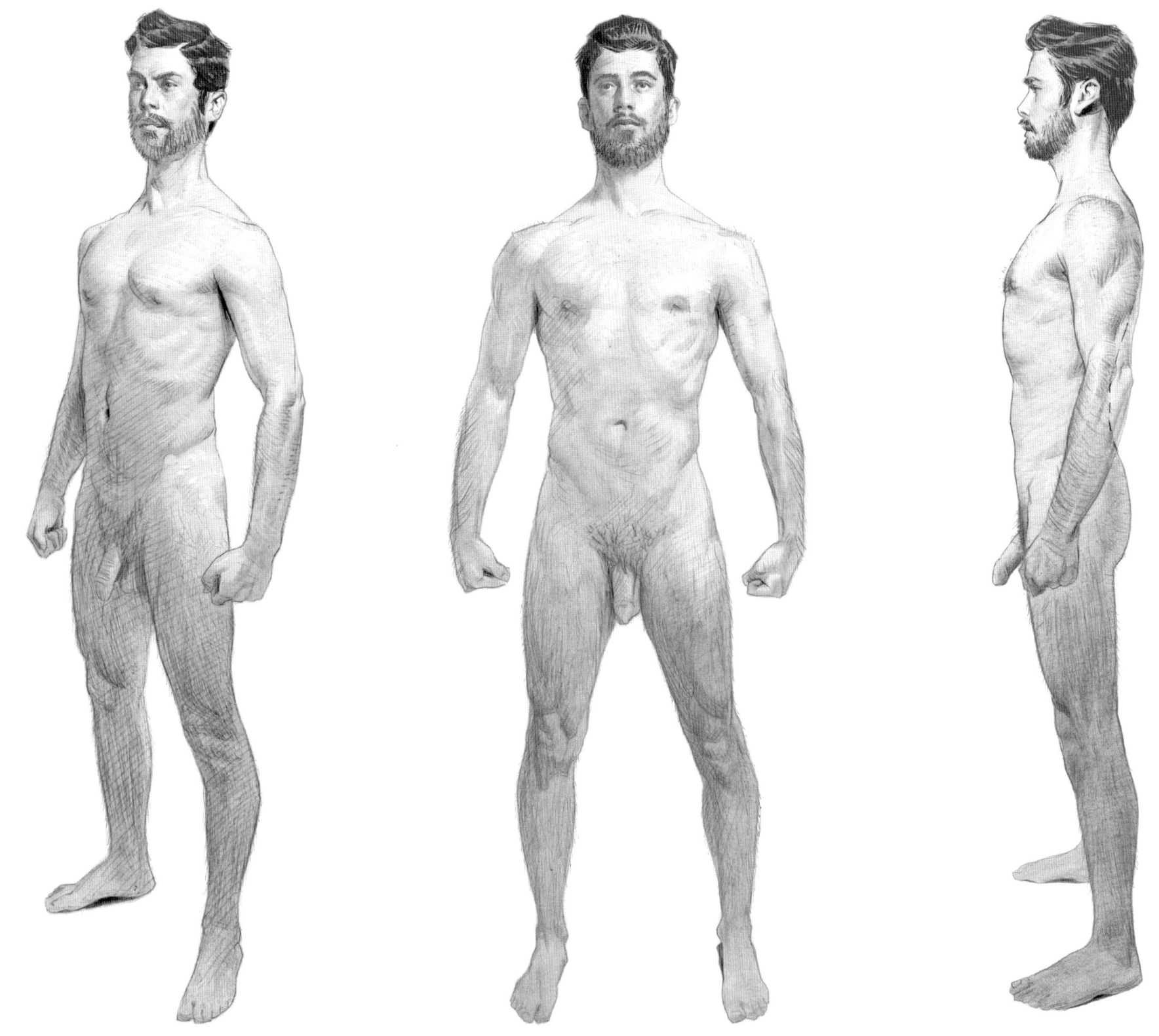

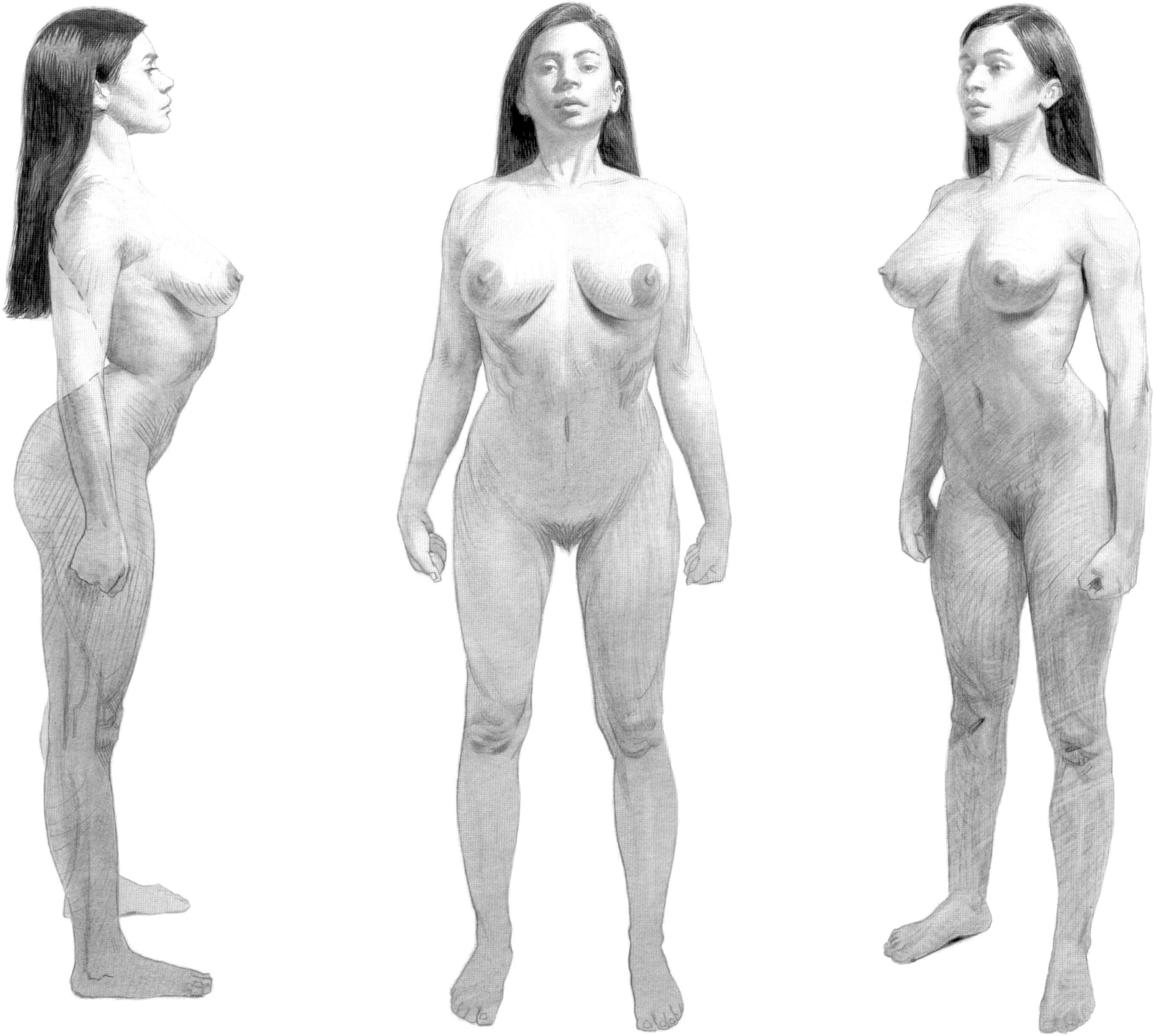

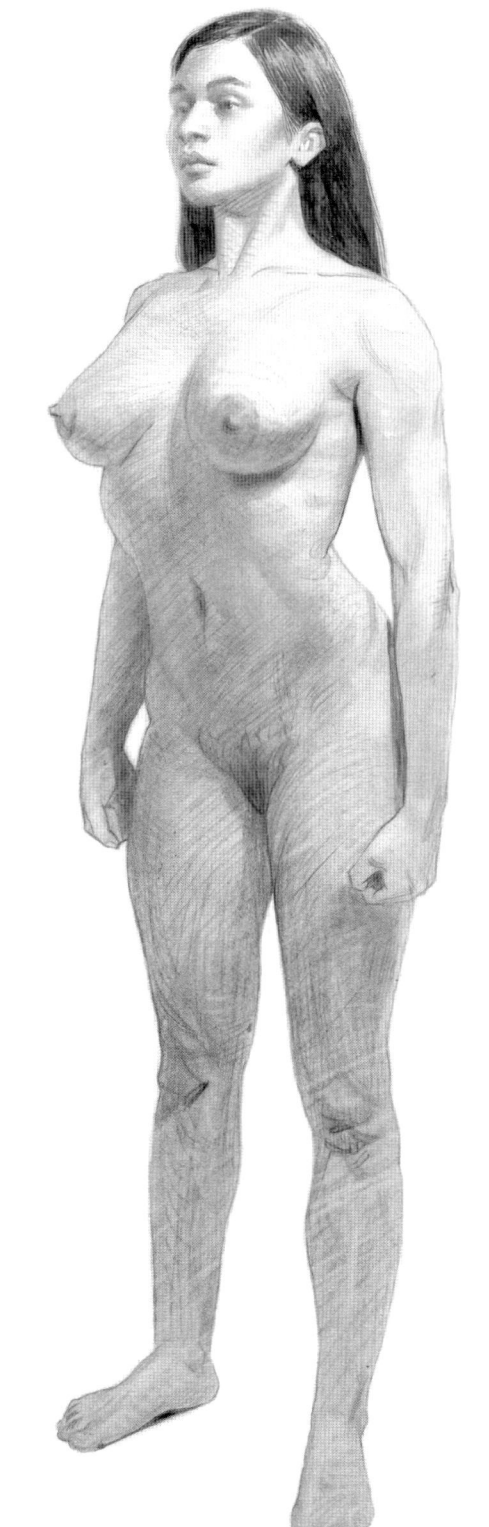

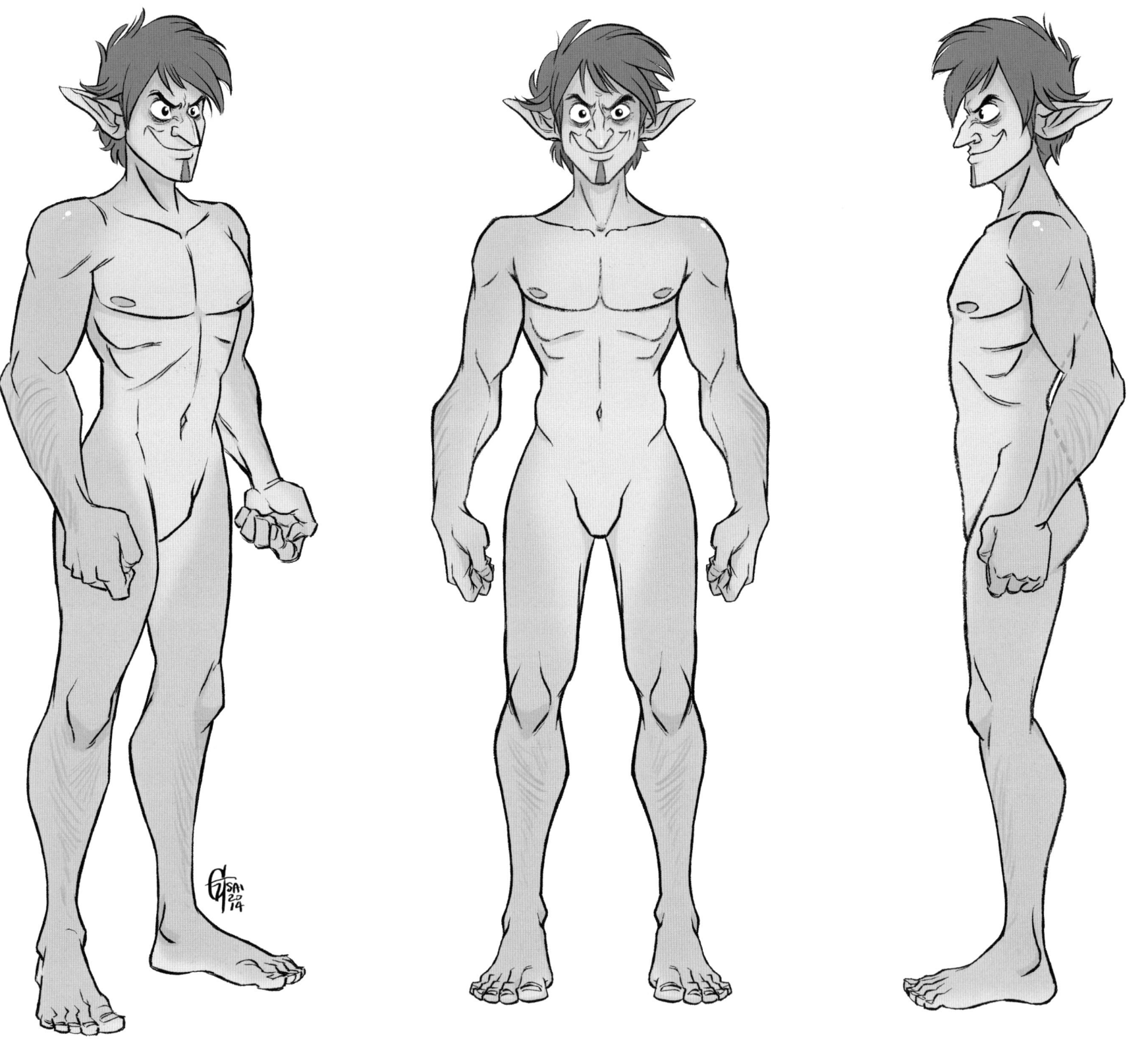

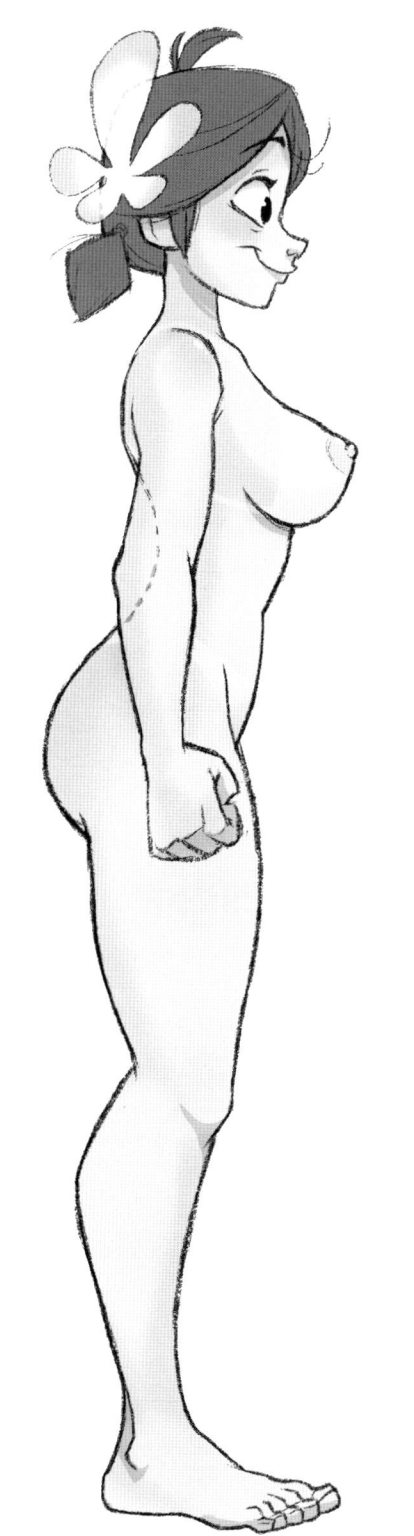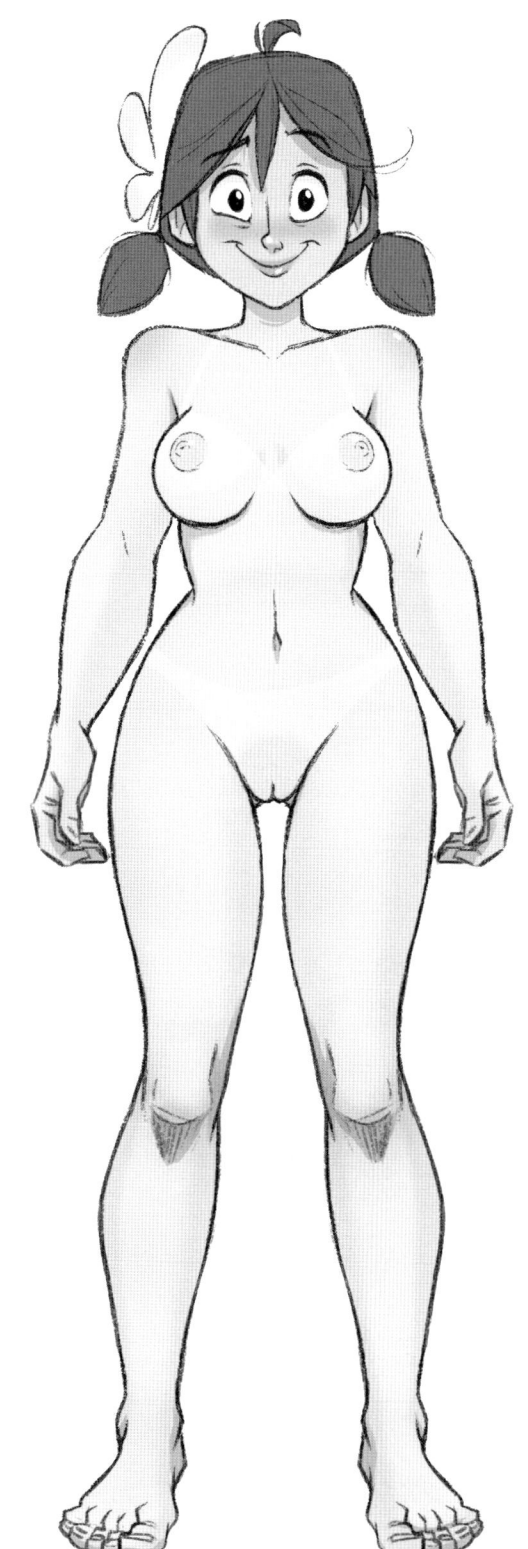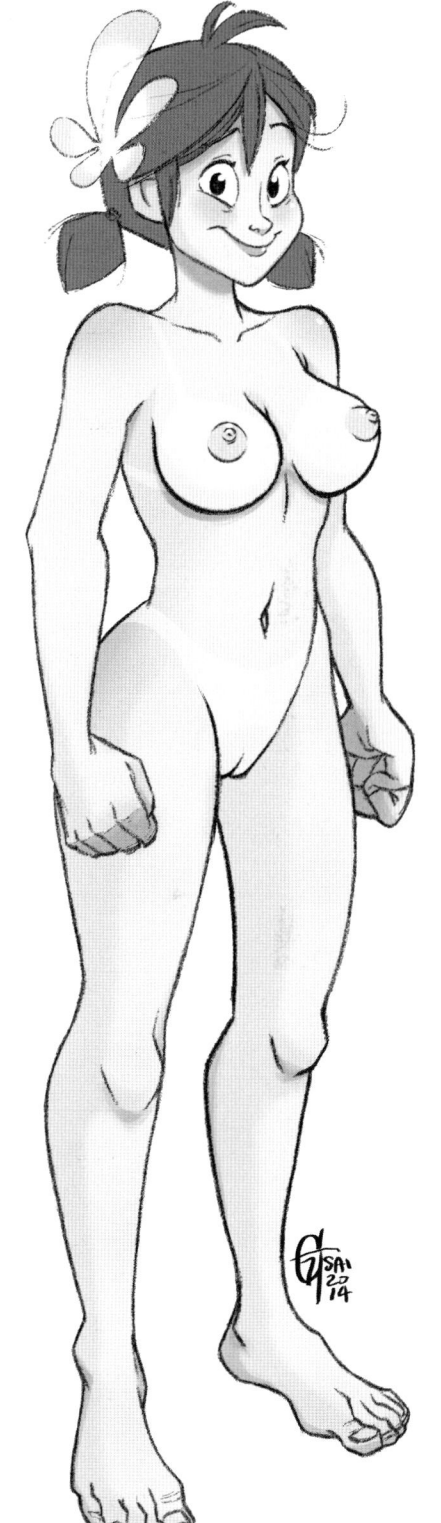

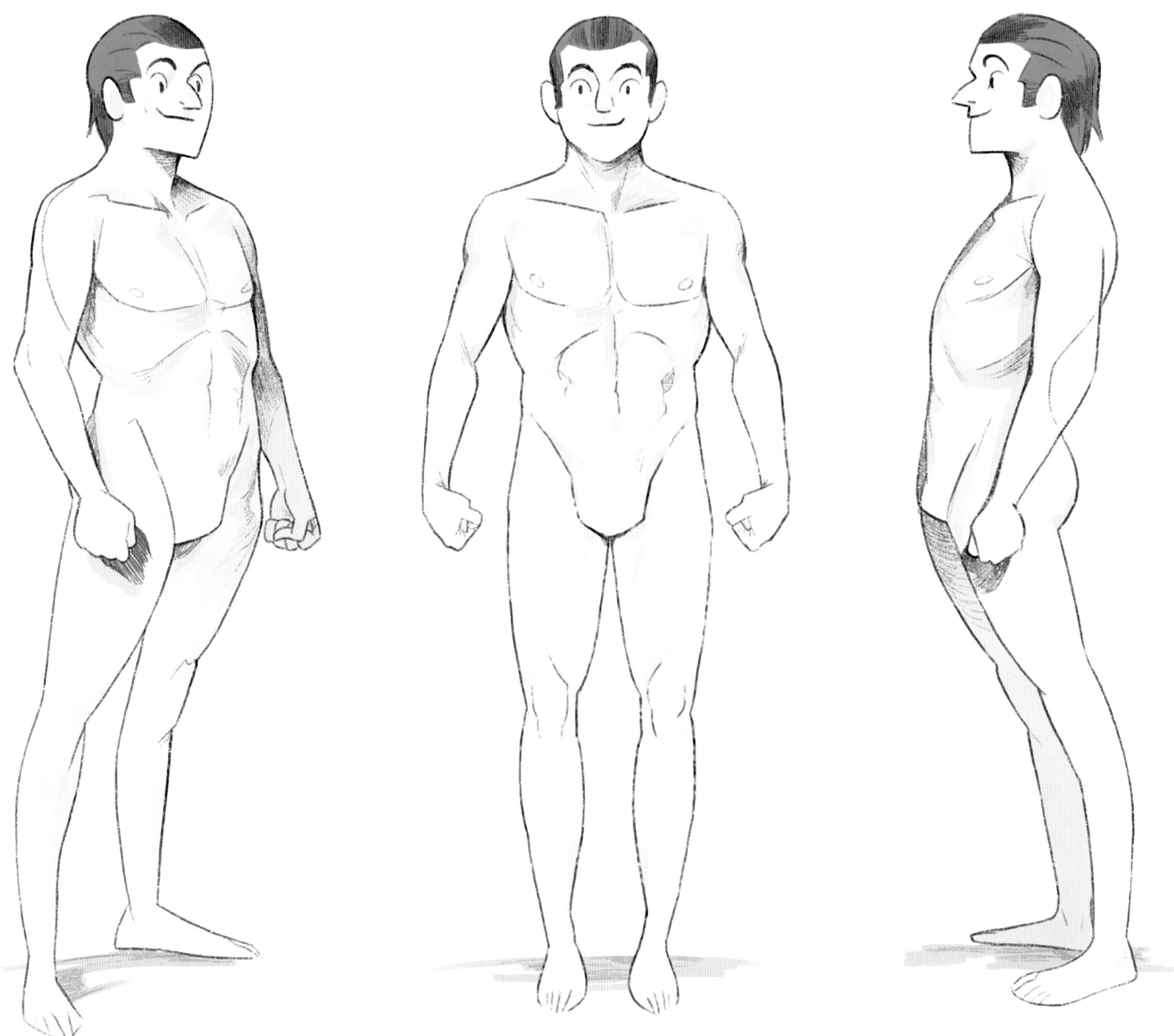

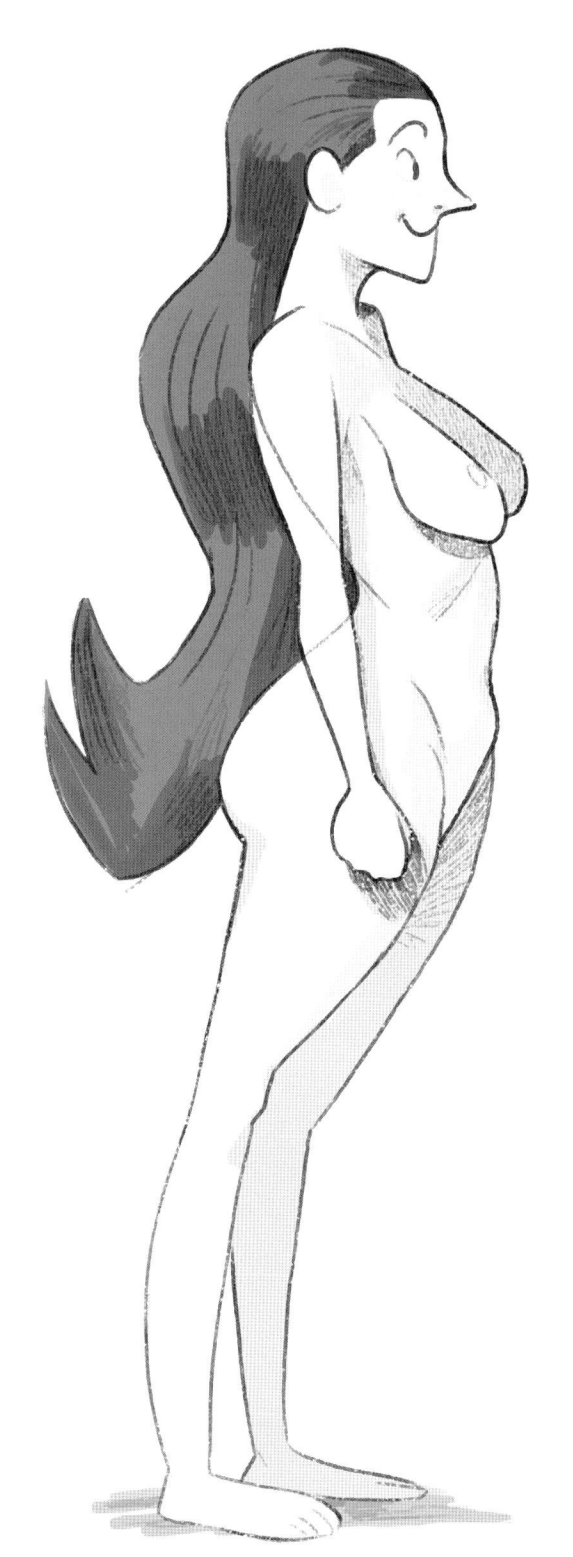
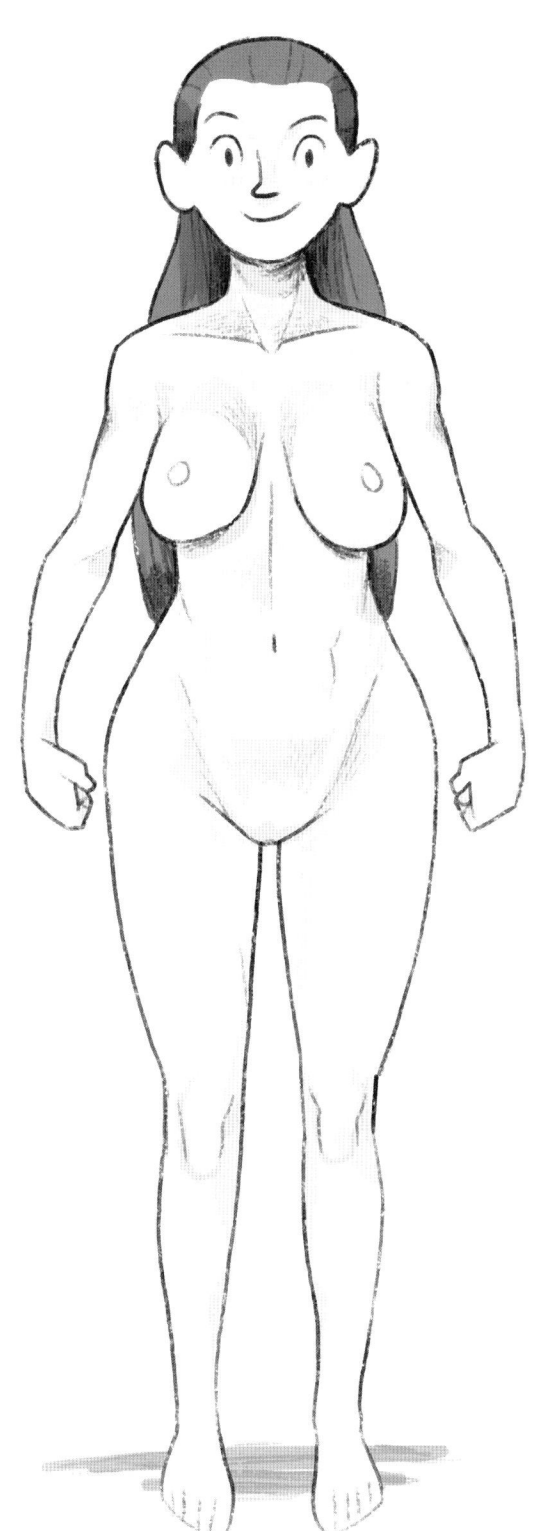

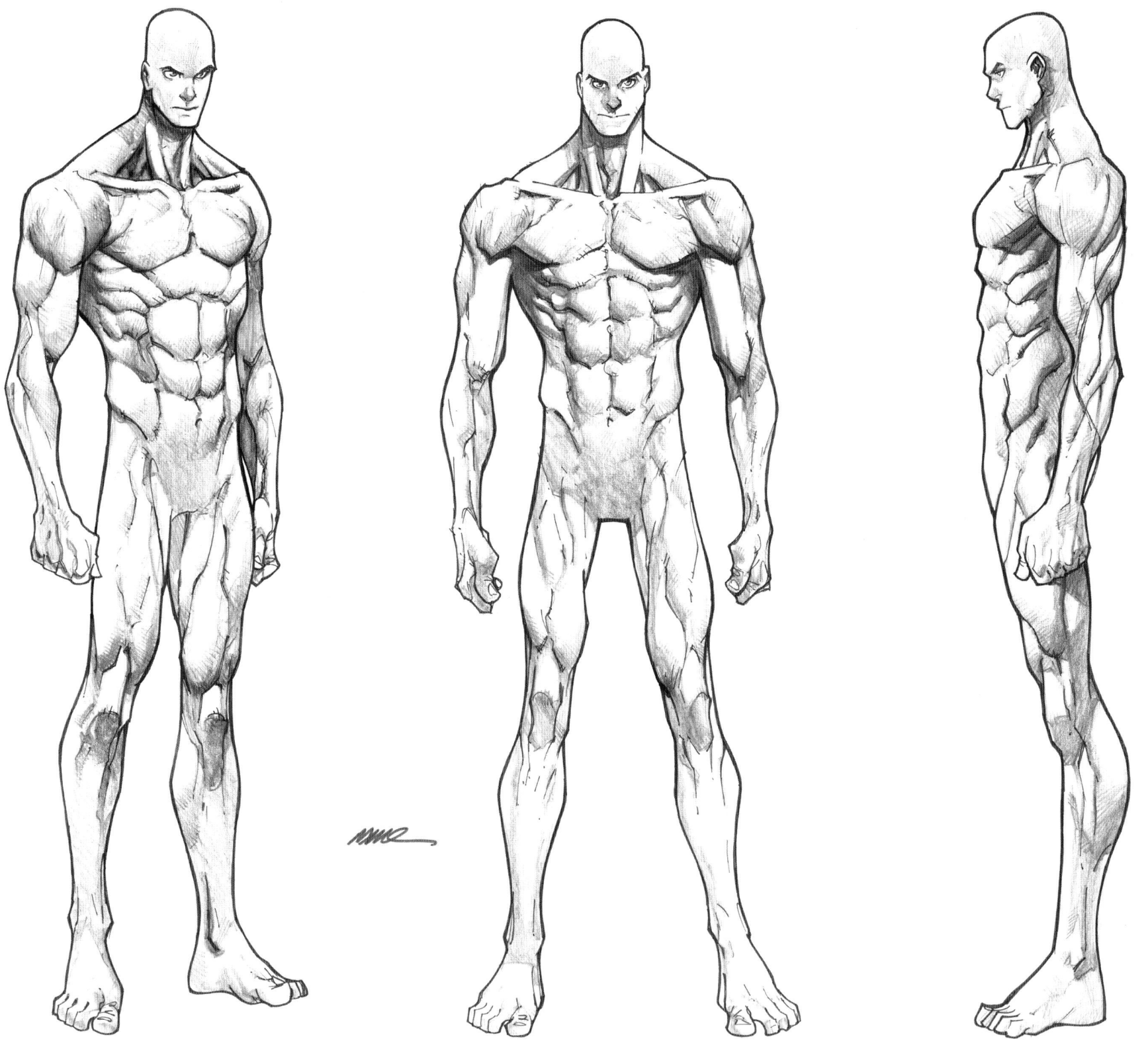

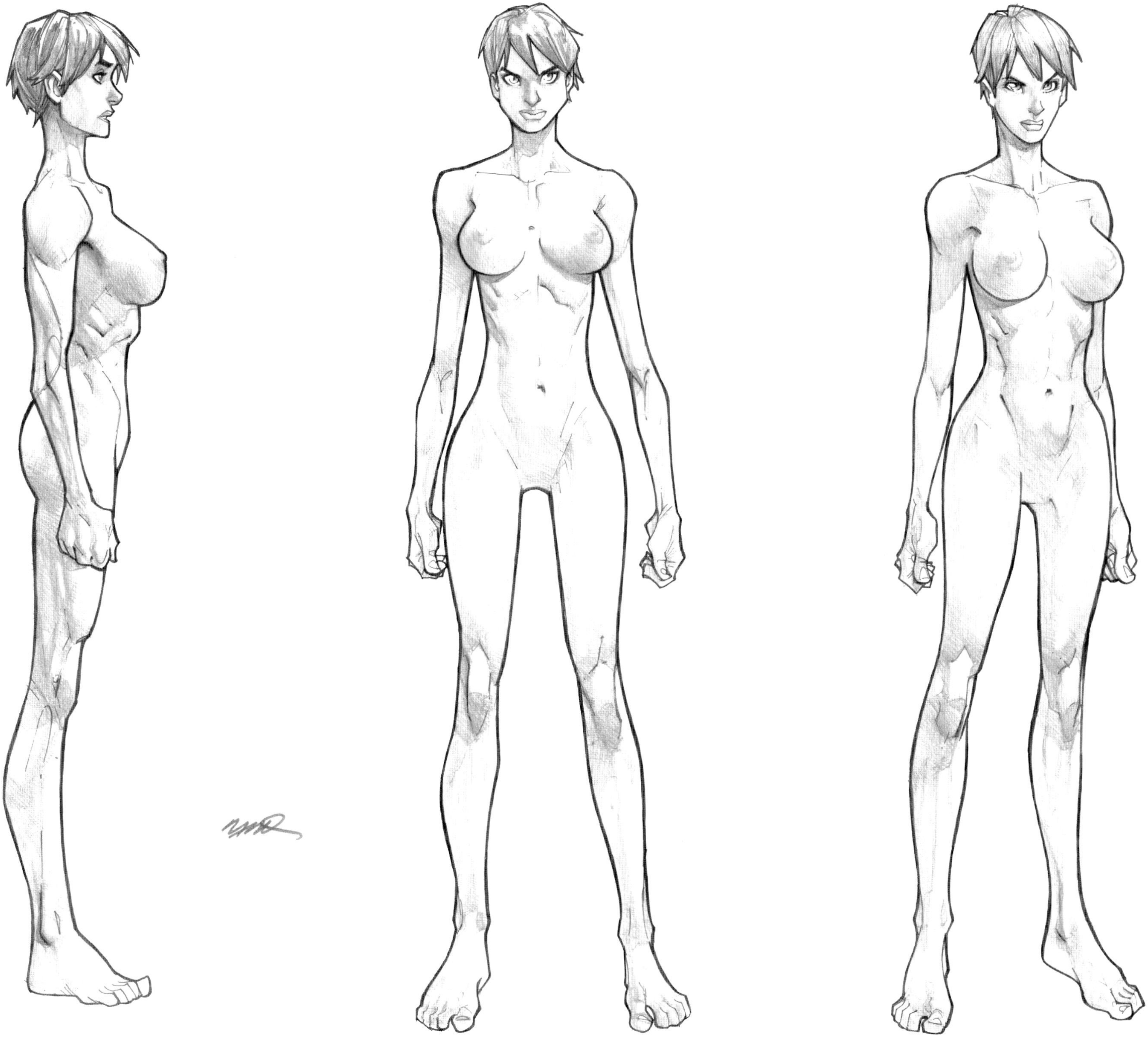

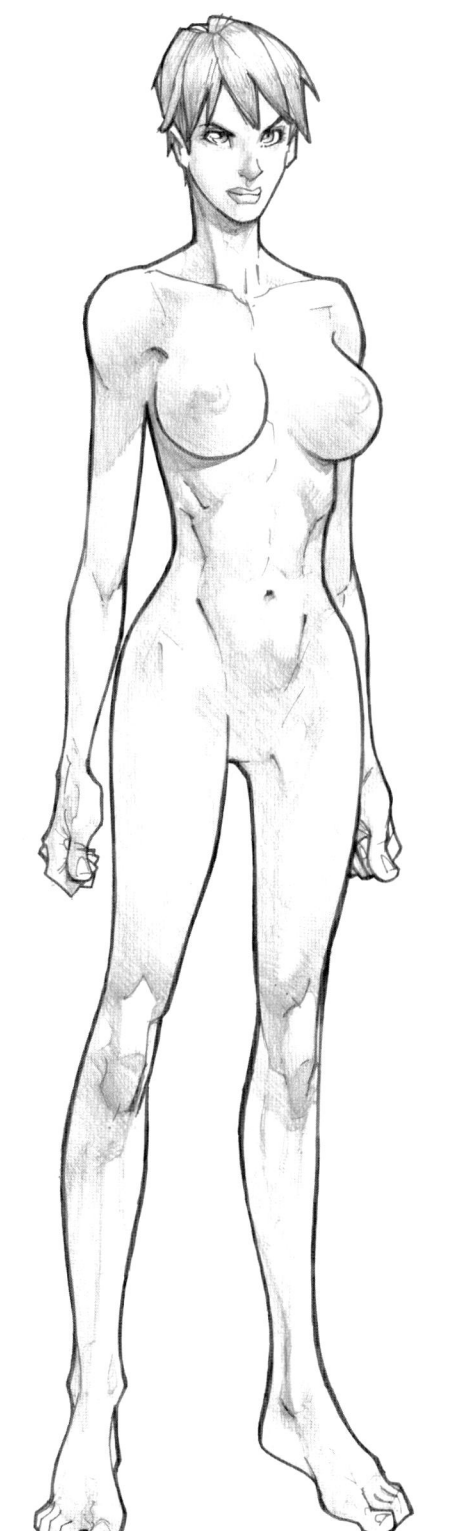

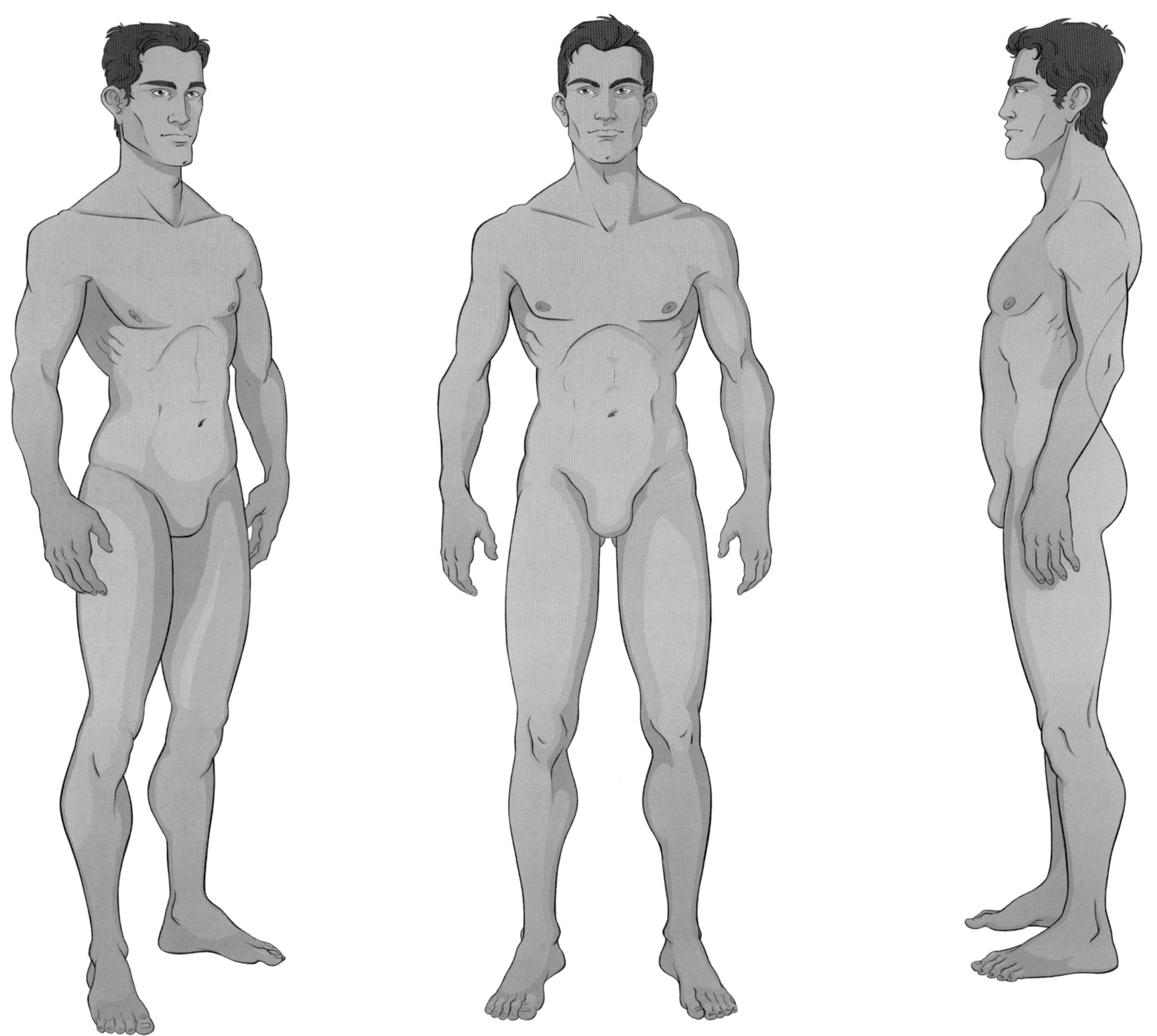

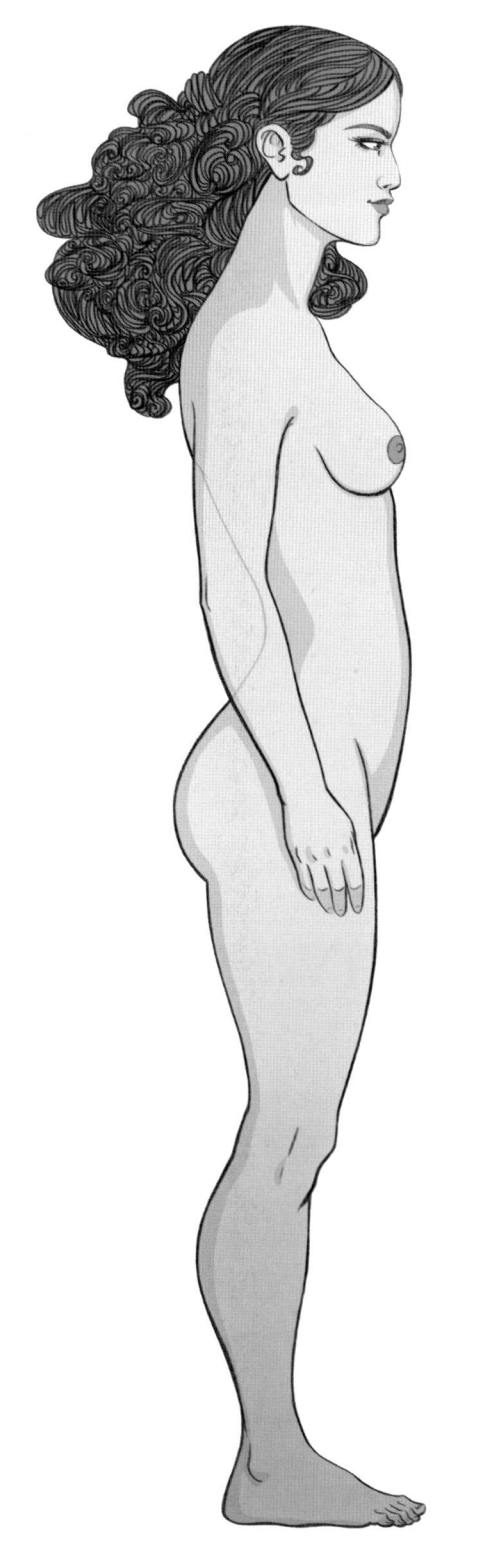
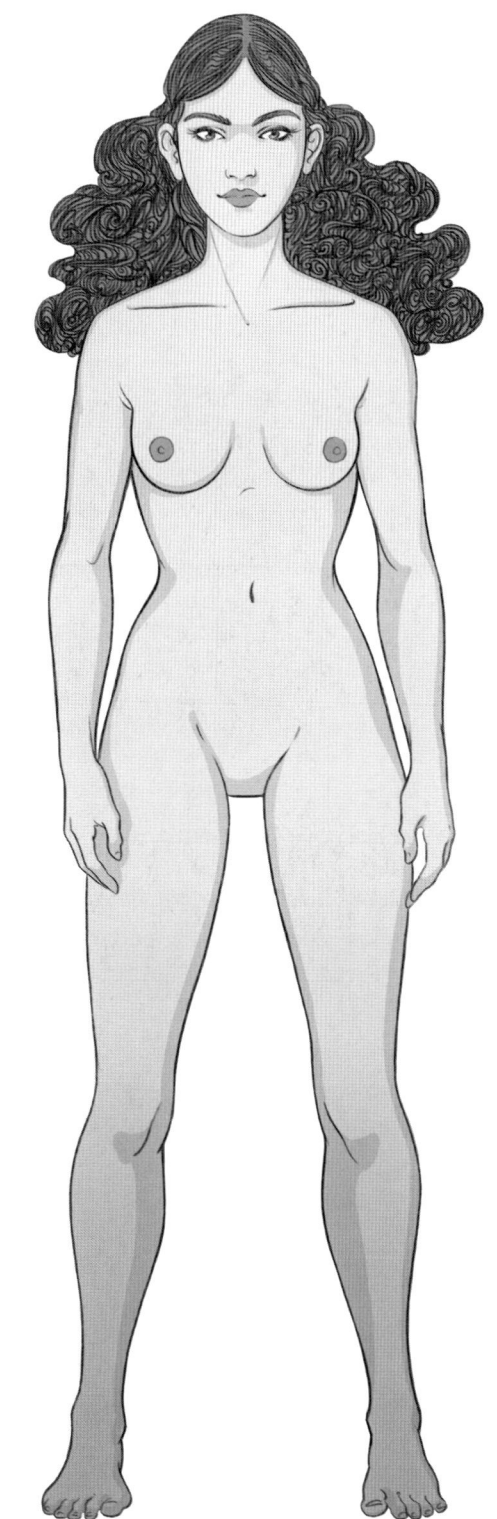
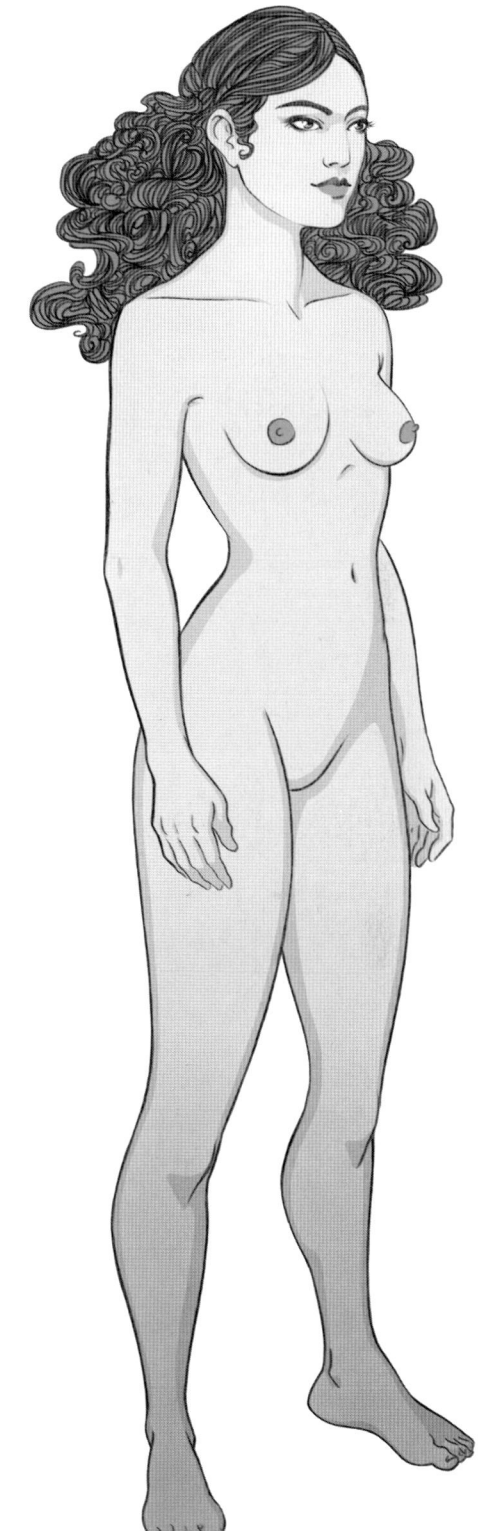

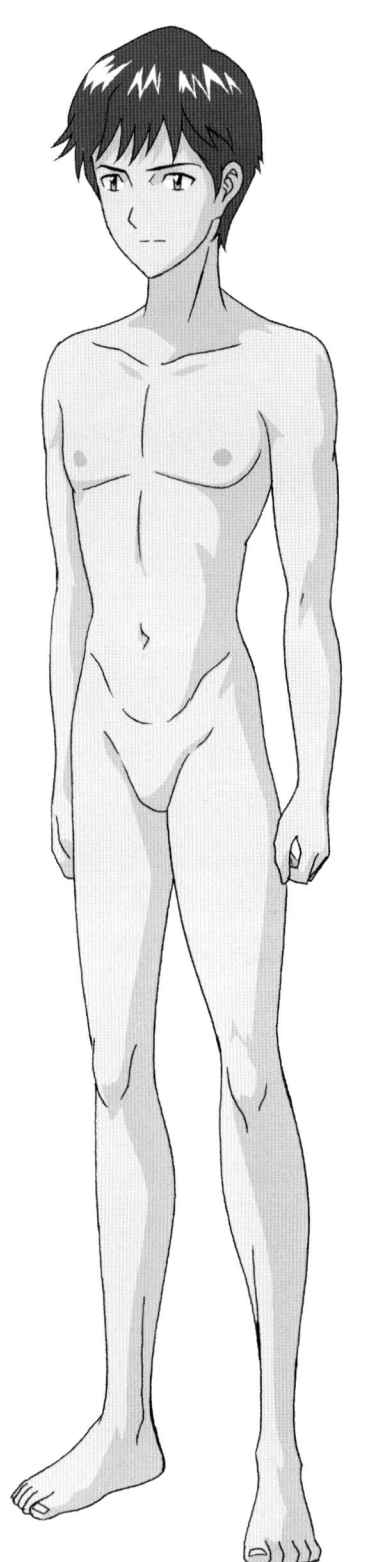
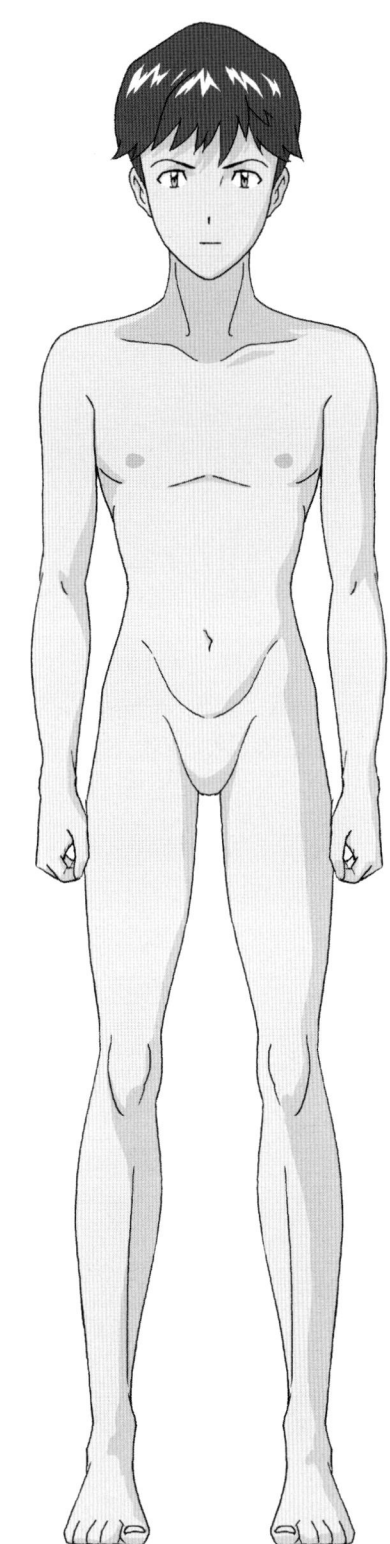
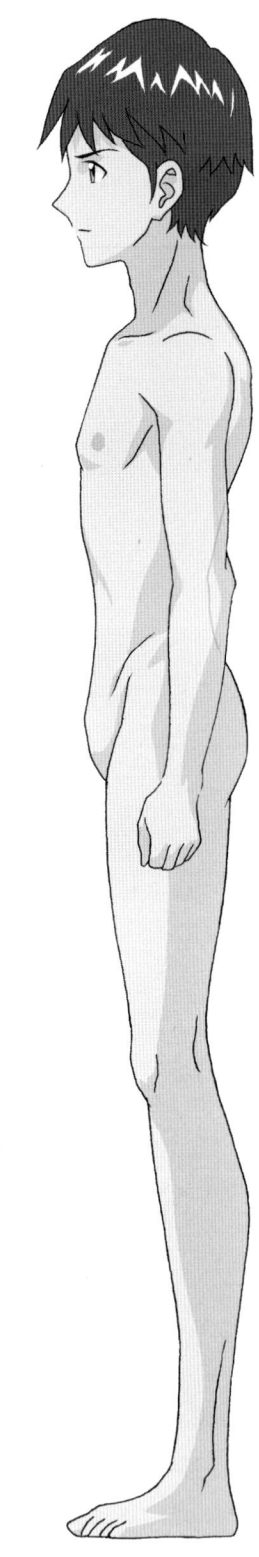

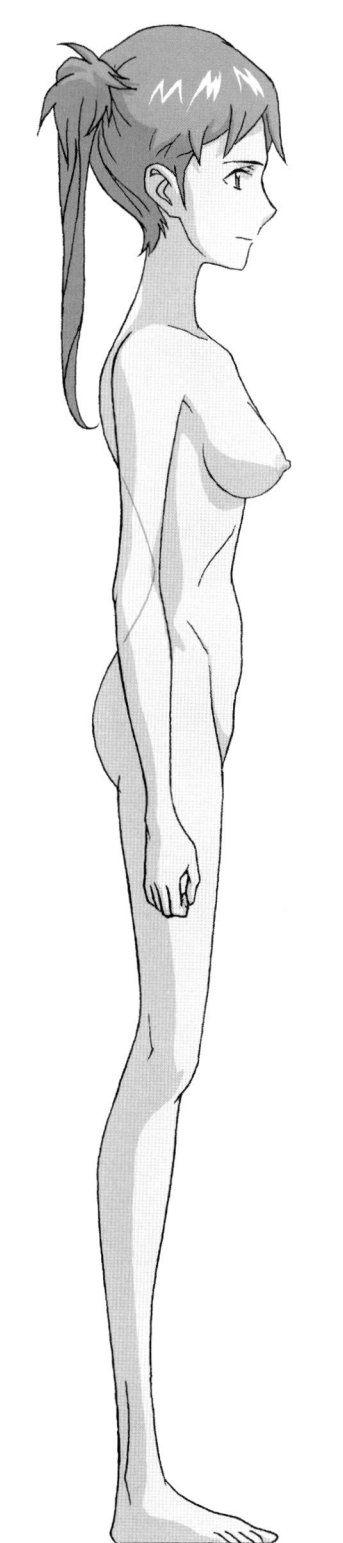
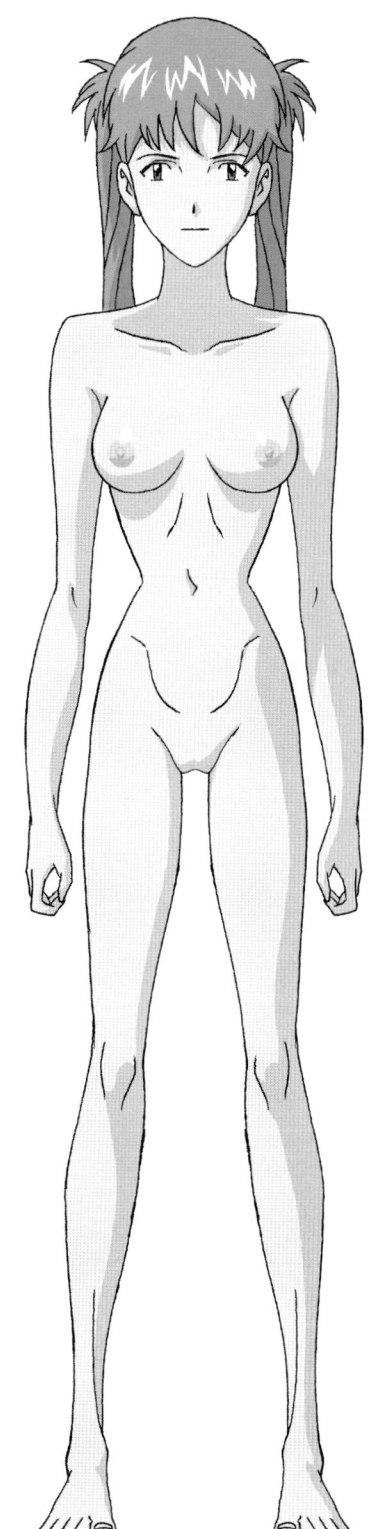
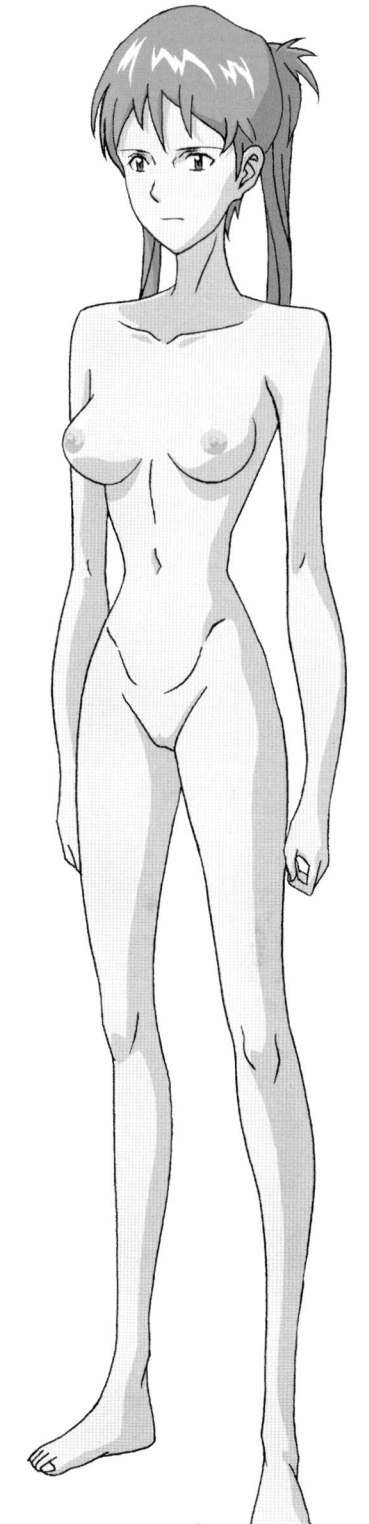

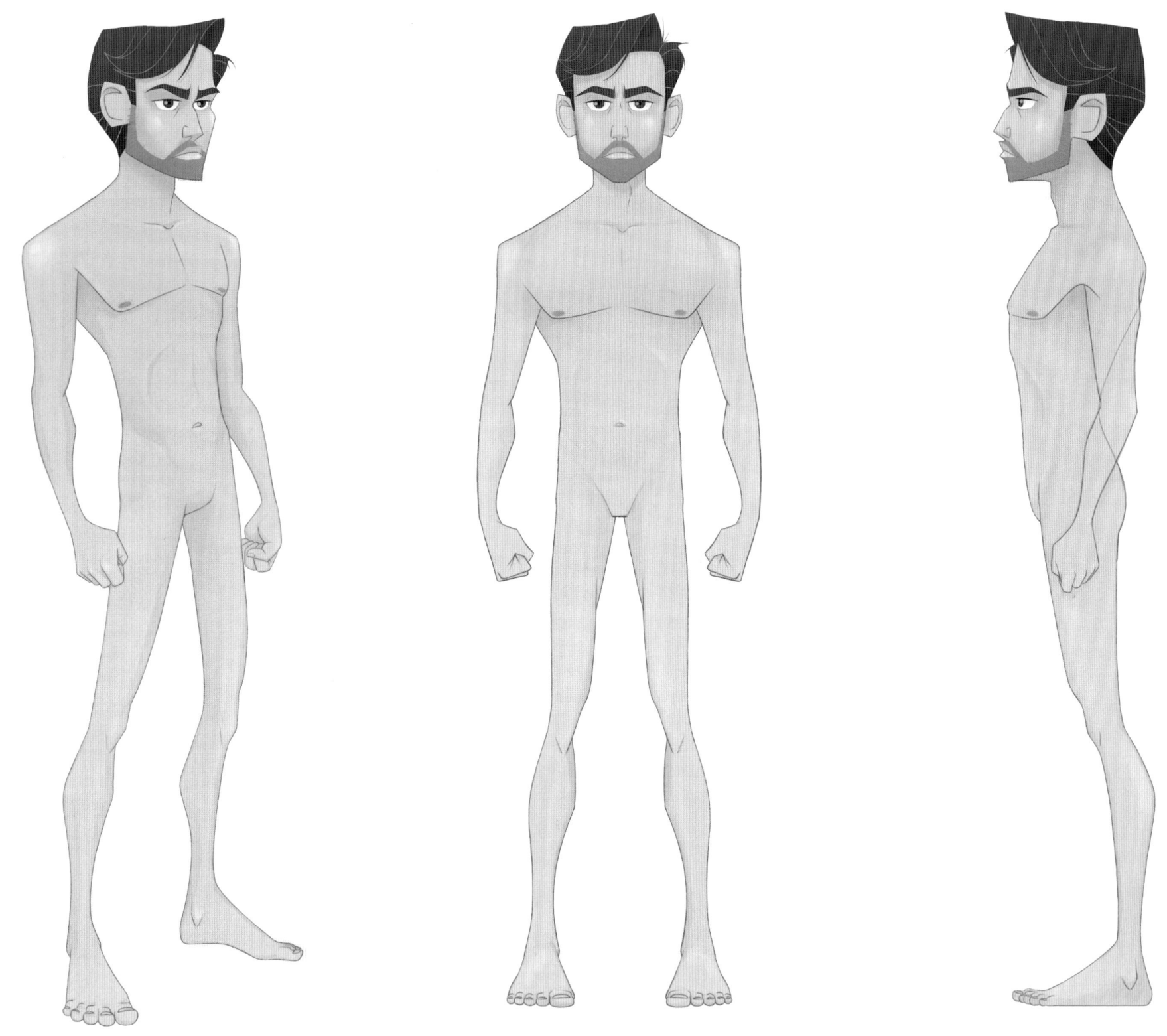

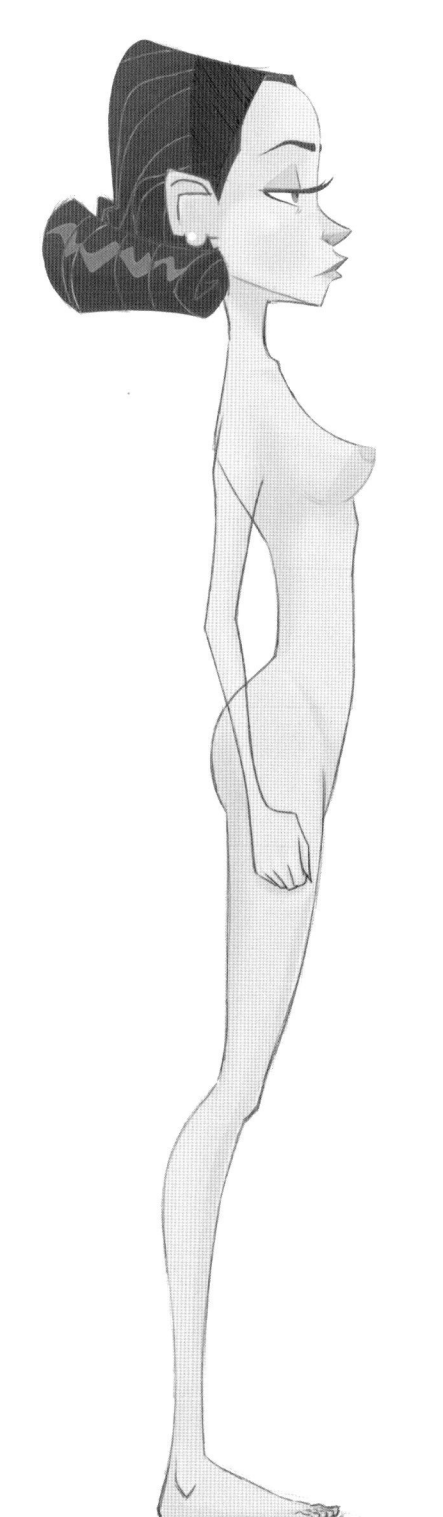
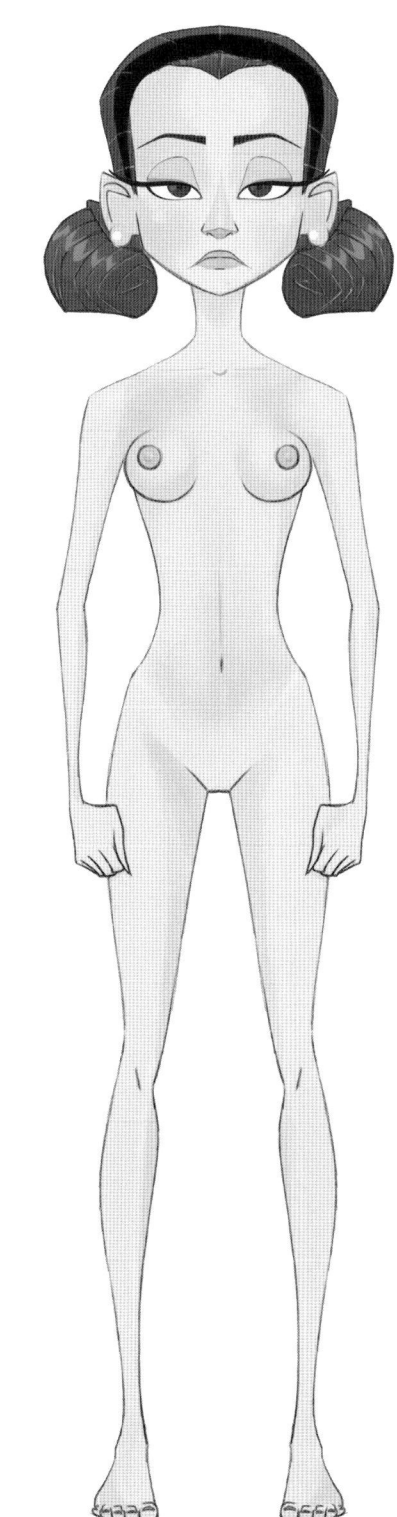
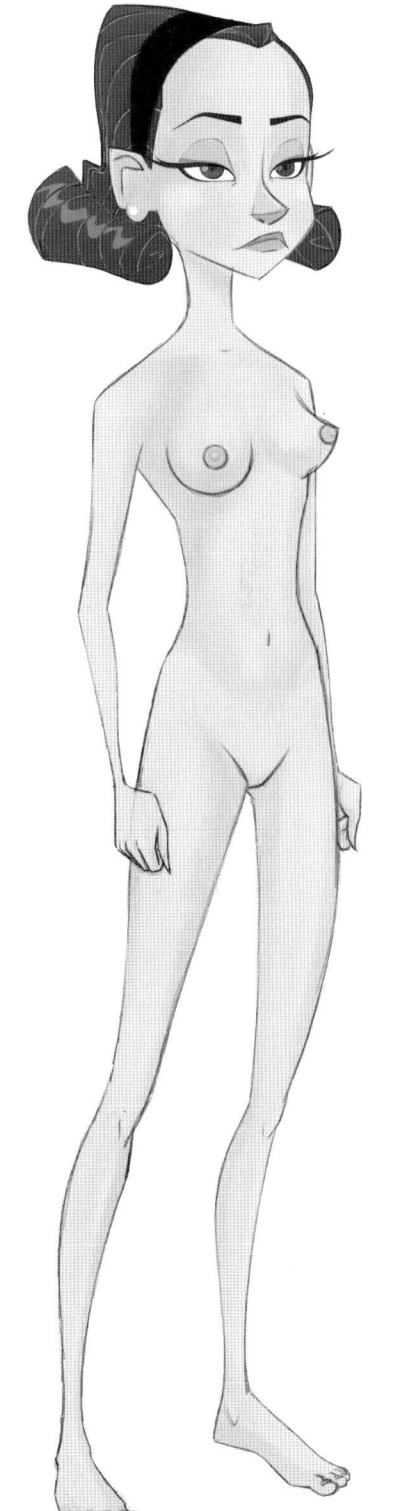

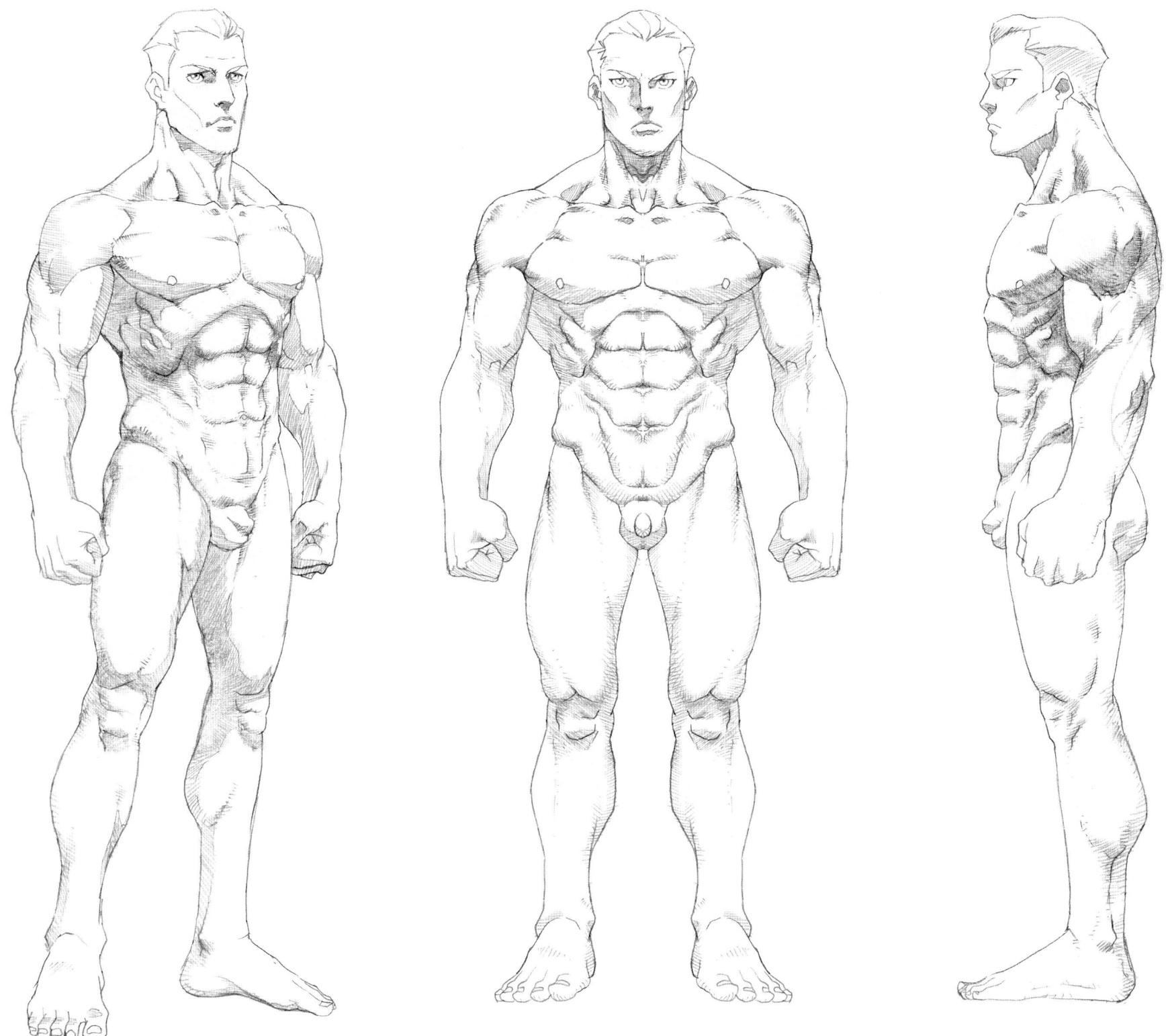

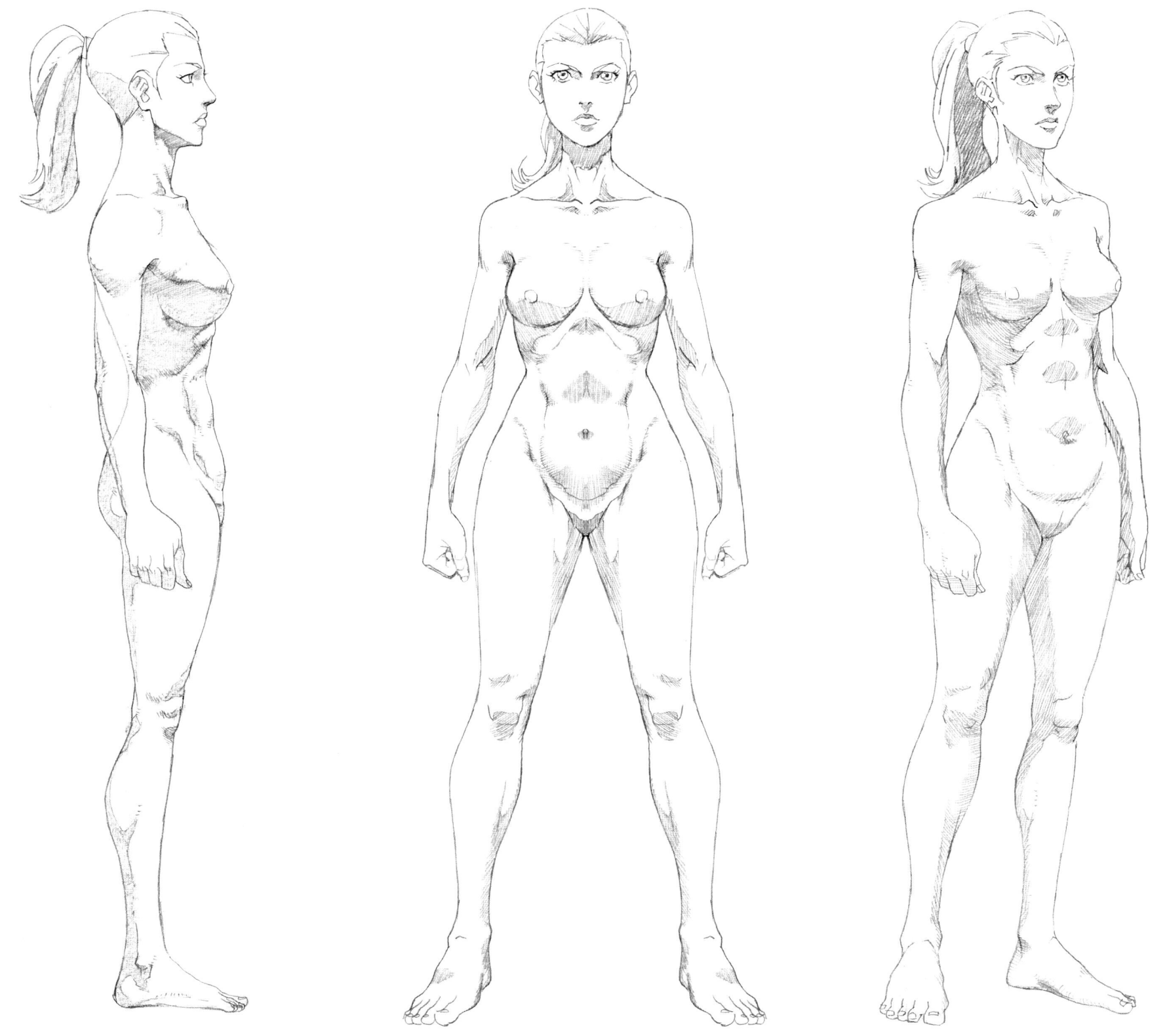

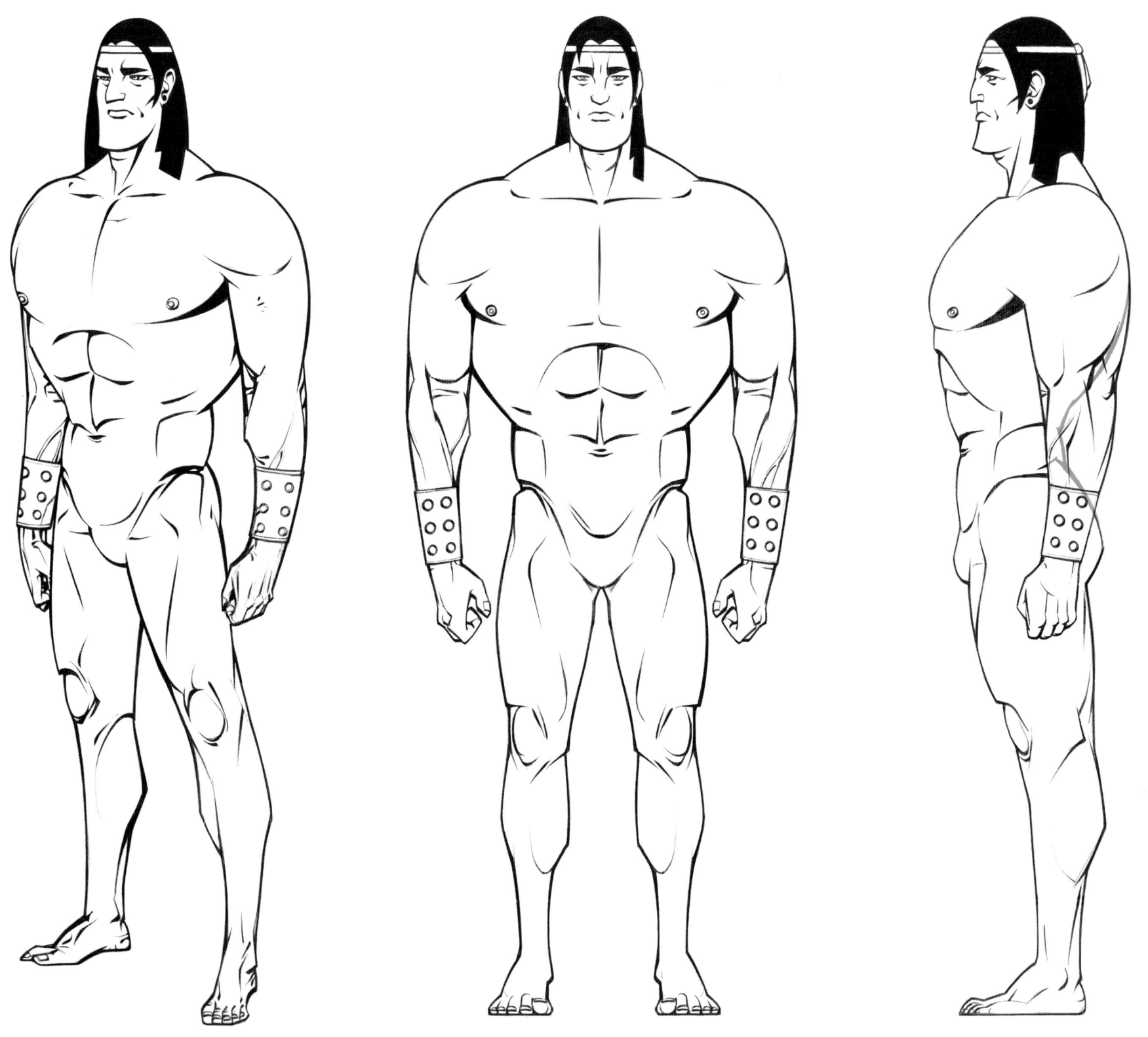

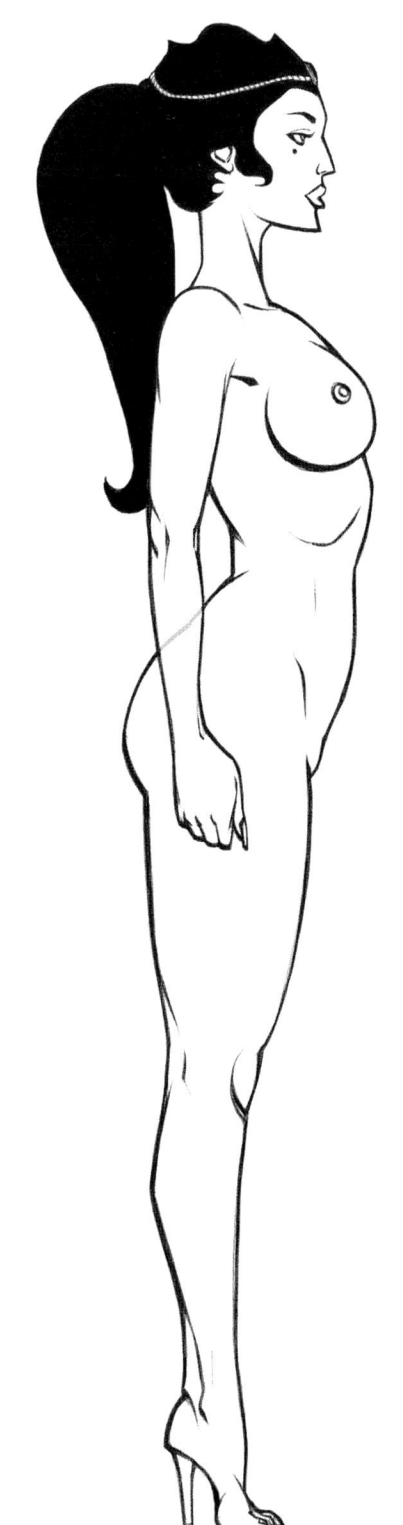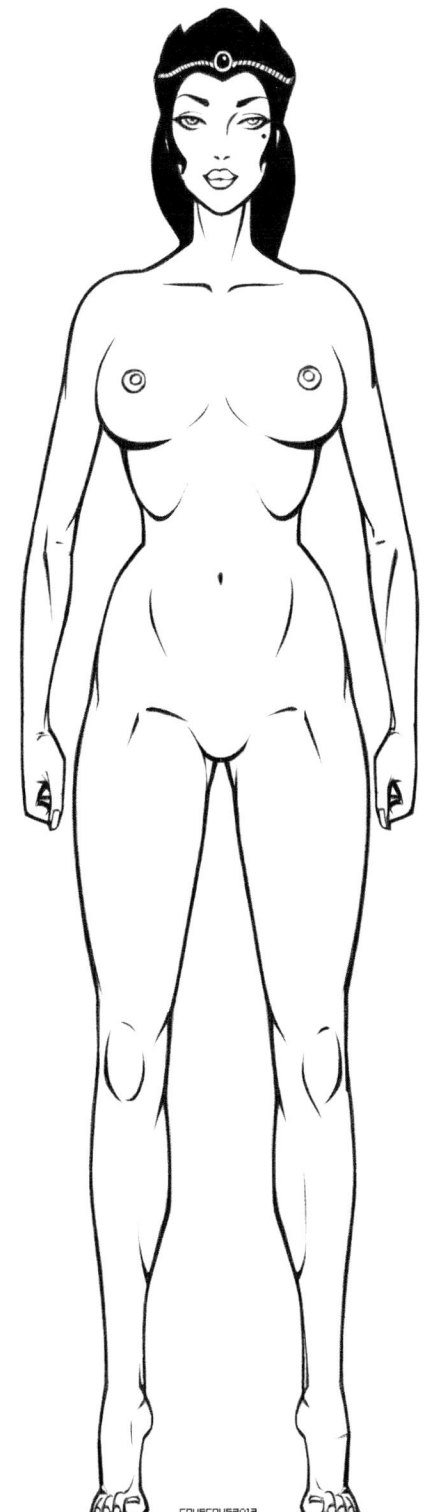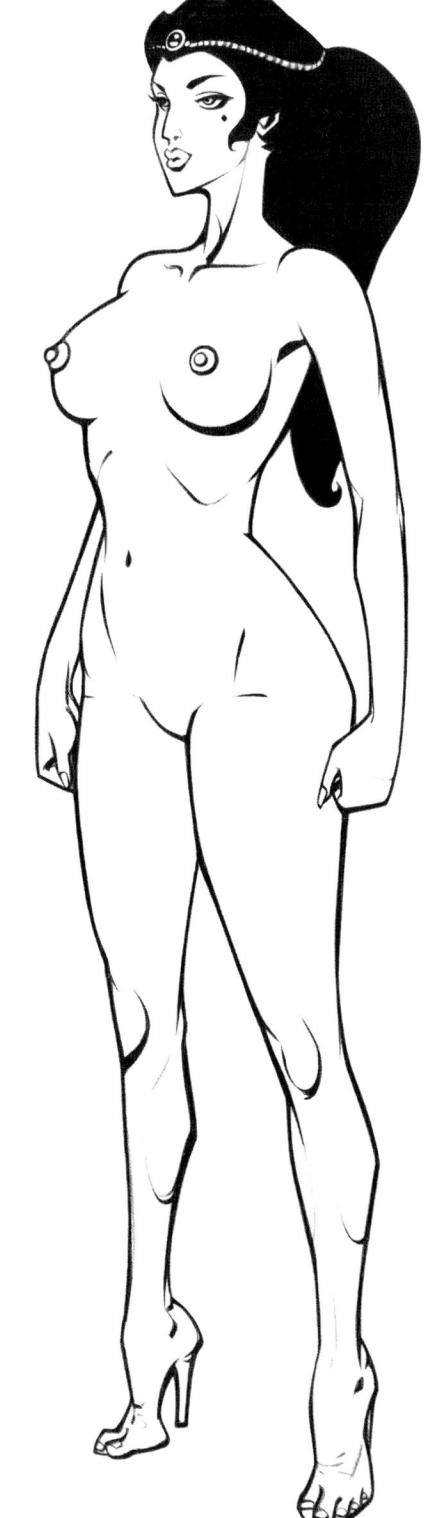

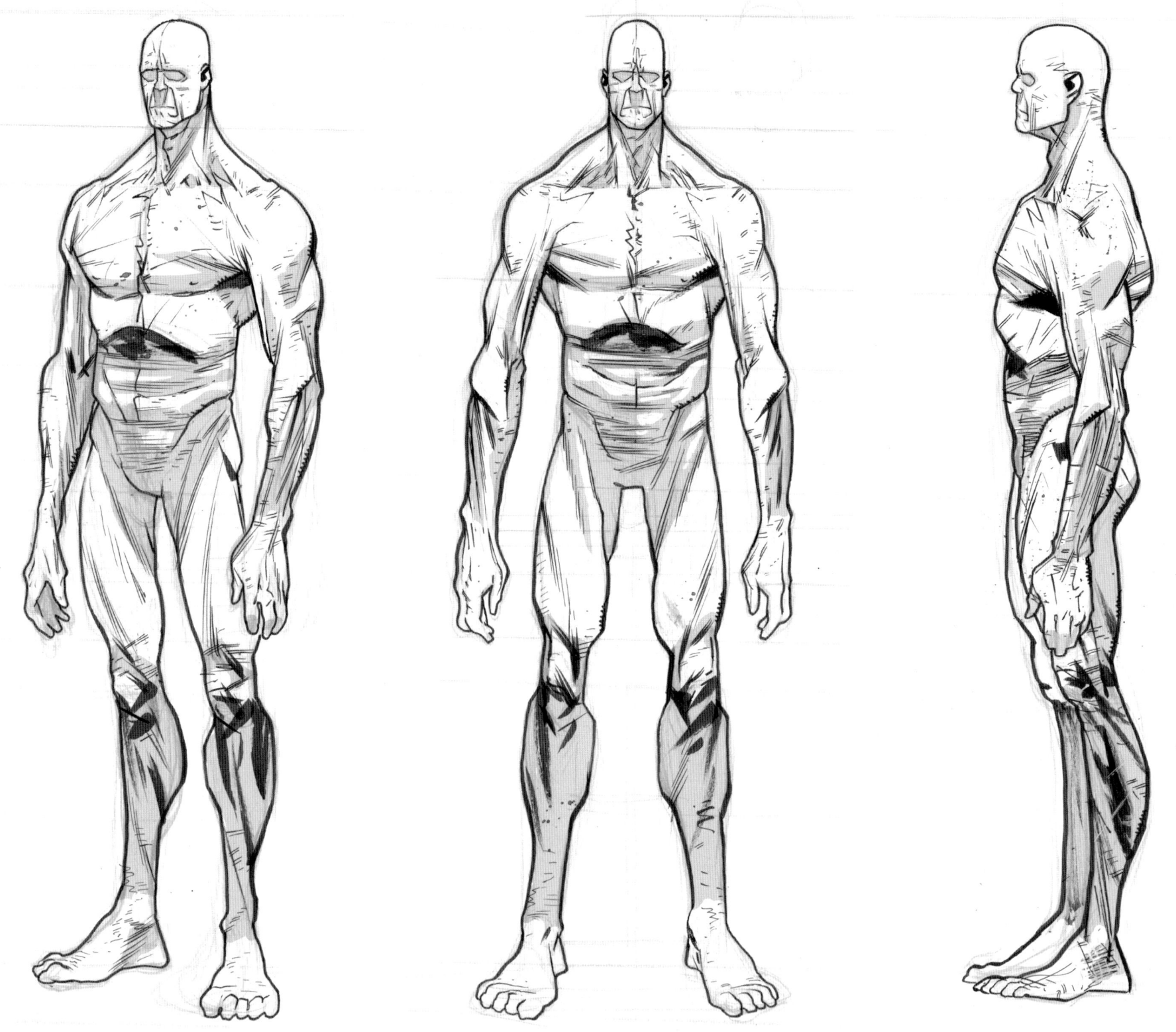

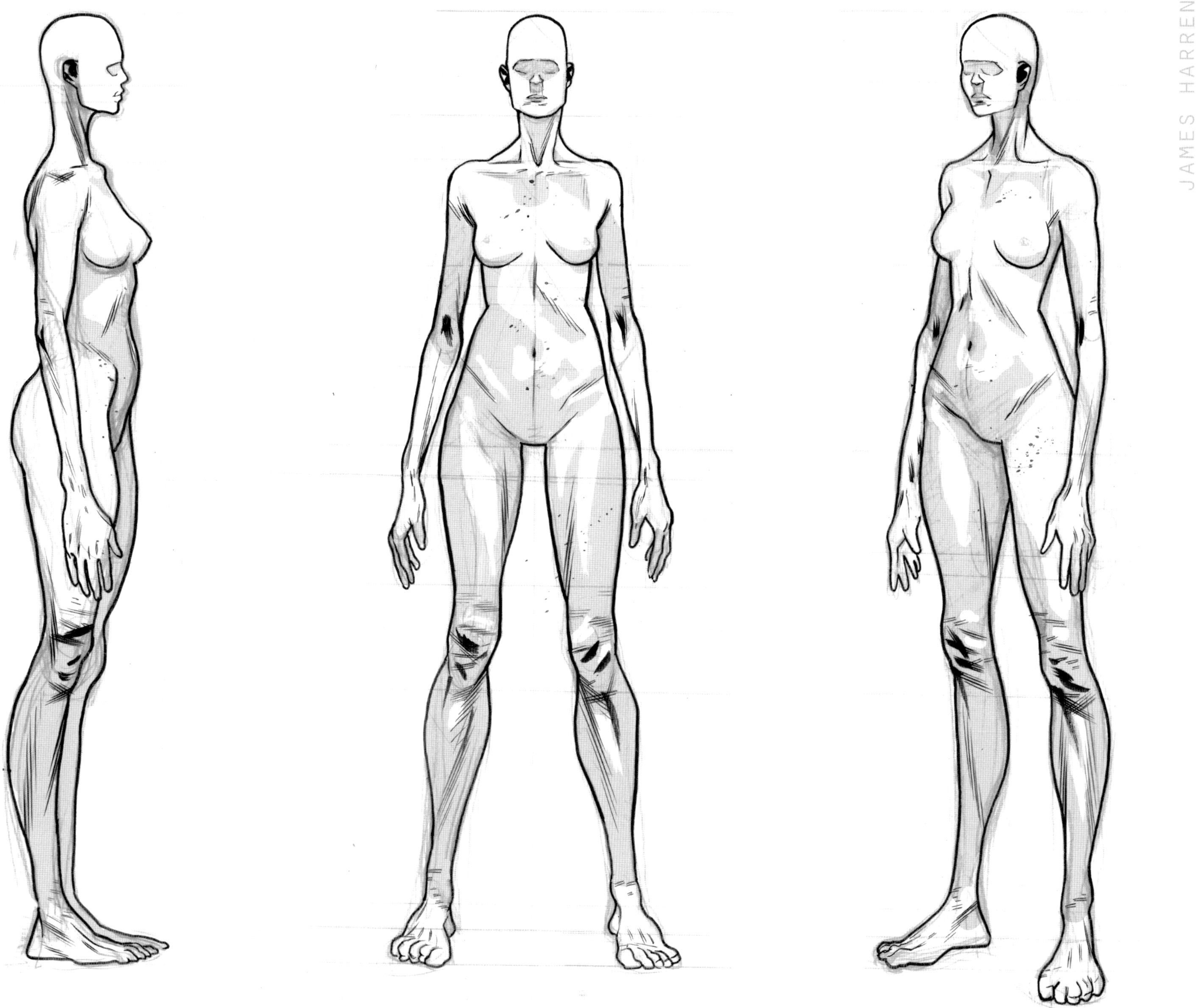

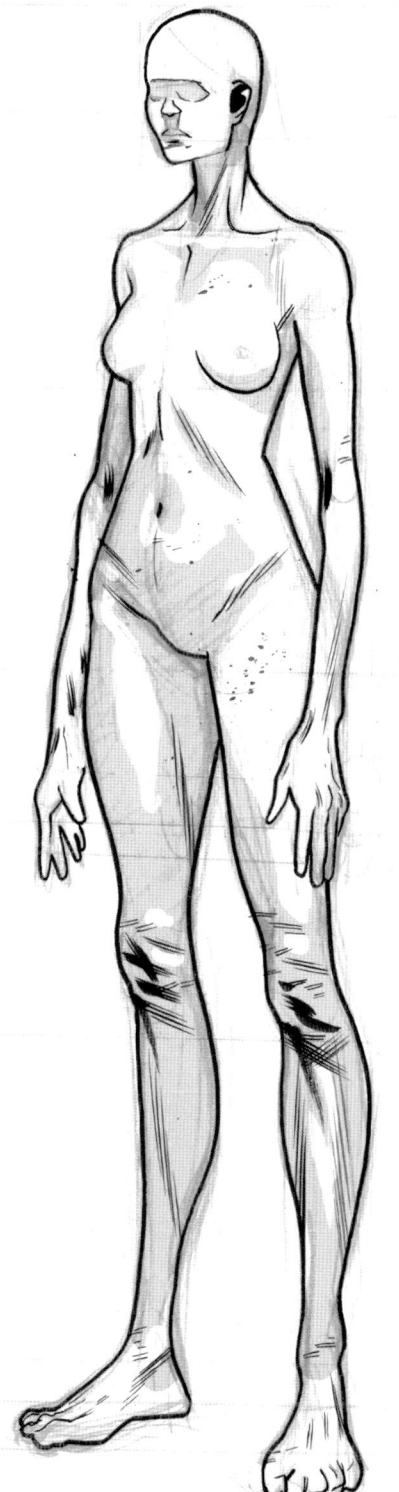

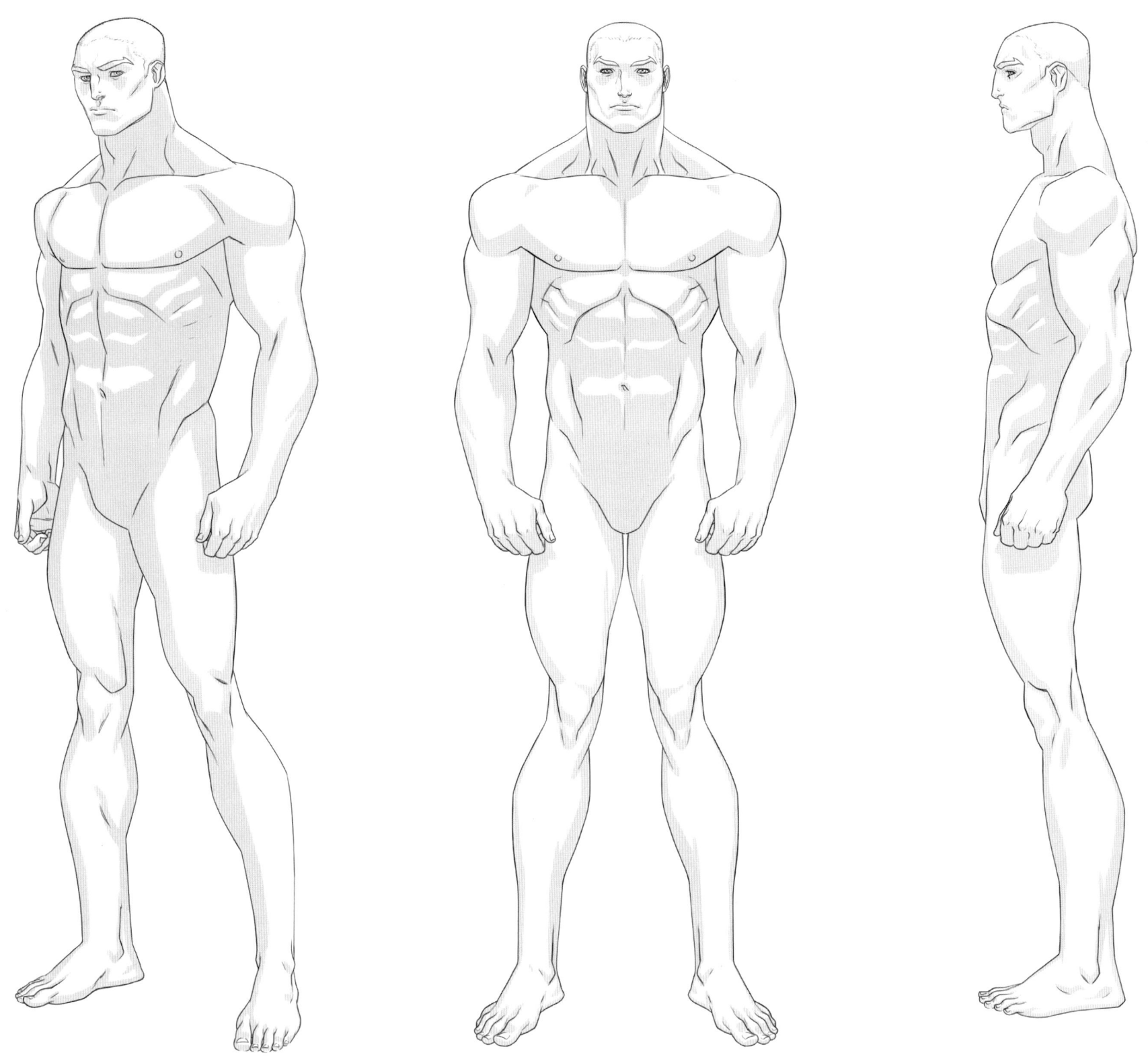

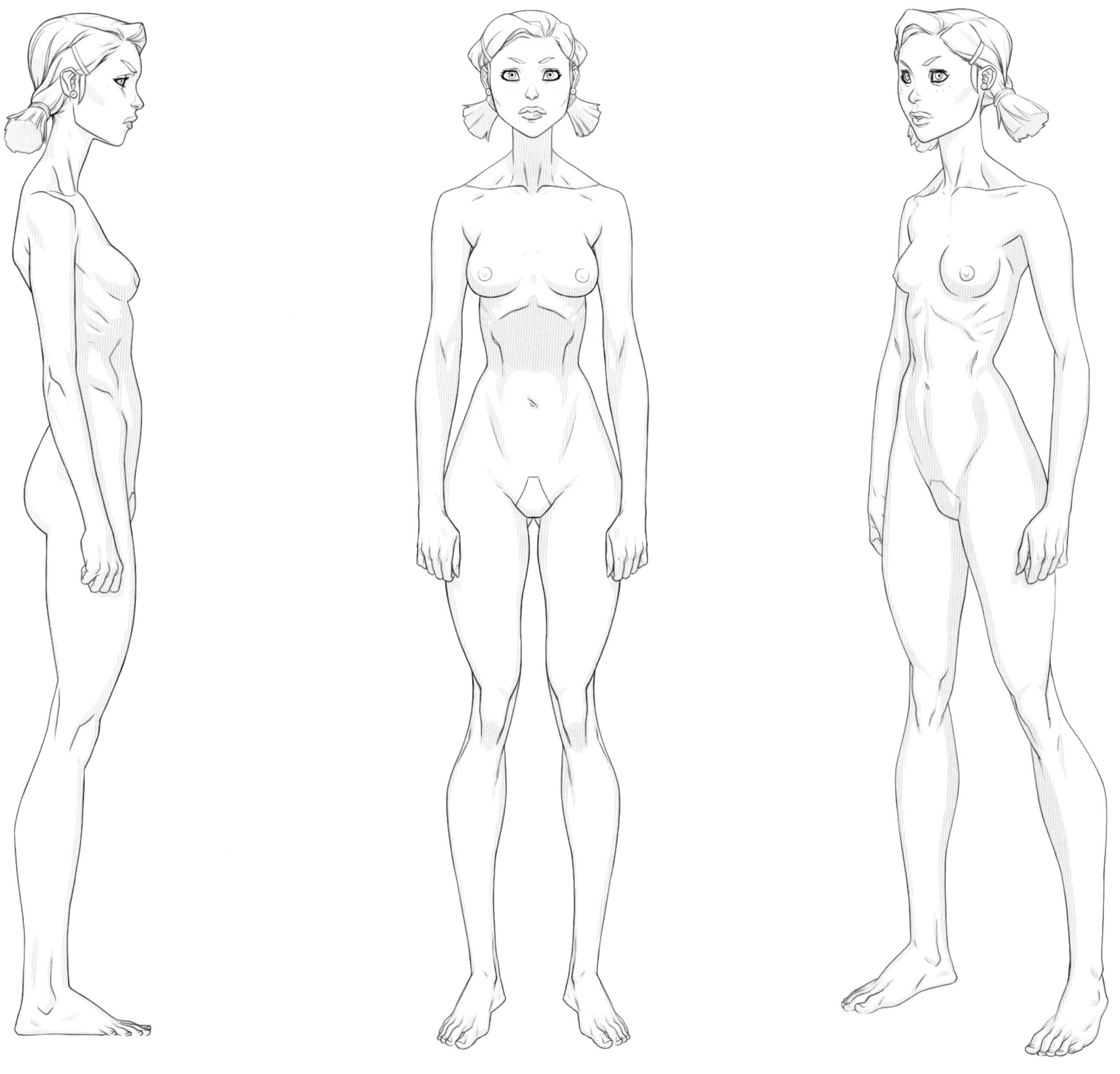

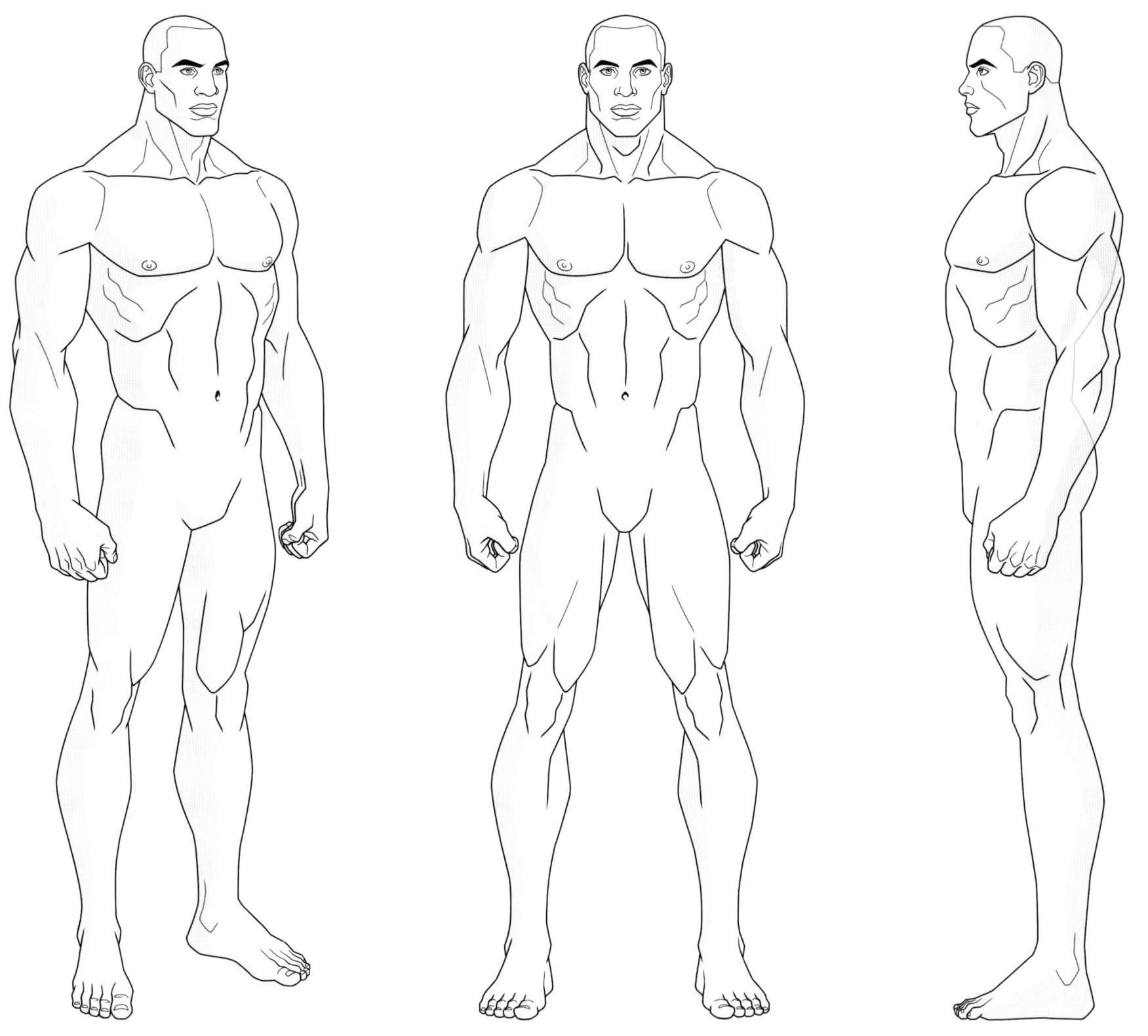

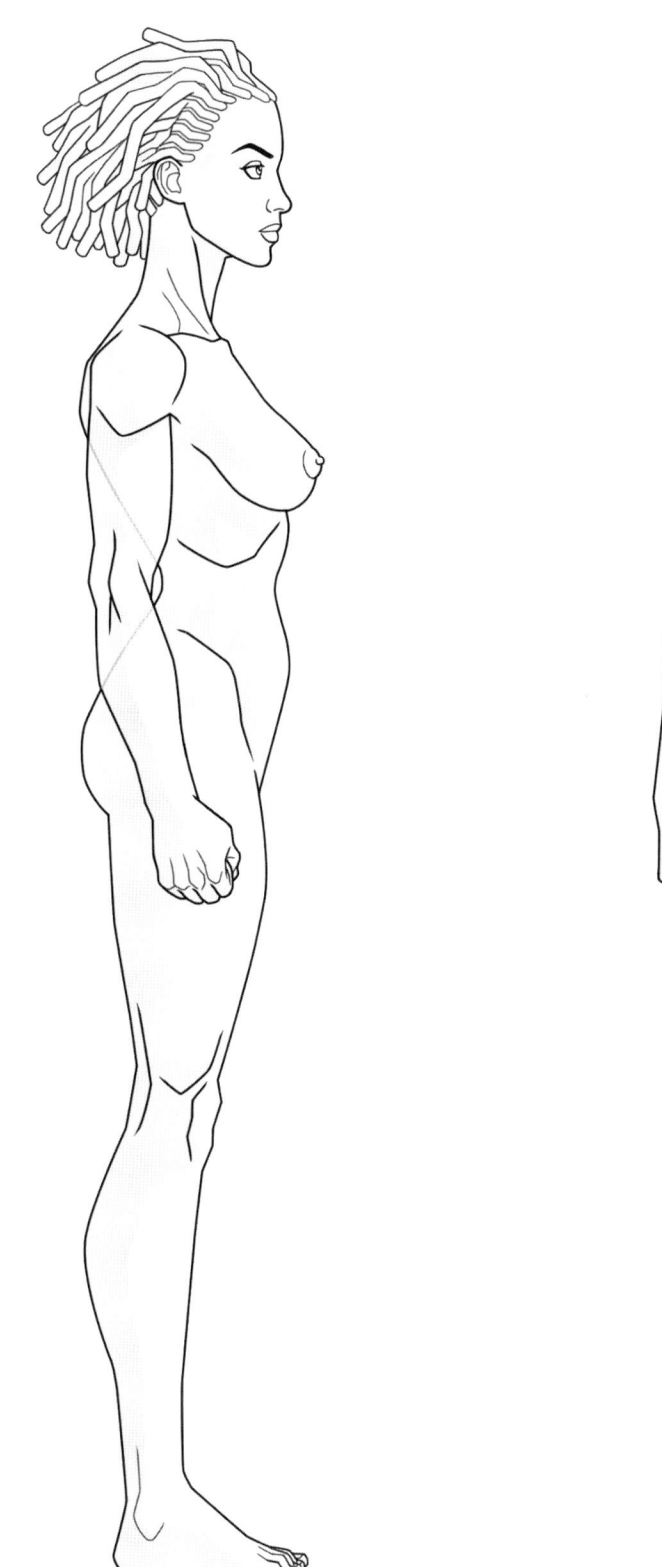
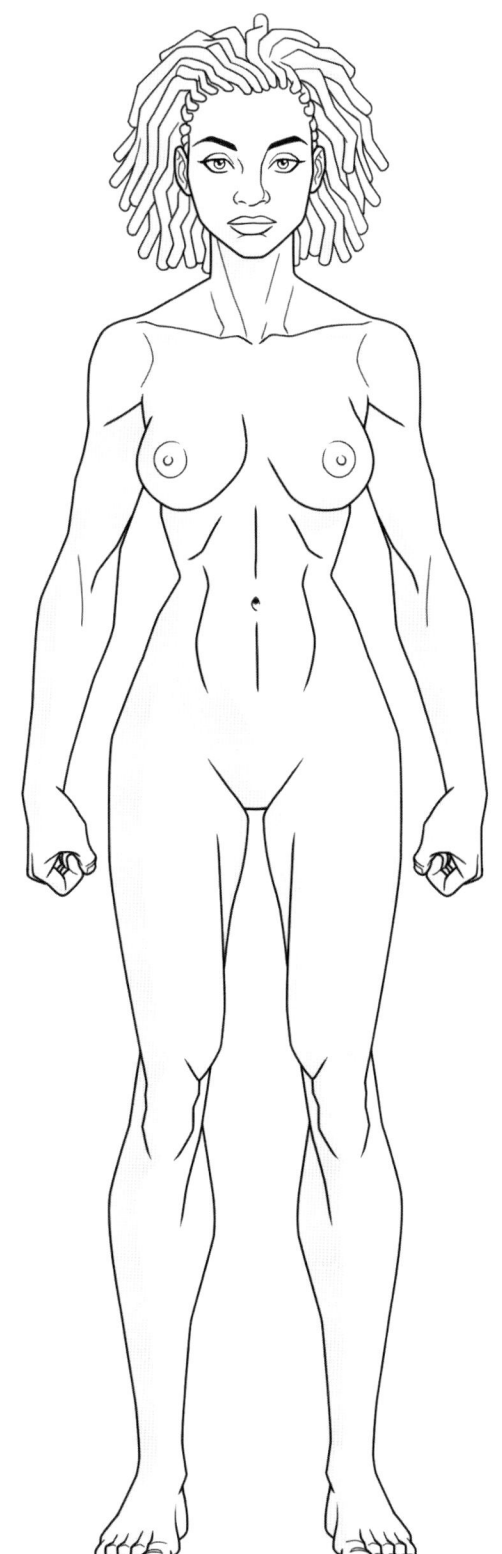
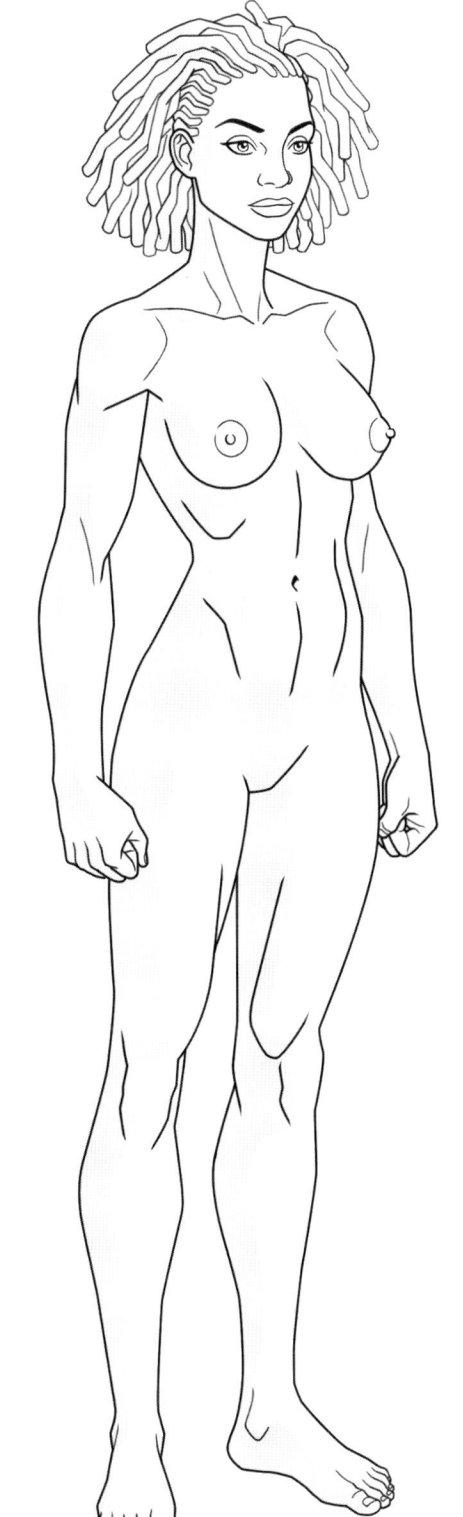

JEROME K. MOORE

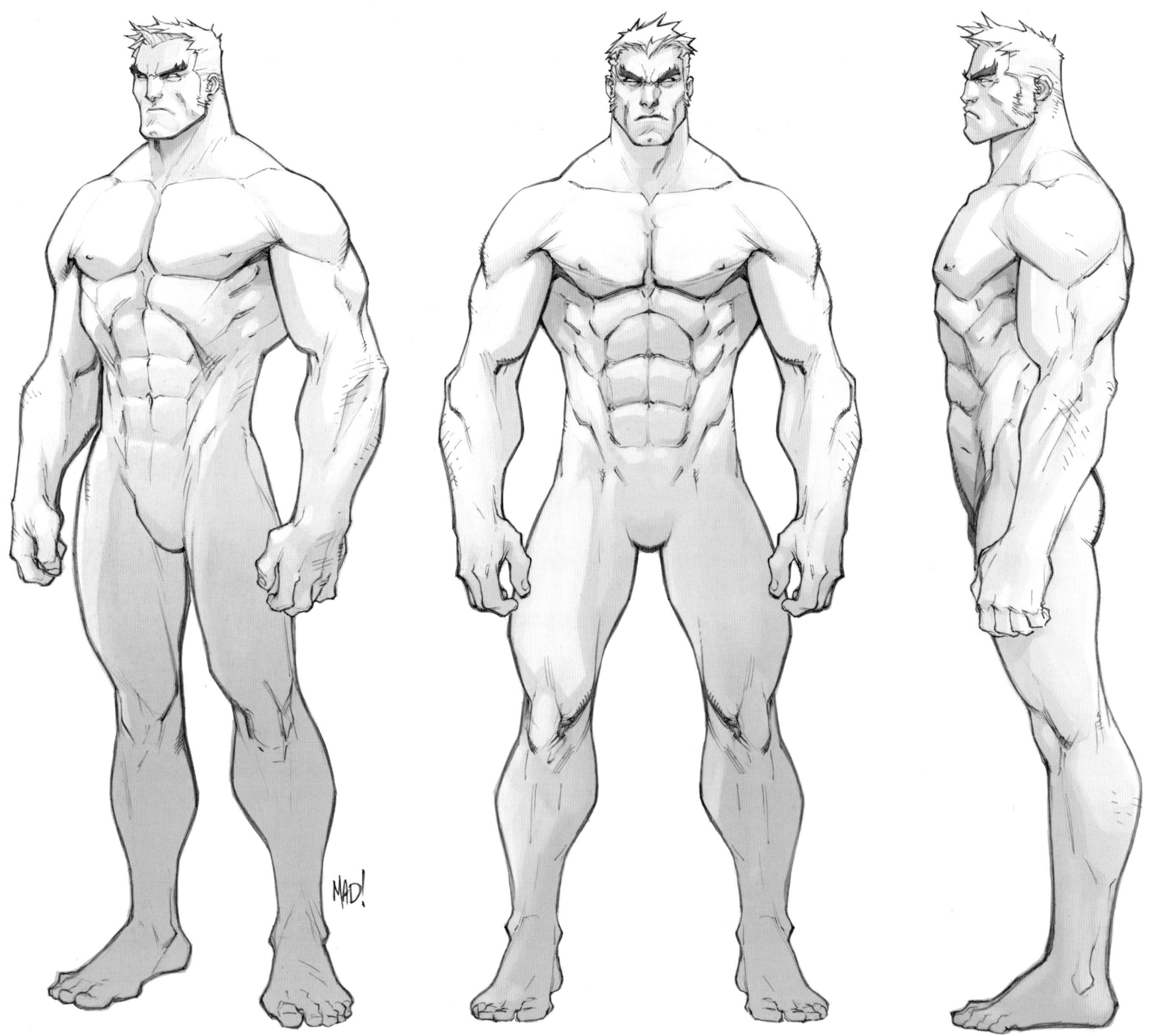

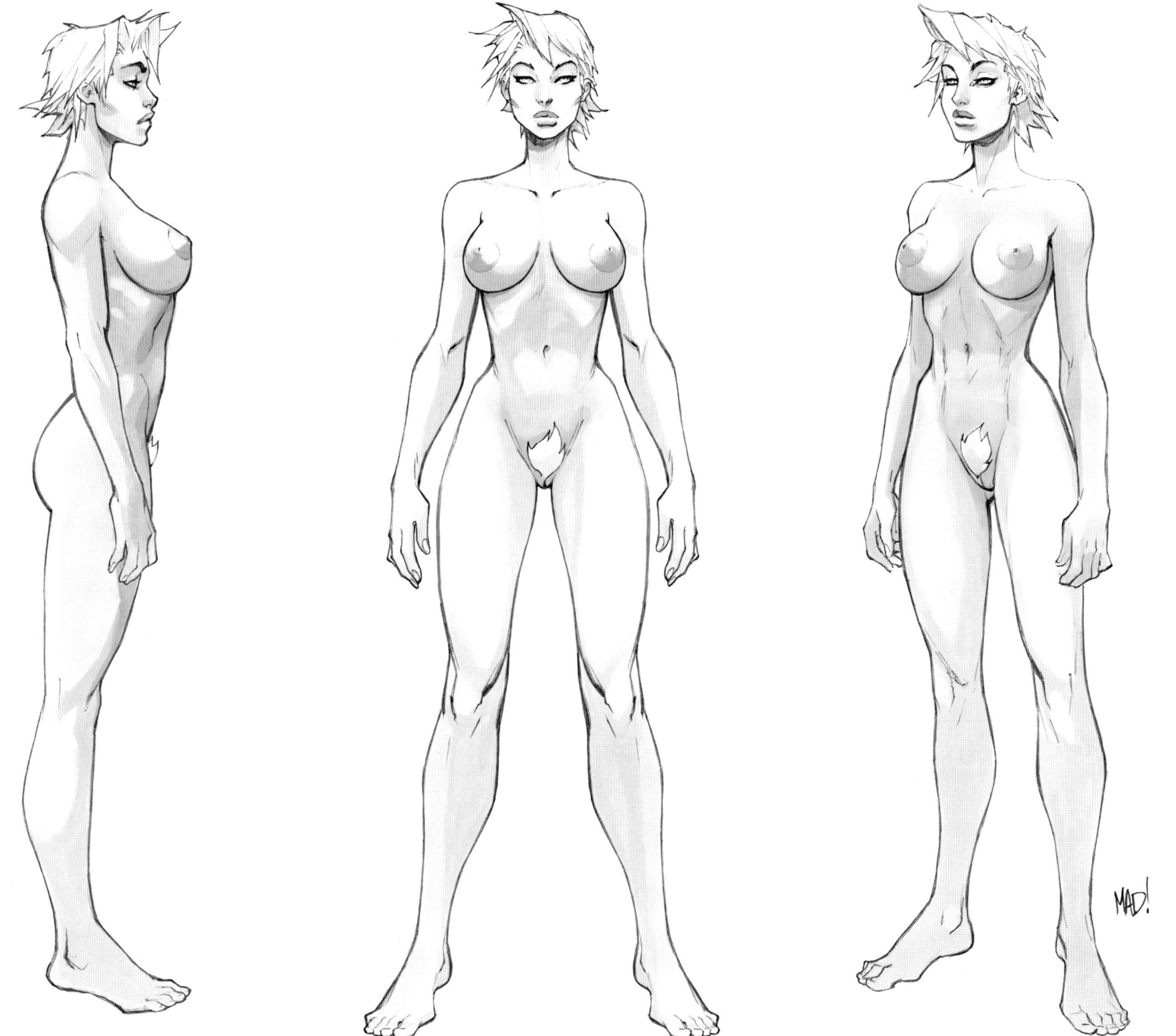

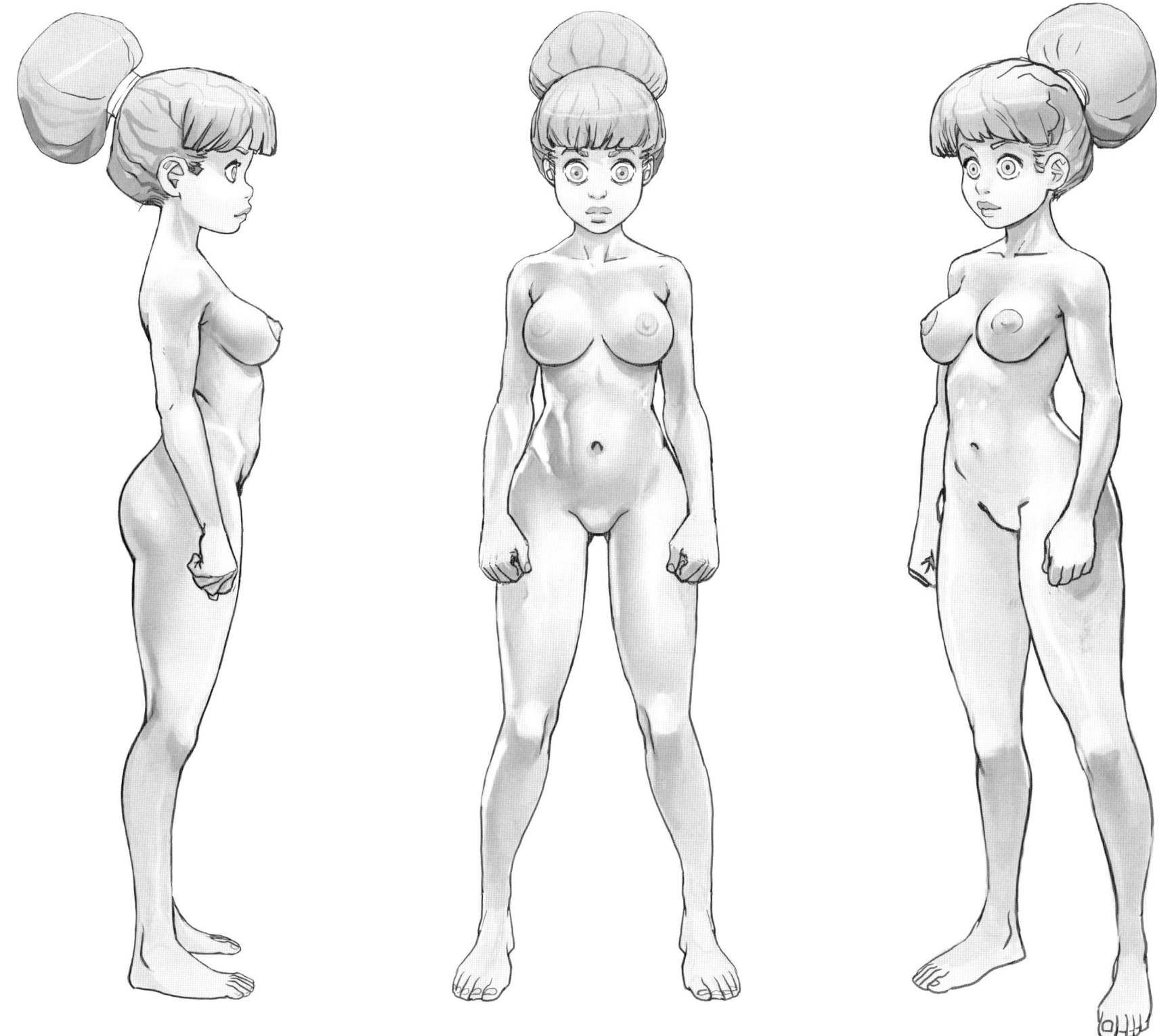

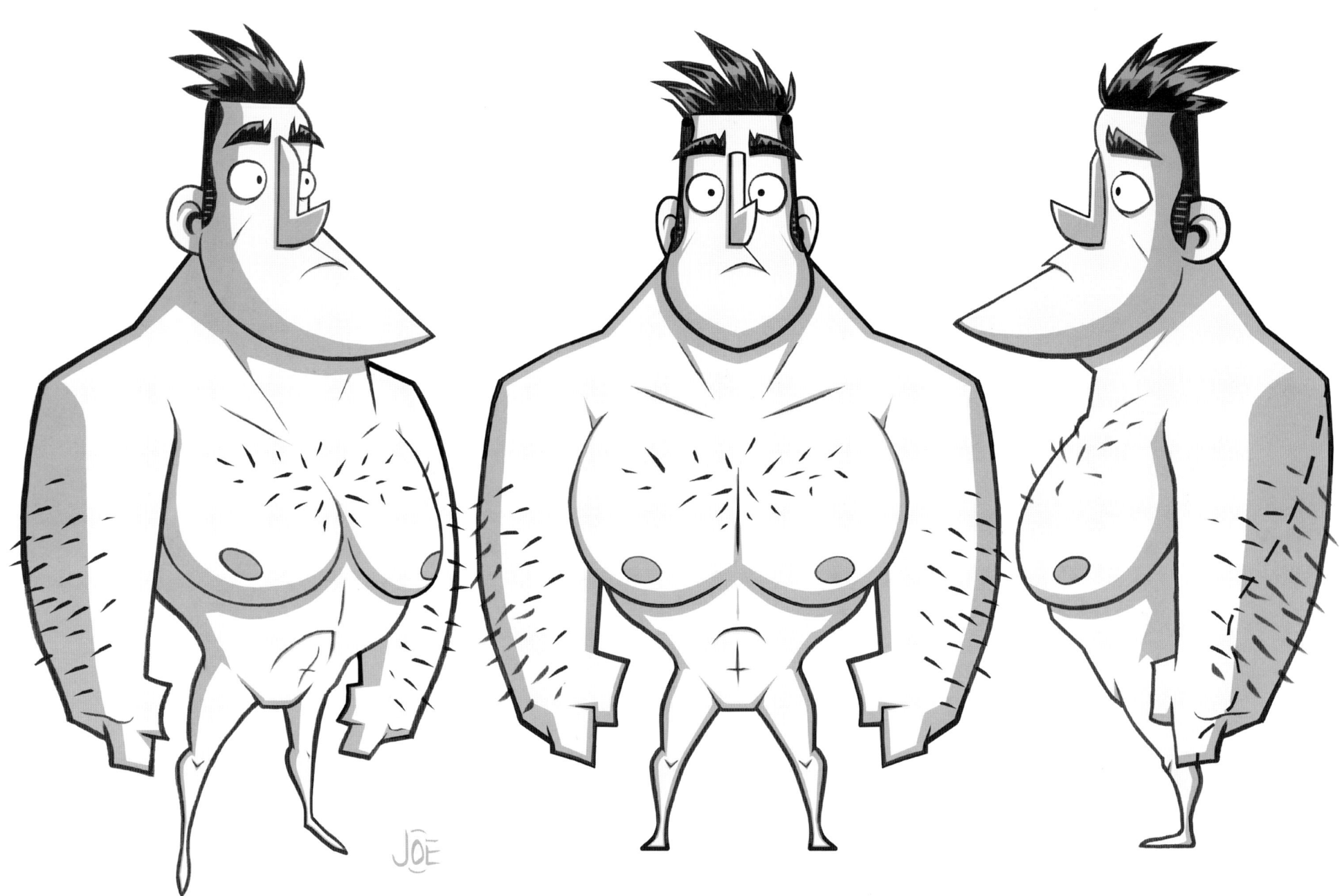

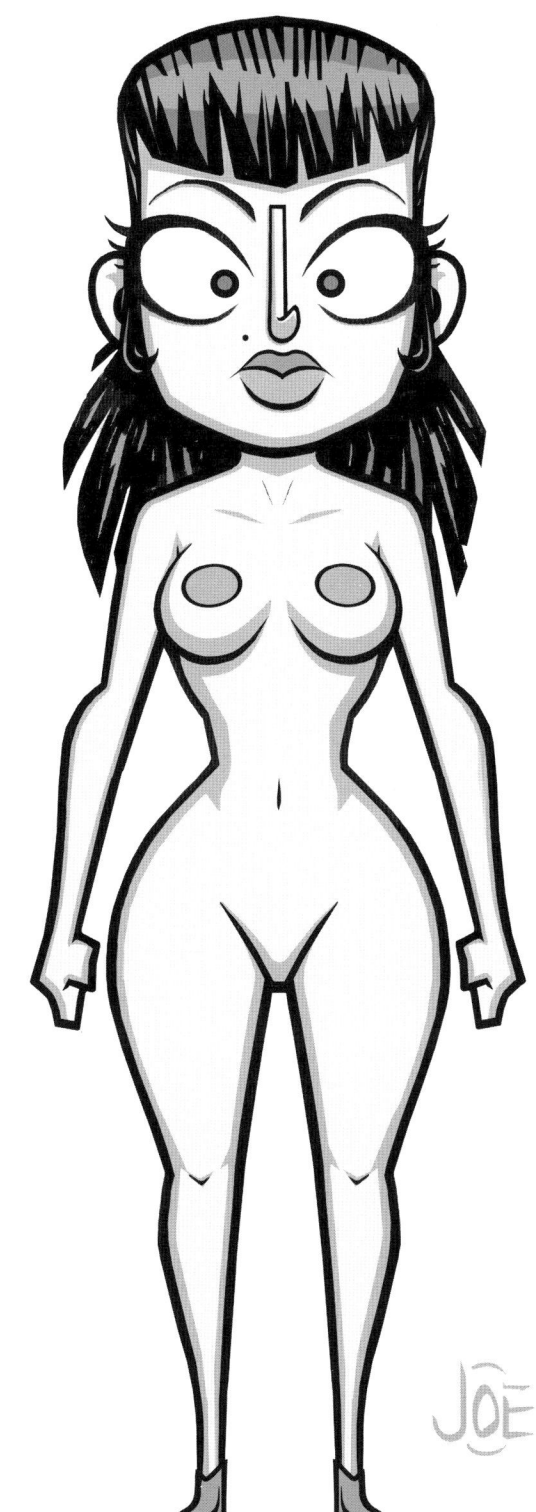
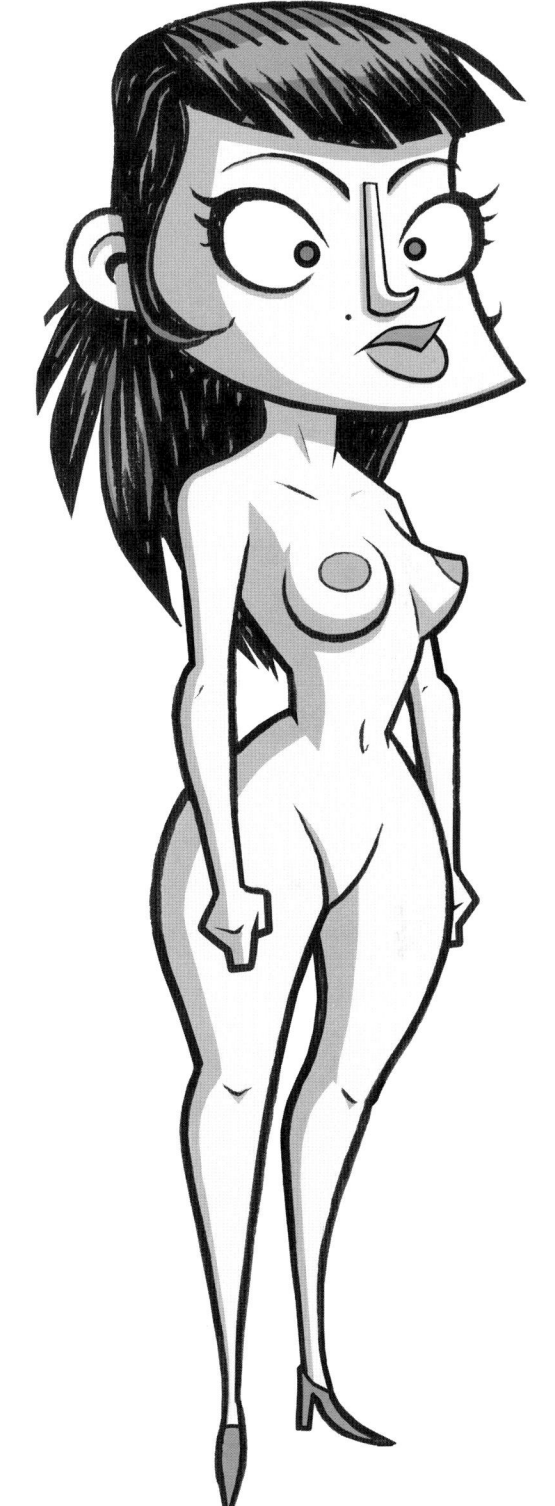

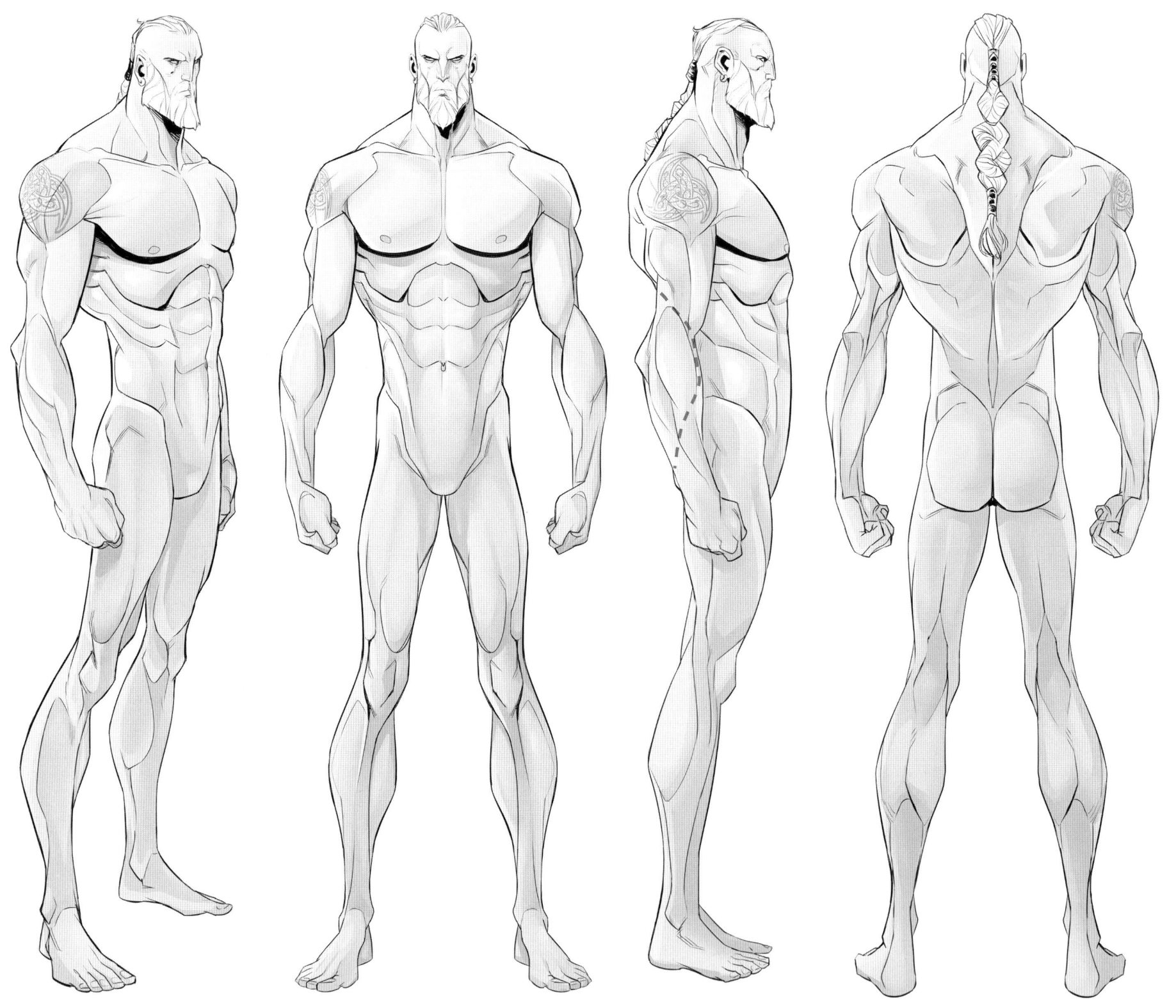

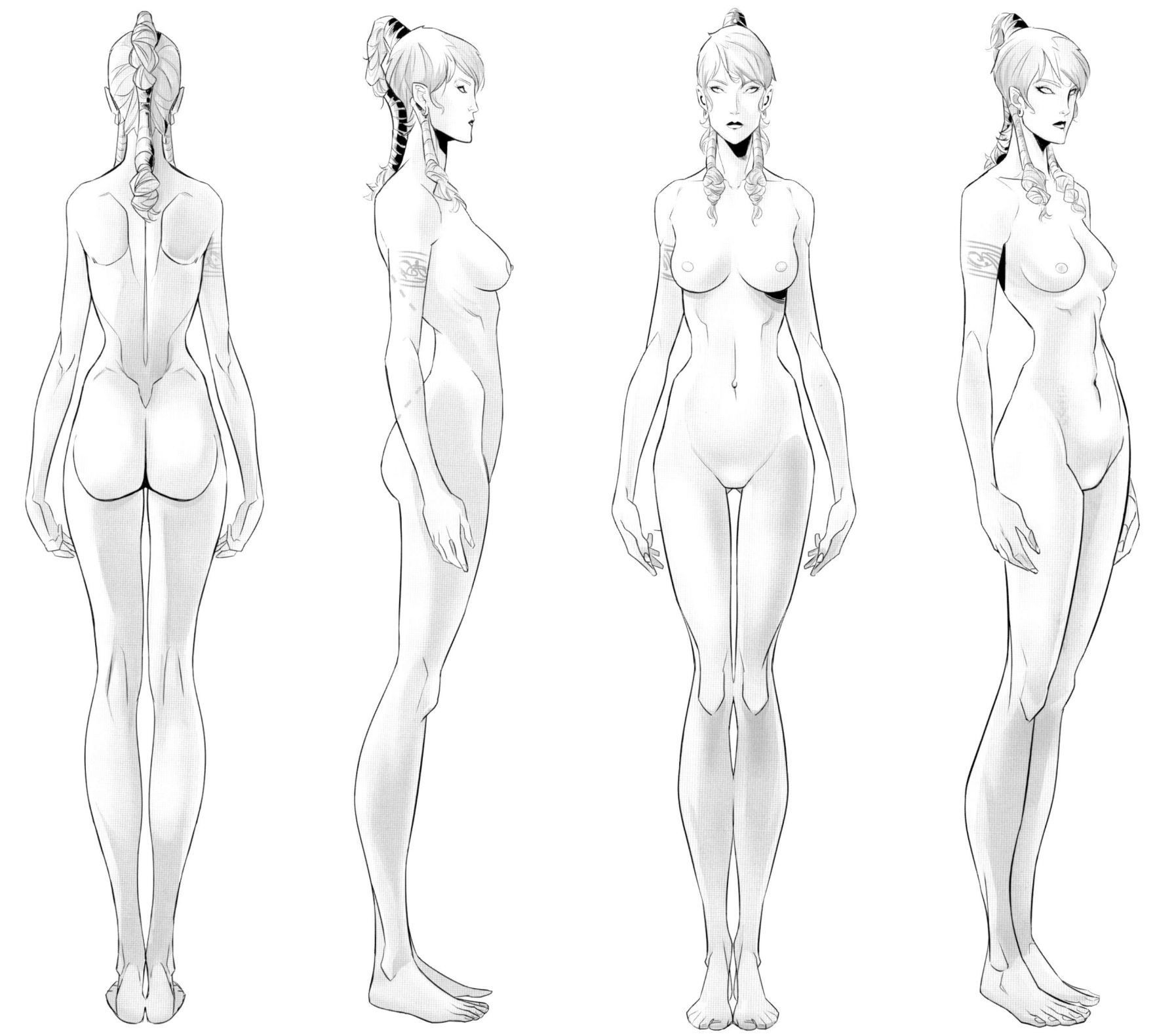

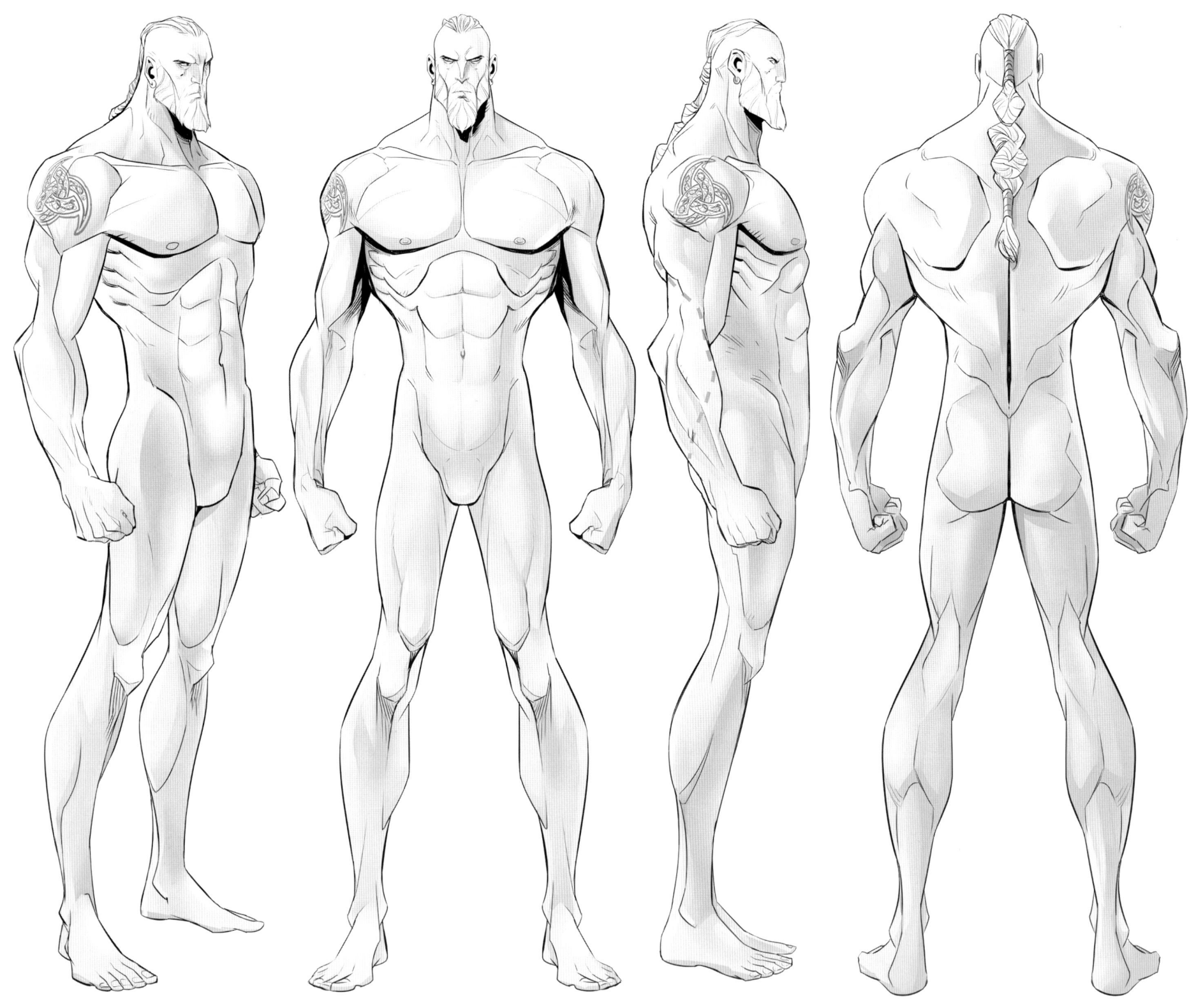

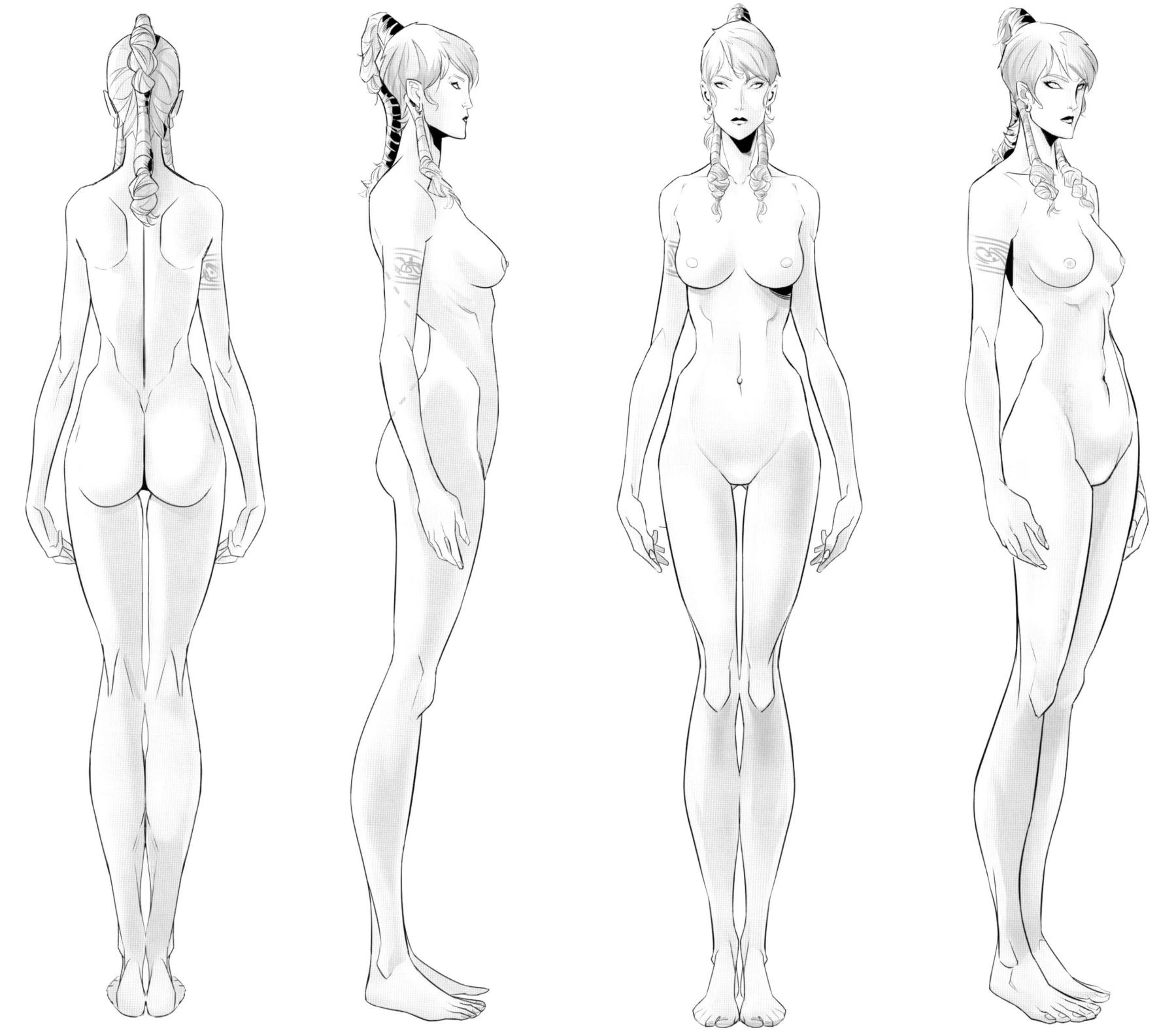

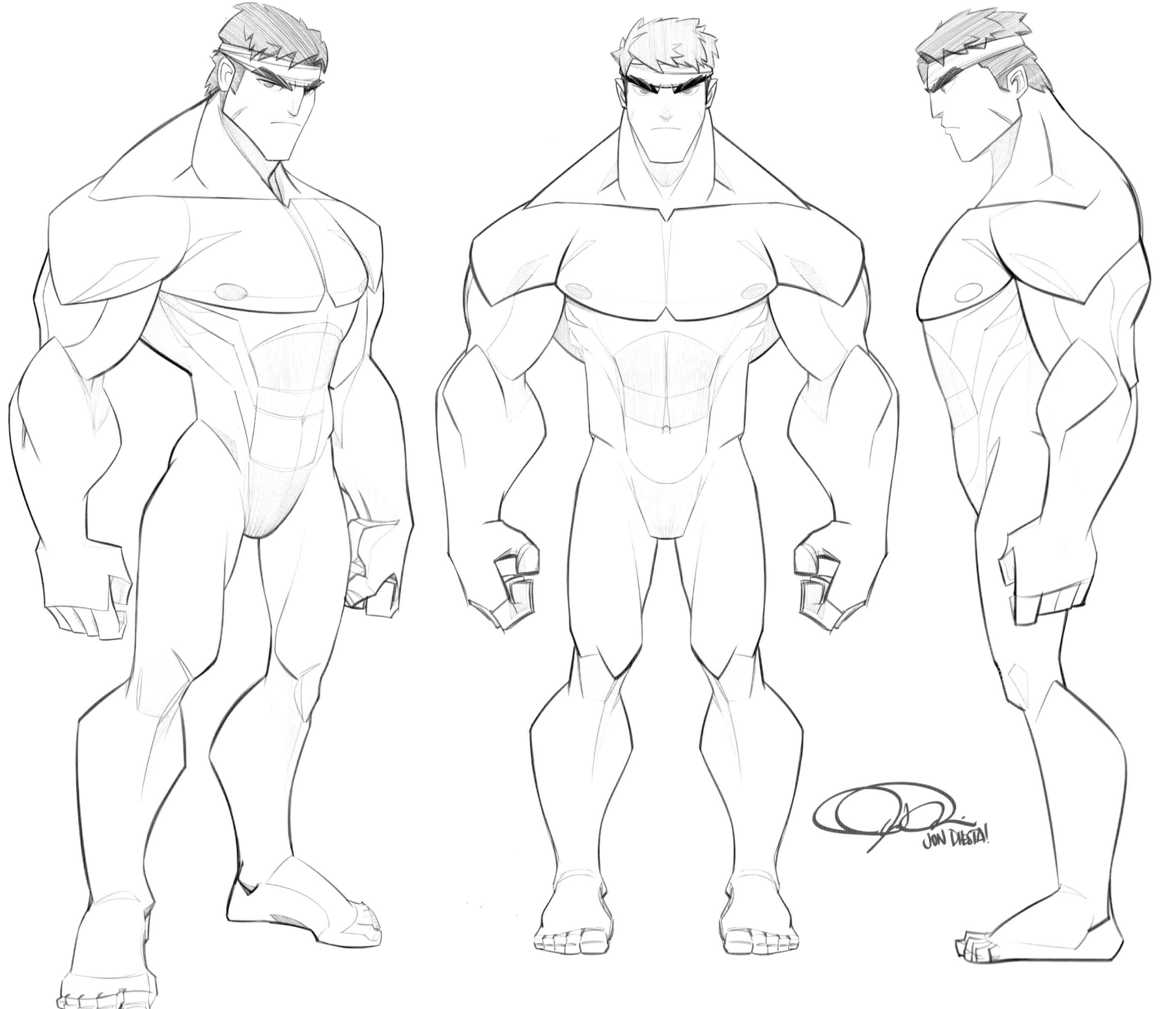

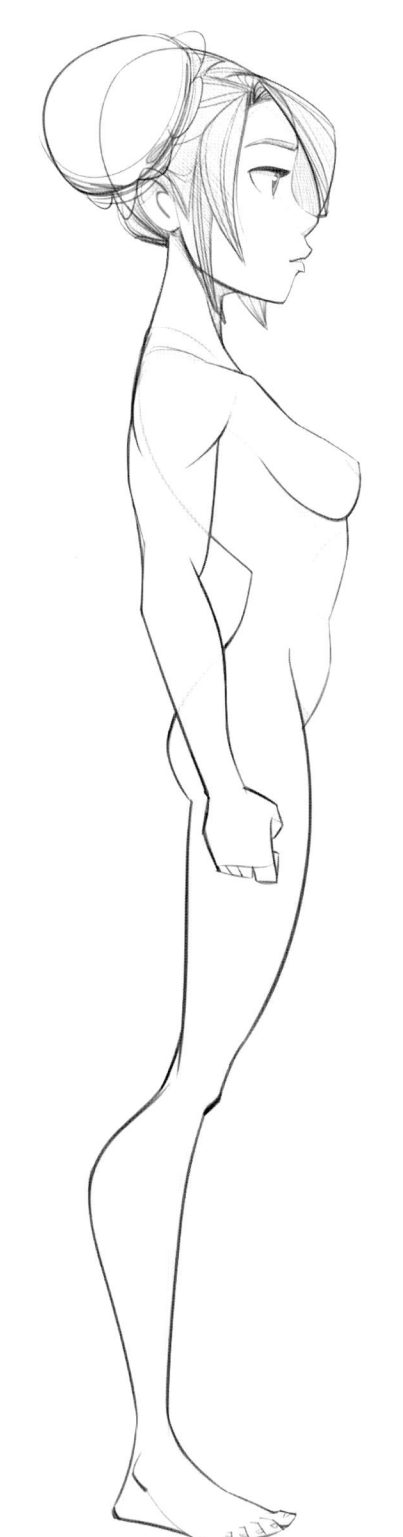
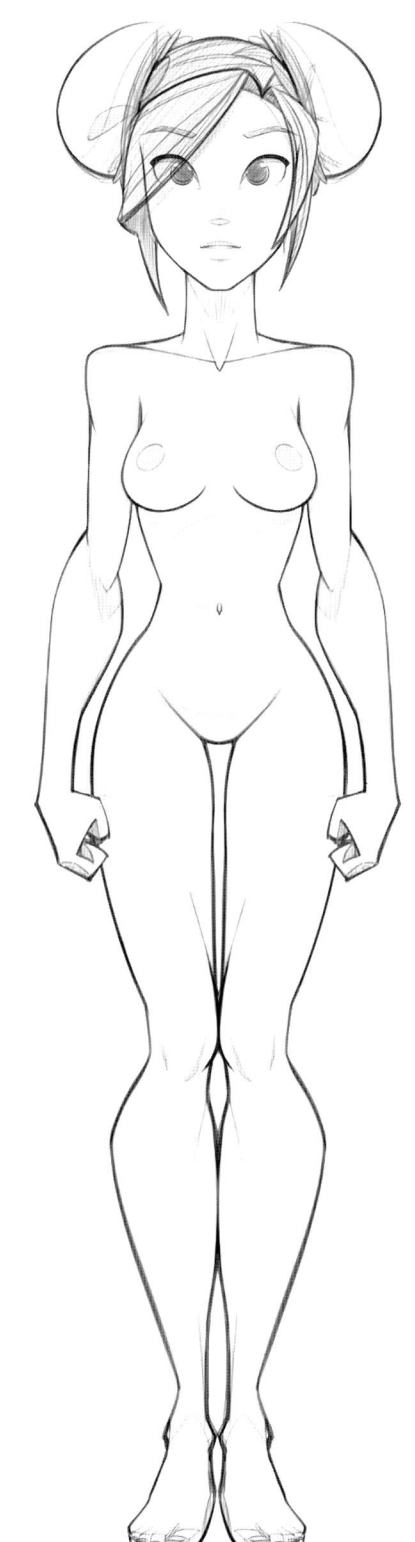
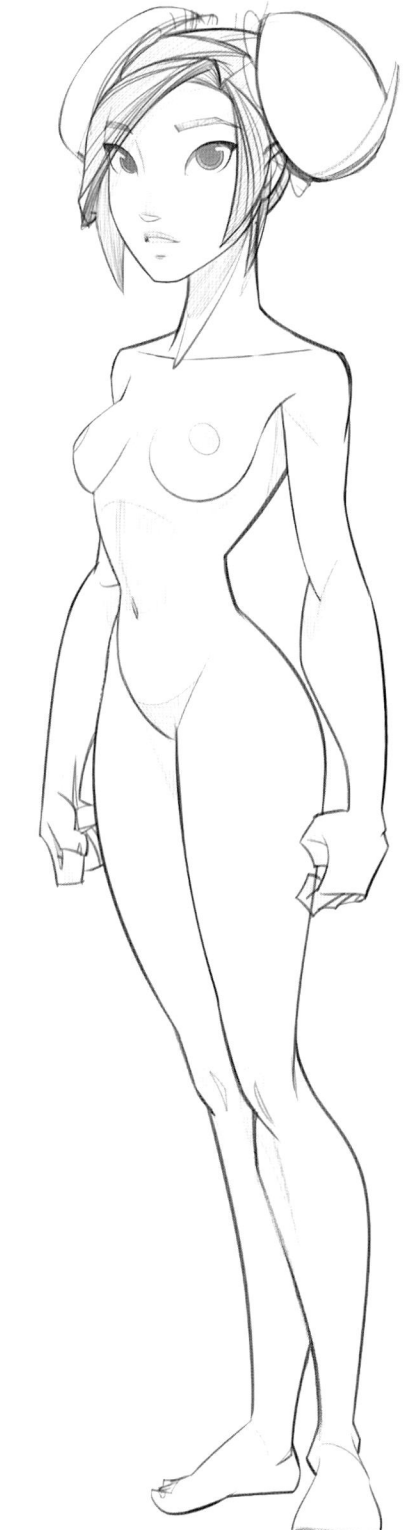

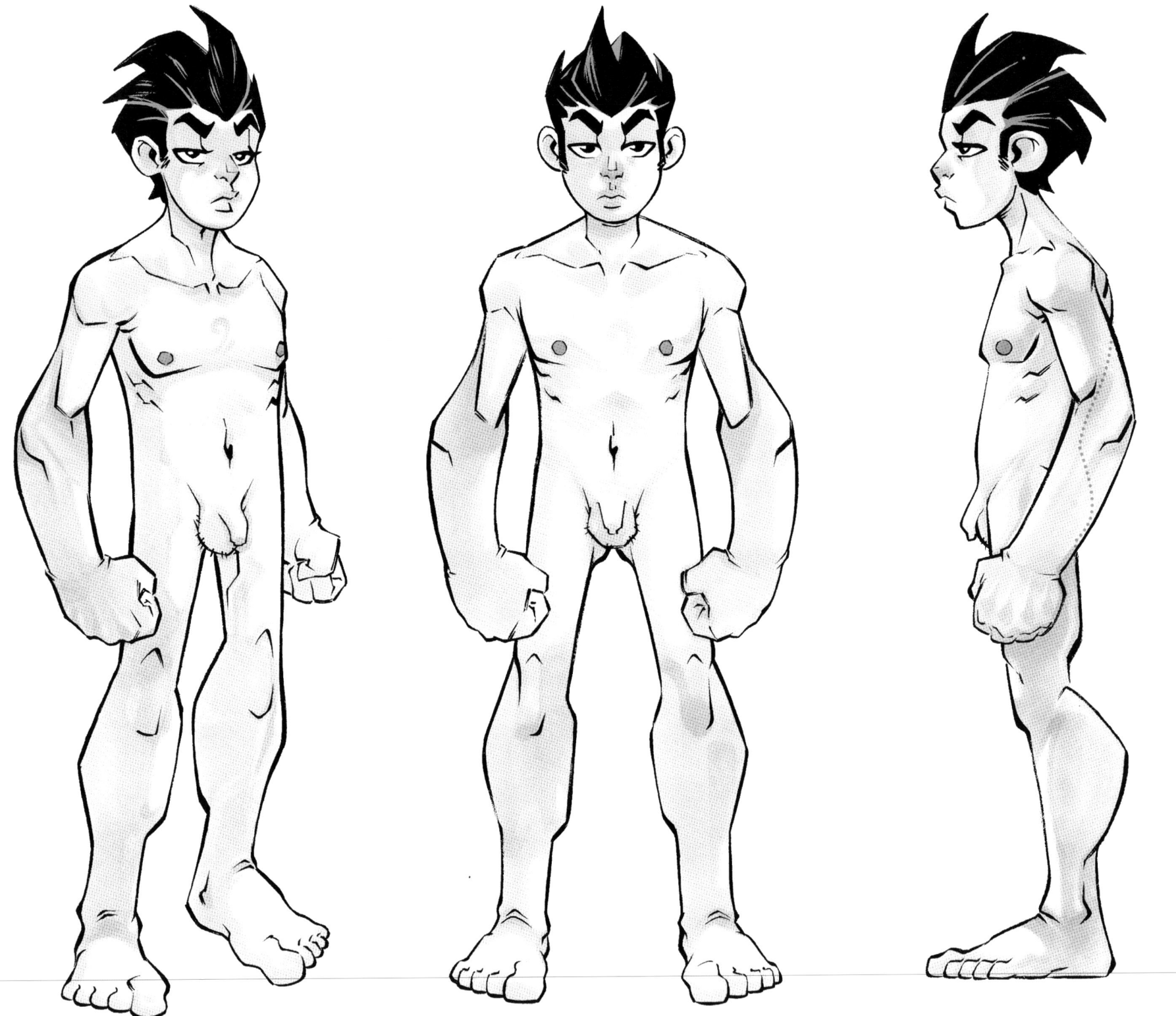

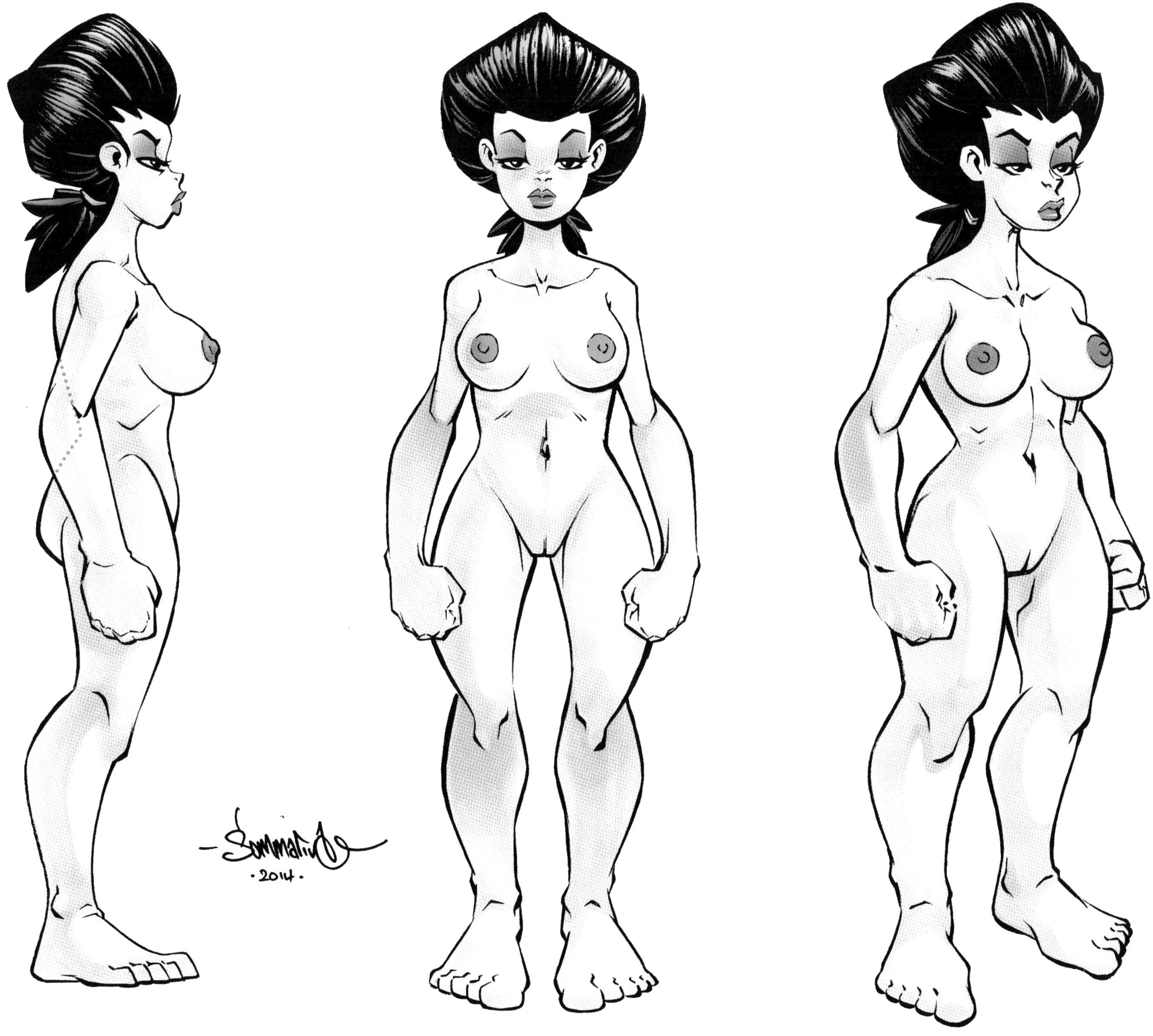

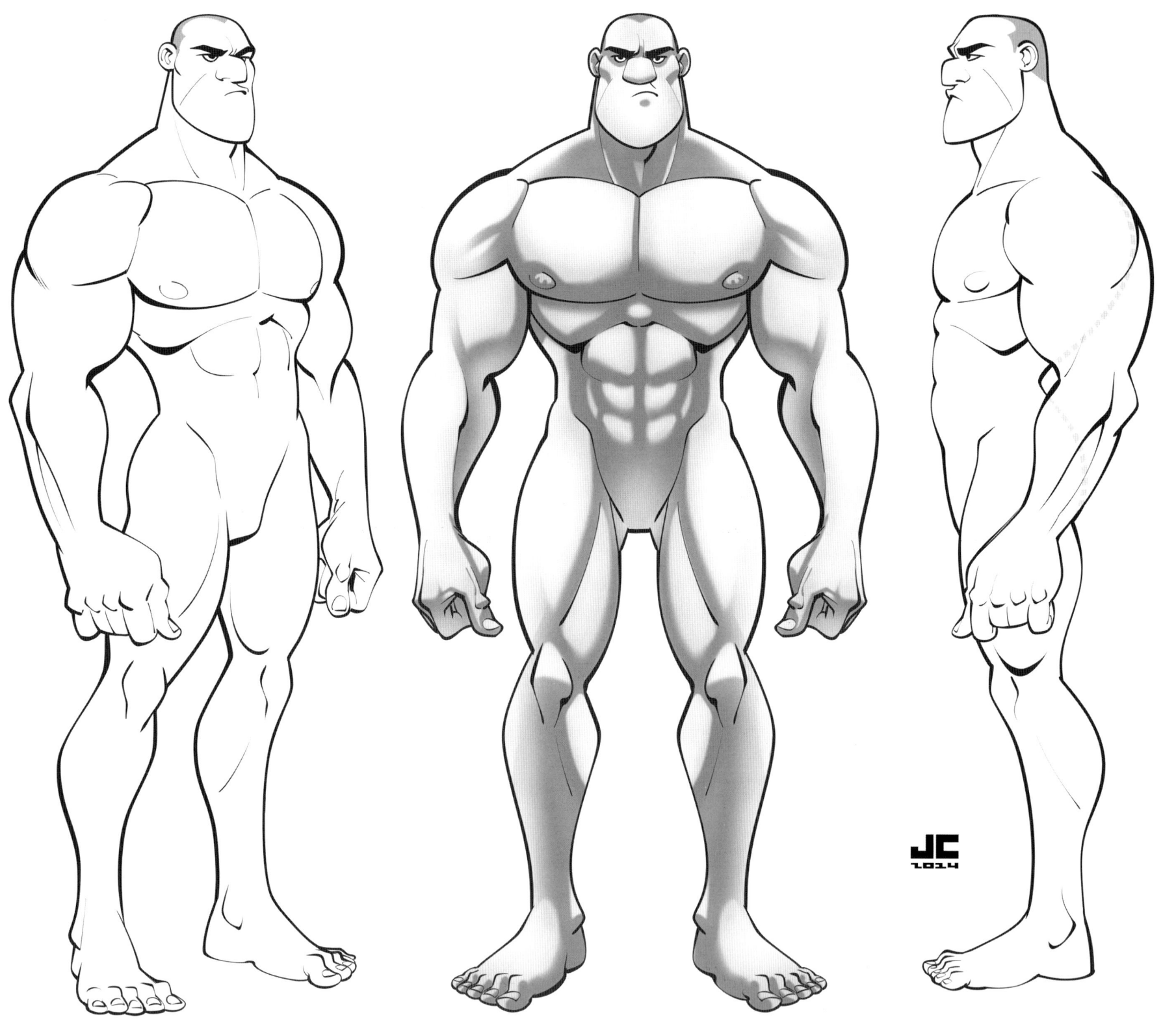

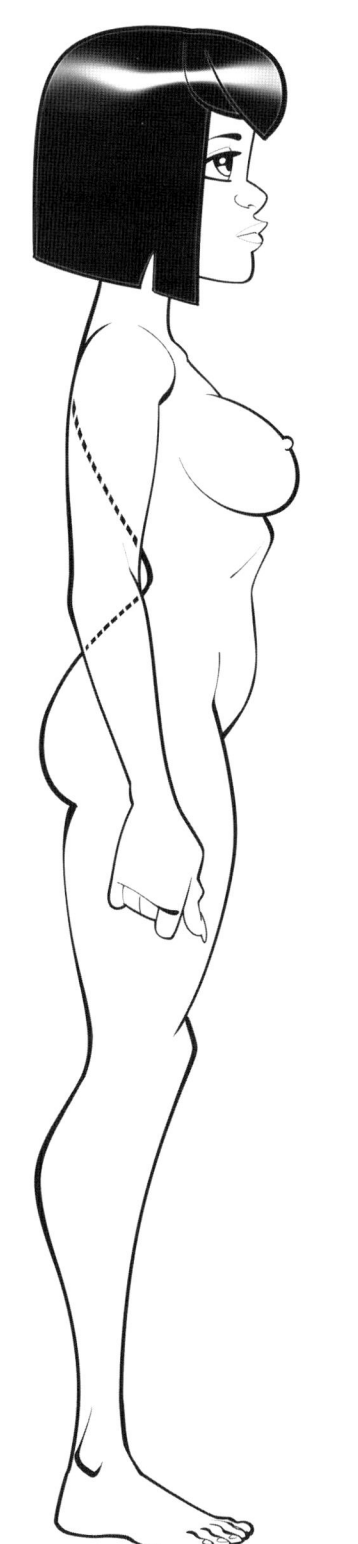
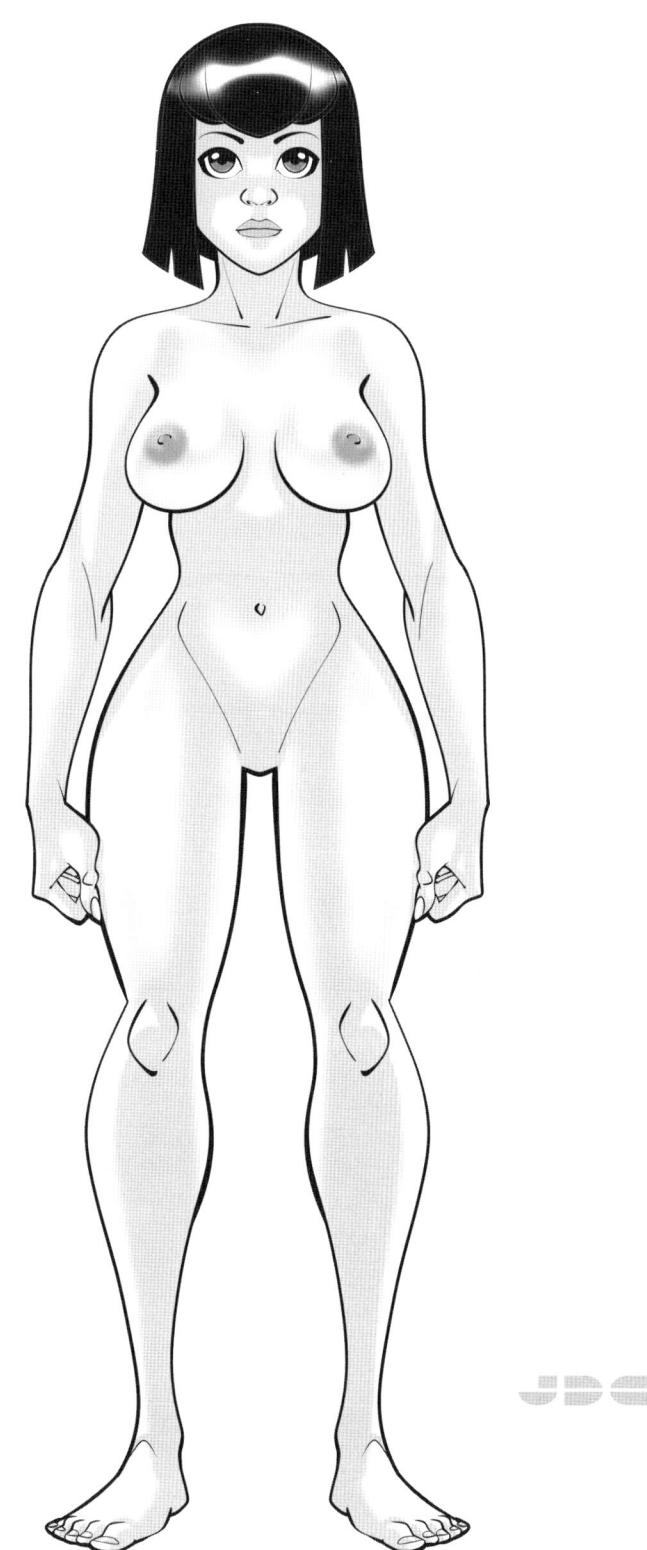
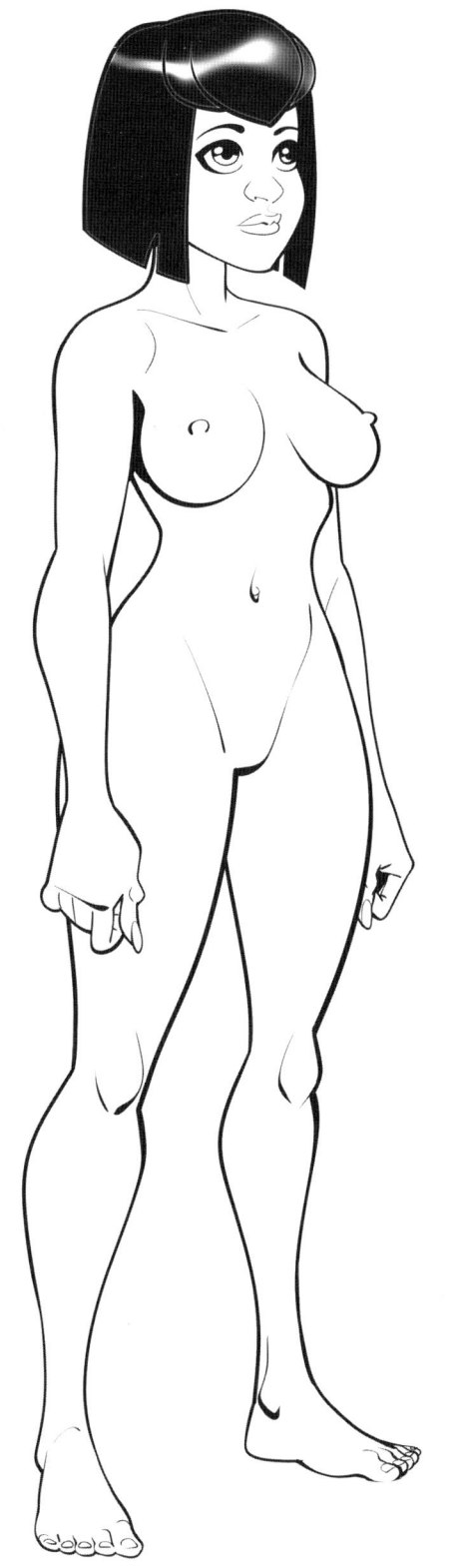

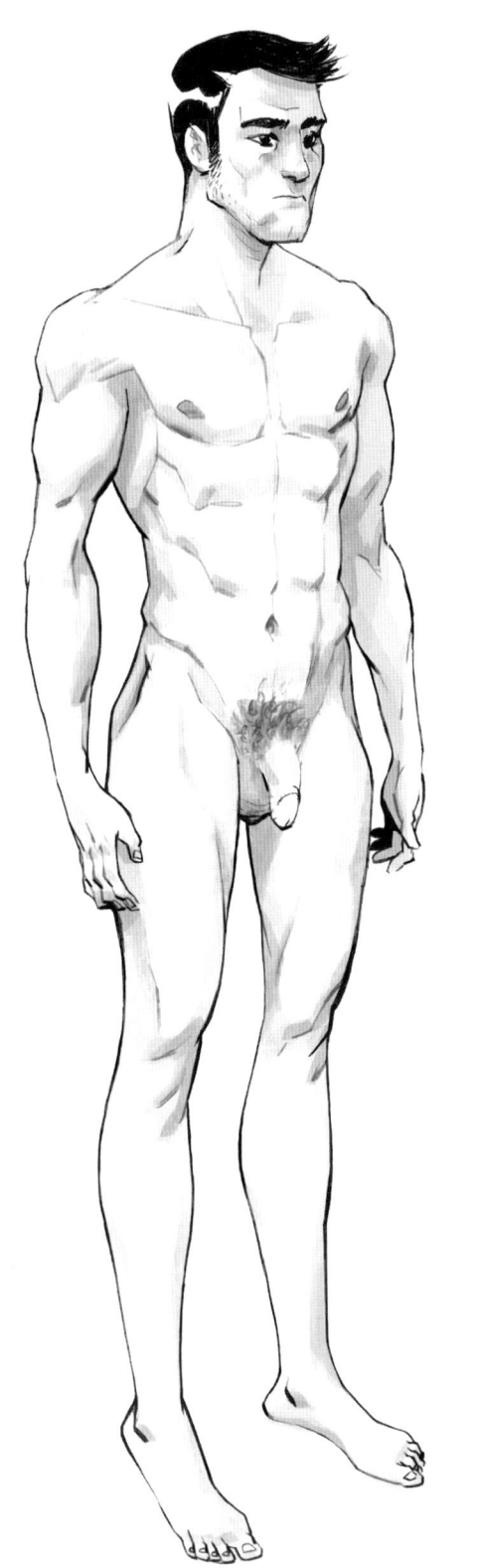
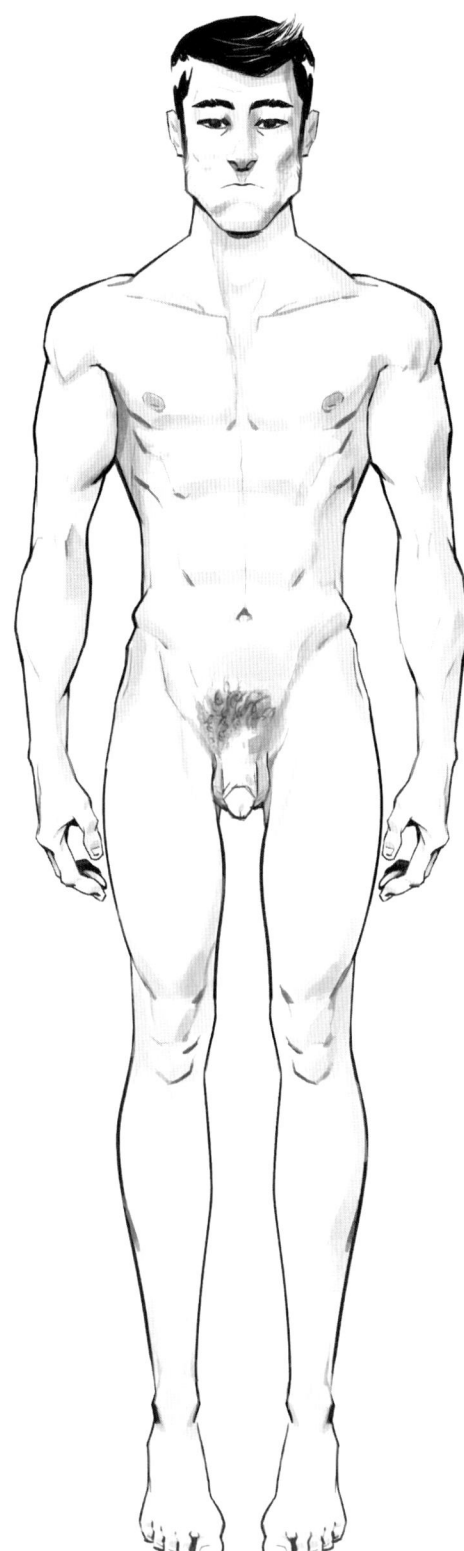
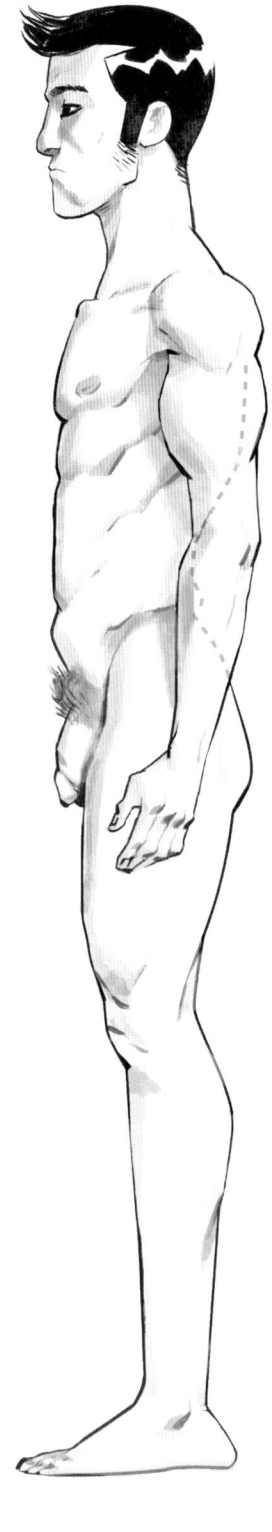

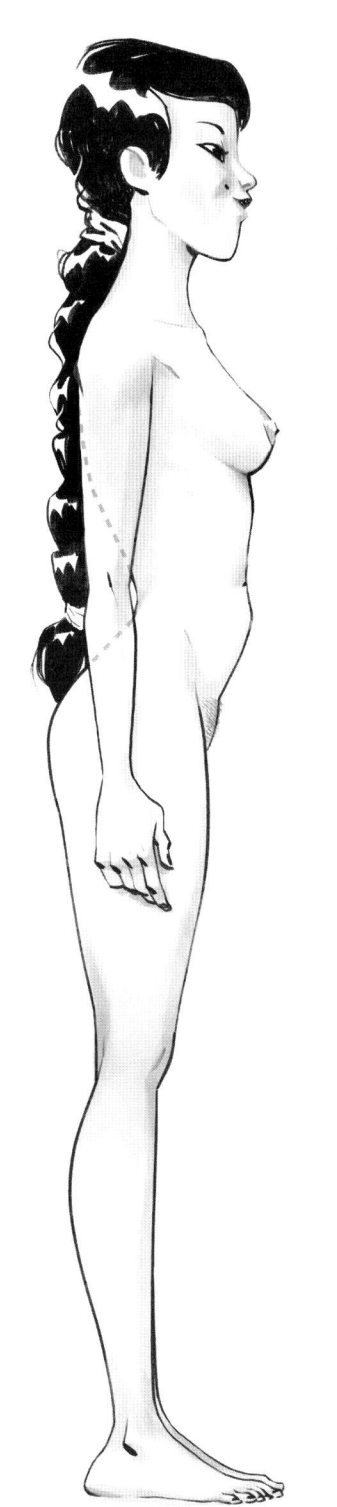
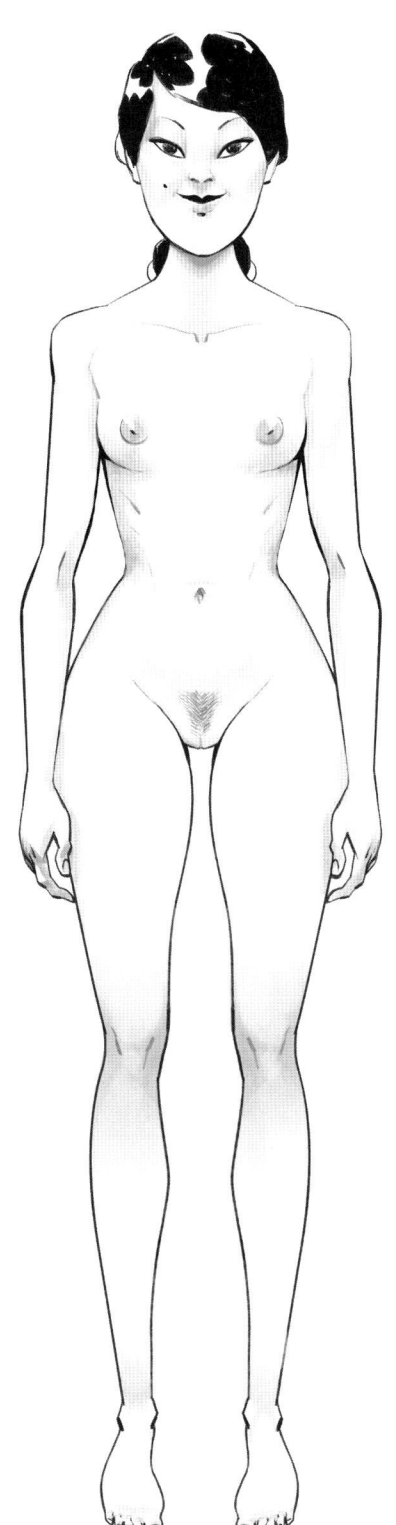
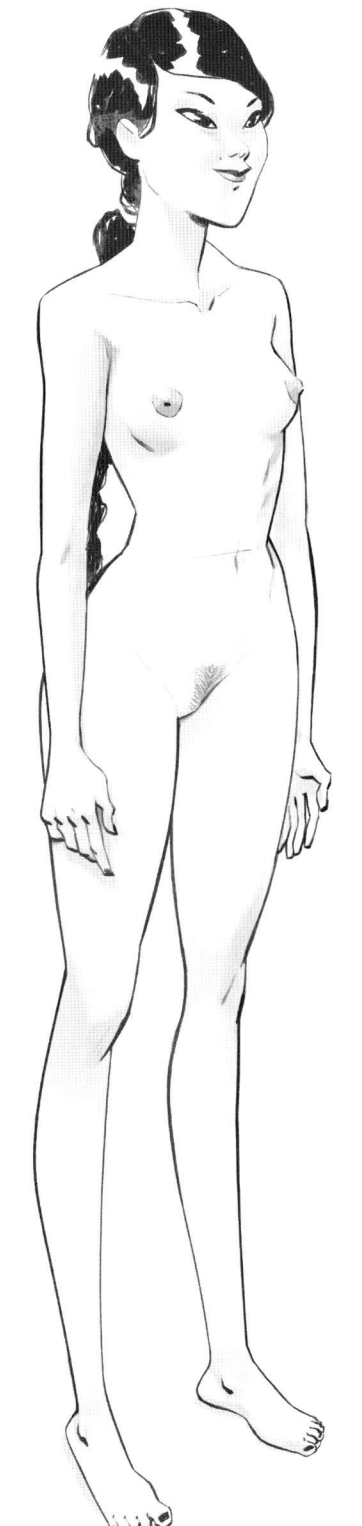

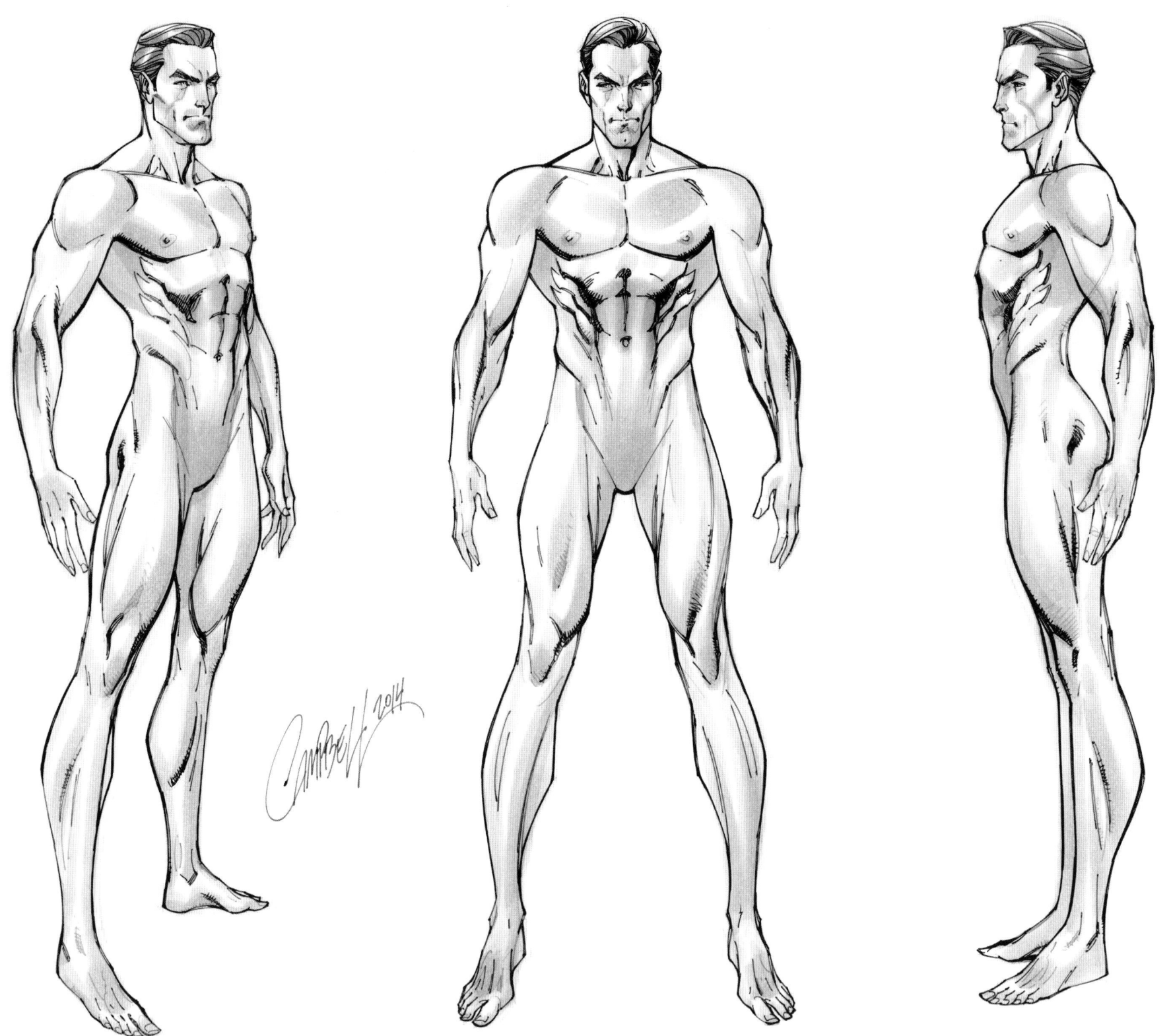

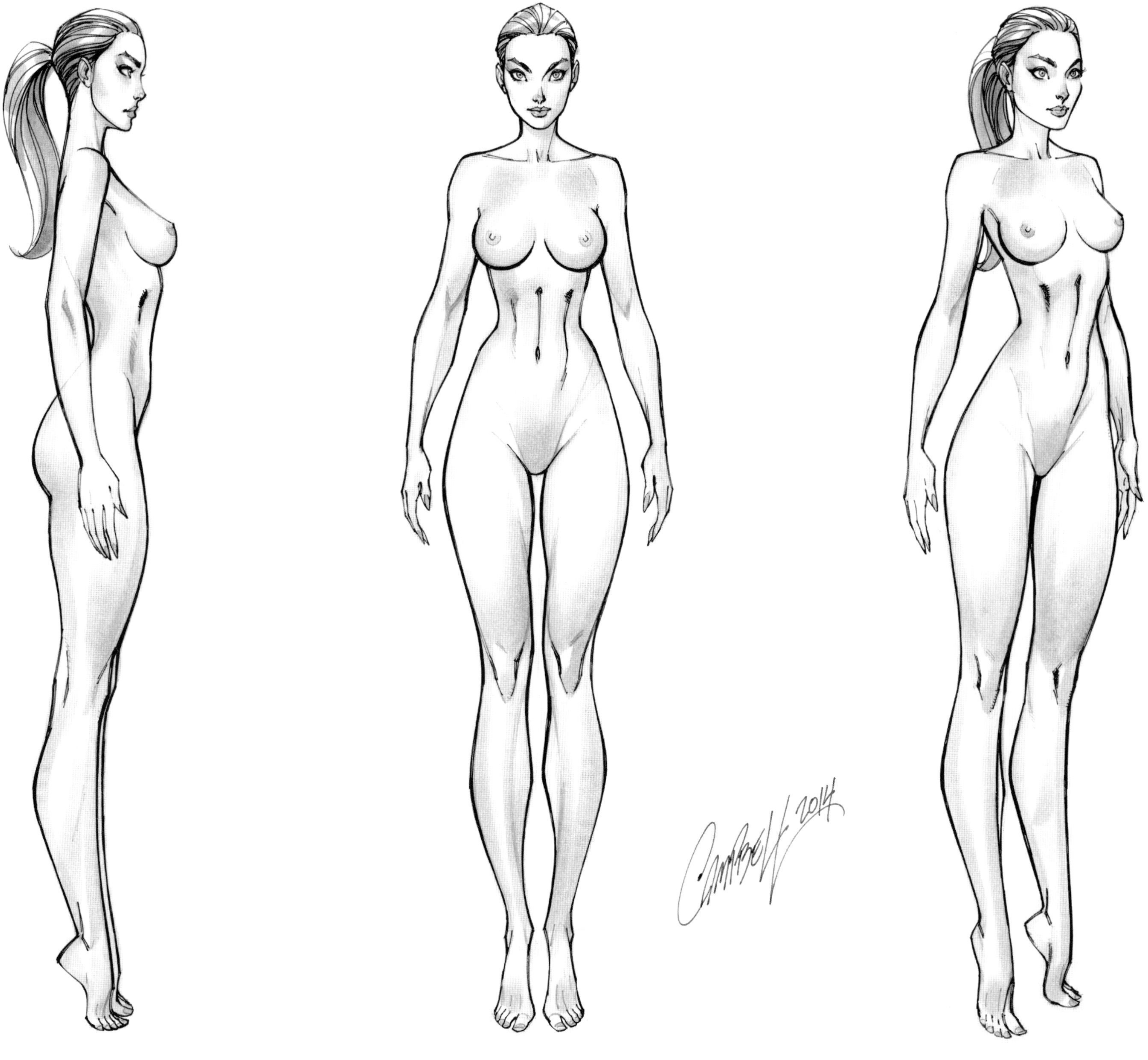

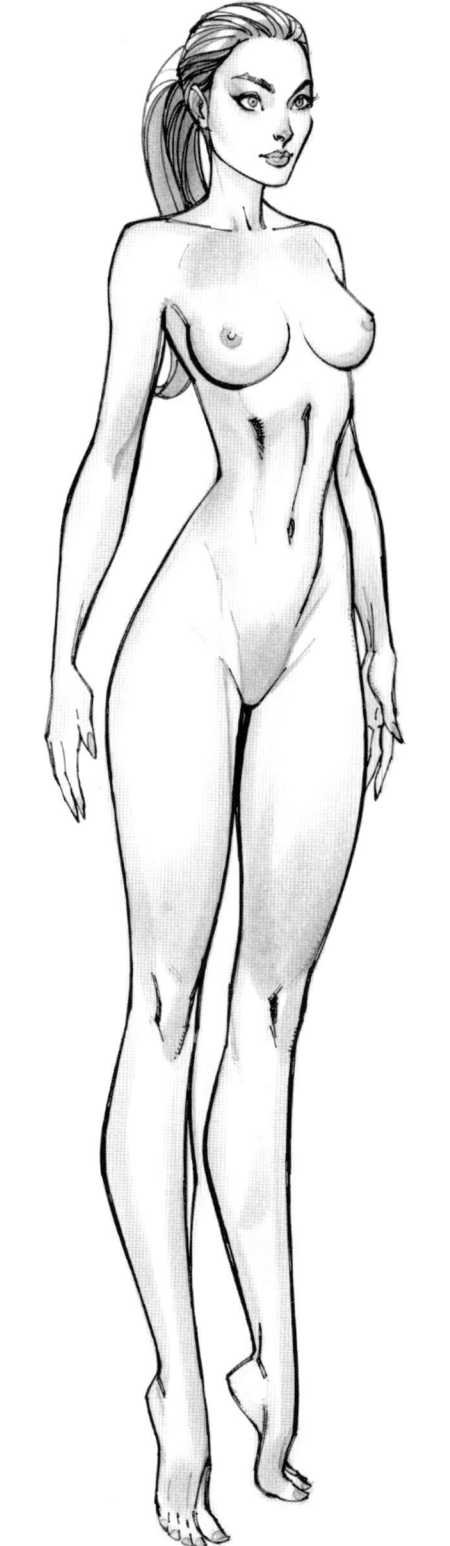

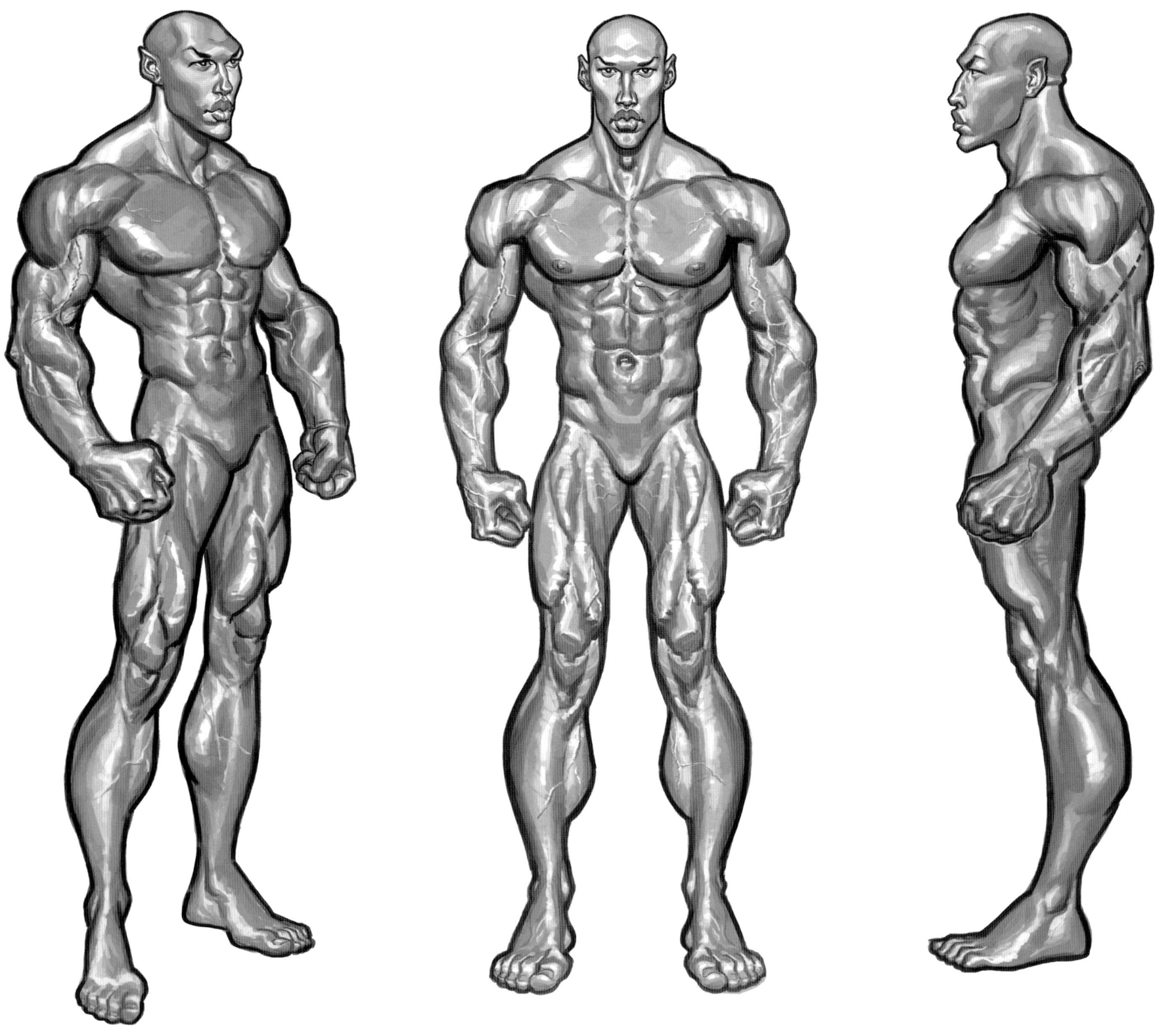

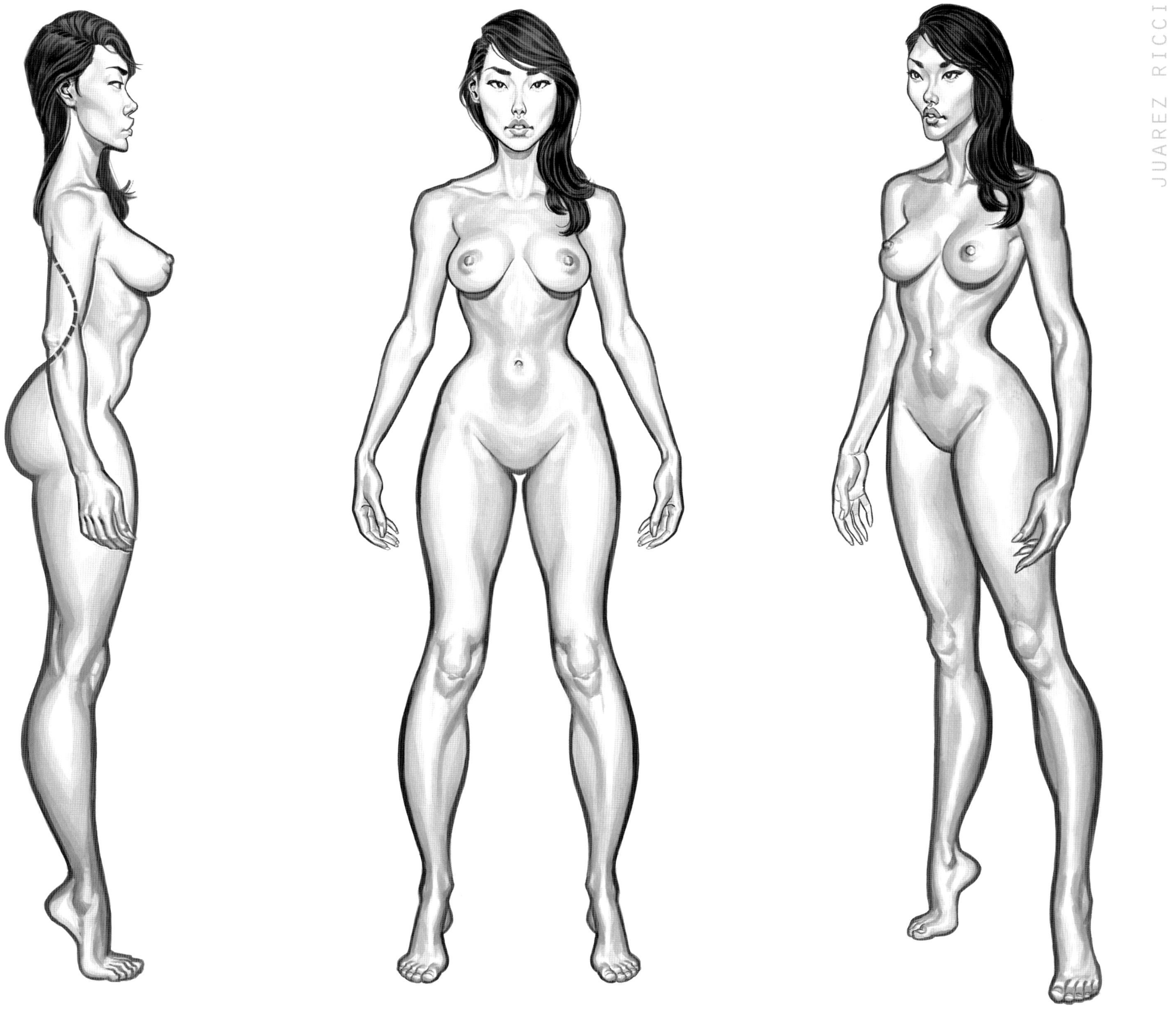

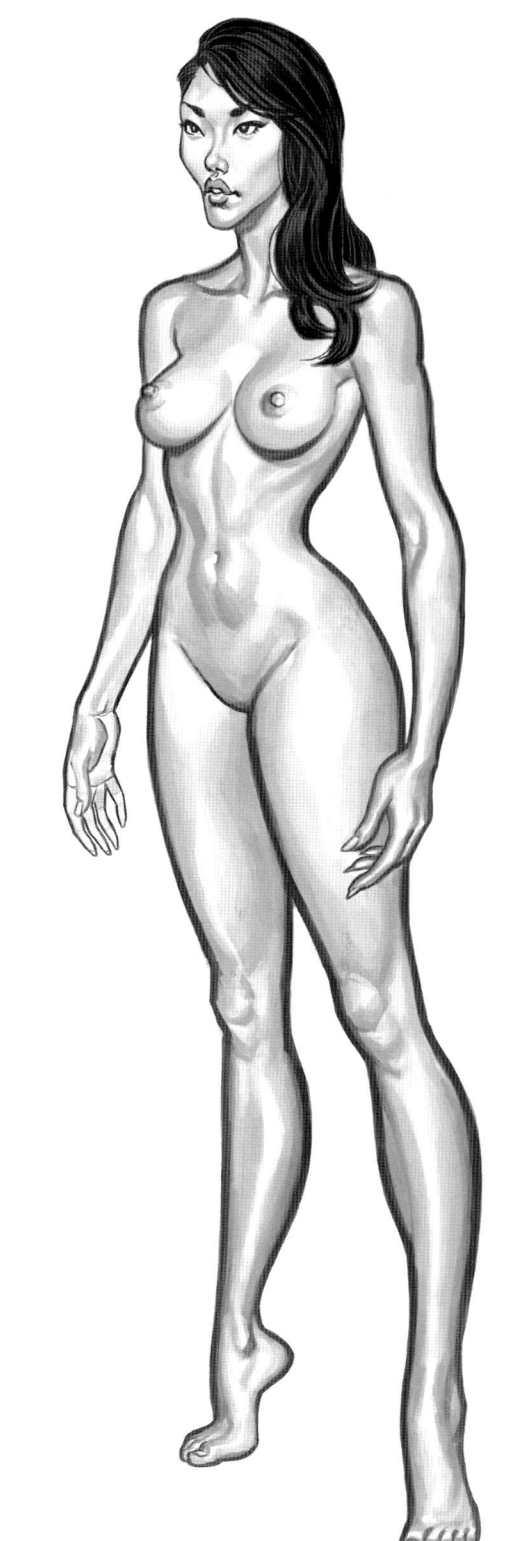

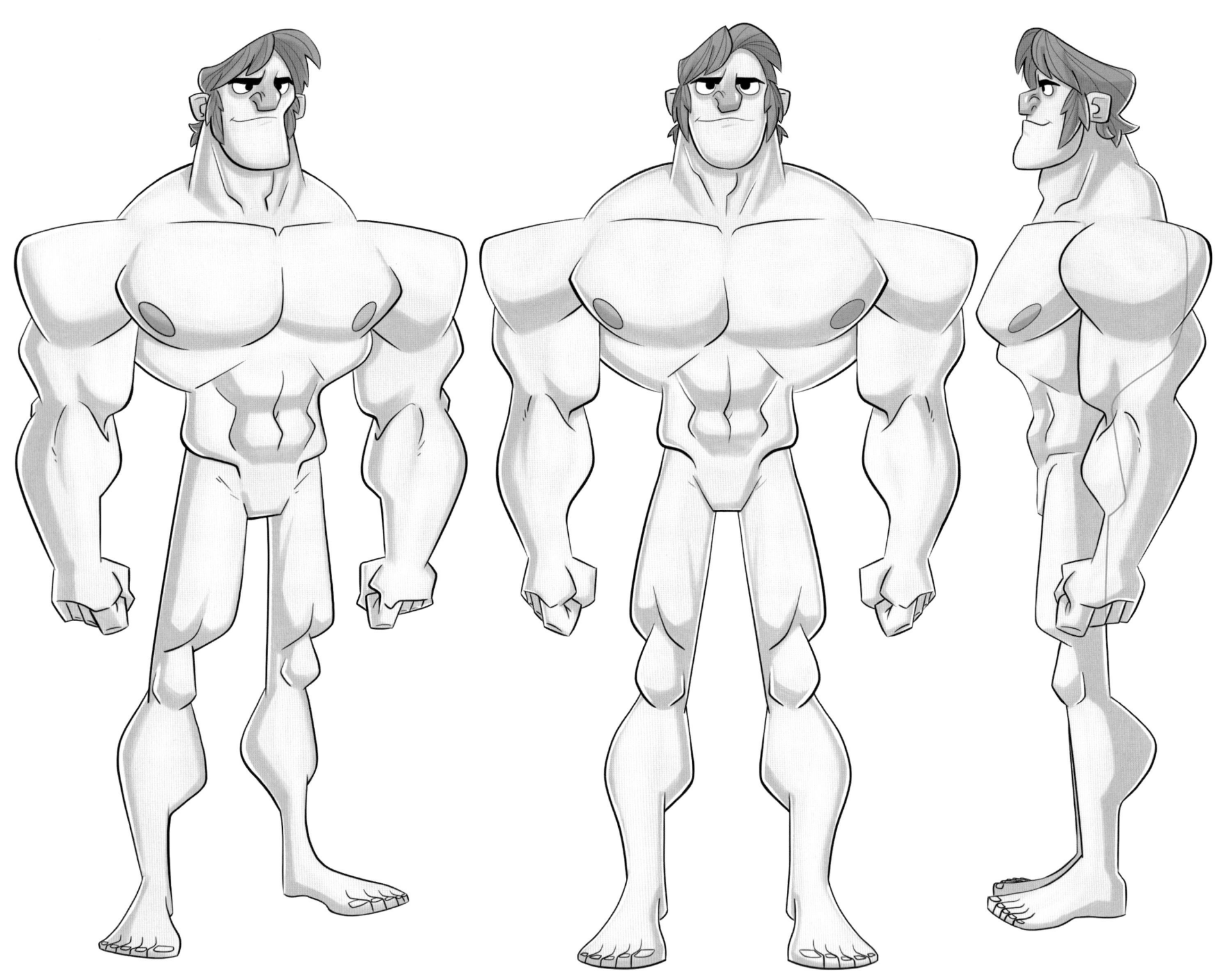

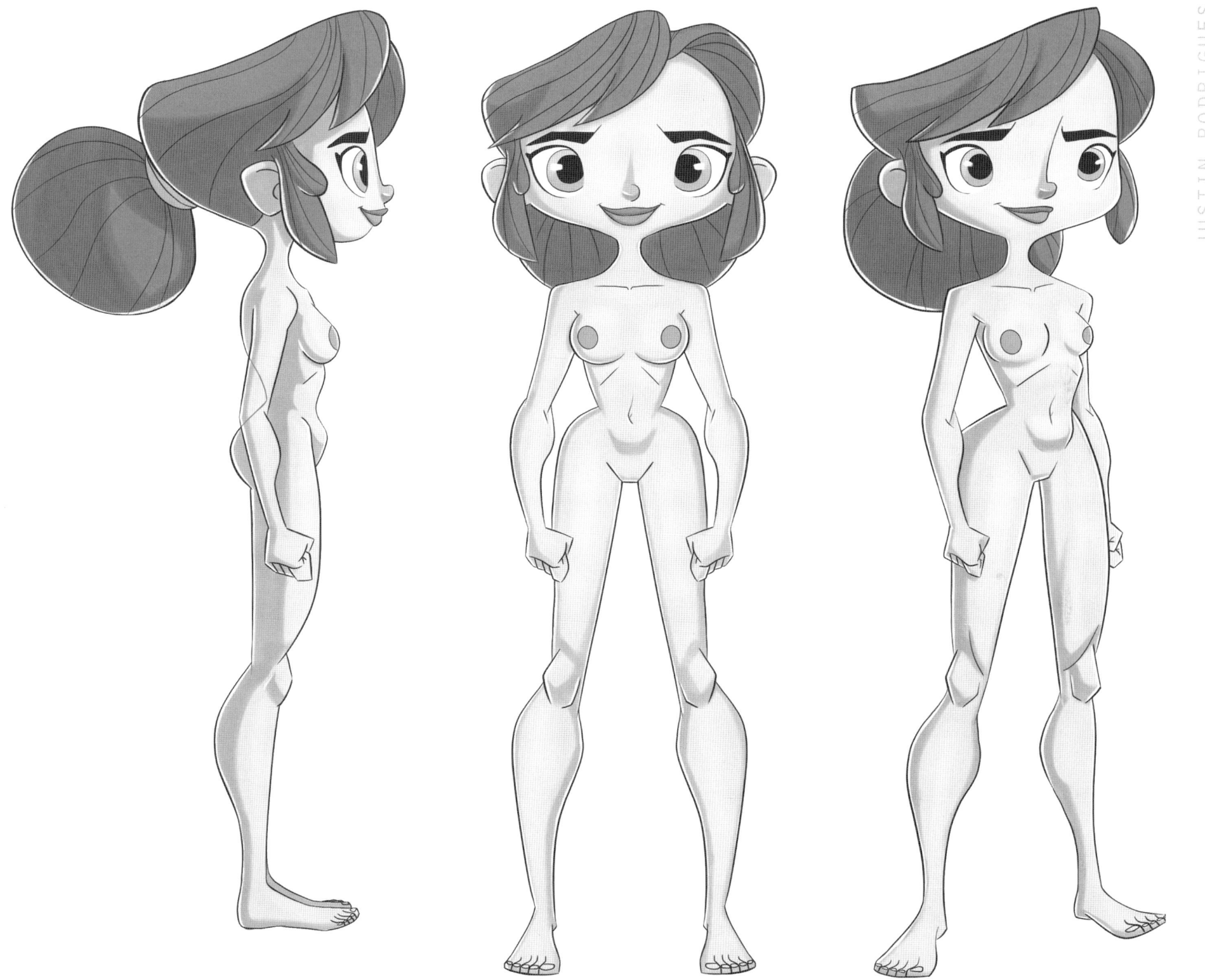

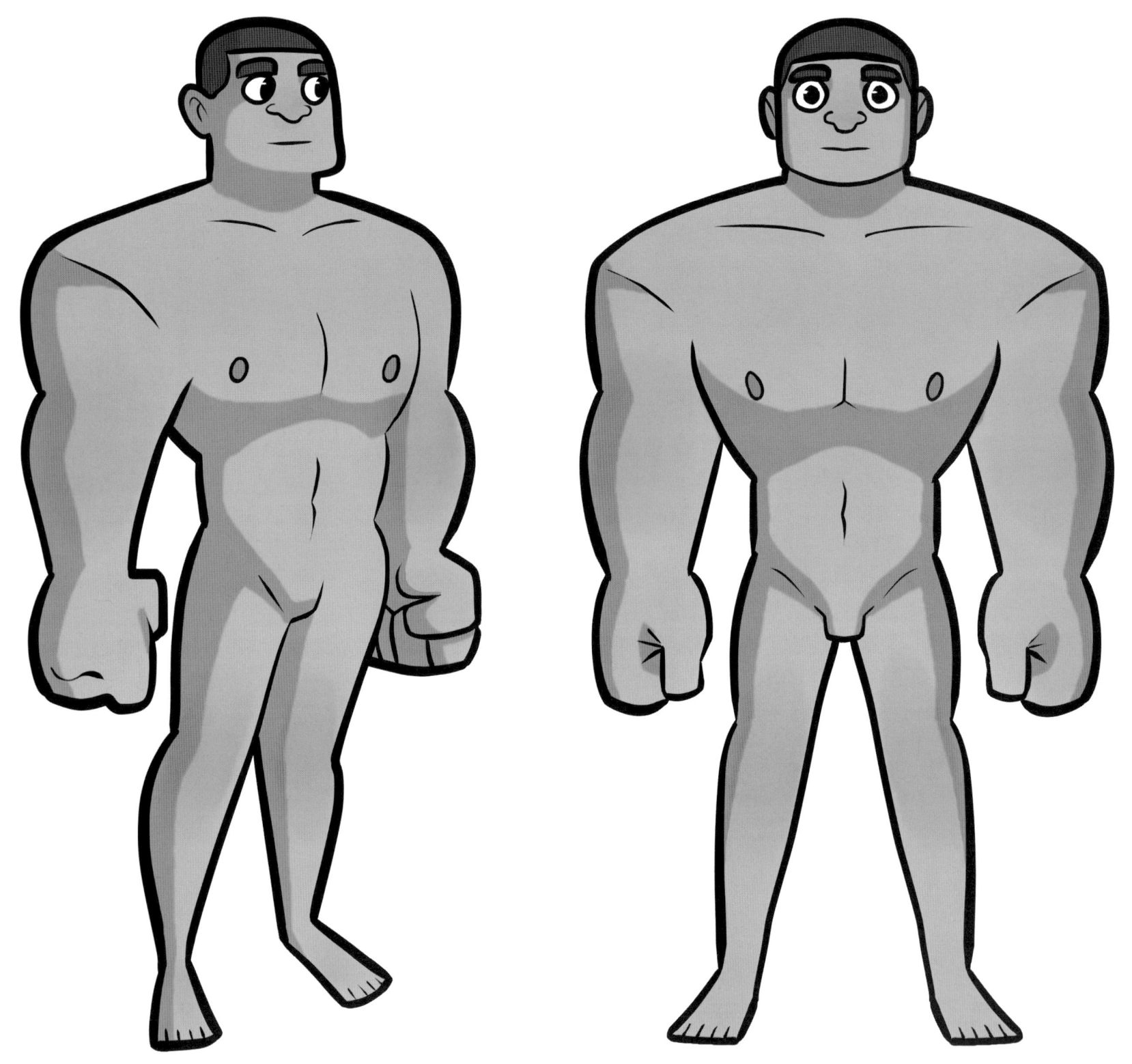

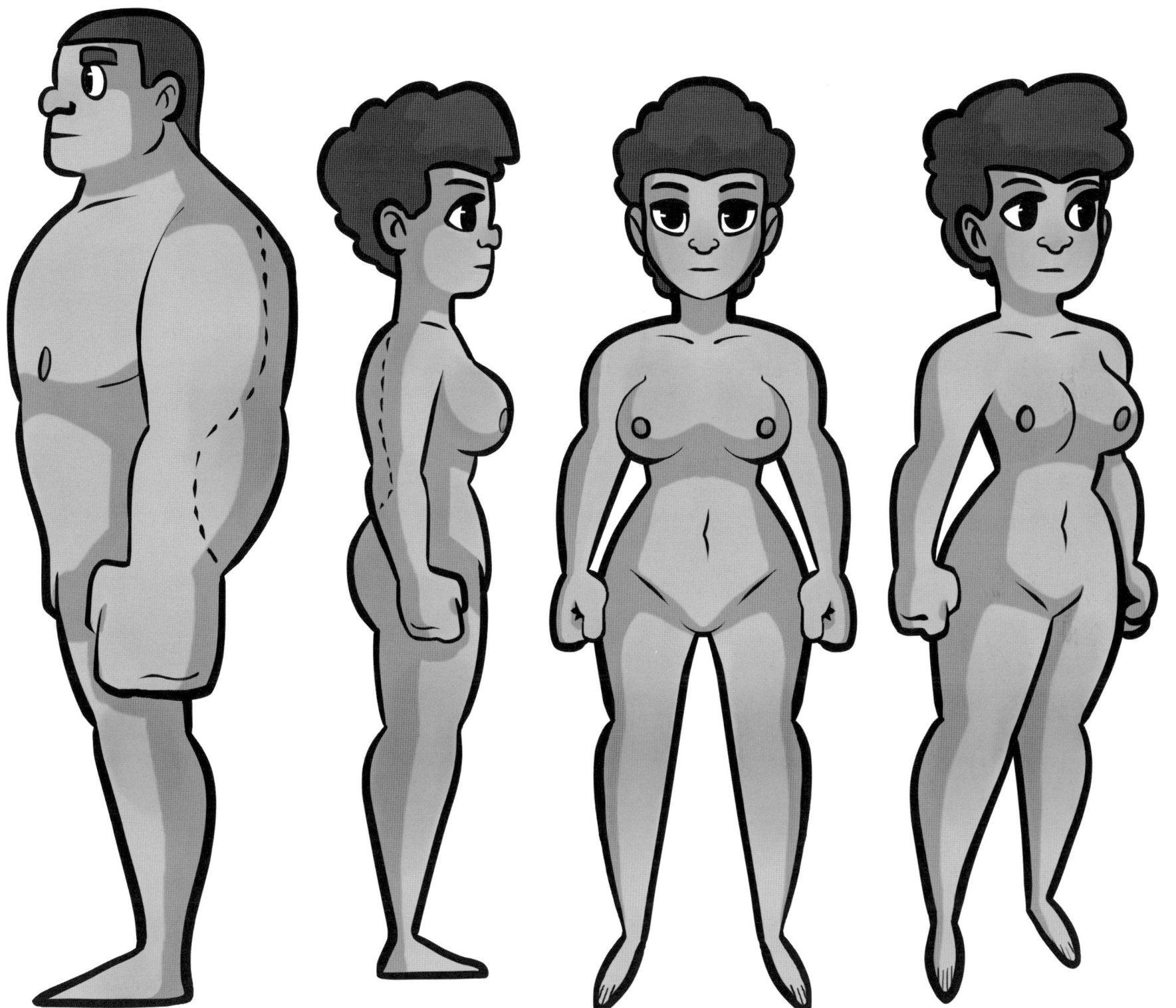

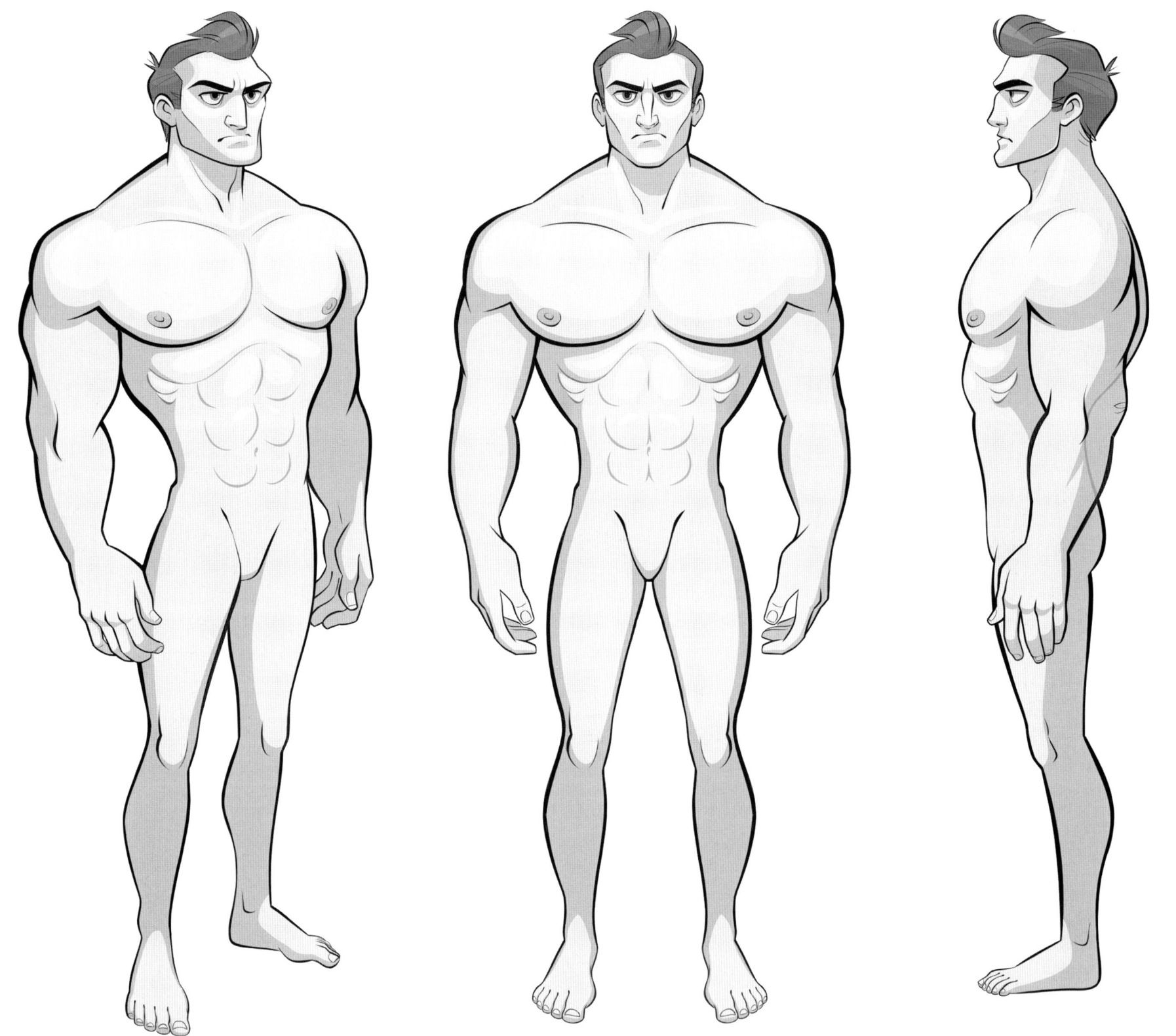

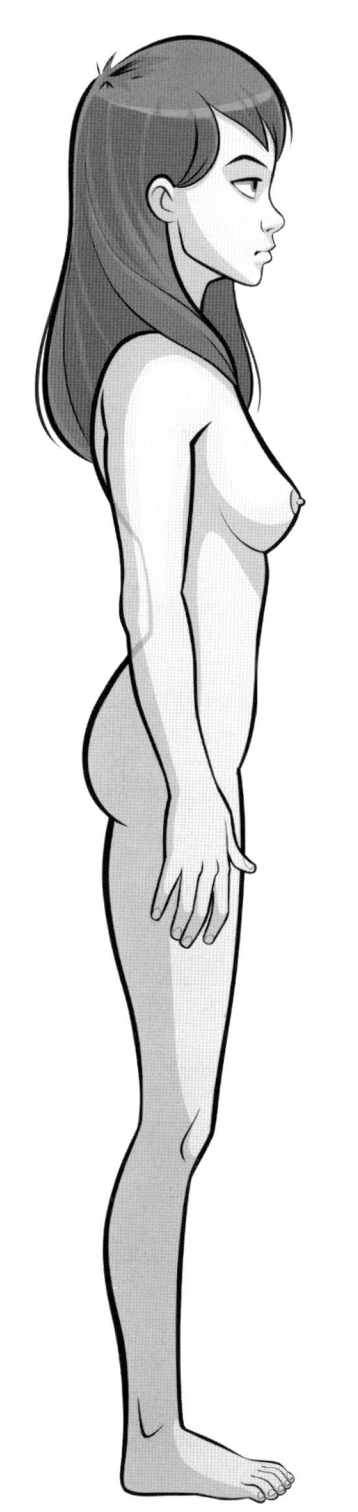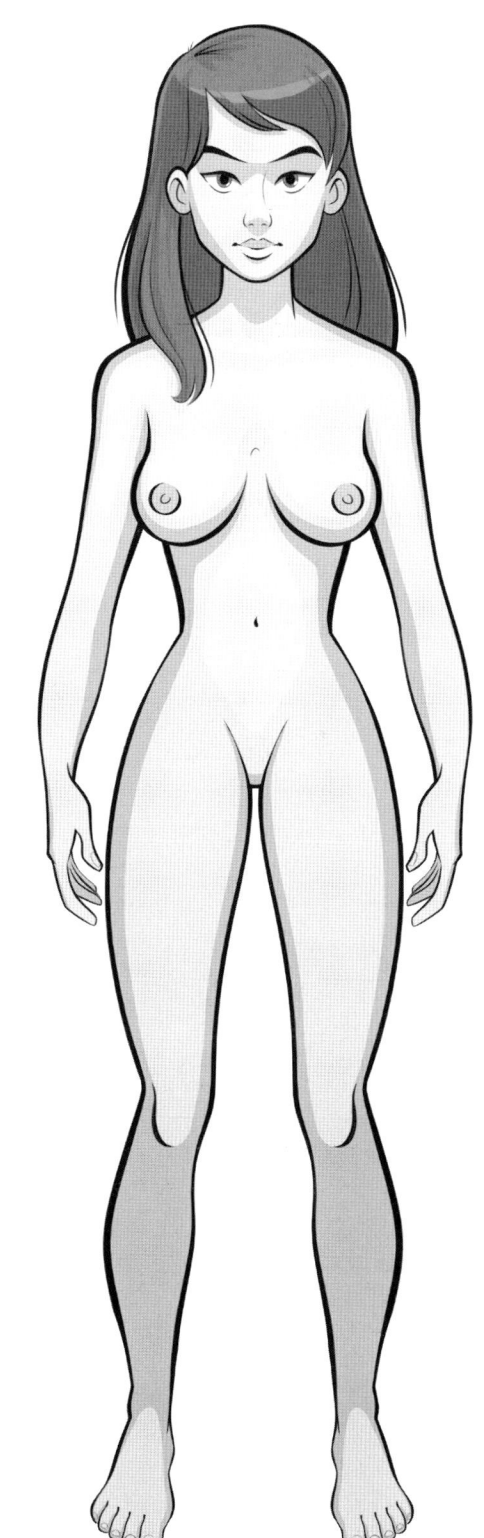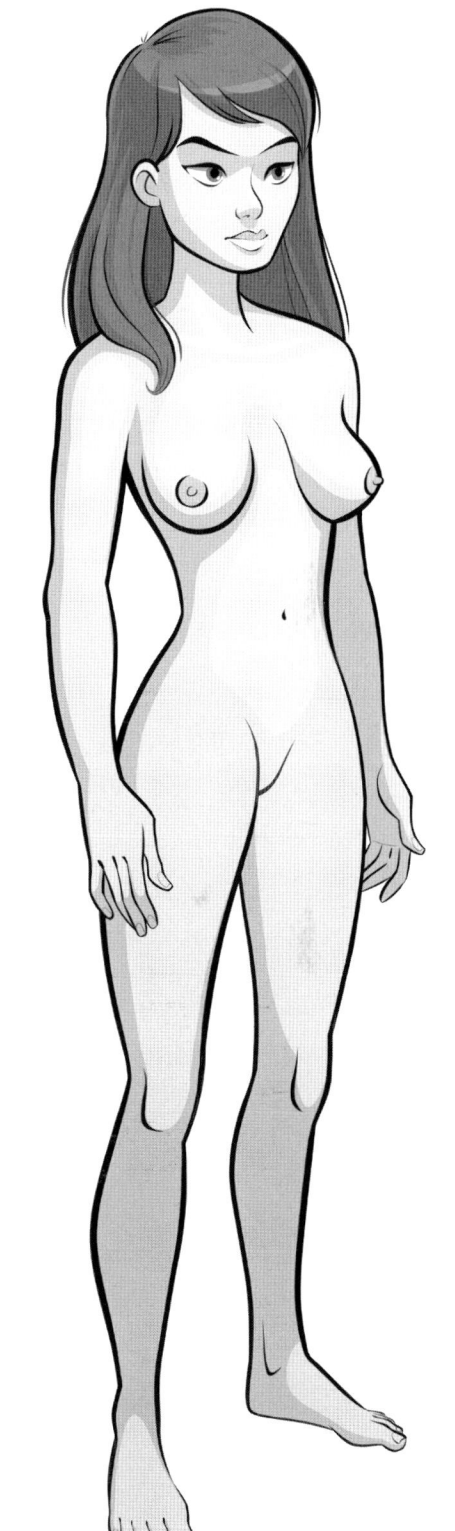

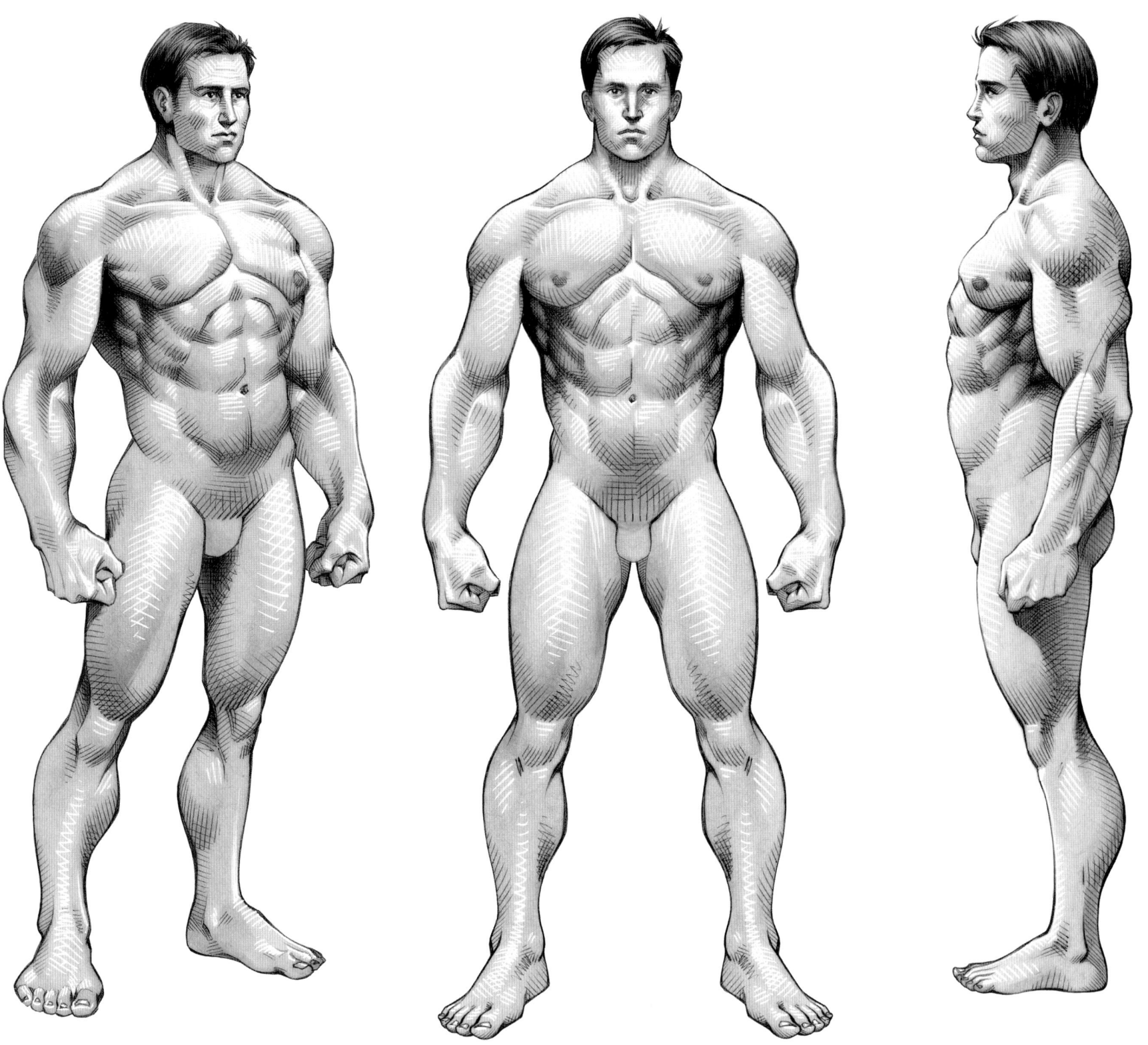

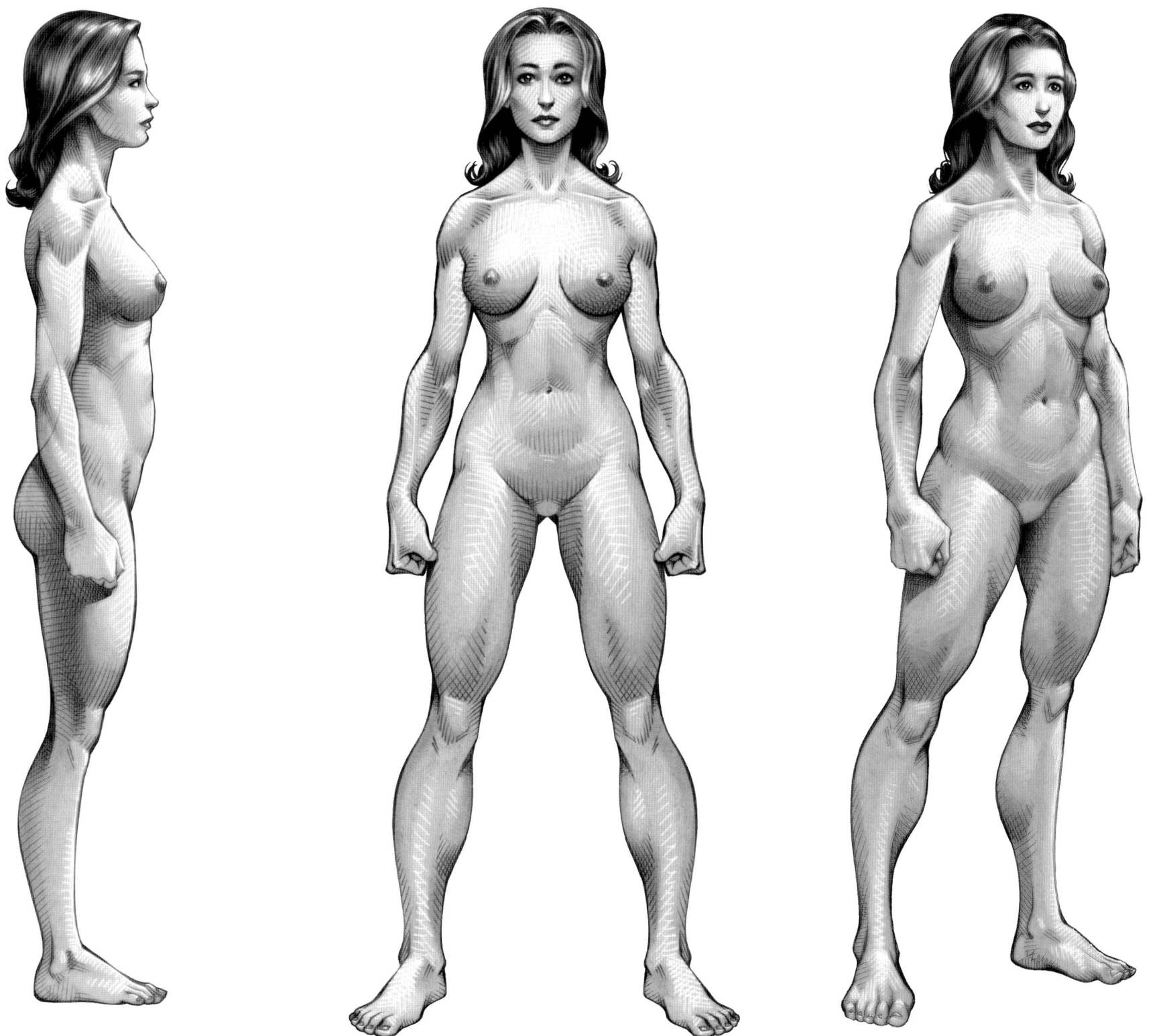

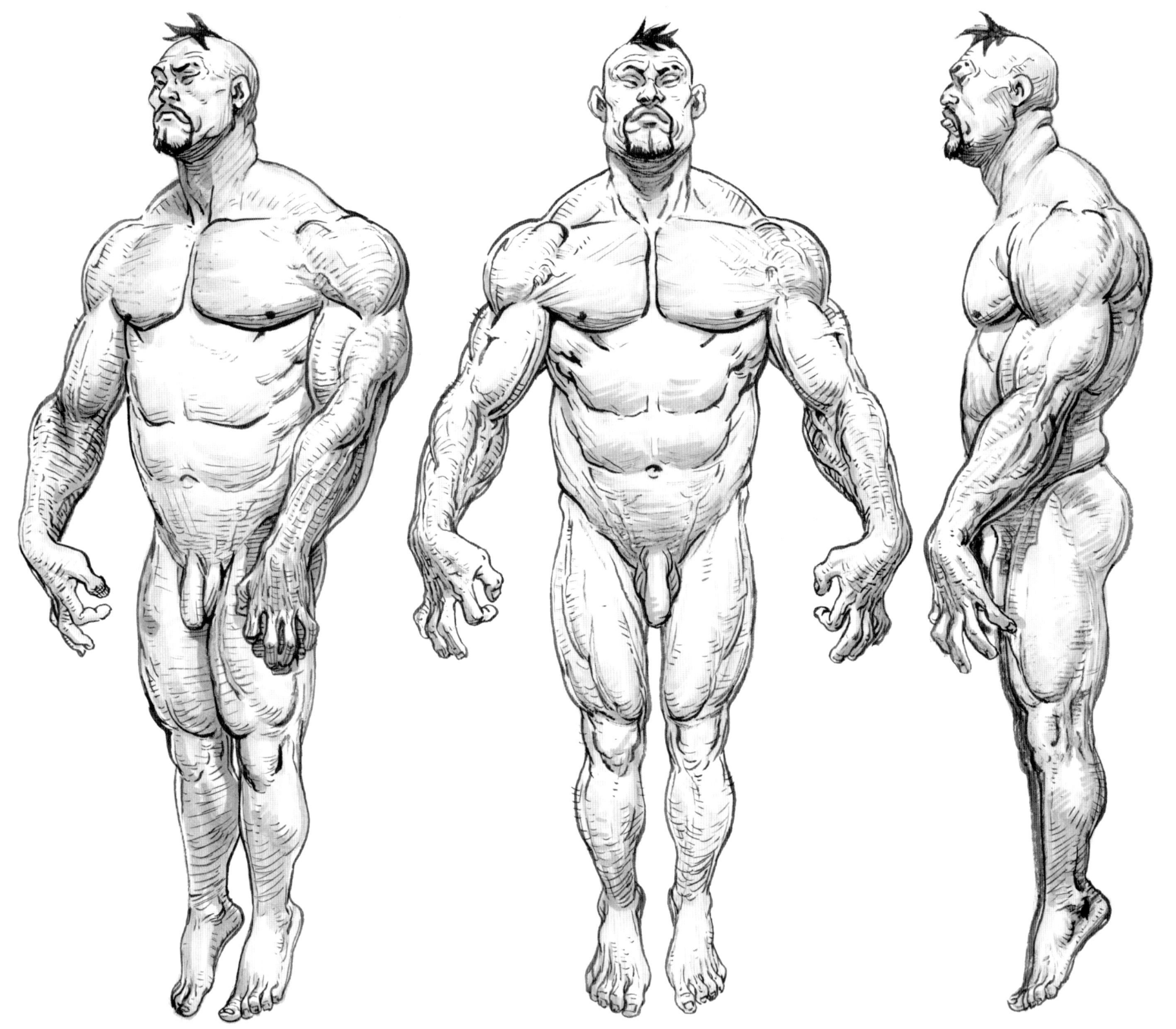

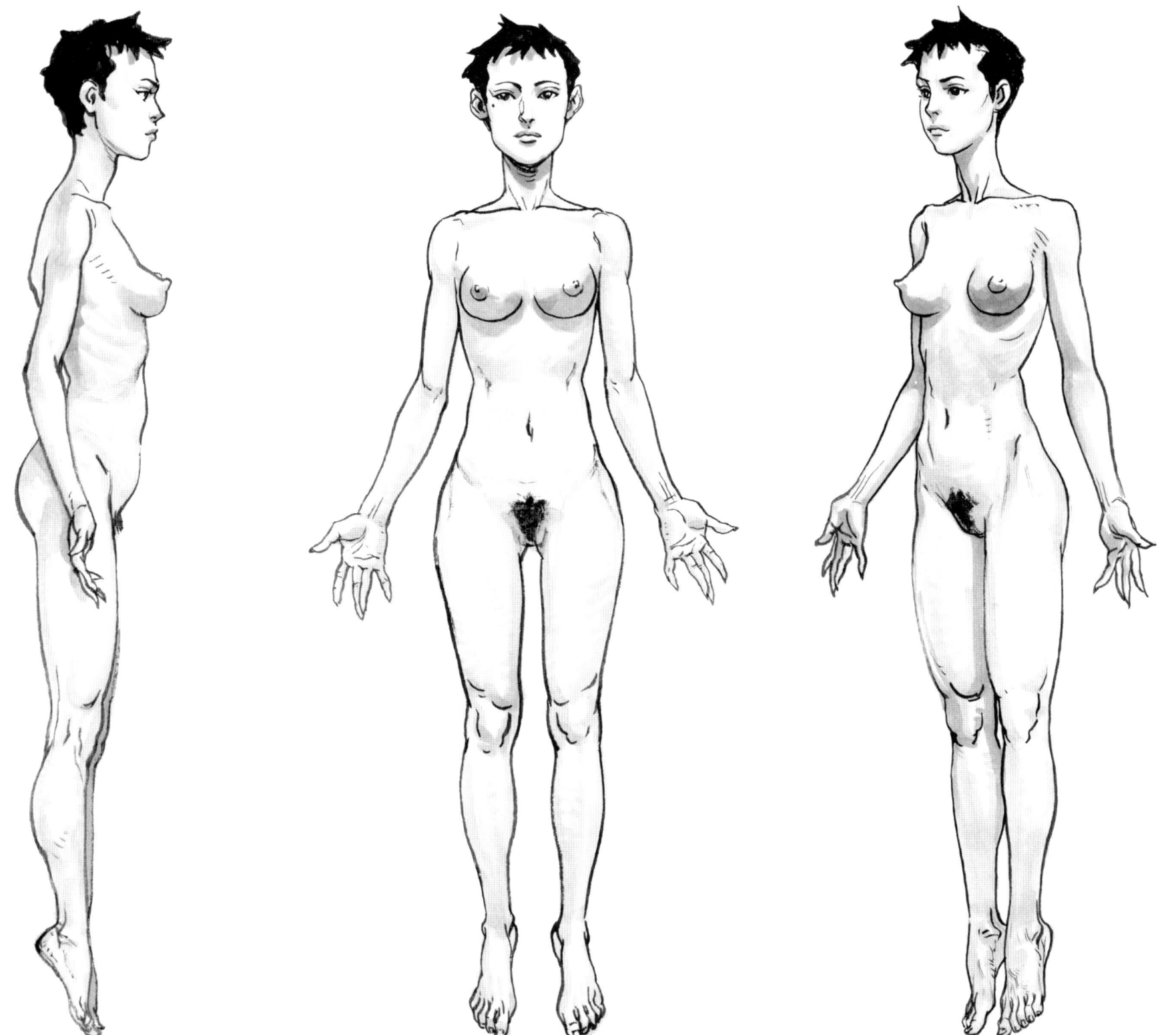

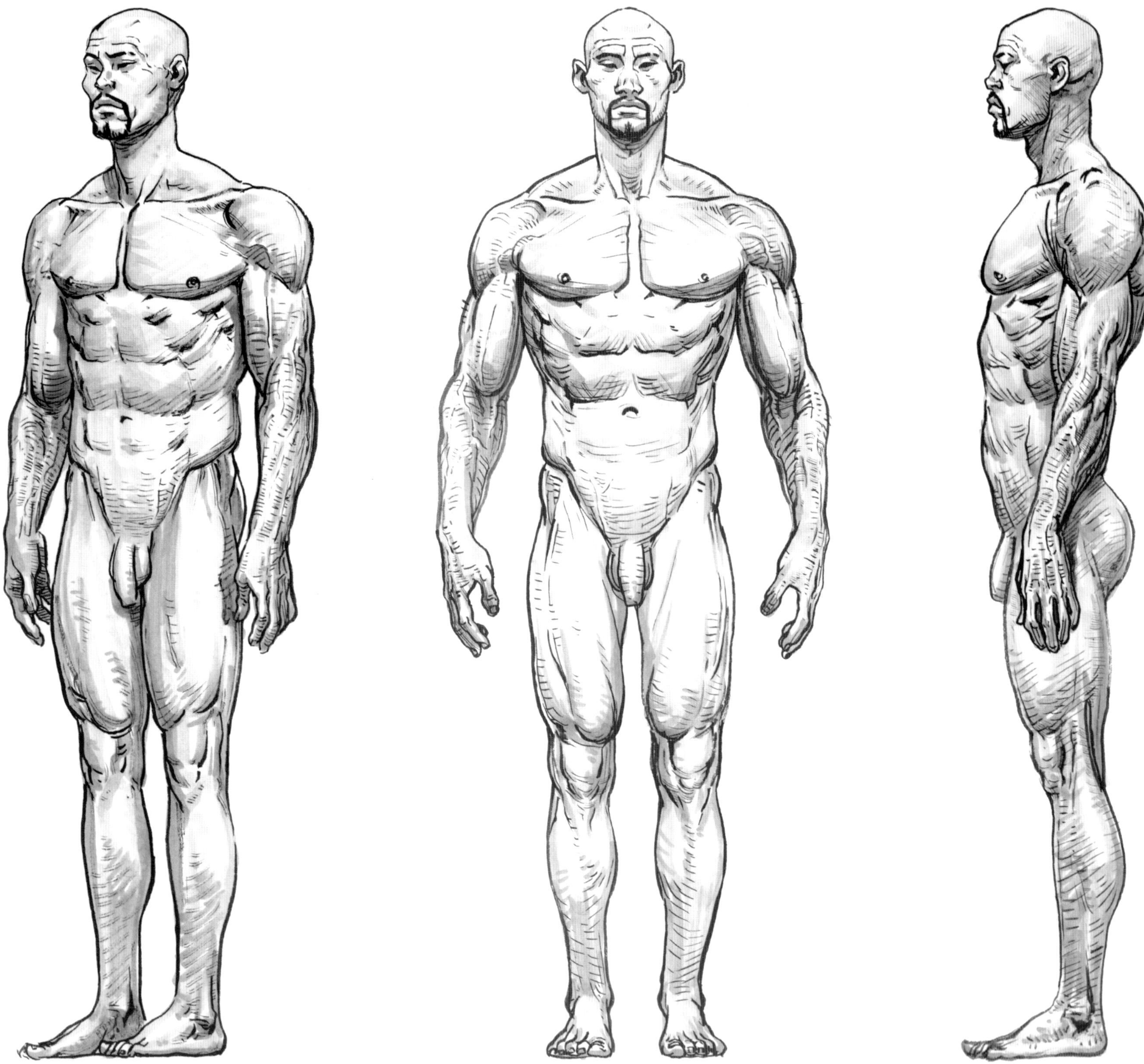

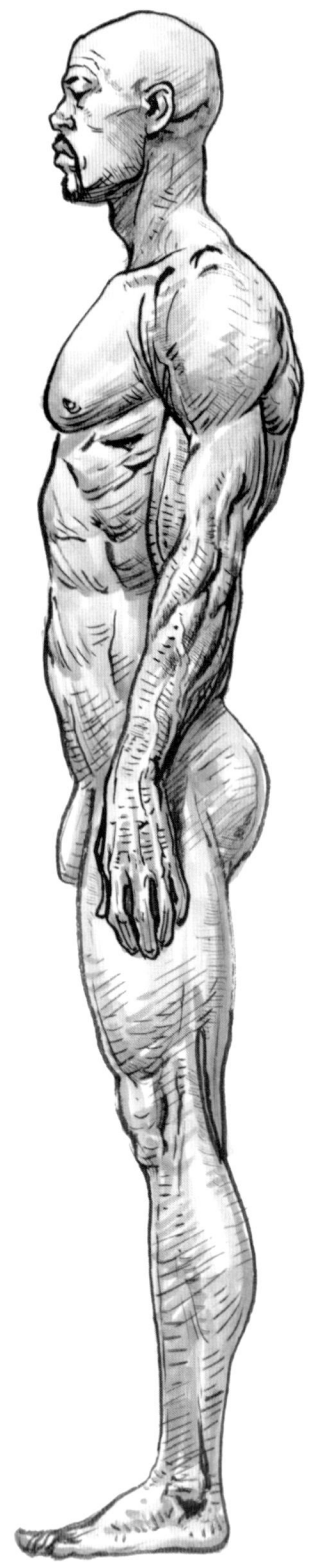

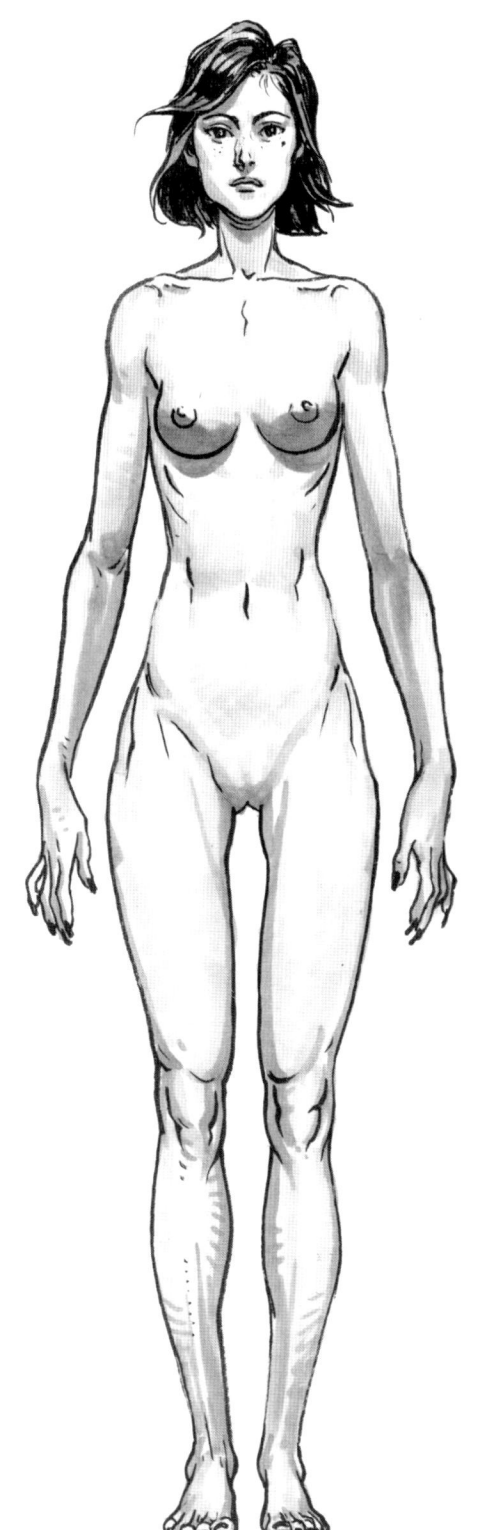
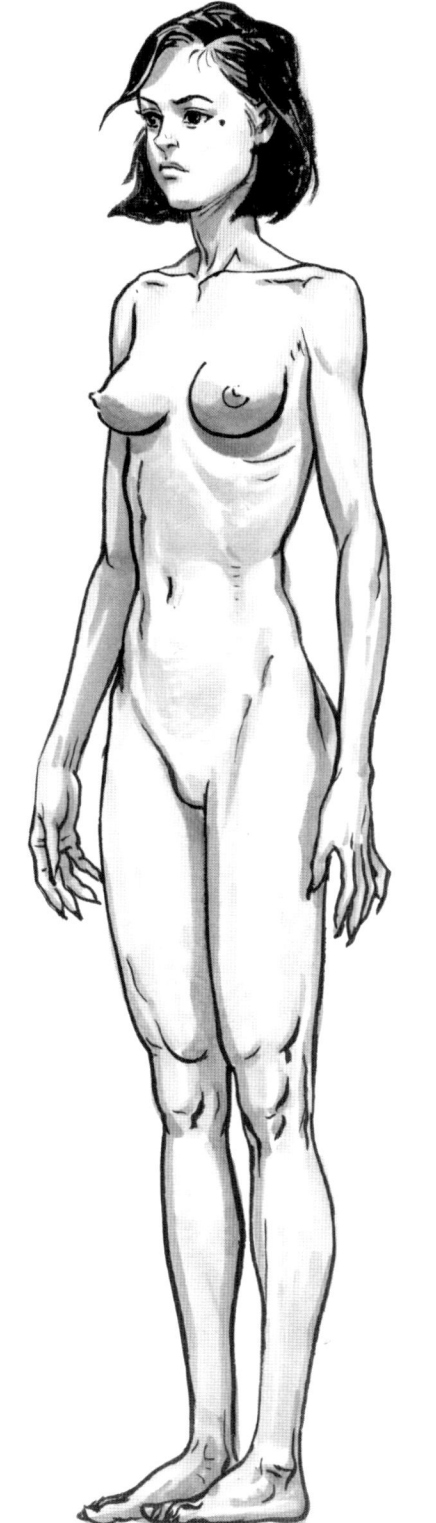

KIM JUNG GI

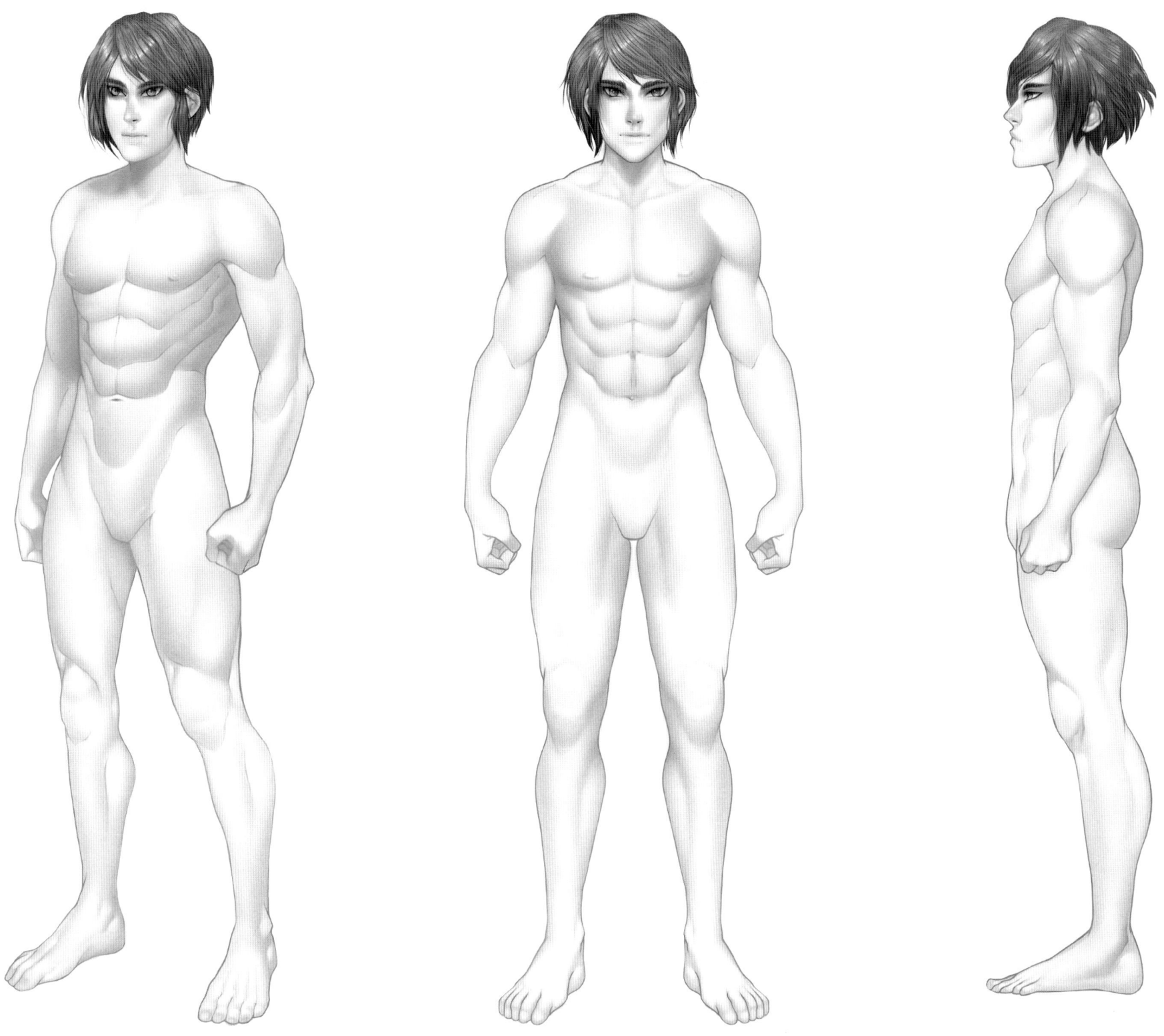

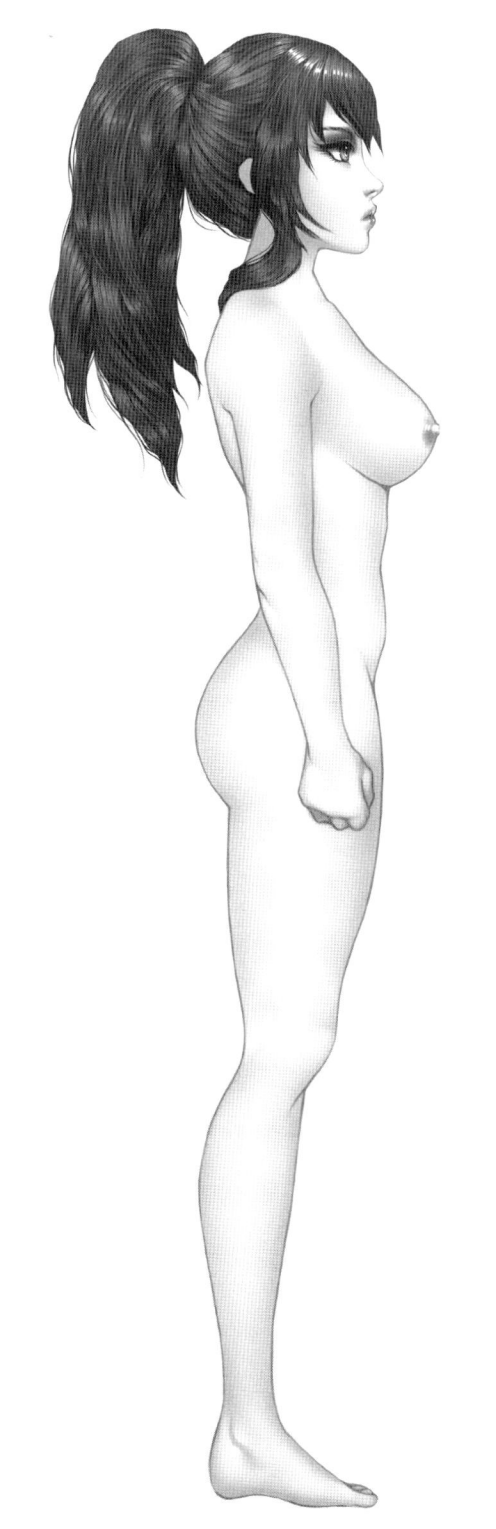
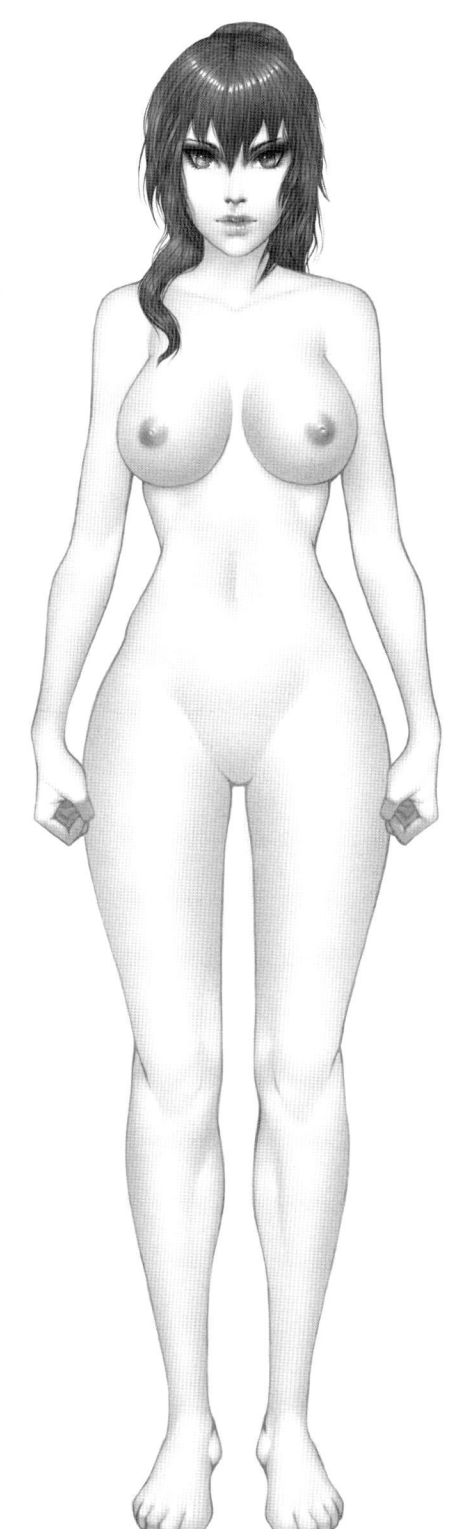
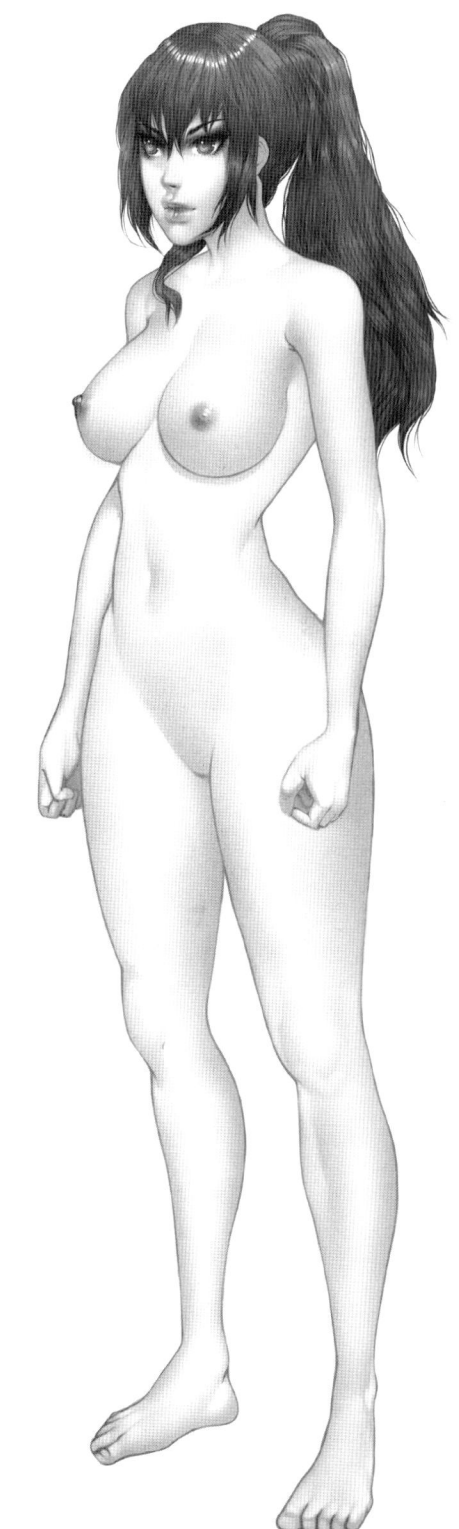

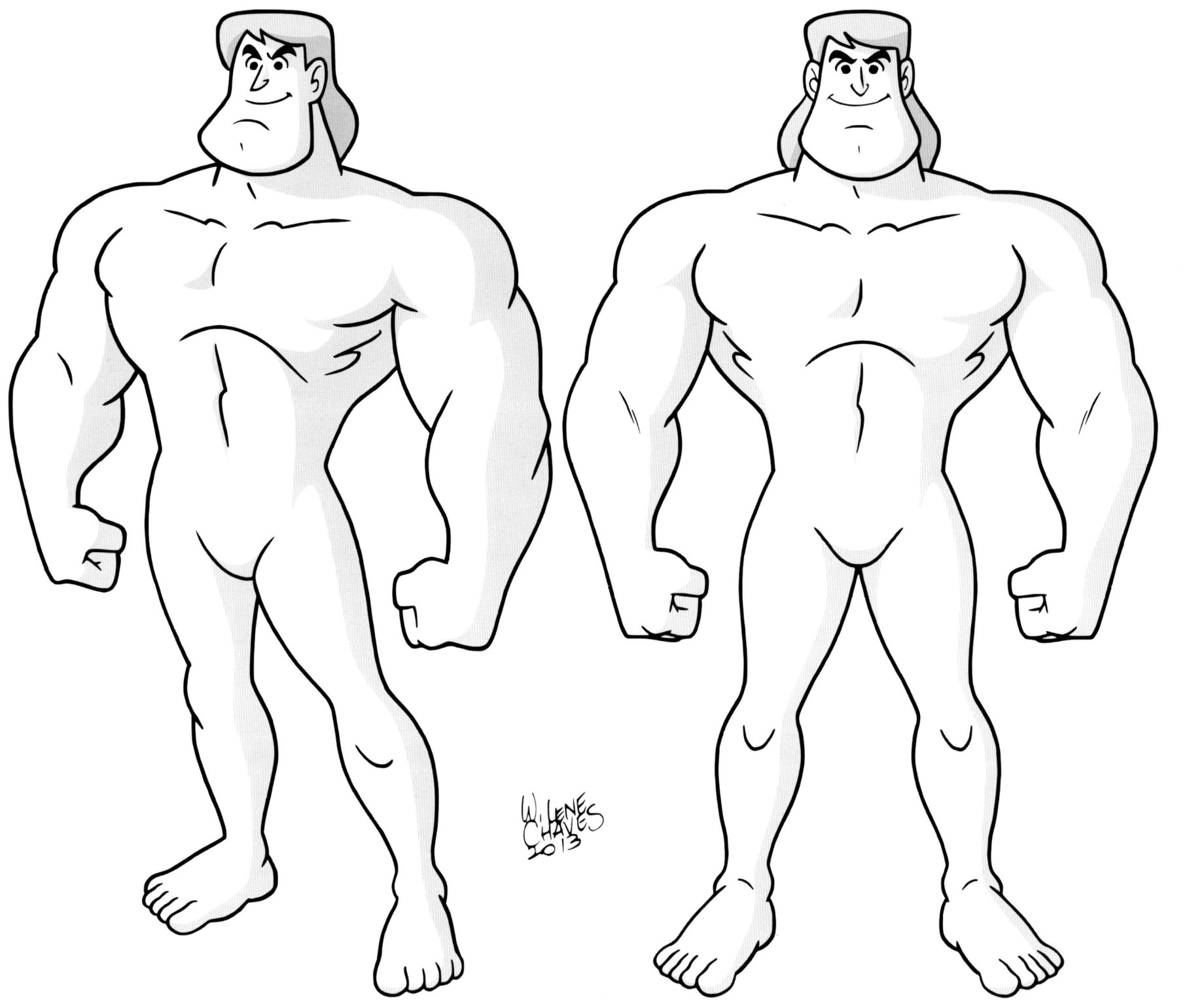

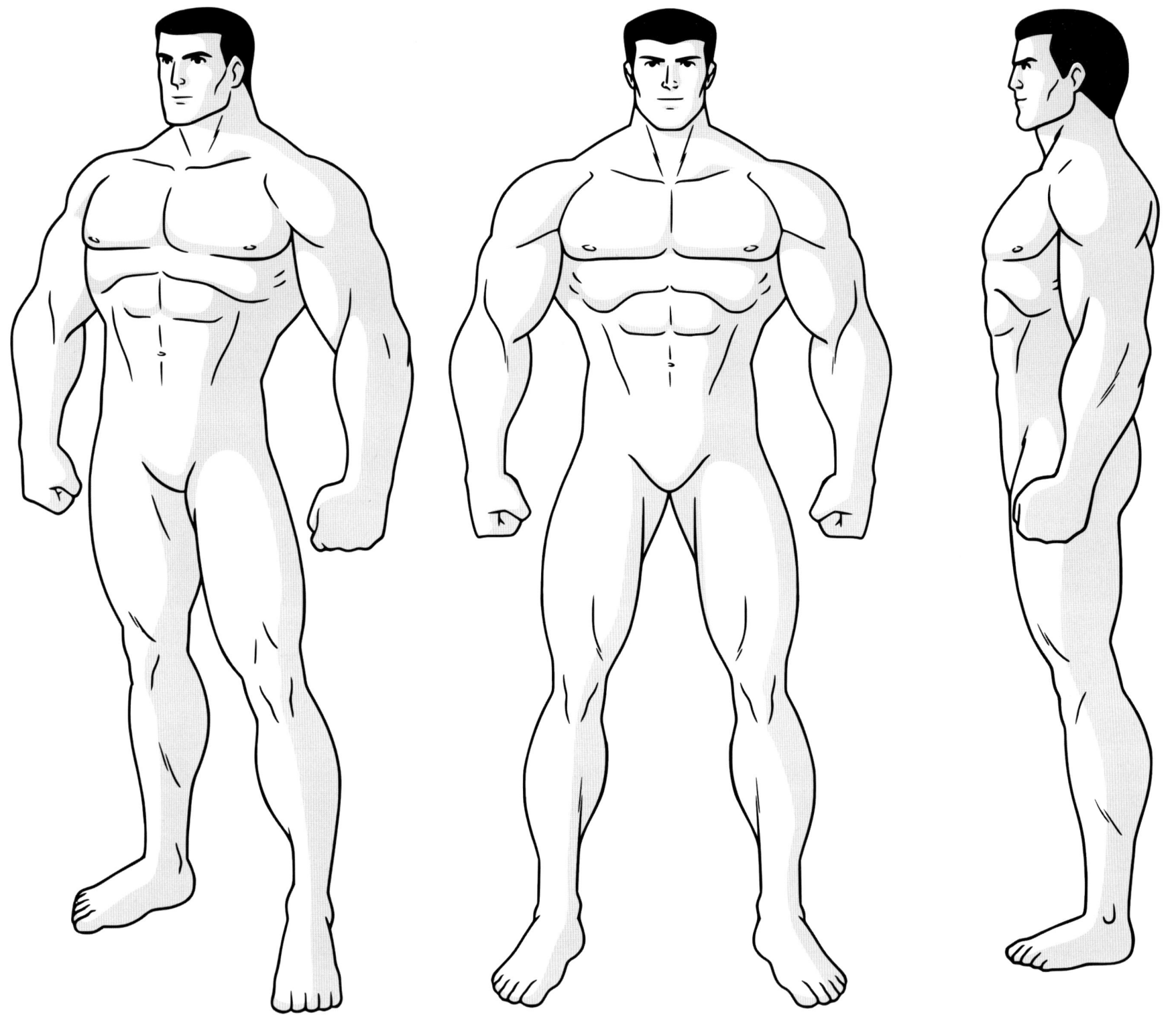

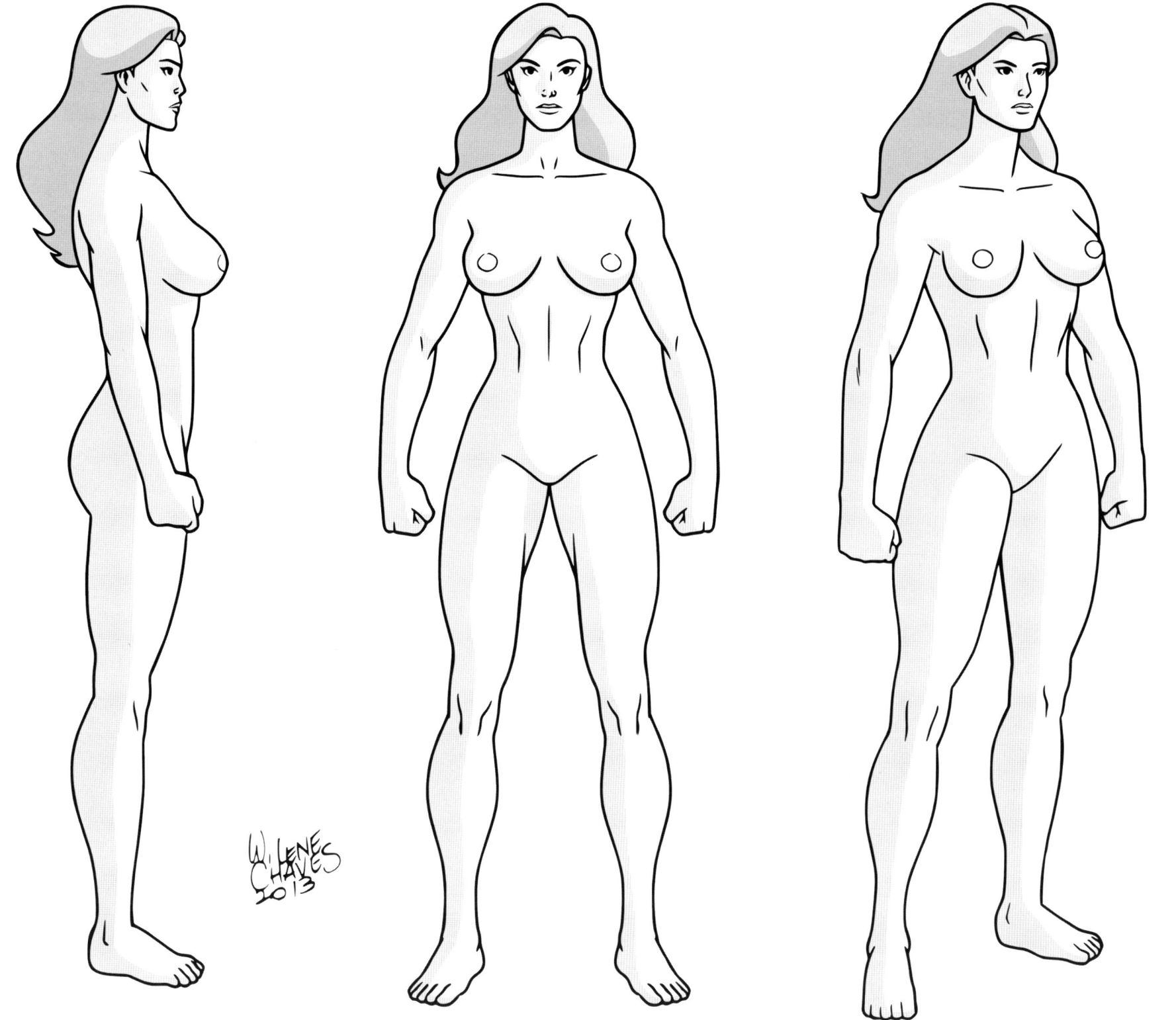

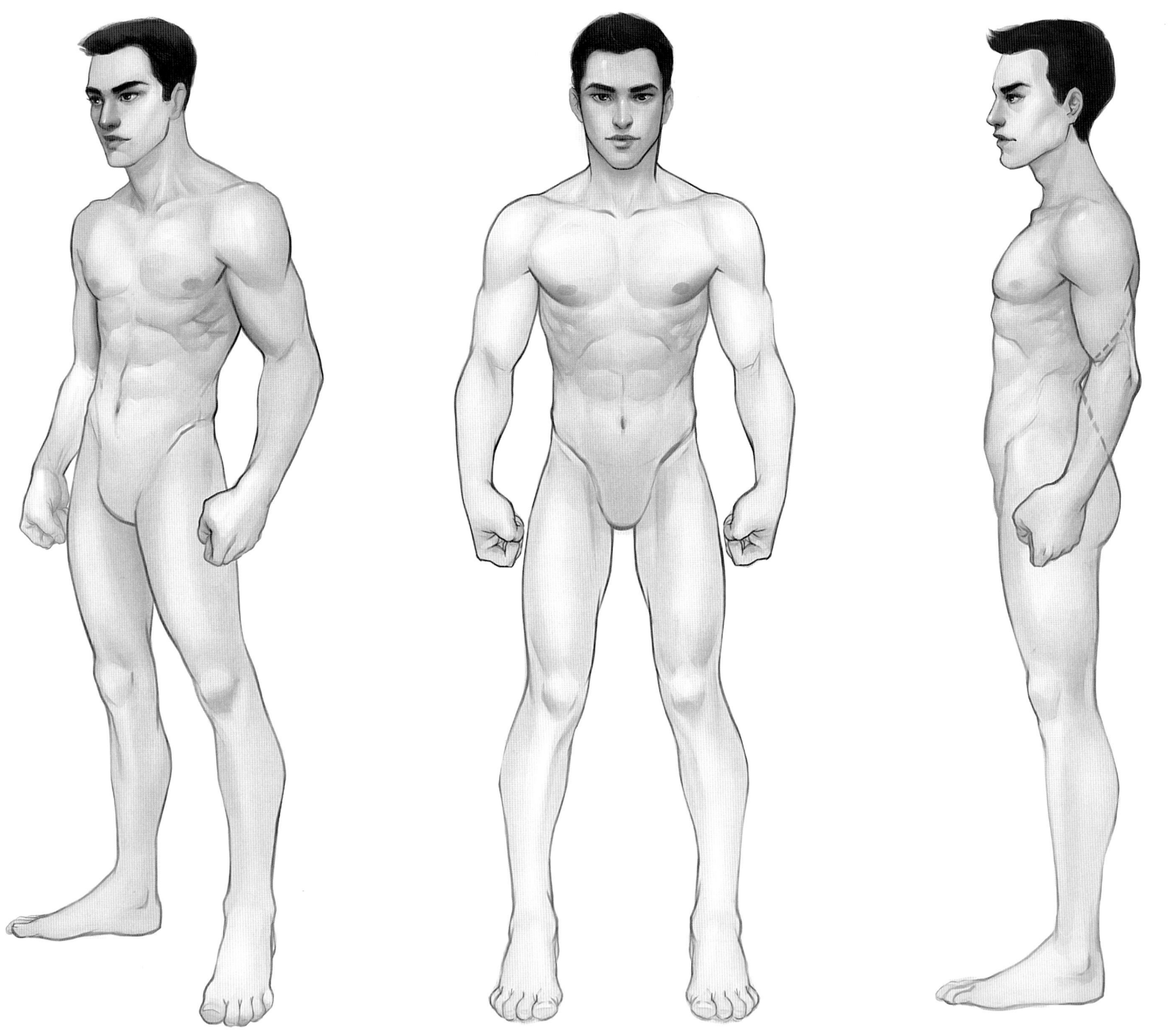

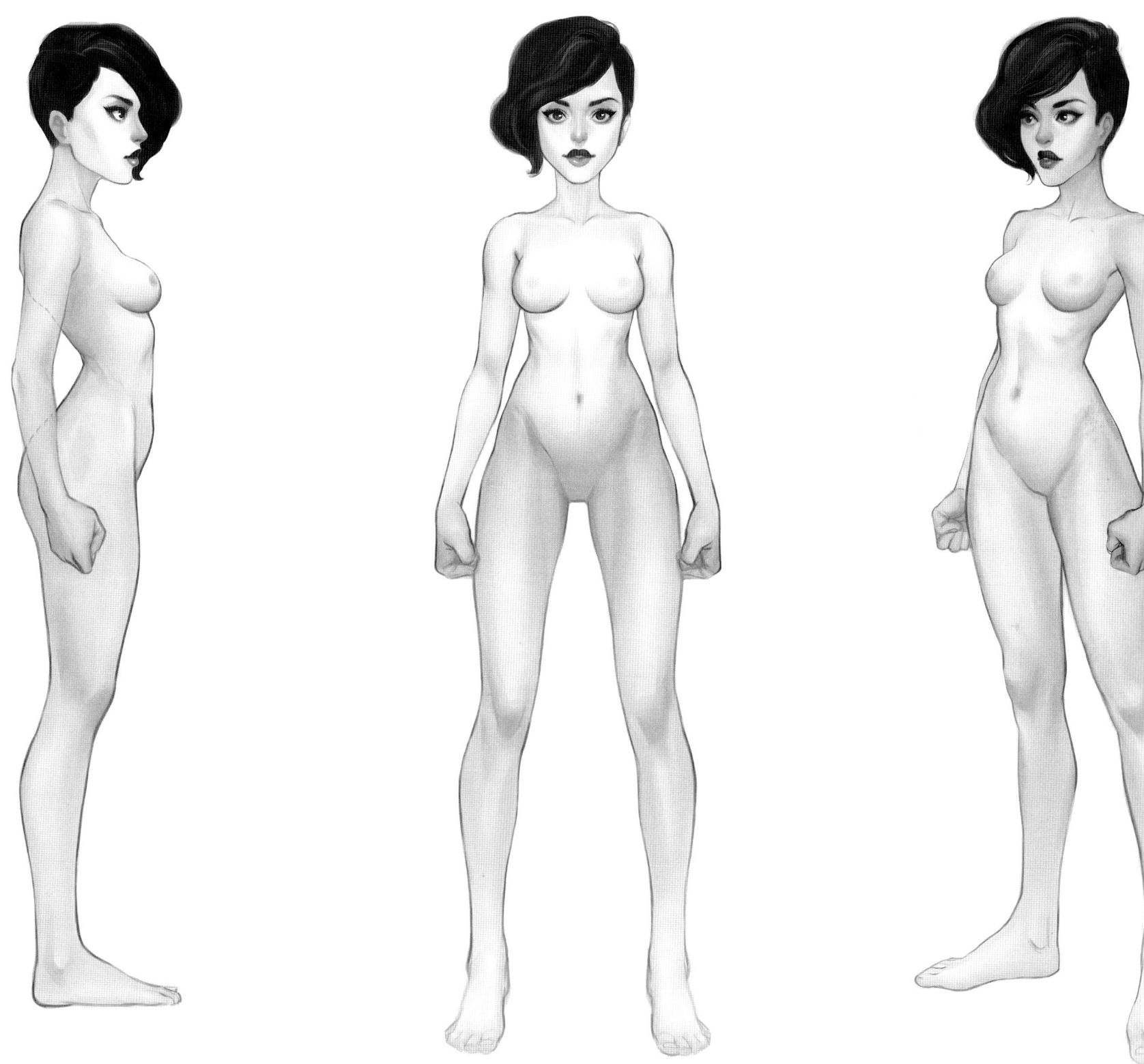

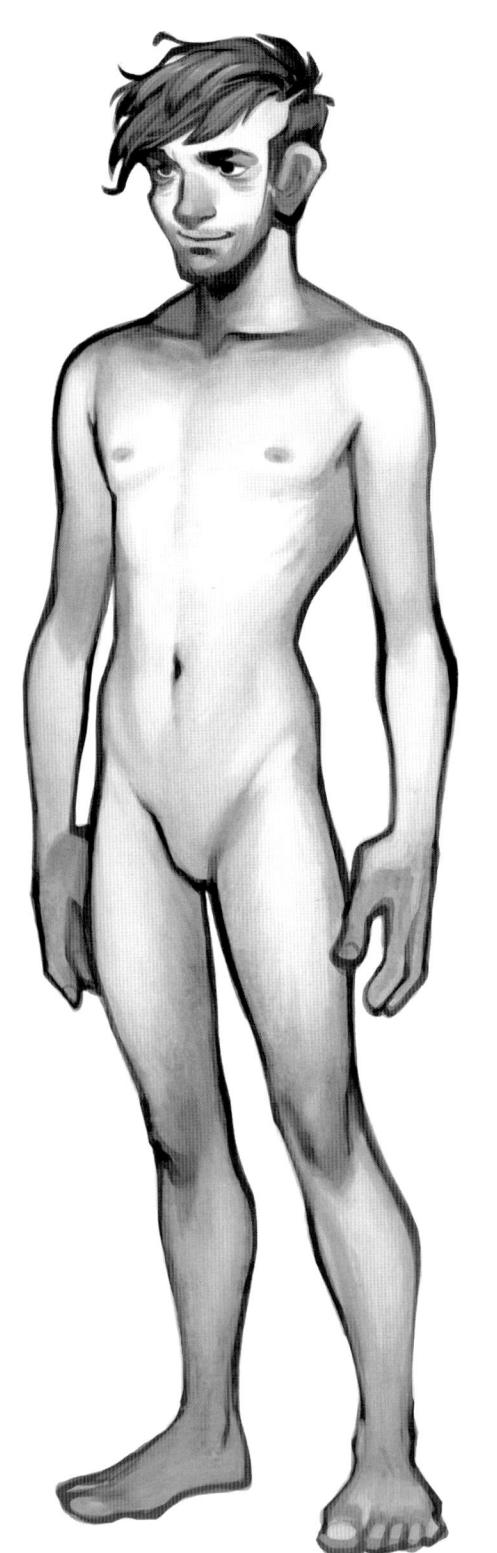
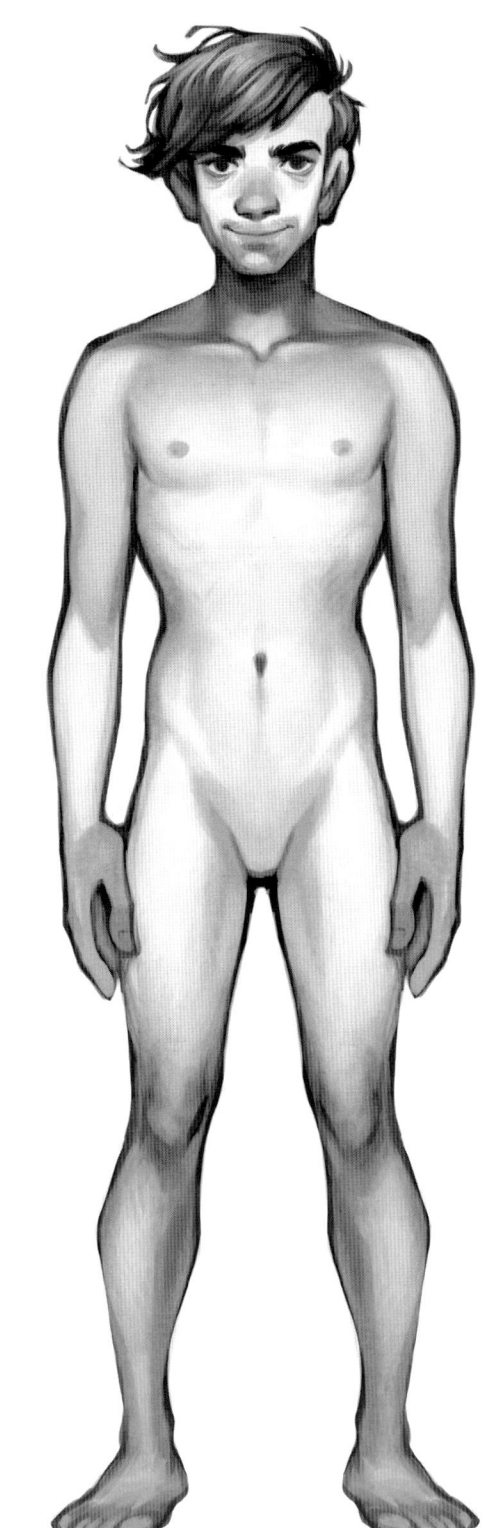
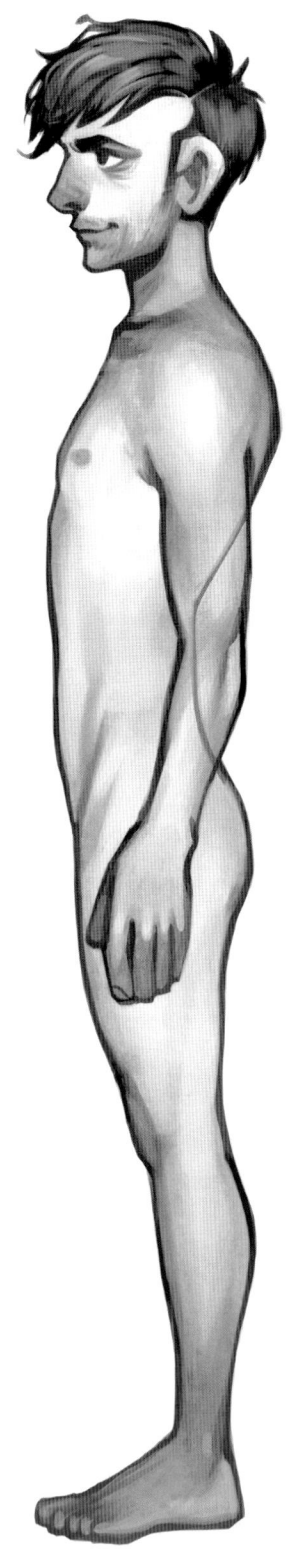

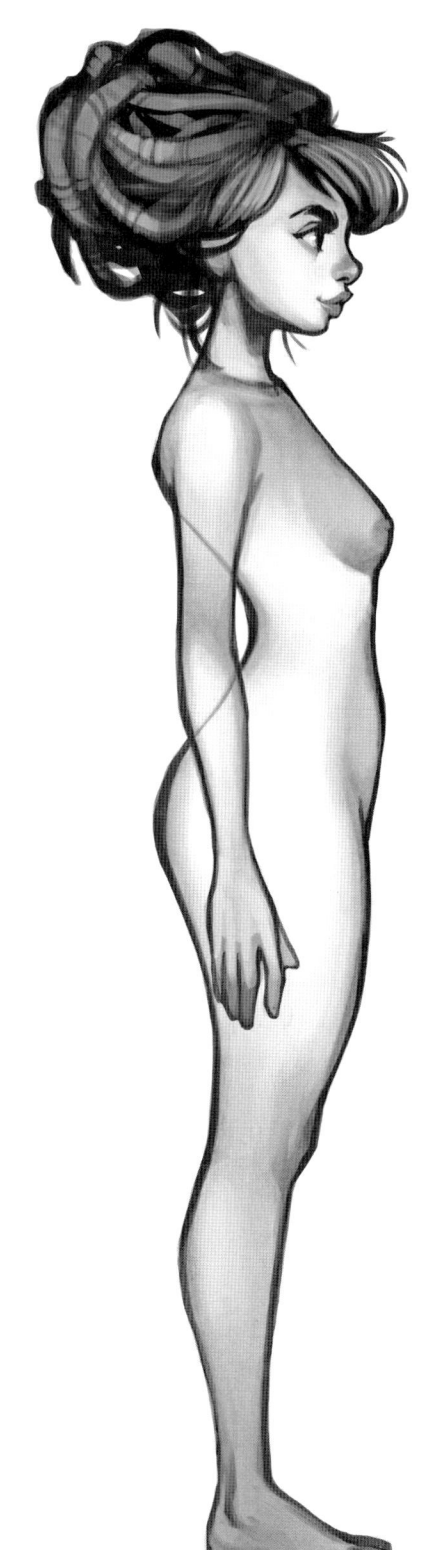
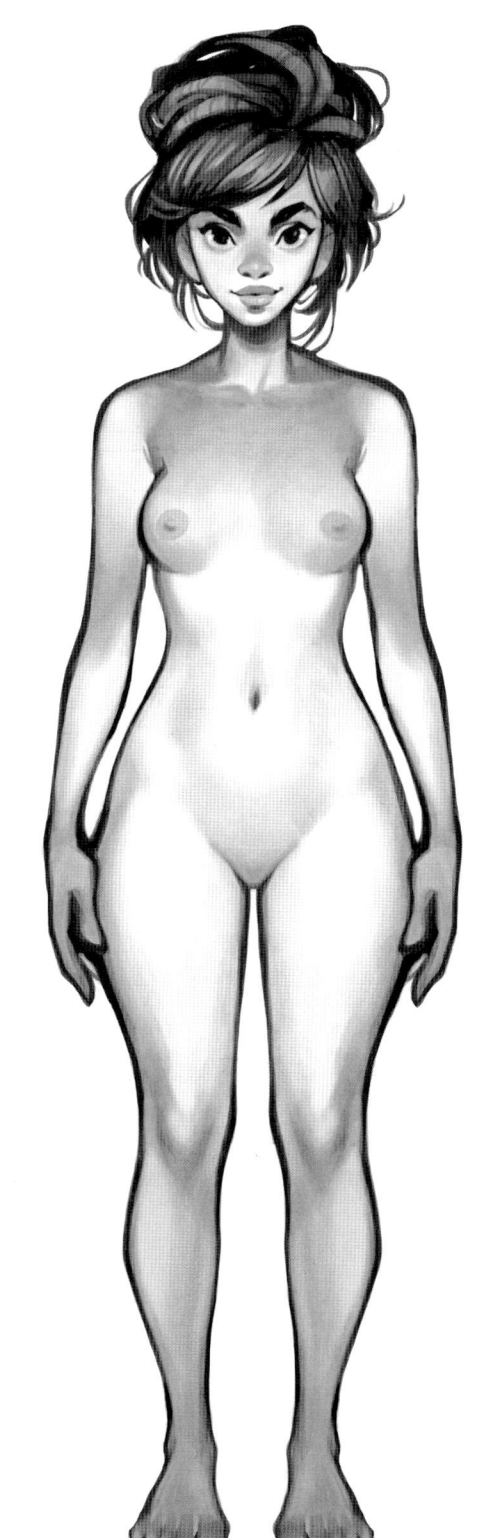
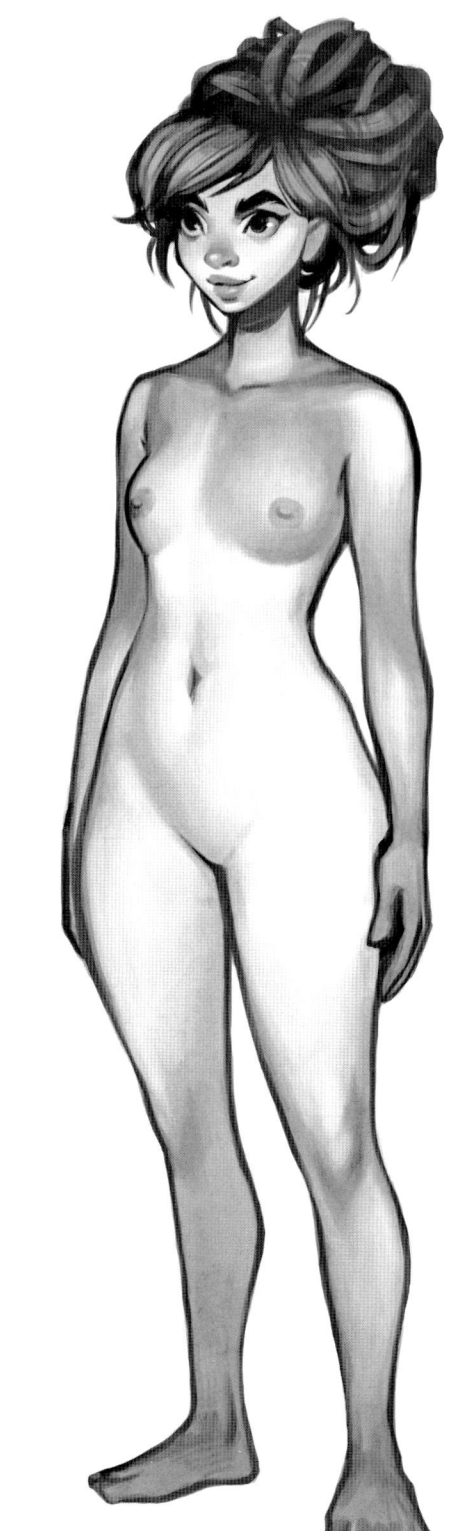

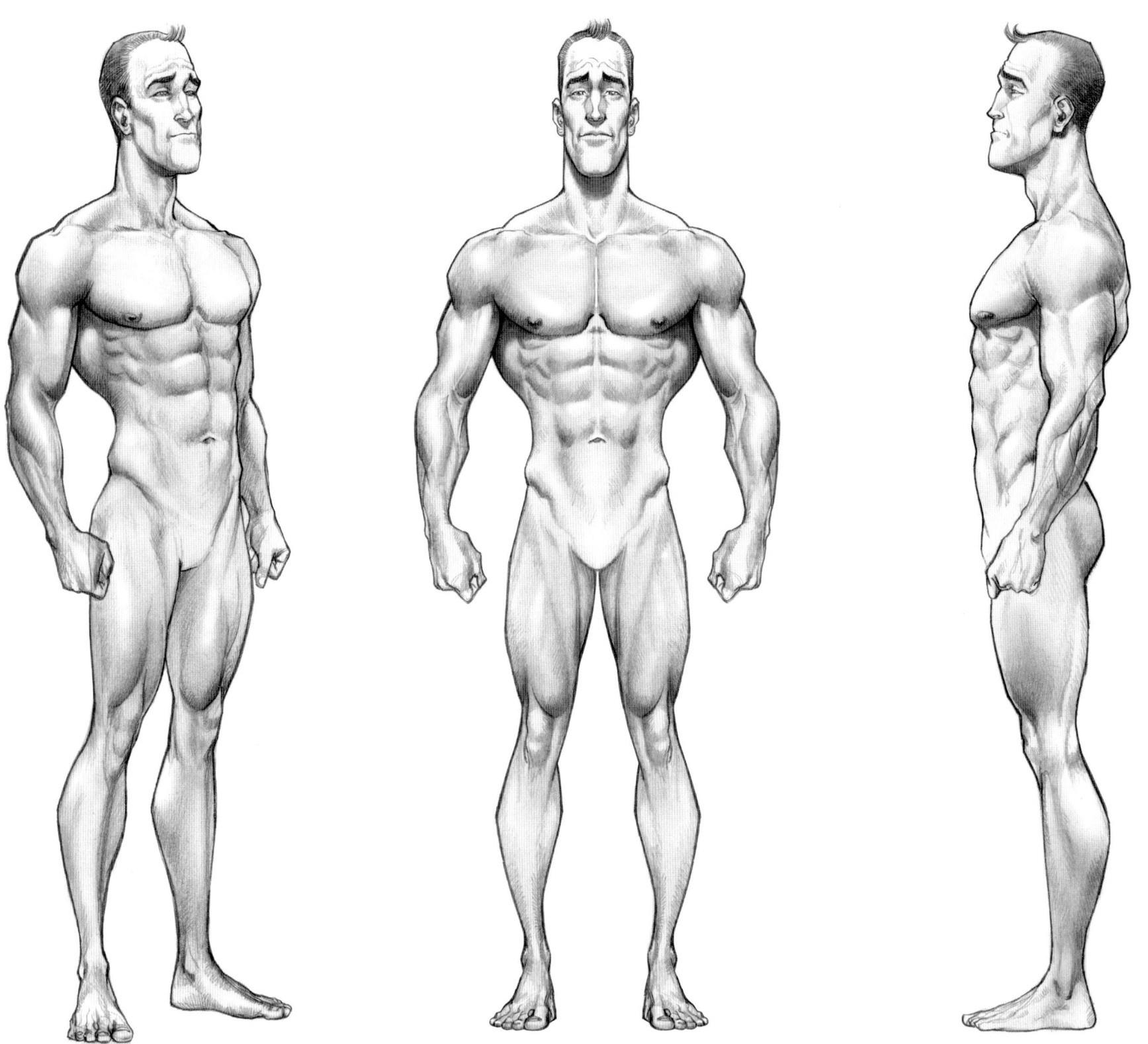

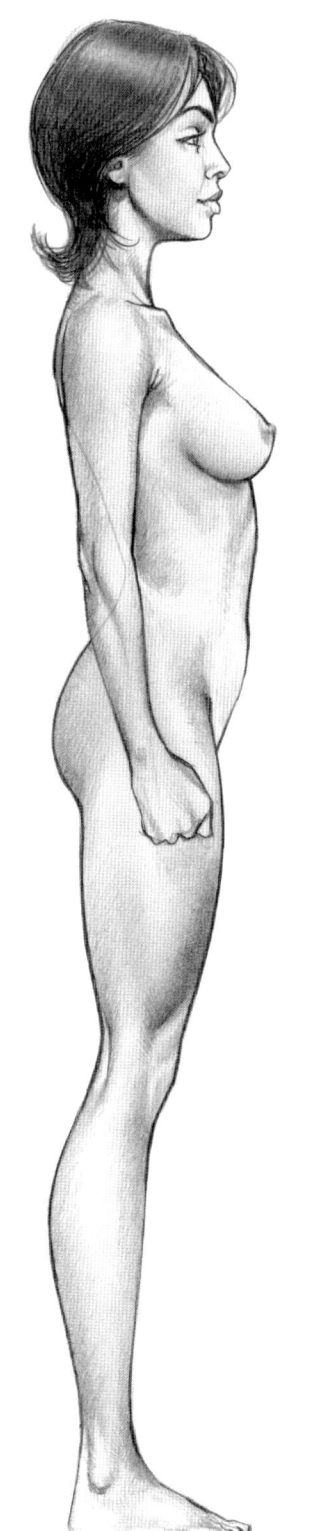
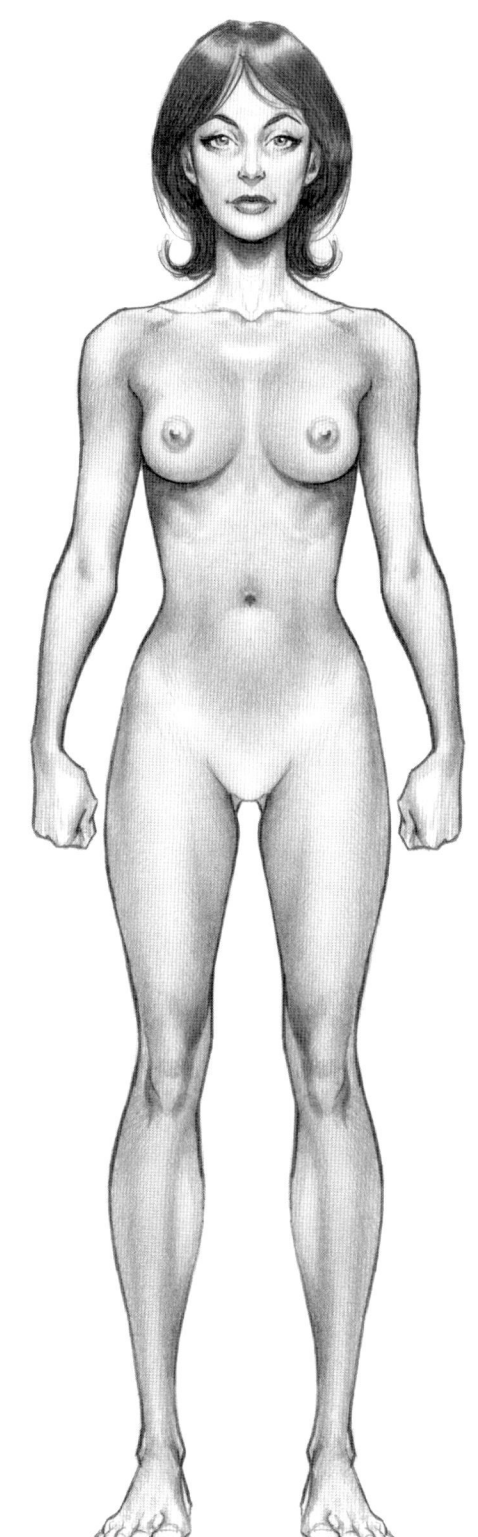
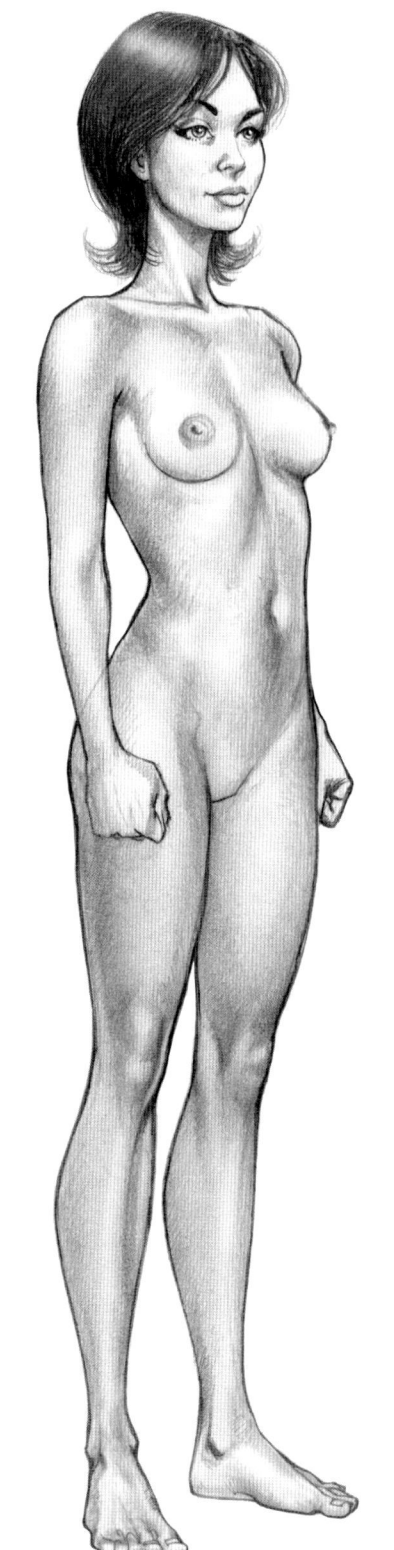

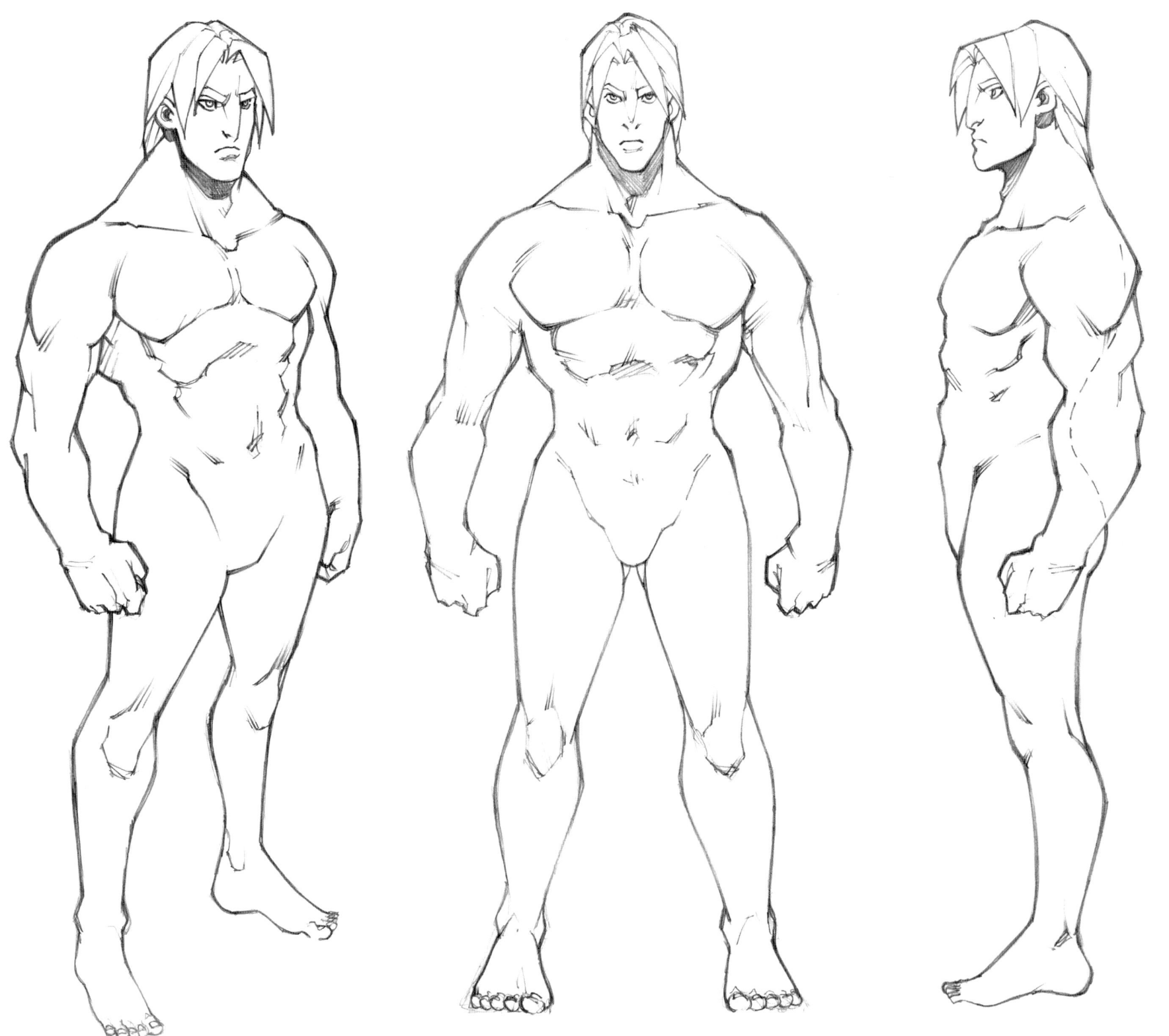

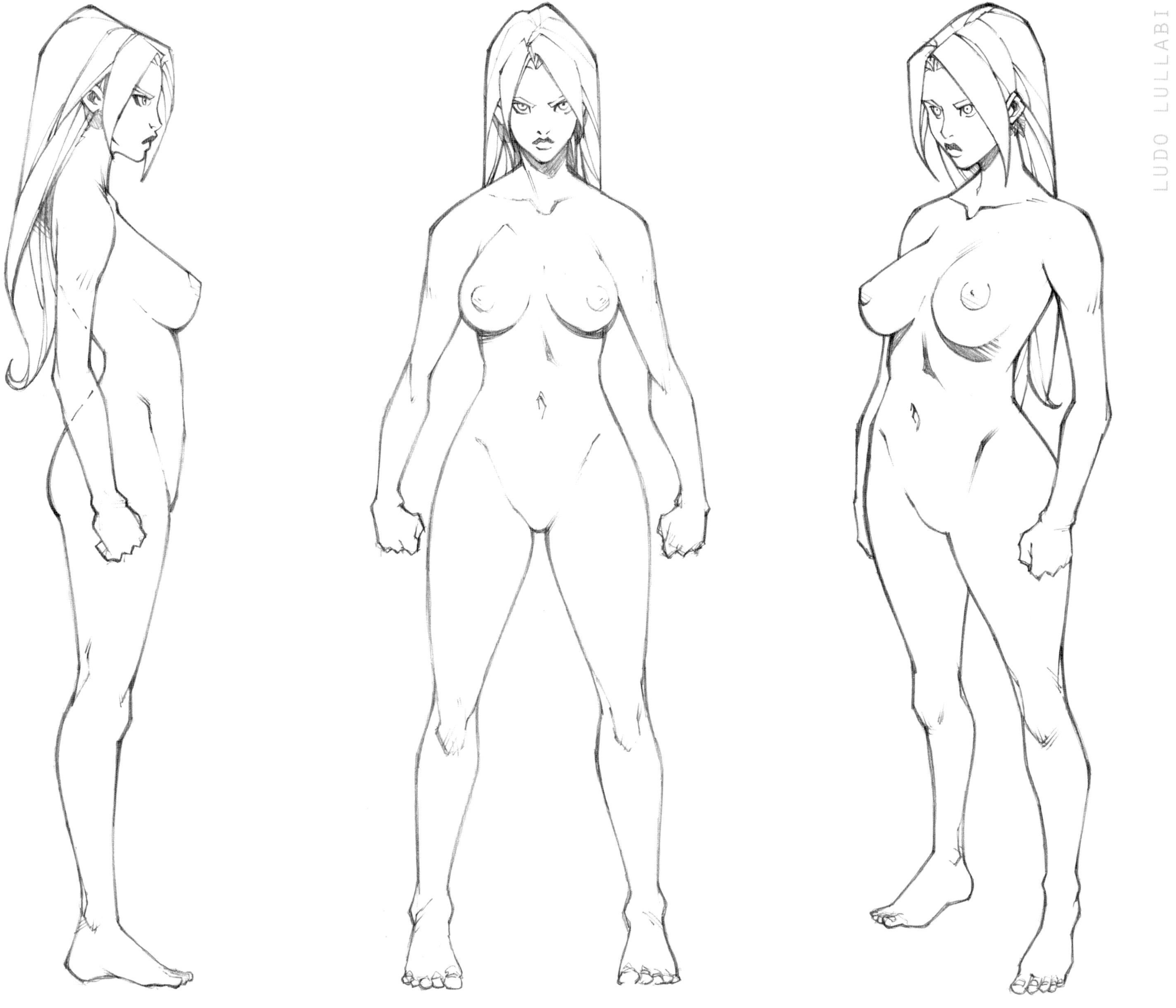

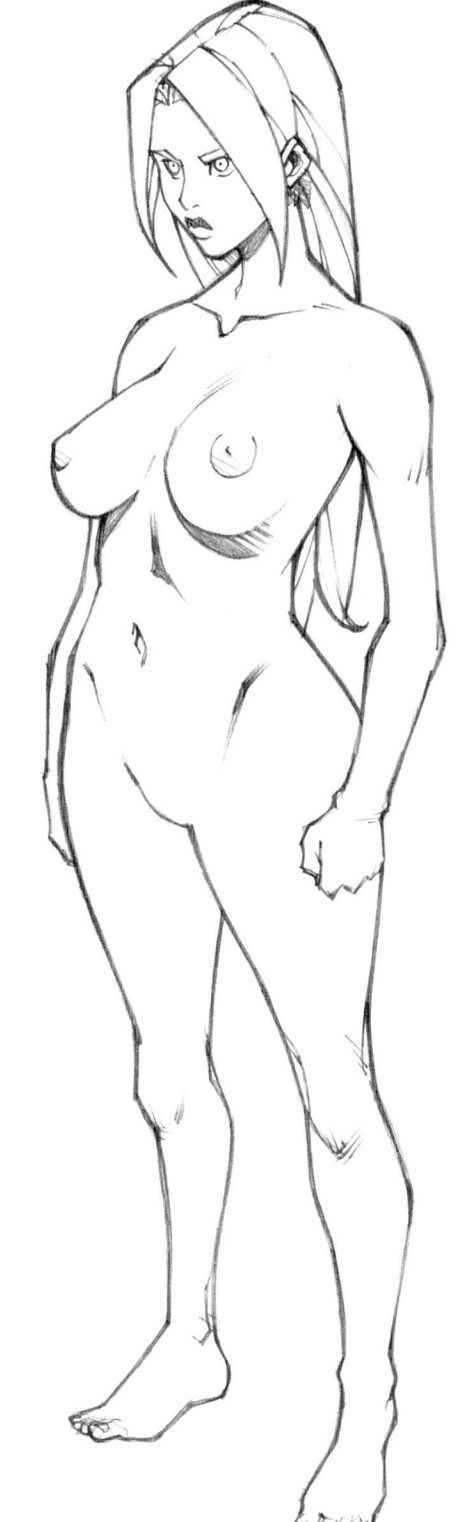

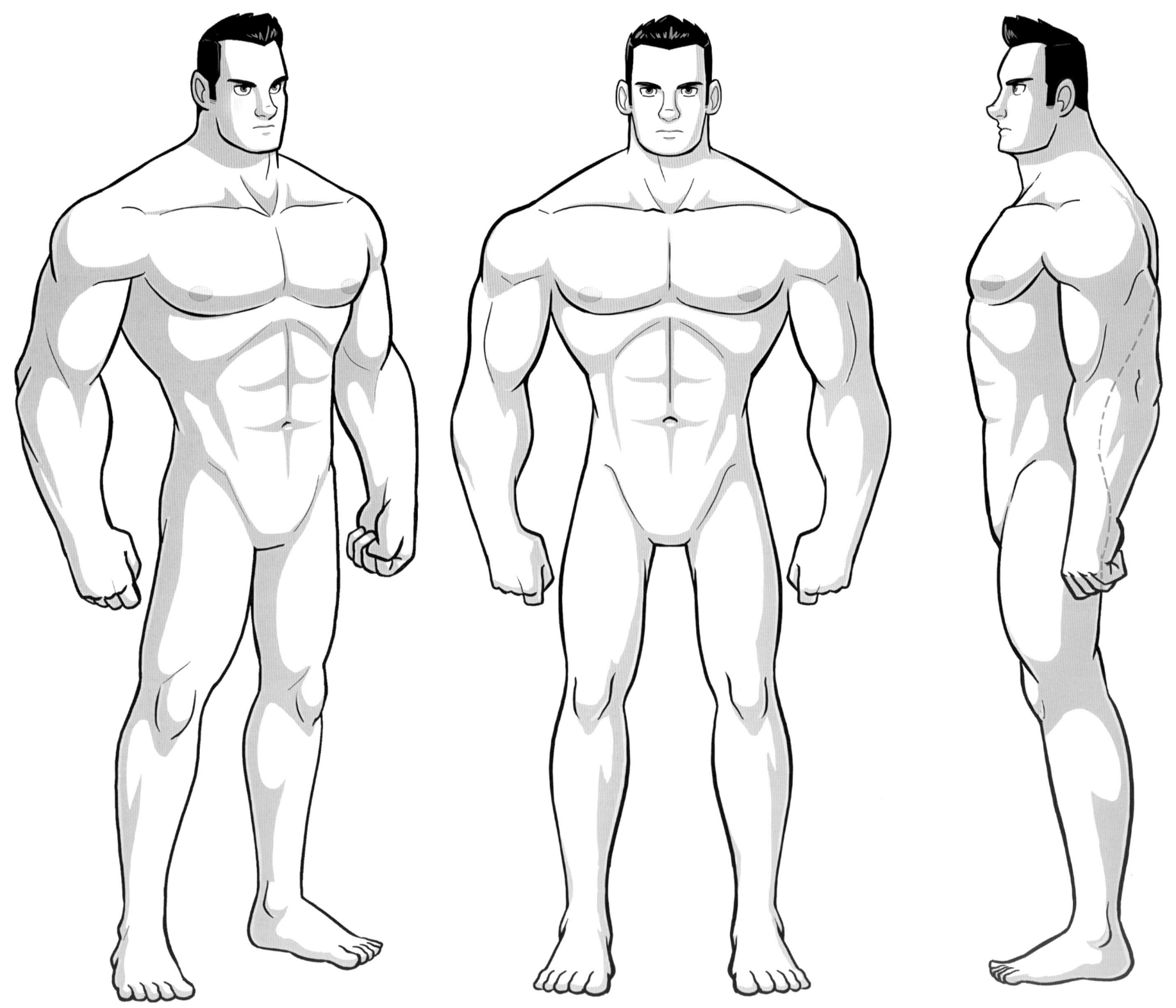

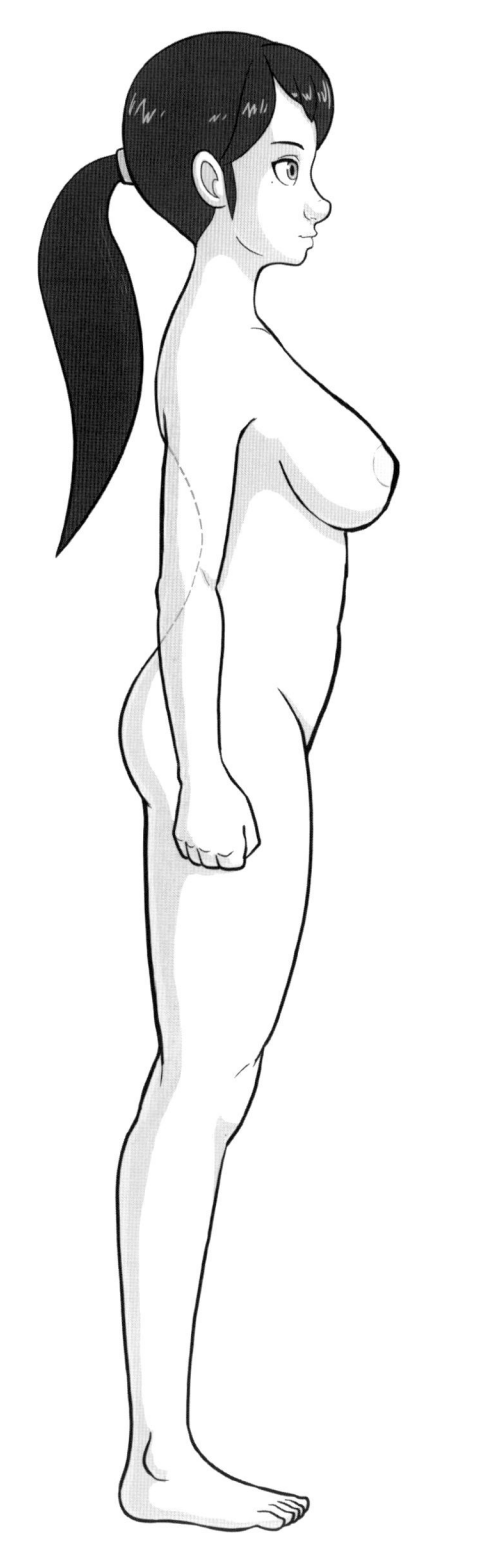
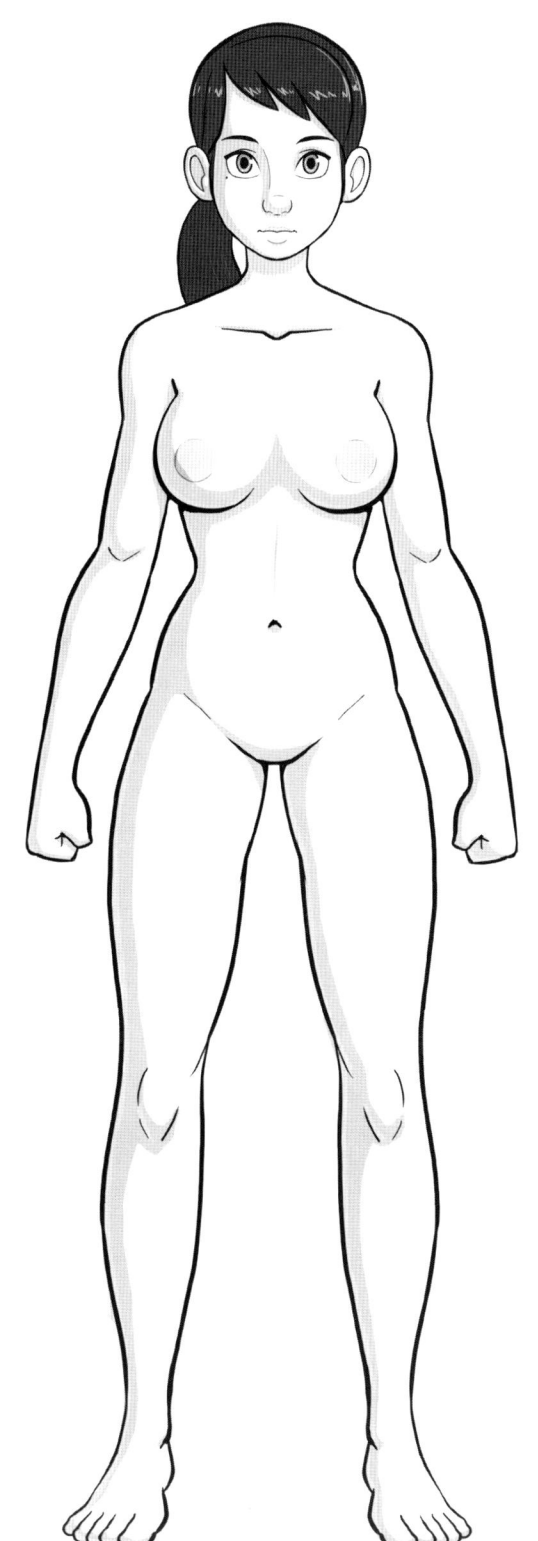
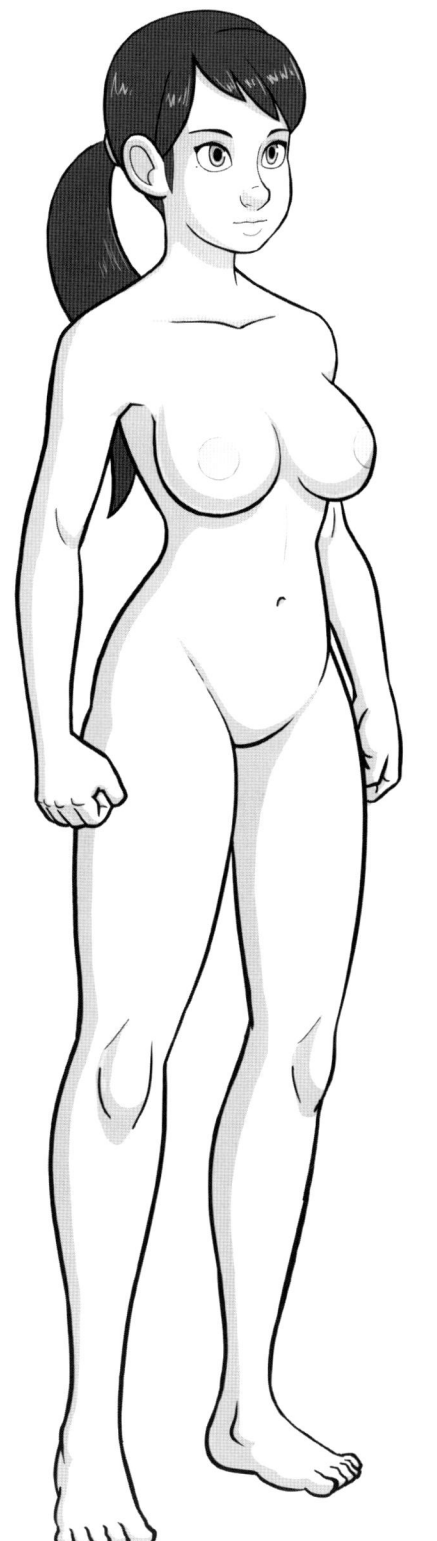

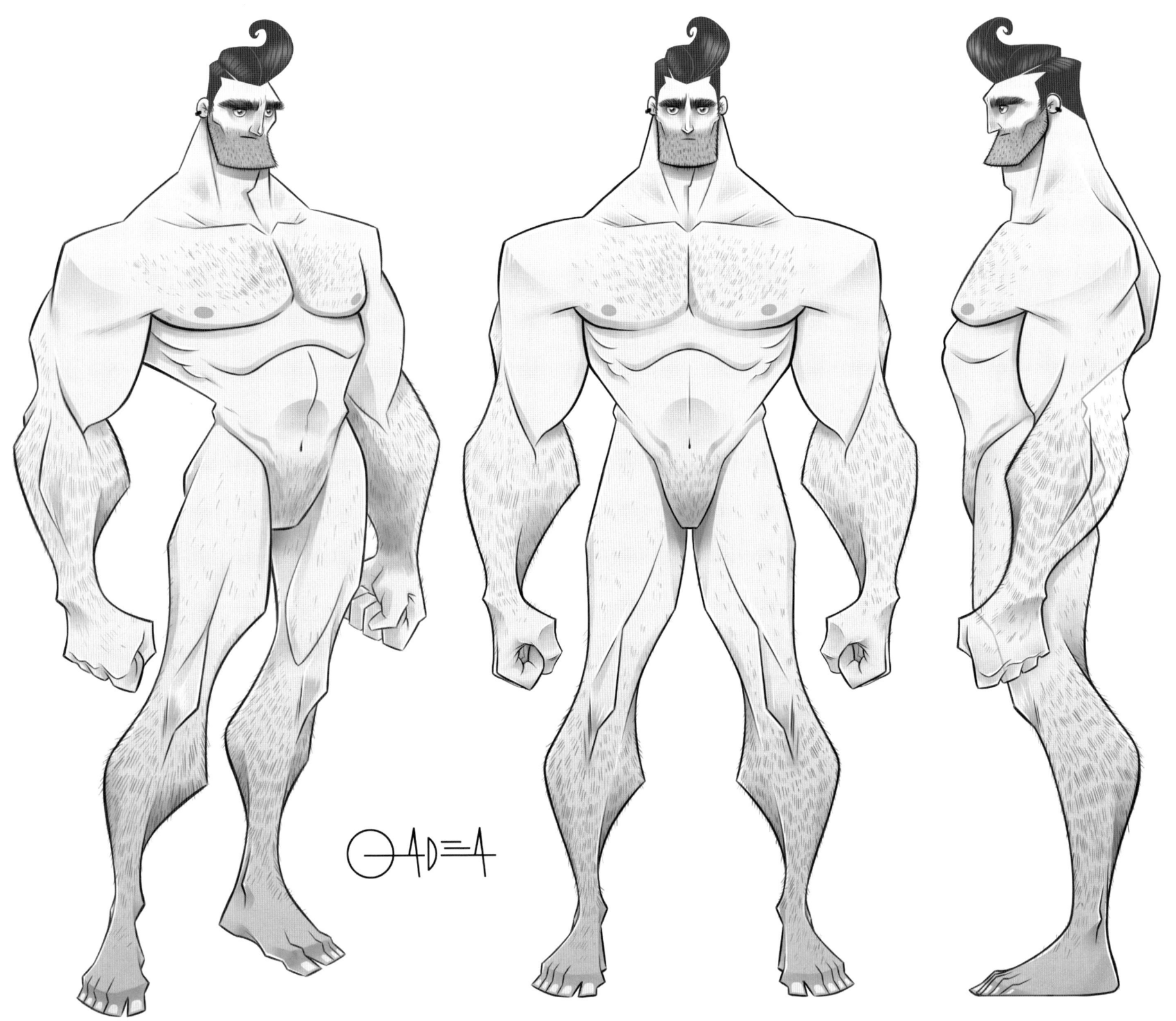

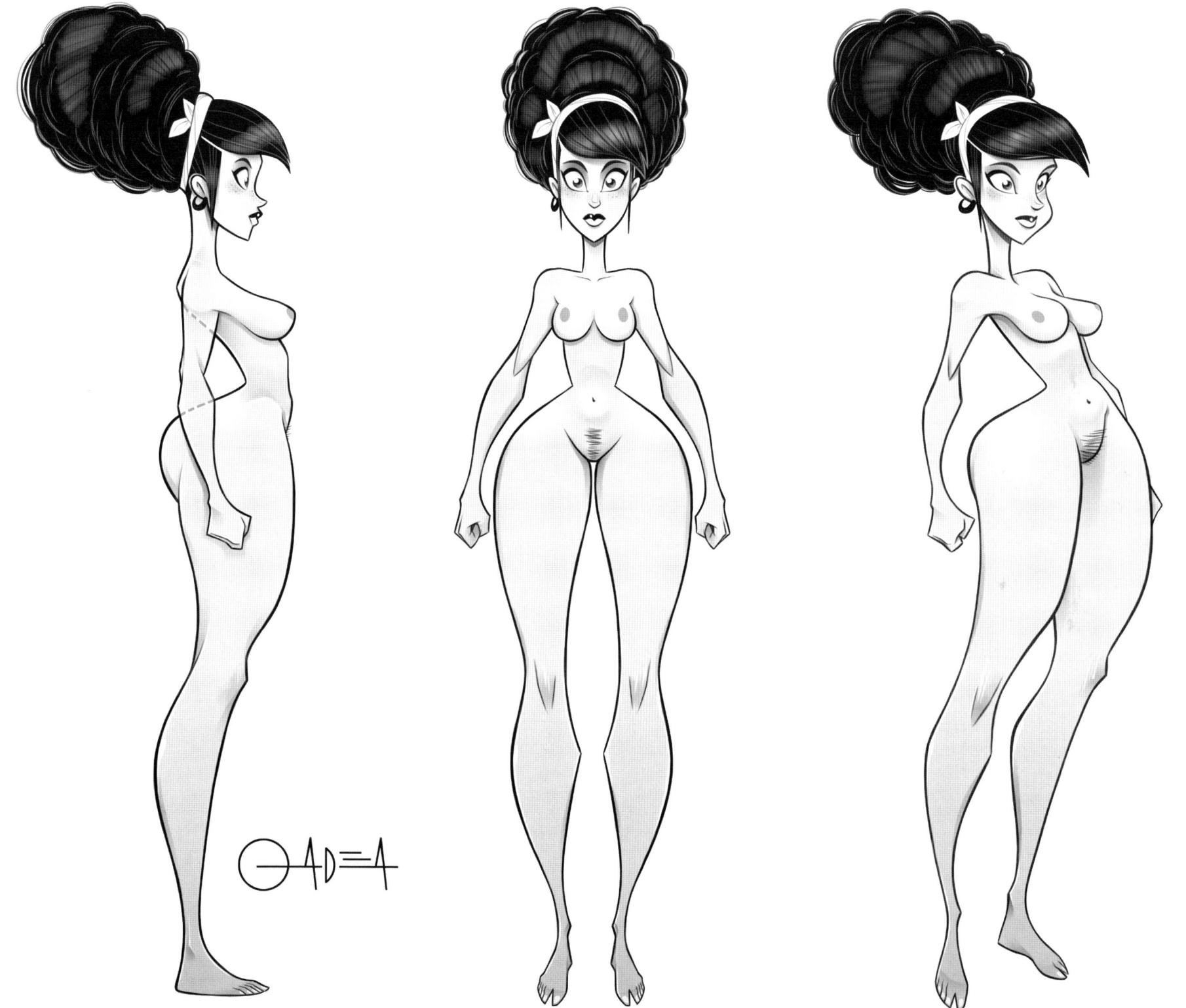

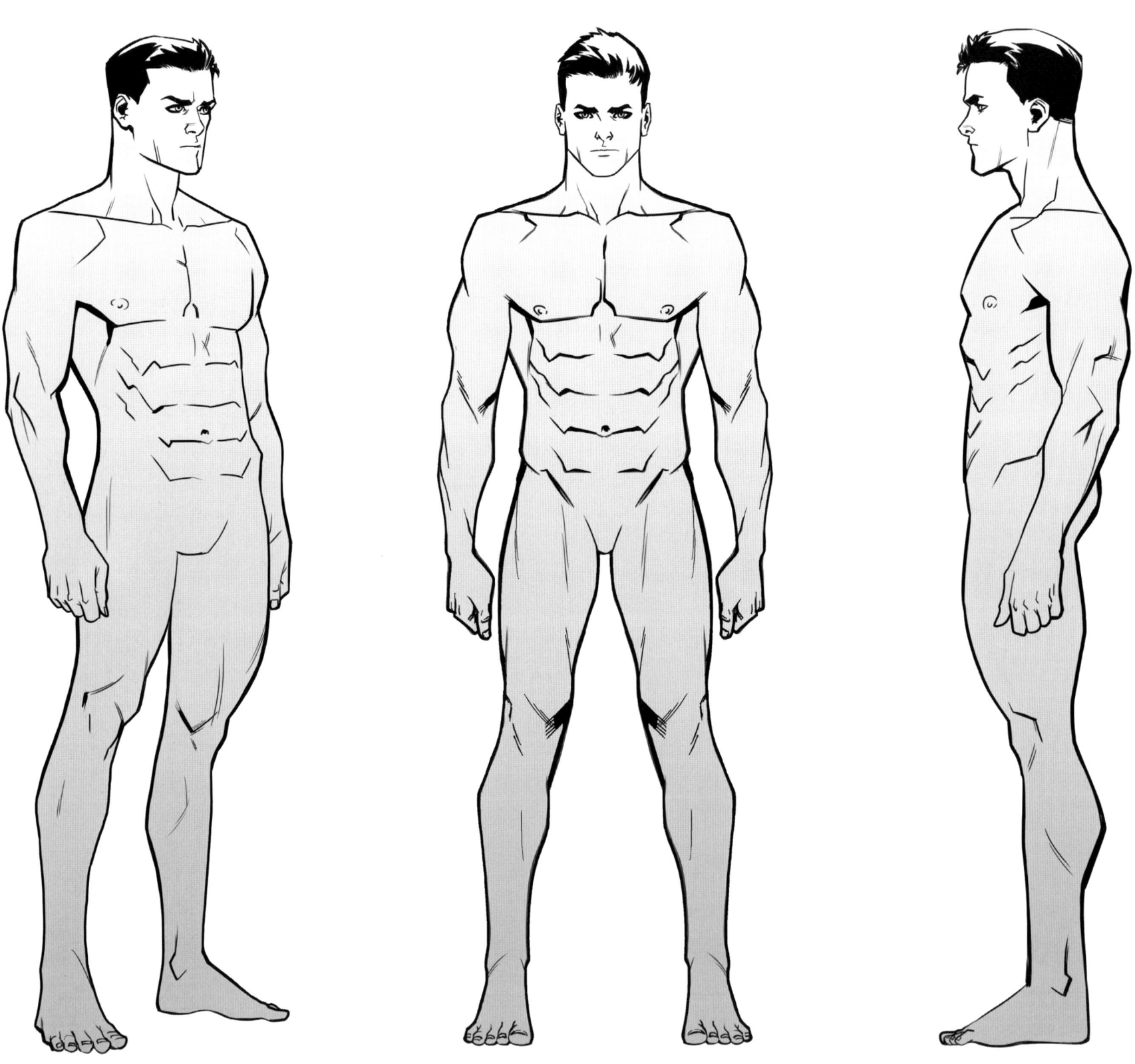

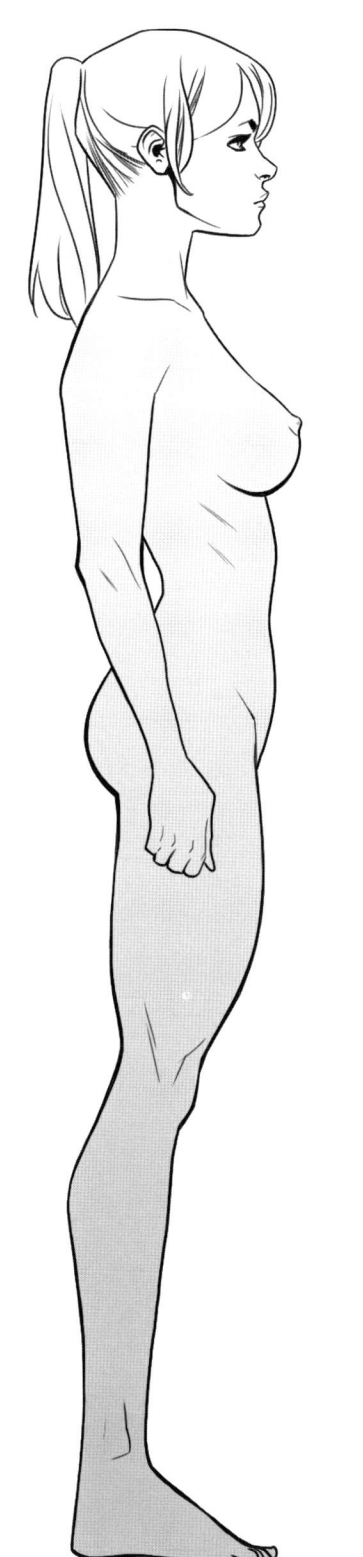
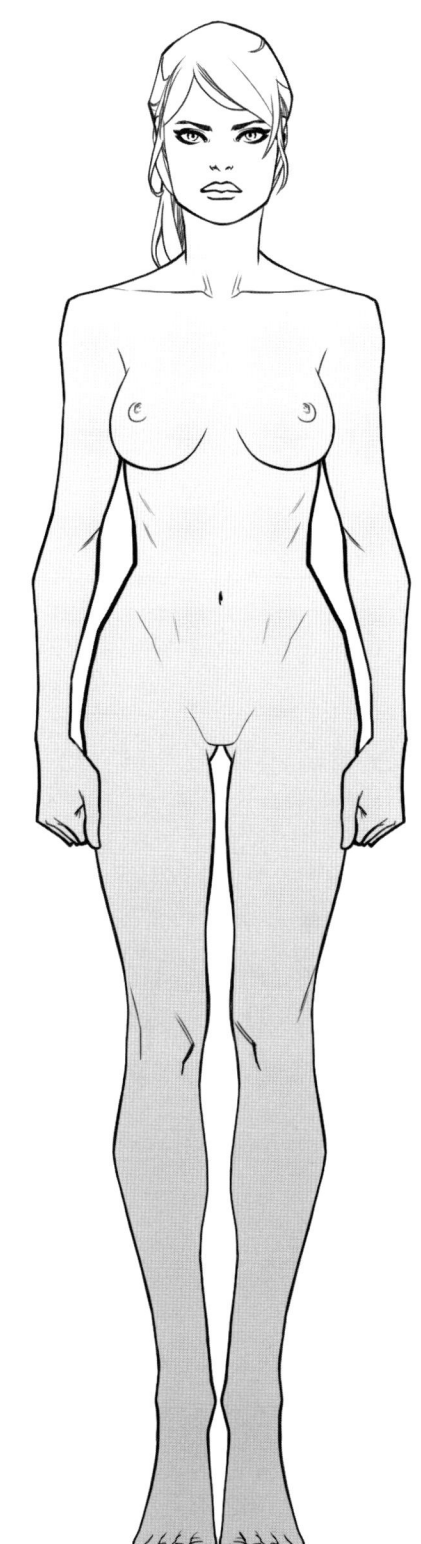
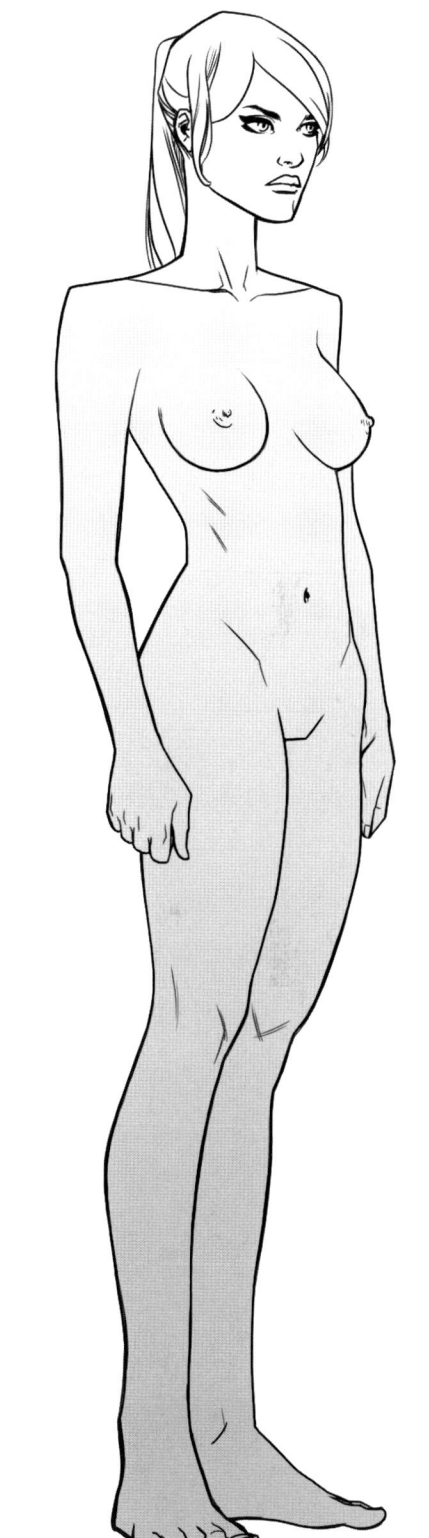

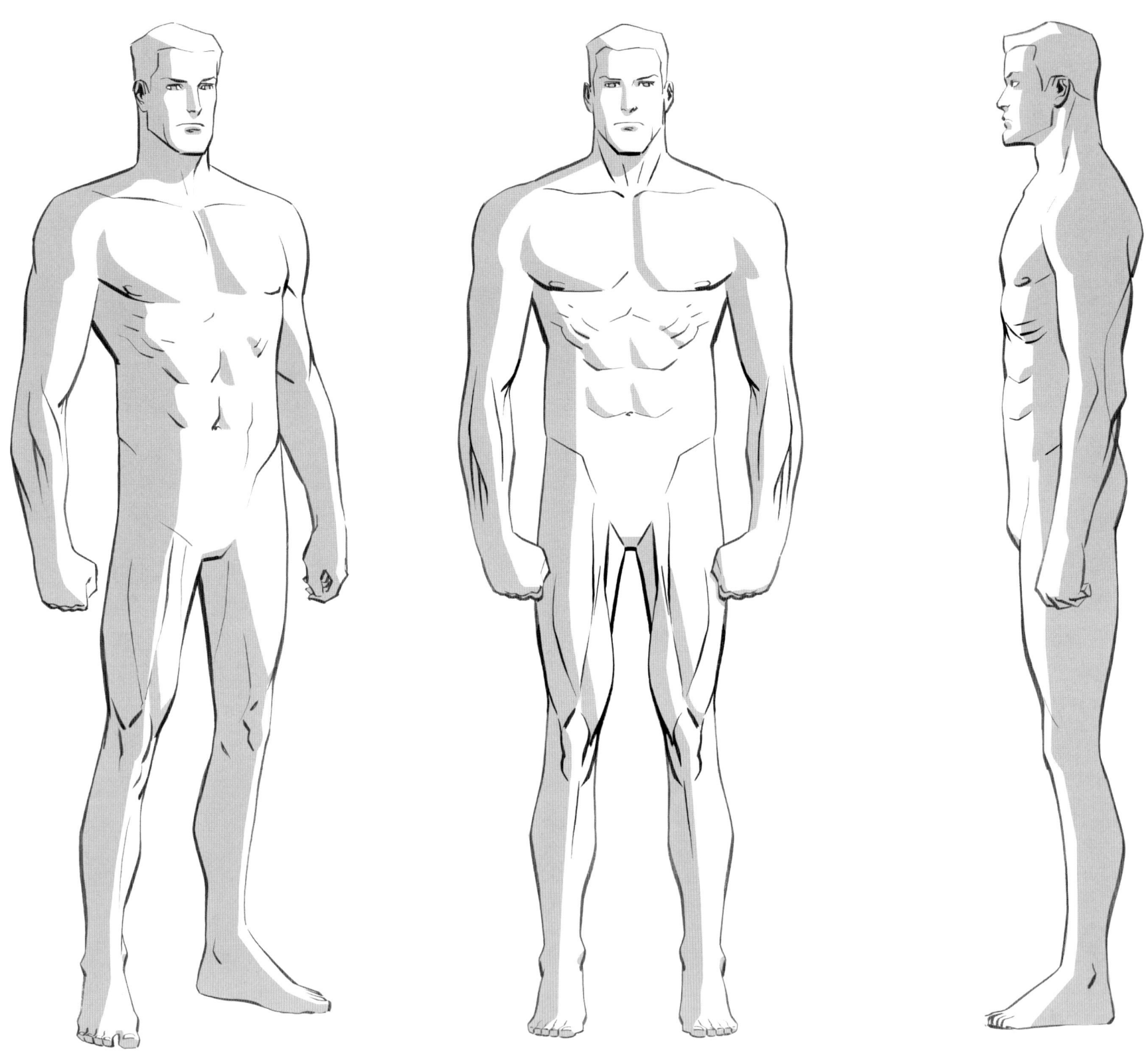

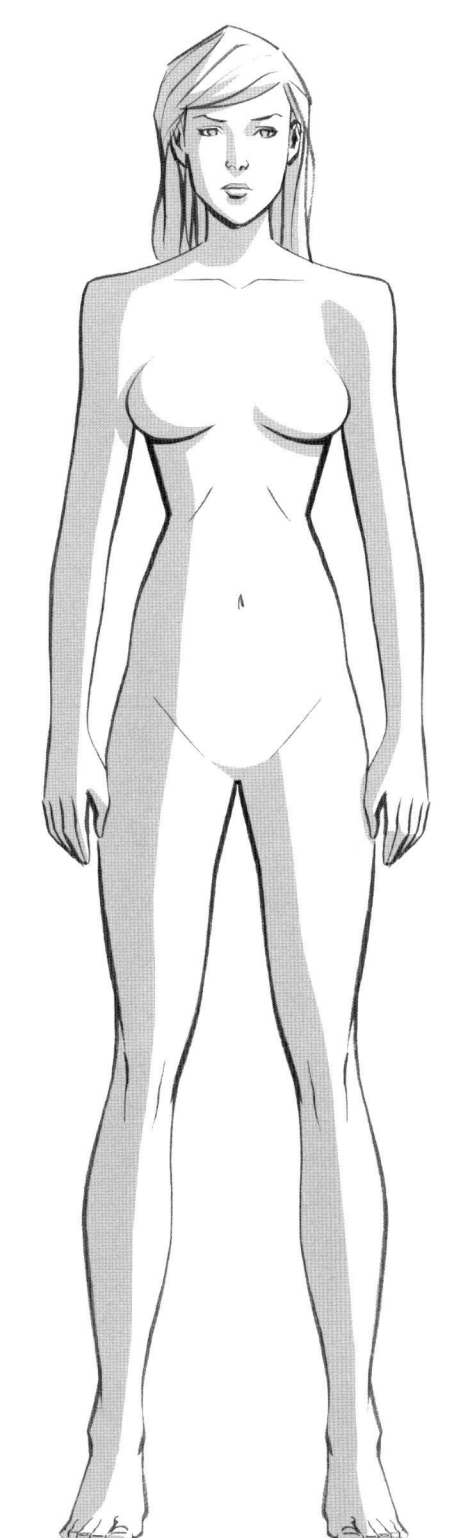
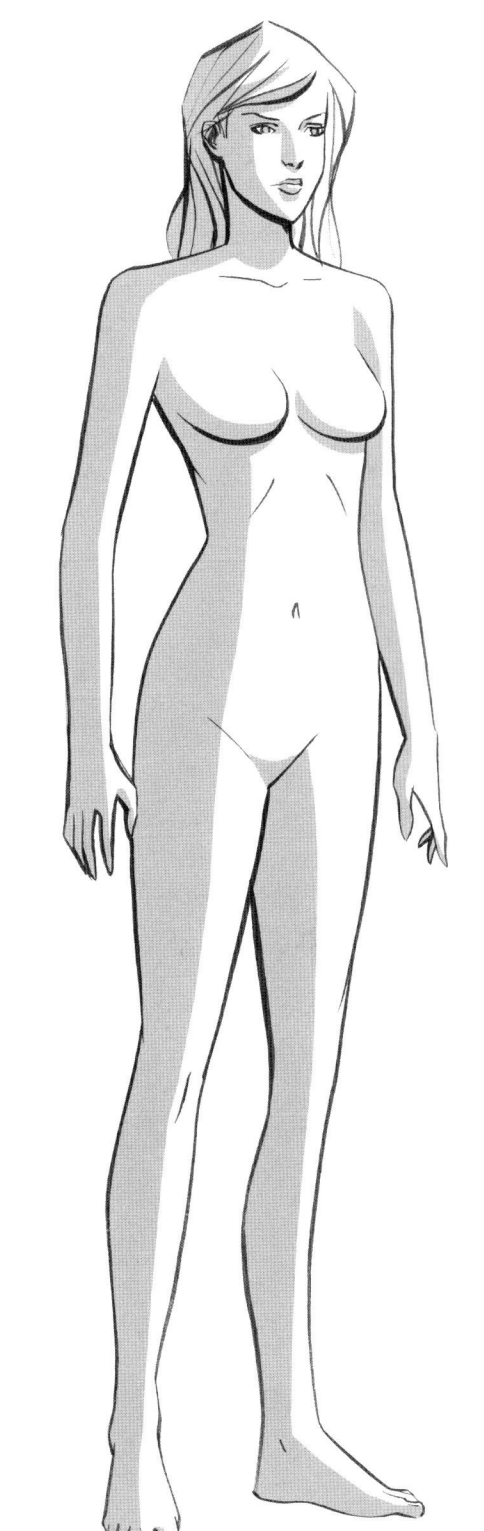

MARCIO TAKARA

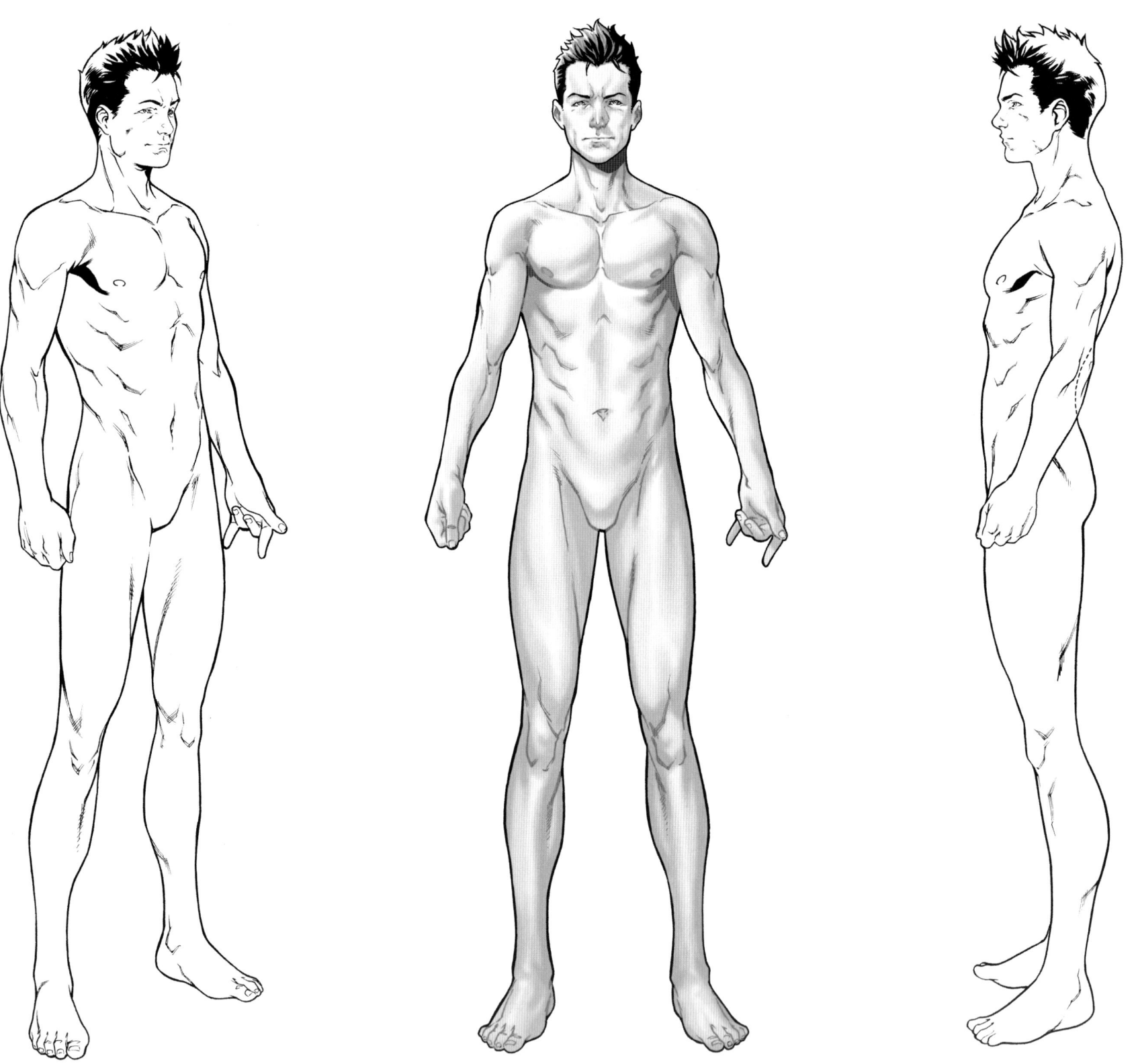

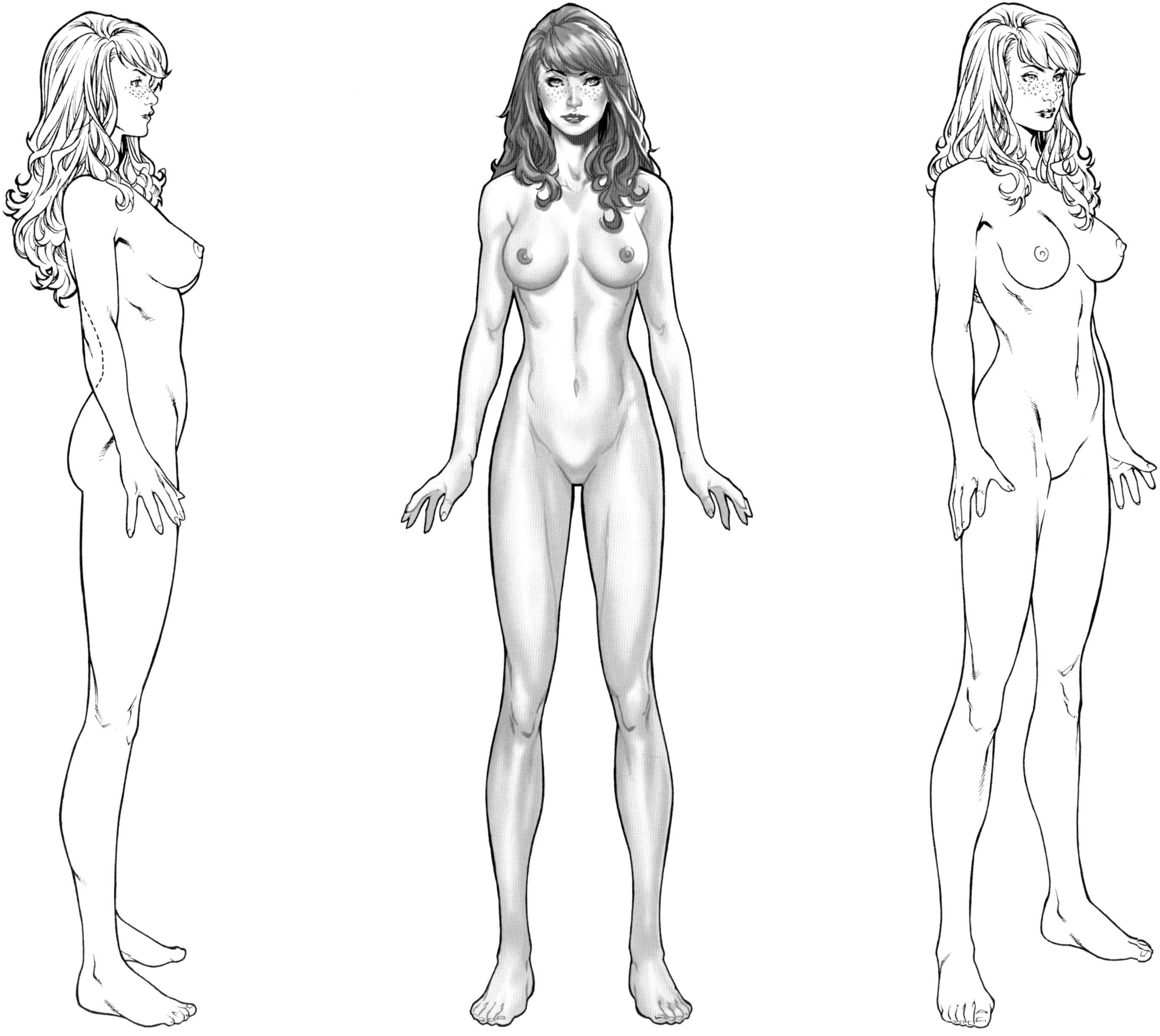

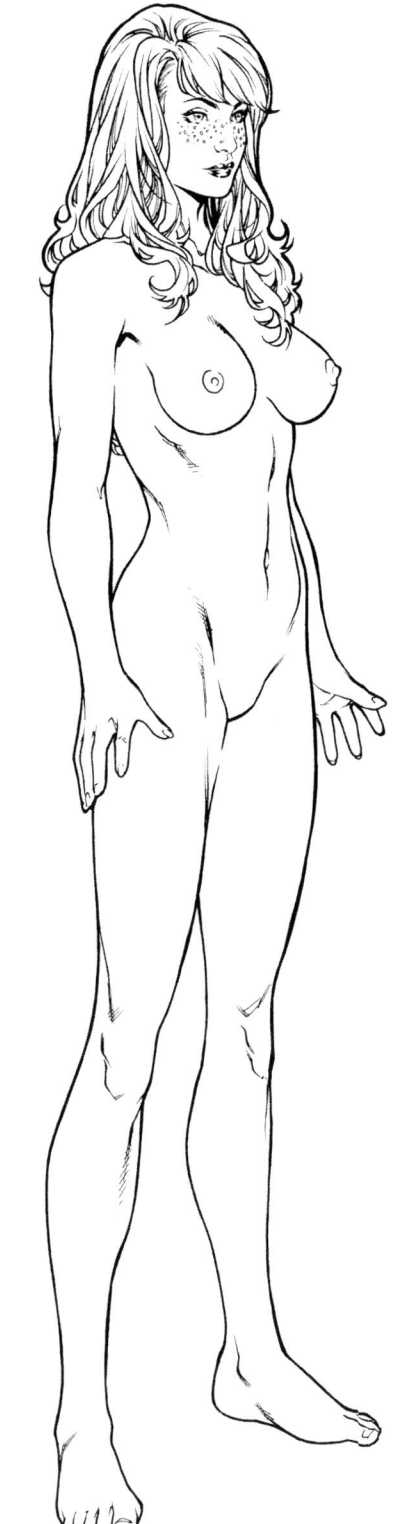

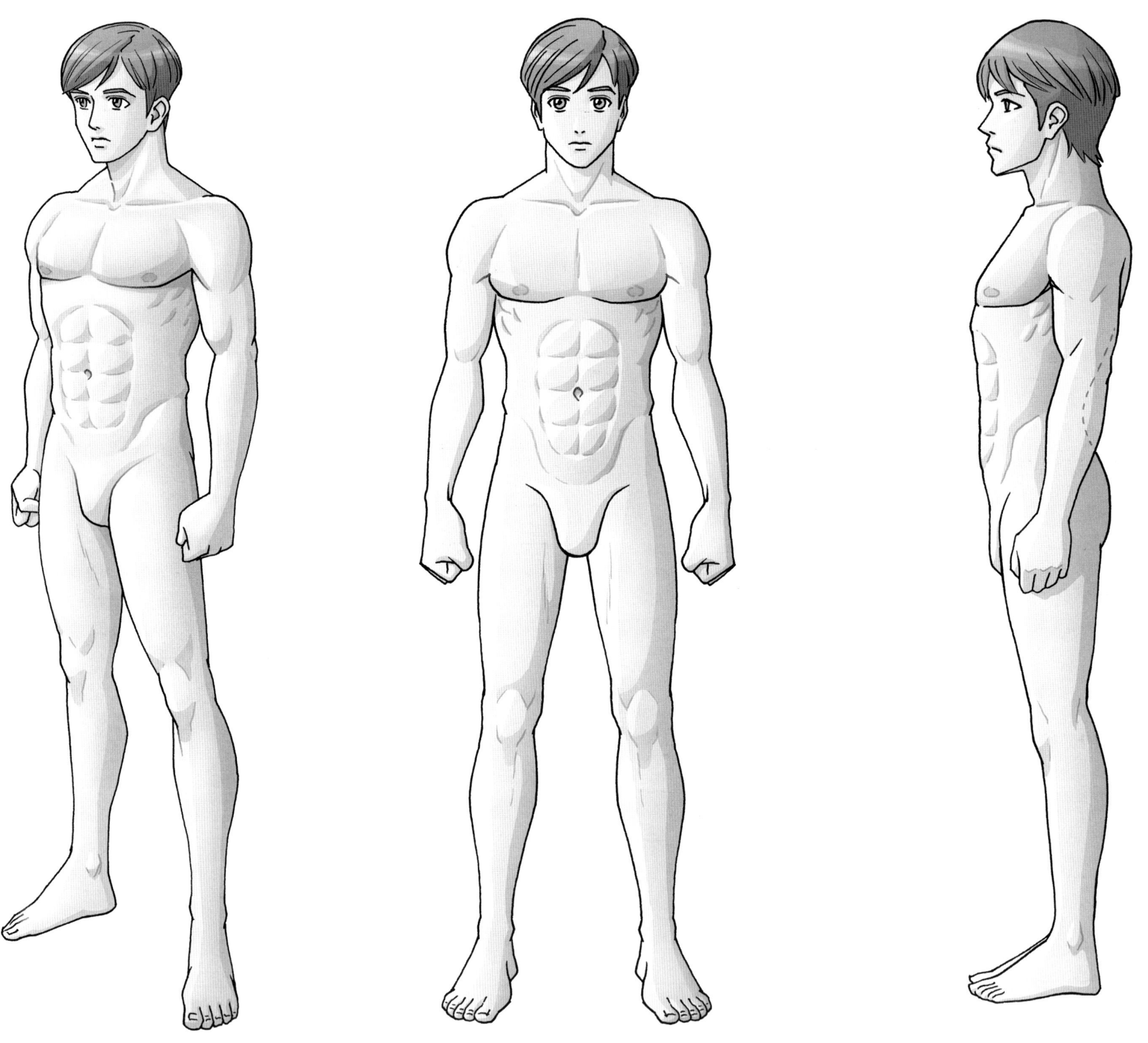

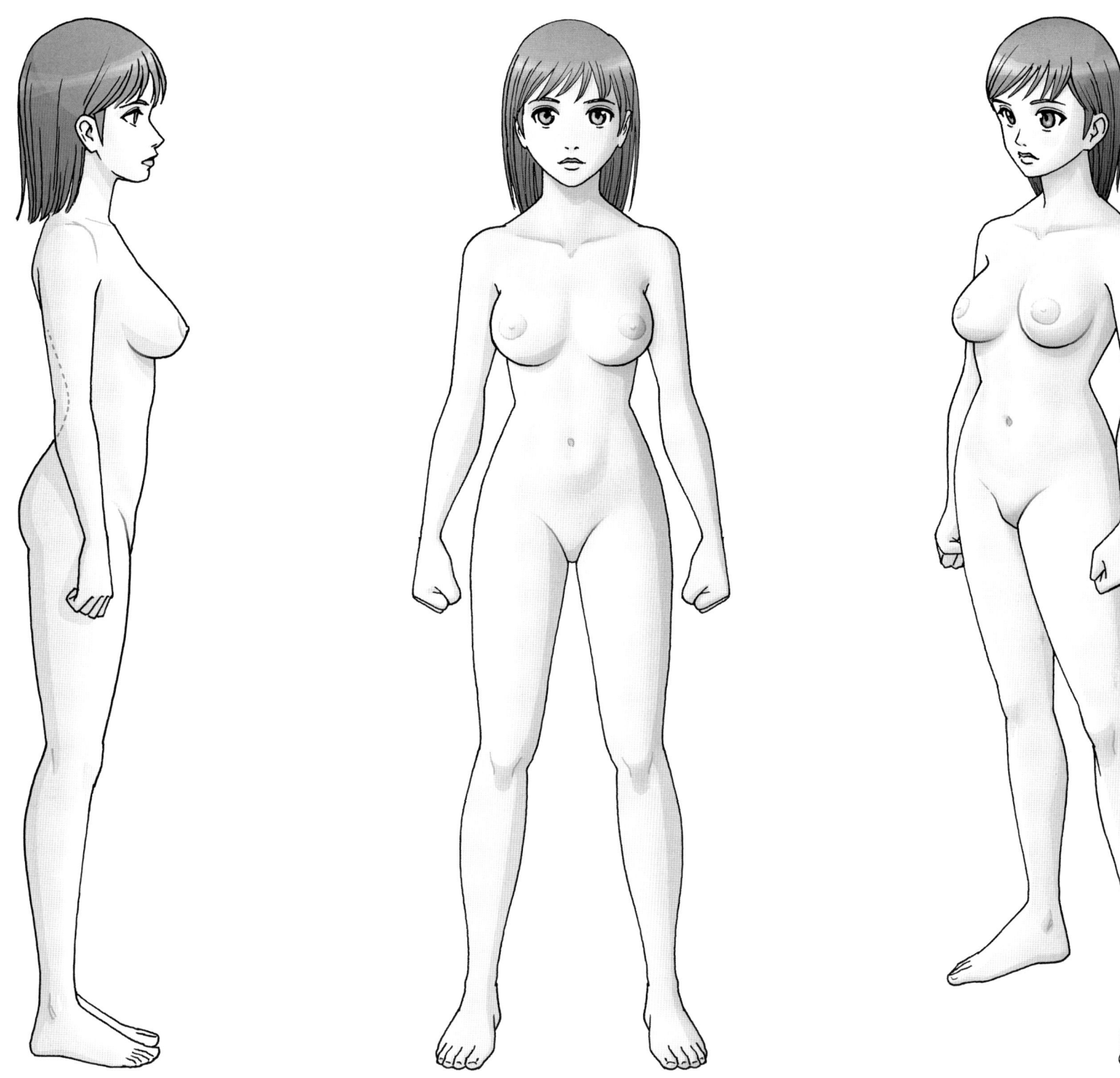

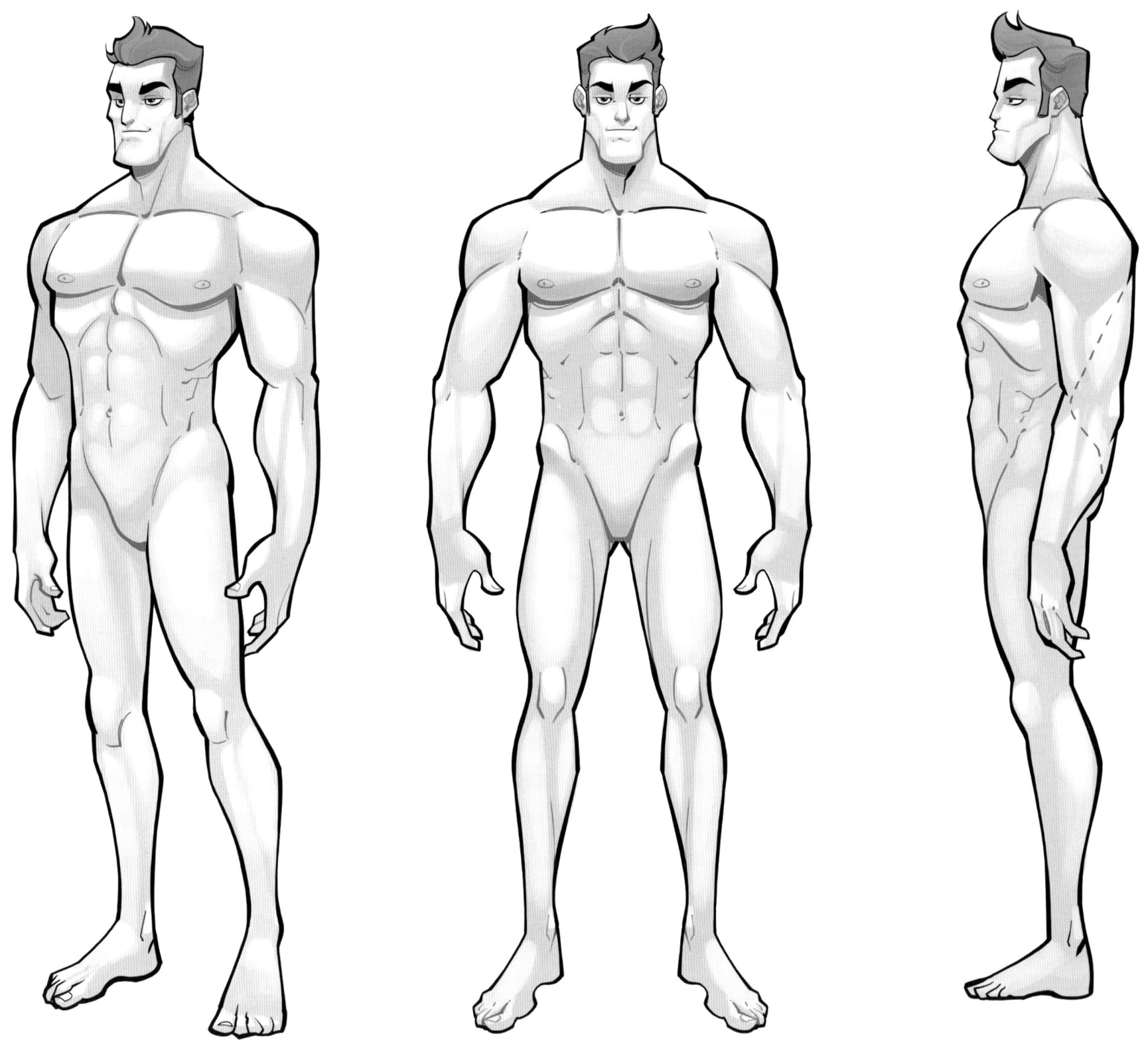

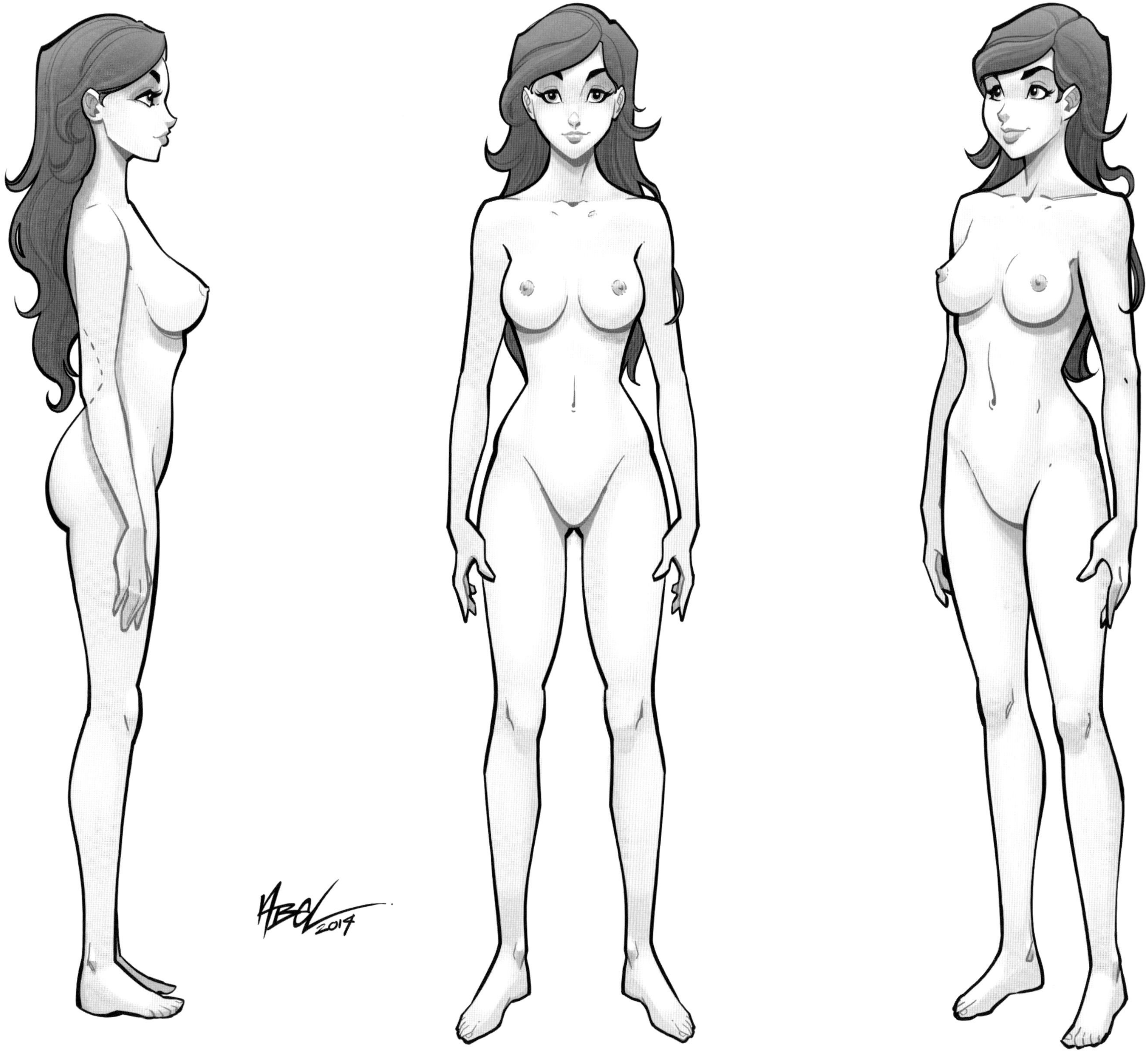

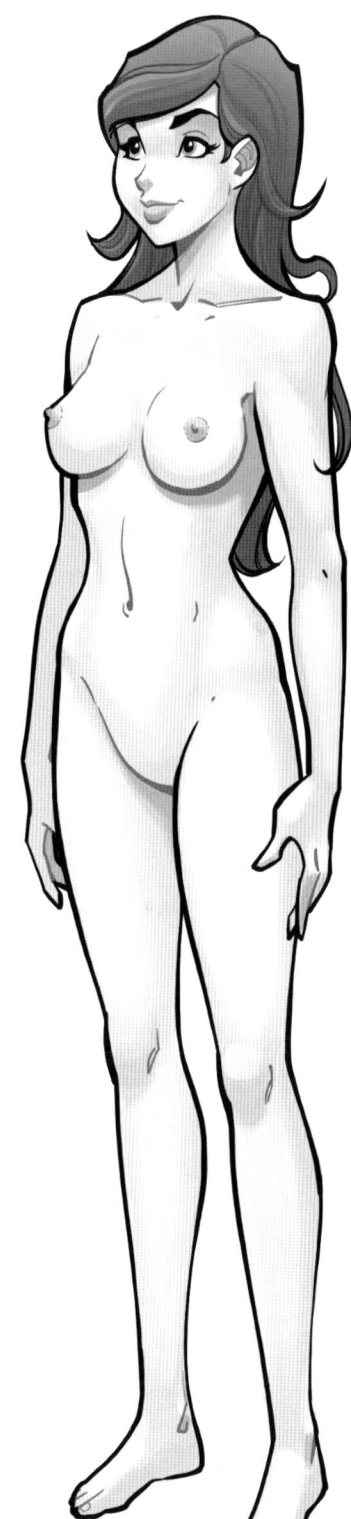

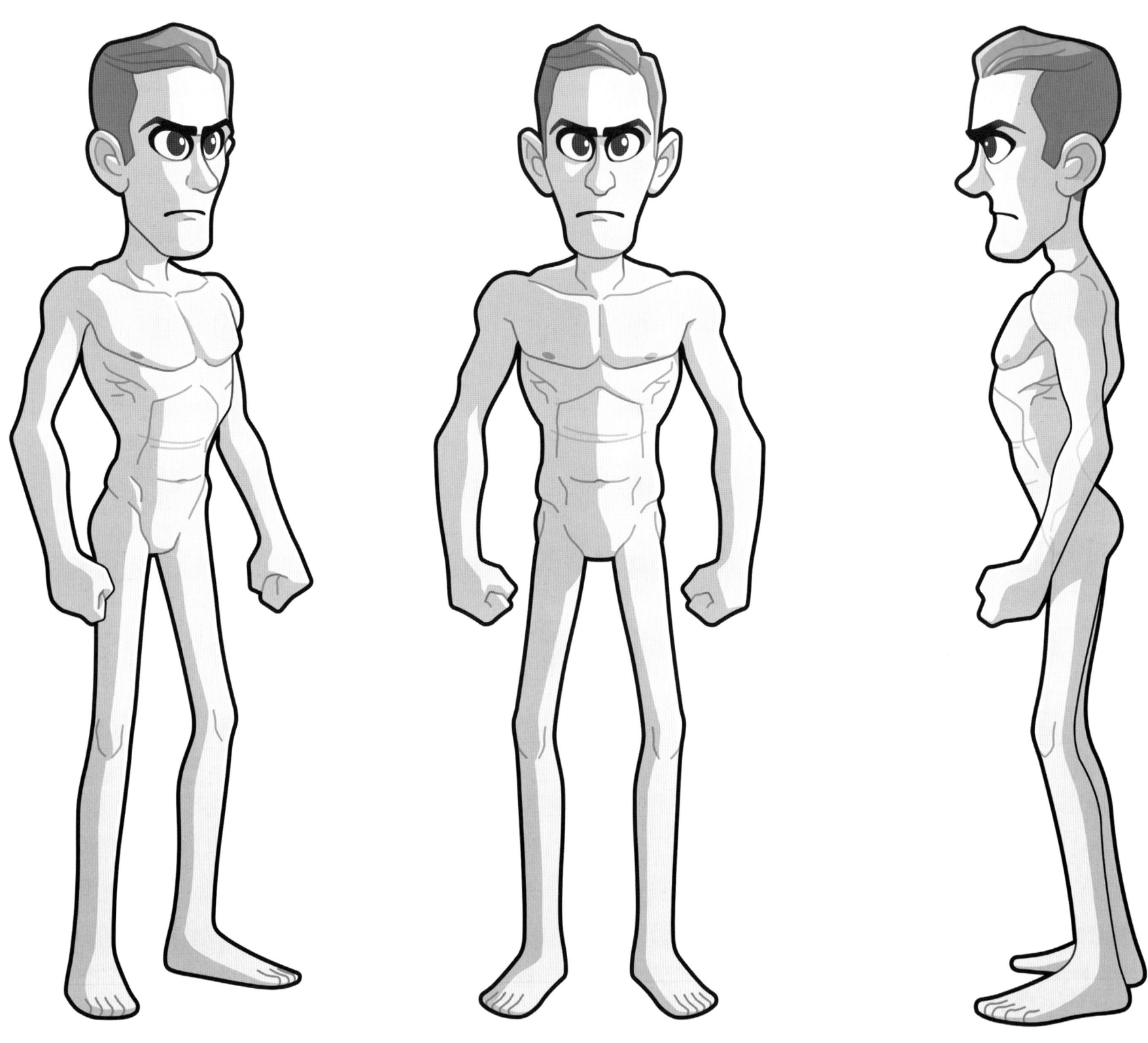

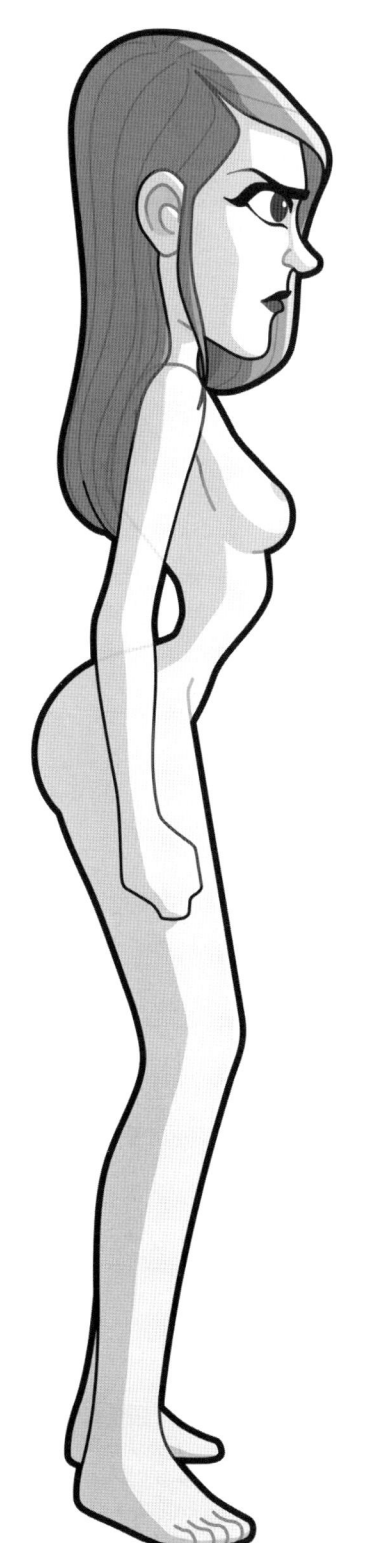
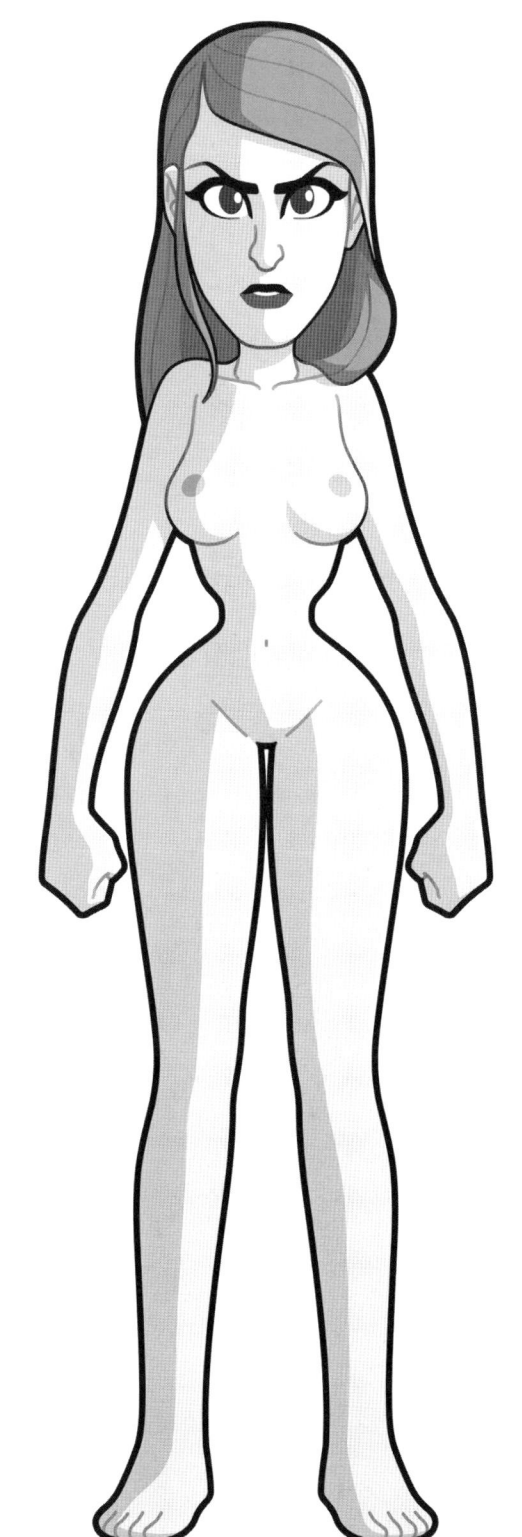
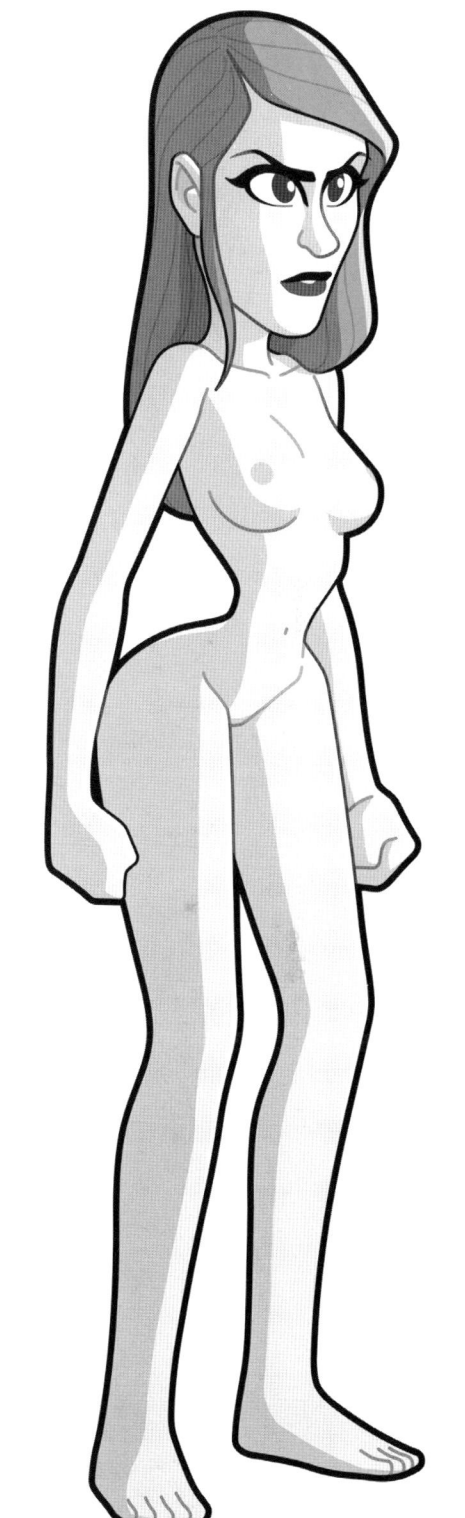

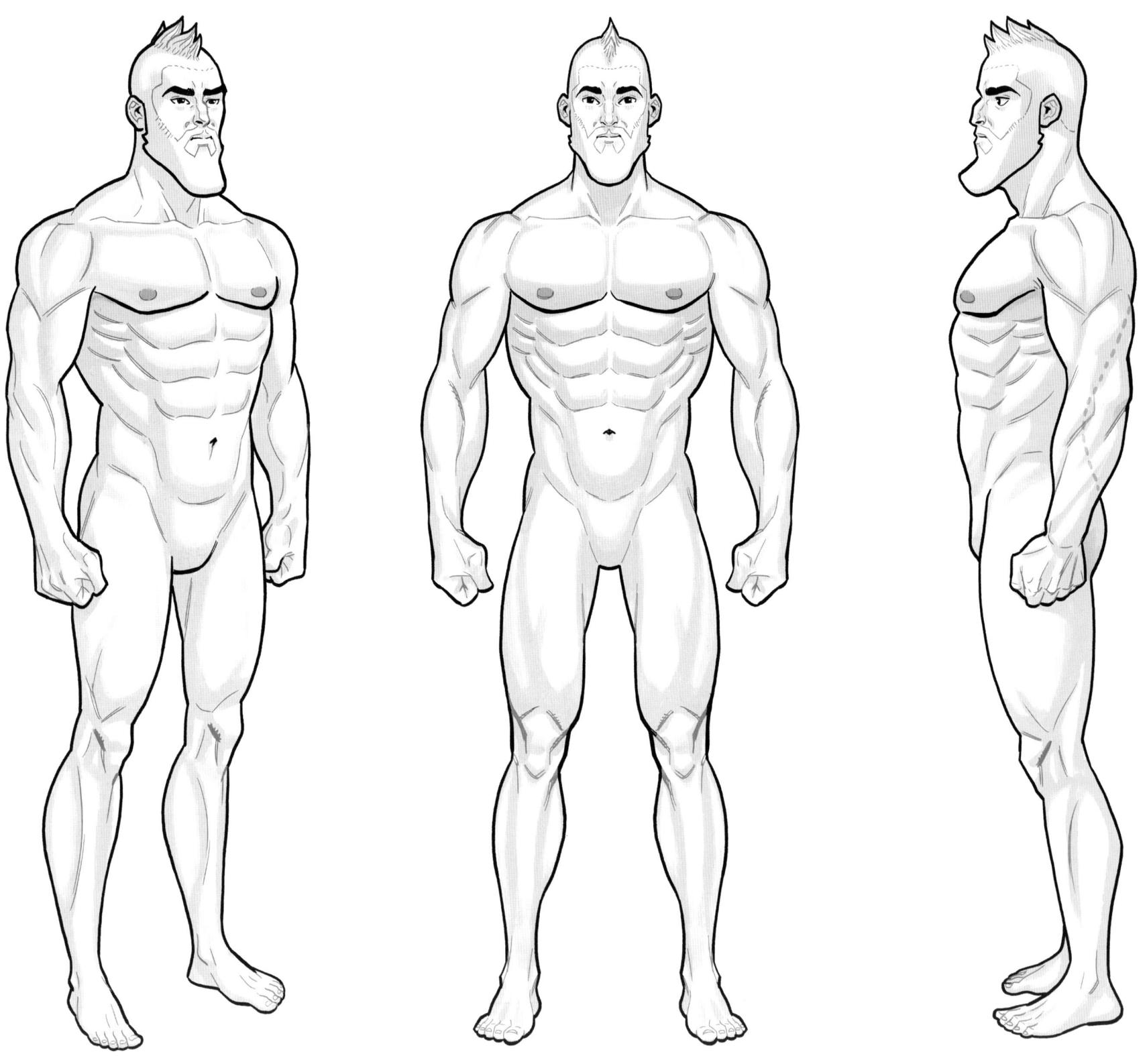

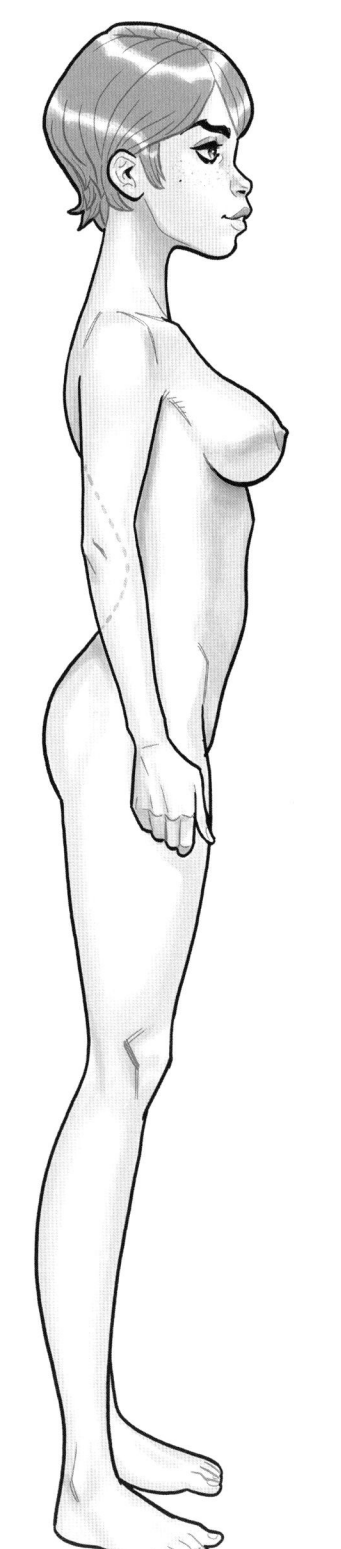
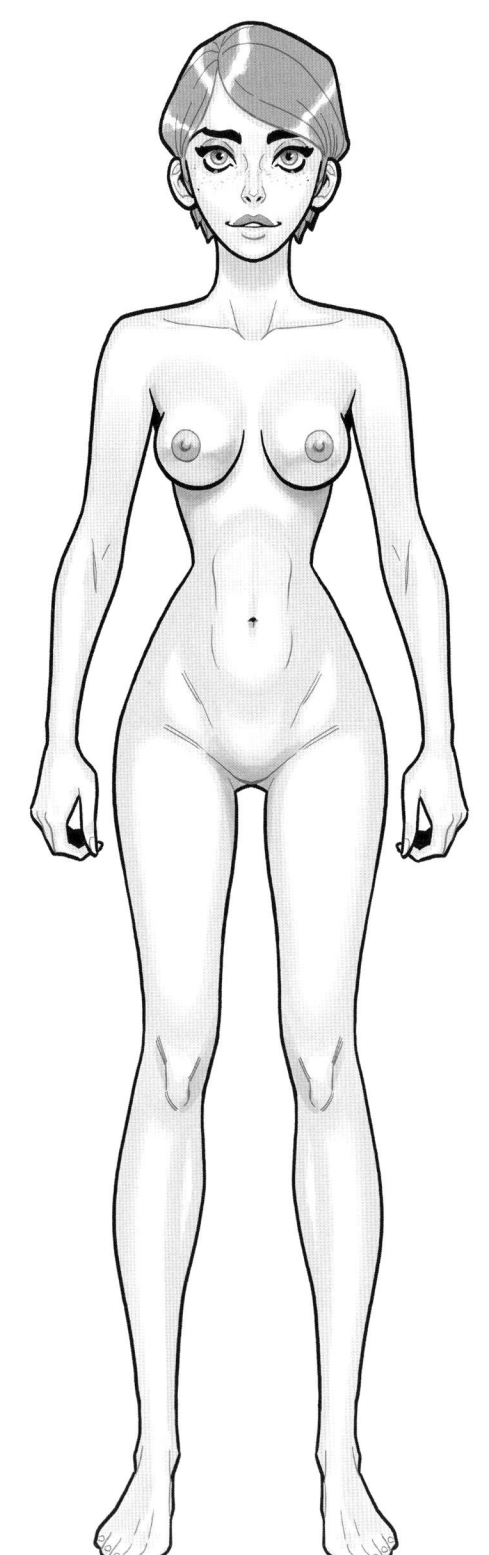
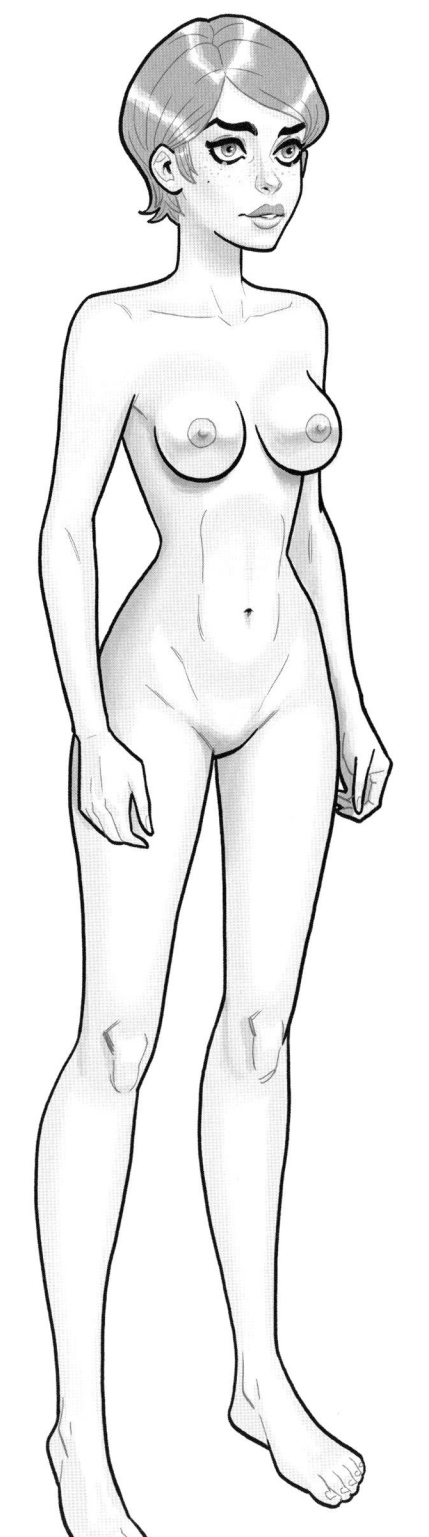

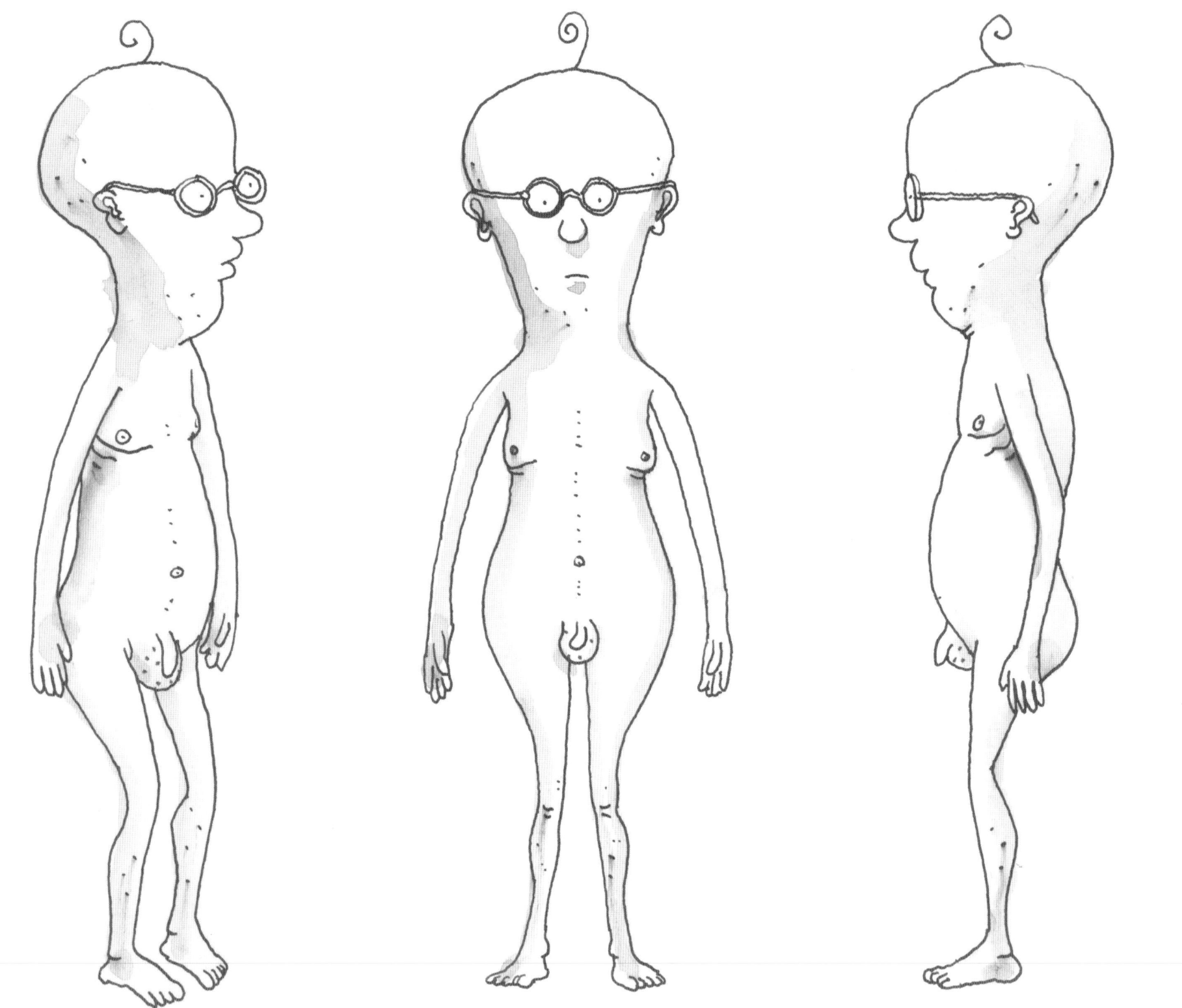

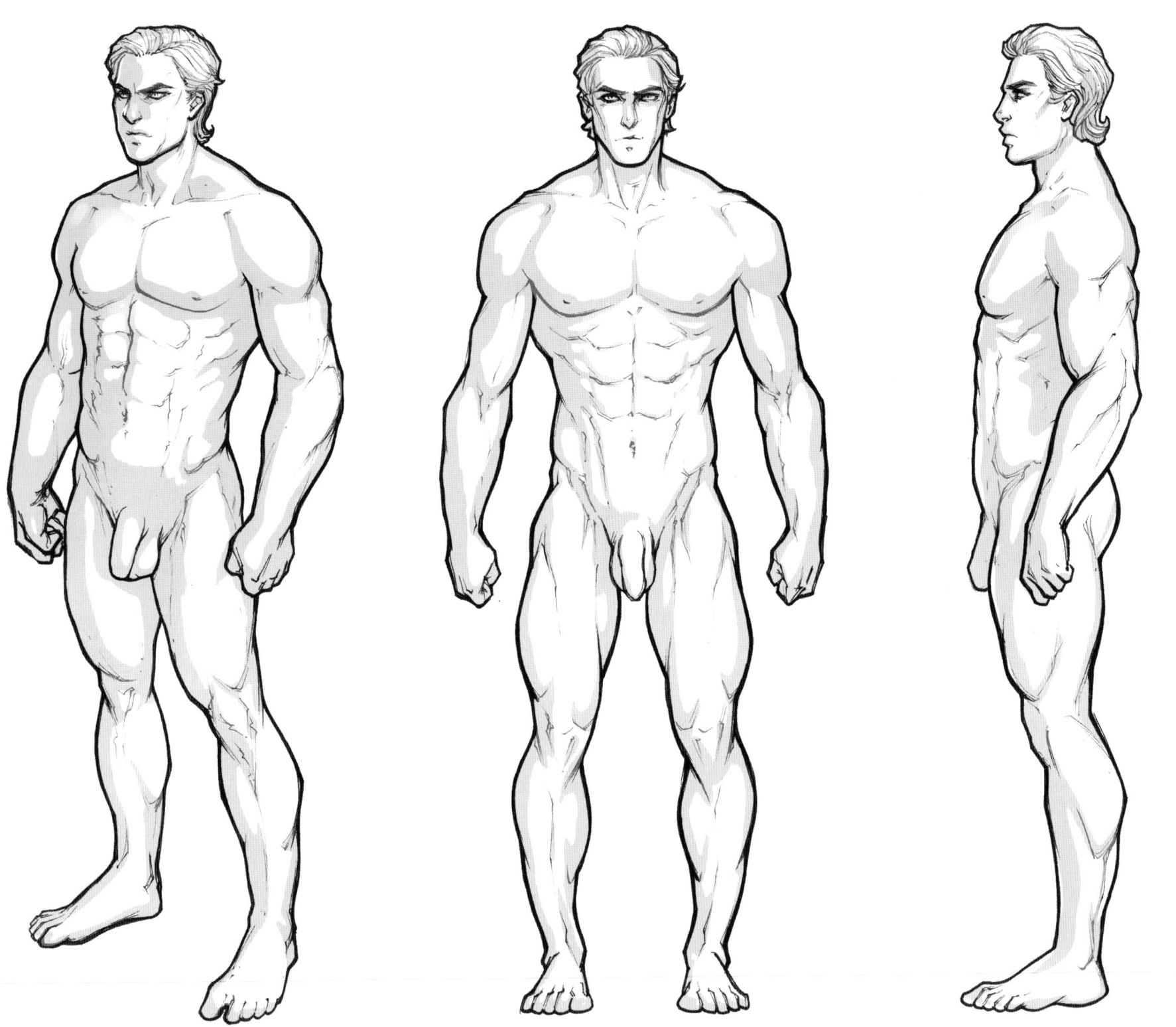

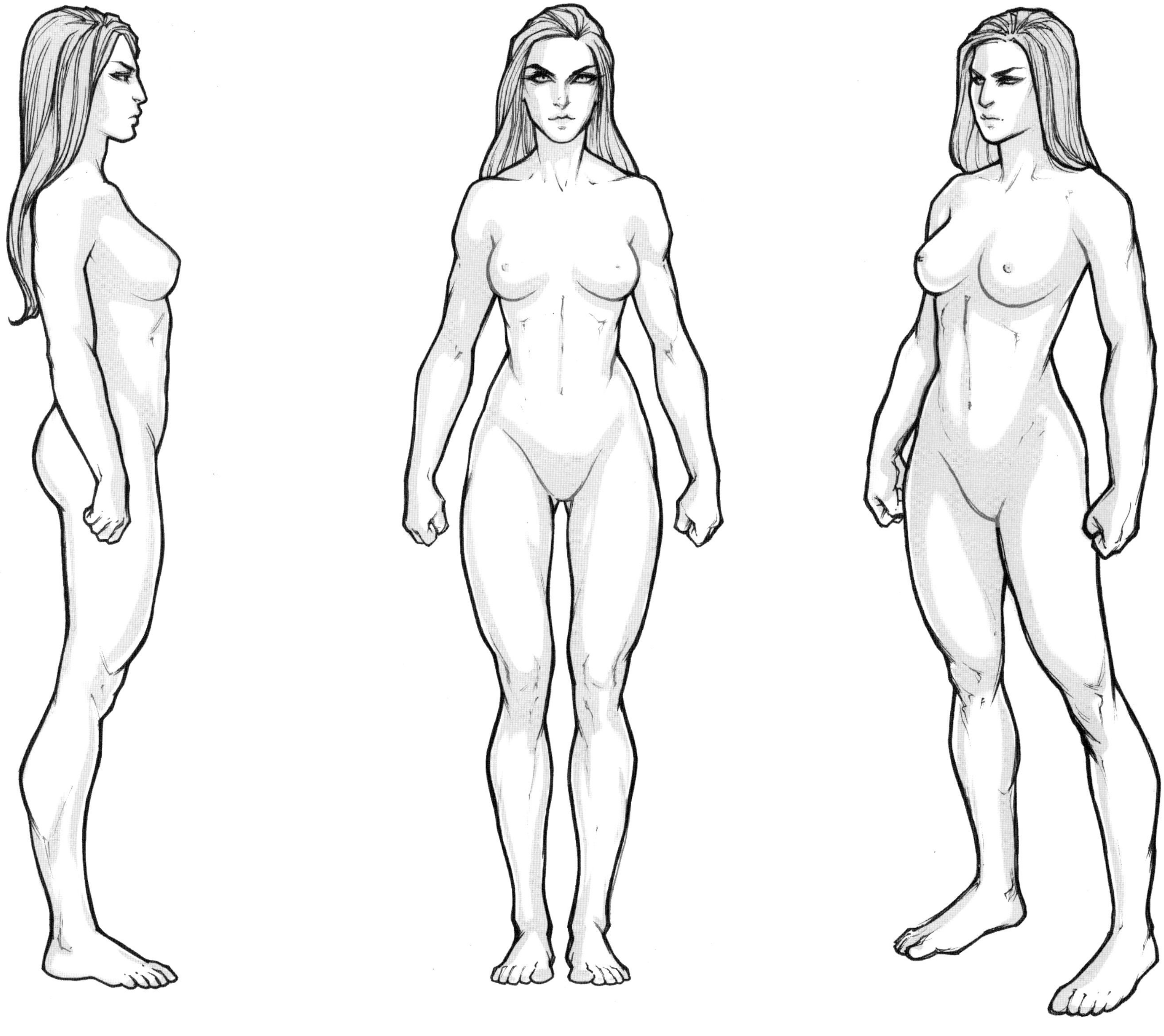

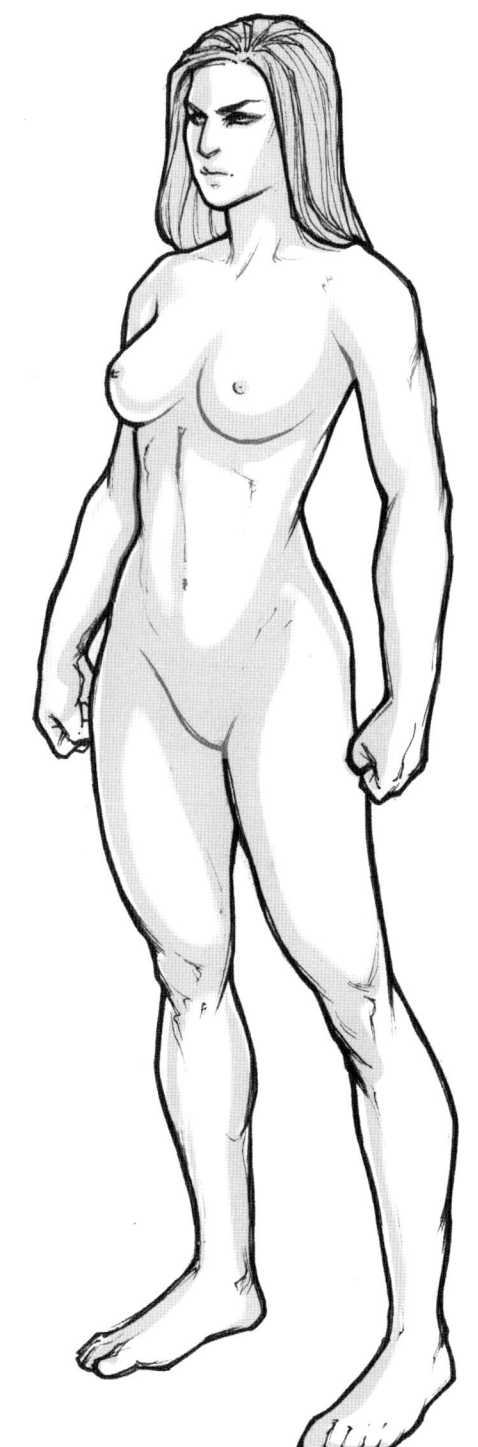

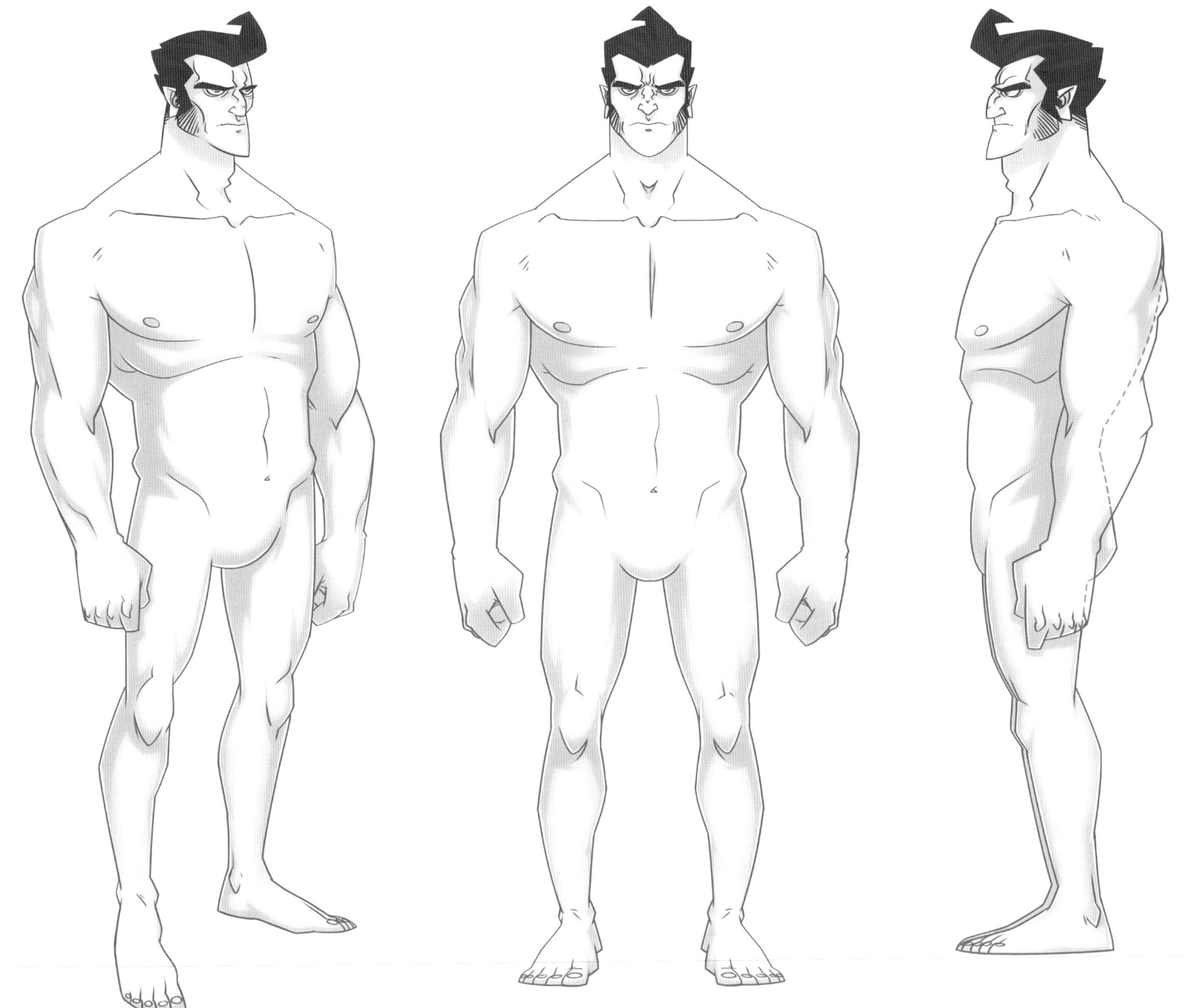

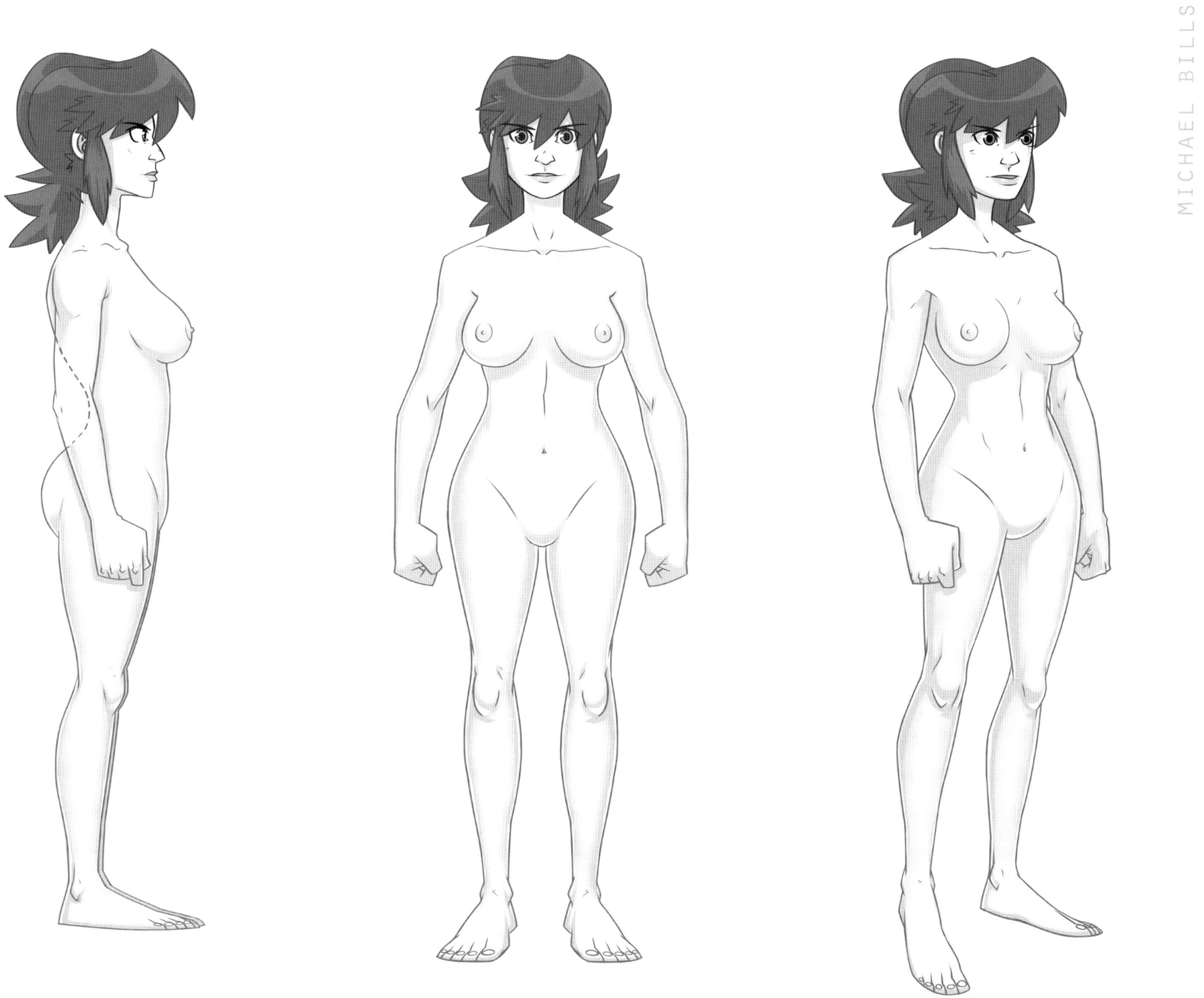

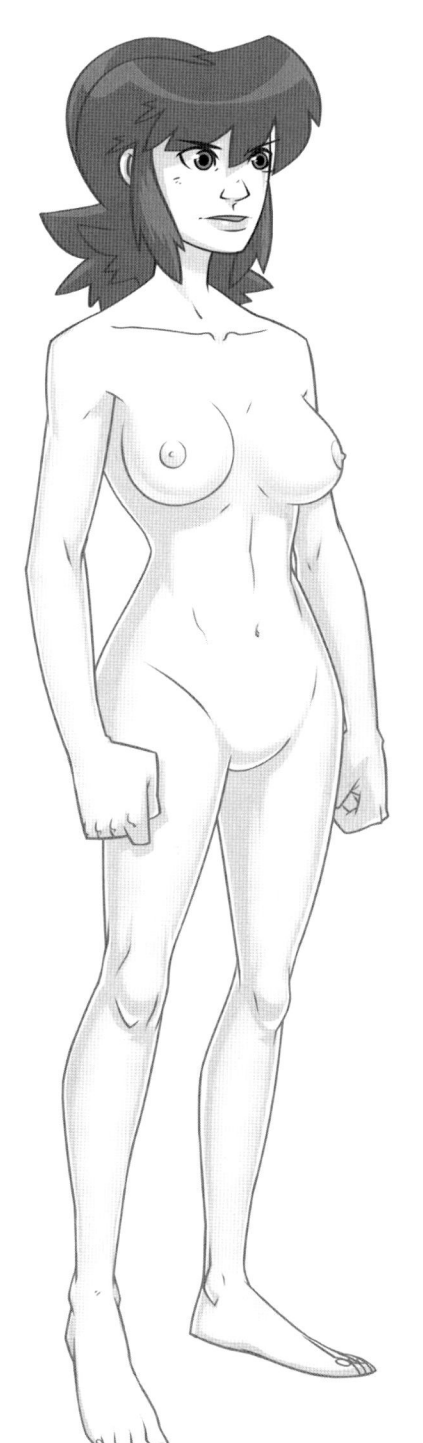

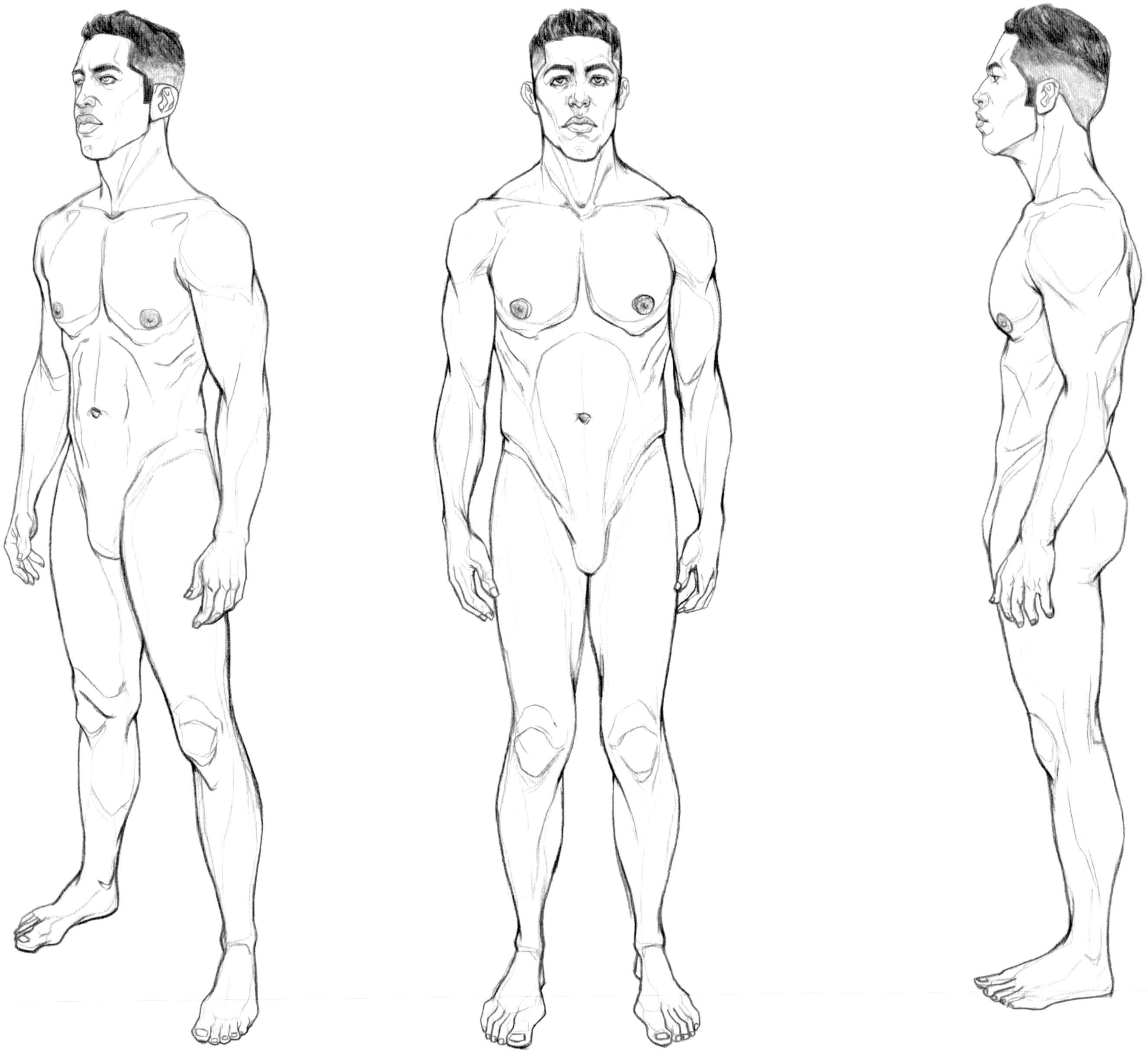

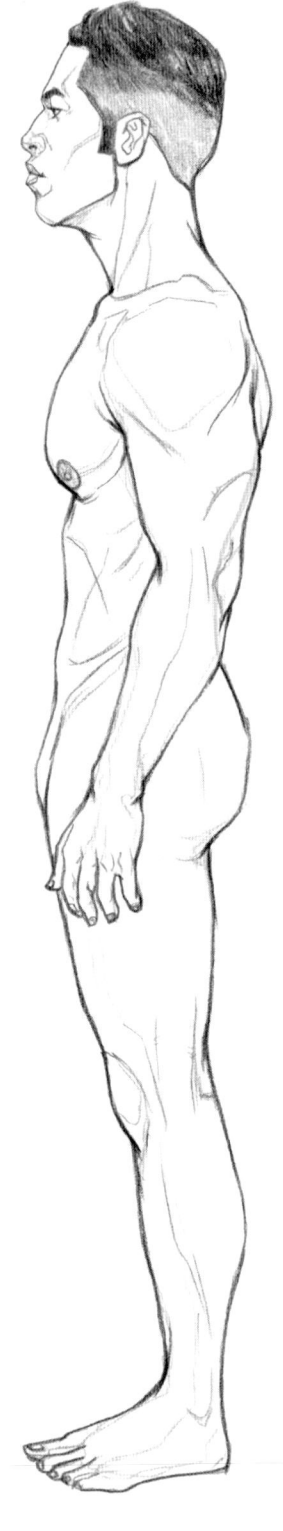

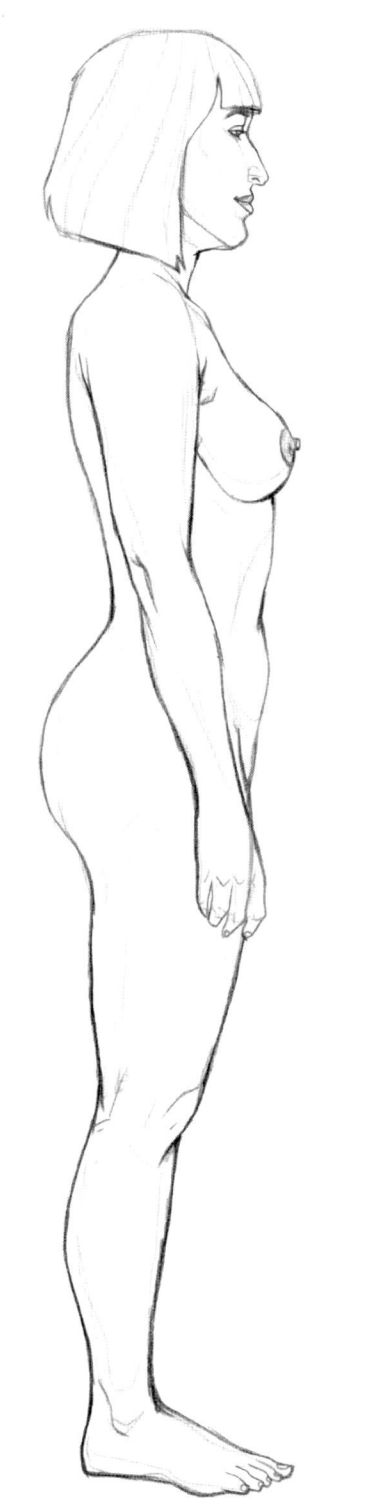
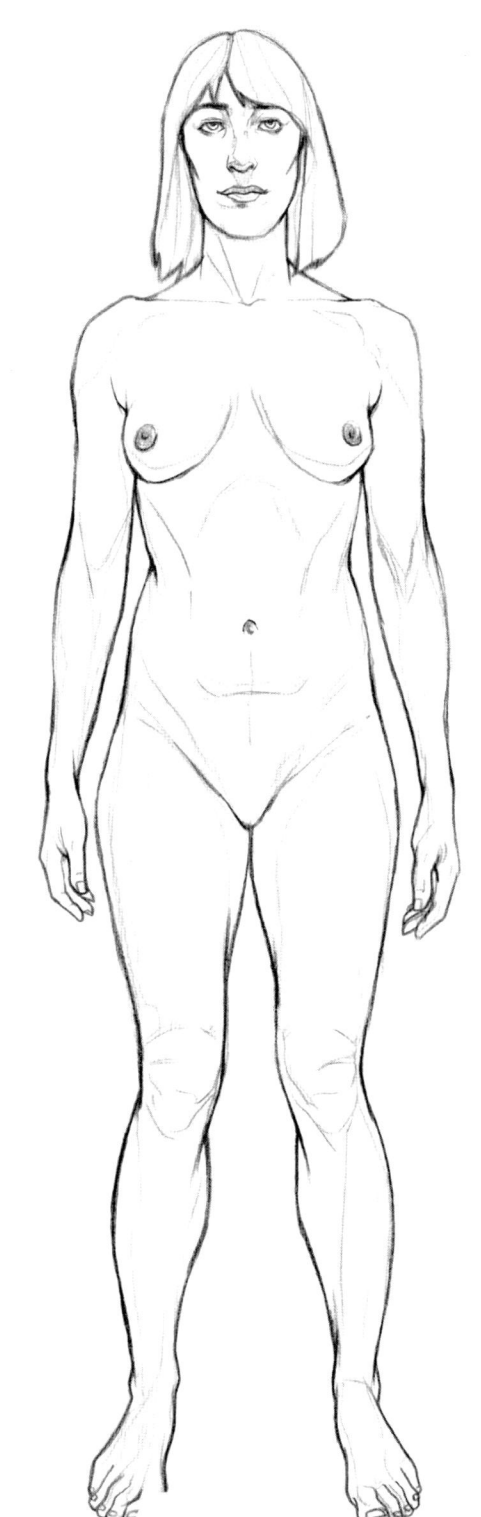
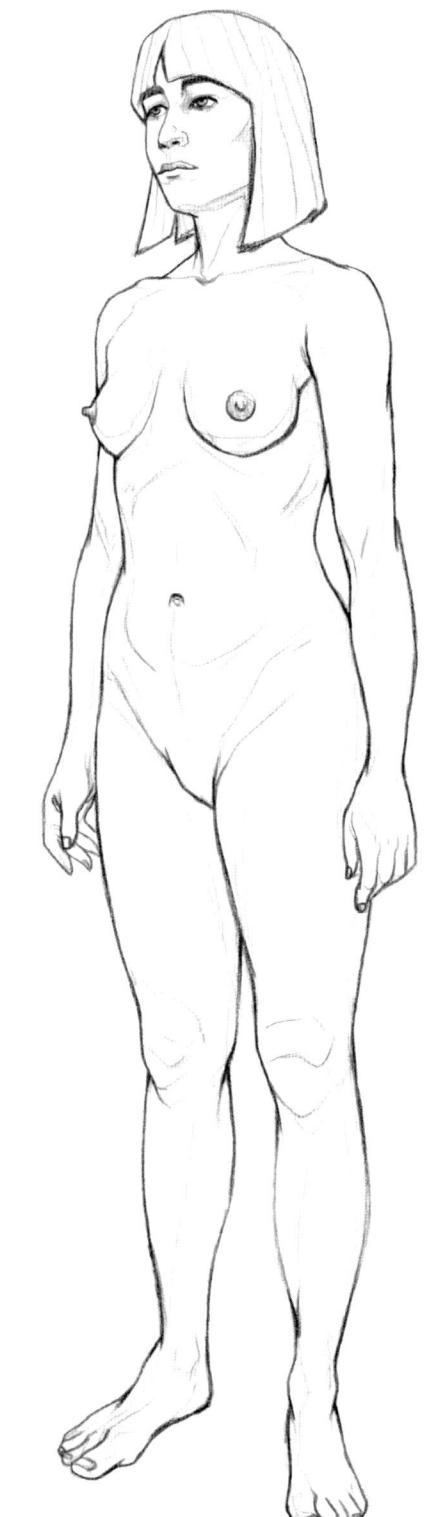

MICHAEL BUFFINGTON JR

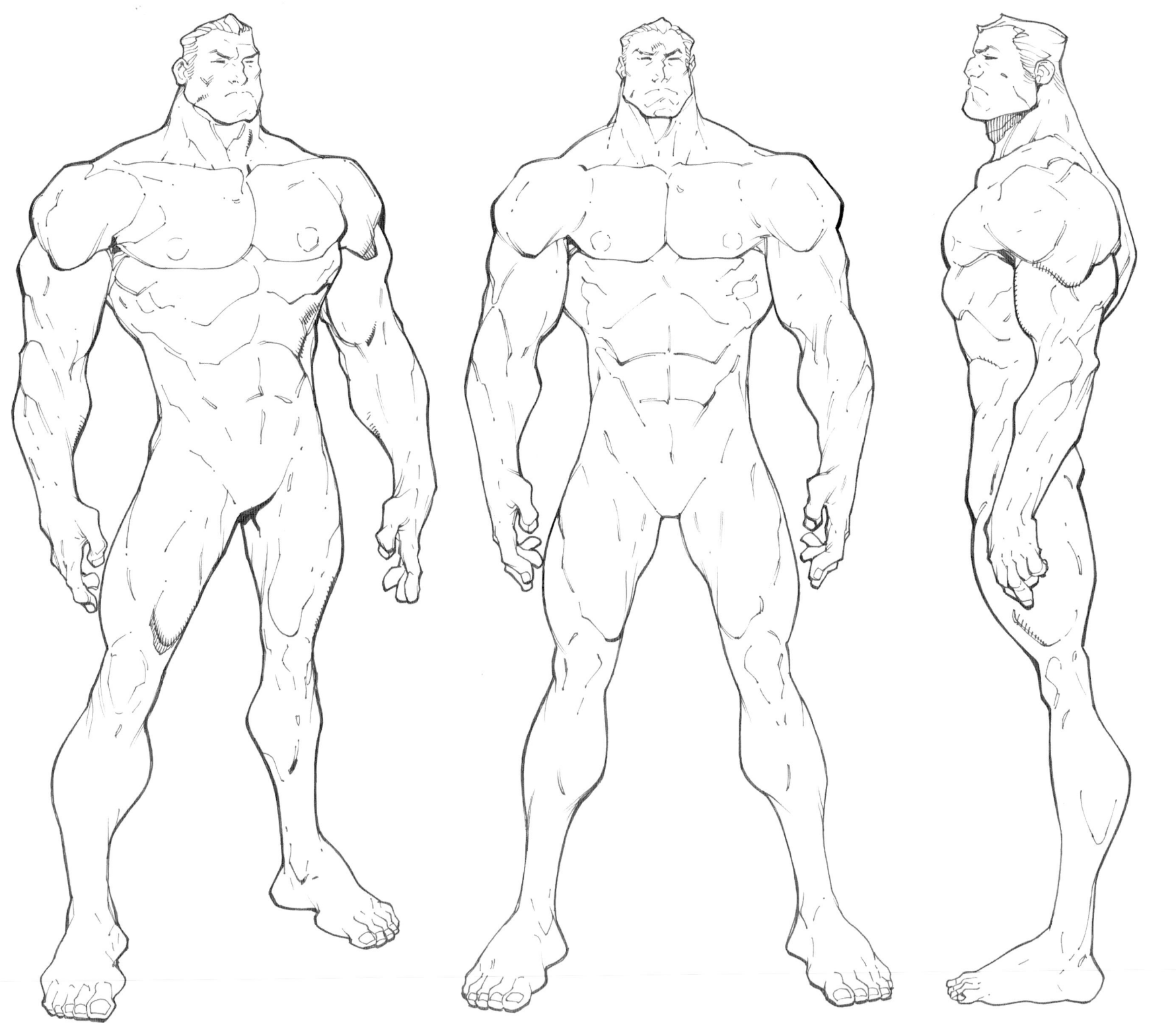

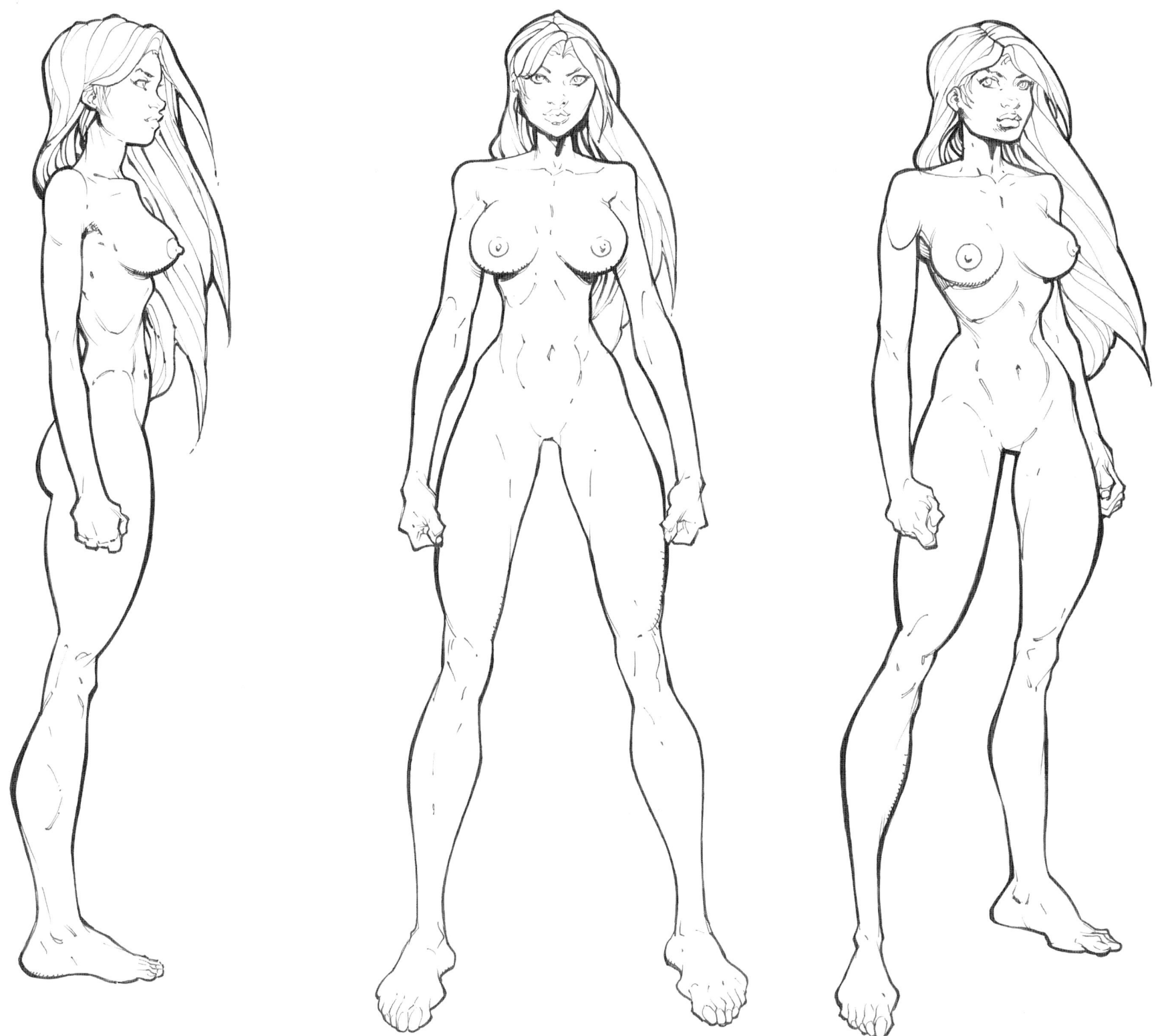

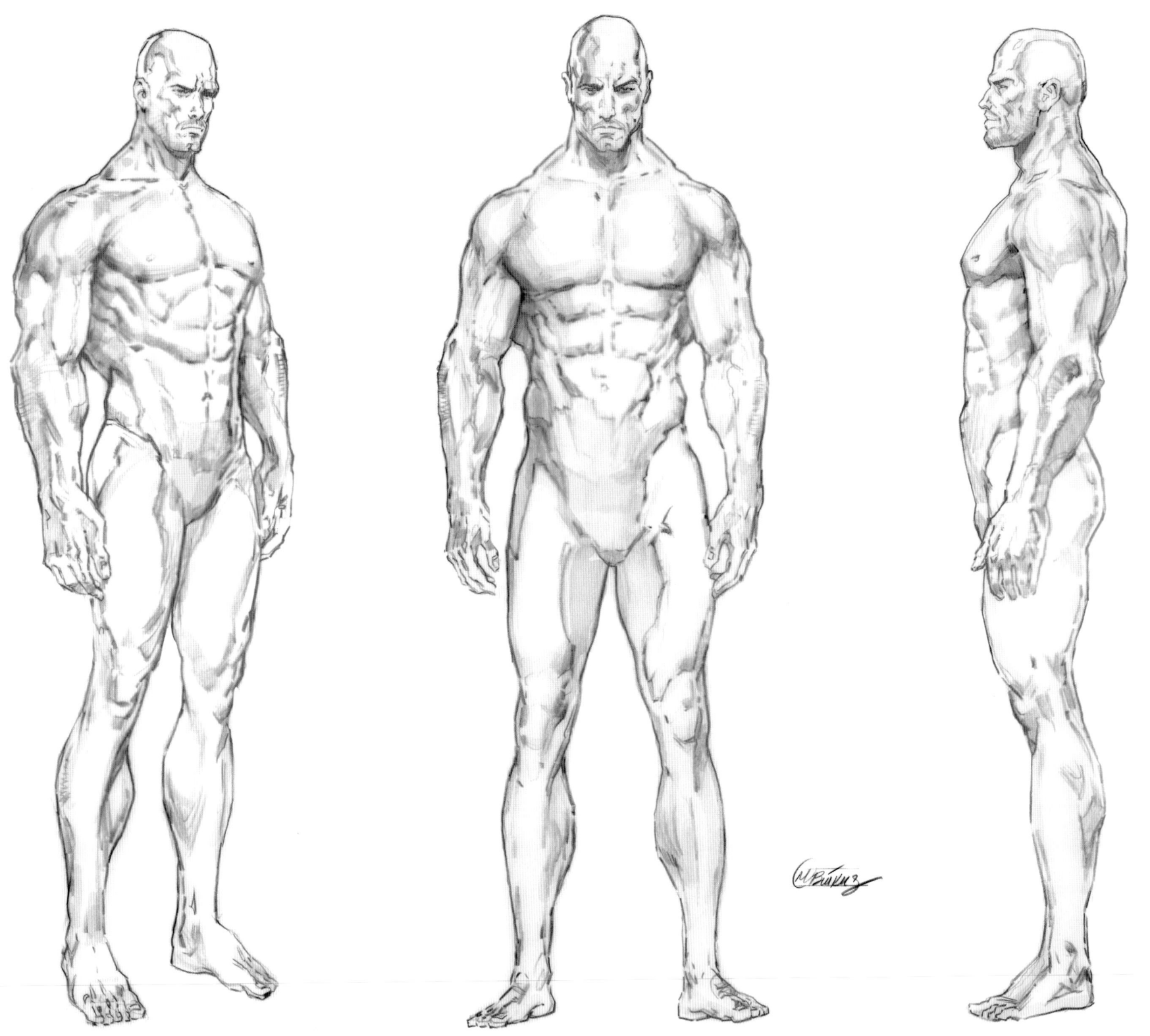

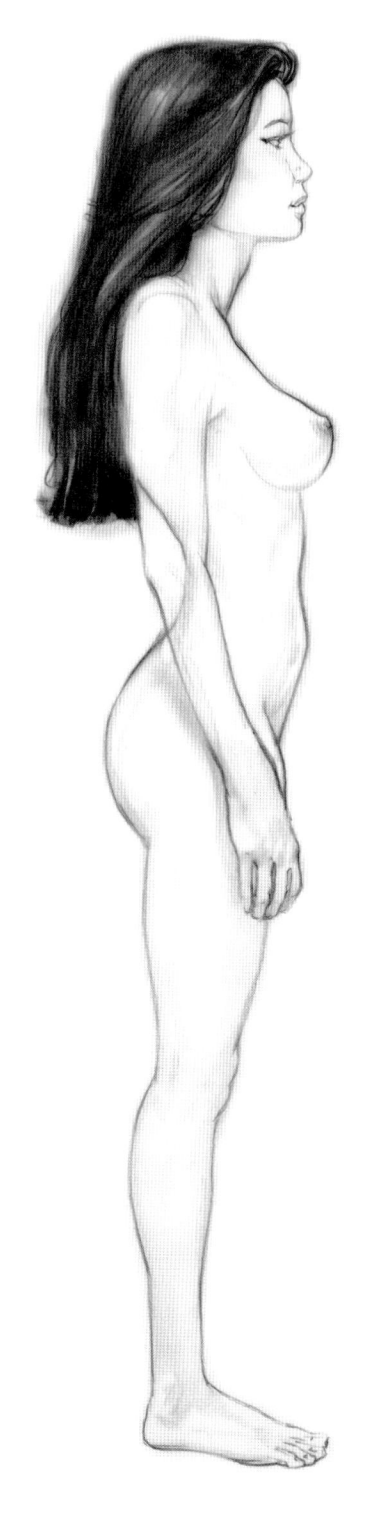
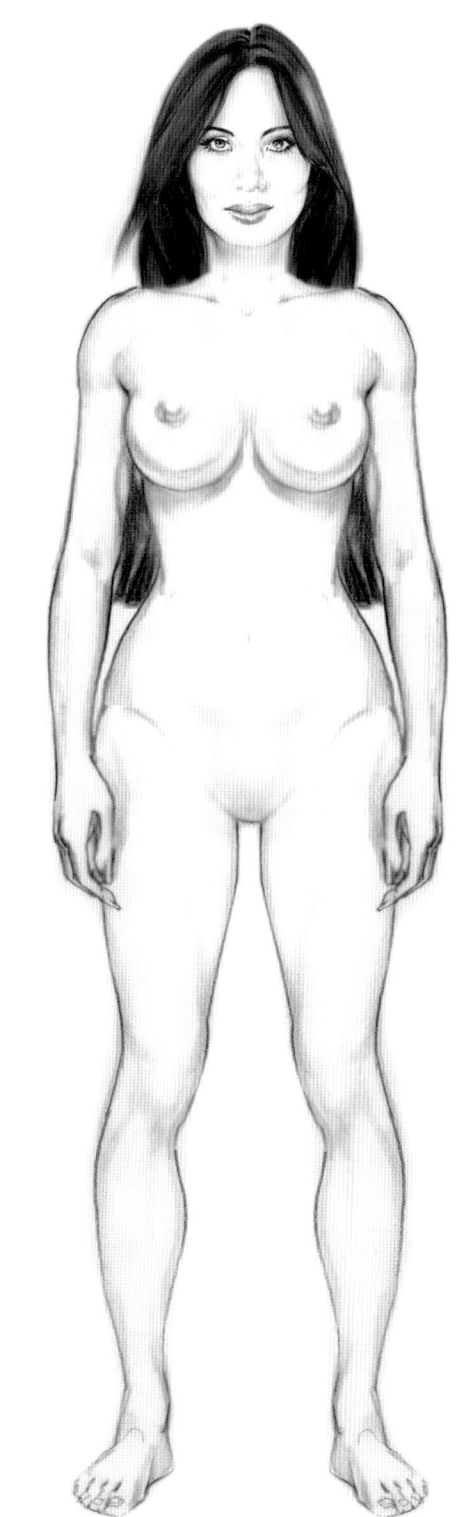
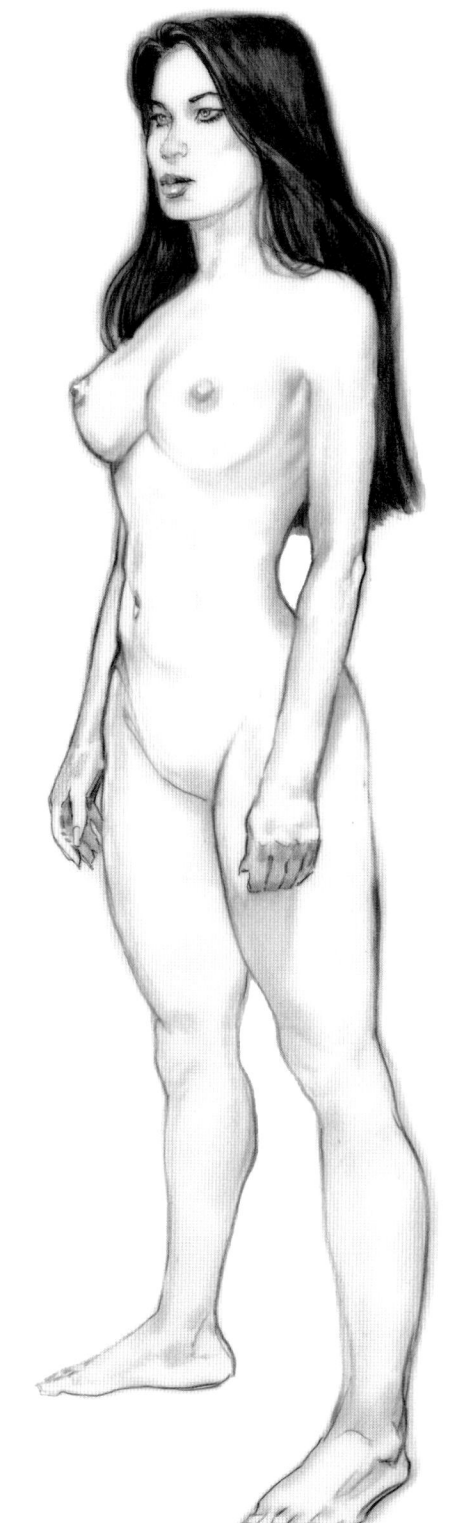

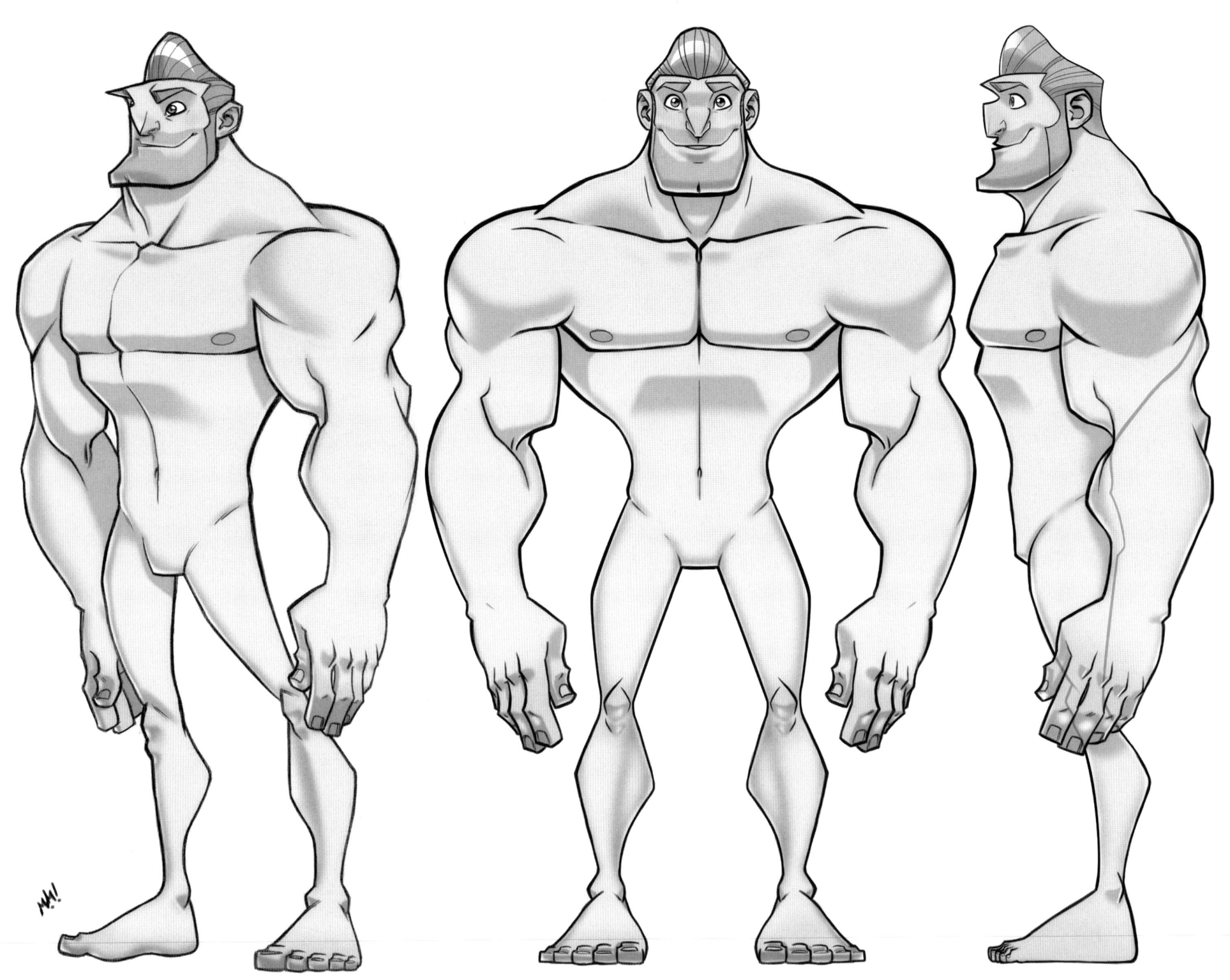

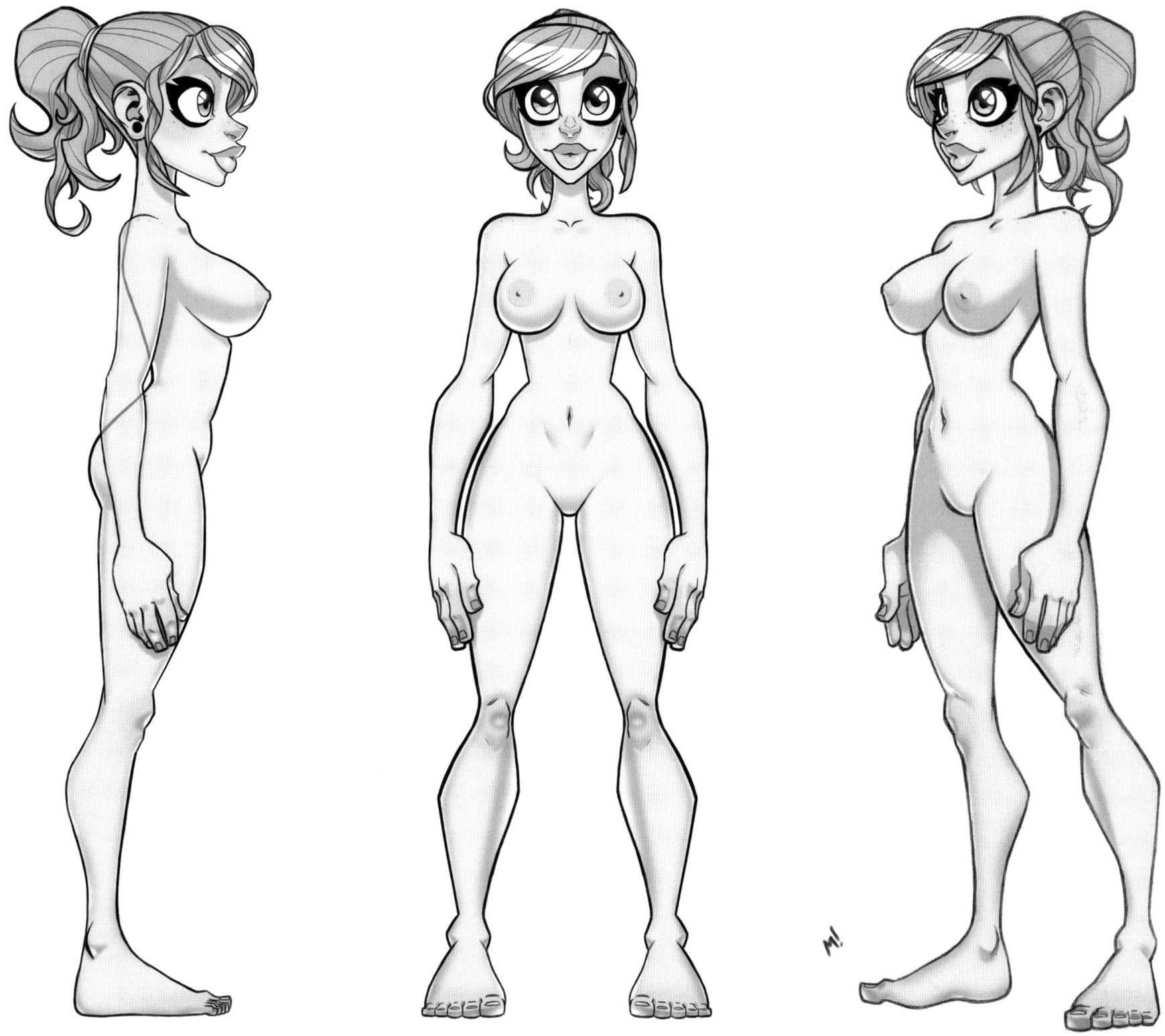

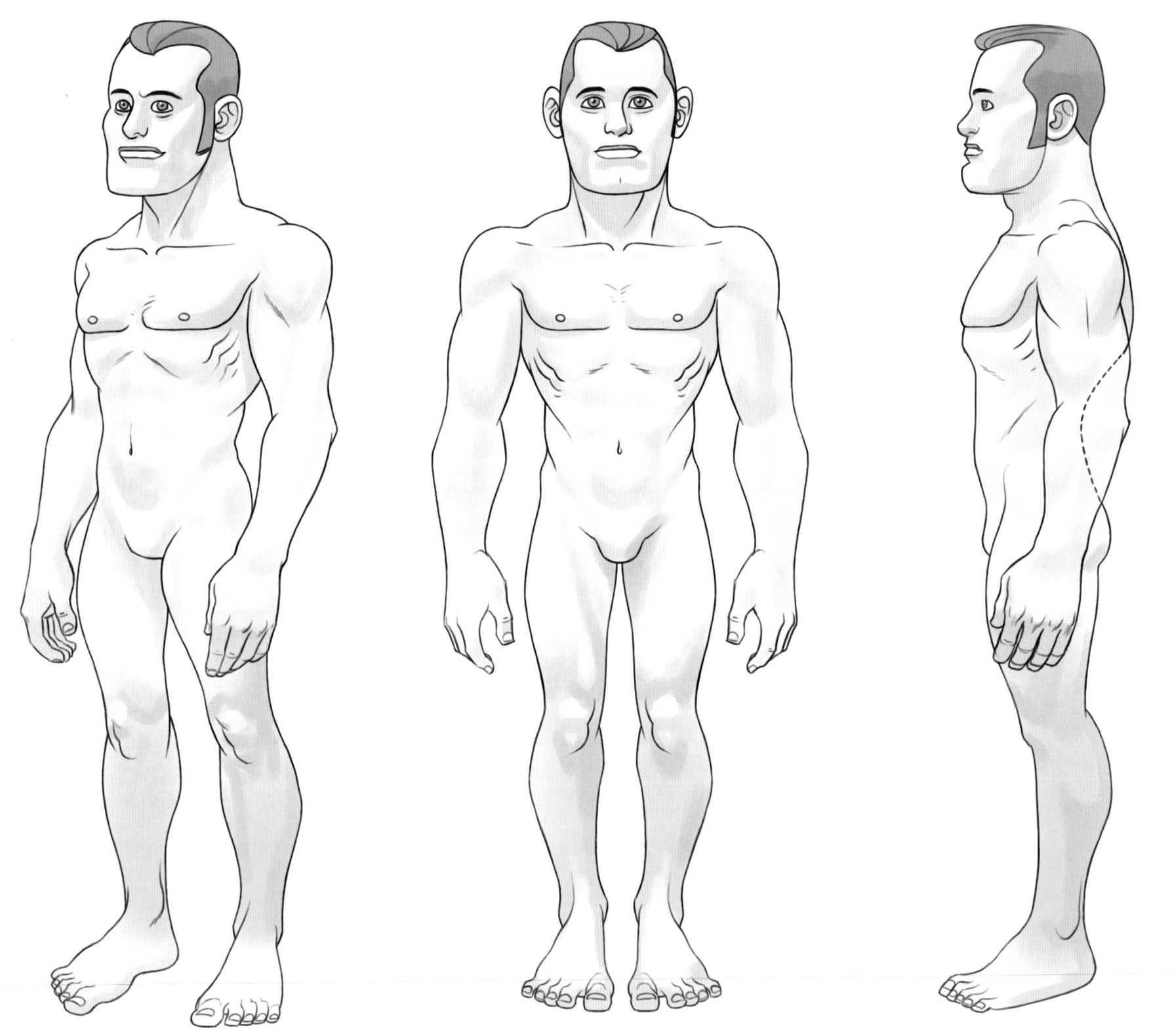

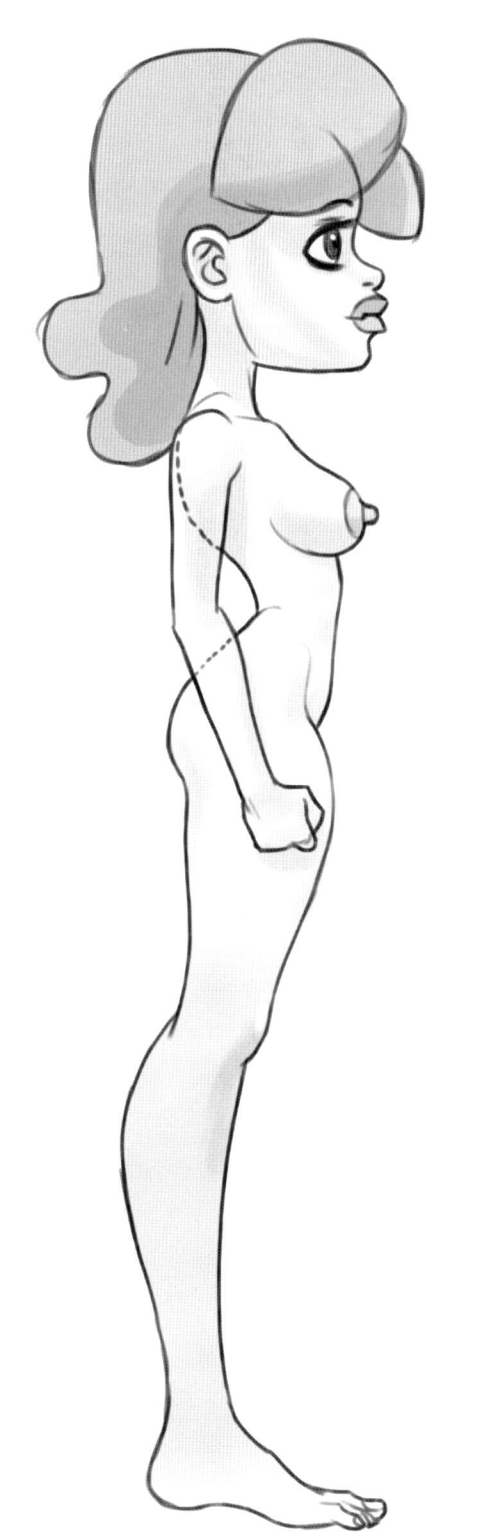
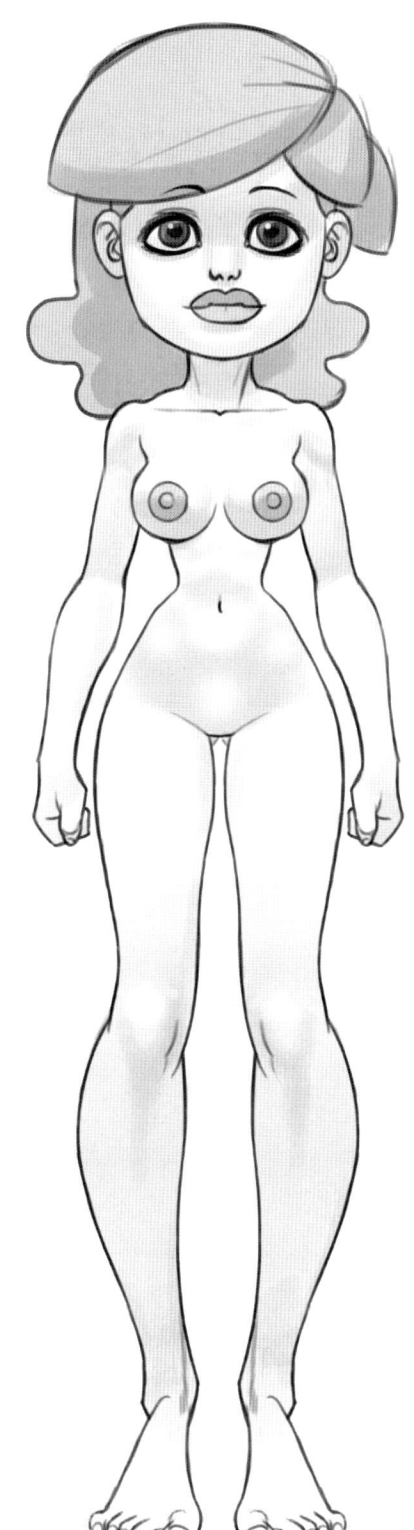
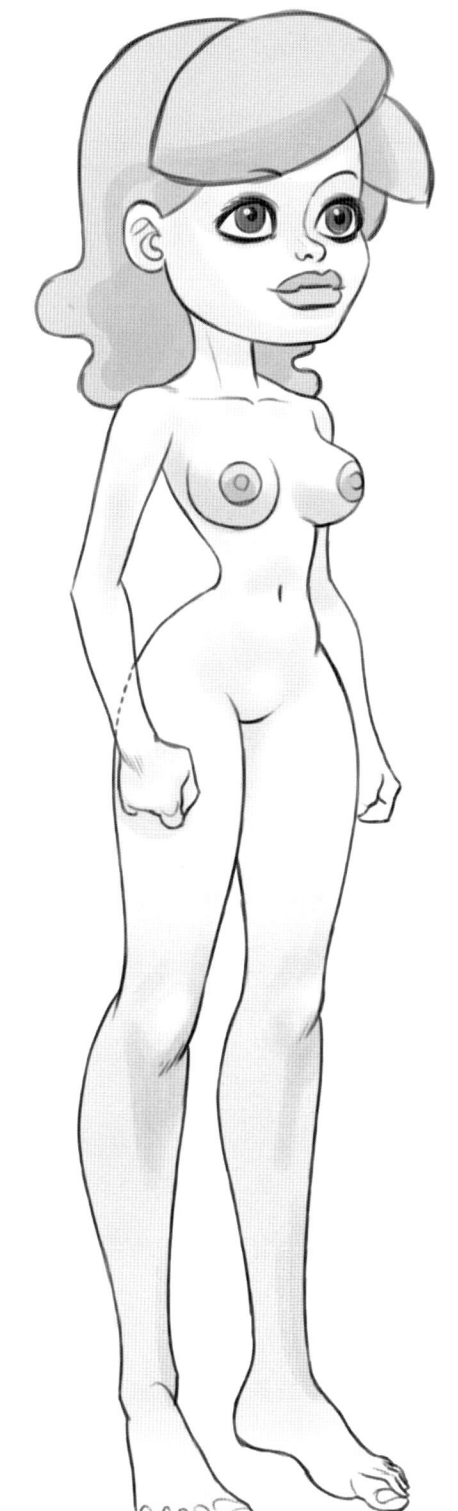

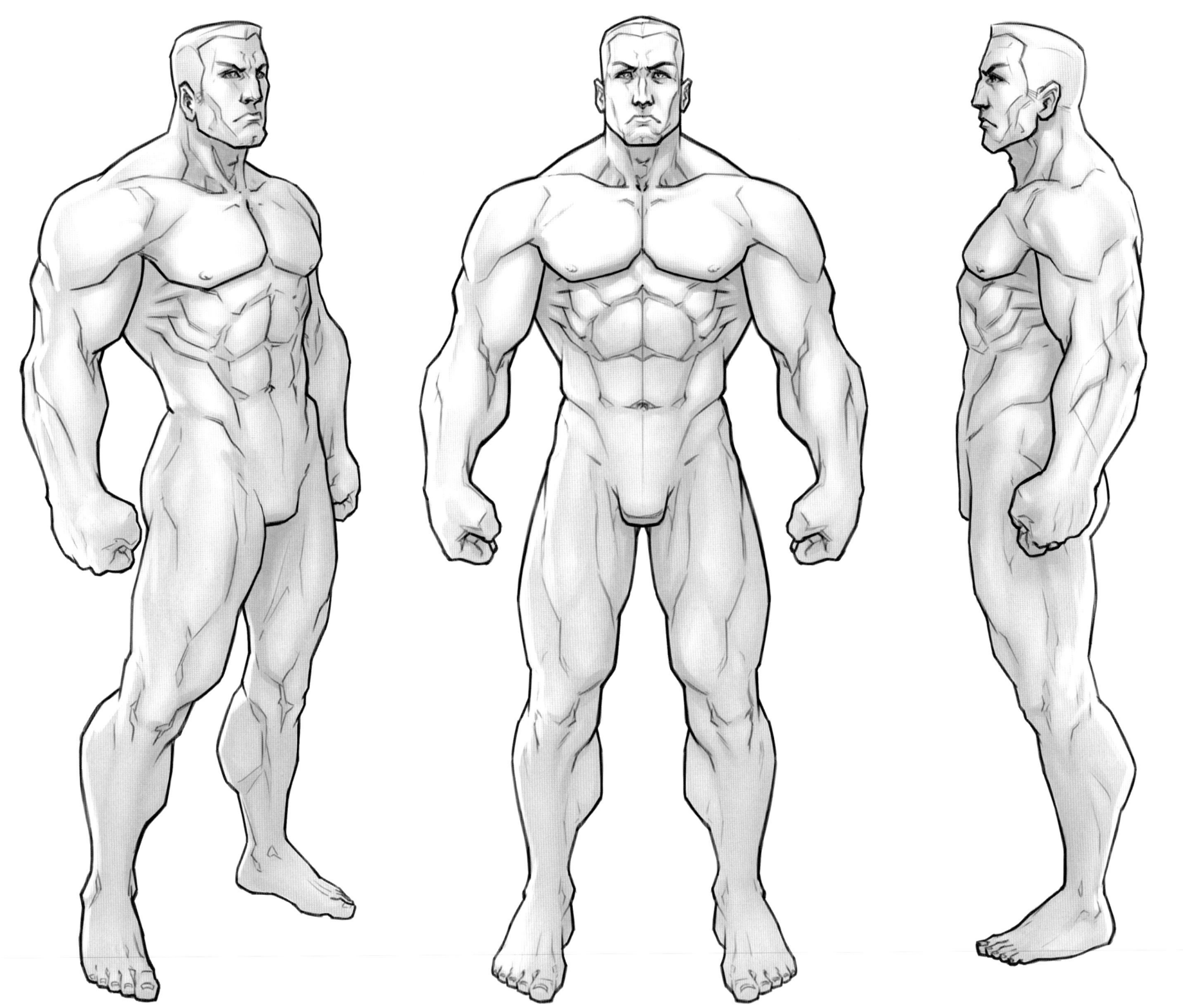

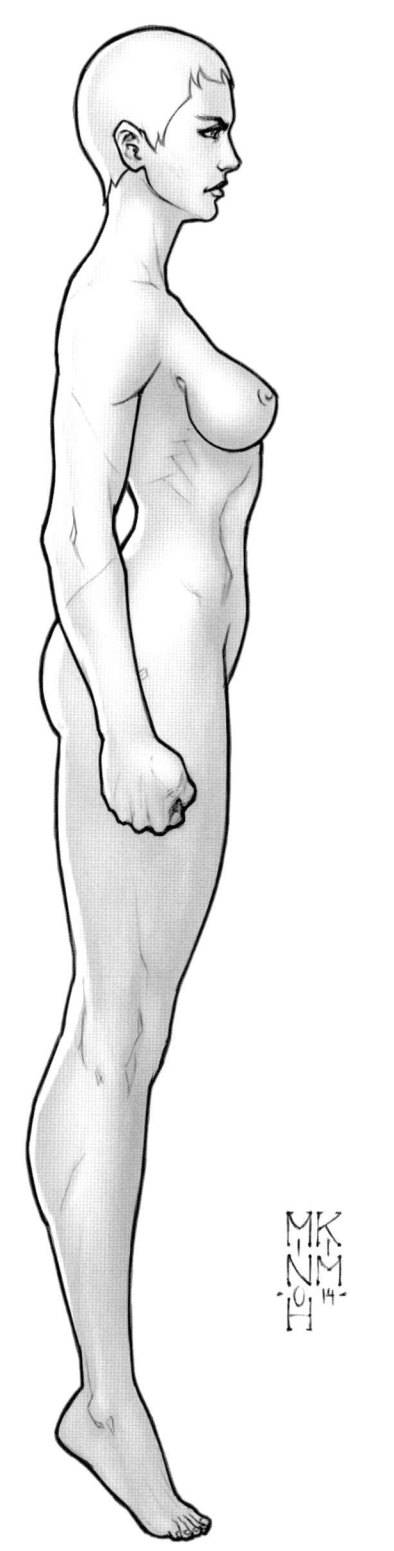
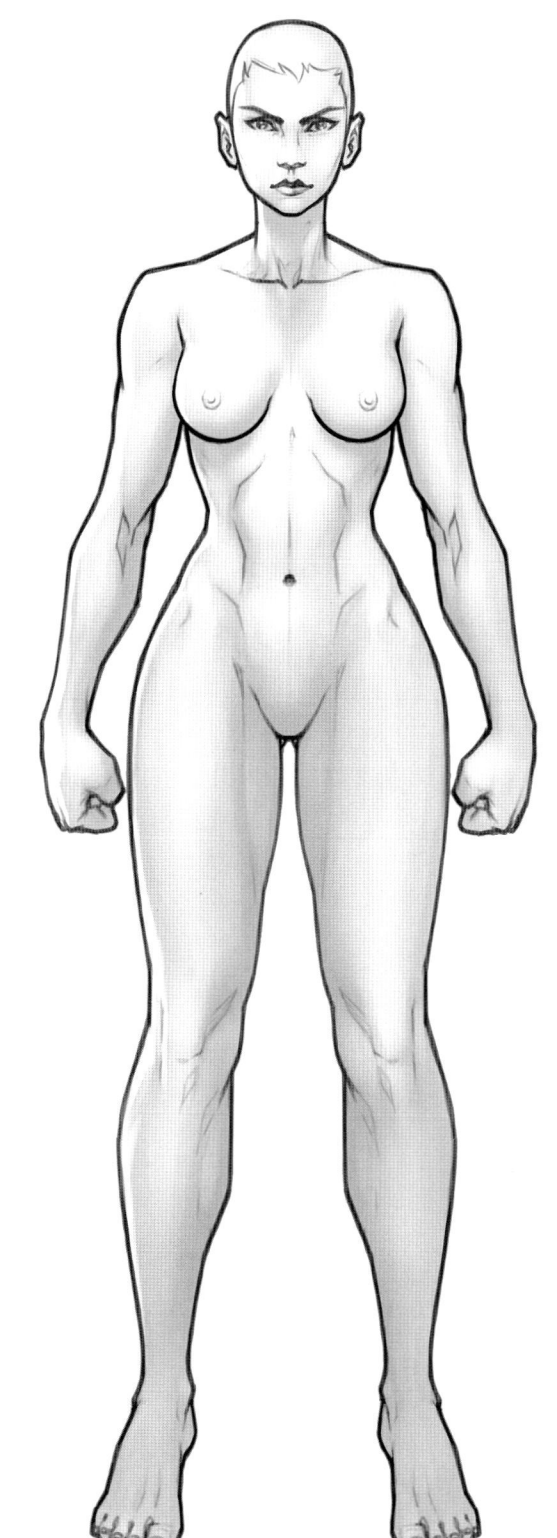
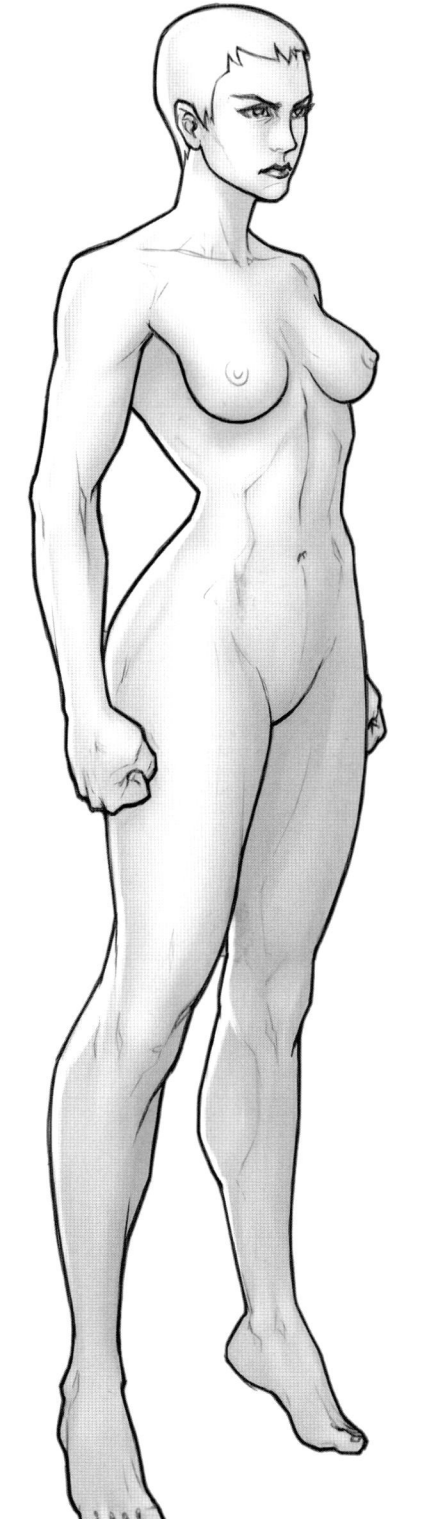

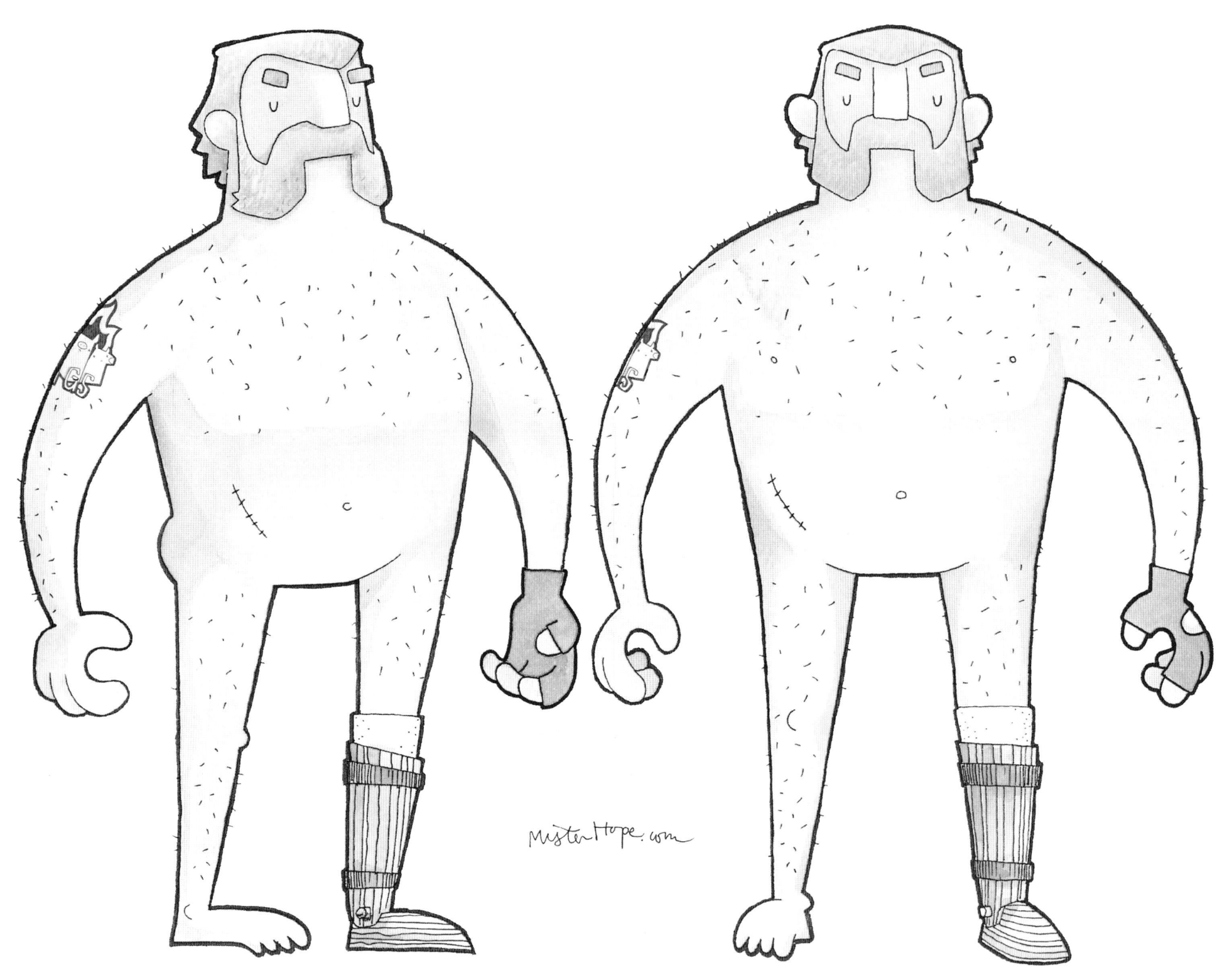

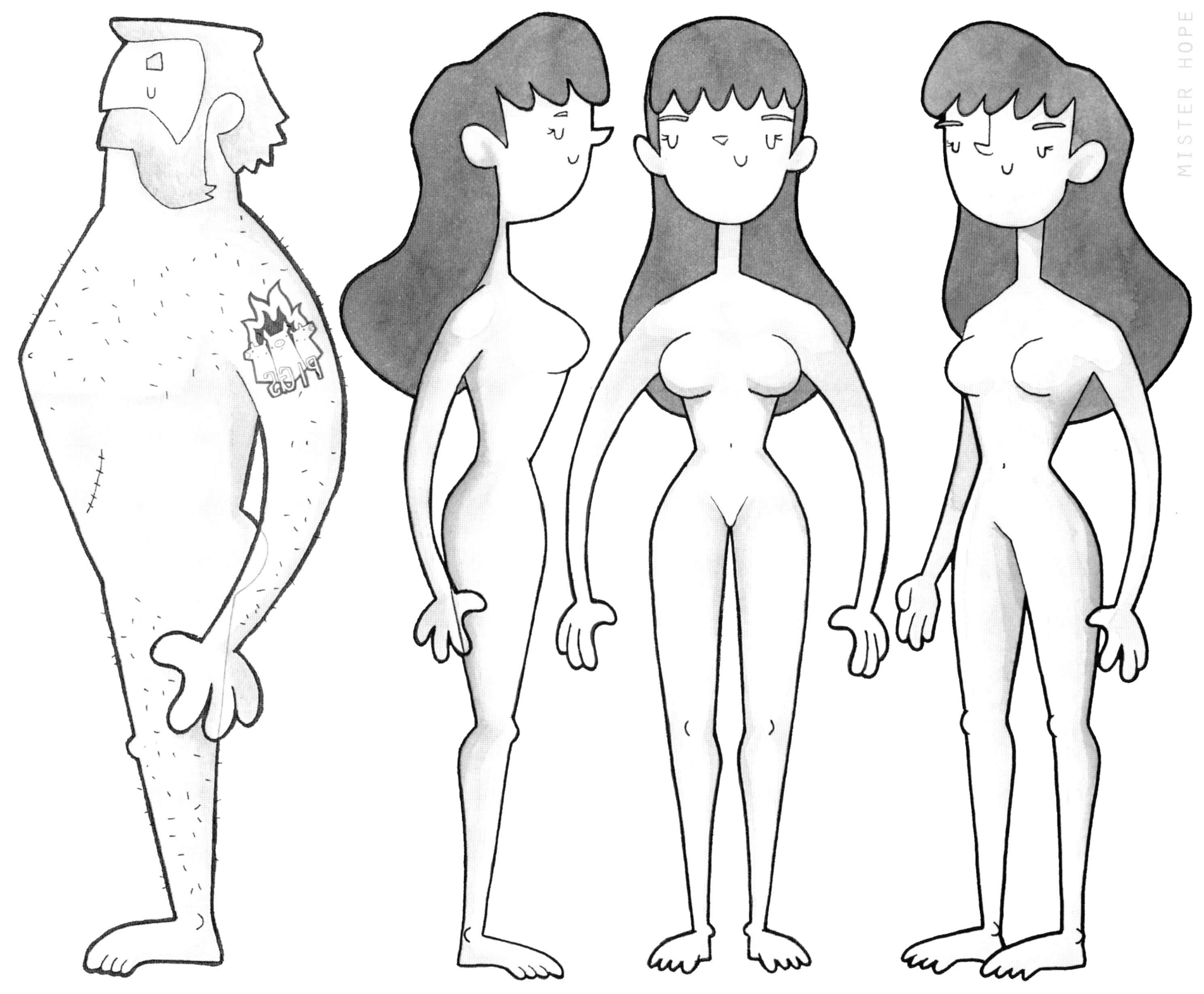

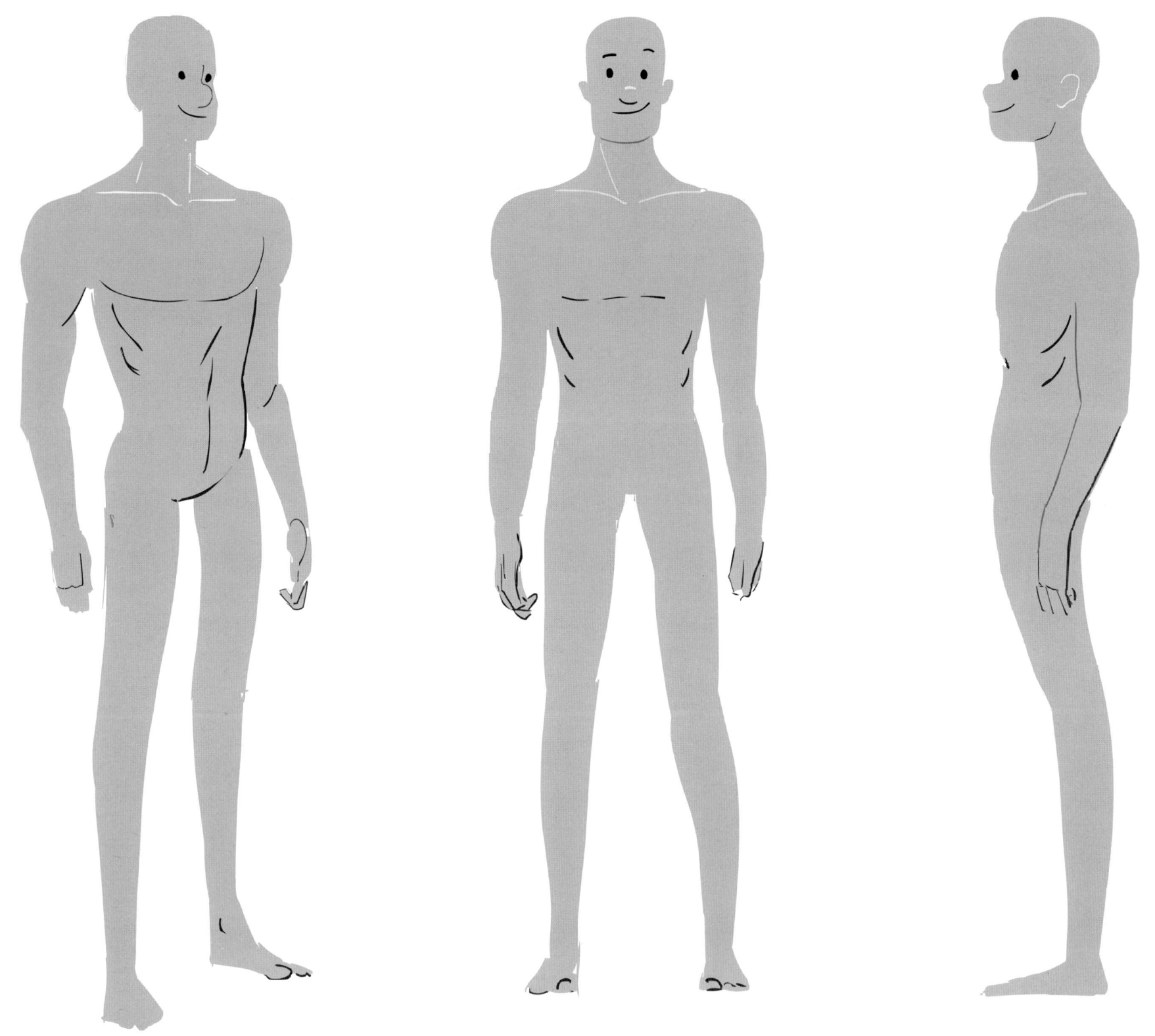

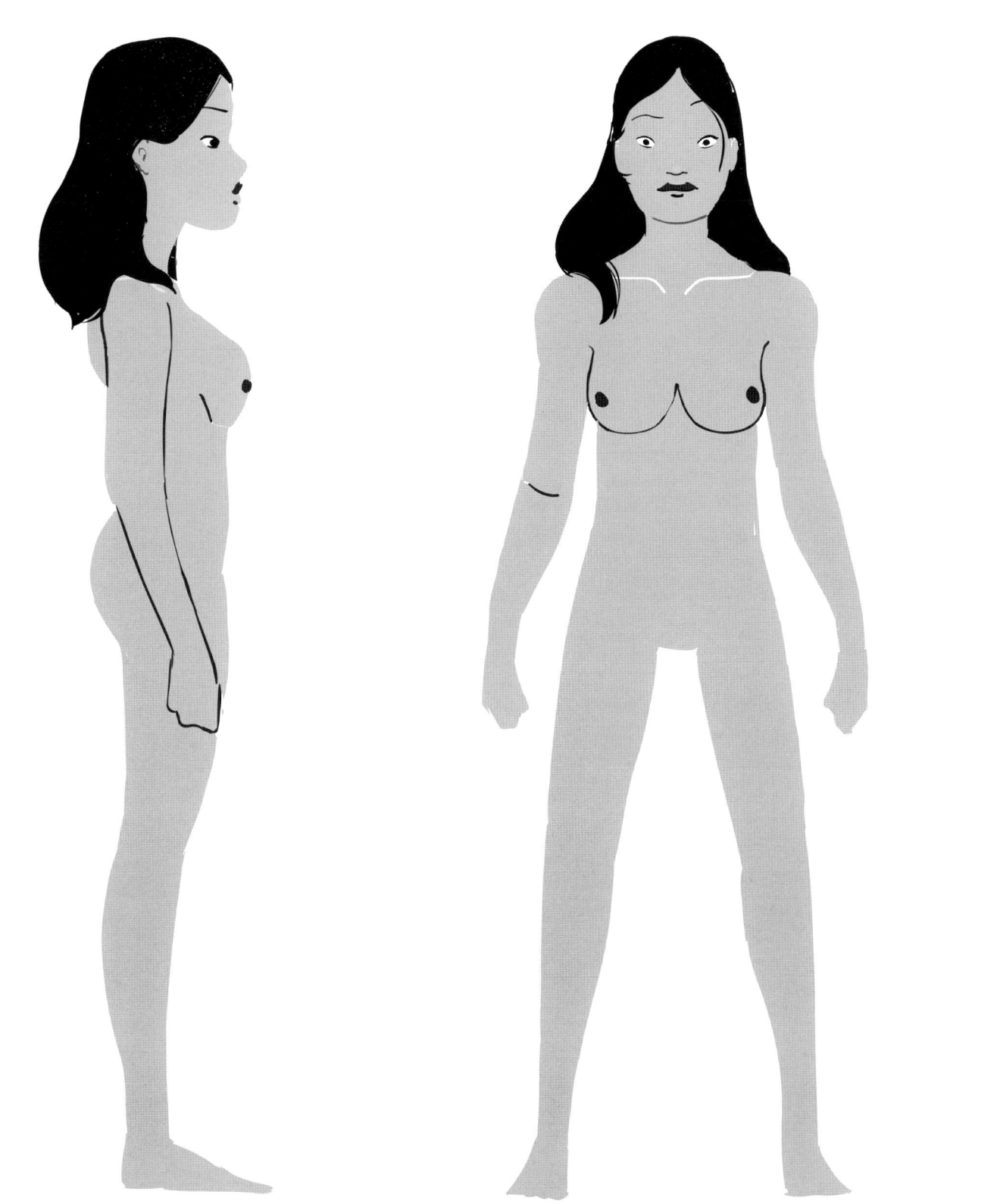

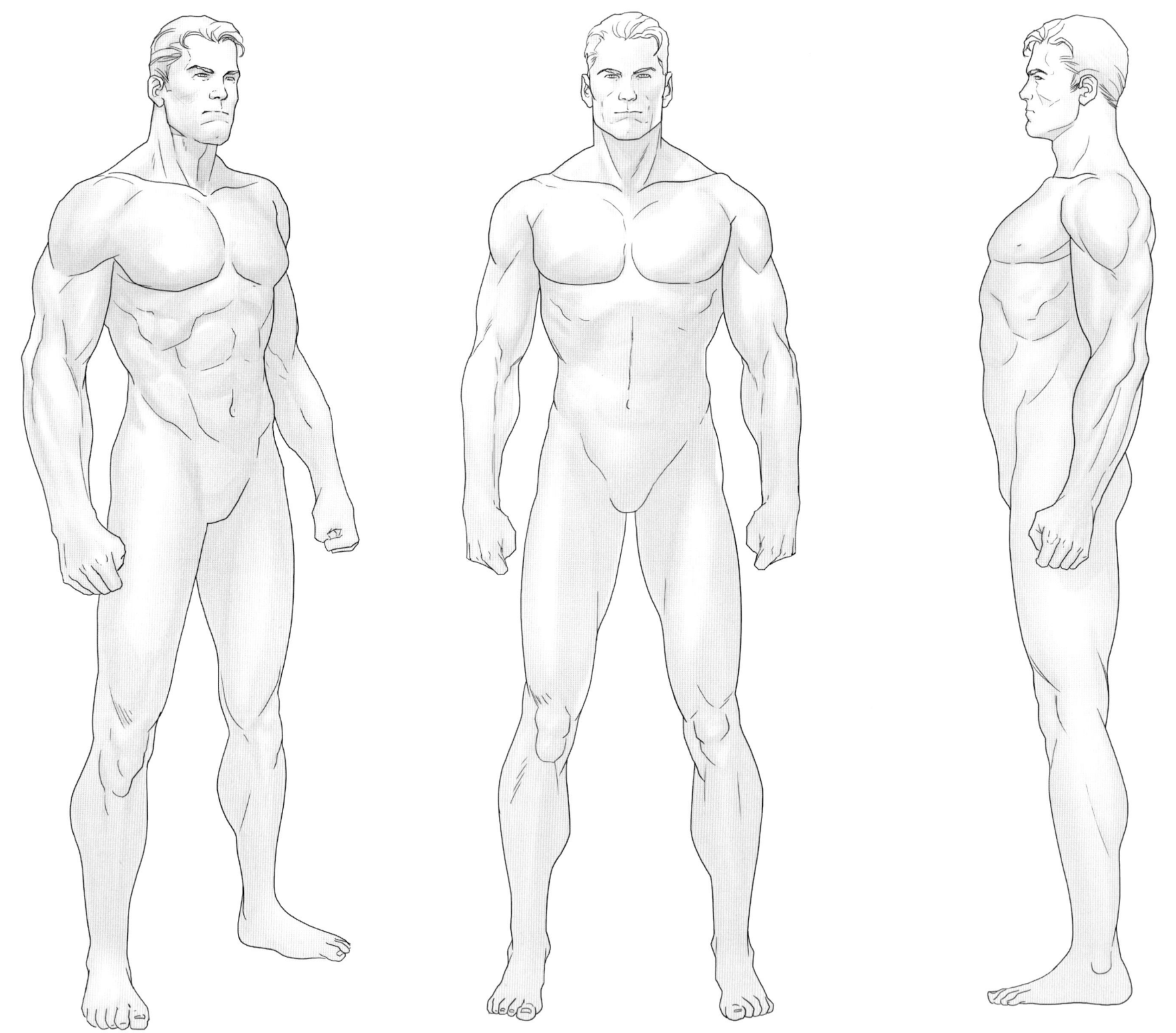

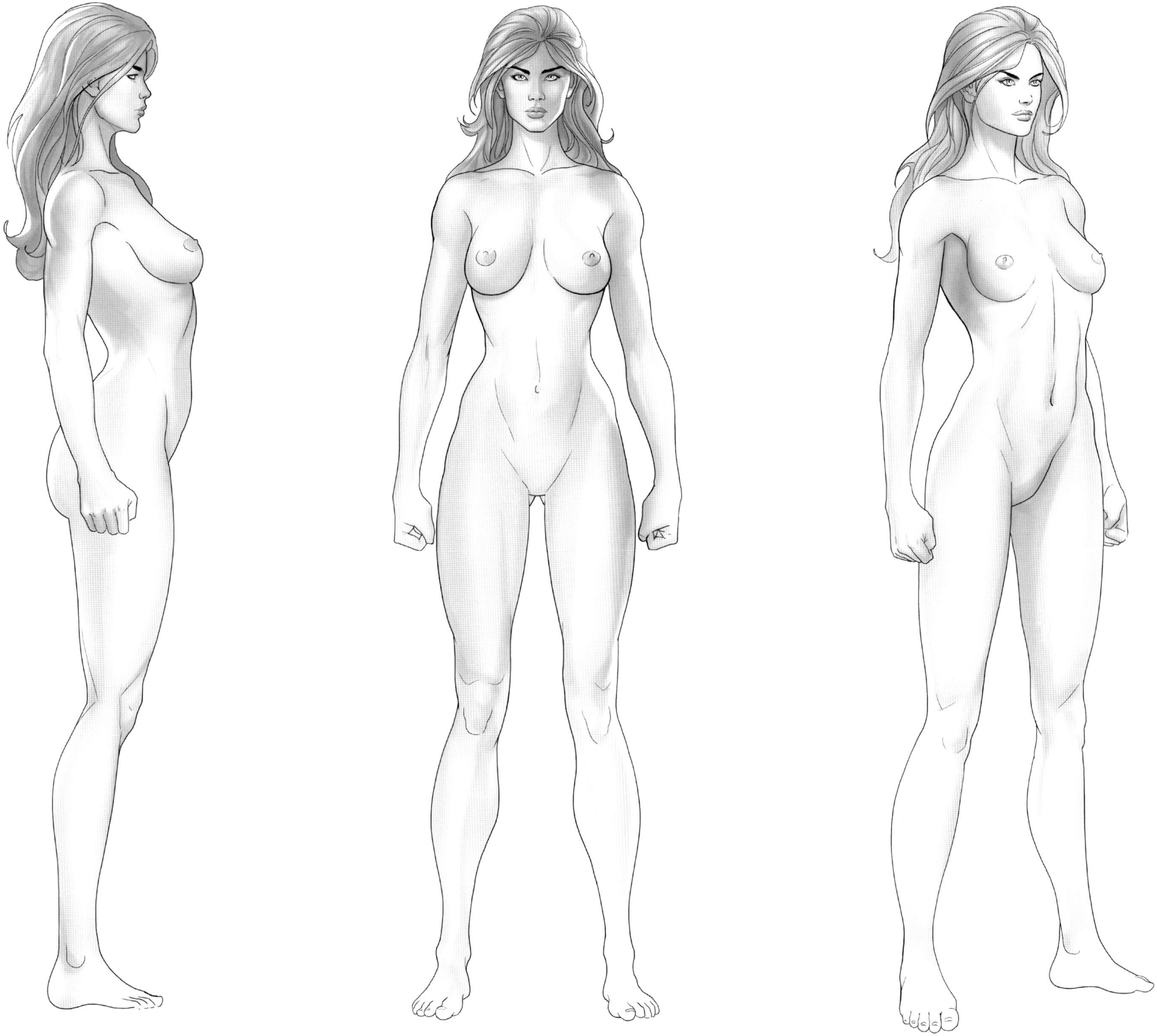

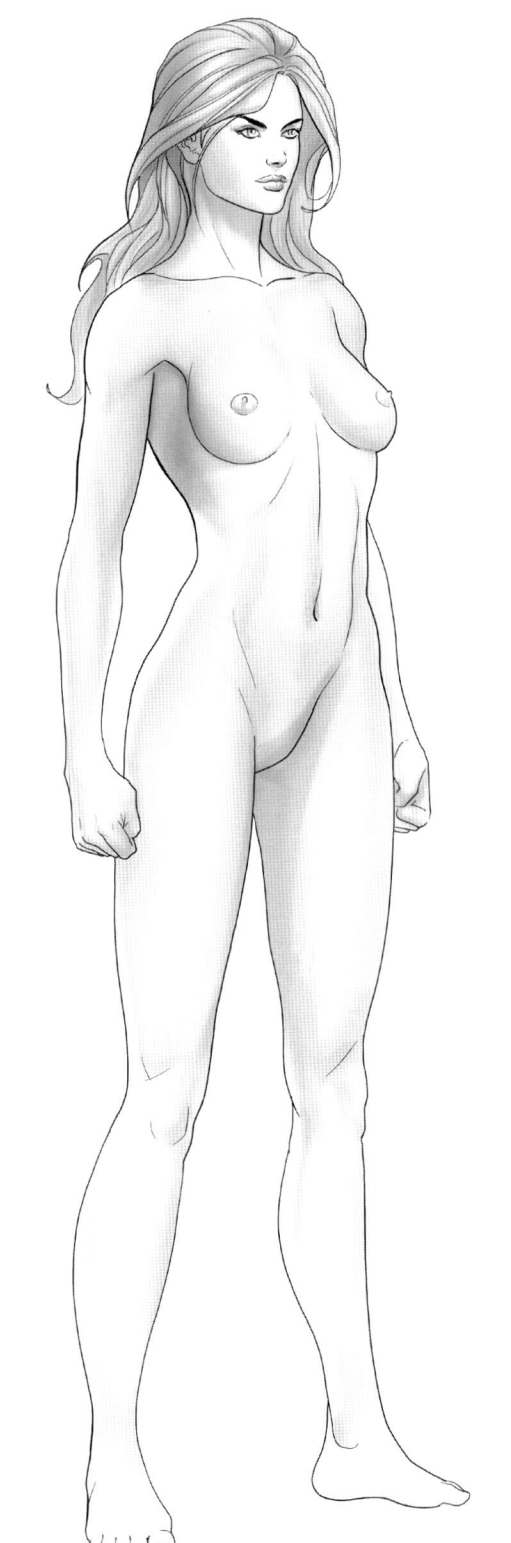

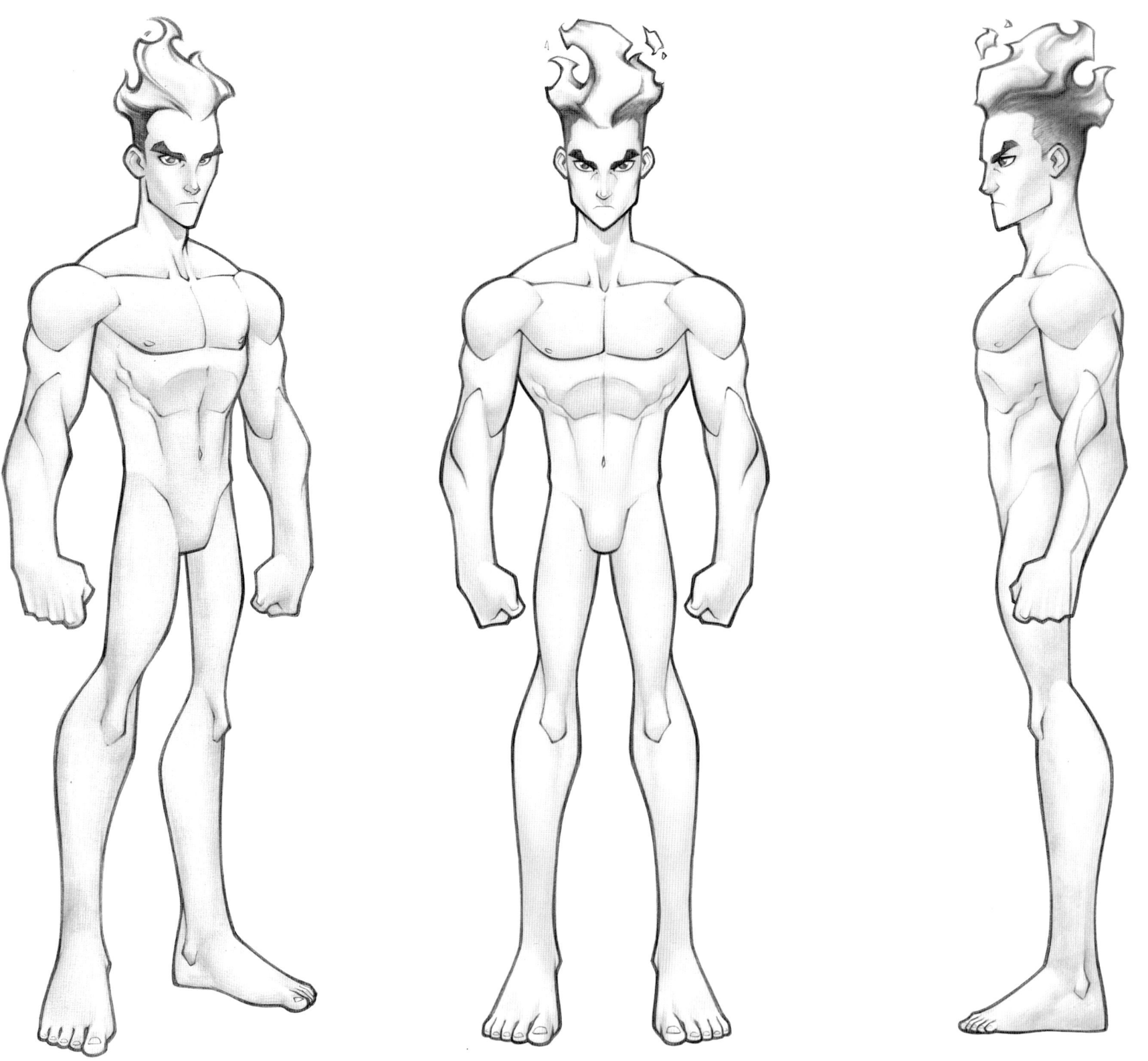

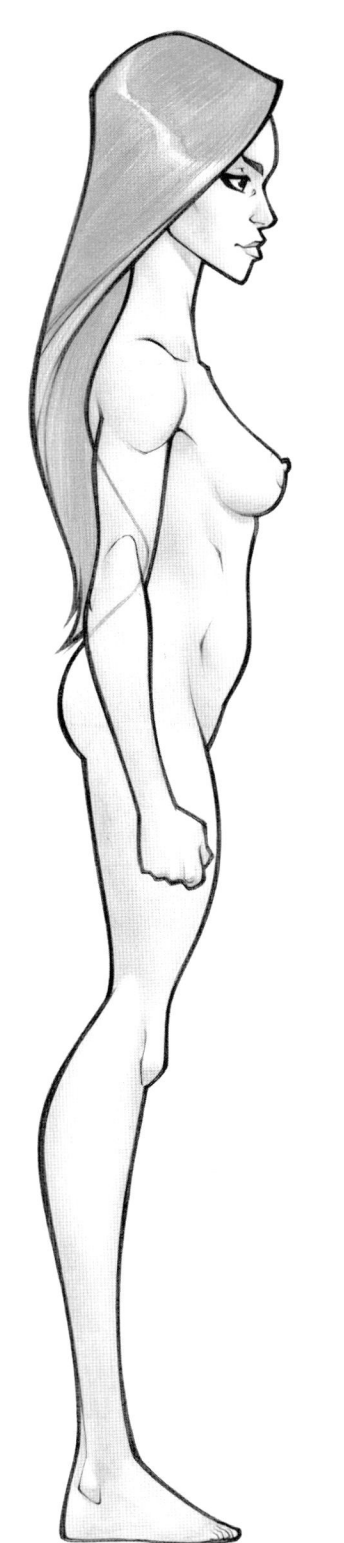
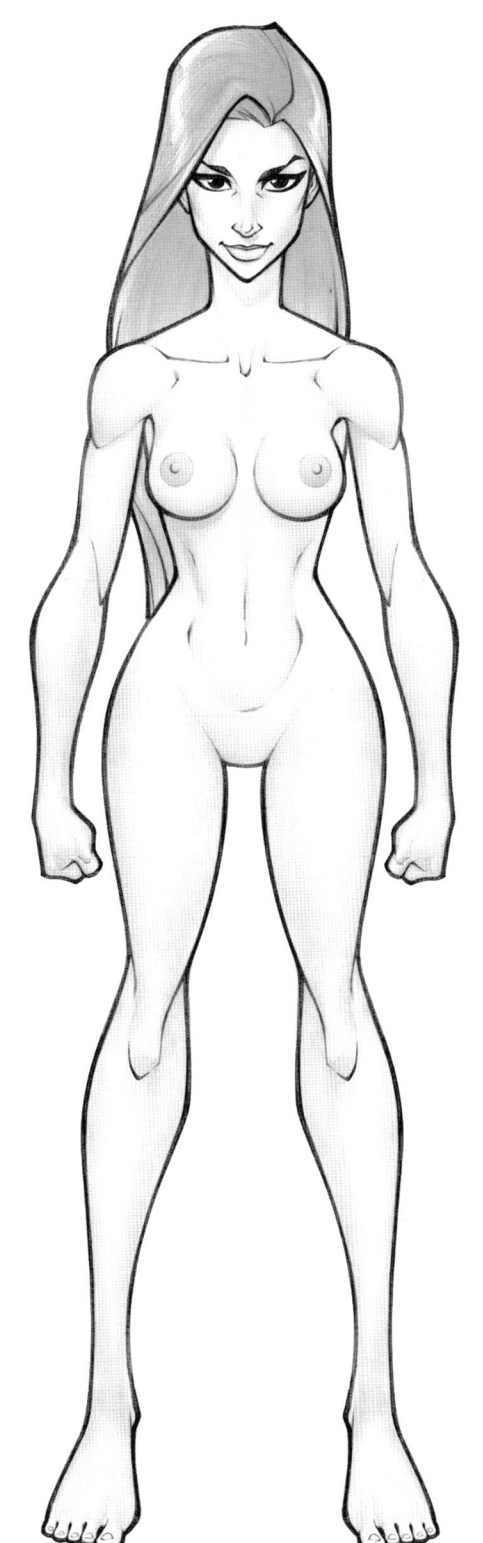
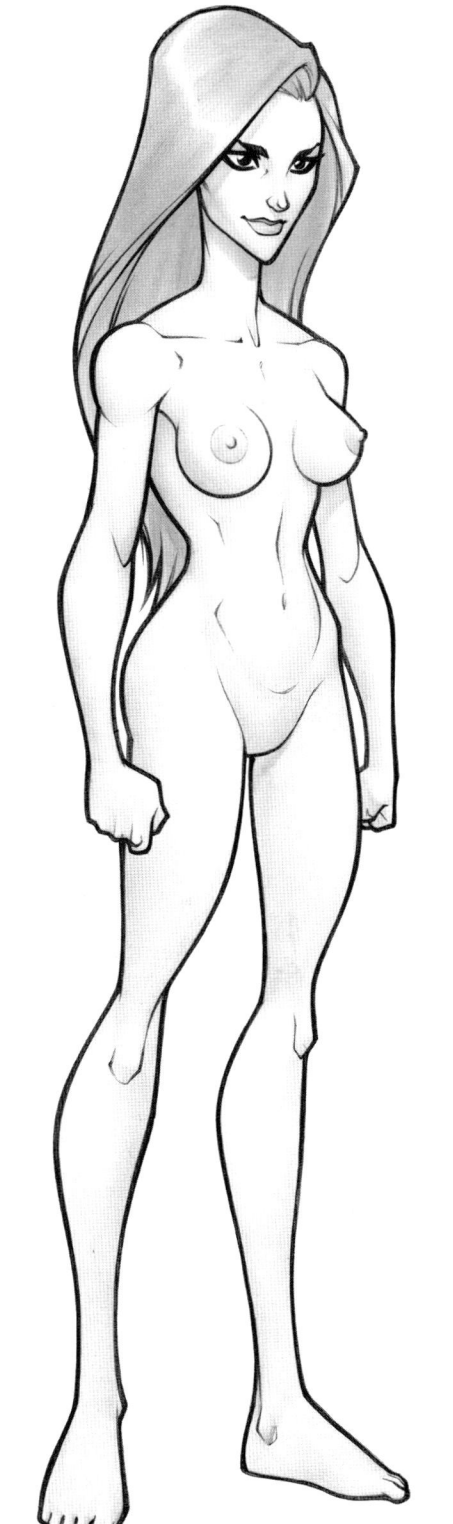

PEDRO DELGADO

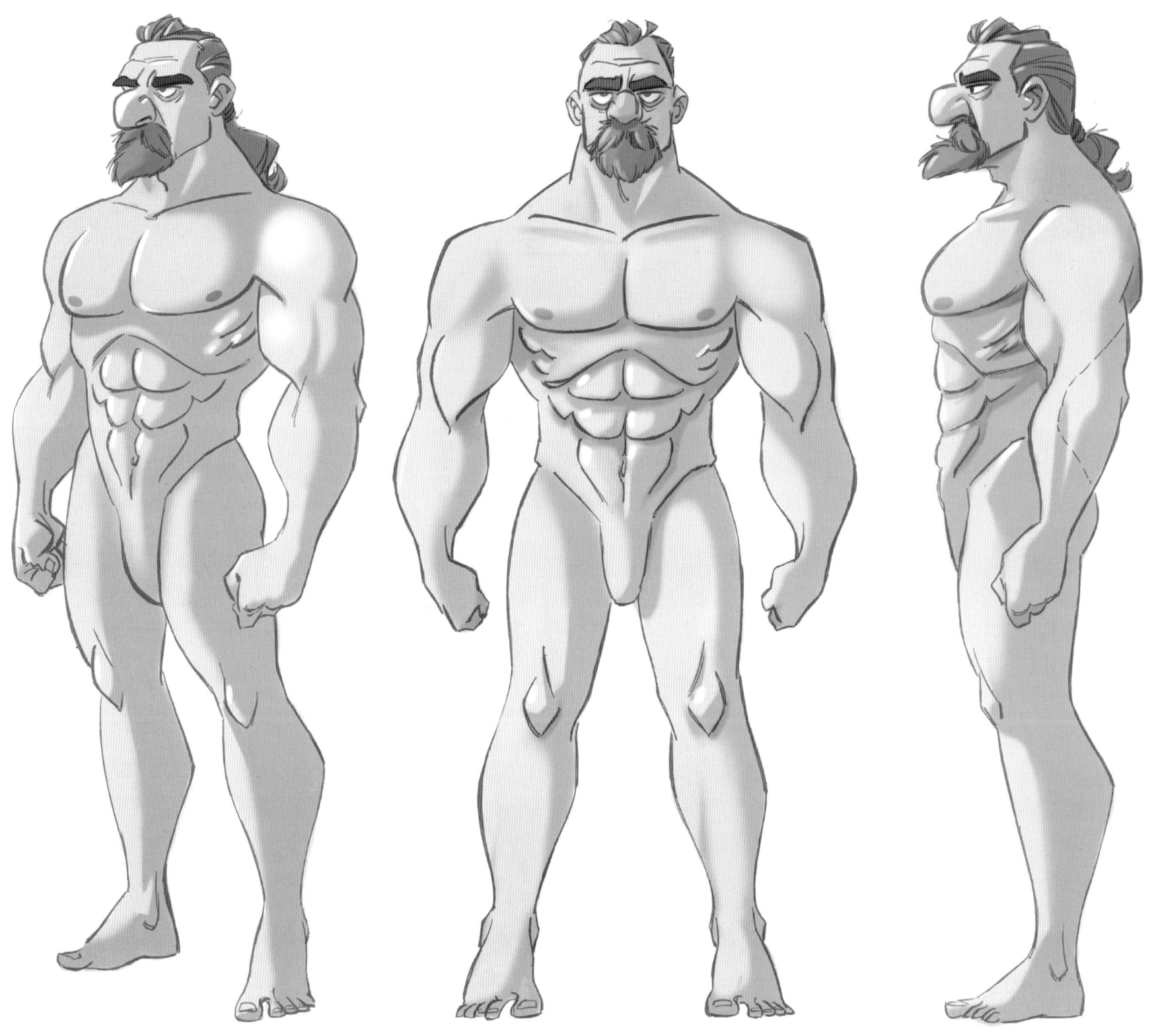

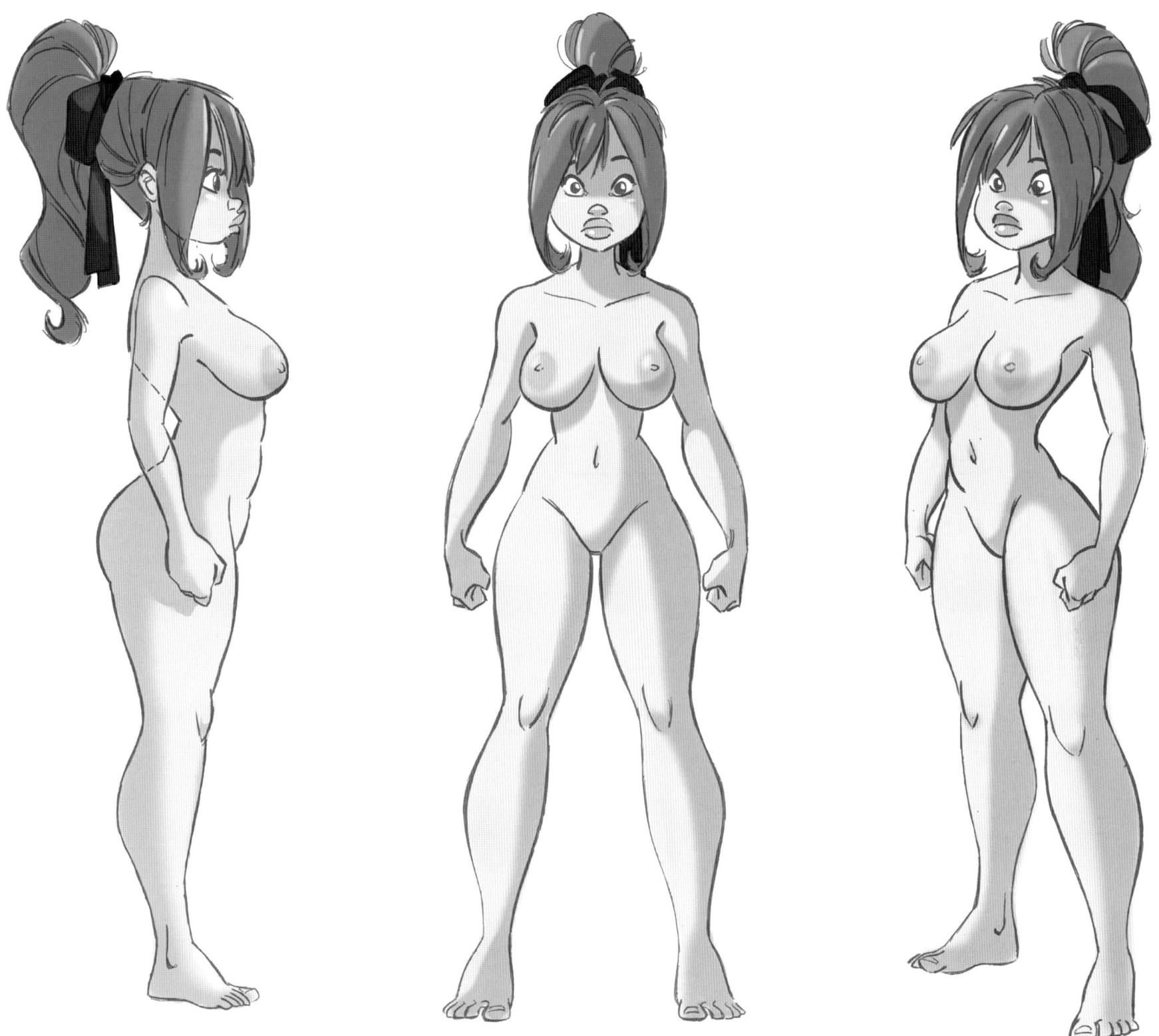

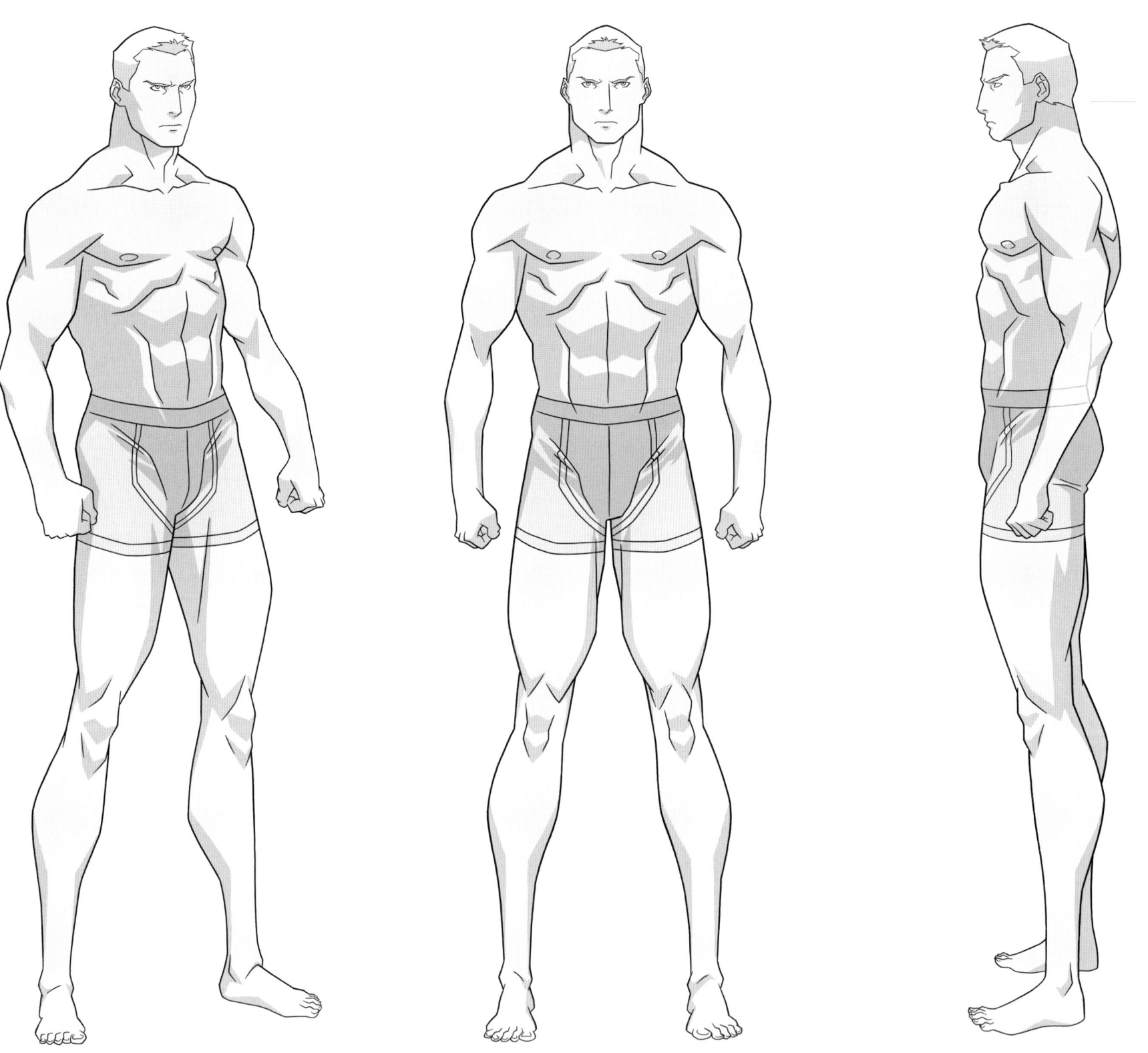

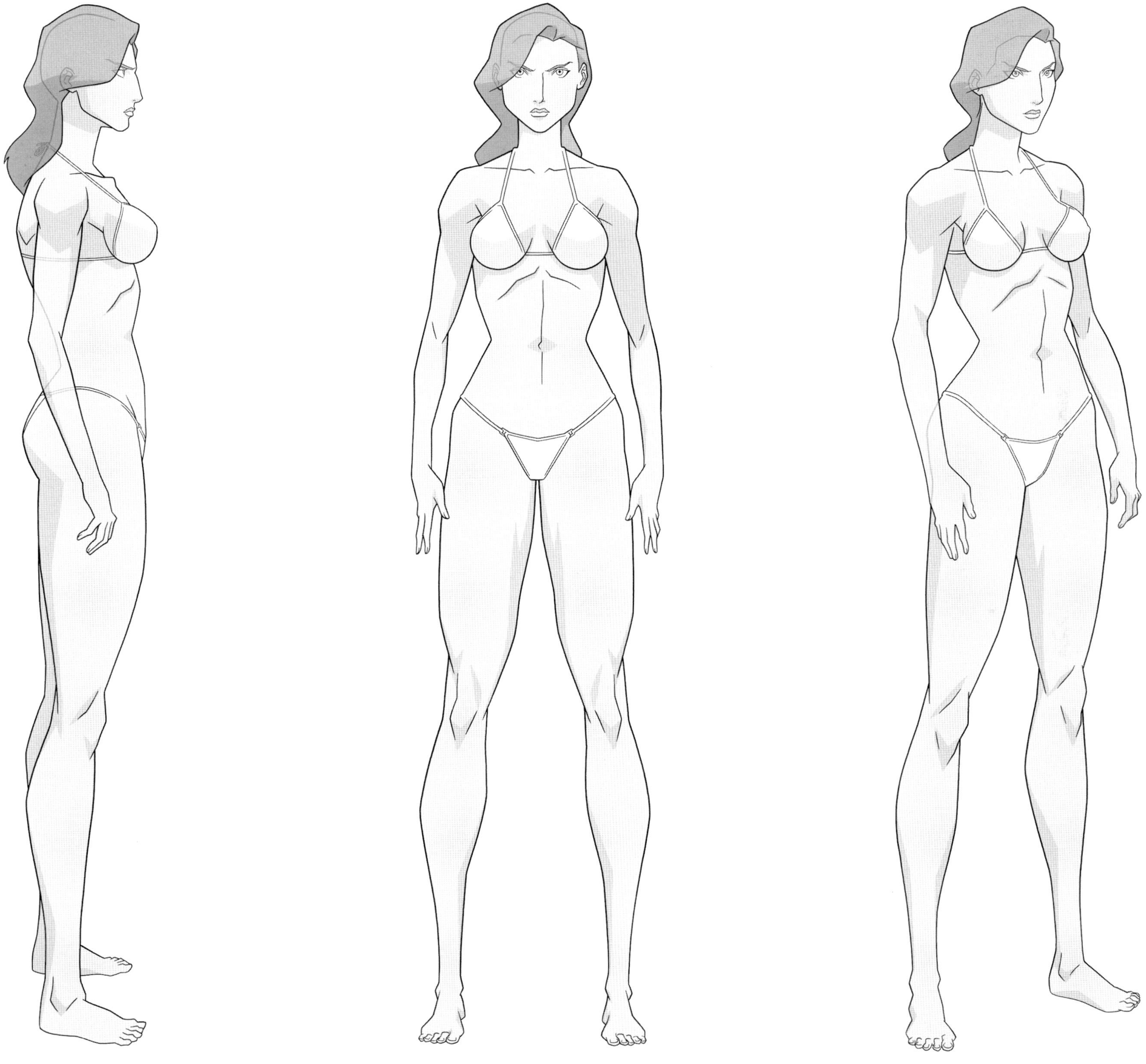

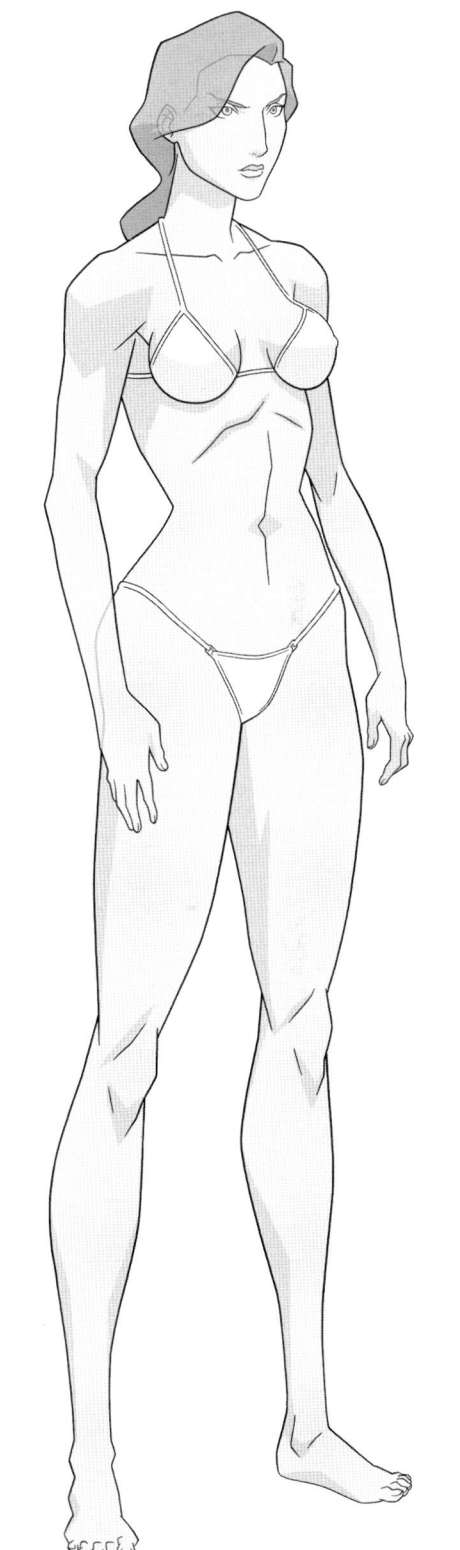

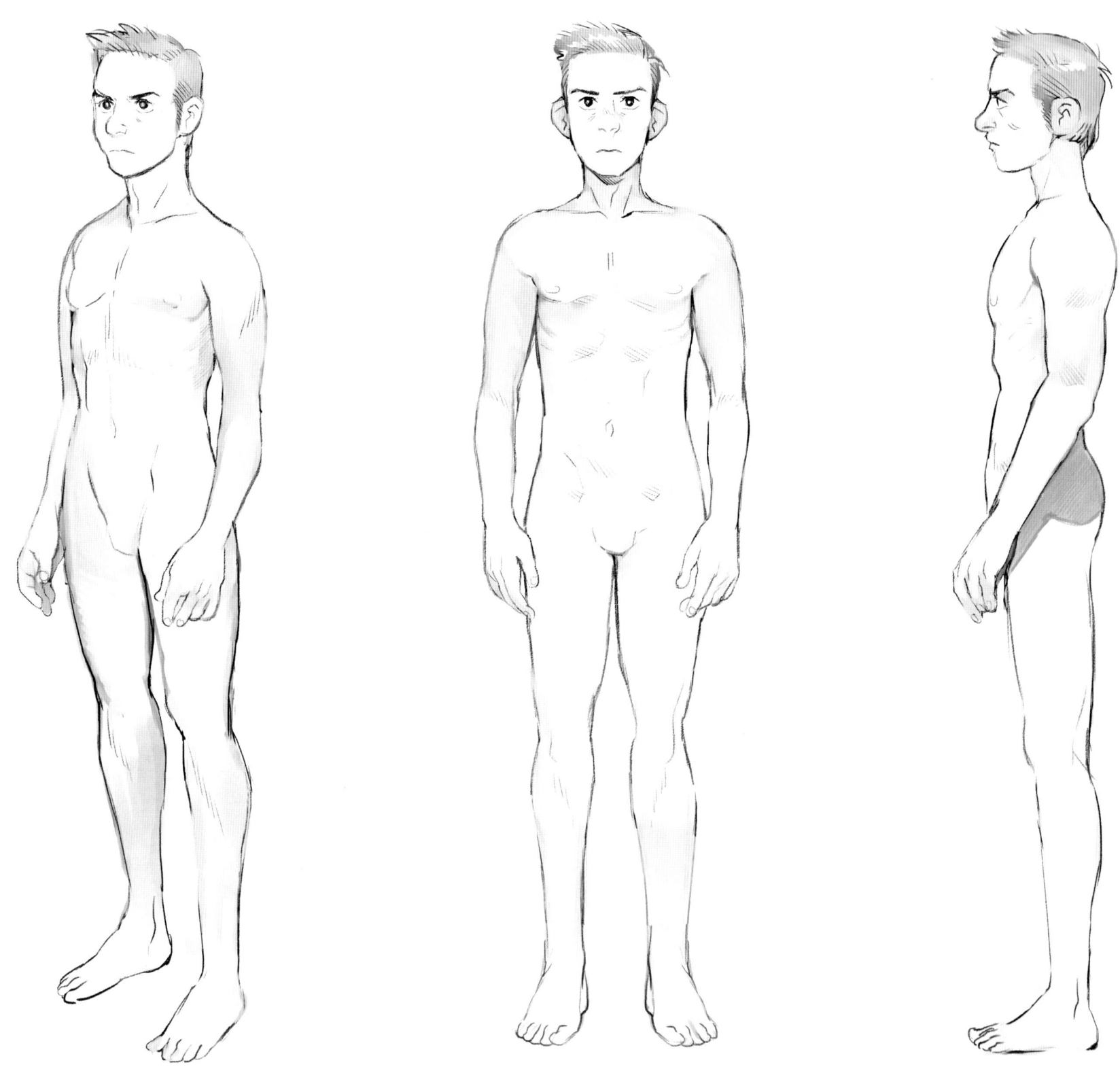

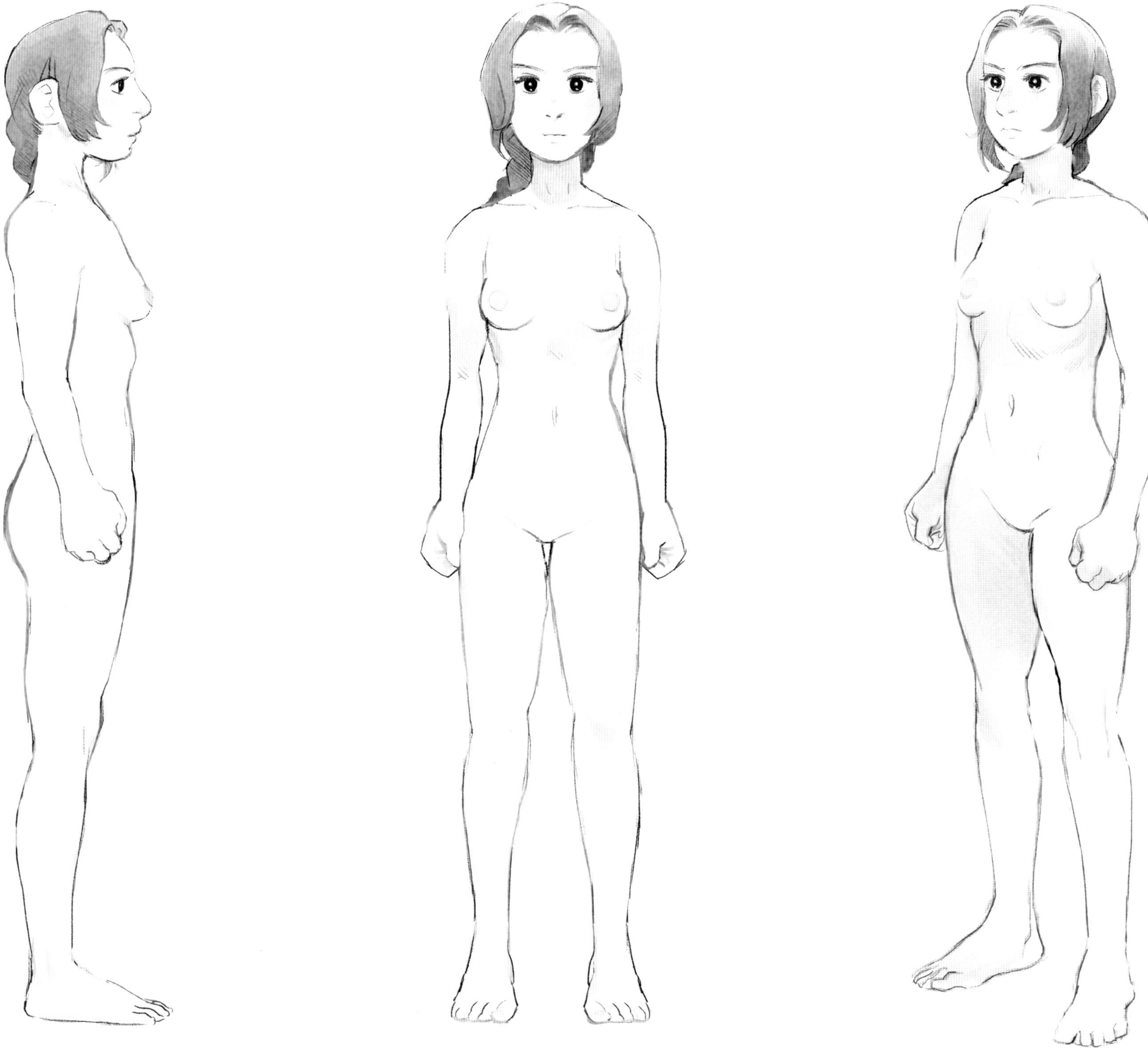

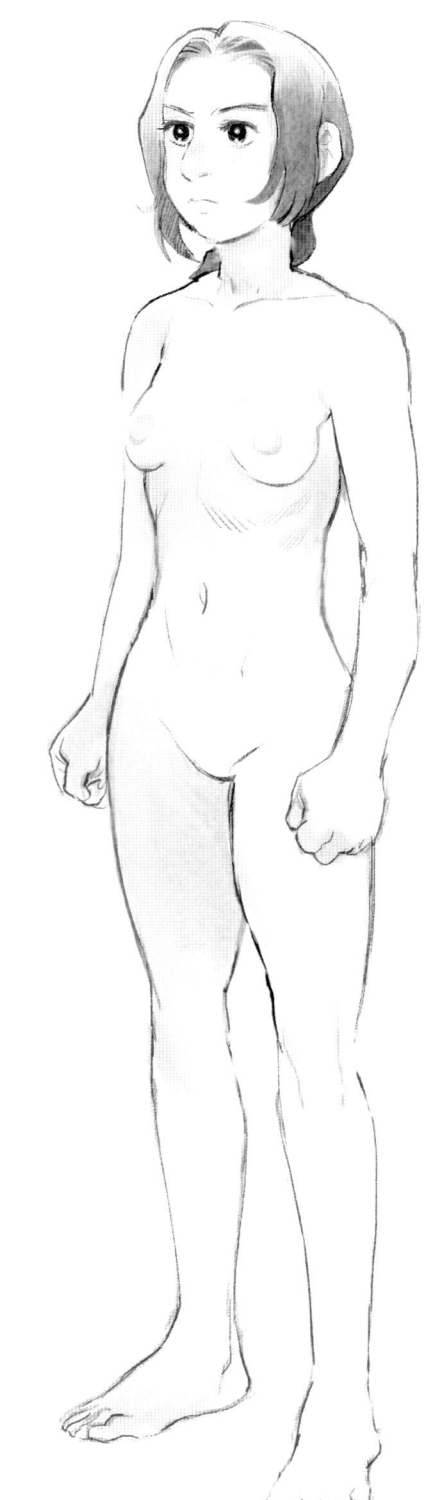

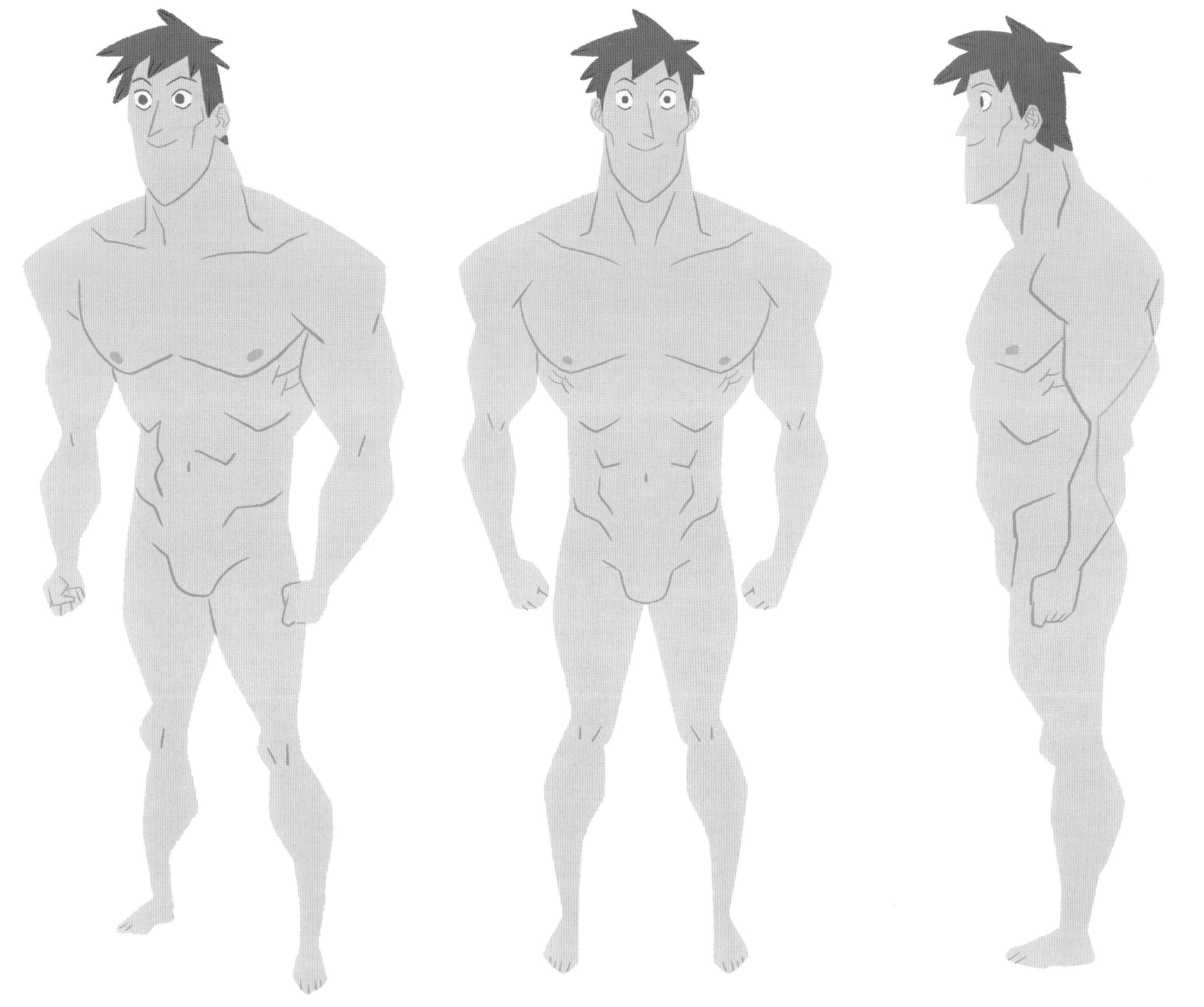

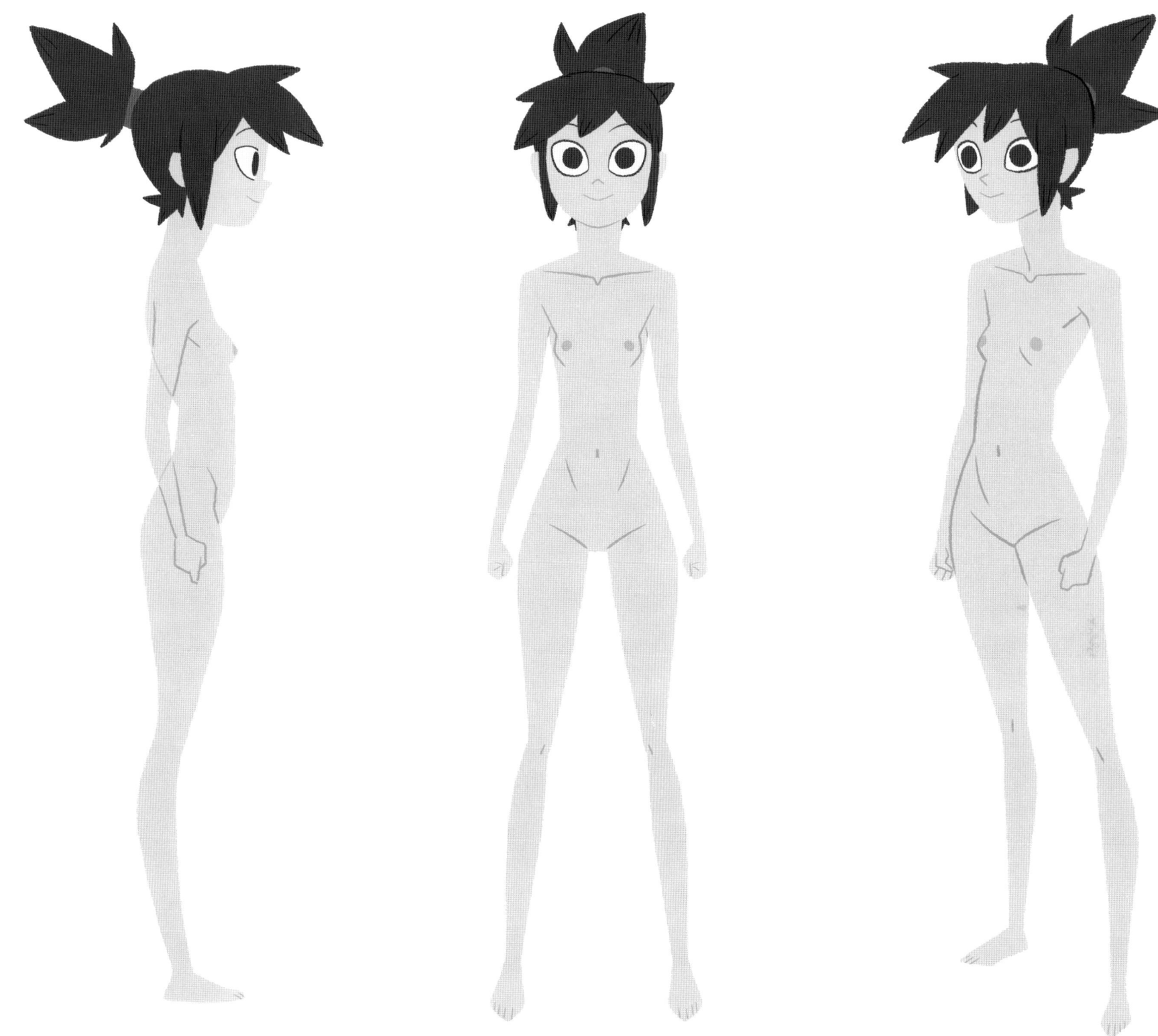

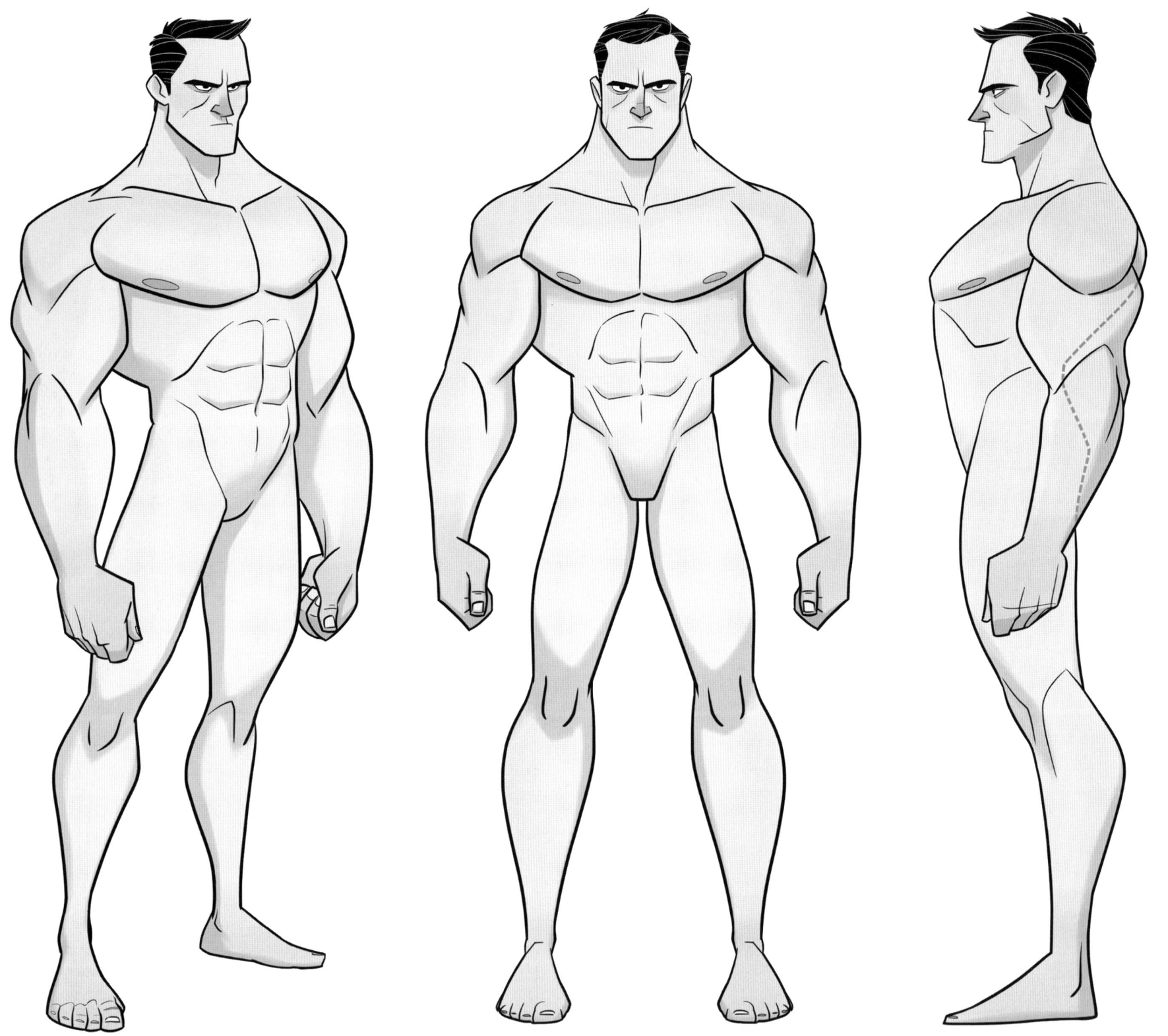

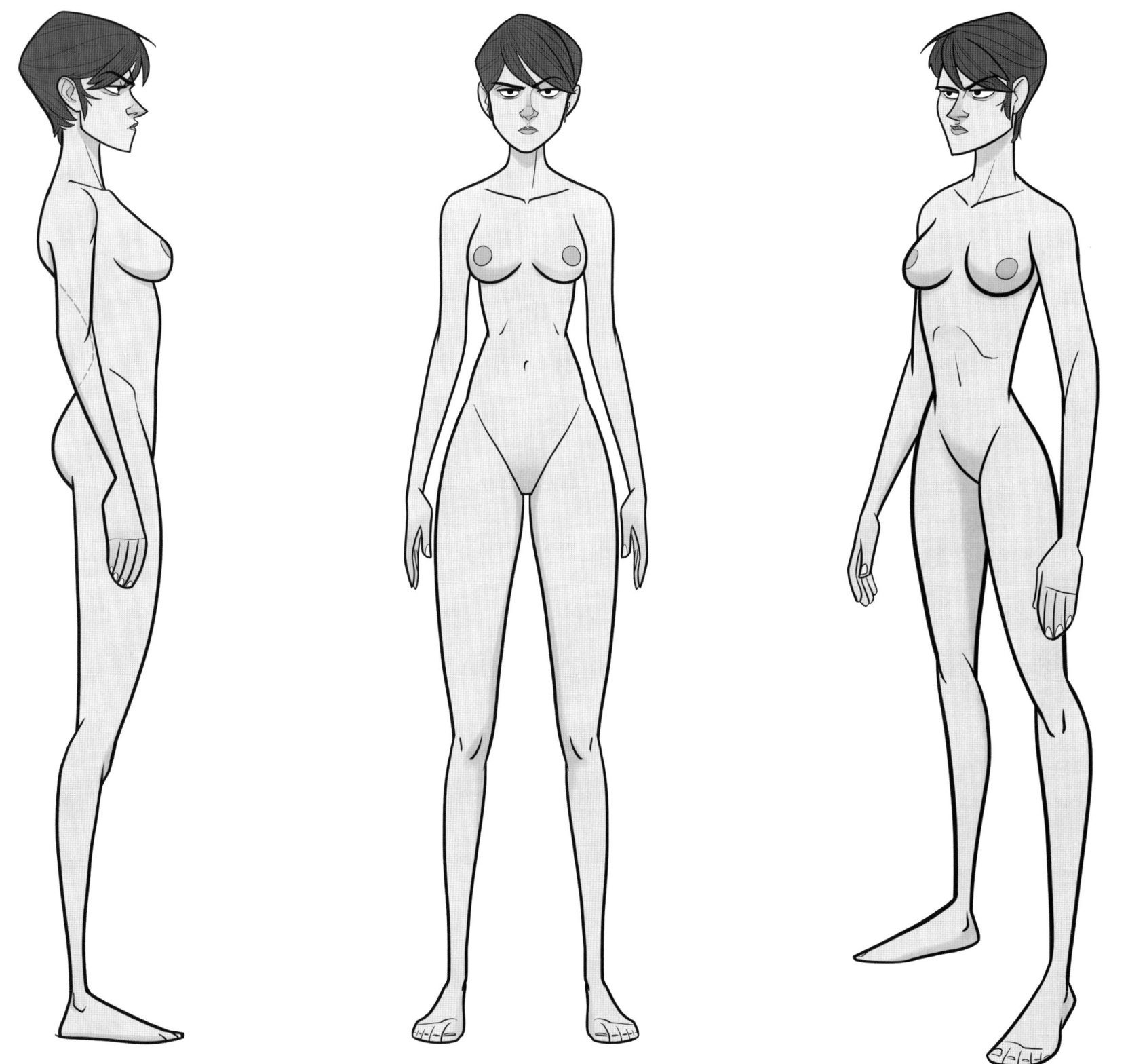

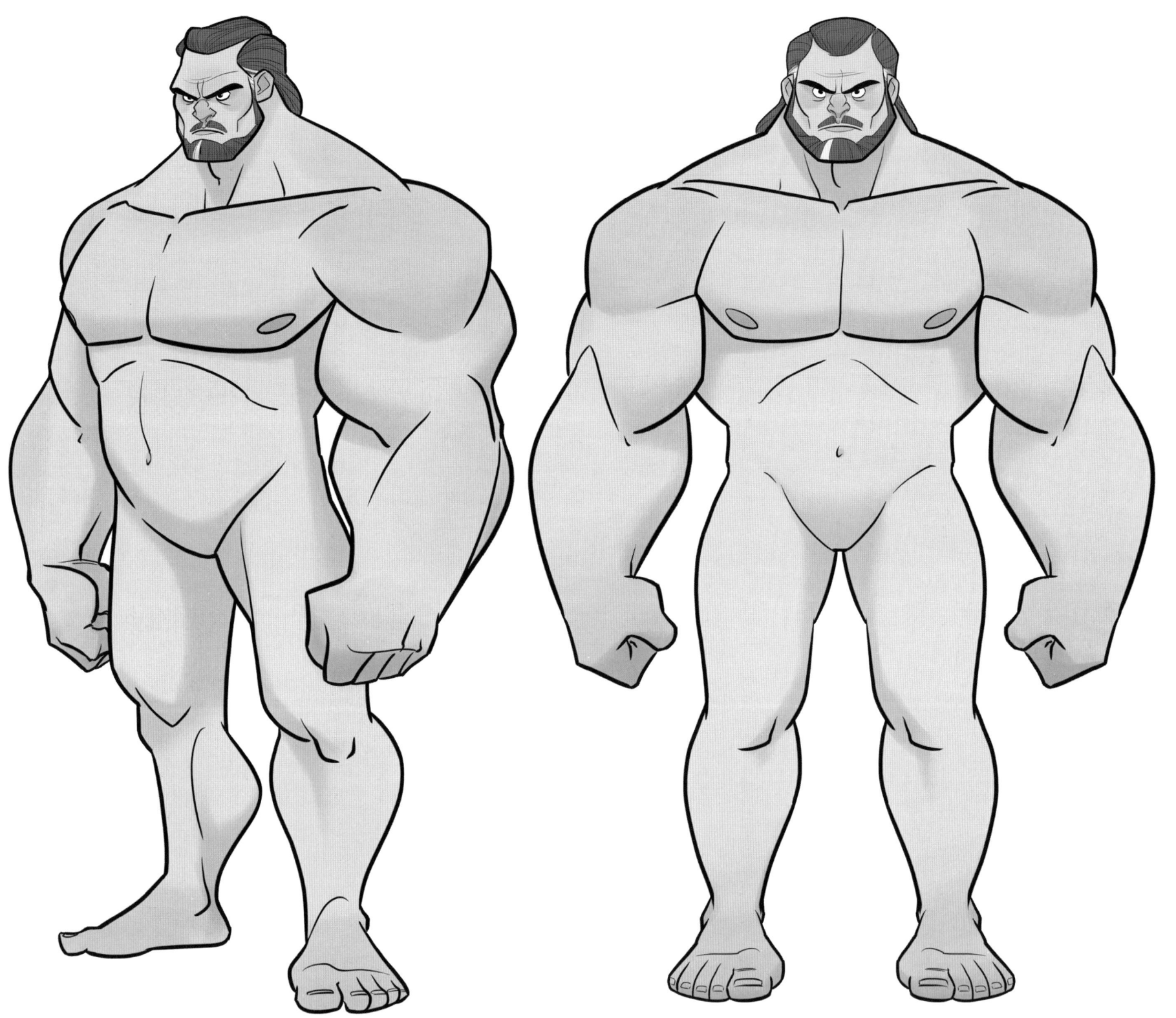

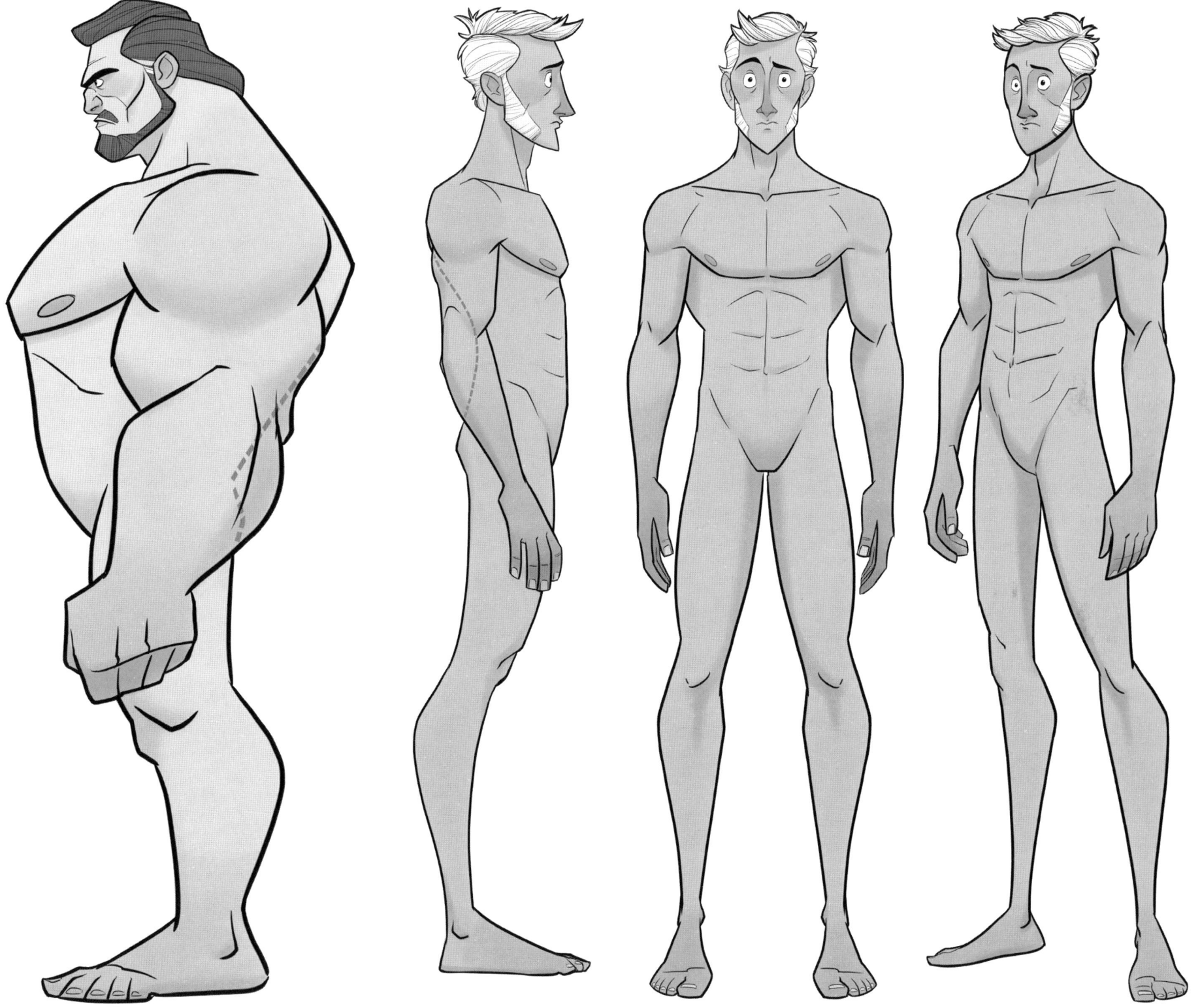

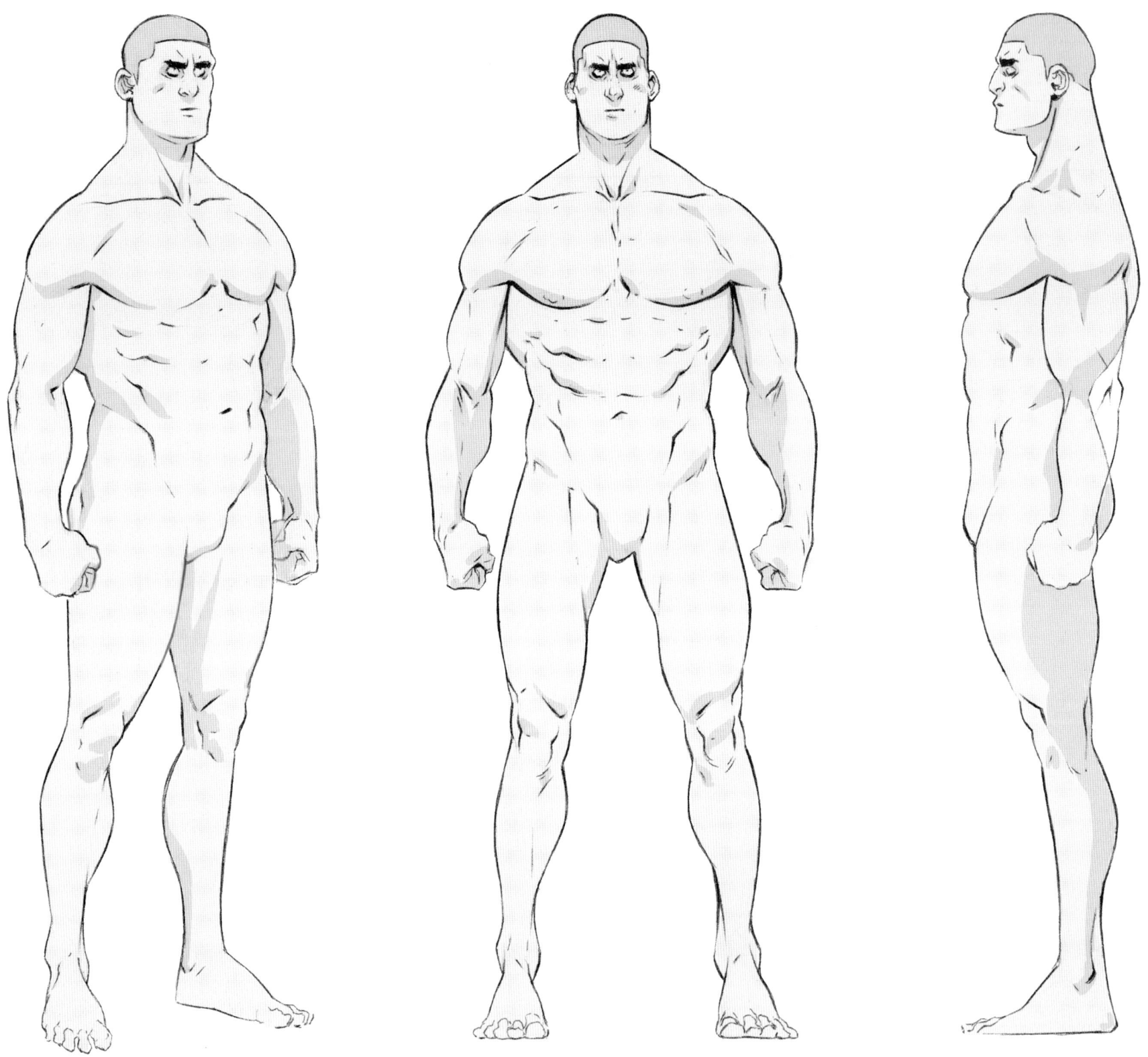

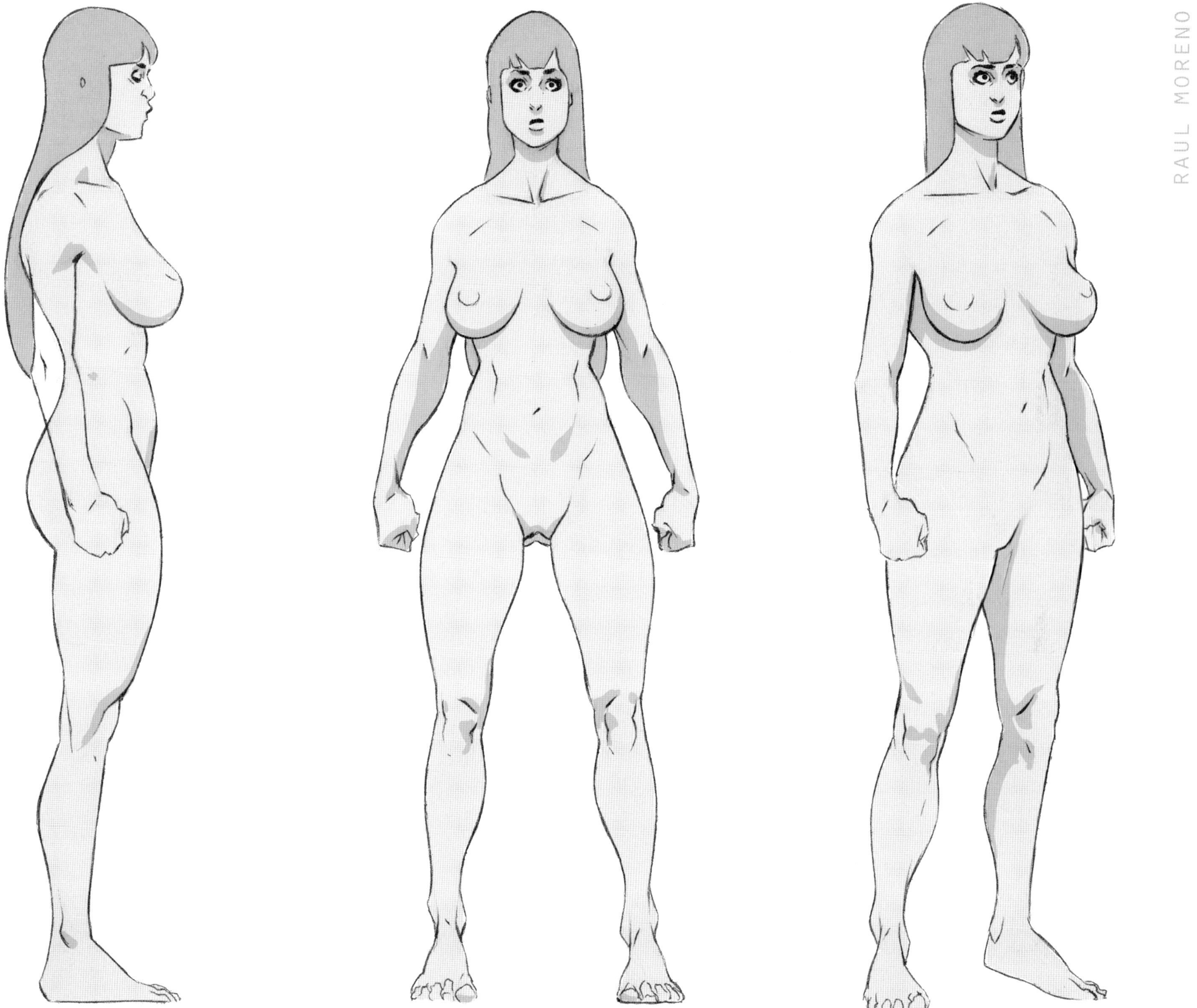

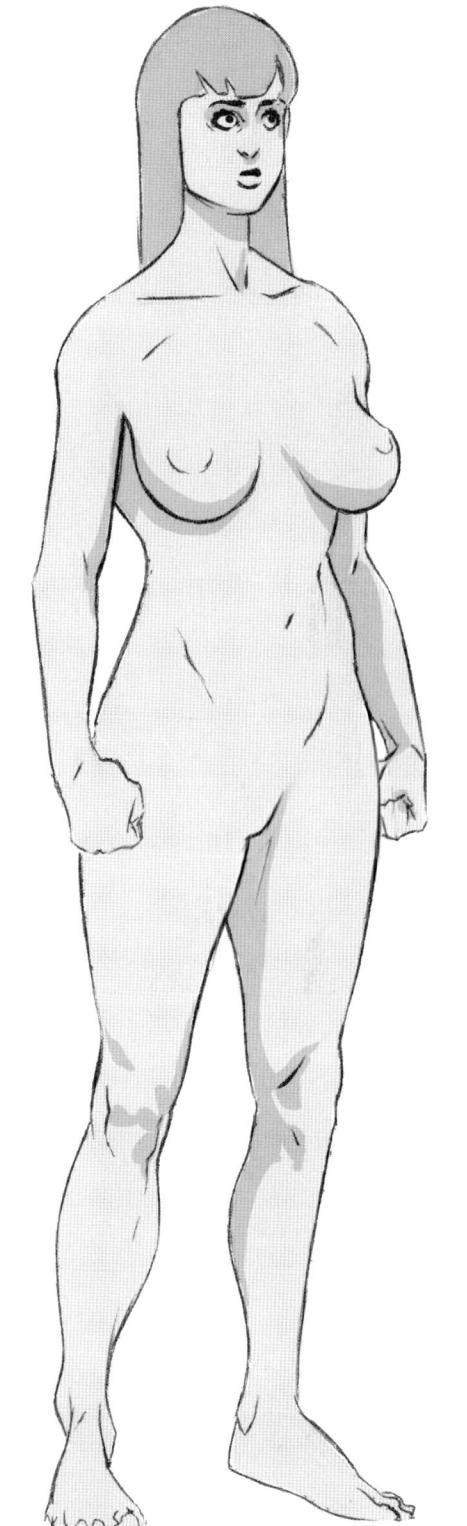

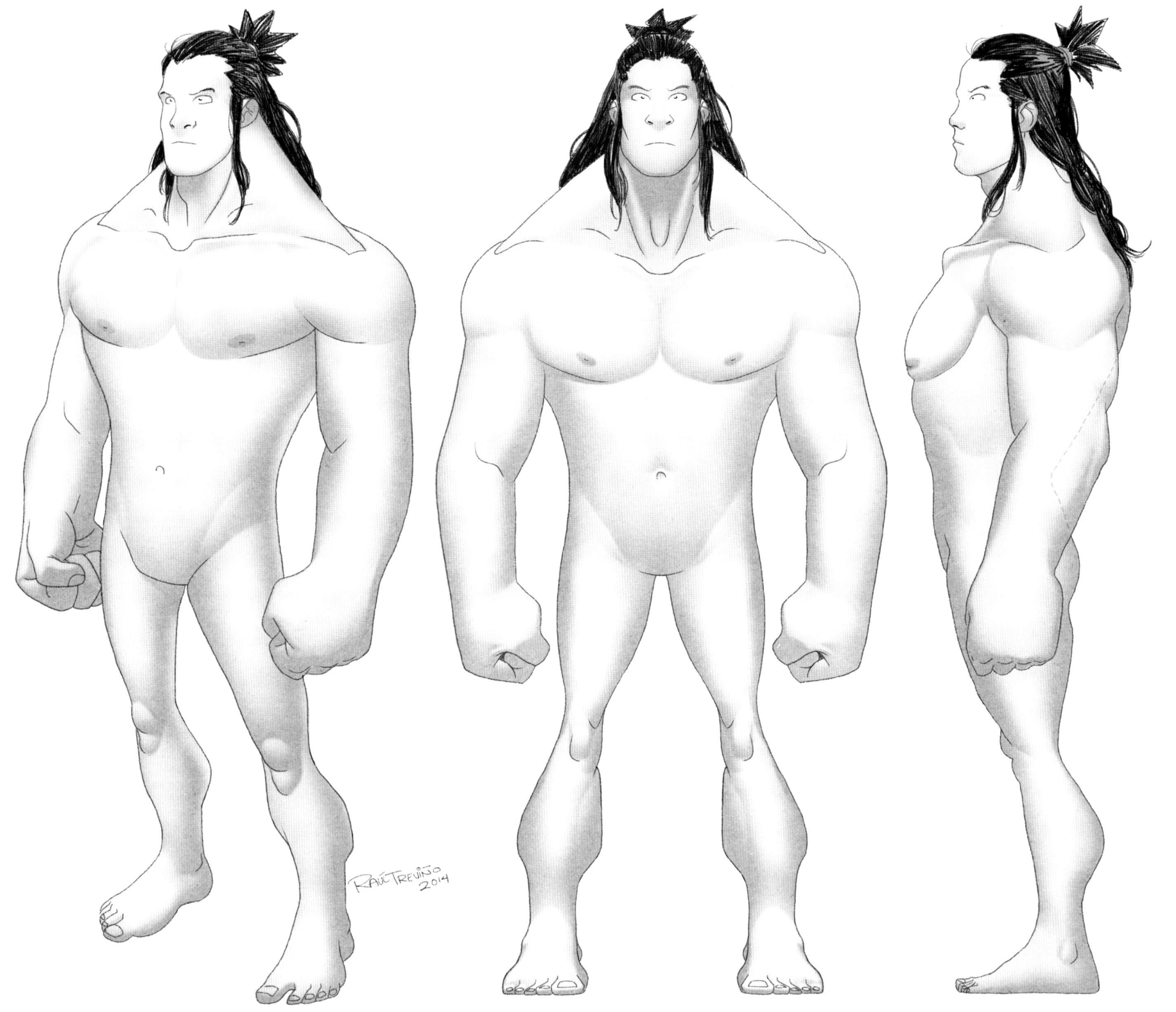

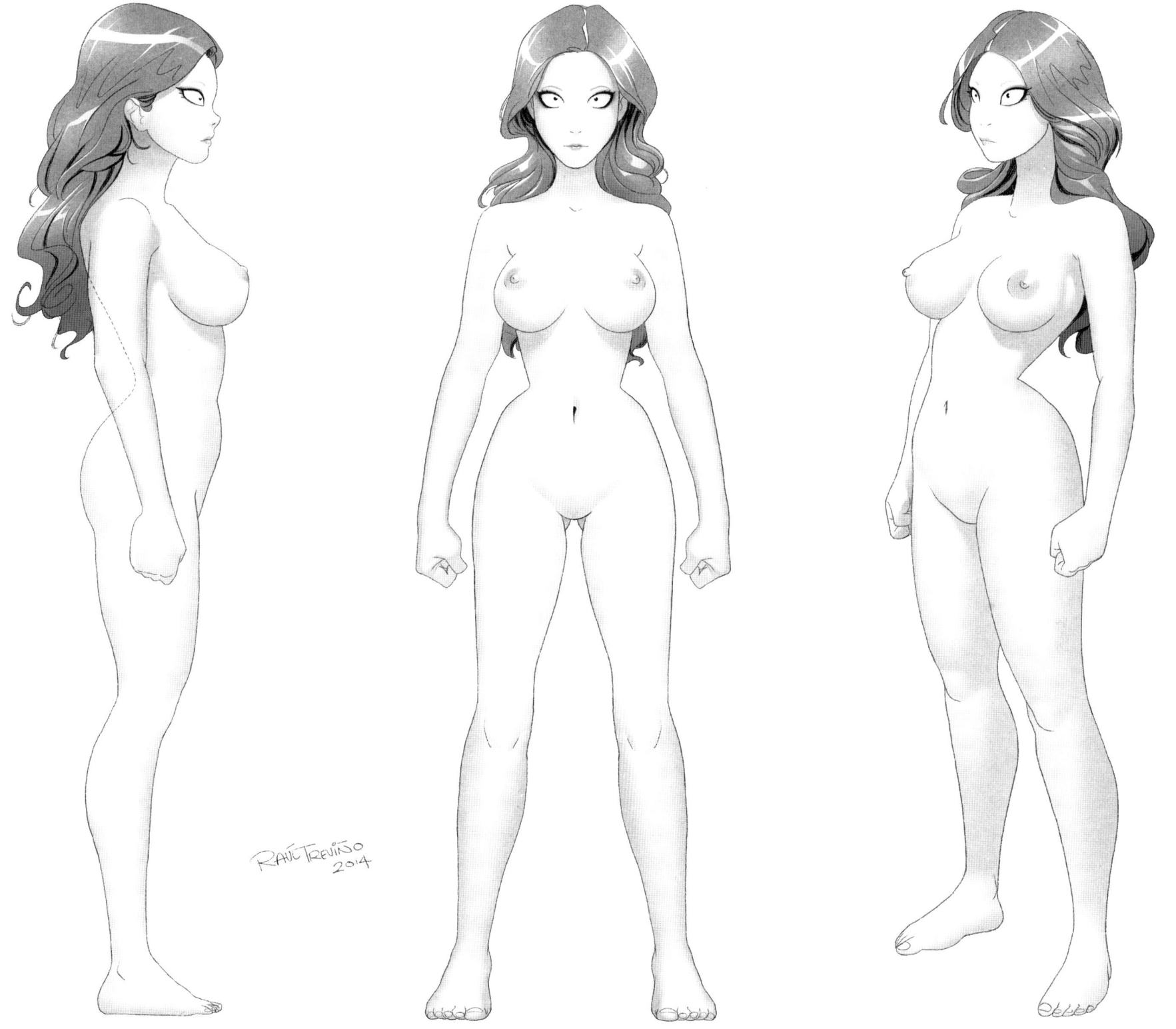

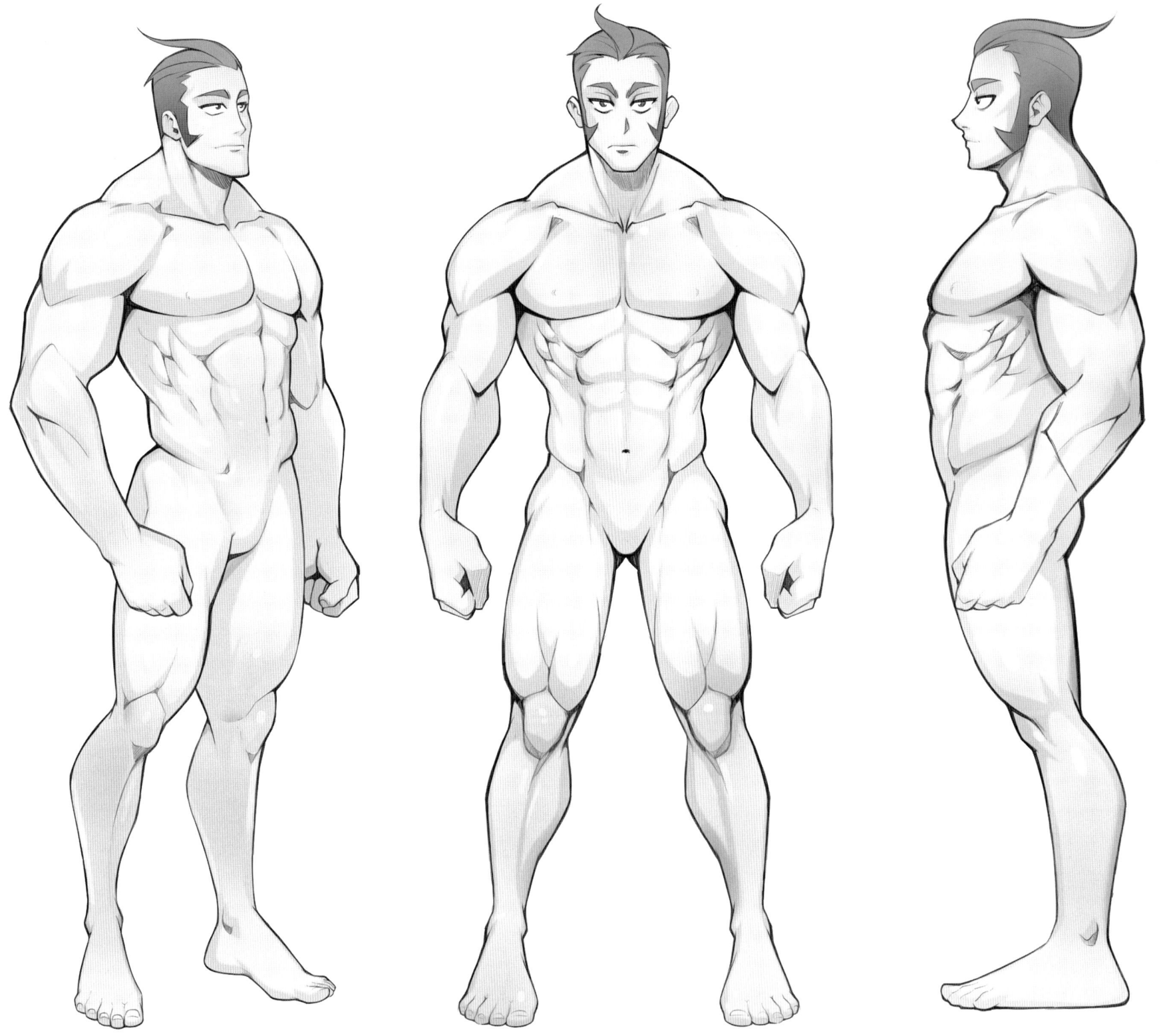

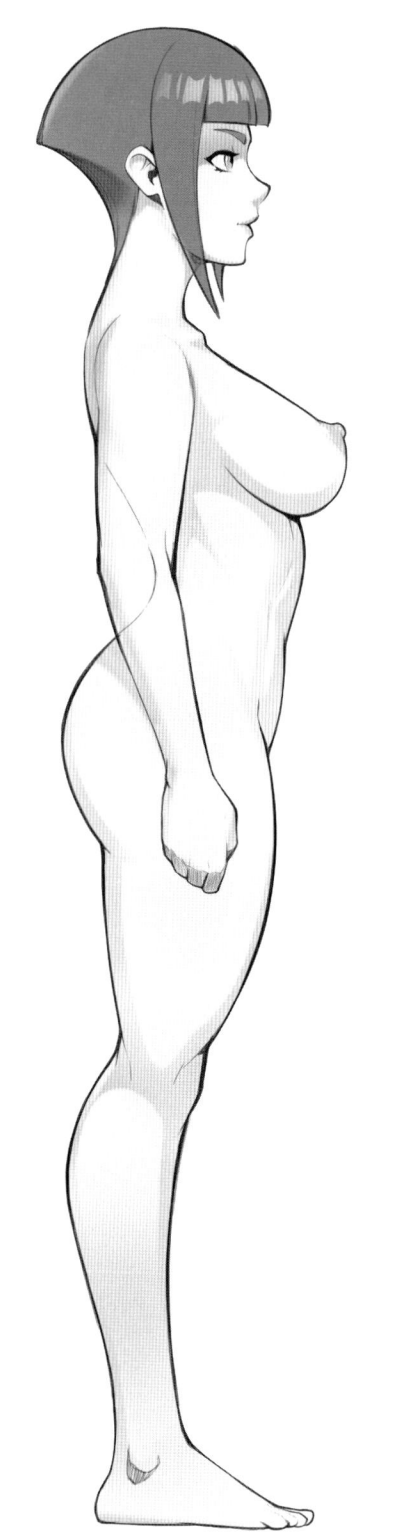
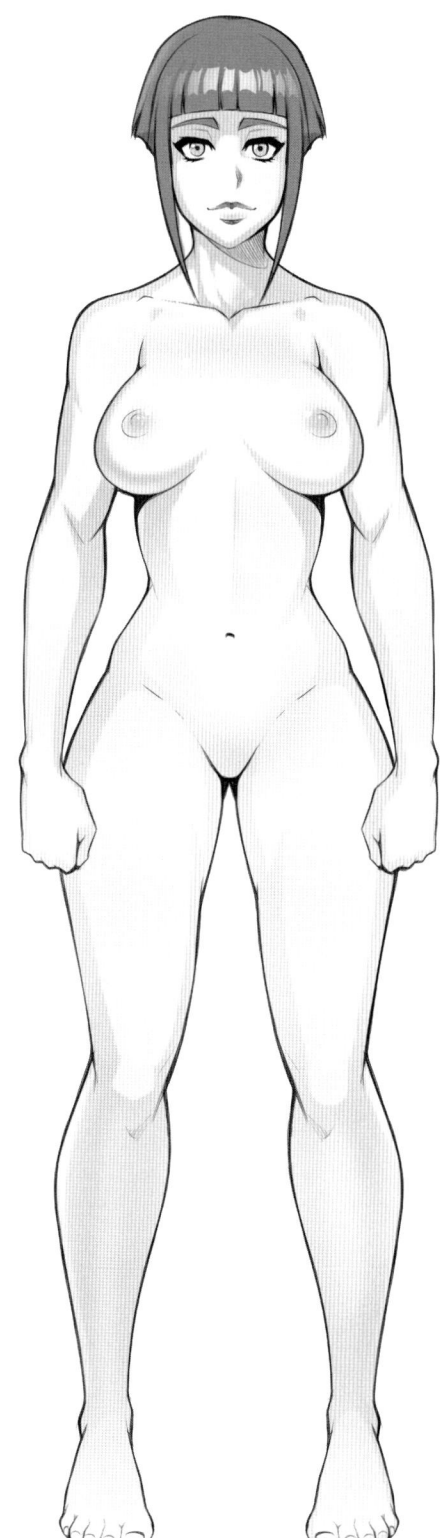
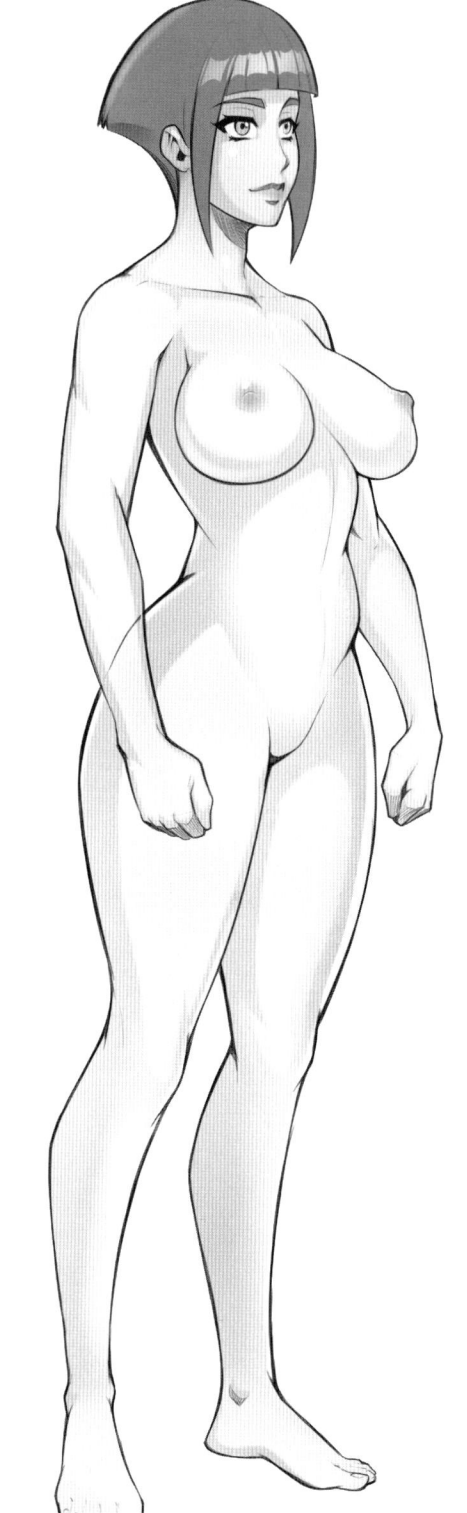

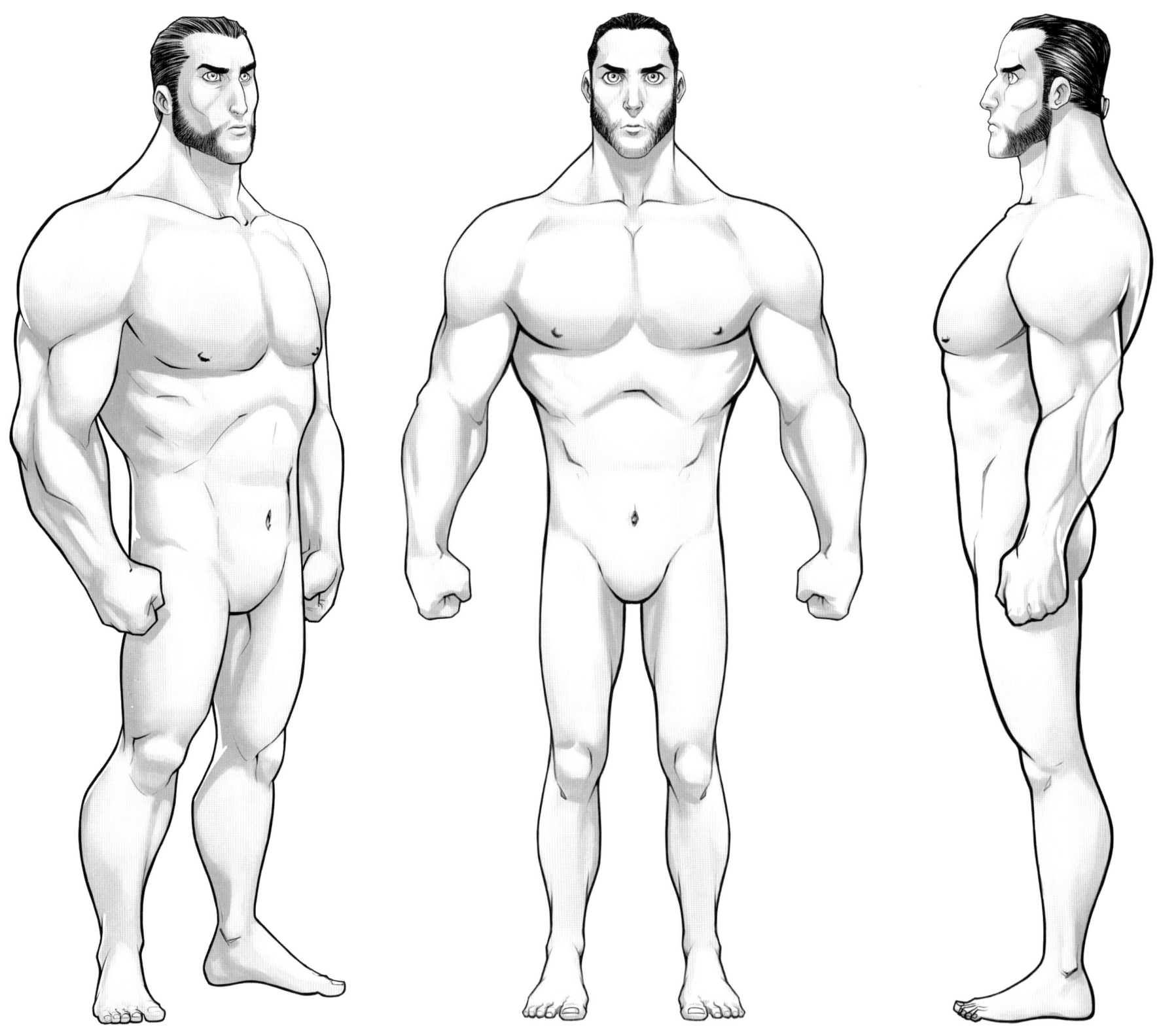

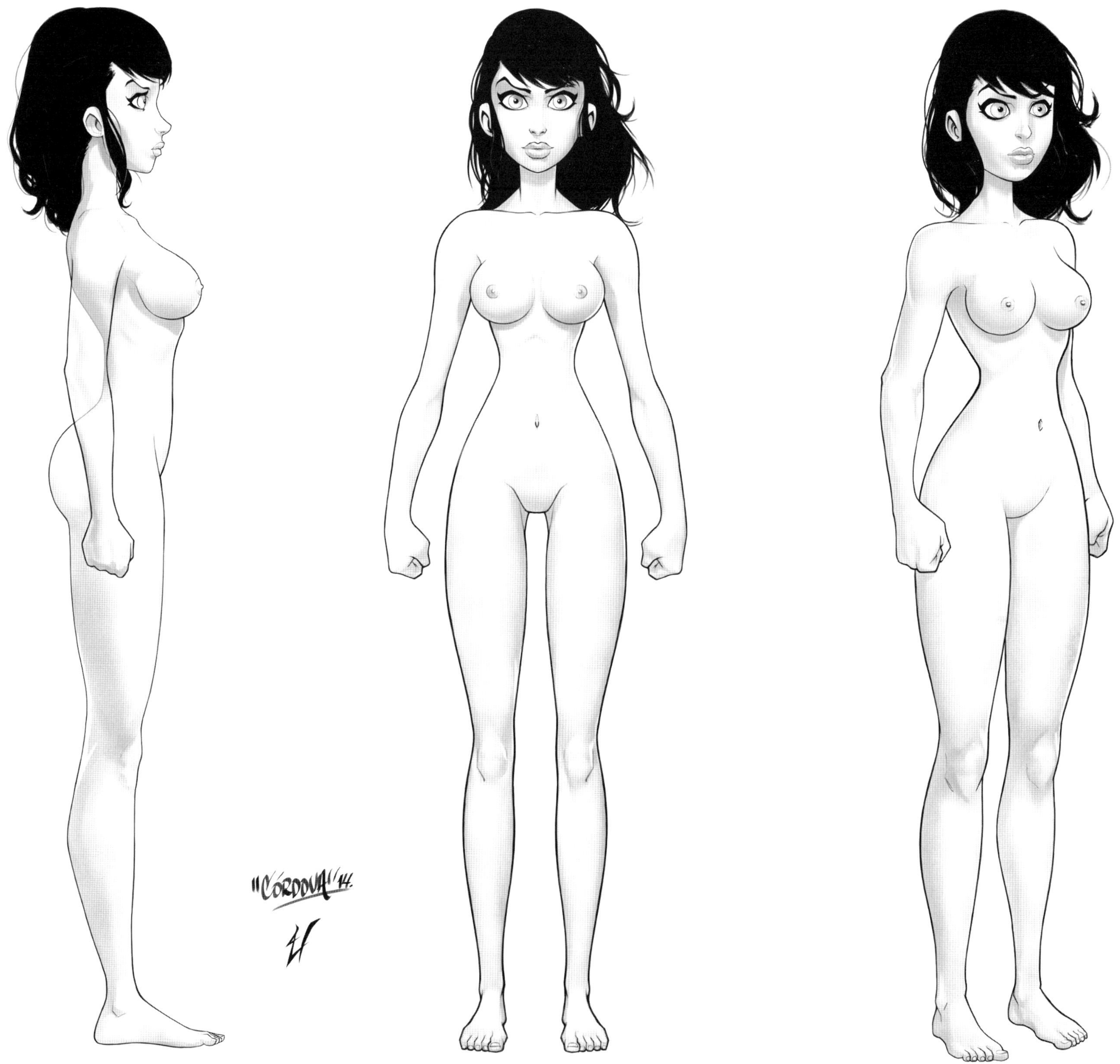

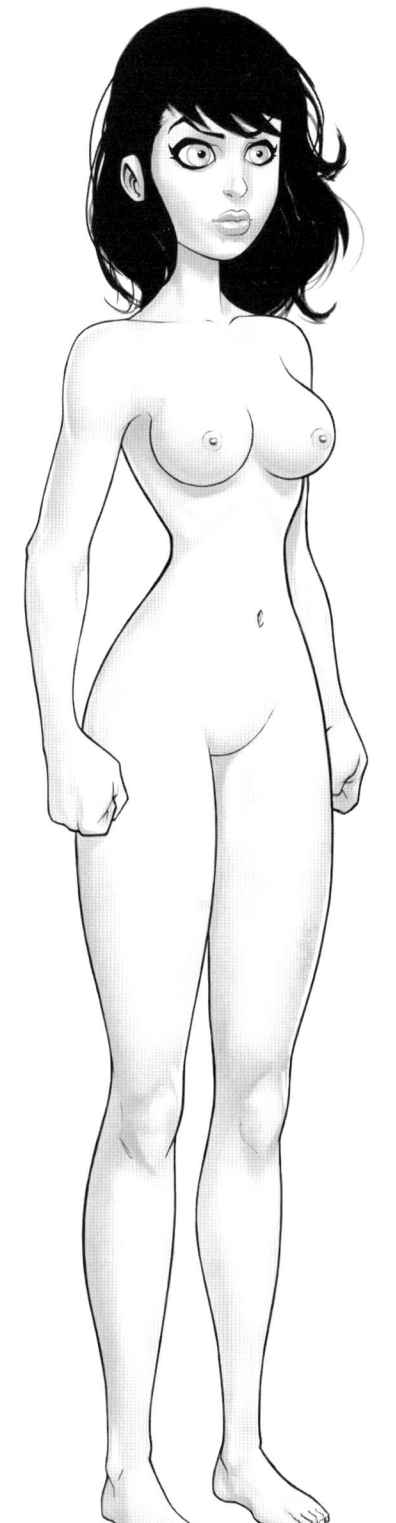

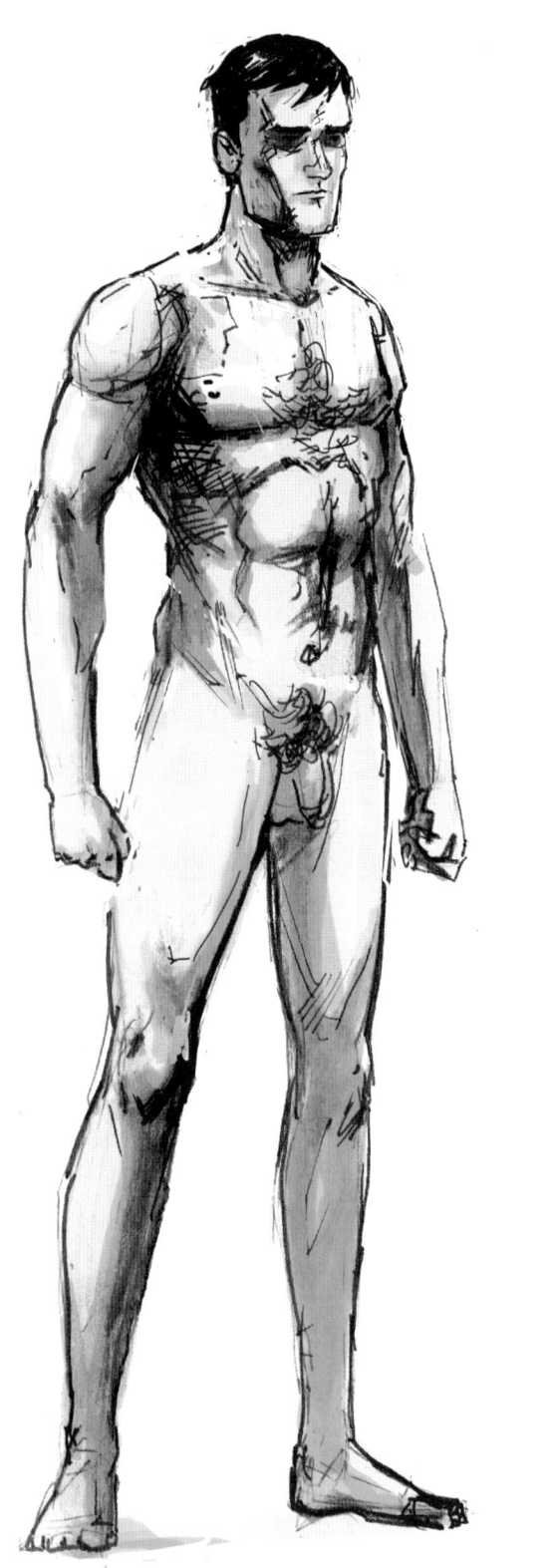
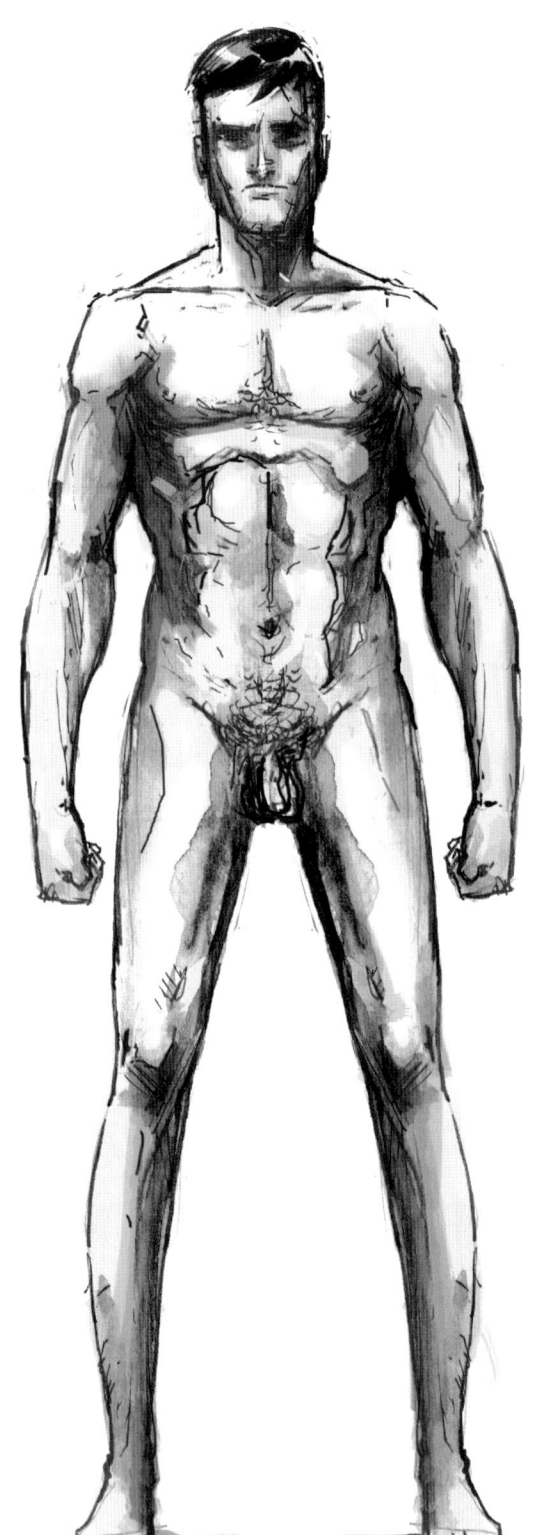

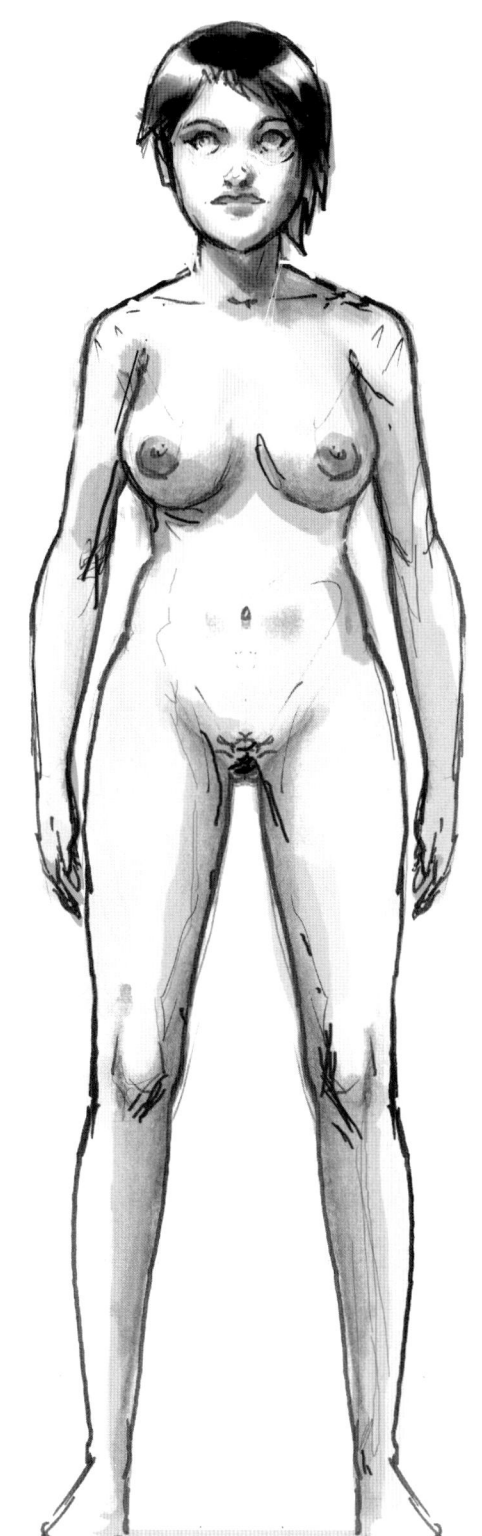
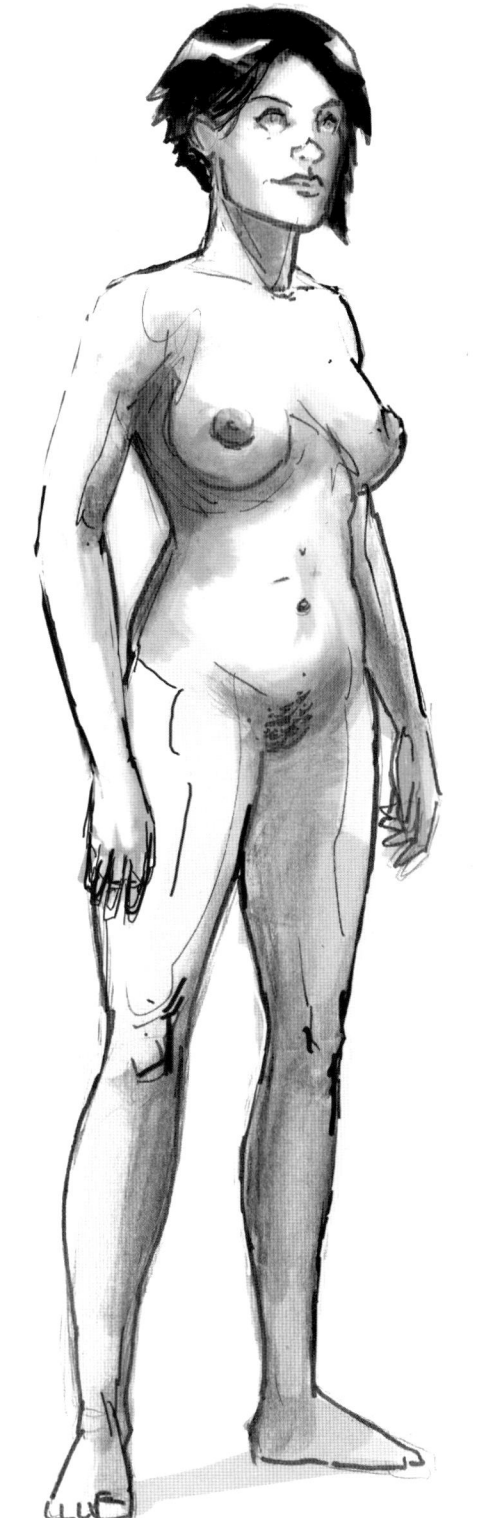

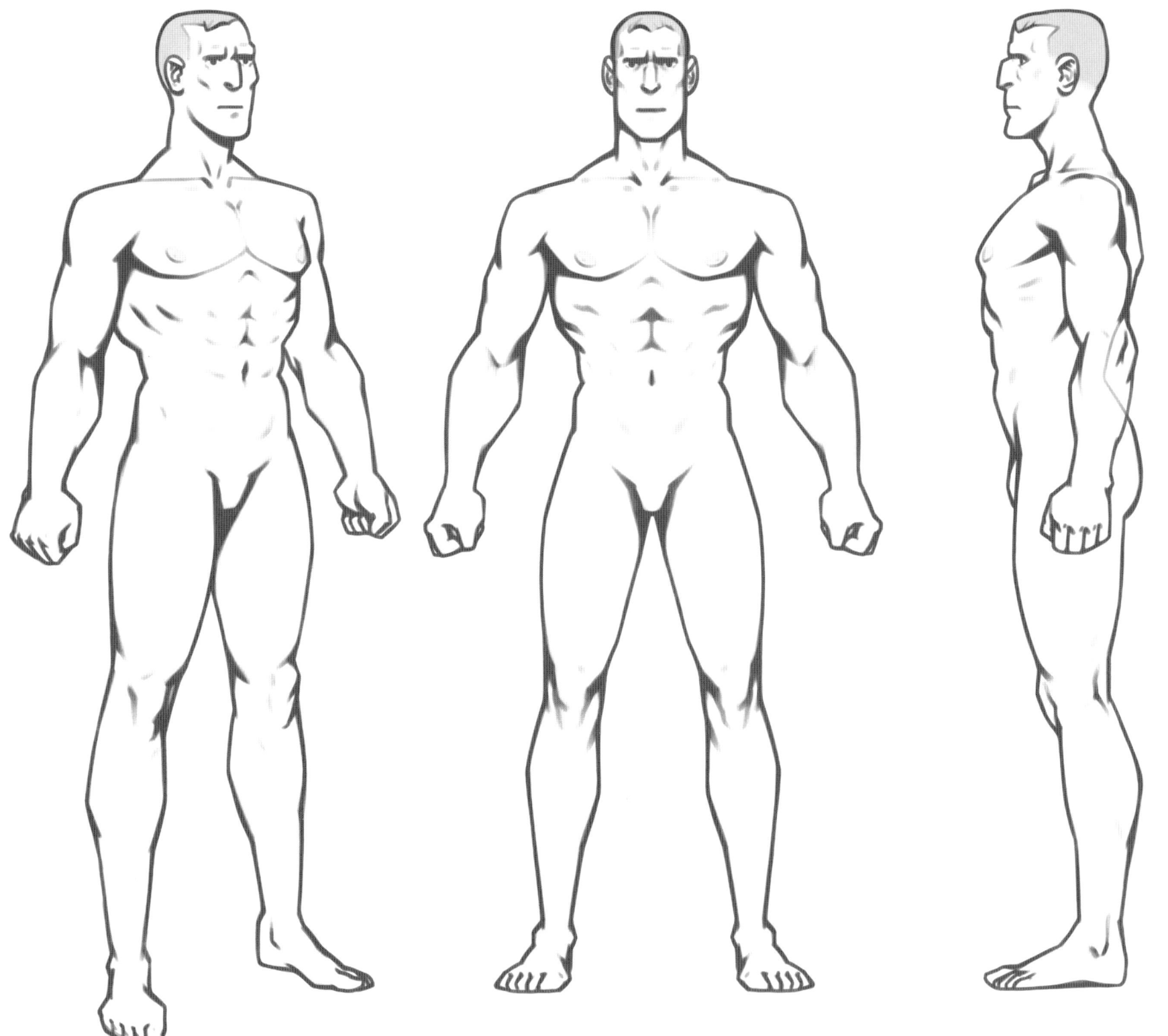

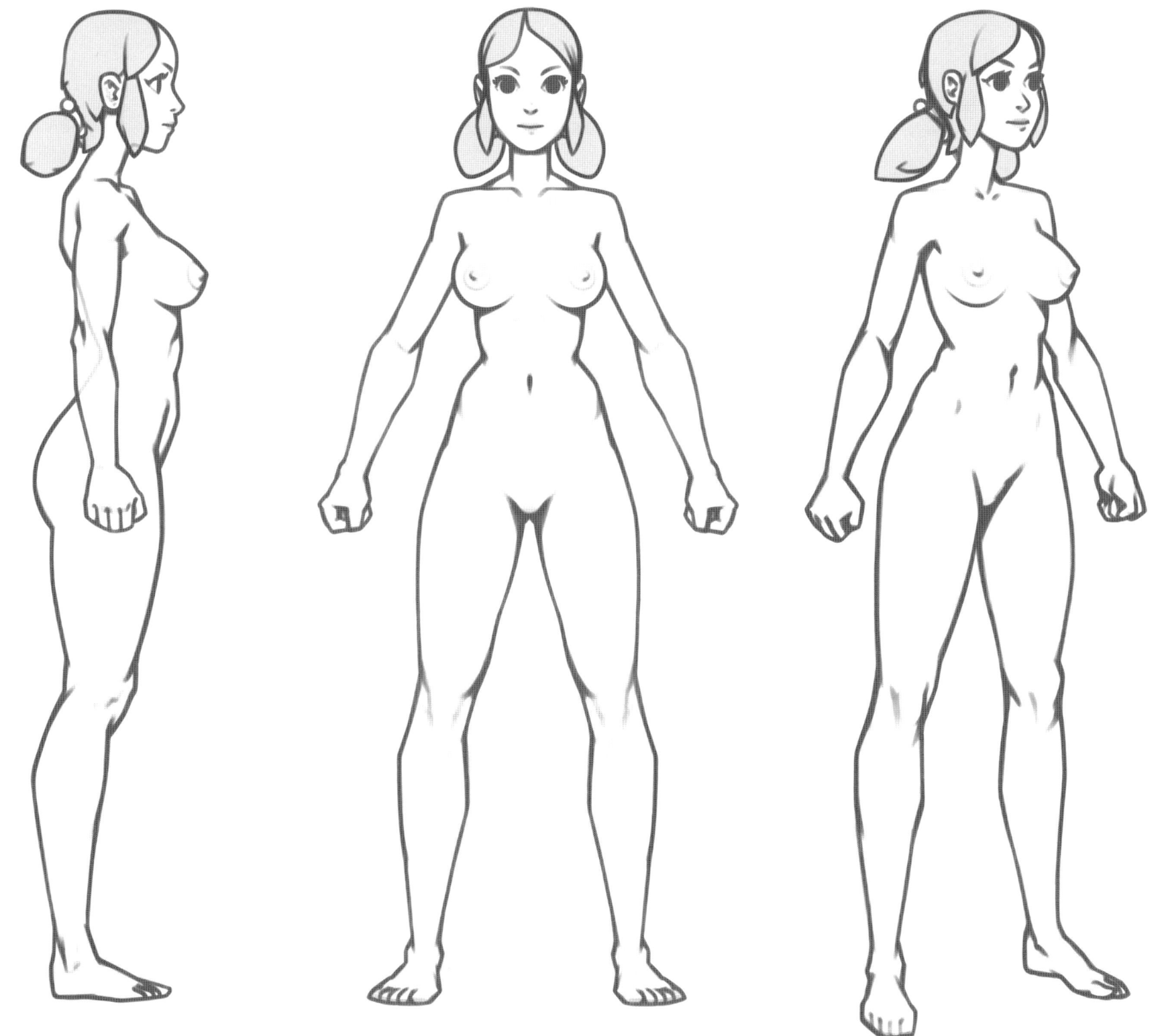

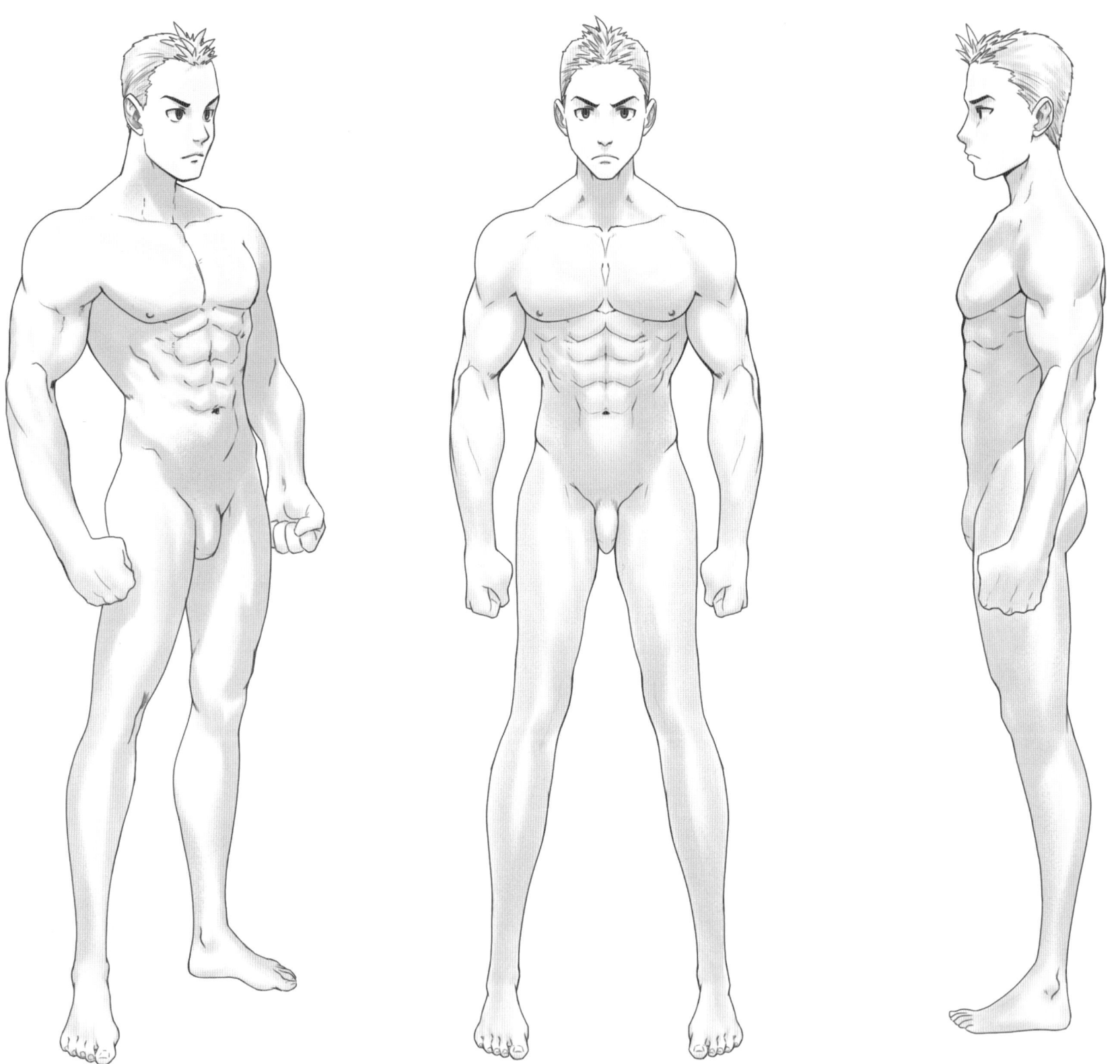

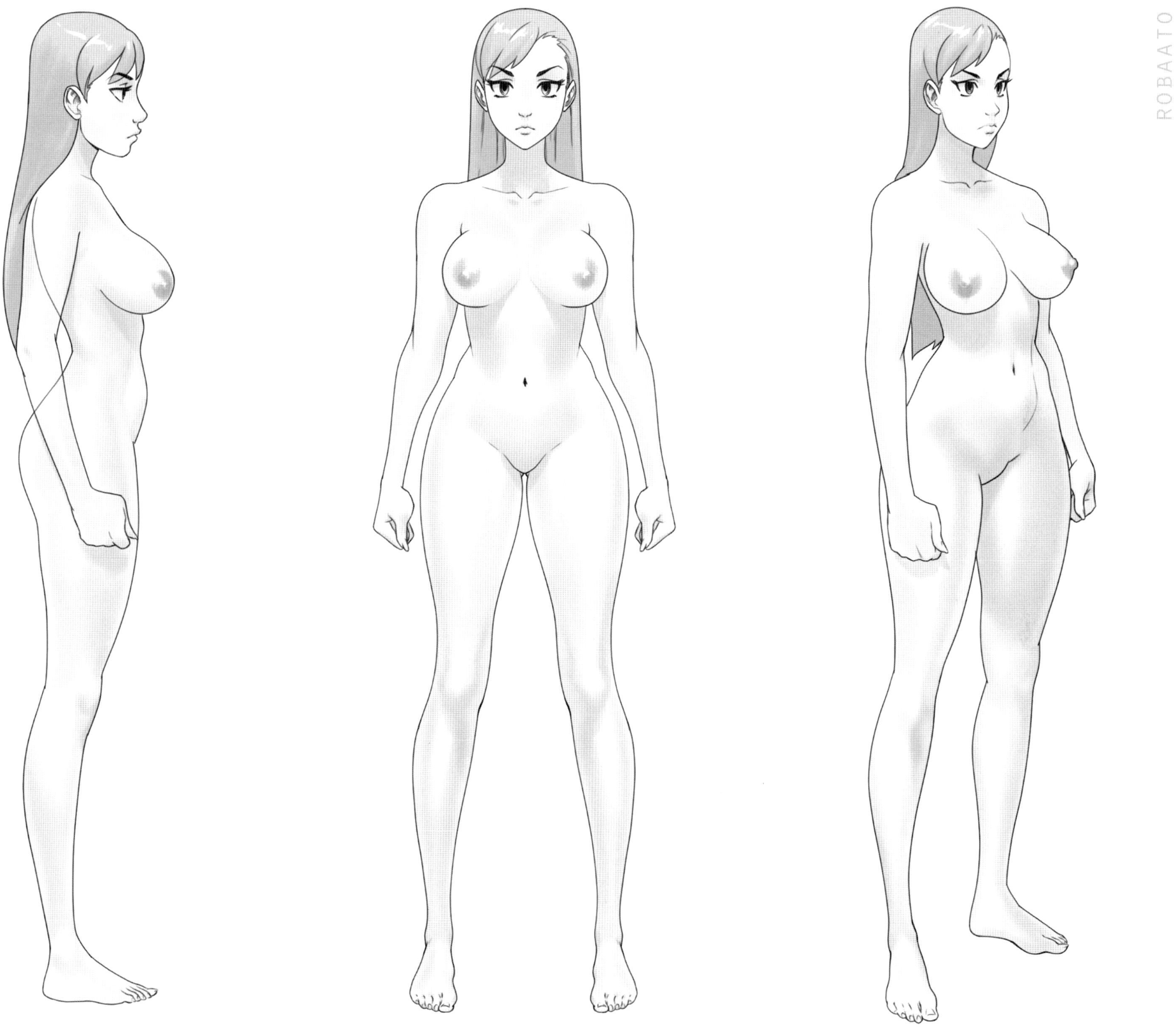

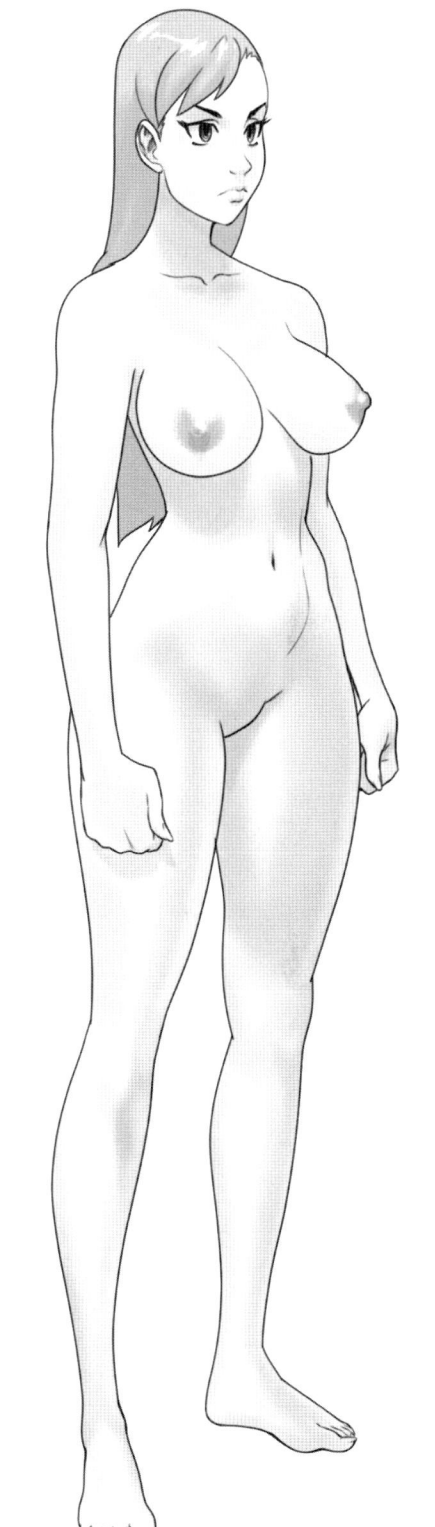

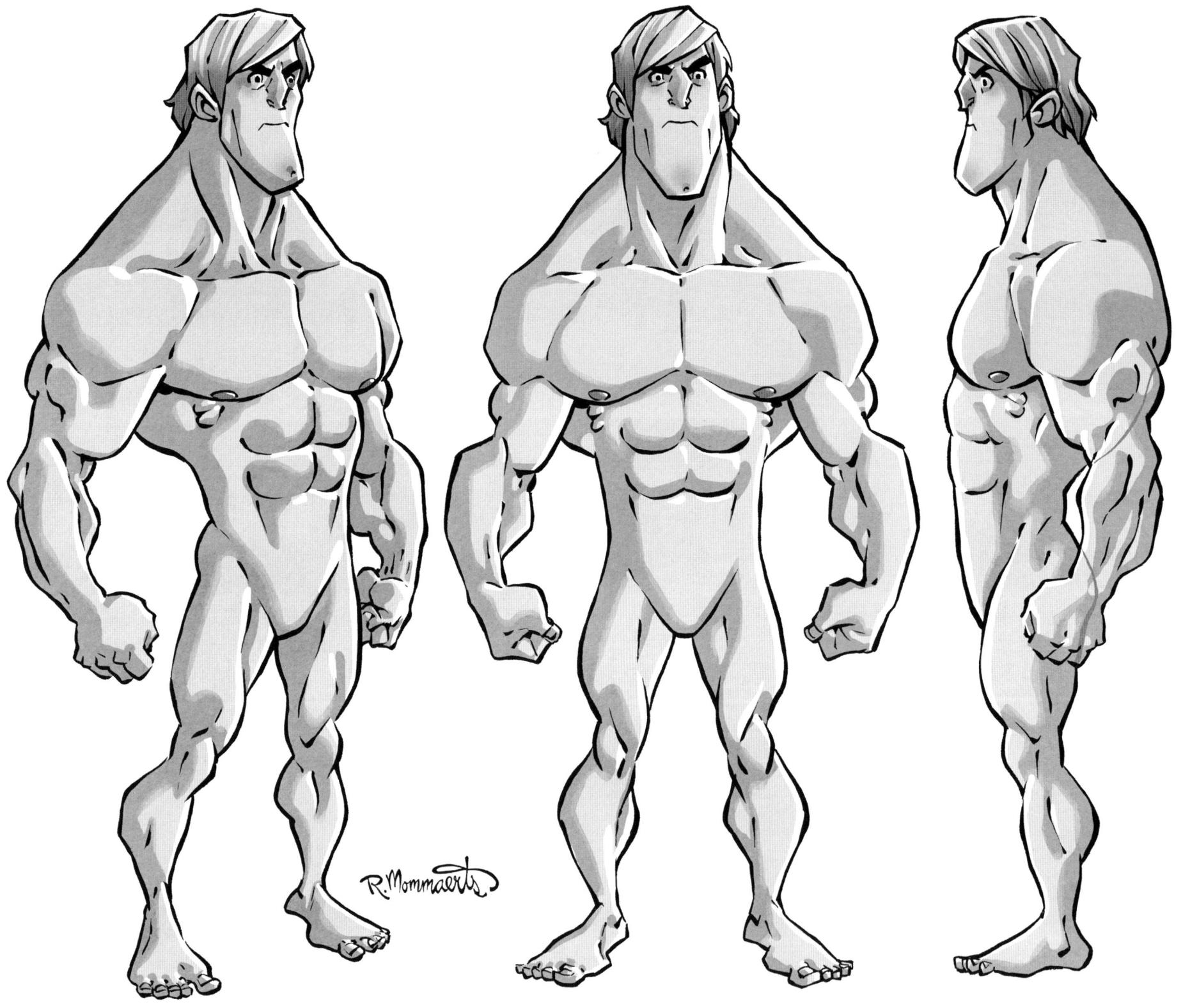

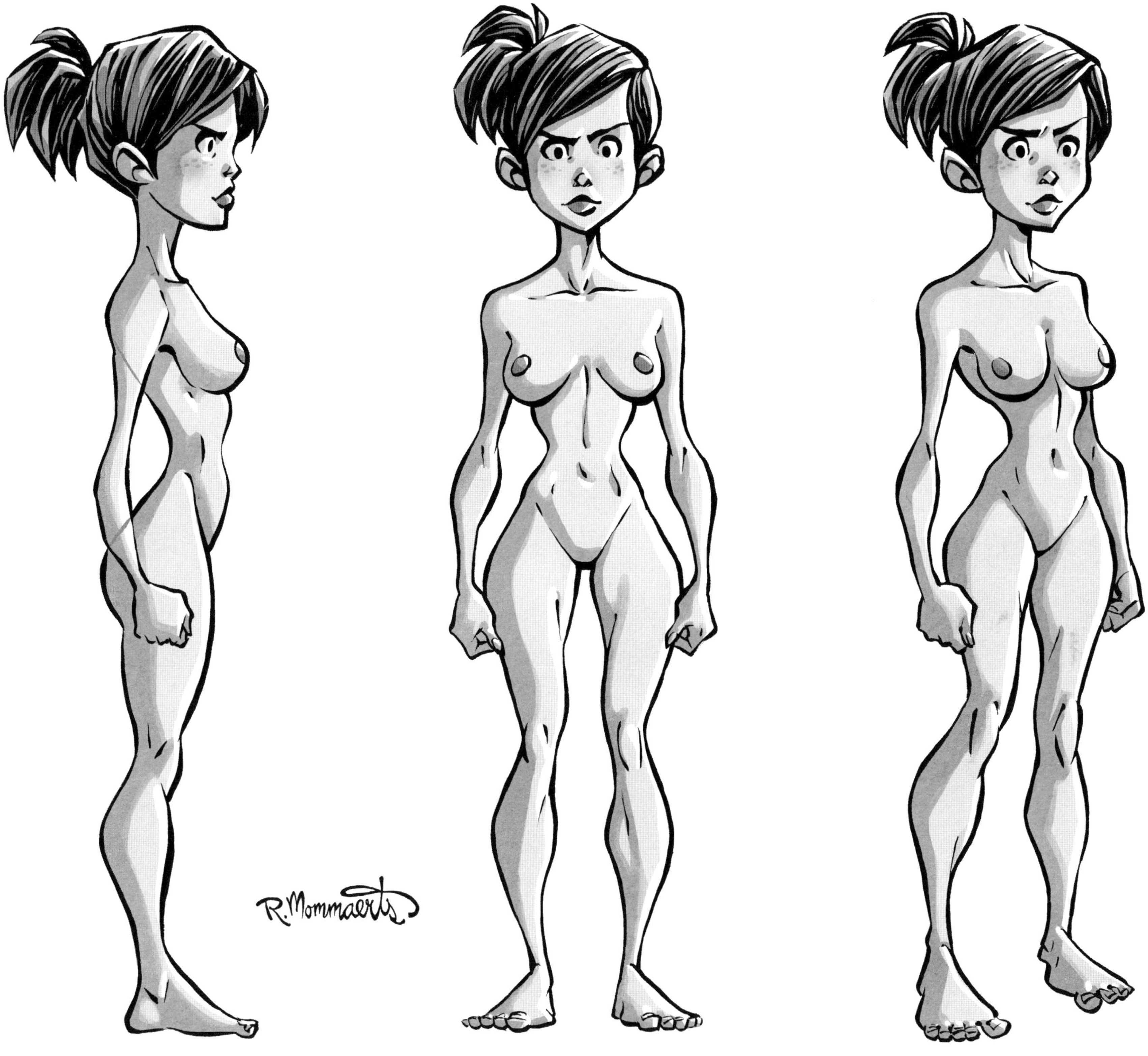

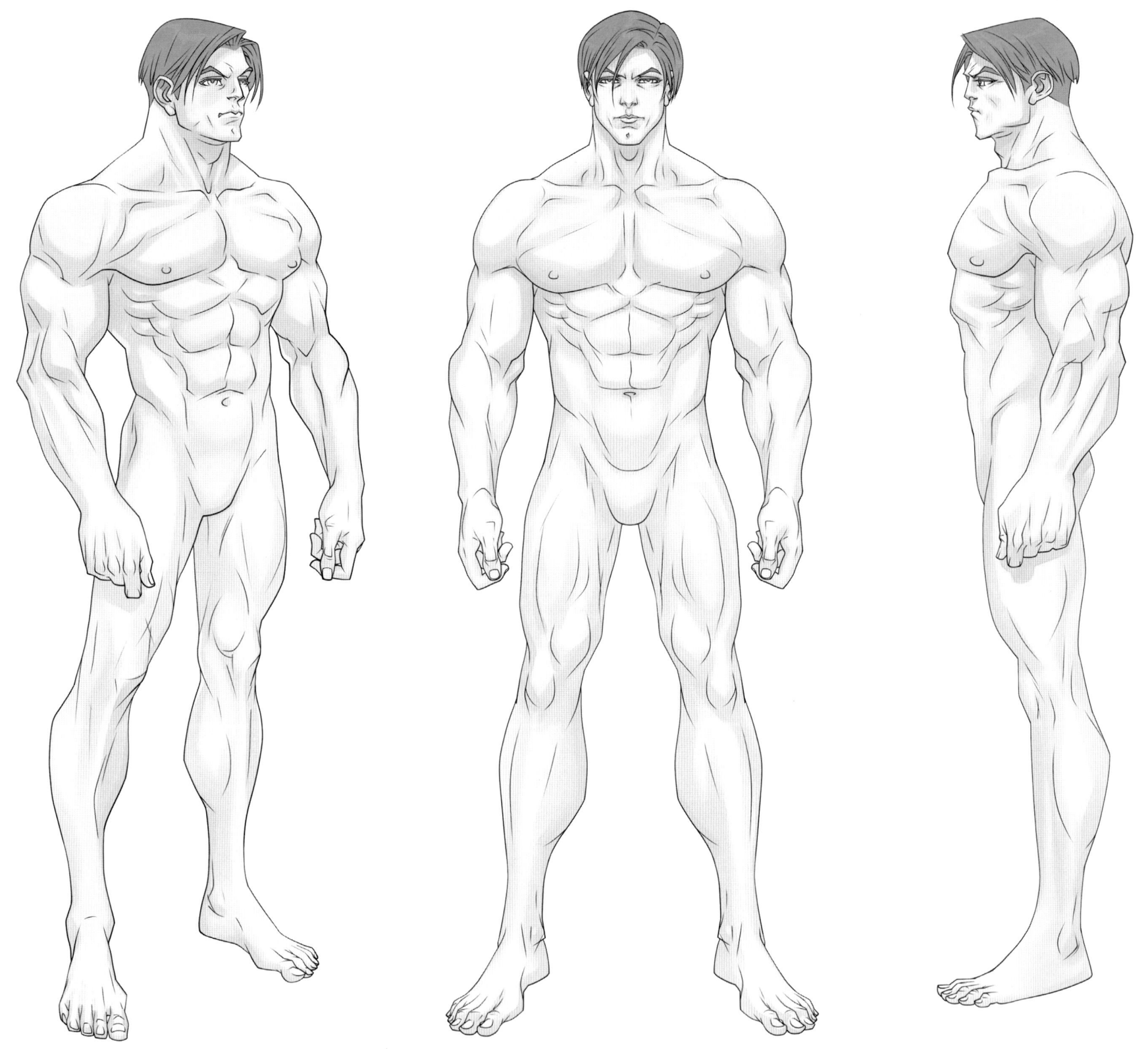

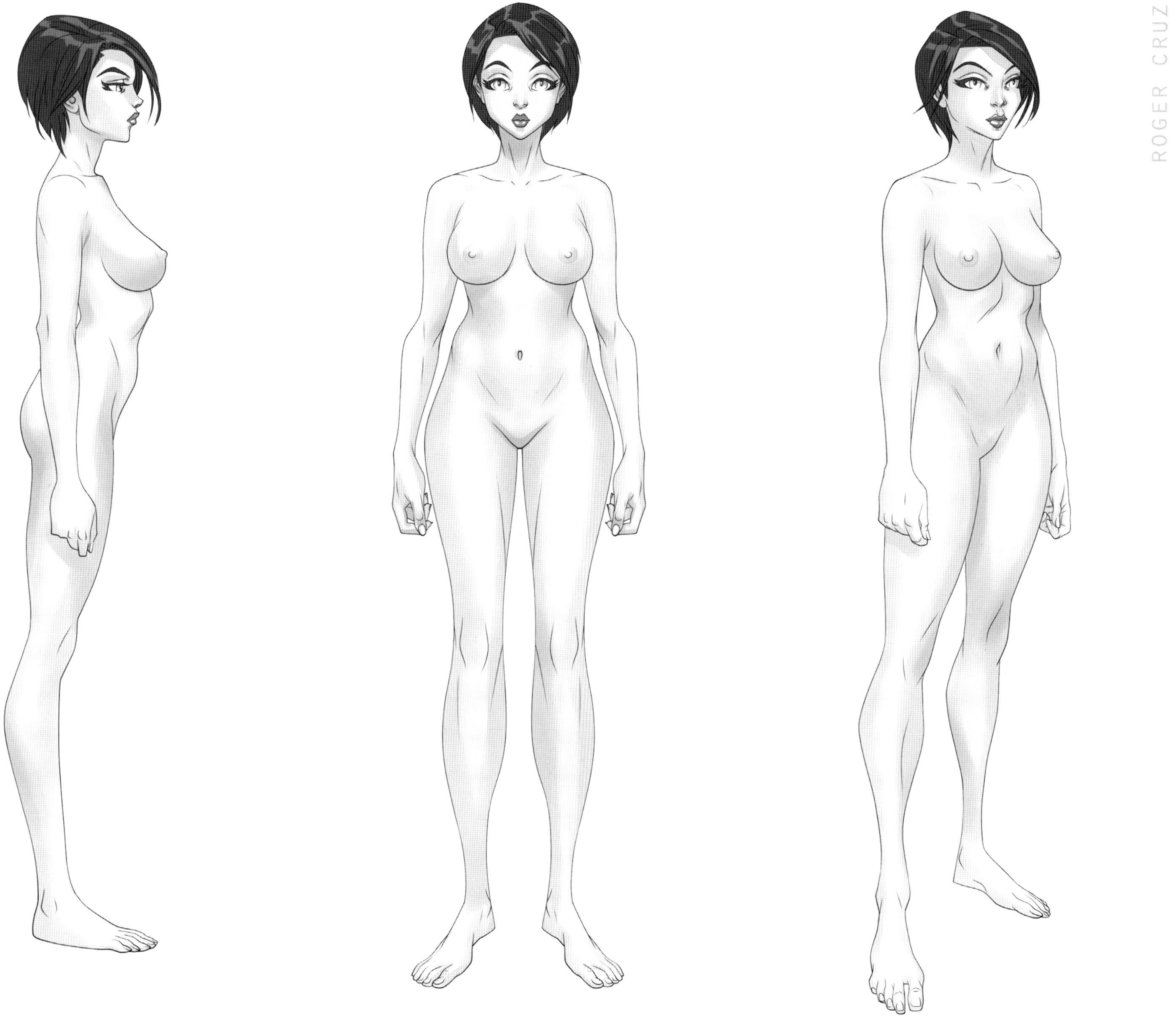

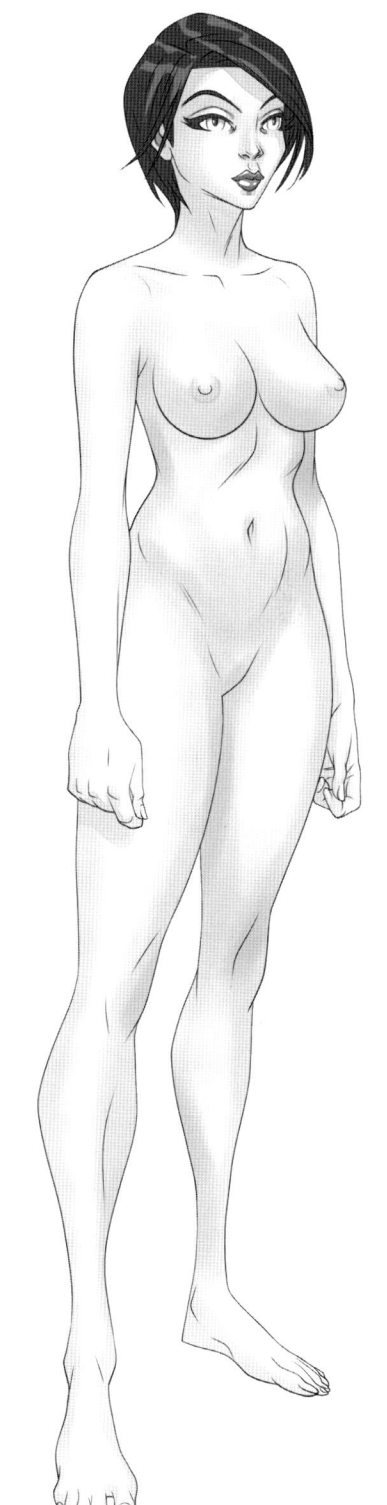

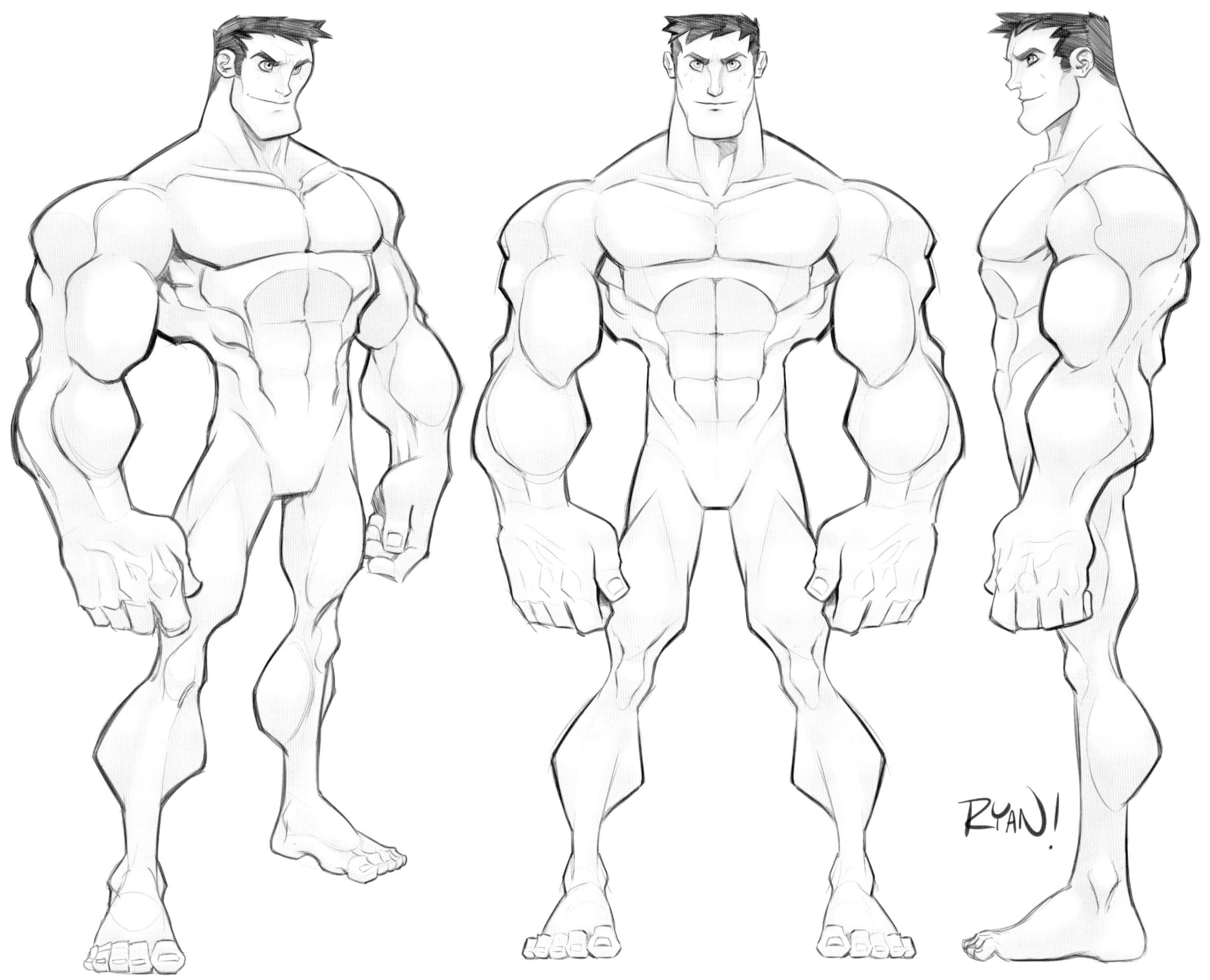

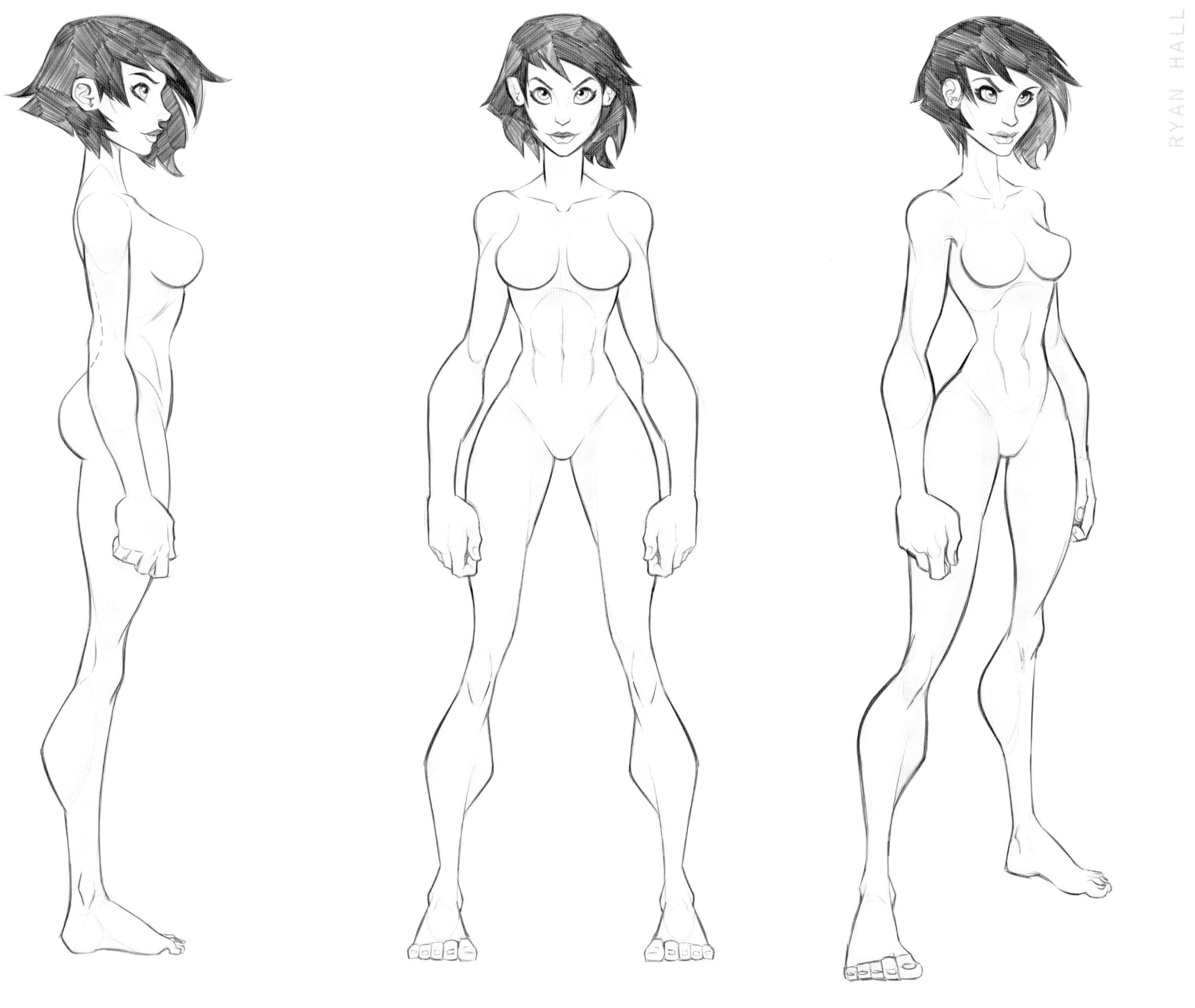

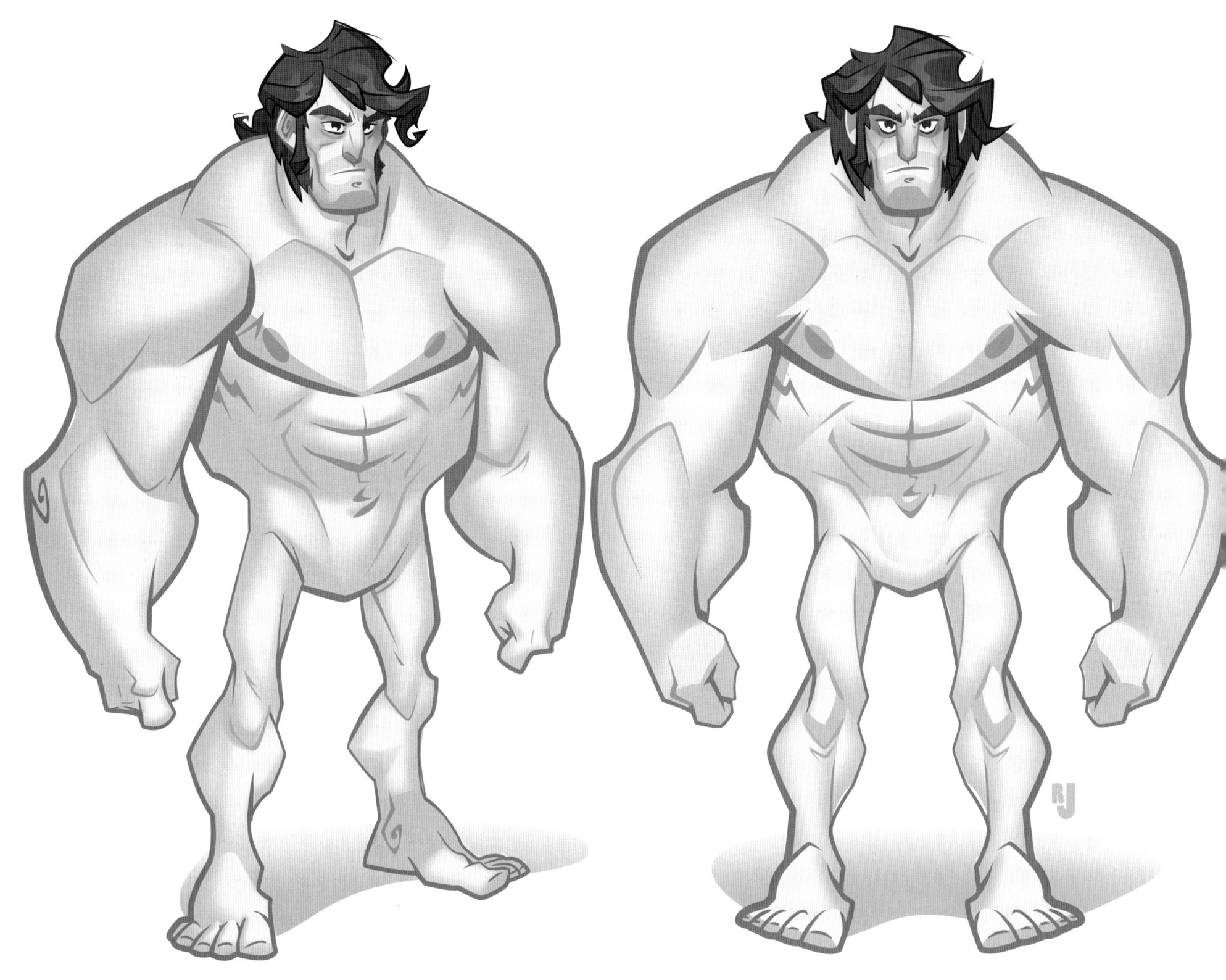

RYAN DAVID JONES

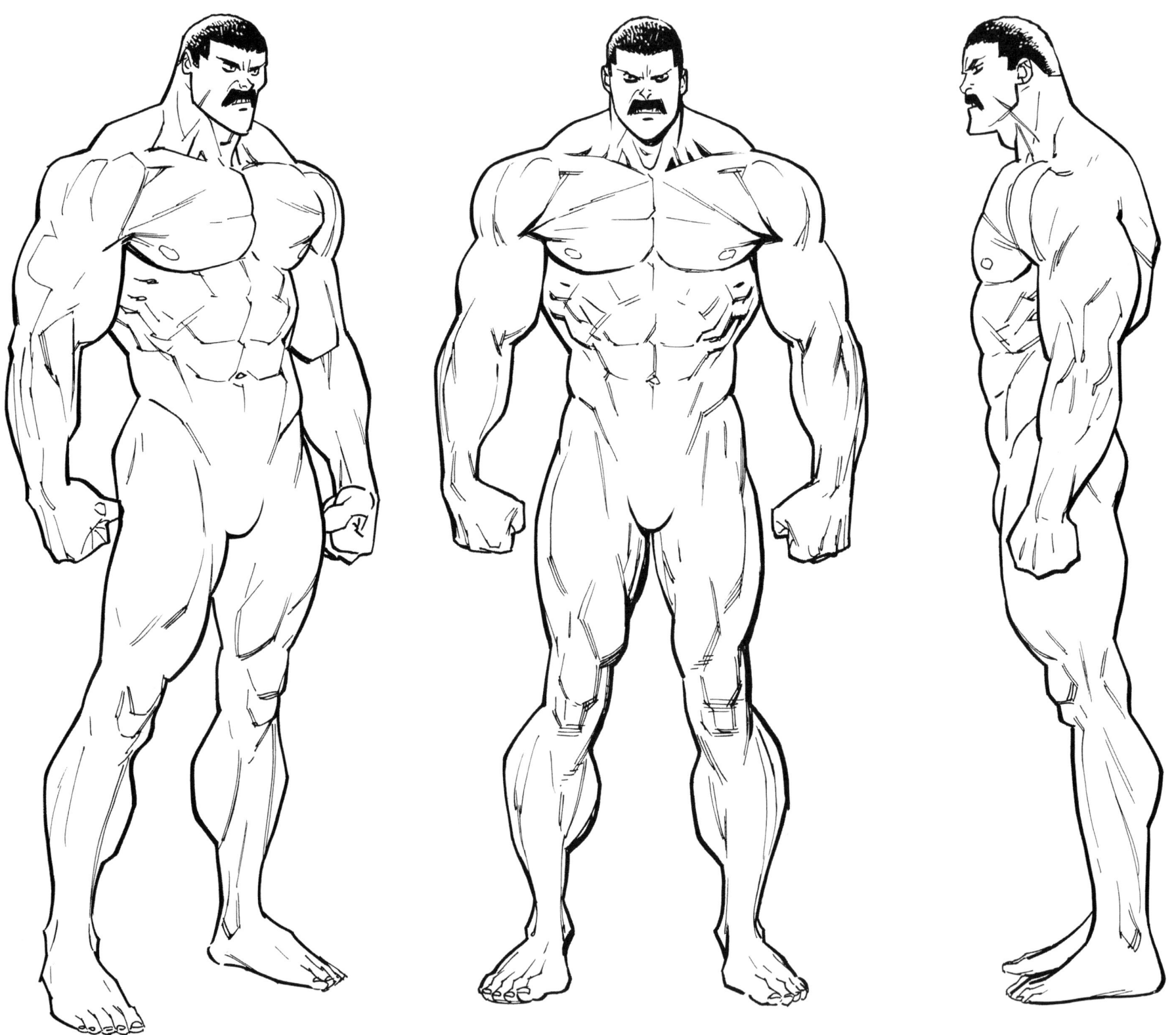

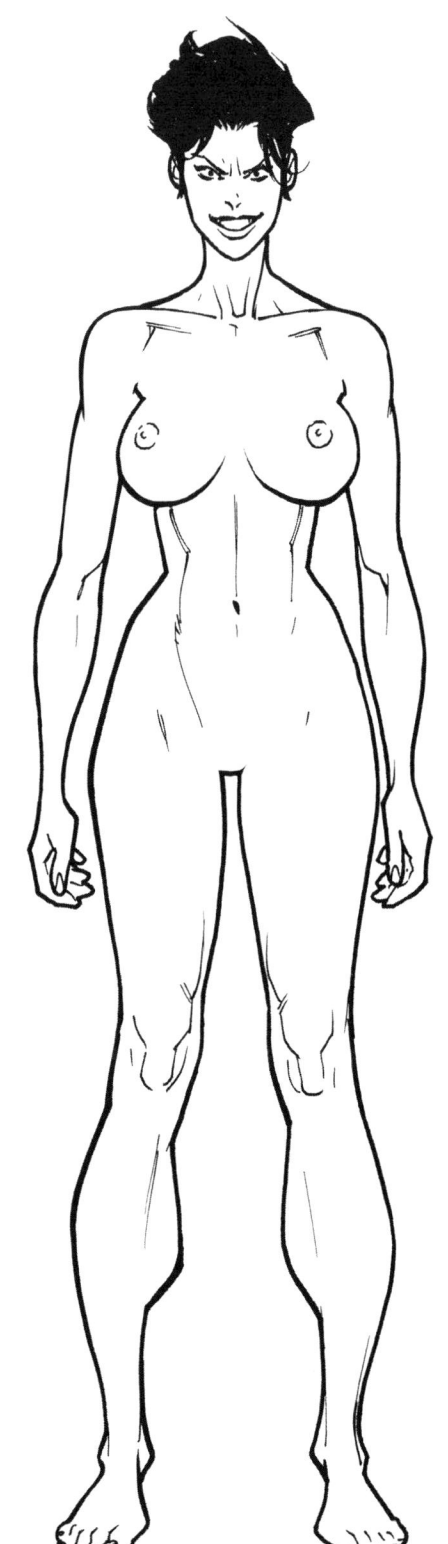
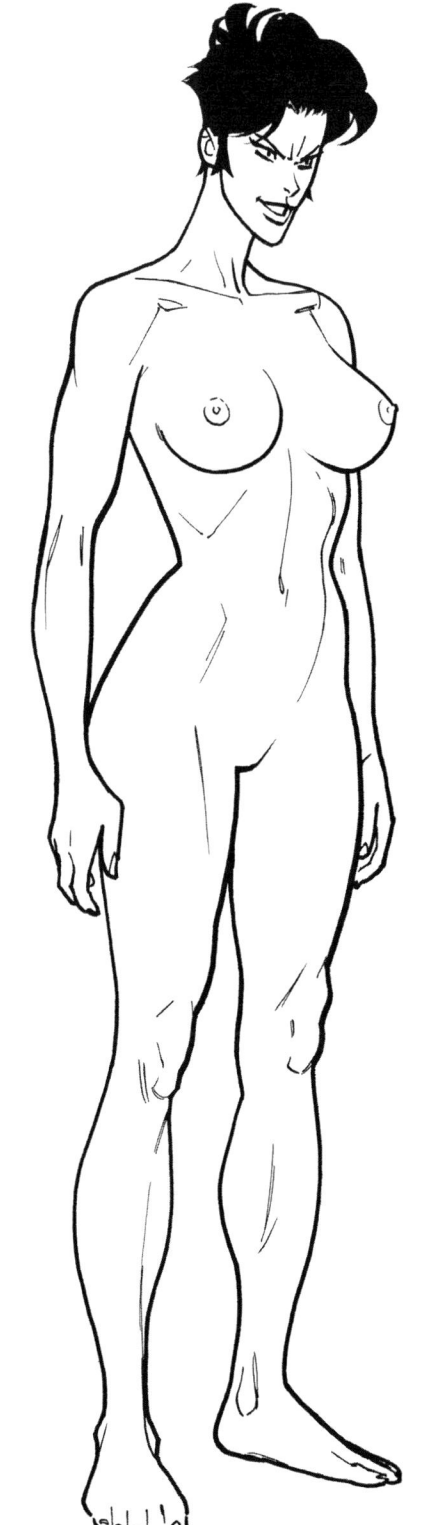

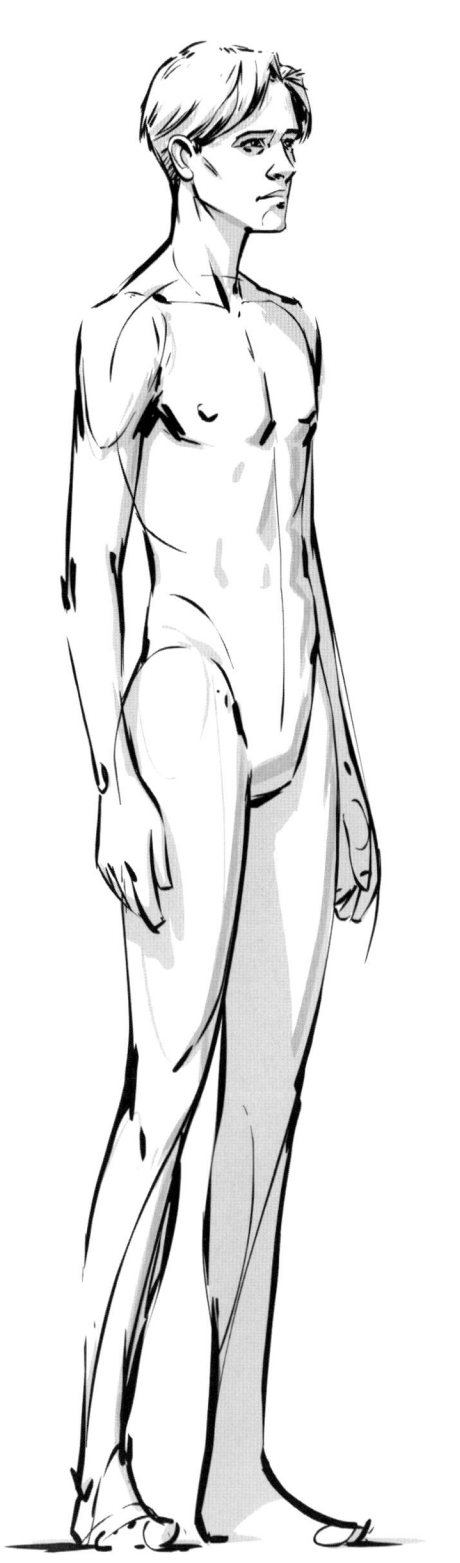
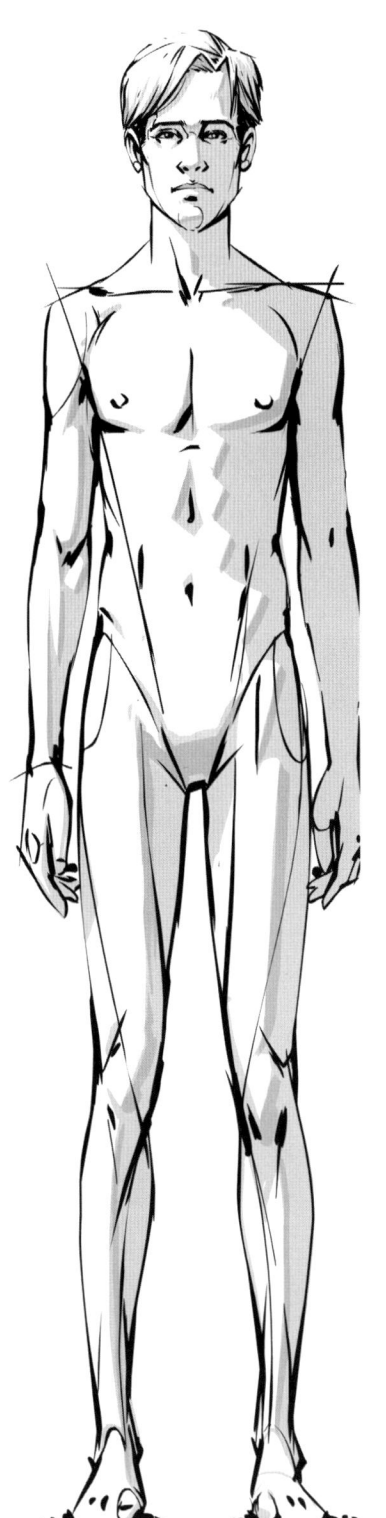
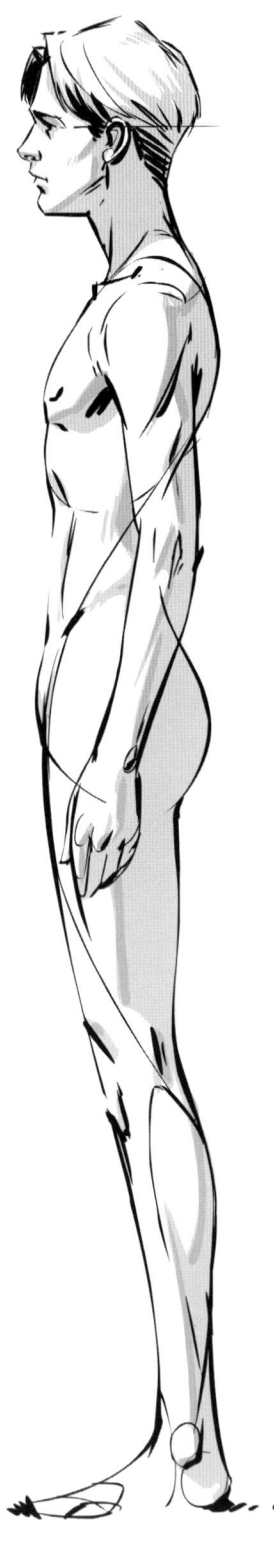

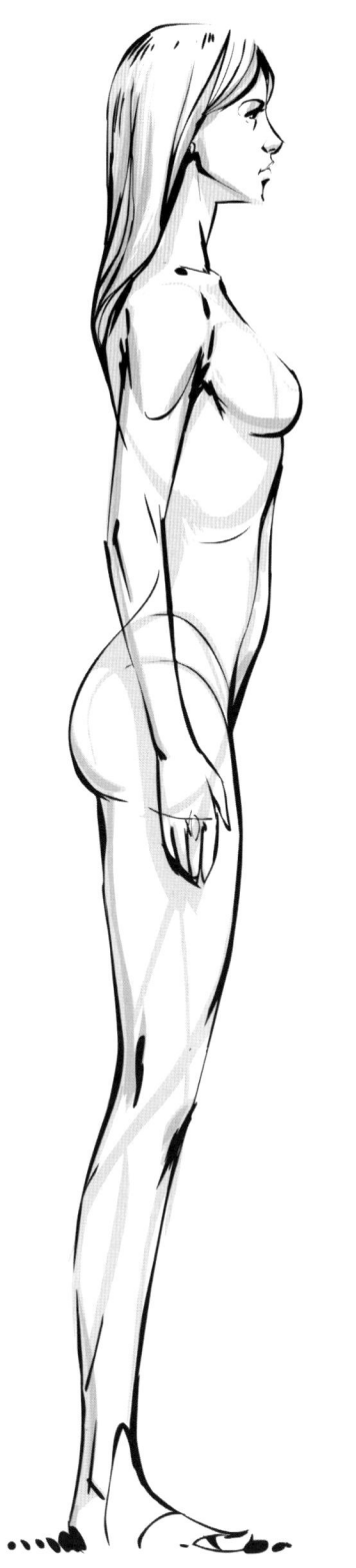
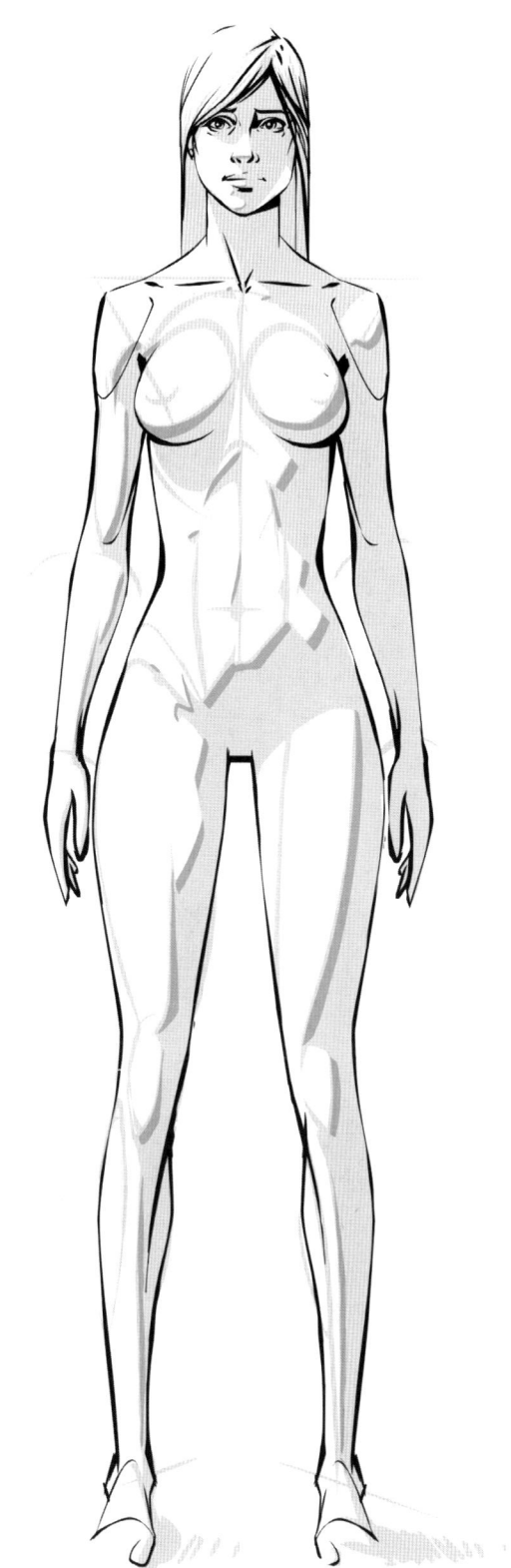
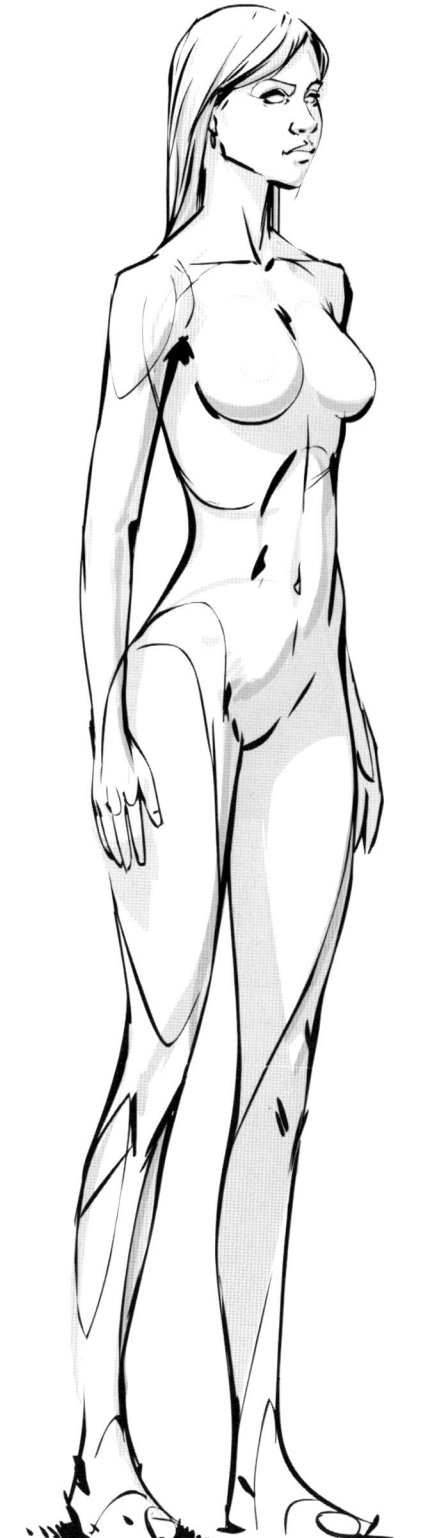

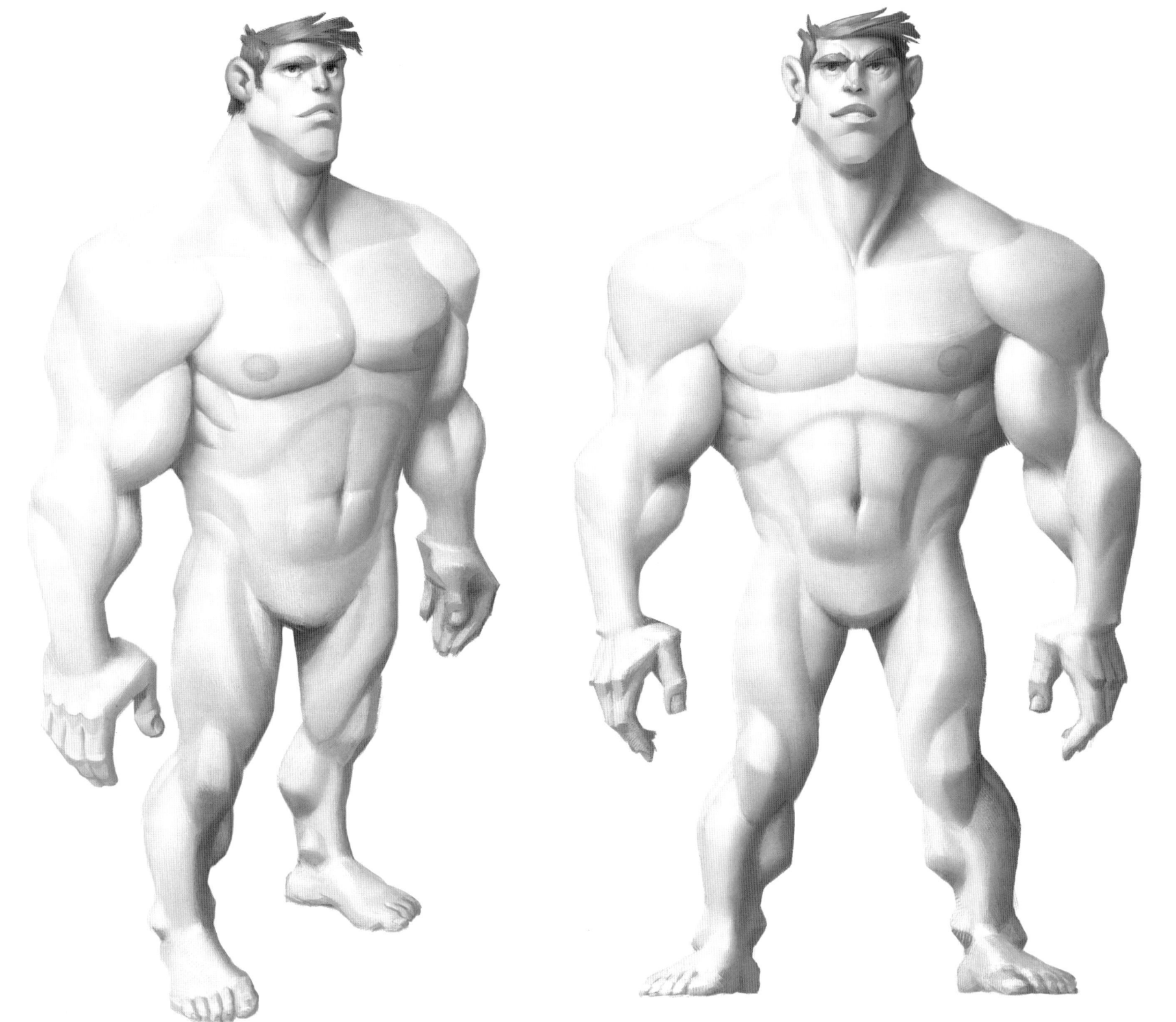

SAM NIELSON

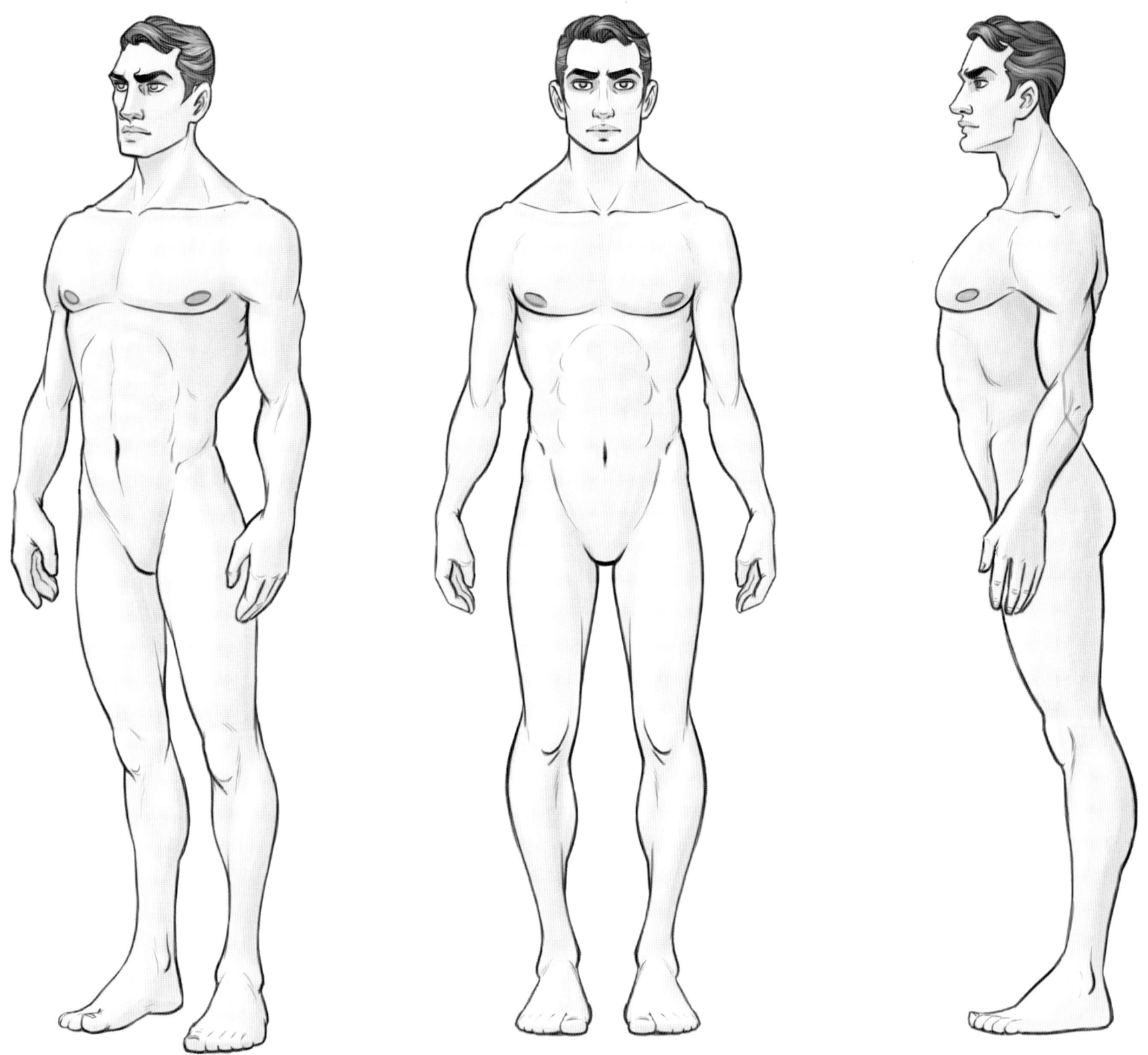

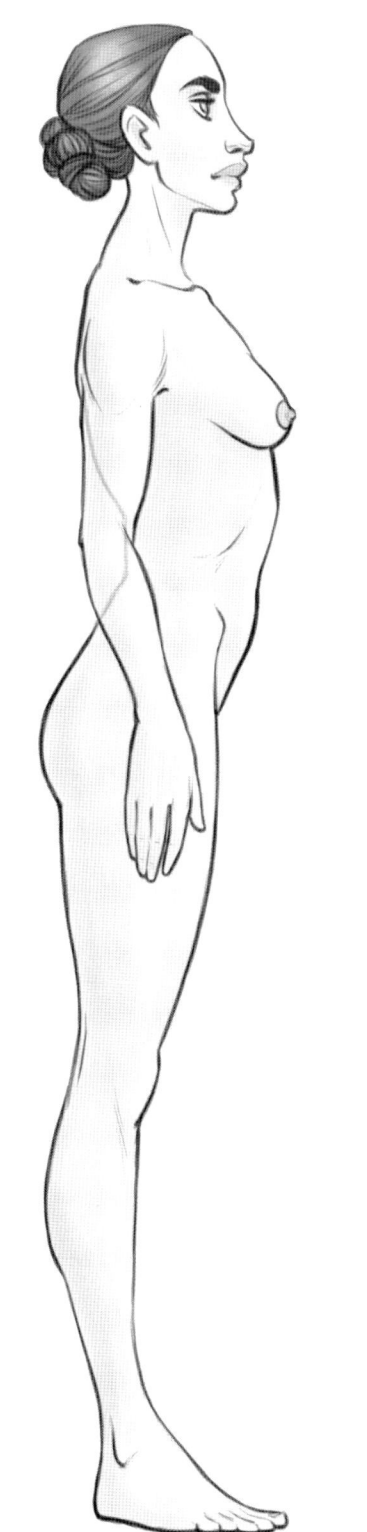
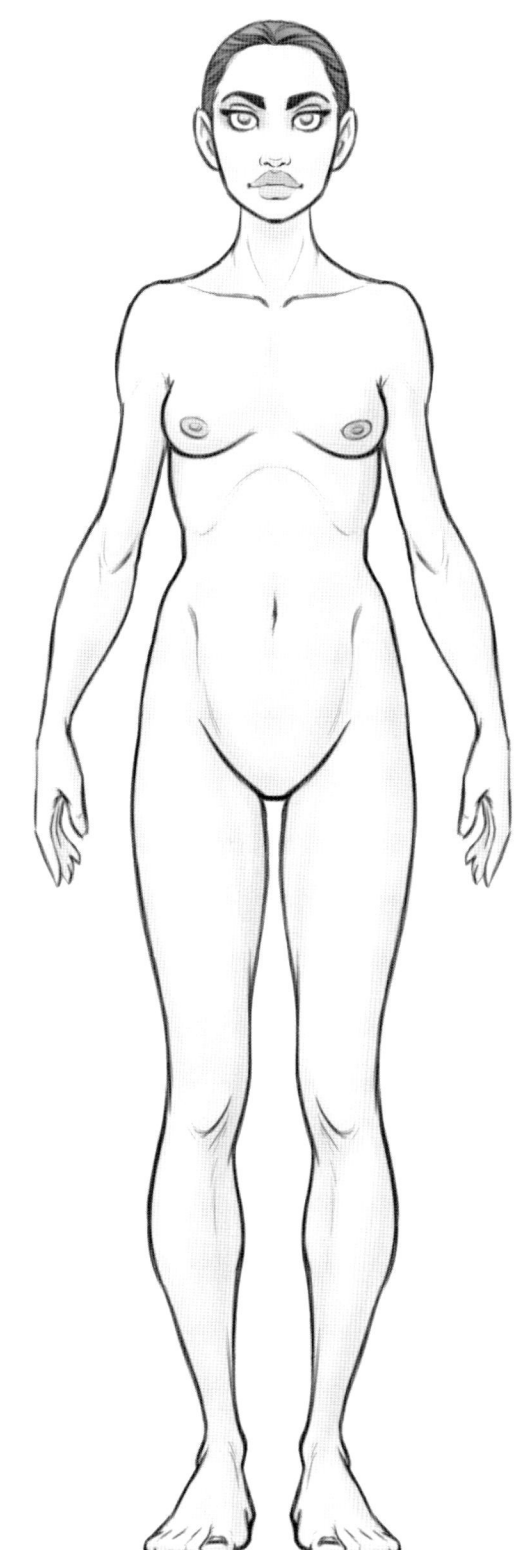
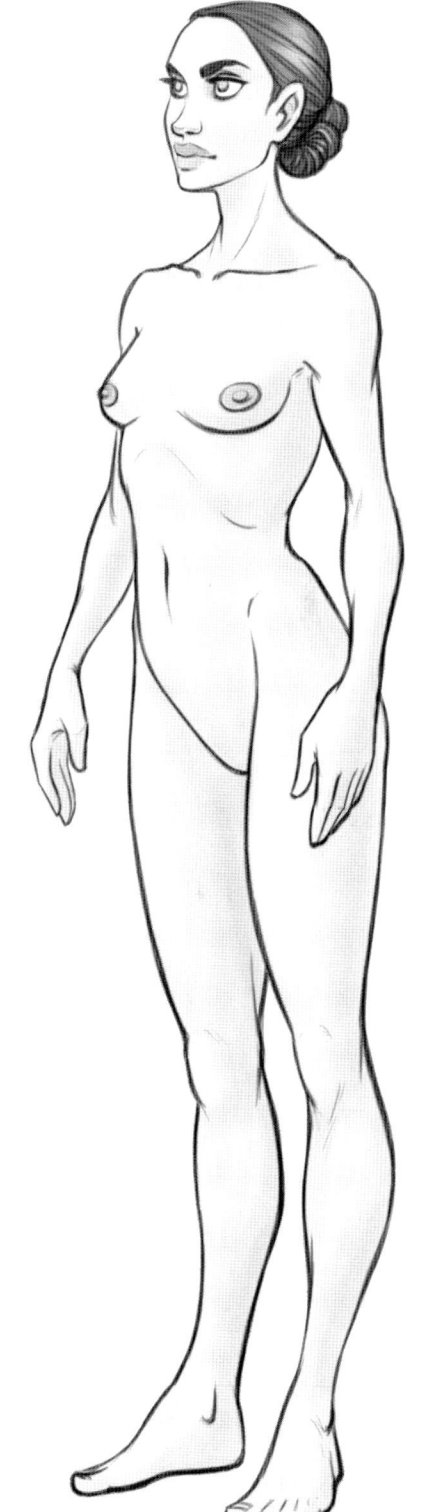

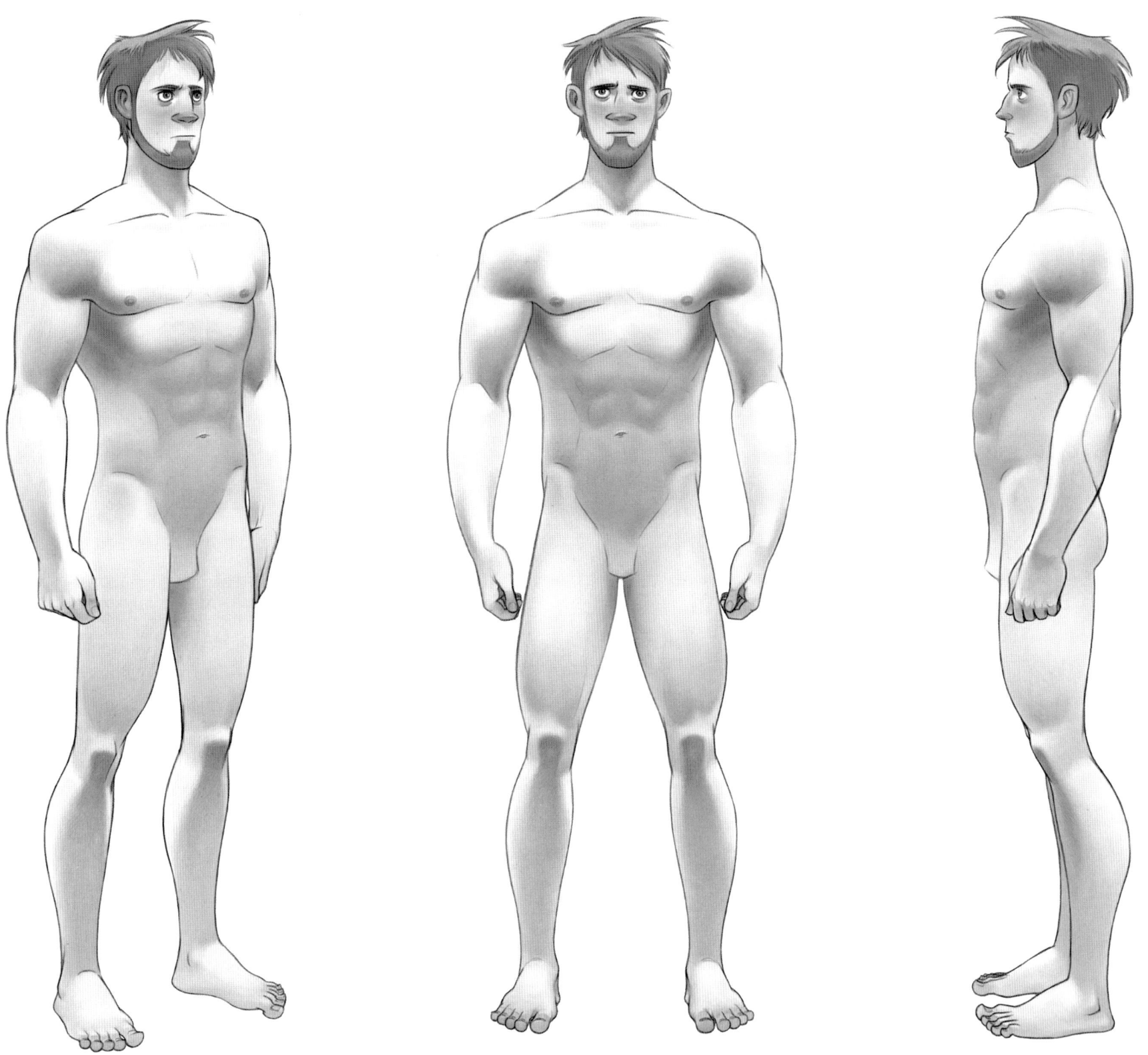

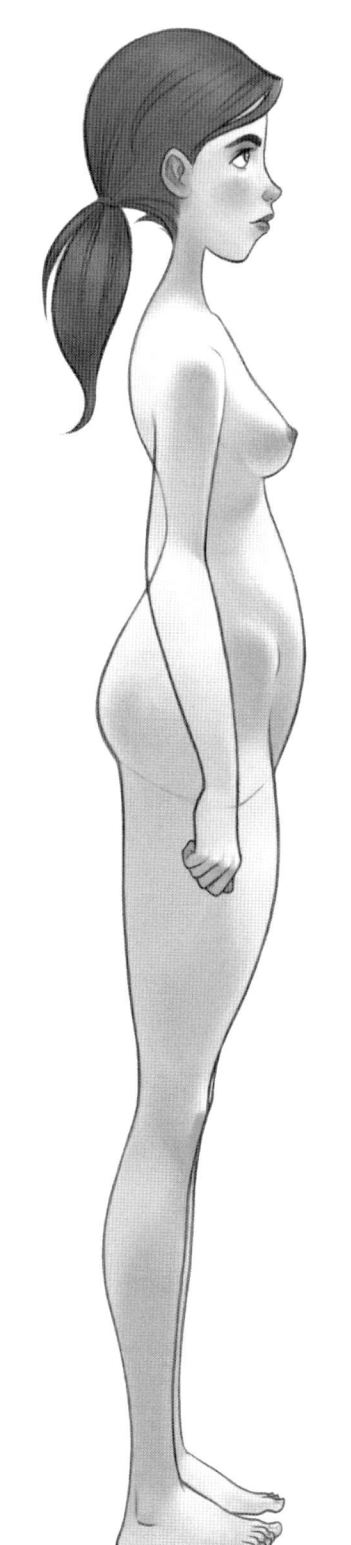
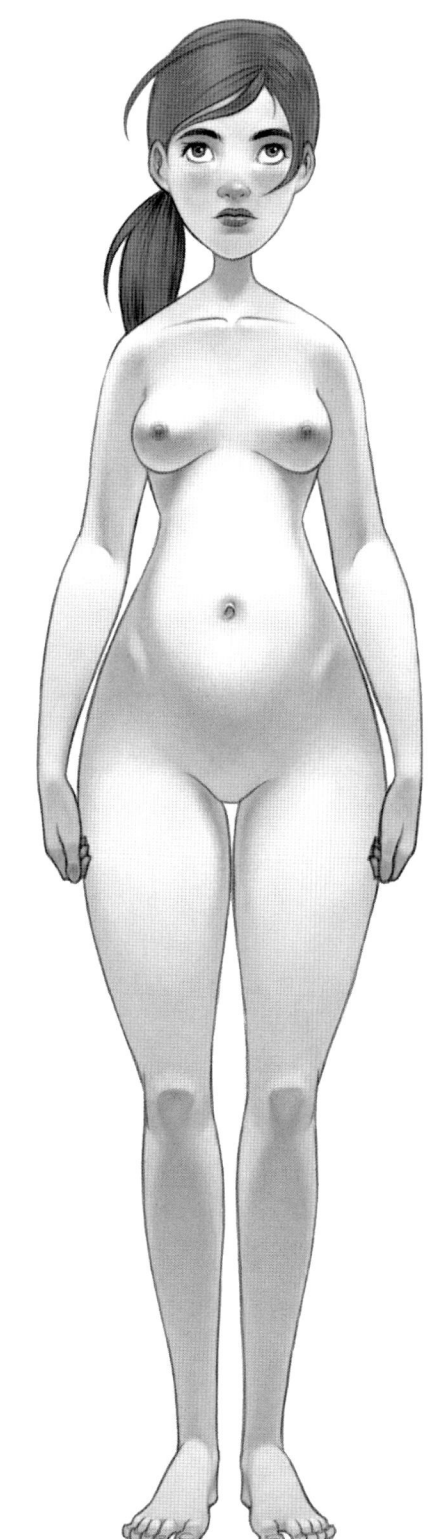
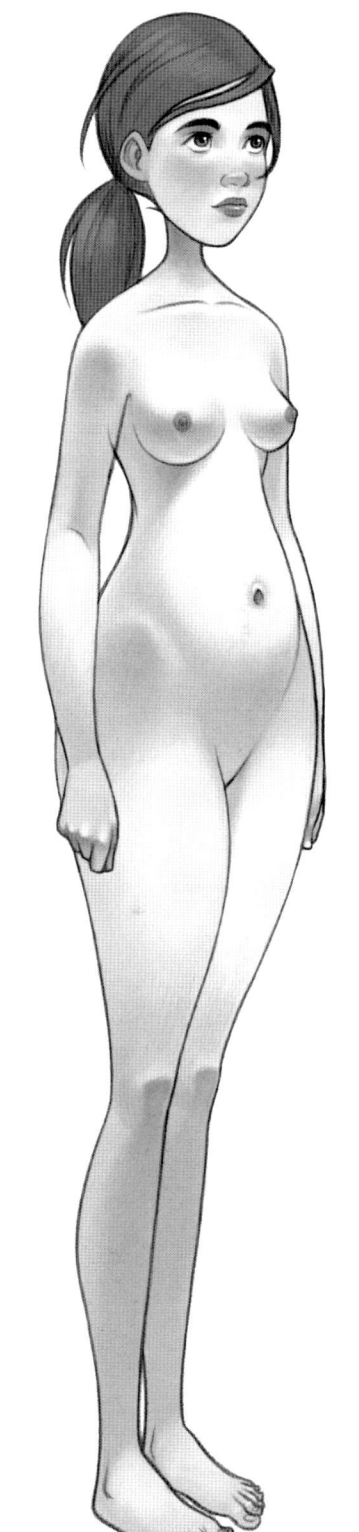

SARAH MENSINGA

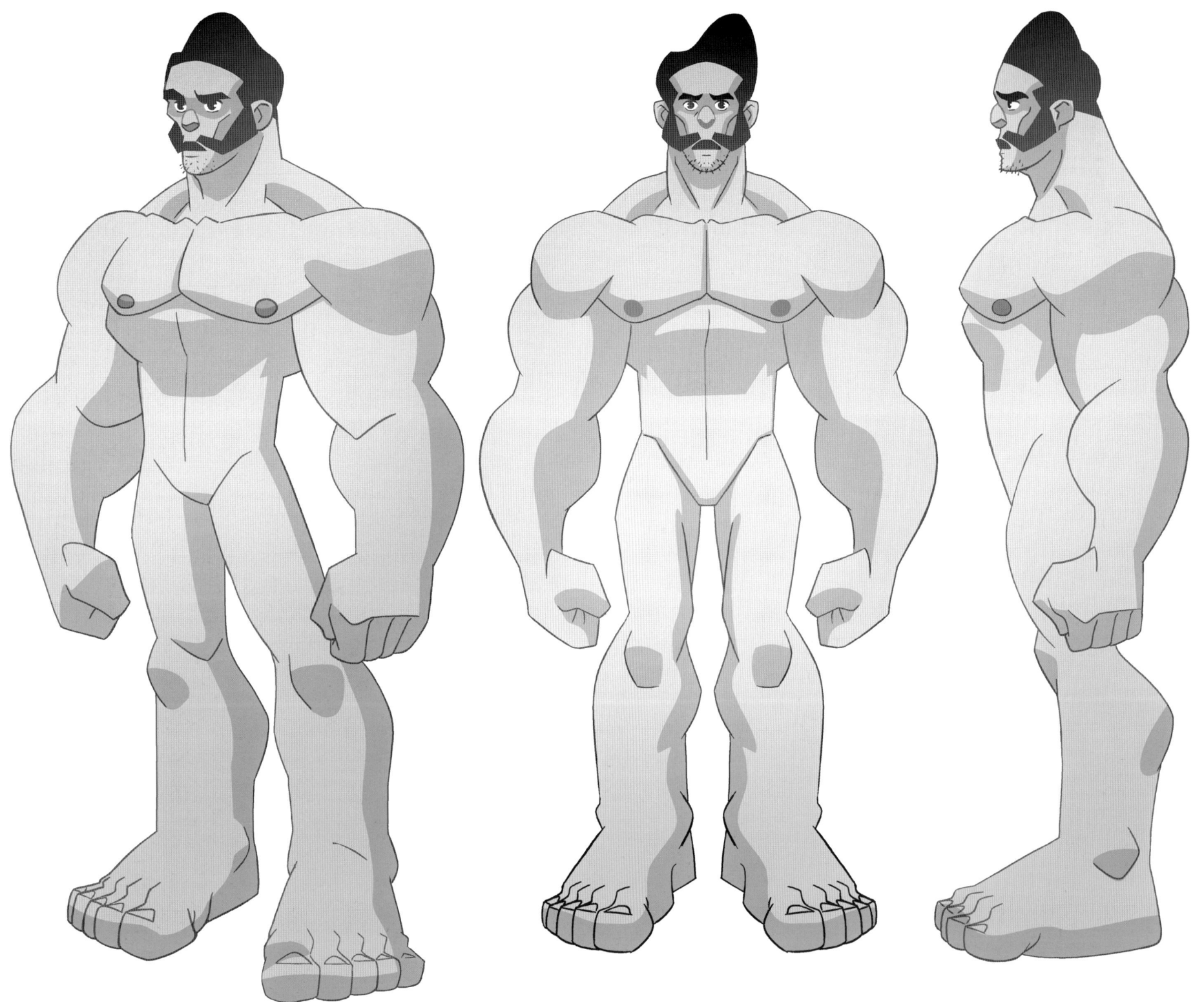

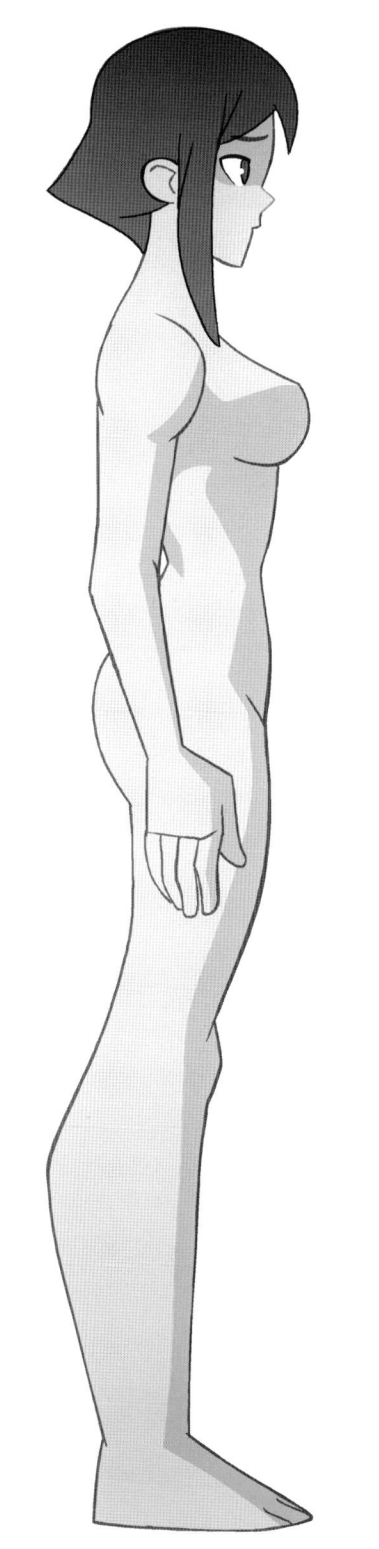
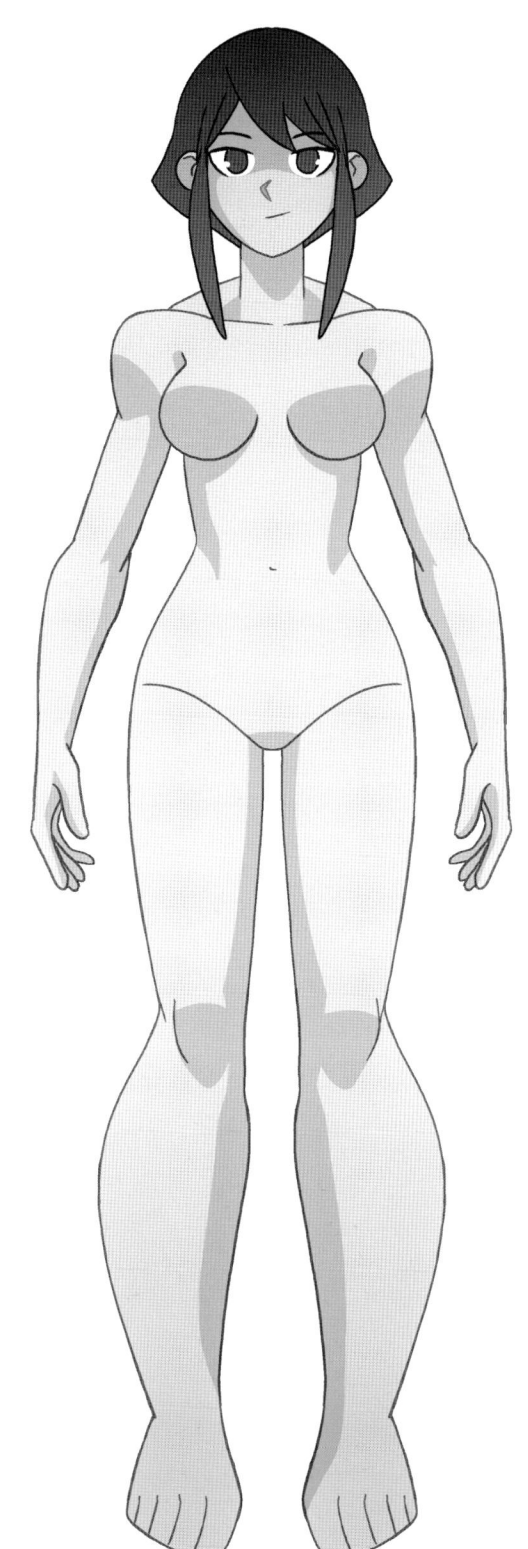
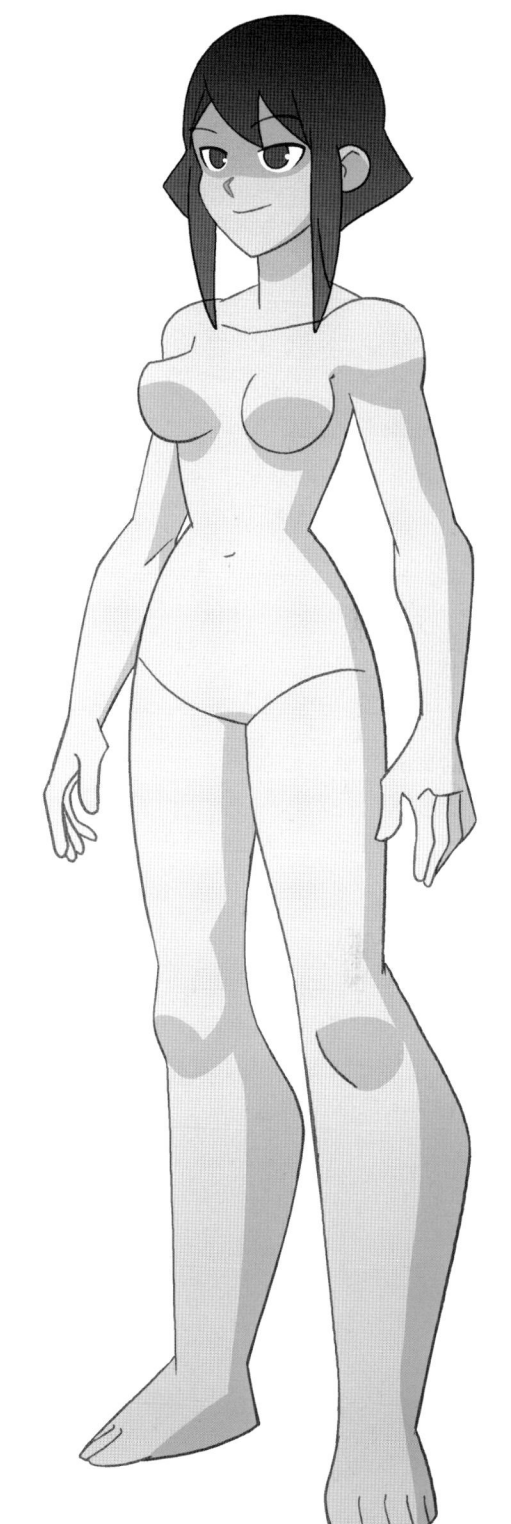

SEAN GALLOWAY

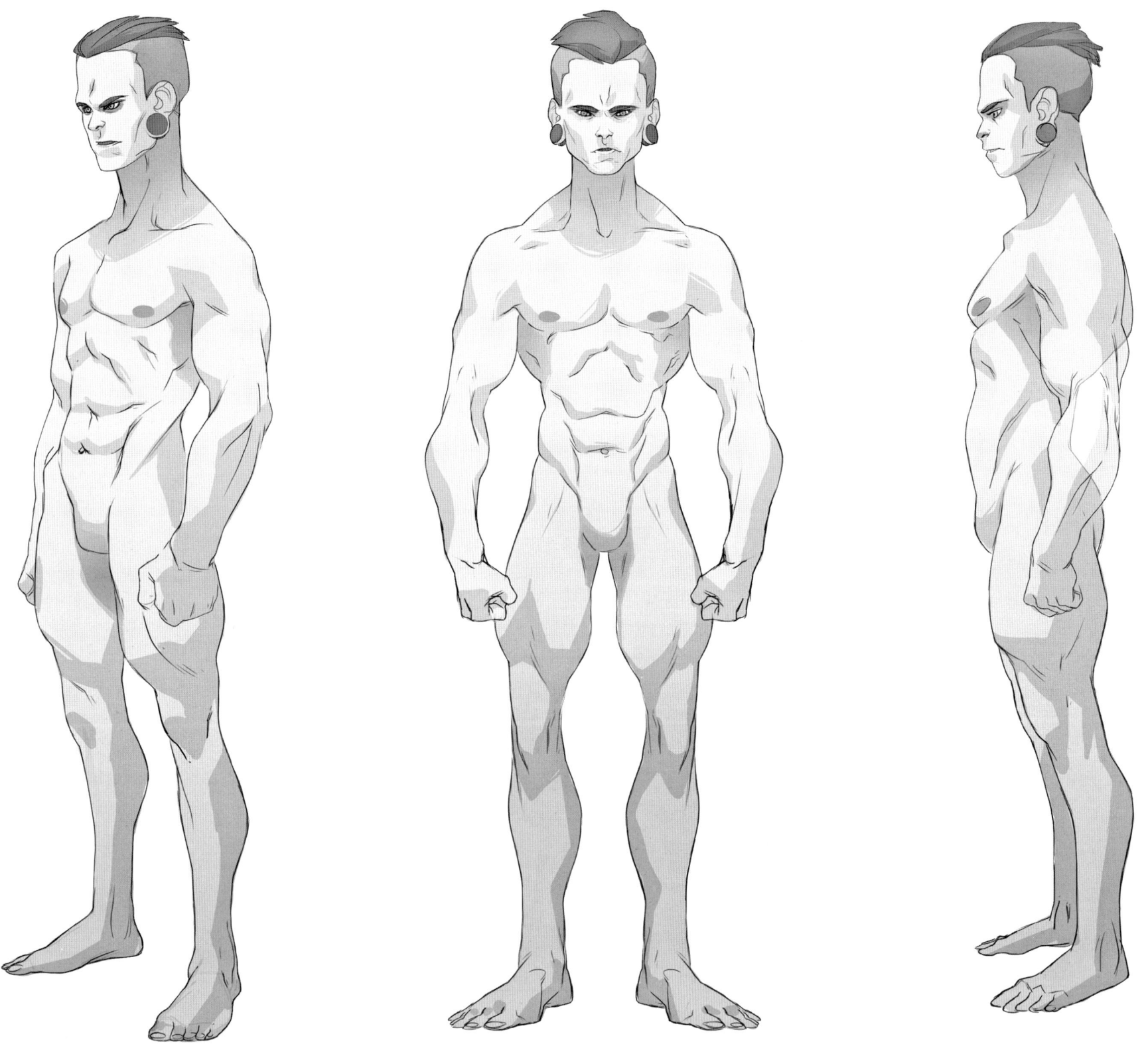

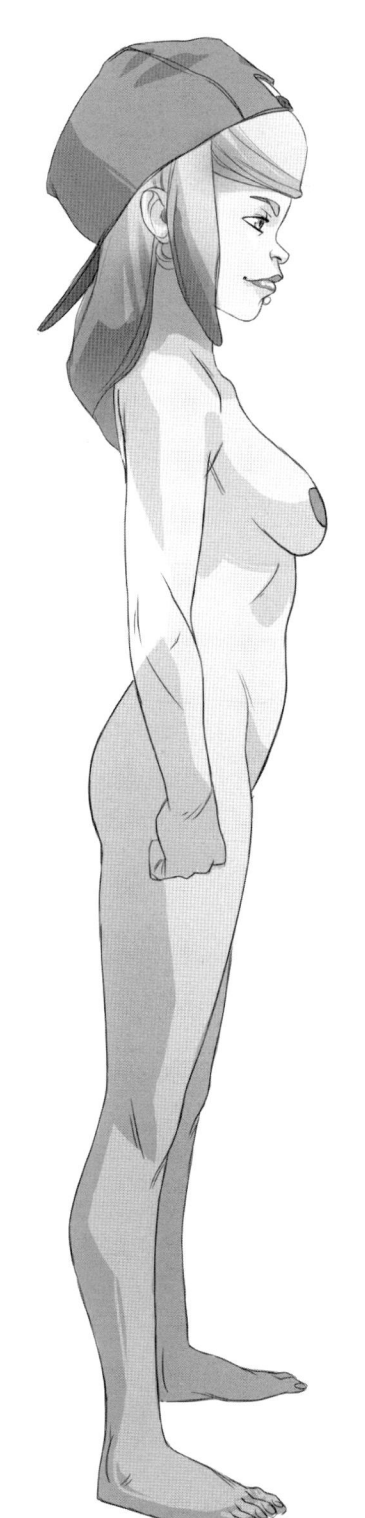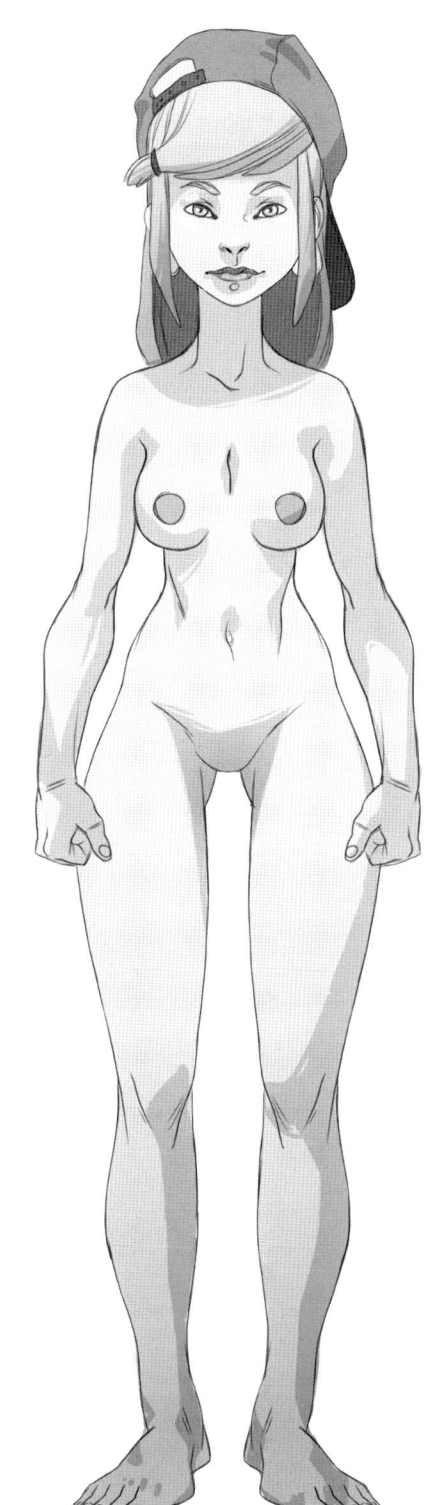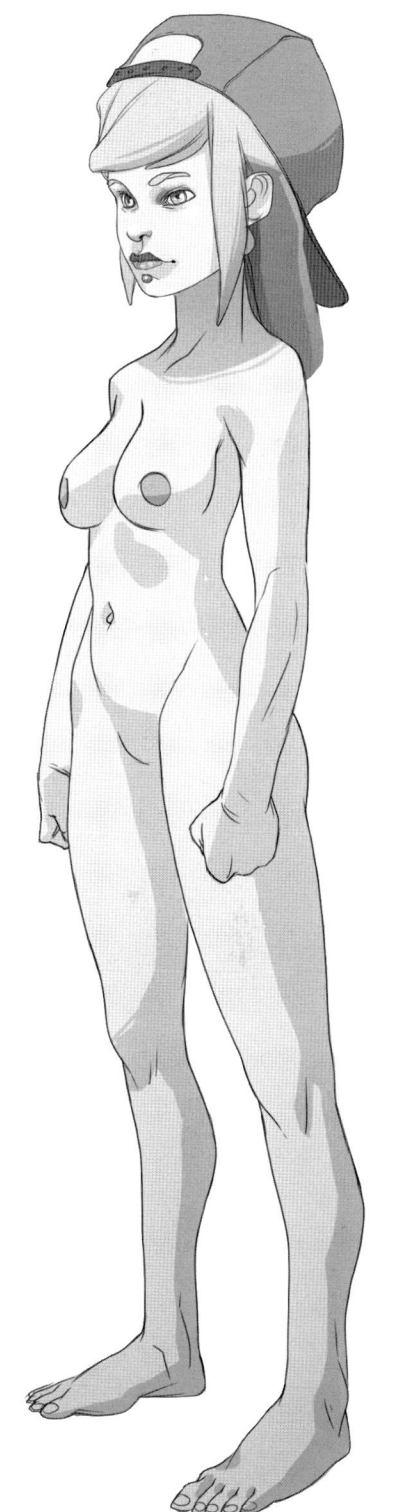

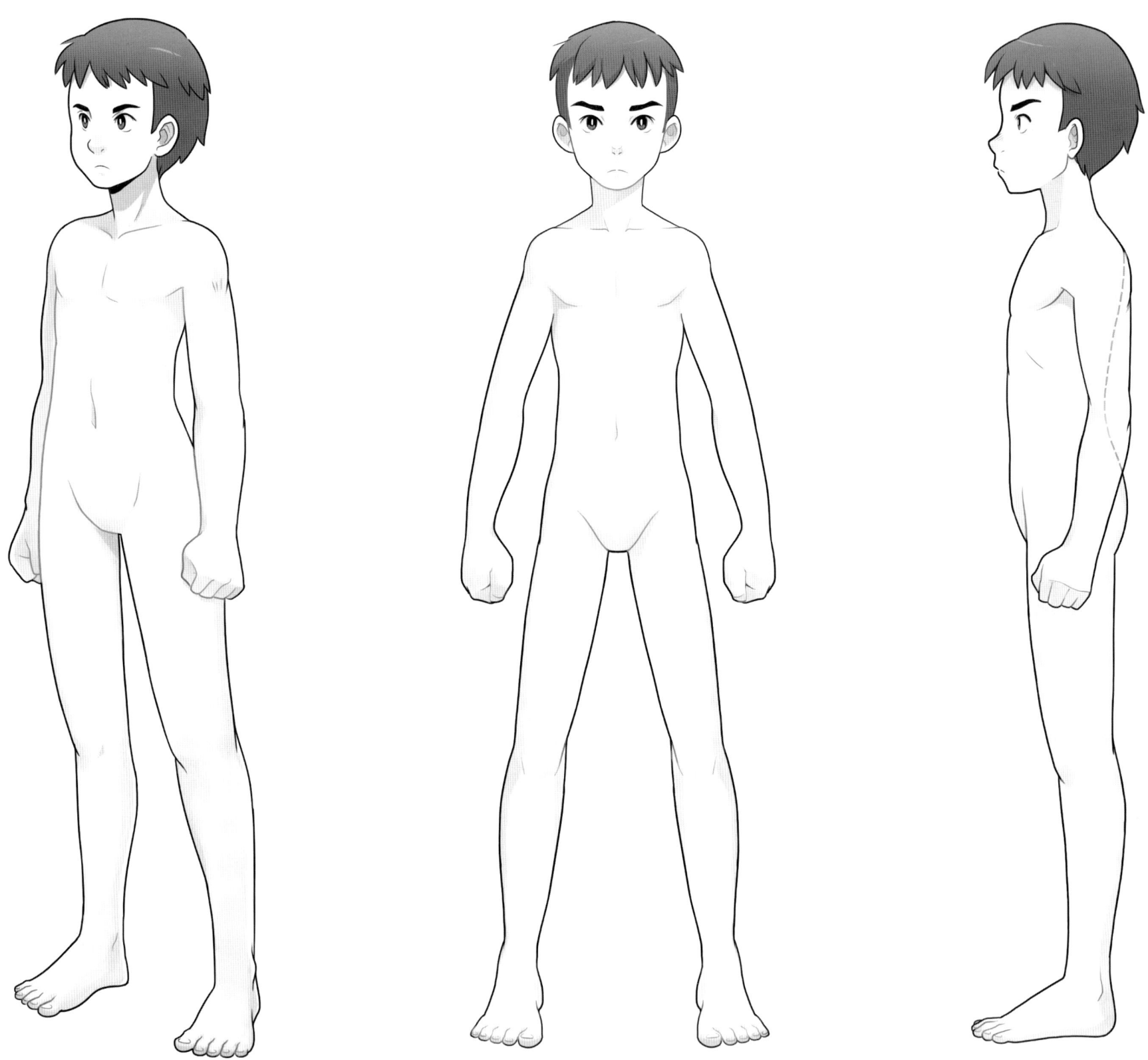

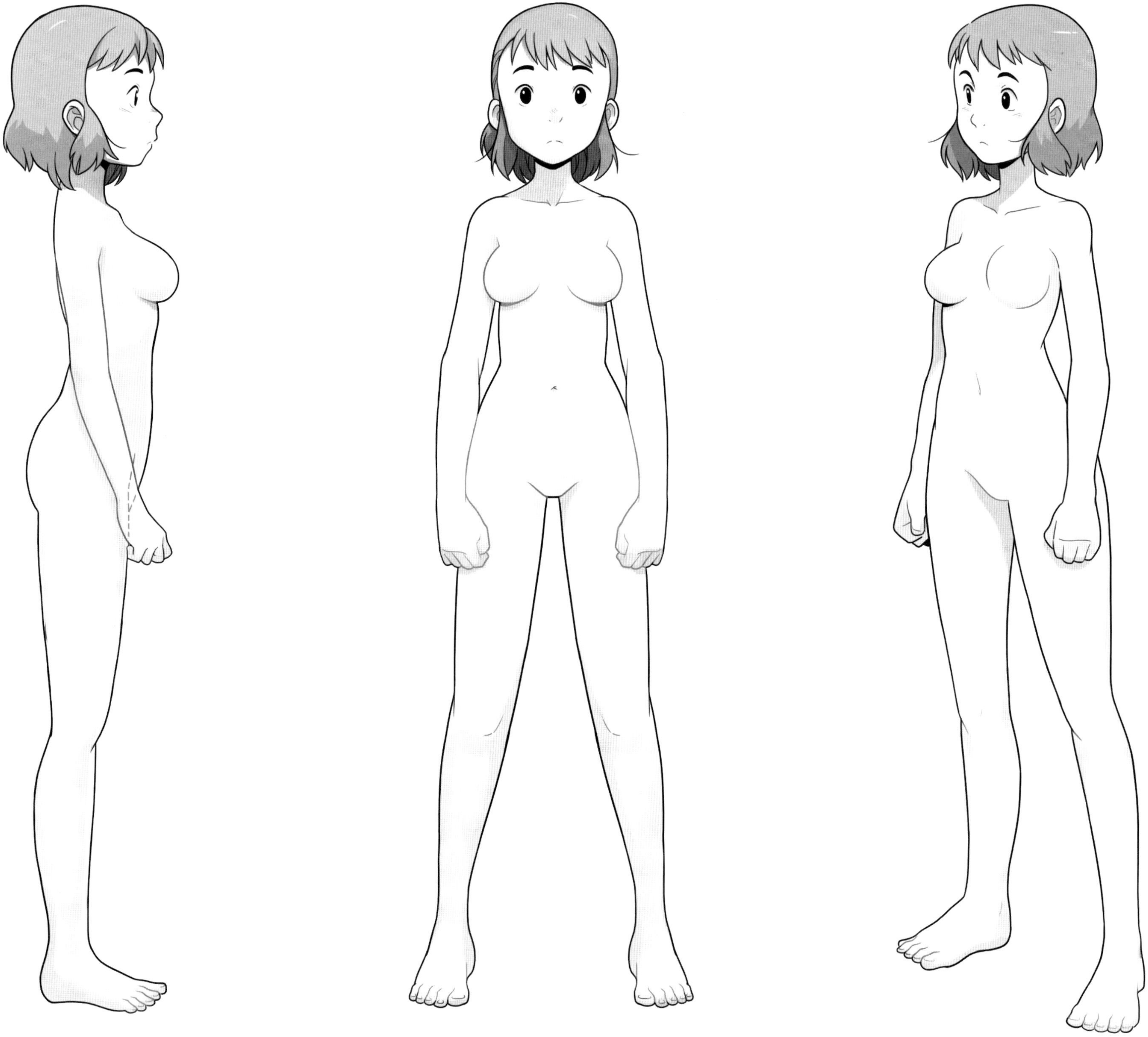

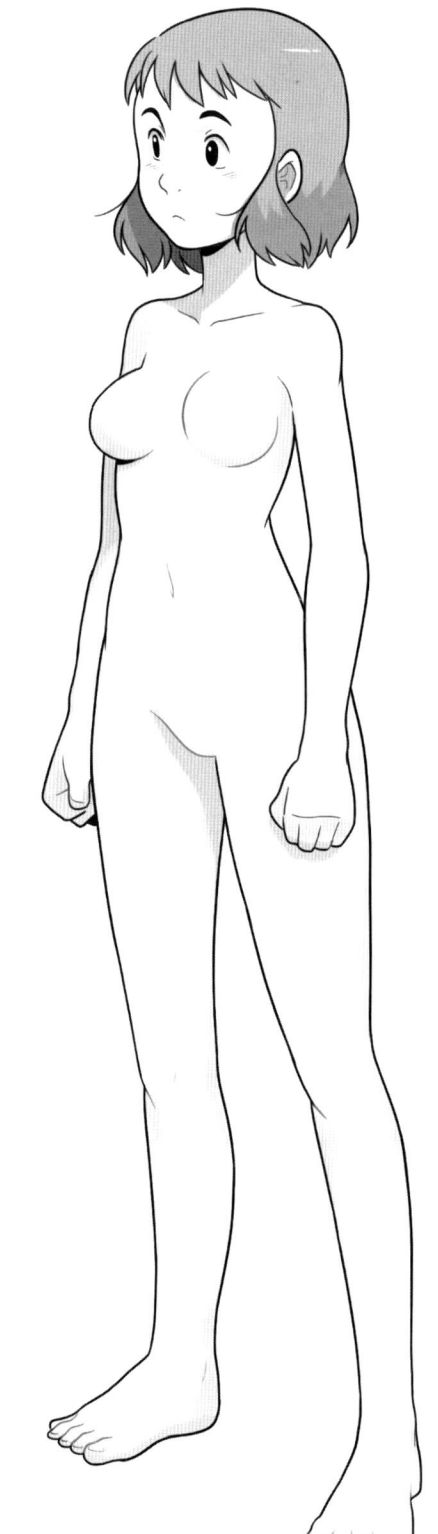

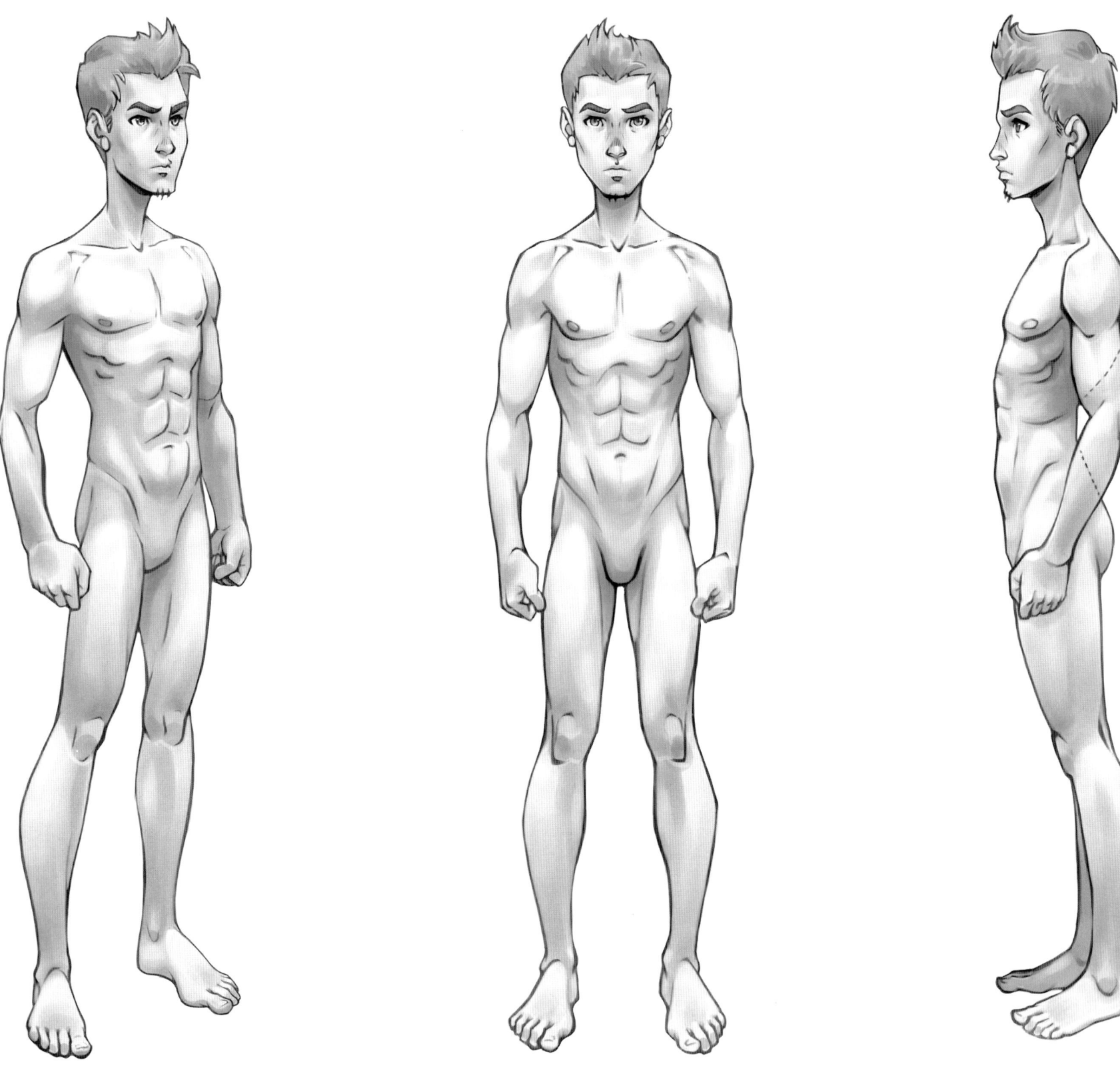

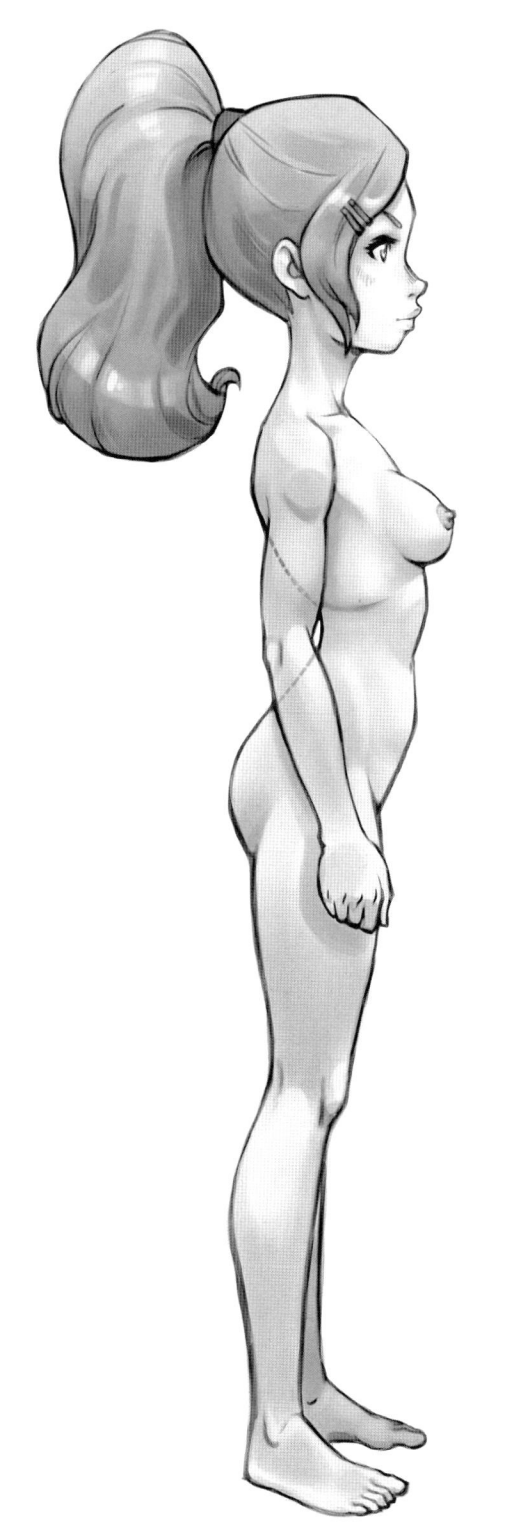
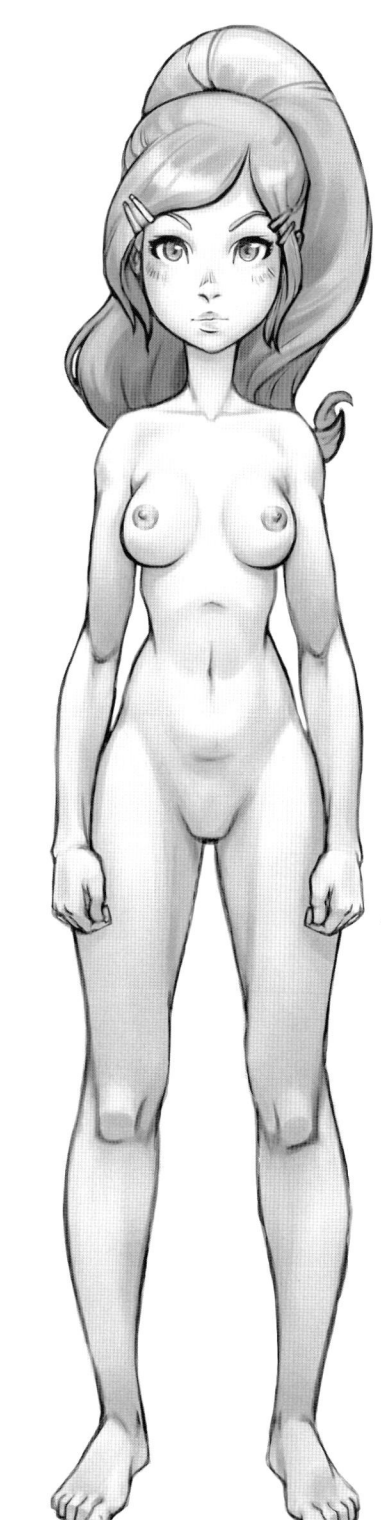
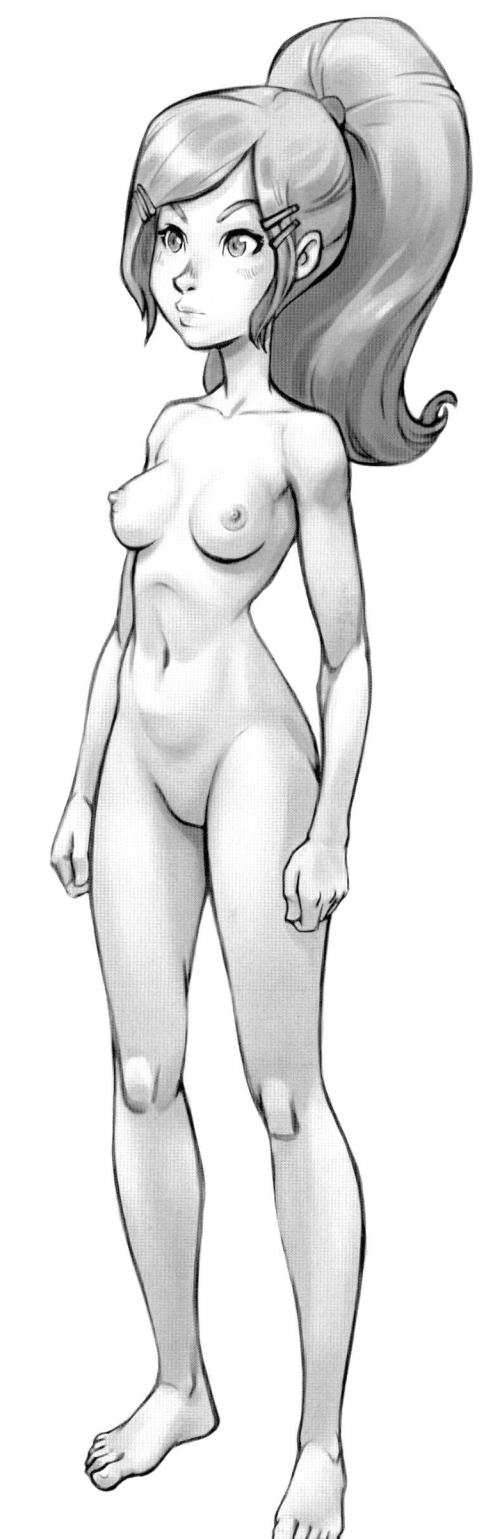

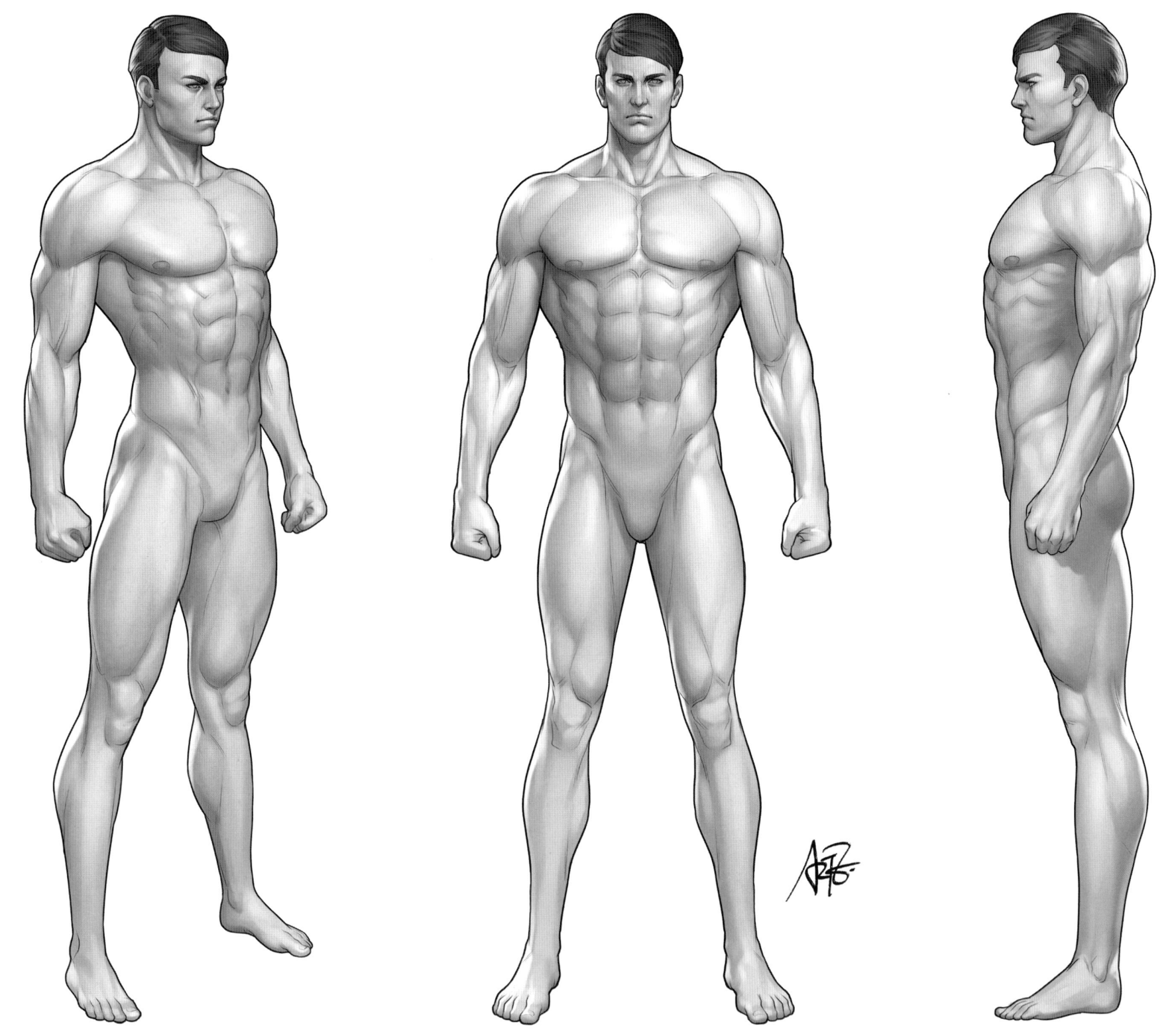

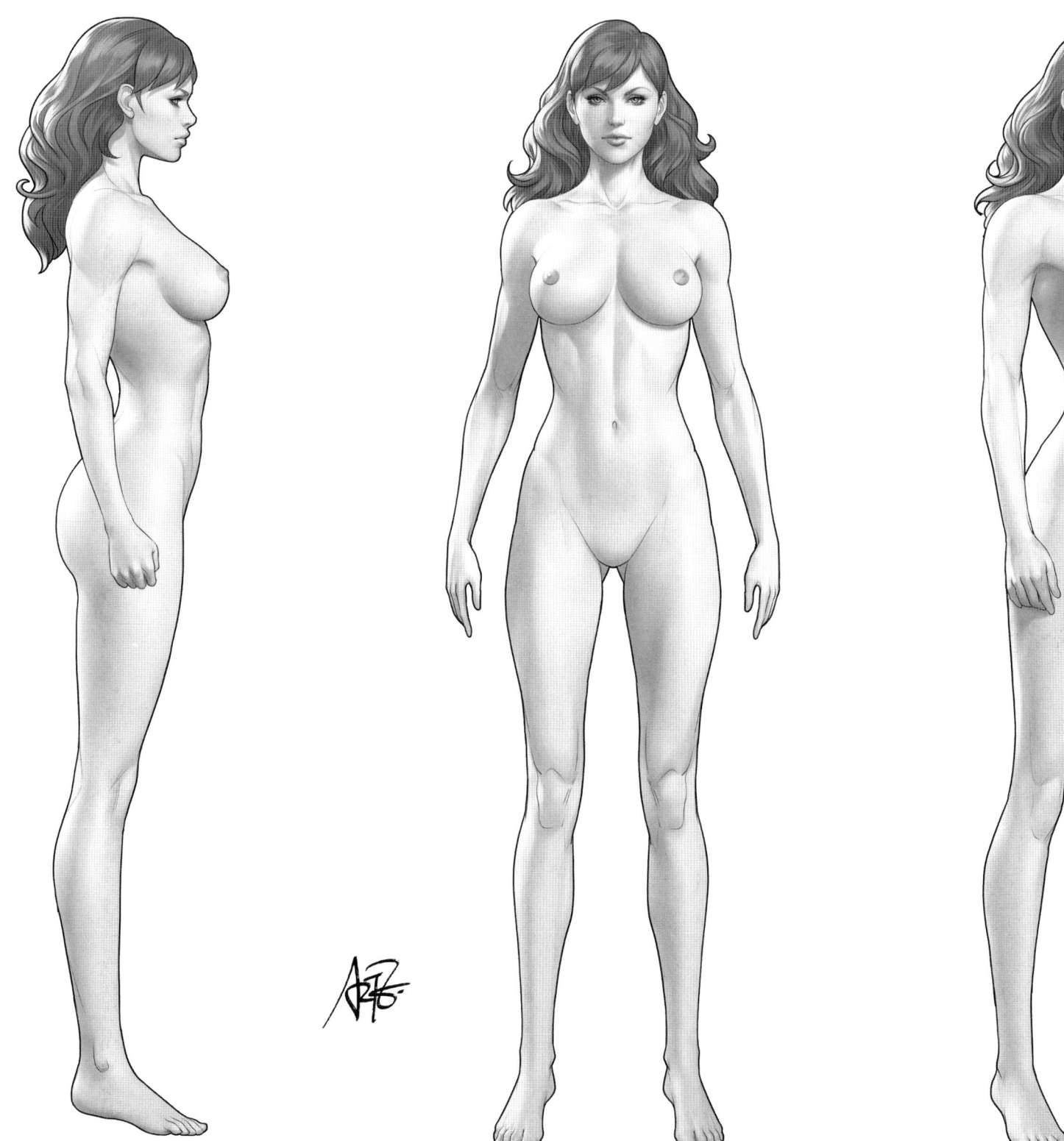

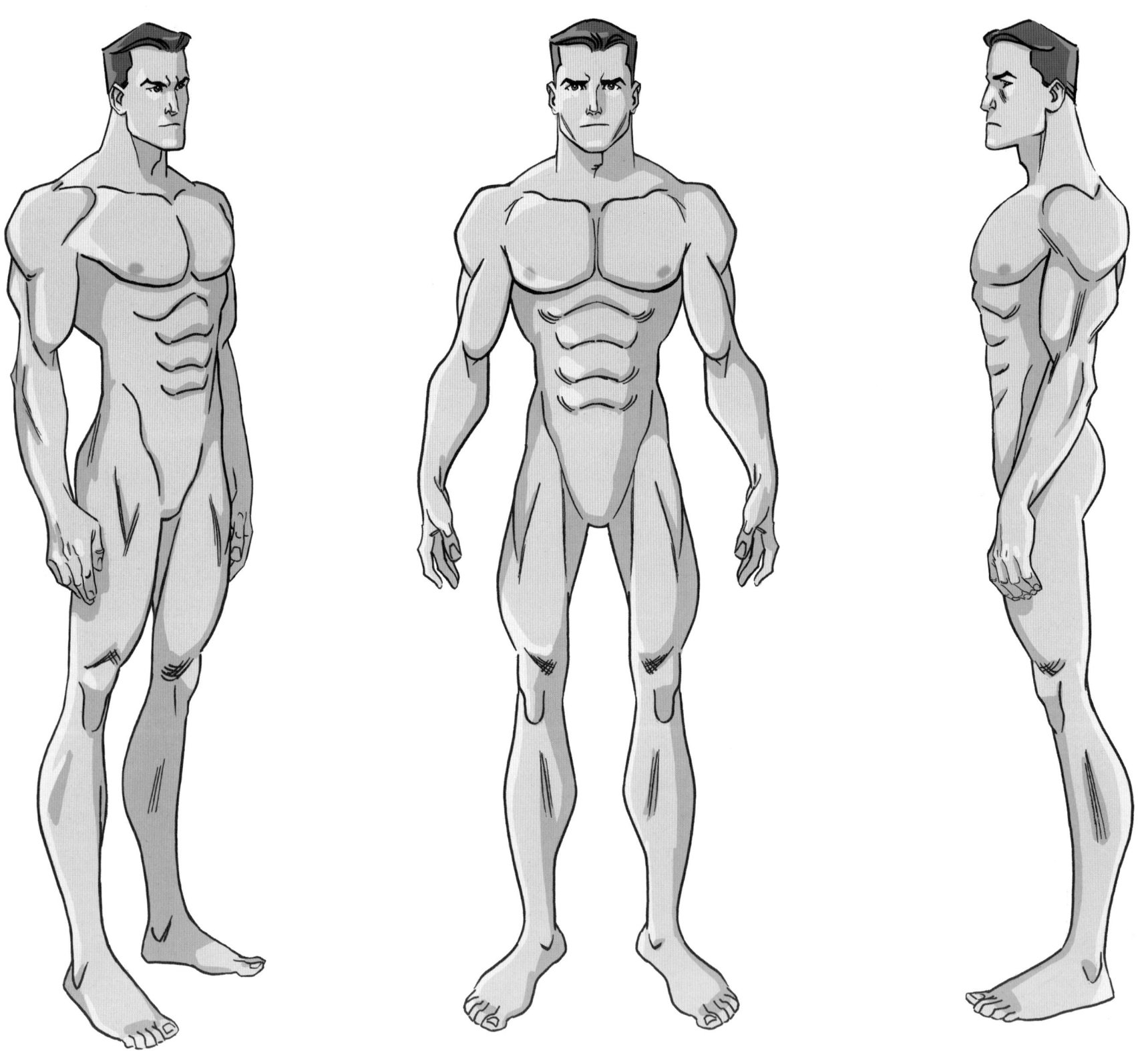

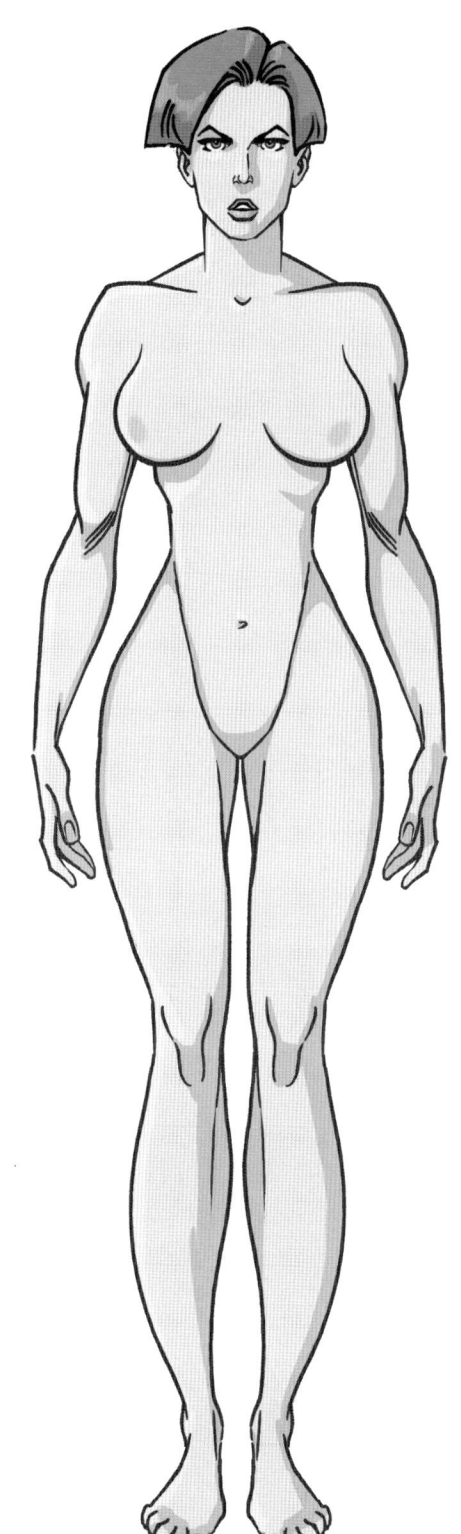
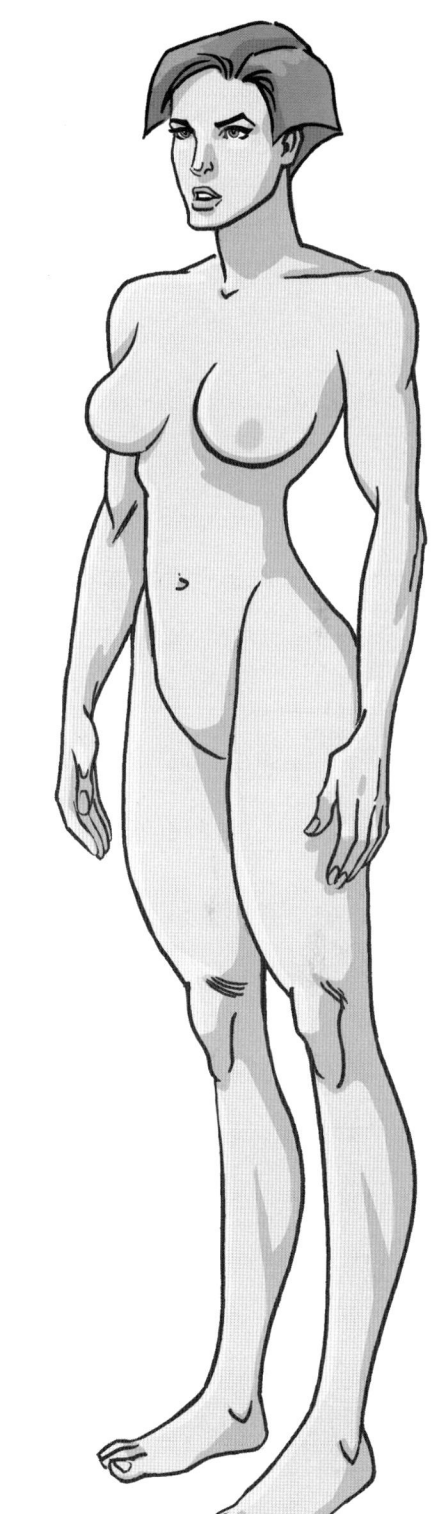

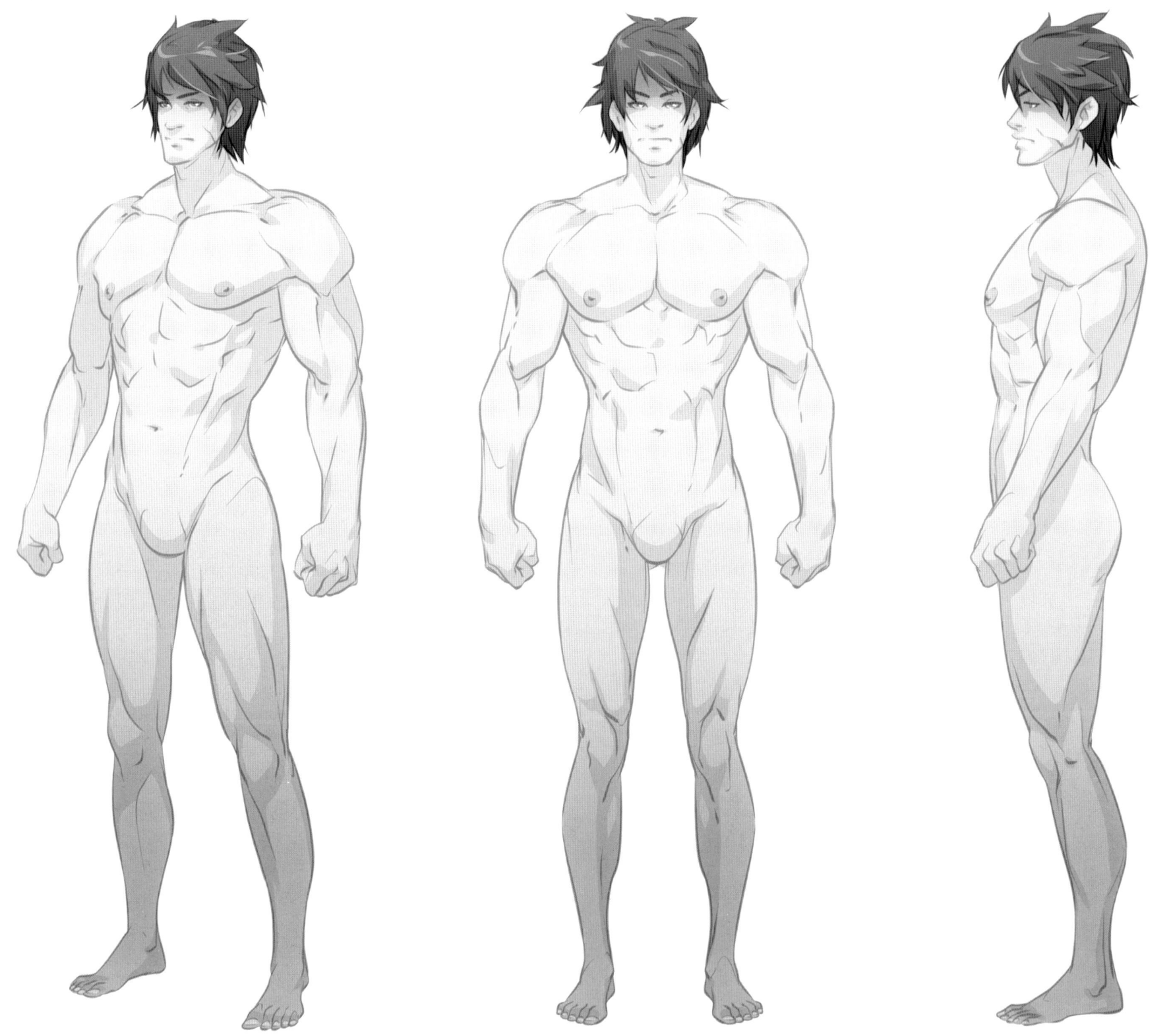

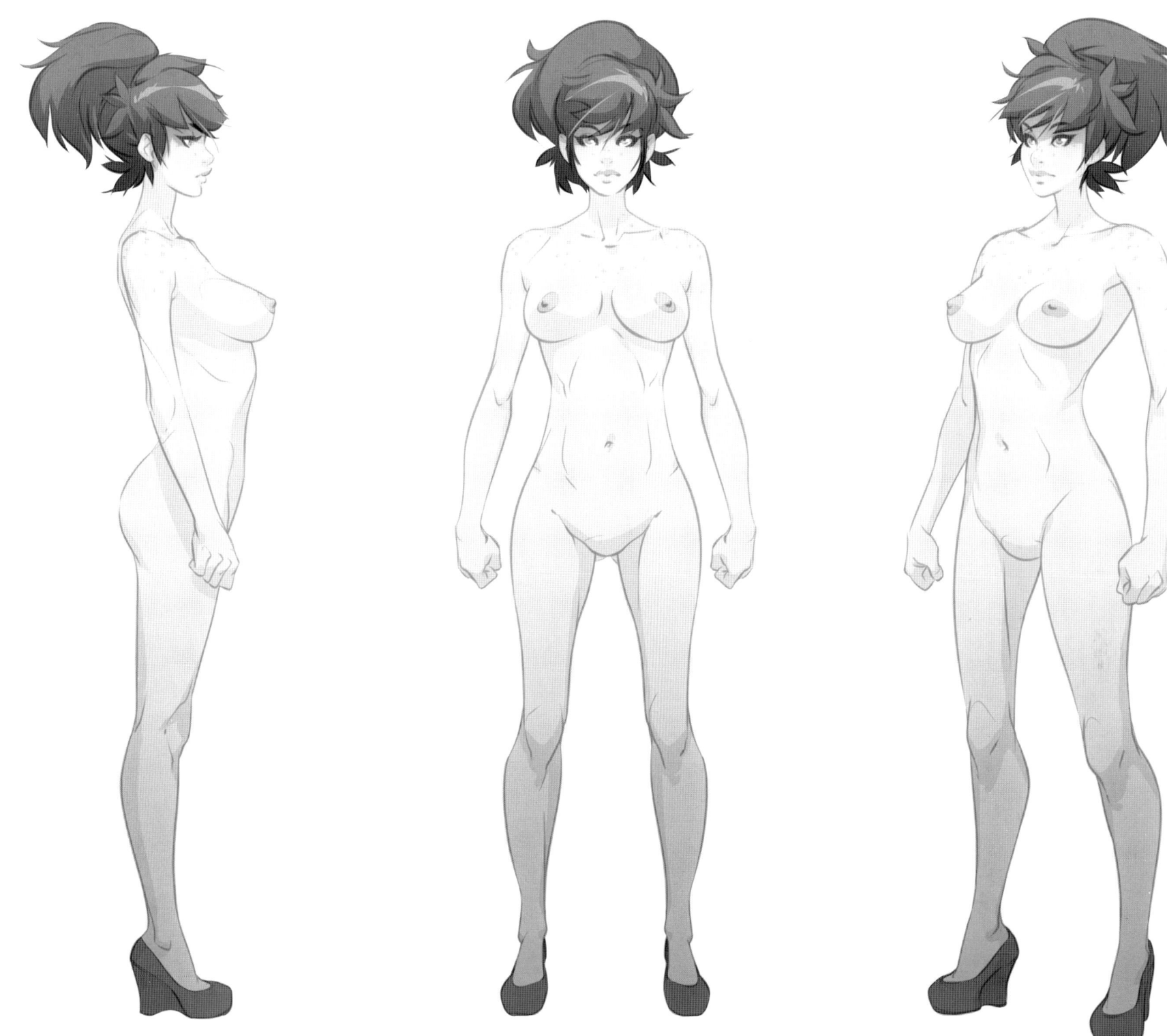

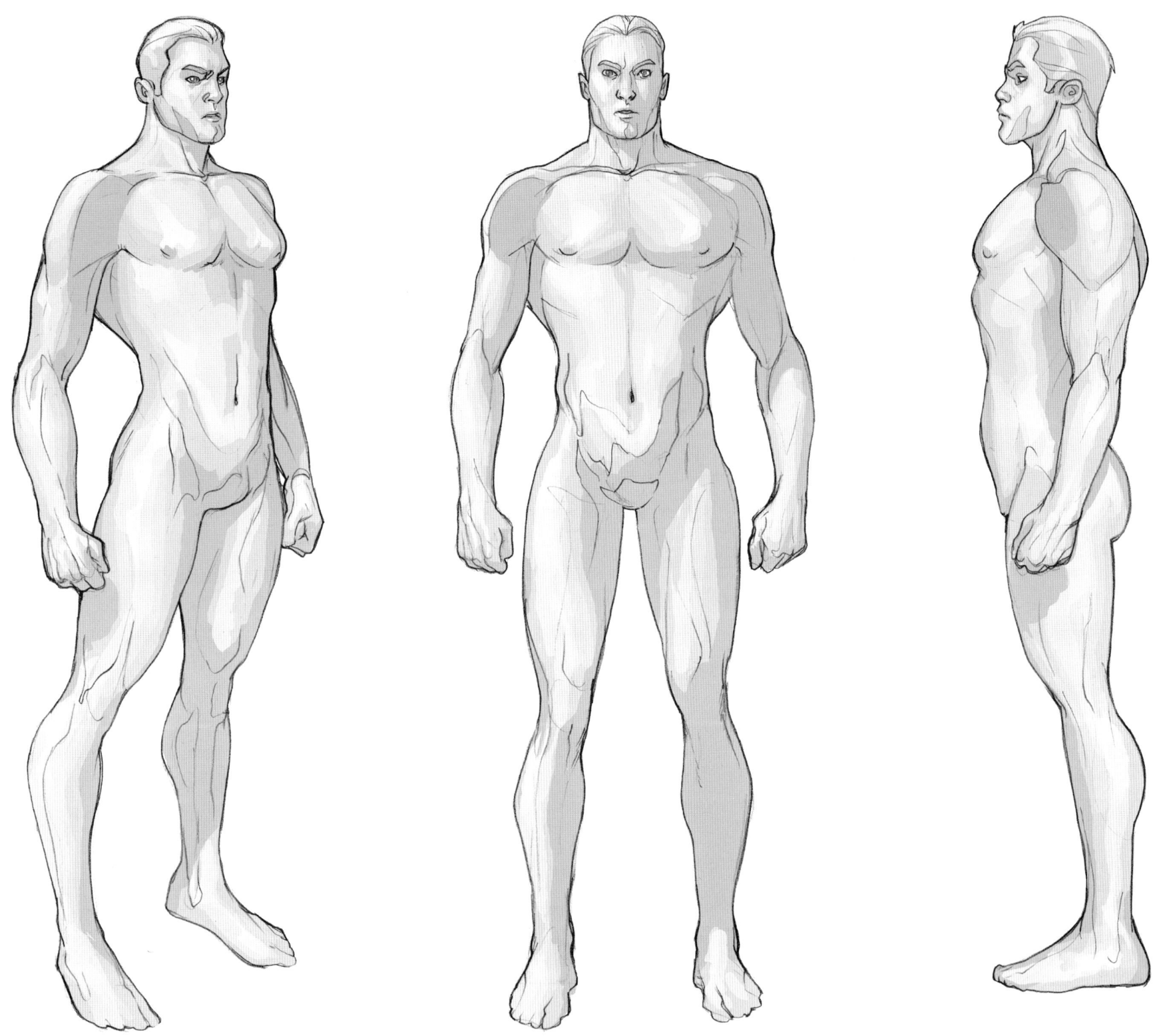

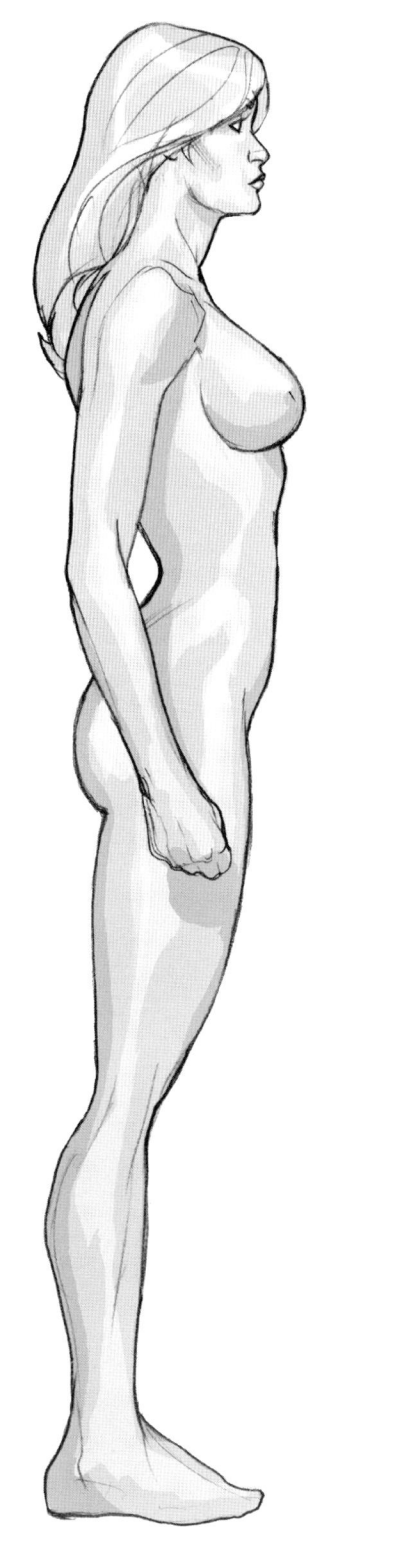
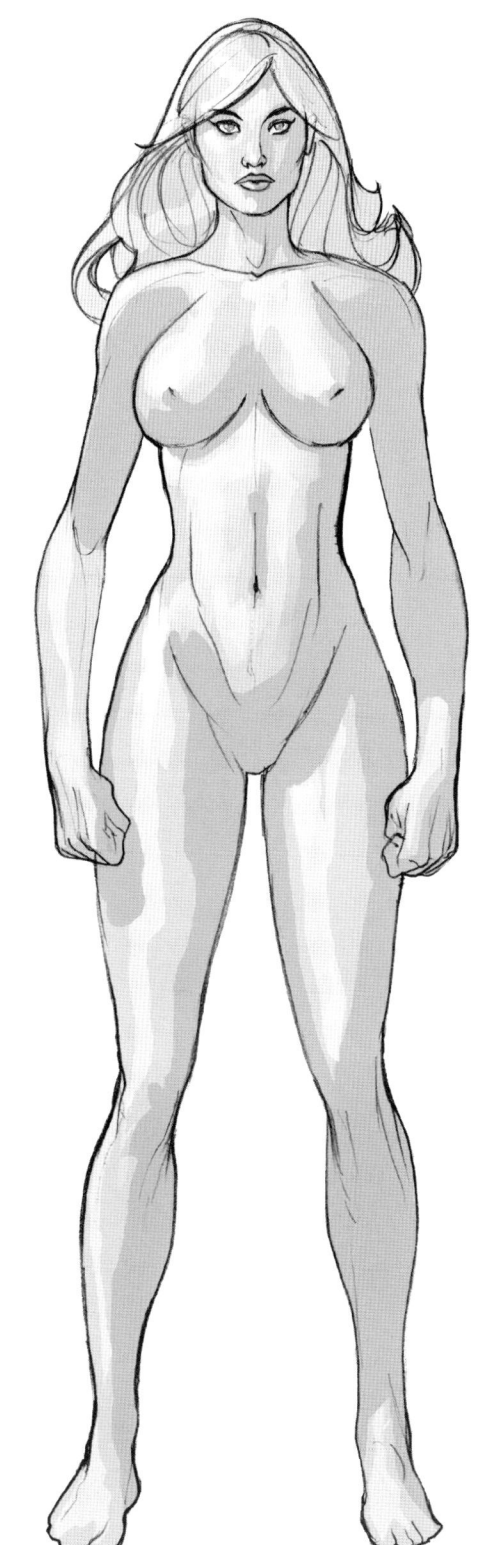
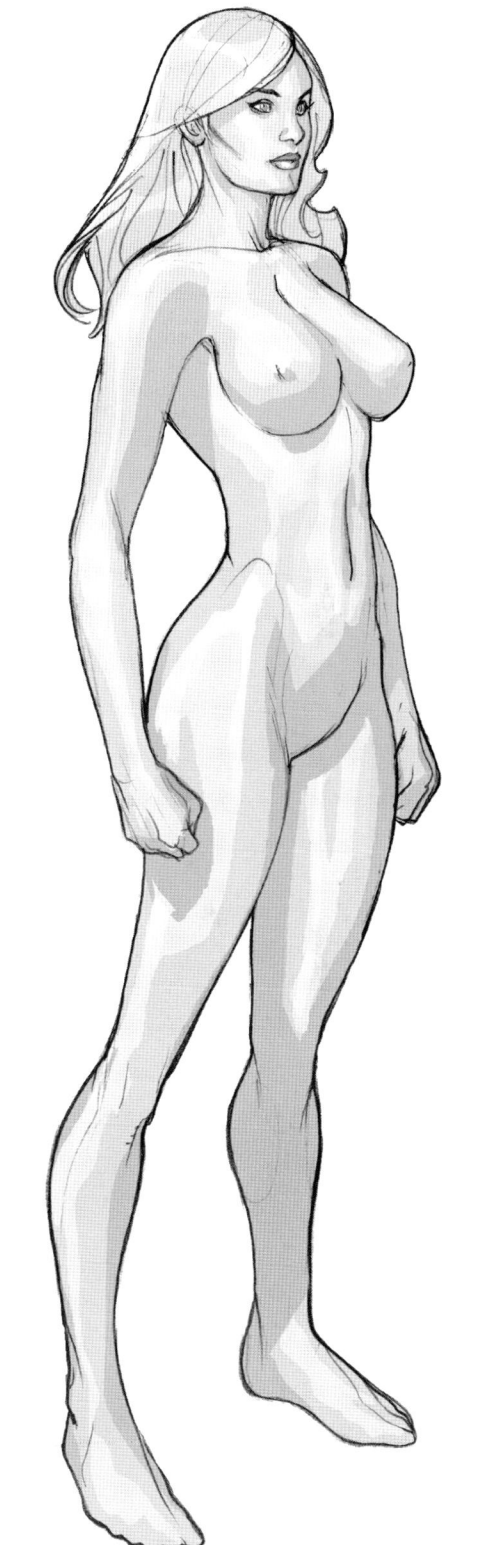

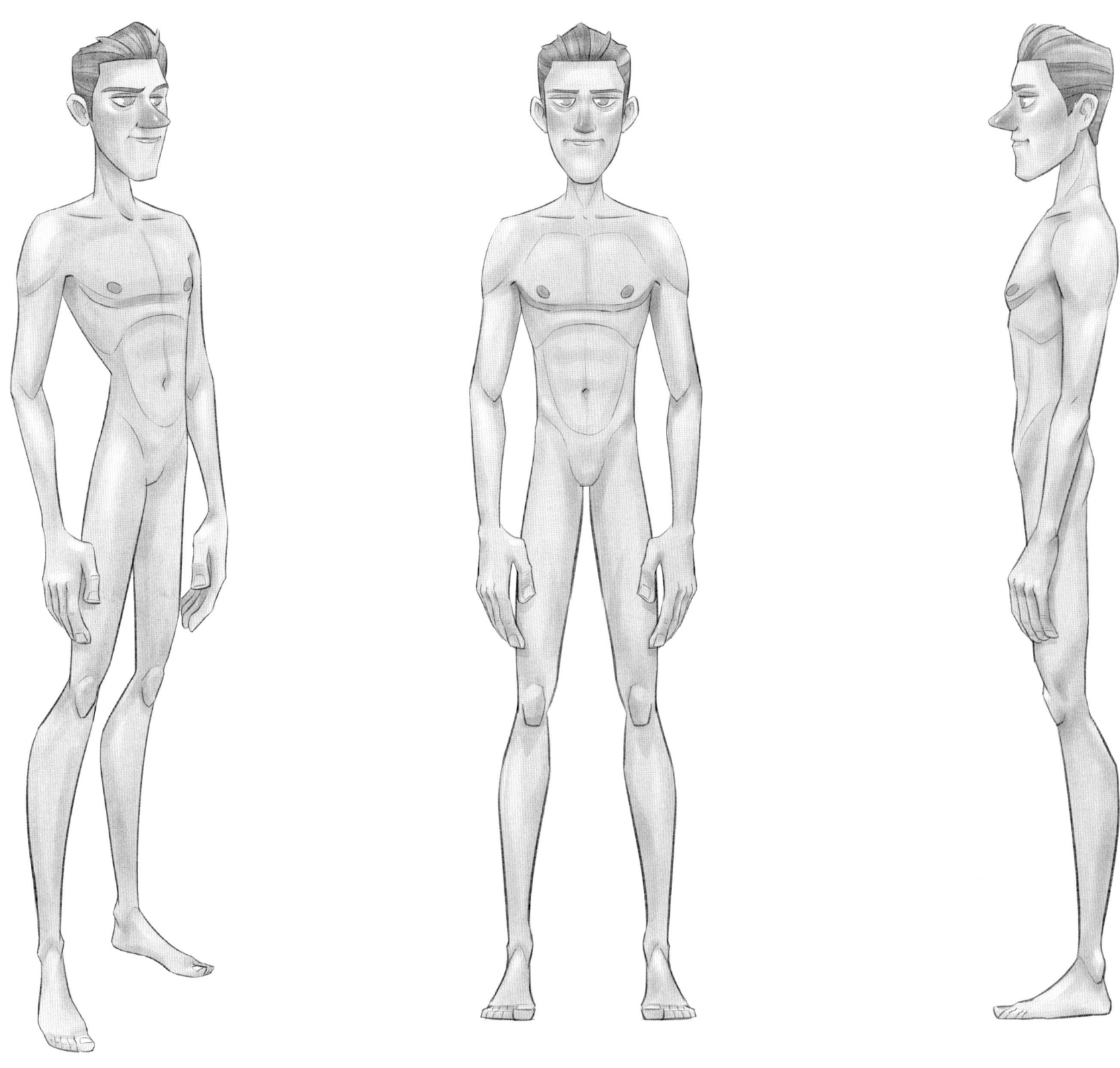

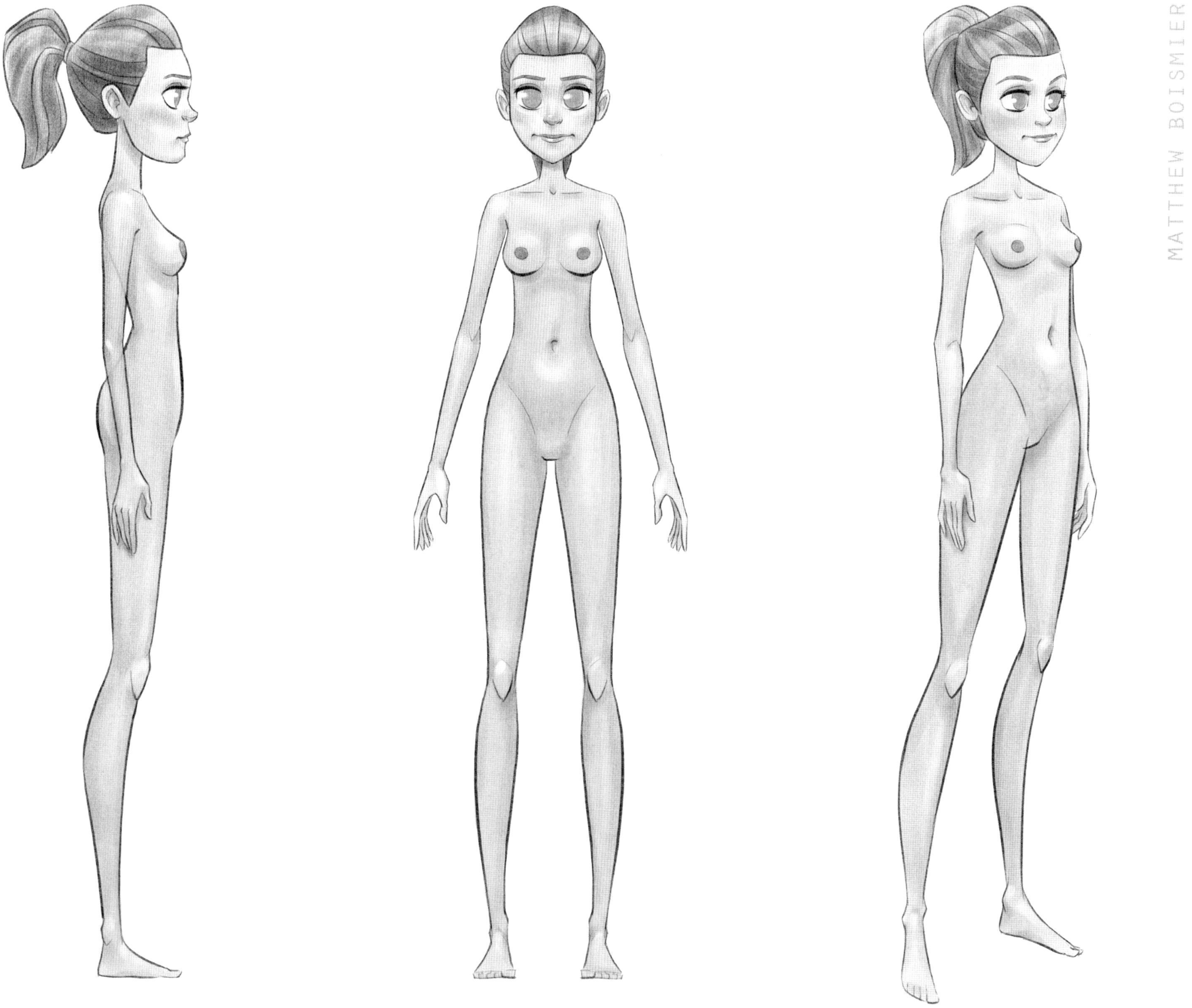

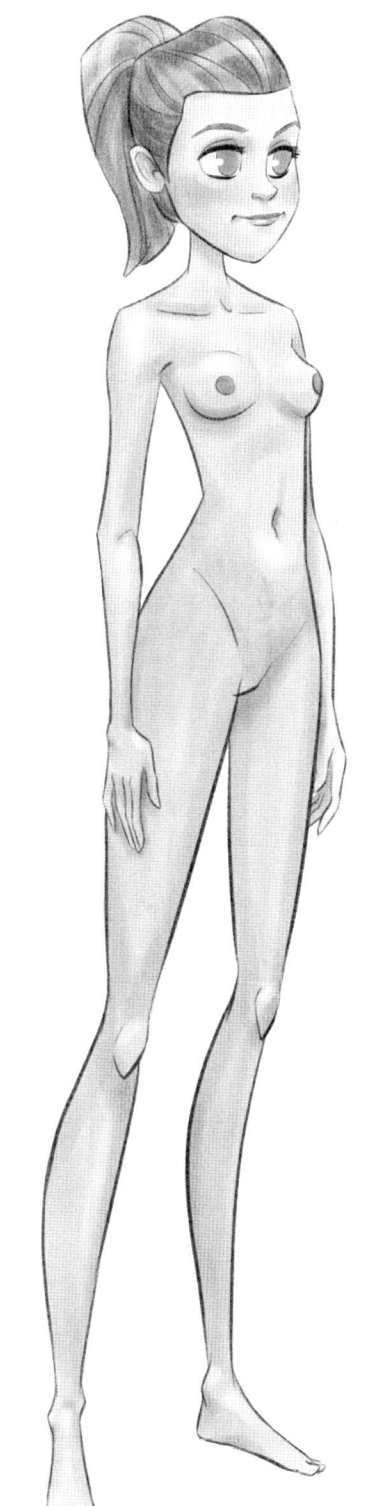

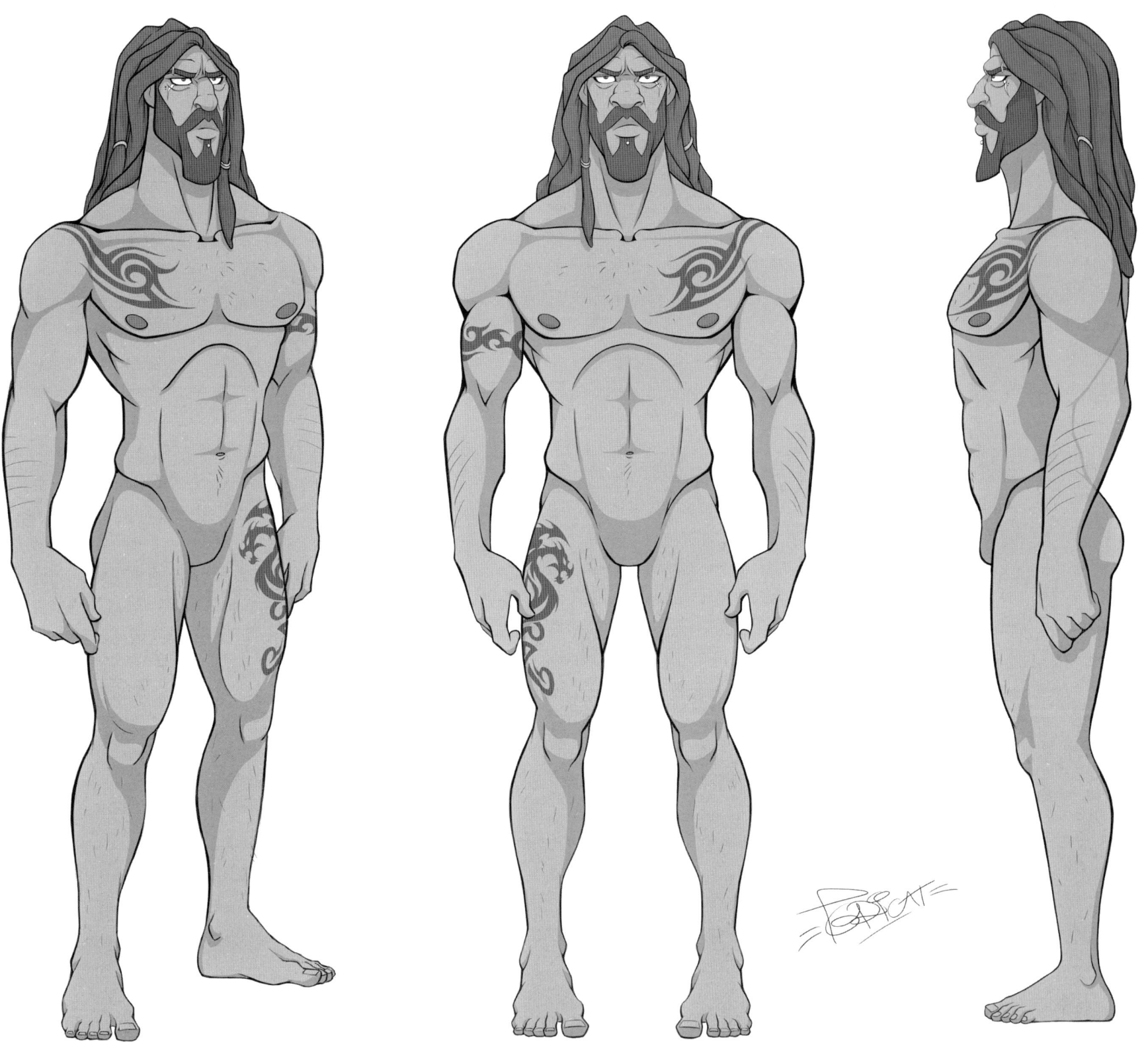

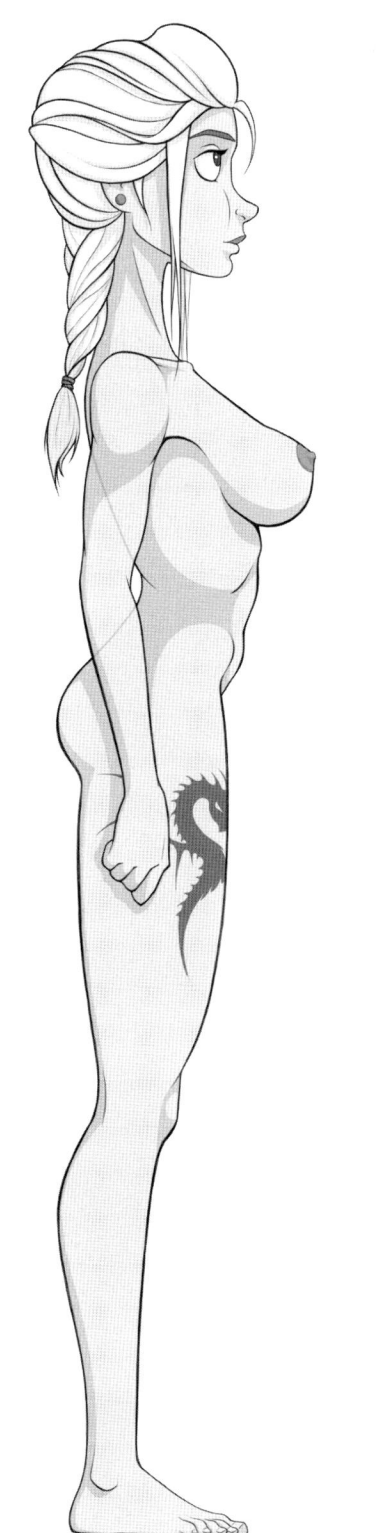
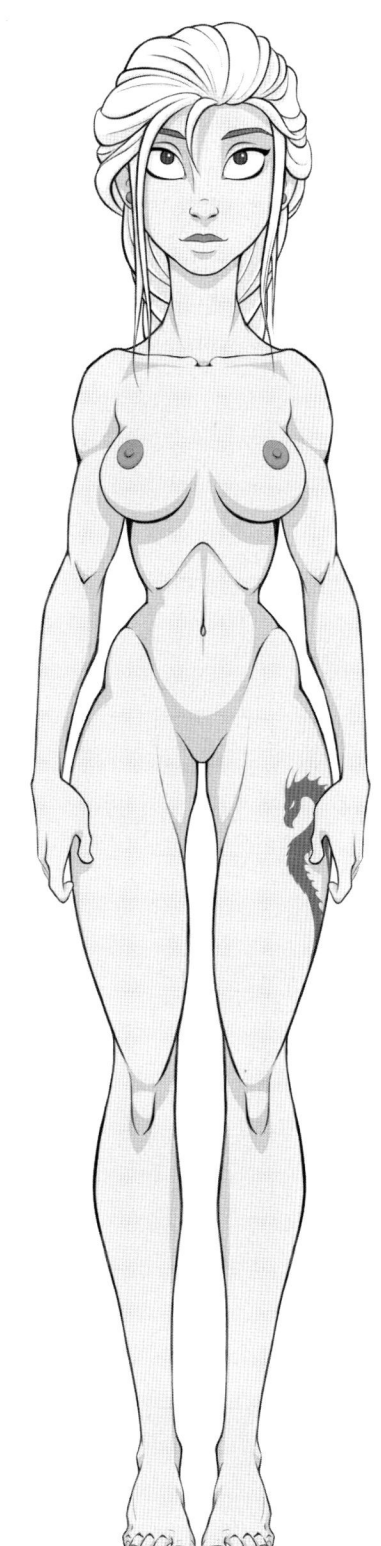

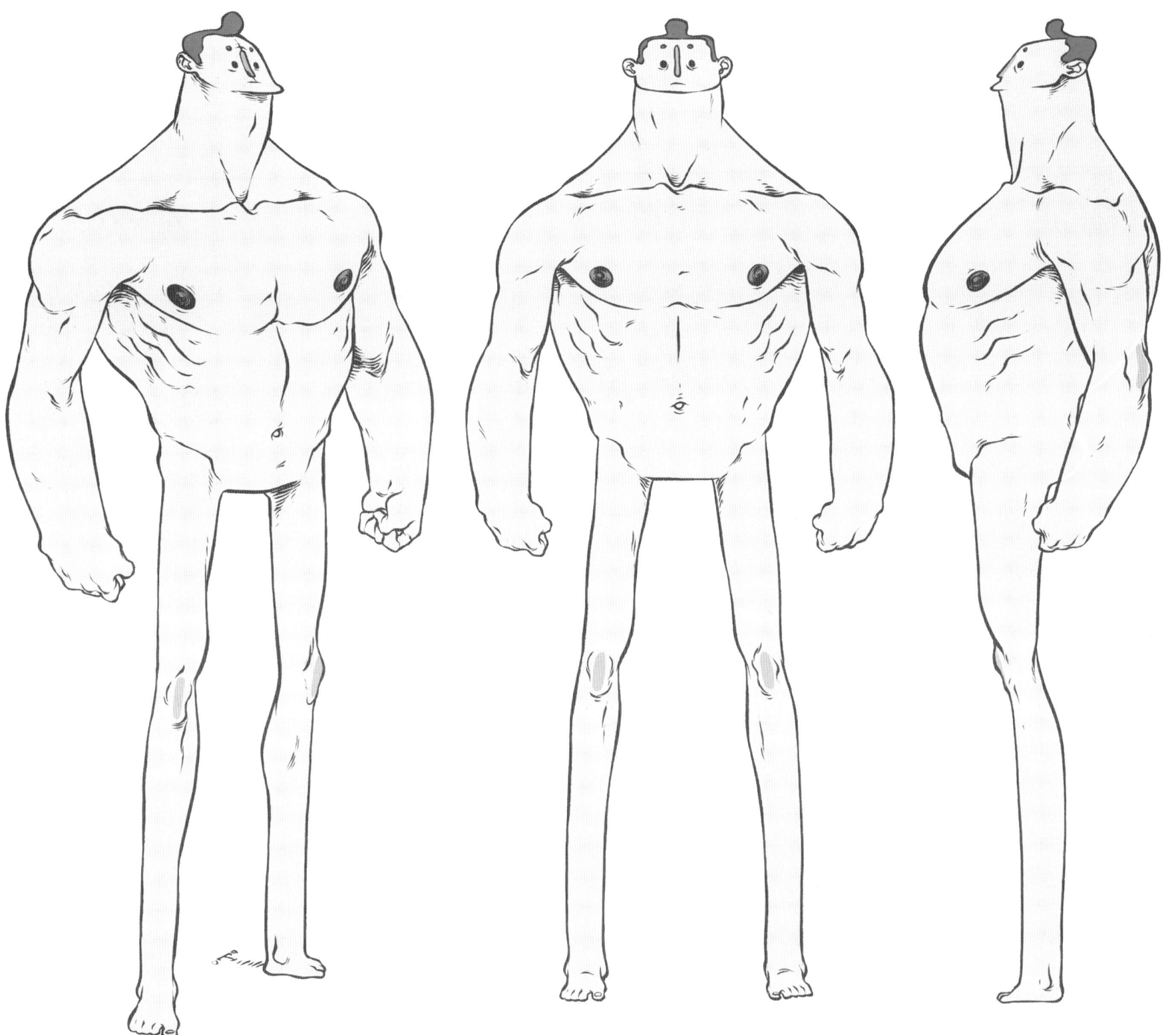

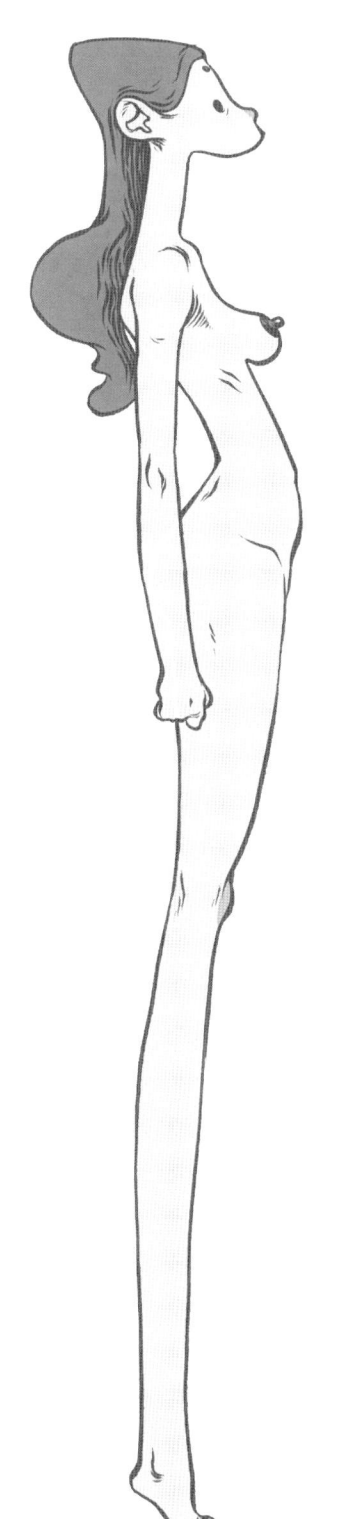
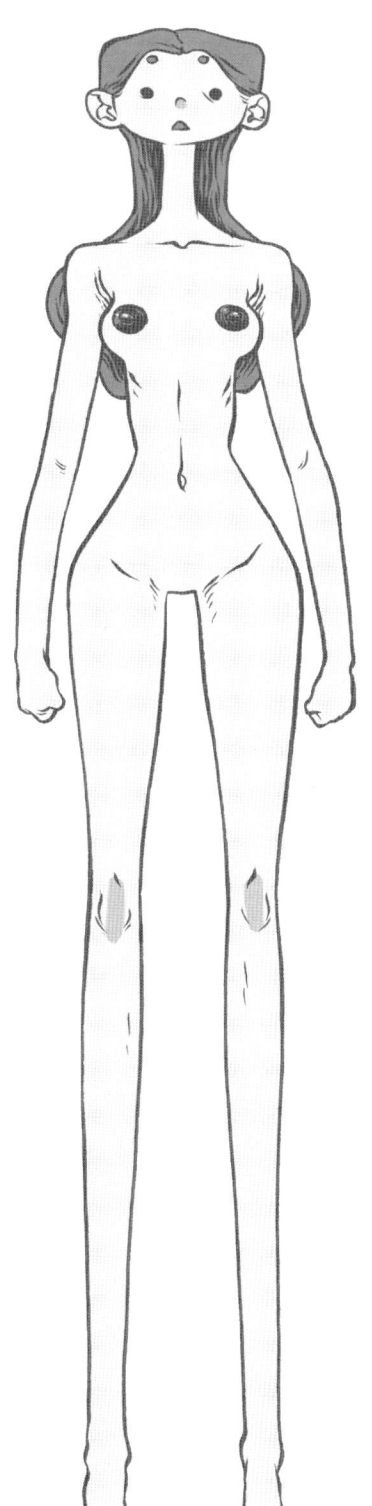

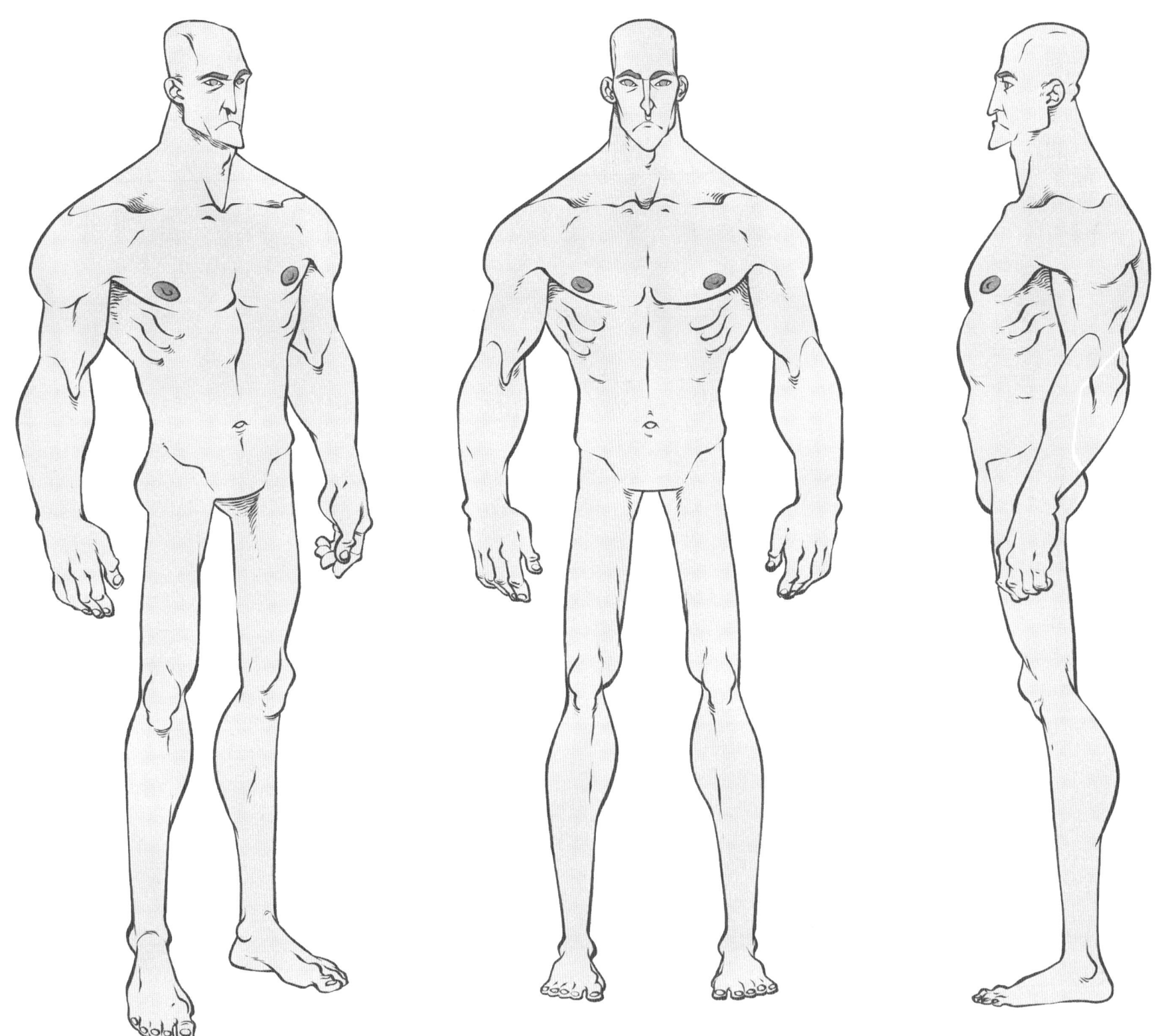

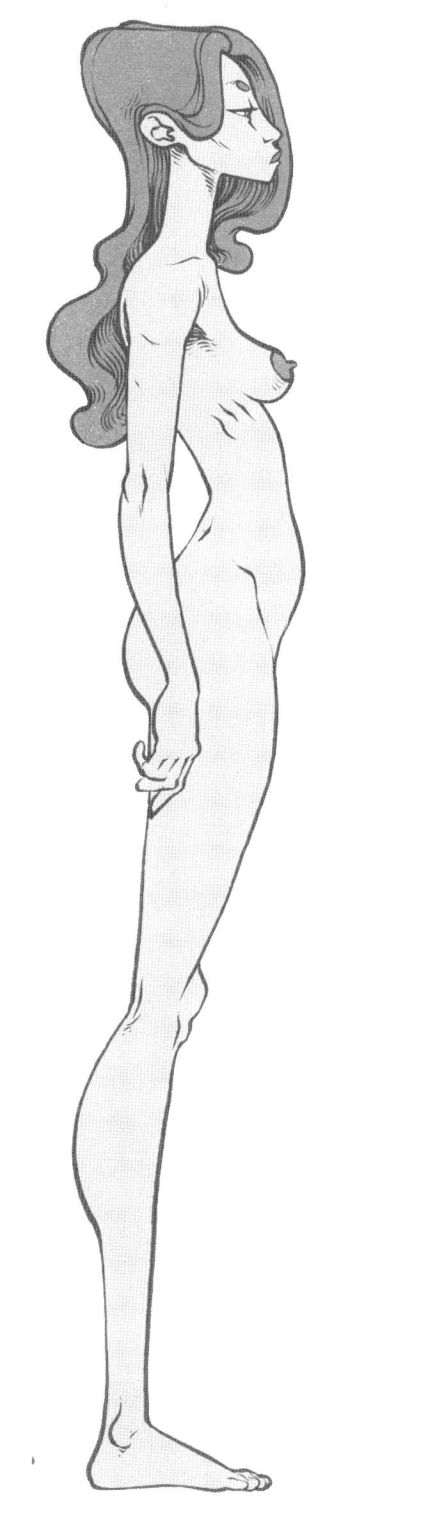
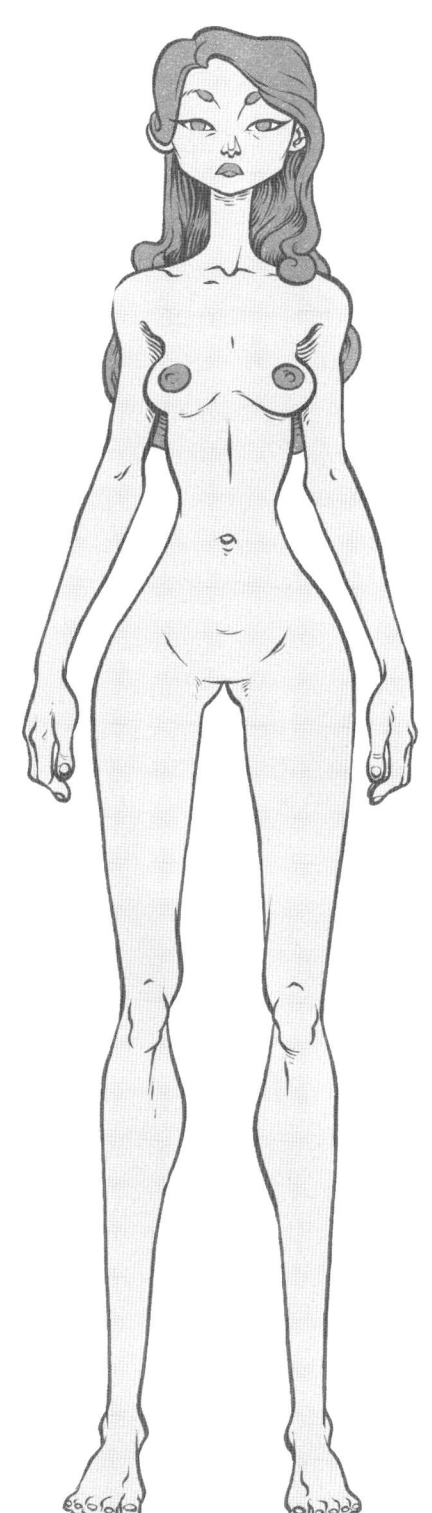
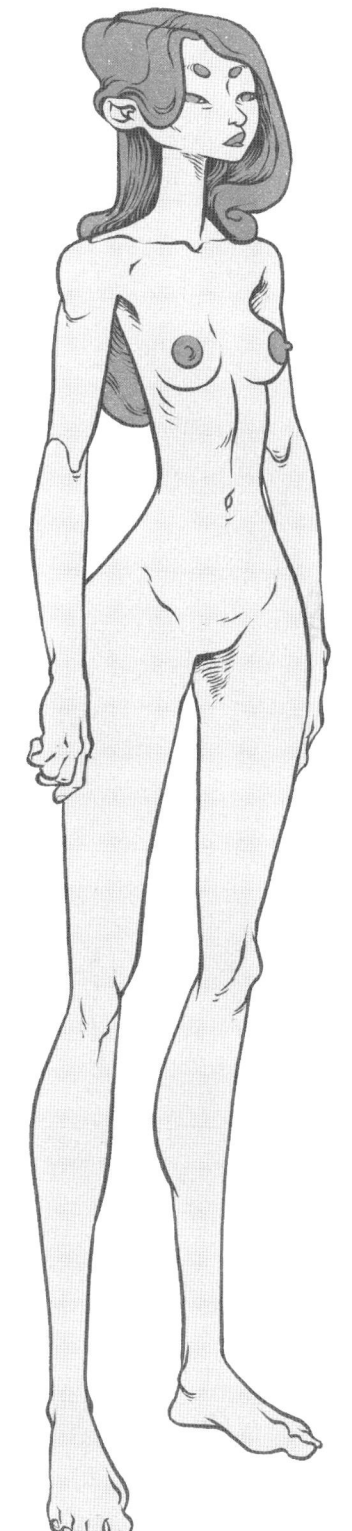

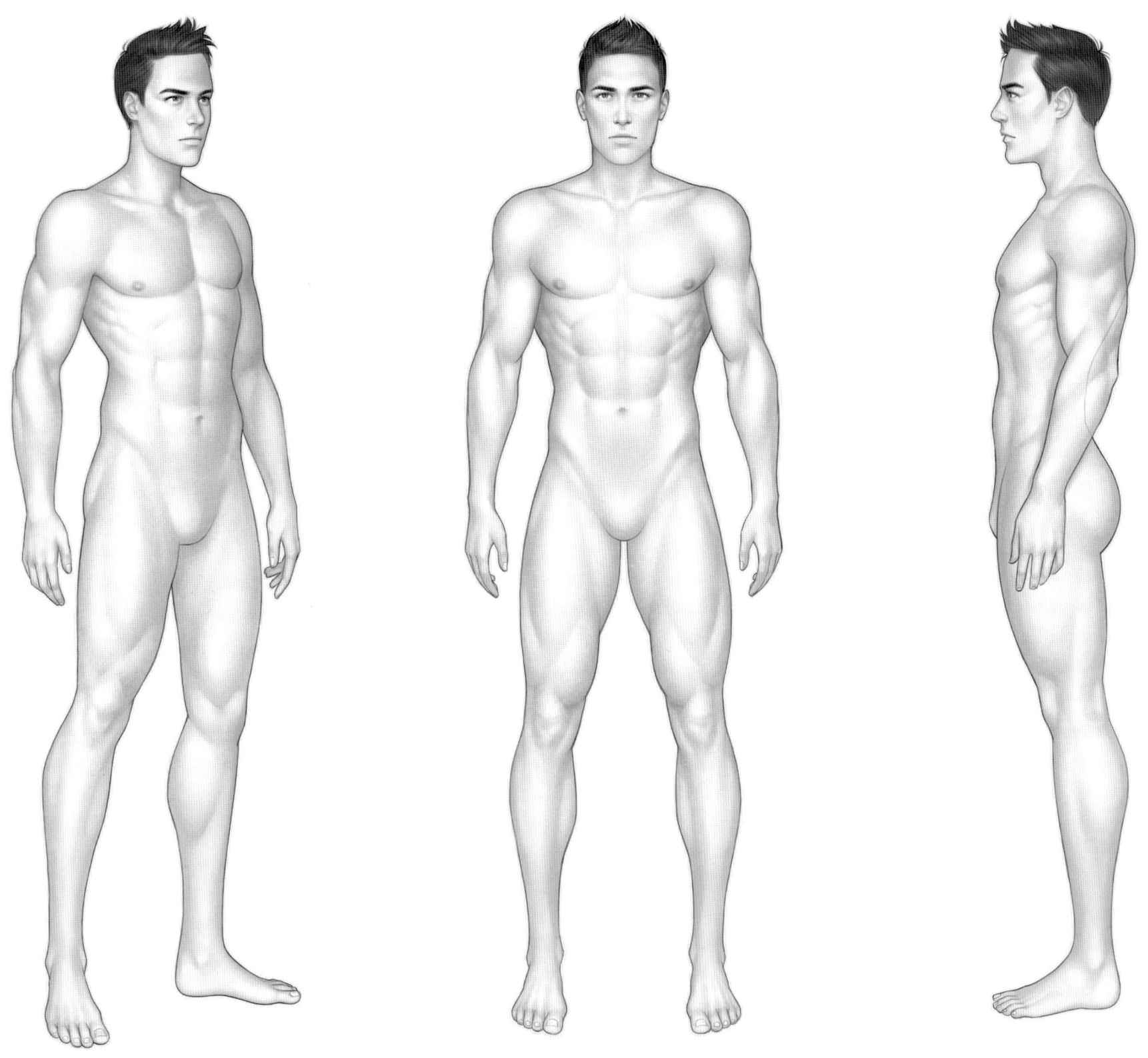

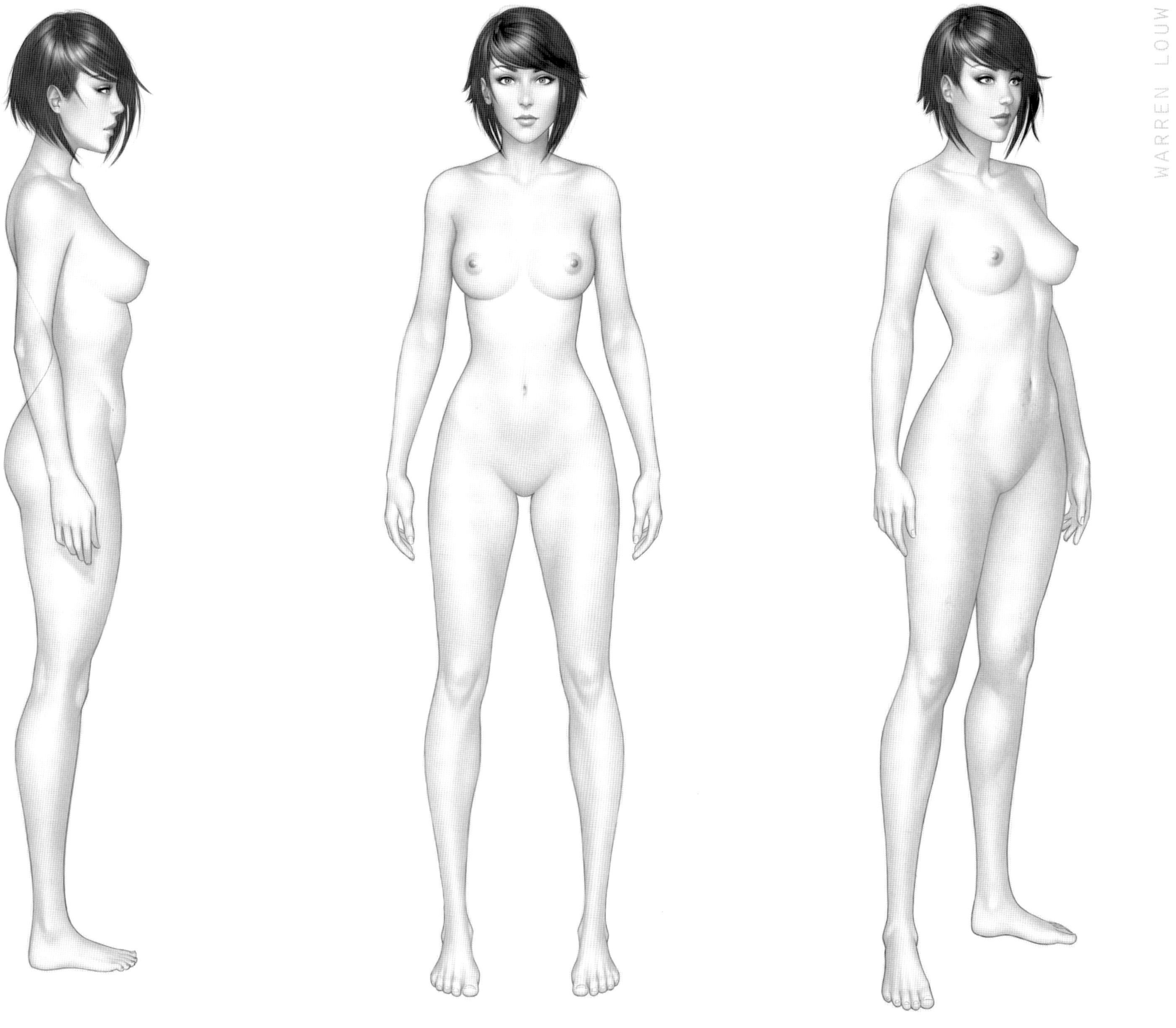

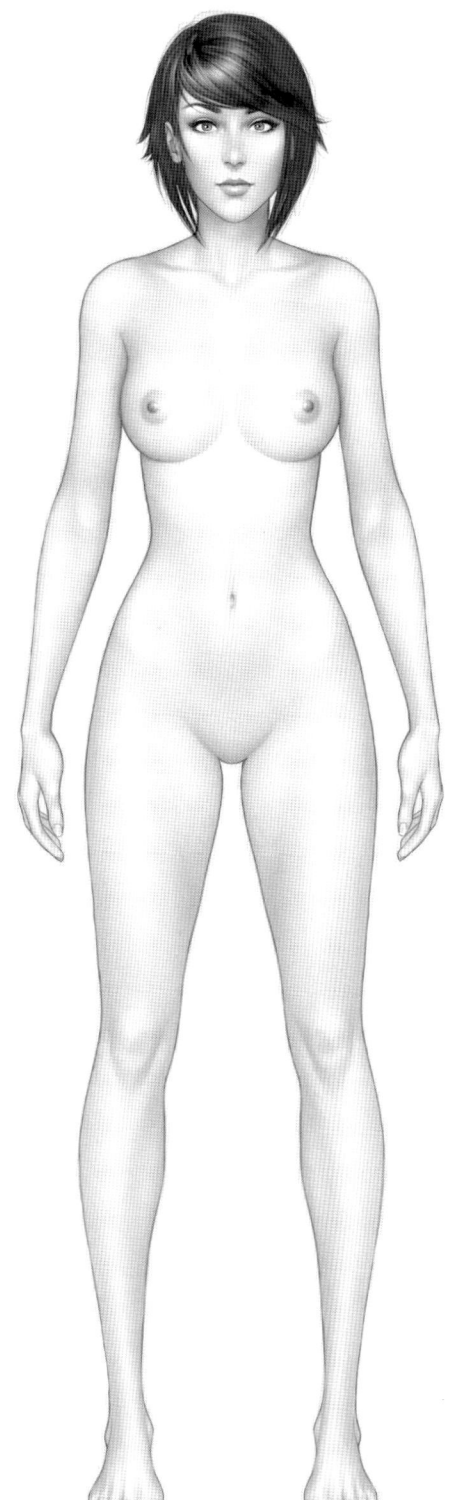
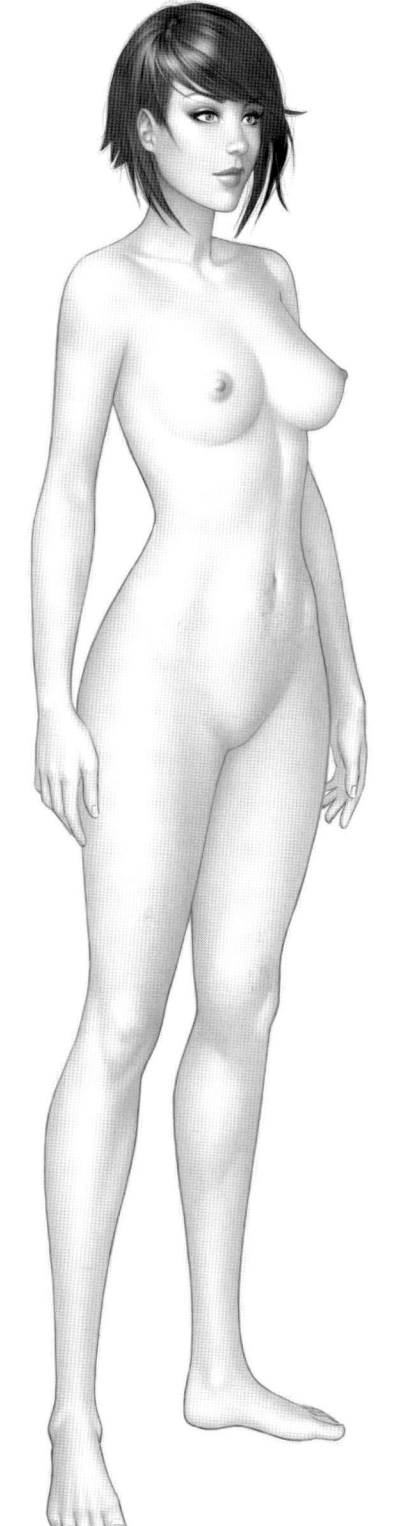

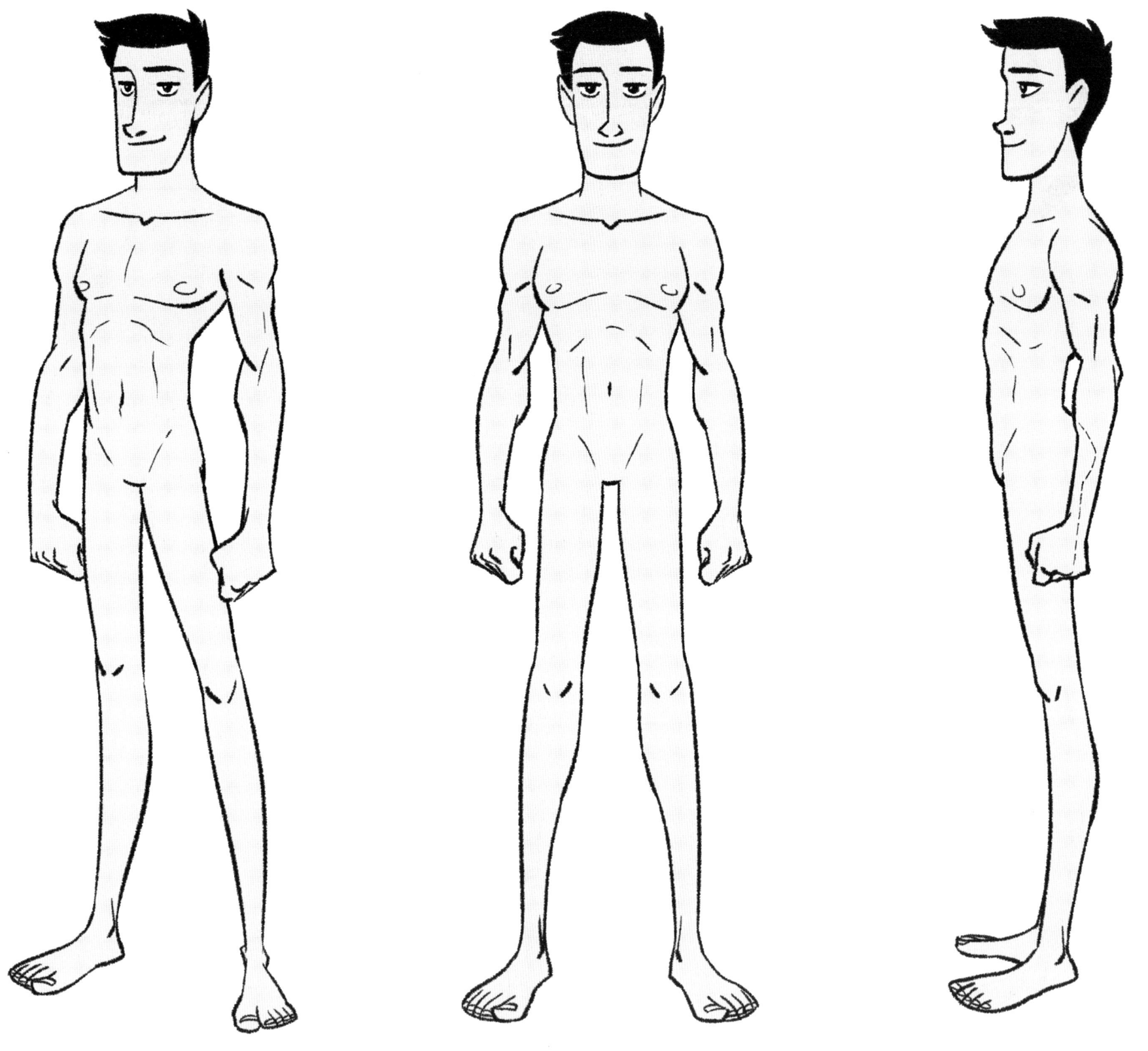

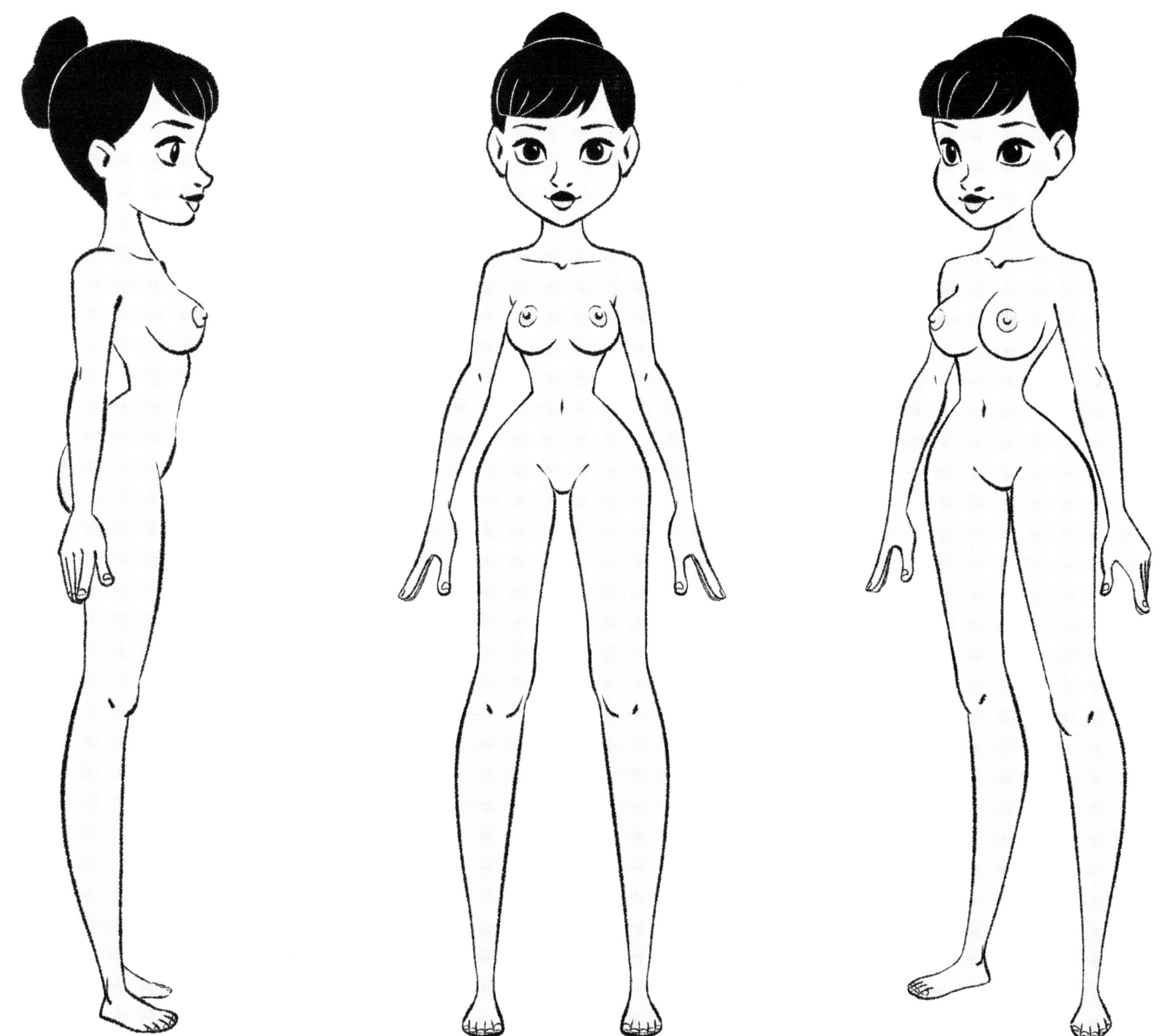

Masters Of Anatomy is a publishing company devoted to the art of character design and artistic anatomy. Working with some of the most famous and talented artists in the world, our goal is to help students expand their knowledge of appealing design and empower them to develop their own artistic style.

Questions or Comments? We'd love to hear from you! Send any and all questions to support@mastersofanatomy.com. For more information about **Masters Of Anatomy** visit http://www.mastersofanatomy.com.

MASTERS OF ANATOMY BOOK 2 : FACES IN CHARACTER DESIGN